# The
# New International
# Lesson Annual

## 2016–2017

### September–August

Abingdon Press
Nashville

The New International Lesson Annual 2016–2017

*Copyright © 2016 by Abingdon Press*

ISBN 978-1-4267-9681-4

ISSN 1084-872X

16 17 18 19 20 21 22 23 24 25—10 9 8 7 6 5 4 3 2 1

MANUFACTURED IN THE UNITED STATES OF AMERICA

# PREFACE

Welcome to the global community of Bible students and teachers who study resources based on the work of the Committee on the Uniform Series, known by many as the International Lesson Series. *The New International Lesson Annual* is designed for teachers who seek a solid biblical basis for each session and a step-by-step teaching plan that will help them lead their classes. *The New International Lesson Annual* can be used with any student curriculum based on the International Lesson Series. In many classes, both the students and teacher rely on *The New International Lesson Annual* as their companion to the Bible.

Over the four quarters of the 2016–2017 Sunday school year we will explore the themes of *God's sovereignty*, *creation*, *love*, and *call*. During the fall quarter we will examine Isaiah, Hebrews, and Revelation to see how these books reveal the Sovereignty of God. Luke's Gospel, selected psalms, and Galatians will help us understand Creation: A Divine Cycle, our study for the winter. In the spring we will survey the New Testament and also focus on the Book of Jonah to discover that God Loves Us. We conclude during the summer with God's Urgent Call, a study of the way God spoke to certain judges and prophets of the Old Testament and selected people of the New Testament as recorded in Acts.

*The New International Lesson Annual* provides numerous features that are especially valuable for busy teachers who want to provide in-depth Bible study experiences for their students. Each lesson includes the following sections:

**Previewing the Lesson** highlights the background and lesson Scriptures, focus of the lesson, three goals for the learners, and supplies you will need to teach.

**Reading the Scripture** includes the Scripture lesson printed in both the New Revised Standard Version and the Common English Bible. By printing these two translations in parallel columns, you can easily compare them for detailed study. If your own Bible is another version, you will then have three translations to explore as you prepare each lesson.

**Understanding the Scripture** closely analyzes the background Scripture by looking at each verse. Here you will find help in understanding concepts, ideas, places, and people pertinent to each week's lesson. You may also find explanations of Greek or Hebrew words that are helpful for understanding the text.

**Interpreting the Scripture** looks specifically at the lesson Scripture, delves into its meaning, and relates it to contemporary life.

**Sharing the Scripture** provides you with a detailed teaching plan. Written by your editor, who is a very experienced educator, this section is divided into two major sections: *Preparing to Teach* and *Leading the Class*.

In the *Preparing to Teach* section you will find a devotional reading and probing questions for your own spiritual enrichment, as well as ideas to help you prepare for the session.

The *Leading the Class* portion begins with activities designed to welcome the students and draw them into the lesson. In the Gather to Learn portion the students' stories and experiences or other contemporary stories are highlighted as preparation for the Bible story. The next three headings under *Leading the Class* are the three Goals for the Learners that were introduced in the Previewing the Lesson portion. The first goal always focuses on the Bible story itself. The second goal relates the Bible story to the lives of the learners. The third goal encourages the students to take action on what they have learned. These goals are foundational for each session, but they are by no means exhaustive, since we trust that students will leave the sessions with many ideas to reinforce and expand their knowledge, beliefs, and actions as Christian disciples. To that end, you will find diverse activities to appeal to a wide variety of learning styles. These activities may suggest listening, reading, writing, speaking, singing, drawing, researching, interacting with others, meditating, and other possibilities. The lesson ends with Continue the Journey, where you will find closing activities, preparation for the following week, and ideas for students to commit themselves to action during the week so that they can put into practice what they have learned.

In addition to these weekly features, each quarter begins with the following helps:

- **Introduction to the Quarter** offers you a quick survey of each lesson to be studied during the quarter. You will find the title, background Scripture, date, and a brief summary of each week's basic thrust. This feature is on the first page of each quarter.
- **Meet Our Writer,** which follows the quarterly introduction, provides biographical information about each writer, including education, pastoral and/or academic teaching experience, previous publications, and family information.
- **The Big Picture,** written by the same writer who authored the quarter's lessons, is designed to give you a broader scope of the materials to be covered than is possible in each weekly lesson. You will find this background article immediately following the writer's biography.
- **Close-up** furnishes additional information, such as a time line, chart, overview, short article, map, or list that you may choose to use for a specific week or anytime during the quarter, perhaps even repeatedly.
- **Faith in Action** describes ideas related to the broad sweep of the quarter that the students can use individually or as a class to act on what they have been studying. These ideas are usually intended for use beyond the classroom.
- **Pronunciation Guide,** a familiar feature that our readers requested, has been moved from the Previewing the Scripture portion of each lesson to a single page before Lesson 1 in each quarter, thereby gathering all words for which pronunciation is provided in one convenient location.

Finally, two annual features are included:

- **List of Background Scriptures** is offered especially for those of you who keep back copies of *The New International Lesson Annual.* This feature, found immediately after the Contents, will enable you to locate Bible background passages used during the current year and refer to them in the future.

- **Teacher enrichment article,** which follows the List of Background Scriptures, is intended to be useful throughout the year. We hope you will read it immediately and refer to it often. This year's article, "All I Really Need to Know I've Learned by the Grace of God," is a recollection of lessons I have learned over decades of teaching Sunday school and Bible study classes. I hope you will find these lessons helpful for your own faith journey and work with your students.

I want to personally thank you for supporting *The New International Lesson Annual* during my tenure as editor. Whether this is your first copy, or whether you've been with us since I began editing the entire book and writing the Sharing the Scripture portion in the 1995–1996 edition, it has been my privilege to share God's word with you. I, of course, cannot possibly do this job alone. We have a dedicated team of publication experts based at The United Methodist Publishing House in Nashville, as well as a cadre of biblical scholars and pastors across the United States who regularly contribute to this resource. I will miss you all! Although I am scaling back to semi-retirement, I plan to continue to make occasional contributions to other United Methodist publications.

My retirement also signals the retirement of *The New International Lesson Annual.* The popular *Adult Bible Studies* student and teacher books will continue to be available through Cokesbury. I trust you will use these invaluable quarterly resources as you prepare your weekly lessons. Two other adult publications based on the International Lesson Series are also available through Cokesbury. Lessons and daily Bible readings are found in the quarterly magazine titled *Christian Living in the Mature Years. Daily Bible Studies,* a quarterly publication based on daily home Bible readings, will also help leaders and students to delve deeper into texts leading up to Sunday's lesson.

I have been motivated and inspired by our journey together over the years. All who use *The New International Lesson Annual* are blessed by the collective community of readers. You have truly been a blessing to me! Our entire *New International Lesson Annual* team prays that you and your study partners will be transformed by the Word of God and the power of the Holy Spirit so as to be conformed to the image of our Lord and Savior Jesus Christ.

Nan Duerling, Ph.D.
Editor, *The New International Lesson Annual*

# CONTENTS

List of Background Scriptures........................................ 12
Teacher Enrichment: All I Really Need to Know I've
    Learned by the Grace of God .................................. 13

## First Quarter: Sovereignty of God
## September 4, 2016—November 27, 2016

Introduction: Sovereignty of God ................................... 19
Meet Our Writer: Dr. Jerry L. Sumney .............................. 20
The Big Picture: God in Isaiah, Hebrews, and Revelation ............. 21
Close-up: Comparison of Priestly Types ............................. 25
Faith in Action: Living in the Light of the Sovereignty of God ........... 27
Pronunciation Guide ............................................... 28

### UNIT 1: THE SOVEREIGNTY OF GOD
### (September 4–September 25)

LESSON      PAGE
1.      The Peaceful Kingdom .................................... 29
           September 4—Isaiah 11:1-9
2.      The Mountain of God ..................................... 38
           September 11—Isaiah 25:6-10a
3.      Foundations of the Earth ................................. 47
           September 18—Isaiah 40:21-31
4.      Everlasting Covenant ..................................... 56
           September 25—Isaiah 61:1-4, 8-11

### UNIT 2: THE SOVEREIGNTY OF JESUS
### (October 2–October 30)

5.      The Imprint of God ...................................... 65
           October 2—Hebrews 1
6.      Builder of the House ..................................... 74
           October 9—Hebrews 3:1-6; Matthew 7:24-29
7.      The Great High Priest .................................... 83
           October 16—Hebrews 4:14–5:10
8.      The High Priest Forever .................................. 92
           October 23—Hebrews 7:1-3, 19b-28
9.      Pioneer and Perfecter of Our Faith........................ 101
           October 30—Hebrews 12:1-13

## UNIT 3: ALPHA AND OMEGA
### (November 6–November 27)

10.      Everything Is Brand New ................................. 110
         November 6—Revelation 21:1-8
11.      I See a New Jerusalem .................................. 119
         November 13—Revelation 21:9-14, 22-27
12.      Living Waters ......................................... 128
         November 20—Revelation 22:1-7
13.      Alpha and Omega .................................... 137
         November 27—Revelation 22:12-21

## Second Quarter: Creation: A Divine Cycle
## December 4, 2016–February 26, 2017

Introduction: Creation: A Divine Cycle ............................. 147
Meet Our Writer: Rev. John Indermark ............................. 148
The Big Picture: Creation and New Creation ......................... 159
Close-Up: The Psalms ............................................. 153
Faith in Action: Acting as a Cocreator with God .................... 154
Pronunciation Guide ............................................. 155

### UNIT 1: THE SAVIOR HAS BEEN BORN
### (December 4–December 25)

1.      God Promises a Savior .................................. 156
         December 4—Luke 1:26-38
2.      The Affirmation of the Promise .......................... 165
         December 11—Luke 1:39-56
3.      God Promised Zechariah a Son .......................... 174
         December 18—Luke 1:8-20
4.      God's Promised Savior Is Born ........................... 183
         December 25—Luke 2:8-20

### UNIT 2: PRAISE FROM AND FOR GOD'S CREATION
### (January 1–January 29)

5.      Praising God the Creator ................................ 192
         January 1—Psalm 33:1-9
6.      All Creation Overflows with Praise ...................... 201
         January 8—Psalm 96:1-6, 10-13
7.      Praise God the Provider ................................ 210
         January 15—Psalm 65:1-2, 9-13
8.      Praise God the Creator ................................. 219
         January 22—Psalm 104:1-4, 24-30

9.         All Creation Praises God . . . . . . . . . . . . . . . . . . . . . . . . . . . . . . . 228
           January 29—Psalm 148

## UNIT 3: THE BIRTHING OF A NEW COMMUNITY
### (February 5–February 26)

10.      Re-created to Live in Harmony . . . . . . . . . . . . . . . . . . . . . . . . . . . 237
           February 5—Galatians 3:26–4:7
11.      New Birth Brings Freedom . . . . . . . . . . . . . . . . . . . . . . . . . . . . . 246
           February 12—Galatians 4:8-20
12.      Freedom in Christ . . . . . . . . . . . . . . . . . . . . . . . . . . . . . . . . . . . . 255
           February 19—Galatians 5:1-17
13.      Christ Creates Holy Living . . . . . . . . . . . . . . . . . . . . . . . . . . . . . 264
           February 26—Galatians 5:18–6:10

# Third Quarter: God Loves Us
# March 5, 2017–May 28, 2017

Introduction: God Loves Us . . . . . . . . . . . . . . . . . . . . . . . . . . . . . . . . . 274
Meet Our Writer: Rev. David Kalas . . . . . . . . . . . . . . . . . . . . . . . . . . . 275
The Big Picture: God's Love for Us . . . . . . . . . . . . . . . . . . . . . . . . . . . 276
Close-up: Jonah and His Story . . . . . . . . . . . . . . . . . . . . . . . . . . . . . . . 280
Faith in Action: Revealing the Love of God . . . . . . . . . . . . . . . . . . . . . 282
Pronunciation Guide . . . . . . . . . . . . . . . . . . . . . . . . . . . . . . . . . . . . . . 283

## UNIT 1: GOD'S ETERNAL, PRESERVING, RENEWING LOVE
### (March 5–March 26)

1.       The Source of All Love . . . . . . . . . . . . . . . . . . . . . . . . . . . . . . . . 284
           March 5—1 John 4:7-19
2.       God's Overflowing Love . . . . . . . . . . . . . . . . . . . . . . . . . . . . . . . 293
           March 12—Ephesians 2:1-10
3.       God's Love Manifested. . . . . . . . . . . . . . . . . . . . . . . . . . . . . . . . 302
           March 19—John 15:1-17
4.       God's Love Restores . . . . . . . . . . . . . . . . . . . . . . . . . . . . . . . . . . 311
           March 26—Joel 2:12-13, 18-19, 28-32

## UNIT 2: GOD'S CARING, SAVING, AND UPHOLDING LOVE
### (April 2–April 30)

5.       God as Our Shepherd . . . . . . . . . . . . . . . . . . . . . . . . . . . . . . . . 320
           April 2—Psalm 23
6.       God's Saving Love in Christ . . . . . . . . . . . . . . . . . . . . . . . . . . . . 329
           April 9—John 3:1-16
7.       God's Love as Victory over Death. . . . . . . . . . . . . . . . . . . . . . . . 338
           April 16—John 19:38-42; 20:1-10; 1 Peter 1:3-9

8.       God's Reconciling Love ................................... 347
          April 23—Romans 5:6-11; 8:31-39
9.       God's Preserving Love .................................. 356
          April 30—John 10:1-15

### UNIT 3: GOD'S PERVASIVE AND SUSTAINING LOVE
#### (May 7–May 28)

10.      God's Sustaining Love ................................... 365
          May 7—Jonah 1:7-17
11.      God's Love Preserved Jonah ............................. 374
          May 14—Jonah 2
12.      God's Love for Nineveh ................................. 383
          May 21—Jonah 3
13.      God's Pervasive Love ................................... 392
          May 28—Jonah 4

## Fourth Quarter: God's Urgent Call
## June 4, 2017–August 27, 2017

Introduction: God's Urgent Call ..................................... 401
Meet Our Writer: Dr. Jerome Creach ................................ 402
The Big Picture: The Call of God ................................... 403
Close-up: The Judges .............................................. 408
Faith in Action: Hearing and Heeding the Call ...................... 409
Pronunciation Guide .............................................. 410

### UNIT 1: CALLED TO BE STRONG
#### (June 4–June 25)

1.       Deborah and Barak ..................................... 411
          June 4—Judges 4:1-10
2.       Gideon's Call .......................................... 420
          June 11—Judges 6:11-18
3.       Jephthah Answers the Call .............................. 429
          June 18—Judges 11:4-11, 29-31
4.       Samson's Call .......................................... 438
          June 25—Judges 13:1-7, 24-25

### UNIT 2: CALLING OF PROPHETS
#### (July 2–July 30)

5.       Moses and the Burning Bush ............................ 447
          July 2—Exodus 3:1-12

6.     Isaiah in the Temple ........................................ 456
      July 9—Isaiah 6:1-8
7.     Jeremiah's Call and Commission .......................... 465
      July 16— Jeremiah 1:4-10
8.     Ezekiel's Call ............................................. 474
      July 23— Ezekiel 3:1-11
9.     Amos's Call............................................... 483
      July 30—Amos 7:1-17

## UNIT 3: CALLS IN THE NEW TESTAMENT
### (August 6–August 27)

10.    Called to Witness....................................... 492
      August 6—Acts 6:1-8
11.    Called to Break Down Barriers .......................... 501
      August 13—Acts 8:26-39
12.    Called to Preach....................................... 515
      August 20—Acts 9:10-20
13.    Called to Be Inclusive ................................. 519
      August 27—Acts 10:19-33

# LIST OF BACKGROUND SCRIPTURES, 2016–2017

## Old Testament

| | | | |
|---|---|---|---|
| Exodus 3 | July 2 | Isaiah 11:1-9 | September 4 |
| Judges 4, 5 | June 4 | Isaiah 25 | September 11 |
| Judges 6–8 | June 11 | Isaiah 40 | September 18 |
| Judges 11 | June 18 | Isaiah 61 | September 25 |
| Judges 13–16 | June 25 | Jeremiah 1 | July 16 |
| Psalm 23 | April 2 | Ezekiel 1–3 | July 23 |
| Psalm 33:1-9 | January 1 | Joel 2 | March 26 |
| Psalm 65 | January 15 | Amos 7 | July 30 |
| Psalm 67:6-7 | January 15 | Jonah 1 | May 7 |
| Psalm 96 | January 8 | Jonah 2 | May 14 |
| Psalm 104 | January 22 | Jonah 3 | May 21 |
| Psalm 148 | January 29 | Jonah 4 | May 28 |
| Isaiah 6 | July 9 | Nahum 1–3 | May 21 |

## New Testament

| | | | |
|---|---|---|---|
| Matthew 7:19-29 | October 9 | Romans 8:31-39 | April 23 |
| Luke 1:1-23, 51=66 | December 18 | Galatians 3:26–4:7 | February 5 |
| Luke 1:26-38 | December 4 | Galatians 4 | February 12 |
| Luke 1:39-56 | December 11 | Galatians 5:1-17 | February 19 |
| Luke 2:1-21 | December 25 | Galatians 5:18–6:10 | February 26 |
| John 3:1-21 | April 9 | Ephesians 2:1-10 | March 12 |
| John 10:1-15 | April 30 | Hebrews 1 | October 2 |
| John 15:1-17 | March 19 | Hebrews 3:1-6 | October 9 |
| John 19:38-42 | April 16 | Hebrews 4:14–5:10 | October 16 |
| John 20:1-10 | April 16 | Hebrews 7 | October 23 |
| Acts 1 | August 6 | Hebrews 12:1-13 | October 30 |
| Acts 6 | August 6 | 1 Peter 1:3-9 | April 16 |
| Acts 7 | August 6 | 1 John 4:7-19 | March 5 |
| Acts 8 | August 13 | Revelation 21:1-8 | November 6 |
| Acts 9:1-31 | August 20 | Revelation 21:9-27 | November 13 |
| Acts 10 | August 27 | Revelation 22:1-7 | November 20 |
| Romans 5:1-11 | April 23 | Revelation 22:8-21 | November 27 |

# TEACHER ENRICHMENT: ALL I REALLY NEED TO KNOW I'VE LEARNED BY THE GRACE OF GOD

Best-selling author and Unitarian minister Robert Fulghum charmed us with his delightful book, *All I Really Need to Know I Learned in Kindergarten*. While I appreciate his wisdom, my journey has been different. My parents, extended family, church, and school certainly taught me much during my formative years, but many of the most important lessons have been learned by living a long, rich life—a life that included the privilege of leading church school classes. In this article I would like to share some things that have I have discovered by leading Bible study classes and by walking daily with Jesus. My prayer is that you may find some manna for your own journey.

**Everyone has a story.** I started my Sunday school teaching career as an aide in the kindergarten class when I was in ninth grade. Throughout the years I've occasionally worked with children but, since my collegiate education and professional experiences were in secondary and college education, I have worked mostly with teens and adults. No matter what the age or stage in life, each person has a story to tell and a back story that helped to shape the person who walked into the classroom today. Looking back to my early years as a teacher, I was probably so focused on "teaching the lesson" that I had carefully prepared that I fear I may not have listened as carefully as I might have to what people were saying about their own lives.

Over the years I've learned that the Christian education setting becomes electrified when students realize that the Bible story jumps off the page and has something to say to their own lives, when they can imagine themselves as certain biblical characters, and recognize how their story and the Bible story intersect. *Knowing about* God the Father, Son, and Holy Spirit is essential. But that knowledge pales in comparison to *knowing* this awesome God of ours. Stories enable us to see how we are in a loving, personal relationship with the one who created, redeemed, and sustains us. Class time cannot, of course, become just a time to tell personal stories, but carefully chosen activities with clear connections to the day's Bible readings can help students connect the dots between their lives and the lives of those biblical people who were touched by God.

**It's up to me as the leader to create a trusting environment where everyone feels safe.** Putting together a lecture is not really a daunting task. Many resources can help any teacher who is willing to spend time studying to present a credible lesson with intellectual integrity. The real challenge comes when the teacher is willing to invite the students into a discussion, to let them share their insights and stories and to raise questions for which there are no scripted answers. For a teacher to admit that he or she doesn't have readily available answers is not a sin. But to shut down people or belittle them or in some way devalue their comments—or allow other class members do the same—is, in my view, catastrophic to the health and well-being of the group. In contrast, if people feel that they can be heard with respect (even if not with agreement) and that whatever is said in the classroom stays in the classroom, then they are going to be willing to speak from their hearts and share their authentic selves with others. My role as the leader is always to ensure that people feel that their ideas, questions, and personal stories are being handled with the same love and care that Jesus would use.

**If I want the class to stay fresh and invigorating, I need to take the risk of trying something new.** Most class members I've worked with over the years quickly get into a pattern of relating to one another, to me as the leader, to the material we are studying, and to the way that we study it. Trying a new kind of activity can be threatening for some people, especially adults. But I've learned that with a bit of cajoling most groups are willing to try something different—as long as I solicit feedback. *How did this work for you? Would you like to do this again? What changes could we make to enhance the activity so as to make it more helpful to you?* In my younger years I was very averse to failure. Everything had to work out well for all participants. It was so much easier to play things safe, to do what I thought everyone would approve of. Yes, I could fail if I tried something new, but the fact of the matter is that seldom happened. Instead, class members learned new things not only about the topic at hand but also about themselves, their relationship with one another, and their relationship with Jesus. They could broaden their horizons by stretching their intellects and their spirits. "I don't want to try that" was often replaced by "I learned something new and had fun in the process." But such new insights would not have surfaced if I as the leader had not taken the risk to challenge the proverbial seven last words of the church: "We've never done it that way before."

**The people who seem the most difficult are the ones who need you and their classmates the most.** Have you ever had a student—of any age—whom you secretly prayed would not show up this week? I sure have. The child who felt displaced by a new sibling who called attention to himself by throwing blocks (and anything else he could find), biting other children, and screaming when he wanted to be noticed. The teenager whose parents were in the throes of a bitter divorce who expressed her rage by making sniping comments to other students. The adult who lost a long-held job and consequently tried to turn whatever discussion we were having to the question of why God lets bad things happen to good Christians. The opinionated student who insisted that his or her understandings were "correct" and any other viewpoints were somehow "wrong" or "inferior" or only held by those who were spiritually immature.

Let's be honest: Such people are difficult to deal with. Especially if you are trying to have a discussion with teens or adults, a person clamoring for attention by getting the class off track or lobbying for the absolute correctness of a specific interpretation can be very disruptive. Instead of smiling while inwardly stewing about such distracting behavior, I came to understand that Jesus allowed himself to be interrupted, even while he was trying to rest. His concern was for those who needed to know that God loved and cared about them. Once I learned that I needed to be interruptible—and that the lesson could withstand a short diversion—I could more gracefully handle the situation and then steer the group back on course. Class members seemed to tune in to the difficult person's problem and help me do that. In a few situations I felt led to spend some time beyond class to support a particular adult student as best I could.

**Most people want to be part of a caring community, not just a class.** While it's true that people who go through high school or college together may remain friends over the years or just appear every five or ten years for a reunion, a Sunday school class is different. It is a community of faith where people voluntarily gather together not just to study but also to rejoice and weep with others, to fellowship with others, and to act corporately as the people of God. Most adult classes have fellowship time, often around a refreshment table. They also take time to hear joys and concerns and then pray for one another. They likely send greeting cards. They may have an occasional potluck dinner at someone's home. Members visit in hospitals and nursing homes and pay respects at funeral homes. In other words, they go far over and beyond what would happen in a secular classroom in terms of taking care of one another. I had to learn to take time for these caring activities and recognize how important they are to the upbuilding of the community of faith. Yes, the planned lesson is the main reason we attend a class, but these caring activities demonstrate that we know how to practice what we are learning.

**People who are really serious about their faith not only want to study but also want to act on their beliefs.** I've always firmly believed that a disciple's walk has to be in sync with his or her talk. Although it's important to say, for example, that people who live in substandard housing need a safe place to stay, it's quite a different matter to do something to assist such people get into appropriate housing. Some years ago, my Sunday school class studied a Habitat for Humanity curriculum. We learned the biblical foundations for this global organization that enables people who need a helping hand to become homeowners who pay their mortgage and maintain the house in which they have invested sweat equity. As we finished our study we asked, "What can we do?" and from that question we formed ecumenical partnerships to build several homes in our county and to contribute to an equal number of houses being built around the world. The class was not sure we could do this, but with a lot of prayer, fund-raising, and getting other believers excited about what we were doing, we were able to act on what we had learned. Those experiences not only helped those who needed housing but also empowered us to grow spiritually when we saw firsthand how God came through time and time again to accomplish the tasks that God wanted done and had entrusted to us.

**Everyone has great and equal value in God's sight. Therefore, we need to help all people feel as if they belong**. For many years my family and I were members of a church that participated in an ecumenical shelter for those who were homeless. During the winter months, churches in our county would bring in people who had nowhere to go, shelter them overnight, give them breakfast there and a bag lunch to take with them, and return them to the church later that evening. Each church had an assigned week. One thing my Sunday school class did was to provide the evening meal for one night during our guests' stay. We'd eat and talk with our guests. Sometimes people were homeless due to bad choices they had made. But it seemed more often than not that a life challenge— loss of a job, serious illness, financial reversals due to unemployment or illness, a death, or break-up of a family, just to name a few reasons—were often at the root of this homelessness. These people did not want to be homeless and were trying to find ways to return to a normal life. More folks than I'd care to remember had served our country but now as veterans could not get the help they needed. The same was true for people suffering from mental illness who had been "main- streamed" into the community without the proper tools to fend for themselves. All of our guests were created in the image of God and were entitled to be treated with dignity and respect. I could not begin to imagine how overwhelming it must be not to have access to the things I so take for granted—a drink of water, a snack or meal, a regular haircut, a bathroom in which to privately bathe and use the toilet.

I learned that our guests were very appreciative of even the smallest kind- ness. I would issue a personal, low-key invitation to our guests to attend Sun- day school and worship with us. Some seemed eager to be a part of a class or congregation. My class eagerly welcomed them, and I think we made them feel at home. During class we heard some truly heartbreaking stories. But my most unforgettable moment was when I saw one of our guests put money in the offering plate during worship. His gratitude and faith reminded me not to take for granted the kind of community that others wish they could be part of on a regular basis.

**Everyone has God-given gifts and talents that need to be recognized and affirmed.** How often have you heard people say, "I'm nobody special, or I don't have any particular gifts that God can use"? I've learned that just telling someone that God has graciously gifted all of us—as true as that is—is just not enough. People need to hear what their own gifts are and the impact they have on the lives of others. I once had a student who could see everyone's gifts except his own. It wasn't until I reminded him of how special he made worshipers feel when he was ushering that he began to recognize that God had gifted him for ministry. The class chimed in to support my remarks and added stories of their own about this man's service. Although he was a modest person, I think that he was quite sincere about his low assessment of his capabilities. Yet I noticed that his demeanor changed when so many people affirmed his gift of hospital- ity and his many contributions to the church. He realized that he was not just "doing a job" but was engaged in a real ministry of service to which God had called him and for which God had equipped him.

**God is in charge and always present, no matter how things seem.** For years I said these words and truly believed them, at least on an intellectual level. But it was not until 1996 when I had two angioplasties and urgent bypass surgery— all within three months of one another when I was forty-nine years old—that I could say these words with absolute certainty, tested in the crucible of a near- death experience: God's gracious, comforting presence is always with me. A life-threatening illness can put things into perspective. No longer was I willing to waste precious time fretting over small stuff that within a few hours wouldn't make any difference anyway. If I had a problem with someone else, I'd do whatever I could to restore our relationship as quickly as possible. I recognized that God was constantly with me and so could say, "This too shall pass."

As I reach the end of my journey as the writer of the Sharing the Scripture portion and editor of *The New International Lesson Annual*, I am grateful to be able to look back over my decades of teaching and involvement with curriculum. I am especially grateful for the lessons that my students and you, our readers, have taught me. I wish you Godspeed as you continue your own journey as a leader in the school of Christ.

# FIRST QUARTER
## Sovereignty of God

SEPTEMBER 4, 2016—NOVEMBER 27, 2016

The theme for the fall quarter is God's sovereignty. During these thirteen weeks we will explore images of the authors of Isaiah, Hebrews, and Revelation to discern the sovereign nature of God.

The four lessons of Unit 1, The Sovereignty of God, examine Isaiah's rich images of God as the one who rules the whole universe. We will discover the world as a peaceful kingdom, a mountain of God, the foundations of the earth, and a new and everlasting covenant. This unit begins on September 4 with The Peaceful Kingdom, based on Isaiah 11:1-9, where we find a world filled with the peace, justice, and righteousness of God. On September 11 we turn to Isaiah 25 to catch a glimpse of The Mountain of God where there is no oppression. Foundations of the Earth, the session for September 18, considers God's ultimate power as seen in Isaiah 40. Isaiah 61, the background Scripture for Everlasting Covenant that we will study on September 25, spotlights promises that God makes and reliably fulfills.

Unit 2, The Sovereignty of Jesus, stretches over five weeks as we investigate images of the reign of the resurrected Christ found in the Letter to the Hebrews. During these sessions we will encounter images of Jesus as the imprint of God, the owner of a household, the great high priest, a priest forever, and the pioneer and perfecter of our faith. The Imprint of God, based on an image found in Hebrews 1, is the first lesson in this unit that begins on October 2. We turn on October 9 to two background Scriptures, Hebrews 3:1-6 and Matthew 7:24-29, to see how Jesus is portrayed as the Builder of the House. We encounter Jesus as The Great High Priest in the lesson for October 16 from Hebrews 4:14–5:10. Jesus is seen as The High Priest Forever in Hebrews 7, which we will delve into on October 23. This unit ends on October 30 with a lesson from Hebrews 12:1-13 as we learn about Christ as the Pioneer and Perfecter of Our Faith.

The final four lessons, which compose Unit 3, titled Alpha and Omega, look at the metaphors in Revelation of one who makes all things new, a vision of the New Jerusalem, a river of life, and the beginning and end of all things to explore how God reigns. The unit starts on November 6 with Everything Is Brand New, rooted in Revelation 21:1-8. I See a New Jerusalem, the session on November 13, examines the eternal beauty of the heavenly city as seen in Revelation 21:9-27. The Living Water, described in Revelation 22:1-7 in the lesson for November 20, brings life and healing. The unit concludes on November 27 with titles depicting Christ—Alpha and Omega—as found in Revelation 22:8-21.

# MEET OUR WRITER

## DR. JERRY L. SUMNEY

Dr. Jerry L. Sumney is a member of the Society of Biblical Literature and is past president for the Southeastern Region of the society. At the national level, he also served as the chair of the steering committee for the Theology of the Disputed Paulines Group from 1996 through 2001 and currently serves as the chair of the steering committee for the Disputed Paulines Section. He is also currently chair for the Pauline Epistles and Literature Section of the International Meeting of the Society of Biblical Literature. He was elected to membership in the Studiorum Novi Testamenti Societas (SNTS) in 2005.

Dr. Sumney has written six books: *The Bible: An Introduction* (2010); *Colossians: A Commentary*, New Testament Library Series (2008); *Philippians, A Handbook for Second-Year Greek Students* (2007); *Servants of Satan, False Brothers, and Other Pauline Opponents (1999); Preaching Apocalyptic Texts* (coauthored with Larry Paul Jones (1999); and *Identifying Paul's Opponents (1990).* He is editor of *The Order of the Ministry: Equipping the Saints* (2002) and coeditor of *Theology and Ethics in Paul and His Interpreters* (1996), *Paul and Pathos (2001),* and *Romans* in the Society of Biblical Literature Bible Resources series (2012). Dr. Sumney also has written more than thirty articles in journals and books. He also contributed entries to the *New Interpreter's Dictionary of the Bible* and the *Dictionary of the Later New Testament and Its Developments,* and *Dictionary of Scripture and Ethics.* In addition, he is a contributor to *The College Study Bible* and the *CEB Study Bible.*

Prior to joining the faculty of Lexington Theological Seminary (LTS) where he is Professor of Biblical Studies, he taught in the religion department at Ferrum College from 1986 through 1997. He received his B.A. from David Lipscomb University in 1978, his M.A. from Harding University in 1982, and his Ph.D. from Southern Methodist University in 1987.

Dr. Sumney has presented papers at regional, national, and international academic conferences. He has also led numerous workshops for elders and deacons; Bible study workshops and series, including in the Lay School of Theology at LTS and in the school for licensed ministers sponsored by the Kentucky region of the Christian Church. He is the regular teacher of an adult Sunday school class in his home church, Central Christian Church (Disciples of Christ), in Lexington.

Jerry and his wife, Diane, have three daughters: Elizabeth, Victoria, and Margaret.

# THE BIG PICTURE: GOD IN ISAIAH, HEBREWS, AND REVELATION

This quarter's lessons come primarily from three different types of books of the Bible. Each represents a different kind of writing and addresses an audience facing very different questions. So we must look at each one individually.

The book of Isaiah was written over the course of some two hundred to three hundred years by three different prophets, all of whom are referred to as Isaiah. The original Isaiah, who lived in Jerusalem during the eighth century B.C., spoke to the kings and people of Judah. He prophesied during the time that the nation of Israel, also known as the Northern Kingdom, was attacked and defeated by the Assyrians. He saw the threat to Judah and called the people to faithfulness to God, telling them that if they did not repent, the nation would fall. His oracles were collected and began to be set in book form either during or soon after his lifetime. Most of chapters 1–39 are from this original Isaiah.

The second prophet who went by the name Isaiah was active while Judah was in exile in Babylon. We can tell this Isaiah was in Babylon because he contrasted God with the gods of the Babylonians rather than the gods of the Canaanites, as the first Isaiah had done. This prophet proclaimed the good news that the exile was about to end and that the people would be allowed to return to Palestine. This return fulfilled God's promises and showed that the people remained in covenant with God. This prophet emphasized consolation. Prophesying in the final years of the exile (about 545–539 B.C.), this prophet often spoke in long poetic oracles. His work appears in chapters 40–55.

The final section of Isaiah is written after the people of Judah have returned to Jerusalem. It is written by either the same prophet who wrote in exile or someone who adopted his style. Chapters 56–66 are called Third Isaiah because the material in them comes from this later set of circumstances and addresses different concerns. When he wrote, the first wave of exiles had returned home. But the beginning of their new life was not as glorious as what Second Isaiah had envisioned. Things were not all comfortable and they were facing opposition from some who were residents in the area of Jerusalem when they arrived. Third Isaiah assures its readers that God is faithful and that God will save them from their opponents. Thus, they will eventually experience the blessings of God.

Our readings in Unit 1 come from all three Isaiahs. As we will see, all three—chapters 11, 25, 40, and 61—offer hope and call for faithfulness. Our first Isaiah reading (from chapter 11) comes from the original Isaiah who primarily called the people to repent and warned of consequences if they did not. But it is a passage that offers great hope after the time of punishment, if the people repent. Our second Isaiah reading (chapter 25) comes from a section of the book whose style suggests to many interpreters that it is written by yet a different author but included here because the hope it offers is consistent with the message of Isaiah. All parts of the book of Isaiah remind the people that God is faithful to the covenant and that God has the power to fulfill the promised blessings.

Hebrews is one of the most distinctive books of the New Testament. Interpreters have struggled to identify its literary type, with many concluding that it is something like an extended sermon or homily. More than any other book, it relies on quotations from the Hebrew Bible and on its readers' knowledge of Judaism. The primary audience of Hebrews is Jewish Christians. When Jews became members of the church in the earliest days, they remained observant Jews even as they were church members. For these Jews there was no contradiction between being believers in Christ and being faithful members of the synagogue. In fact, the apostles themselves continued to be faithful Jews and to worship and offer sacrifices in the Temple, as well as being regular members of their local synagogues. At some point, some synagogue members who were not in the church began to reject those who were in the church. That trend may have begun when the church began accepting Gentiles without requiring them to convert fully to Judaism or when they began to make more exalted claims about Jesus. This opposition worsened when the Jerusalem Temple was destroyed in A.D. 70. Some Jews who were not in the church may have thought that what they saw as the unfaithfulness of the Jews in the church was part of the reason God had allowed the Temple to fall. After all, early prophets had said that the original Temple would fall because of unfaithfulness, and it had. Later prophets had said that a more glorious Temple and nation would arise when the people were faithful. But now the Second Temple had also fallen—and its fall was interpreted by some as the result of unfaithfulness. Whether Hebrews was written shortly before or after the fall of the Temple (and there is significant debate about which it is), the Jewish church members it is written to are facing increasing rejection from their fellow Jews outside the church.

Hebrews is written to encourage believers who are being pressured to abandon faith in Christ and return to a form of Judaism that does not include Christ. The pressure has gotten to the point that Hebrews sees it as persecution. To combat this pressure, Hebrews tells of the great blessings believers have in Christ and makes a series of comparisons between Judaism and the church. The writer constantly claims that the blessings in Christ are greater than those in Judaism without Christ. He makes these comparisons as stark as he can so that his readers can see that the blessings are greater than the troubles they endure for being in the church. But even as he says that the blessings in Christ are greater, he acknowledges that there are significant blessings in Judaism. Unlike what we find in Paul and other New Testament writers, Hebrews rejects participation in or questions the validity of the Jerusalem Temple services. If Hebrews is written before A.D. 70, his point is to keep Jewish church members from relying on those services rather than on Christ as the means by which they maintain their relationship with God. If the book is written after A.D. 70 (as a majority of scholars think), then the rejection of its services is a way of affirming that the Temple is not needed for Jewish church members to continue their intimate relationship with God. Either way, the constant theme is the superiority of the church over the Temple and Judaism.

These comparisons make Hebrews a dangerous book for us. It is easy for us to denigrate Judaism and simply claim superiority as Christians. But we must remember that this book is written by a Jewish author for Jewish Christians who are doubting their decision to have faith in Christ. They recognize the ways God is present in the Mosaic covenant and they know the blessings and relationship they have with God in it. This book does argue that there are more and better blessings in Christ than in the Mosaic covenant, but it recognizes that there is real relationship with God and substantial blessings in the earlier covenant. In our reading of it, we must celebrate the blessings we have in Christ without denigrating the blessings of the Mosaic covenant.

The third book that a major portion of our texts come from is Revelation. Its literary type is called apocalyptic. Writings of this type have a heavenly being mediate a special message to someone on earth to reveal God's plan to set things right in the world. These writings come from communities in crisis. They appear when it seems that the forces of evil are so great that they will overcome the people and purposes of God. When God's people are being persecuted and evil seems to be overpowering God's will, it suggests that either God is not as powerful as we say God is or else that God is not as loving and just as we say. Apocalyptic texts give assurance that God has the power and the will to defeat evil and to vindicate the faithful. Their most central purpose is to assert that God is the God of power, justice, and love that we say God is. Because God has these characteristics, God will not allow the wicked to prevail. These writings say this will be evident when God acts to bring ultimate salvation and judgment. This literature looks beyond and behind the scenes to tell its readers that God will not let the wicked get away with harming them and that God will vindicate their faithfulness. When all is said and done, the blessings that the faithful receive far outweigh any suffering they endure for the faith. Since this is the final resolution of things, God's justice, love, and power are what determine the character of final existence.

A second important task of apocalyptic writings is to exhort the persecuted to remain faithful. By assuring them about the character of God and about God's determination to act to save the faithful and punish the wicked, these texts remind the faithful that the difficulties they endure will be worth it in the end. God will not allow their suffering to be the last word; they will receive blessings that far outweigh their suffering. The audience of these books is the faithful who may be wavering. These believers are wondering if they had made a mistake when they turned from other gods to the one God. After all, you would think that turning to the true God would mean that your life would get better. But the opposite has been the case. Apocalyptic works argue (and all the New Testament agrees) that evil has taken control of the world, that God is not in immediate control. While God has ultimate power and will one day assert it, at the moment evil is in control. These powers of evil punish faithful people for turning to God. God does not intervene to stop this at the moment, but God's response will come and will be decisive. Then evil will be subdued and God's faithful people will be vindicated. The job of God's people now is to be faithful in the midst of a world dominated by powers that oppose God's will. While this analysis of the world makes us nervous, we can see the truth in it when we think of the ways we are trapped in systems that implicate us in unjust systems. Examples include our participation in an economic system that relies on child labor or near-slave conditions to make tennis shoes and all sorts of clothing (remember the garment factory fires in Bangladesh and Pakistan) or even our tax system that requires us to pay for things we think are wrong (perhaps weapons or some medical procedures or any number of things—few of us think everything the government spends money on advances the kingdom of God). Writers and readers of apocalyptic texts are the recipients of the ill effects of those systems rather than those who benefit from them.

By the time John writes Revelation, there is a two-hundred-year tradition of writing in this style. John draws on that tradition for the imagery he uses. The language is dramatic, even grotesque (for example, chapter 17 or 19:17-18). These images are intended to shock. They must be dramatic enough to illustrate to the oppressed that the power of God is greater than those powers that now tyrannize them and the world. As the literary tradition shows, all of the imagery is symbolic; none is to be taken literally. So as we read Revelation, we must look for what it wants to tell us about salvation or about the defeat of evil without thinking that the descriptions it gives are the literal reality. John is grasping for ways to express how certain God's victory is over evil and how glorious salvation is.

# CLOSE-UP: COMPARISON OF PRIESTLY TYPES

| Category | Levitical Priests | Jesus | Biblical References |
|---|---|---|---|
| Tribe of origin | Levi | Judah | Hebrews 7:14 |
| Kind of person | Sinner | Holy, blameless, undefiled, separated from sinners, exalted | Hebrews 7:26-27 |
| Number of priests | Many | One | Hebrews 7:23-24 |
| Time in priesthood | Temporary, due to mortality | Eternal priest in heaven | Hebrews 7:23-24; 9:12 |
| Frequency of sacrifice | Daily | Once for all | Hebrews 7:27; 9:12 |
| People for whom sacrifice was offered | Offered for the people and for themselves | Offered only for others | Hebrews 7:26-27 |
| Type of sacrifices | Animals | Himself | Hebrews 9:11-14 |
| Place where sacrifices were offered | Tent (tabernacle) made by humans | Holy Place | Hebrews 9:11-12 |
| How appointed to the priesthood | By the law, which appointed people prone to weakness | By God, who appointed a Son made perfect forever | Hebrews 7:28 |

## Biblical References to Melchizedek

| | |
|---|---|
| Referred to as "King of Salem" (likely Jerusalem) | Genesis 14:18; Hebrews 7:1 |
| Name means "king of righteousness" and "king of peace" | Hebrews 7:2 |
| Referred to as "priest of God Most High" | Genesis 14:18 |
| Provided bread and wine for troops returning with Abram | Genesis 14:18 |
| Offered blessing for both God and Abram | Genesis 14:19-20; Hebrews 7:1 |
| Received tithe (ten percent) of spoils of war from Abram | Genesis 14:20; Hebrews 7:2, 4 |
| Jesus said to be a priest "according to the order of Melchizedek" | Hebrews 6:20 |
| Melchizedek has no earthly mother or father or genealogy | Hebrews 7:3 |
| No beginning or end recorded for his life | Hebrews 7:3 |
| Resembles the Son of God | Hebrews 7:3 |
| Melchizedek's priesthood is forever | Hebrews 7:3 |
| Greatness described in relation to Abram and the Levitical priests | Hebrews 7:4-10 |
| Jesus compared to Melchizedek | Hebrews 7:11-22 |
| Jesus is "a priest forever according to the order of Melchizedek" | Psalm 110:4 Partially quoted in Hebrews 7:21 |

# FAITH IN ACTION: LIVING IN THE LIGHT OF GOD'S SOVEREIGNTY

During the fall quarter we have been considering the sovereign nature of God. A sovereign is someone who holds supreme leadership powers. Thus, when we mention the sovereign God we are referring to the one who possesses ultimate power.

Help the students relate to the sovereign God by posting these activities at the beginning of September and encouraging the adults to do as many as they can over the course of this quarter. Plan occasional opportunities during class for participants to report on any activities they have tried.

1. Examine your own behavior. How are you acting in ways that affirm your belief that God is in charge? Which of your behaviors deny God's rightful place as sovereign? What changes will you make?
2. Make a list of people and situations for which intercessory prayer is needed. Pray daily for each person and situation on your list. Trust God to act with supreme power according to the divine will on behalf of each person or situation.
3. Speak with Jesus daily about your own needs and shortcomings. Ask him to intercede on your behalf before God the Father.
4. Ponder your understandings of the Second Coming of Christ. Do you expect him to return to earth in glory? If so, what do you expect to happen when he comes? What are you doing—or could you be doing—to prepare yourself to meet him when he comes again or at your death?
5. Think about changes that you have seen in your congregation, denomination, or the Christian church at large over the course of your lifetime. Which of these changes do you find positive? Why? Which do you find negative? Why?
6. Skim through the Book of Revelation. Jot down any images that seem to have meaning for you. Try to locate some artwork depicting these images. Spend time with this art so as to allow God to teach you through these images.
7. Help someone who is going through one of life's storms to find patience, endurance, and the self-discipline necessary to weather the crisis. Support this person in prayer. Also offer whatever hands-on assistance this person seems willing to accept.
8. Take action to be a good steward of the water of life. Do whatever you can to conserve water and keep water free from contamination. Encourage others to also be good stewards of this essential resource for life.

9. Recall from the lesson for November 6 that our sovereign God promises to make all things new. What needs to be made new in your church? For example, are there toys or furnishings in the church nursery or Sunday school rooms that need to be replaced? Work with others to throw a "baby shower" or "birthday party" to collect new toys and supplies while also providing an entertaining afternoon for the children of the church.

# PRONUNCIATION GUIDE

apocalyptic (uh pok uh lip' tik)
*archēgos* (ar khay gos')
*maranatha* (mair uh nath' uh
   OR mahr uh nath' uh)
Melchizedek (mel kiz' uh dek)
Parousia (puh roo' zhee uh)

UNIT 1: THE SOVEREIGNTY OF GOD
# The Peaceful Kingdom

---

## PREVIEWING THE LESSON

**Lesson Scripture:** Isaiah 11:1-9
**Background Scripture:** Isaiah 11:1-9
**Key Verse:** Isaiah 11:9

### Focus of the Lesson:
We live in a world full of divisions, hatred, trouble, and chaos. Will we ever experience harmony? Isaiah's prophecy reveals that the sovereign God will bring about a world of peace.

### Goals for the Learners:
(1) to identify the ways God acts as well as the key descriptors of God's peaceful kingdom.
(2) to look forward to the day when Christian communities will be known for their godly life of peace.
(3) to identify an area of church or community life that does not meet God's intention for peace and develop a strategy to address it.

### Supplies:
Bibles, newsprint and marker, paper and pencils, hymnals, optional index cards

---

## READING THE SCRIPTURE

NRSV
Lesson Scripture: Isaiah 11:1-9
¹A shoot shall come out from the
    stump of Jesse,
  and a branch shall grow out of
    his roots.
²The spirit of the LORD shall rest
    on him,
  the spirit of wisdom and

CEB
Lesson Scripture: Isaiah 11:1-9
¹A shoot will grow up from the
    stump of Jesse;
  a branch will sprout from his roots.
²The LORD's spirit will rest upon him,
  a spirit of wisdom and
    understanding,
  a spirit of planning and strength,

understanding,
  the spirit of counsel and might,
  the spirit of knowledge and the
    fear of the LORD.
³His delight shall be in the fear of
    the LORD.
He shall not judge by what his
    eyes see,
  or decide by what his ears hear;
⁴but with righteousness he shall
    judge the poor,
  and decide with equity for the
    meek of the earth;
he shall strike the earth with the rod
    of his mouth,
  and with the breath of his lips he
    shall kill the wicked.
⁵Righteousness shall be the belt
    around his waist,
  and faithfulness the belt around
    his loins.
⁶The wolf shall live with the lamb,
  the leopard shall lie down with
    the kid,
the calf and the lion and the fatling
    together,
  and a little child shall lead them.
⁷The cow and the bear shall graze,
  their young shall lie down
    together;
  and the lion shall eat straw like
    the ox.
⁸The nursing child shall play over
    the hole of the asp,
  and the weaned child shall put its
    hand on the adder's den.
⁹**They will not hurt or destroy**
  **on all my holy mountain;**
**for the earth will be full of the**
  **knowledge of the LORD**
  **as the waters cover the sea.**

a spirit of knowledge and fear
  of the Lord.
³He will delight in fearing the LORD.
He won't judge by appearances,
  nor decide by hearsay.
⁴He will judge the needy with
  righteousness,
  and decide with equity for those
  who suffer in the land.
He will strike the violent with the
  rod of his mouth;
  by the breath of his lips he will
    kill the wicked.
⁵Righteousness will be the belt
  around his hips,
  and faithfulness the belt around
    his waist.
⁶The wolf will live with the lamb,
  and the leopard will lie down with
    the young goat;
  the calf and the young lion will
    feed together,
  and a little child will lead them.
⁷The cow and the bear will graze.
  Their young will lie down
    together,
  and a lion will eat straw like an ox.
⁸A nursing child will play over the
    snake's hole;
  toddlers will reach right over the
    serpent's den.
⁹**They won't harm or destroy**
  **anywhere on my holy**
  **mountain.**
  **The earth will surely be filled**
  **with the knowledge of**
  **the LORD,**
**just as the water covers the sea.**

# UNDERSTANDING THE SCRIPTURE

**Introduction.** The first ten chapters of Isaiah consist largely of a series of oracles, though there are narratives that give a context for the oracles. Some oracles are warnings of coming doom for Judah and Israel for their unfaithfulness (1:2-31; 2:5–3:15; 3:16–4:1; 5:1-30). These are relieved with promises of restoration and blessing (2:1-4; 4:2-6). These threatening and reassuring oracles appear in the context of the threat of the Assyrian army. When that great empire conquers the Northern Kingdom of Israel, the small nation of Judah is the only remaining nation comprising predominantly Israelites—and it is under threat. While Isaiah envisions Assyria as the instrument of God's punishment of Israel, he also accuses it of arrogance toward God and of excessive violence (10:5-19, 33-34). Because of this arrogance, Assyria will also be punished by God and so cease to be a threat to God's people. This promise of punishing the Assyrians appears just before our passage. So if Assyria is to be punished, what does that mean for God's people? Our passage is Isaiah's answer.

**Isaiah 11:1-3a.** Chapter 11 describes a glorious time after the end of the oppression by Assyria, a time when God's will is done through God's people. It begins with the image of a shoot growing out of a stump. This is especially appropriate imagery at this point in Isaiah. Isaiah has described the result of God's judgment on God's own people to be that they are cut off with only a stump remaining, a stump that is burned (6:13). But now the word of hope is that God can revive even that stump. Now the

stump stands for the Davidic dynasty. It is called the stump of Jesse because Jesse is David's father. After the devastation, God will bring new life to God's people.

This restoration comes when the Spirit of the Lord comes on the descendant of David. The Spirit was seldom present in this era. It came at times on prophets, judges, and kings, but it did not just stay on them. Its coming was often disruptive, a moment of God breaking into the world in an unusual way. Sometimes it brought a prophecy or insight; other times great strength. But in the new time of restoration, the Spirit stays on this new leader. It is through God's Spirit that the king is given knowledge, wisdom, discernment, and power. These are the attributes of an ideal king. They are attributes that humans only aspire to or pretend to possess. But the Spirit of God bestows them on this king. The characteristic that Isaiah emphasizes most, however, is the "fear of the LORD." He mentions it twice in a row (11:2 and 3a). It is not the Assyrians that the king should fear, but God. Fearing the Lord means more than being afraid, though in a book that has threatened judgment and destruction fear should not be left out. But this fear is more the awe that one experiences in the face of the mighty work God is performing. It acknowledges that God is the one who makes nations powerful and brings them down. This ideal king that Isaiah describes not only fears God but he also takes pleasure in recognizing that it is God's power that establishes a great future for Judah. This understanding is in stark contrast to the arrogant Assyria in the previous chapter that boasted of its own power and was struck down.

**Isaiah 11:3b-5.** One of the characteristics that emperors claimed for themselves in the ancient Near East was that they brought peace and justice to their realm. For example, Hammurabi, an eighteenth-century B.C. king of Babylonia, asserted that he had been commissioned by the gods to bring justice to the land. So the ideal king of Judah will bring social justice to the land. One of the dominant sins that the prophets of Isaiah's time condemned was the oppression of the poor and powerless by the wealthy and powerful. Judah's king, who has the Spirit of the Lord, will enforce justice. The NRSV translation of 11:3 seems strange. It says that the king will not judge by what he sees or hears. The CEB captures the meaning of this expression when it says that "He won't judge by appearances, nor decide by hearsay." Fair and truthful judgment will prevail. This dispensing of justice involves both the raising of the poor and the destruction of the wicked. This text assumes that only a greater power can put an end to the injustice that the wealthy impose on those below them. Such destruction of the wicked is here part of establishing justice. This description of the king concludes by noting that righteousness and faithfulness will be constant aspects of his character and his reign. Again, this is in sharp contrast to the description of the king and the nation in the previous chapters of Isaiah. In those chapters the king and the nation turn from God and so reap injustice and disaster. The king who lives and reigns faithfully in righteousness brings justice and peace.

**Isaiah 11:6-9.** Among the most beautiful descriptions of what God wants for the world appears in these verses. The predator and the prey exist together peacefully; killers become harmless, even to children. All is good and right with the world. This idealized vision of life in harmony with the will of God points back to the time before the Fall in Eden, as the reference to the snake suggests. Isaiah envisions the return of the nation with their ideal king as a return to a time when there was no sin and no consequences of sin in the world. That is how wonderful life will be. This is how certain Isaiah is that the fall of the nation and the exile of the people does not mean that God has deserted them. God's faithfulness means that God will restore them and do so in glorious fashion. Importantly, this time of goodness and life is present because "knowledge of the LORD" (11:9) fills the land. When the people know and live in accord with the will of God, justice and peace are the order of the day.

---

## INTERPRETING THE SCRIPTURE

*The Spirit of the Lord Is with God's People*

One of the outstanding features of Isaiah's poetic vision of the return of Judah from exile is his assertion that the Spirit of God will be with them. The pledge that the Spirit will be with the king promises a more intimate presence of God than the people had known before. The Spirit's presence brings knowledge of God's word and will. It also brings acknowledgment of the awe-inspiring things God does. It is the source of the people's understanding and experience of God. This new understanding of God calls God's people to live together in new ways. They must no longer engage in the practices that brought judgment; this new presence and knowledge of God brings a new way to live in personal, business, and civic life.

In its earliest days, the church proclaimed that the time had come when the Spirit was on all of God's people, not just their leader. It proclaimed that this intimate experience of God was no longer only for leaders and prophets, but for all who turn to God through Christ. The Spirit brings assurance of God's presence and love, but does even more: The Spirit helped the church discern and know the will of God. Further, the distribution of the Spirit to all in the church suggested that all had access to God and that all were one. Thus, all should be treated fairly. As the place of the presence of God, the church should grant no privilege to those whom the rest of the world saw as more valuable. So the church proclaimed that in their community slave and free, and women and men, were of equal status. This is what the indwelling of the Spirit reveals. This understanding of God's will led believers to share their possessions in radical ways. Acts tells of members selling agricultural estates, the common means by which the wealthy made money, to support the poor in their midst (Acts 2:44-45; 6:1-7). The indwelling Spirit calls the church to orient itself in a new way. It must honor those that others denigrate because they lack wealth or power; and they must offer support, including financial support, to church members who need help. After all, they have seen that these members are so valuable that God's Spirit lives in them.

*God Wants Justice for All of God's People*

The leader that Isaiah envisions is, in an important sense, the representative of God's people. He is a leader, but he also embodies what God wants for all people. As leader and representative, he begins to establish what God wants for the world. As we have seen, he is blessed with the Spirit and so with knowledge of God. The direct result of this knowledge of God is that he begins to administer true justice throughout the land. It was common practice in the ancient world for judges to rule in favor of the wealthy. Cases were often determined by bribery or by whether you were a friend of the judge or whether you knew a friend of the judge. The oracles in the first part of Isaiah see disaster coming, in part, because the courts do not give a fair hearing to the poor. But when the kingdom is established with knowledge of God as the guide for how to live, justice will reign. Cases will no longer be decided by the status of the litigants or even by hearsay evidence. The legal system will be just.

It is not just the legal system that fostered injustice; it is the entire social structure. Part of the reason the legal system was such an issue was that it was the means the wealthy used to take possession of the land of the poor. As they amassed more wealth and turned small farmers into tenant farmers, they held more power over them and so could abuse them more. But the kingdom that is established with the knowledge of God renders justice and equity to the poor.

The social system that is pleasing to God, that reflects knowledge of God, will be one that is just. It offers no advantages to those with more wealth or status. All are recognized as the children of God. This acknowledgment of the identity of all as God's children means that those who are the people of God must work beyond the walls of the church to establish structures and institutions that reflect knowledge of God and, therefore, operate on the basis of justice and equity. Isaiah assumes that when God's people know God's will, it leads them to work for a world that reflects what God wants it to be. The world that reflects who God is and what God wants is a world in which justice is given to the poor. The systems of government and commerce that reflect God's will do not give advantages to the rich and well connected.

But there is a threatening aspect to this work. Justice will not flourish unless those who oppose it are disempowered. The wicked will be struck down. The overthrow of unjust systems is not easy work; power must be wrested from them by those who work for justice. This aspect of God's kingdom is difficult for us to think about. We like to think that all people will just be reasonable and see the truth of God's will. But, of course, we know that is not true. The struggles of many in the United States to have their rights acknowledged demonstrate that power has to be exerted to defeat those who would deny justice to all. For righteousness and justice to thrive, unjust social and economic systems must be dismantled. This is part of the work establishing God's kingdom.

### God's Will Is Sure

Just as the ruler, the shoot from the stump of Jesse, is idealized as a king, so also is the result of his reign. Isaiah envisions the coming of God's kingdom as a time that will right all the ills of the world. Things will be as God has always wanted them. Even things that seem so ingrained that they are a part of the natural order will be changed: Lions won't hunt lambs but rather will be herded by children; snakes will no longer frighten or threaten life. Indeed, this is a return to Eden. The time when justice is the order of the day is when the will of God for the world is established. It is a beautiful moment; all that threatens peace and security is transformed. The emphasis on knowledge of God resurfaces at the end of this poetic vision of God's kingdom. The time in which God's peace rules is the time when knowledge of God covers the world. Just as it all began with the ruler having knowledge of God, now its accomplishment indicates that God is known by all.

As much as the coming king will work to accomplish God's purposes, we should note that the power and initiative are from God. God causes the branch to grow and sends God's Spirit. Isaiah can be confident about the coming of such a day of peace because its coming does not merely rely on human effort. This outcome is sure because God is the one who guarantees it.

# SHARING THE SCRIPTURE

## PREPARING TO TEACH

### Preparing Our Hearts

Ponder this week's devotional reading from Psalm 72:1-7. What does the psalmist pray for on behalf of this ideal king? How do the actions of this king affect the people under his rule? What is the psalmist's prayer for the king himself? If you were to pray for an ideal ruler, what traits would you want to see in this person? How would you support this person?

Pray that you and the students will intercede on behalf of those elected to rule over you.

### Preparing Our Minds

Study the background Scripture and the lesson Scripture, which are both from Isaiah 11:1-9.

Consider these questions: *Given that the world is full of divisions, hatred, trouble, and chaos, do you expect to ever experience harmony? If so, under what circumstances?*

Write on newsprint:
❏ information for next week's lesson, found under Continue the Journey.
❏ activities for further spiritual growth in Continue the Journey.

Review The Big Picture and Faith in Action, which immediately precede this lesson. Be prepared to read the portions concerning Isaiah in The Big Picture: God in Isaiah, Hebrews, and Revelation. Post activities found on the page titled Faith in Action: Living in the Light of God's Sovereignty.

## LEADING THE CLASS

### (1) Gather to Learn

❖ Welcome everyone and pray that those who have come today will seek to live in peace.

❖ Invite the adults to call out the names of countries in the world where there is division, hatred, and trouble. List these places on newsprint. Briefly identify reasons for the problems in the places the class has listed. Are there racial or ethnic conflicts? Are people competing for scarce resources, such as water? Is an outside force oppressing the people of the area?

❖ List places in your own region or community that are hotbeds of strife. Again, briefly identify reasons for this unrest.

❖ Read aloud today's focus statement: **We live in a world full of divisions, hatred, trouble, and chaos. Will we ever experience harmony? Isaiah's prophecy reveals that the sovereign God will bring about a world of peace.**

### (2) Goal 1: Identify the Way God Acts as Well as the Key Descriptors of God's Peaceful Kingdom

❖ Read the paragraphs referring to Isaiah in The Big Picture: God in Isaiah, Hebrews, and Revelation to set the stage for the sessions of the first unit, The Sovereignty of God.

❖ Distribute paper and pencils. Ask half of the group to listen for comments about the way God acts as today's Scripture is read and jot down those ideas. Ask the other half to listen for and jot down descriptions of God's peaceful kingdom. Select a volunteer to read Isaiah 11:1-9.

❖ Call on volunteers from the first group to say what they have learned about the way God acts. Fill in gaps by using information in Understanding the Scripture from Isaiah 1:1-3a and 3b-5.

❖ Note that the church has understood these passages to be fulfilled in Jesus and the reign of God that he ushers in.

❖ Ask: **In what ways do you perceive Isaiah 11:1-9 to be fulfilled in Jesus?**

❖ Invite volunteers from the second group to describe God's kingdom. Add to the discussion by using information in Understanding the Scripture from Isaiah 1:6-9.

❖ Ask: **Where do you see evidence of God's kingdom breaking into today's world?**

*(3) Goal 2: Look Forward to the Day When Christian Communities Will Be Known for Their Godly Life of Peace*

❖ Distribute index cards (or half sheets of paper) and pencils. Read: **A new family has moved into the community. They would like to give several churches a try but have been put off because of bad experiences in the past. Those experiences left them feeling that they could live more peacefully and closer to God if they just practiced their faith on their own and steered clear of a church. On your paper, write one reason why a family might choose to stay away from a church.** Collect the cards, shuffle them, and read the responses.

❖ Discuss this question: **What could a church do to change behaviors and attitudes so that visitors and members alike find peace, wholeness, and a real sense of community within the church?**

❖ Point out that as Spirit-filled people, believers have the means to bring about these changes. Read The Spirit of the Lord Is with God's People in Interpreting the Scripture.

❖ **Option:** Ask: **If class members had an opportunity to talk about their own congregation with this family seeking a church, what would they say about how they have found God's peace within this community of faith?**

*(4) Goal 3: Identify an Area of Church or Community Life that Does Not Meet God's Intention for Peace and Develop a Strategy to Address It*

❖ Read or retell God Wants Justice for All of God's People in Interpreting the Scripture.

❖ Repost the newsprint from the Gather to Learn portion where the students named situations in their community that are in need of God's peace. Form several small groups and ask each one to select a situation they would like to tackle. Distribute newsprint and a marker to each group and encourage them to answer this question: **What can we as Christians do to address this issue in ways that will help to solve this problem?**

❖ Call on a representative from each group to identify the situation and comment on how it could be addressed. Post each group's newsprint.

❖ Suggest that groups delve further into the issues to develop a concrete plan of action. Form one or more task forces that will meet outside of class to undertake this work. Set a date for these groups to report back and plan time to include their reports during the class session.

*(5) Continue the Journey*

❖ Pray that as the learners depart, they will go in peace to spread peace to everyone they encounter.

❖ Post information for next week's session on newsprint for the students to copy:

- **Title: The Mountain of God**
- **Background Scripture: Isaiah 25**
- **Lesson Scripture: Isaiah 25:6-10a**
- **Focus of the Lesson: Oppressed people are always looking for relief from their injustices. Who will deliver them? Isaiah's prophecy reveals that the sovereign God will give deliverance from oppression.**

❖ Challenge the adults to grow spiritually by completing one or more of these activities related to this week's session.

(1) **Act as a peacemaker in your home, church, or community this week to bring resolution to a problem that is causing dissension.**

(2) **Recall global situations of disharmony from the Gather to Learn portion. Ponder what these places would look like and how the people would act if God's peaceful kingdom broke in upon them. Pray that God will in fact bless these situations with peace.**

(3) **Think about people you know who are good at mediating conflicts. List any personality traits and skills that enable these people to be effective mediators. Evaluate yourself in light of this list. What skills and traits do you already have? How might you go about developing skills so as to be a more effective mediator?**

❖ Sing or read aloud "O Day of Peace That Dimly Shines."

❖ Conclude today's session by leading the class in this benediction, which is adapted from Hebrews 12:1b-2a, the key verses for October 30: **May we go forth empowered to run with perseverance the race that is set before us, looking to Jesus the pioneer and perfecter of our faith. Amen.**

UNIT 1: THE SOVEREIGNTY OF GOD

# THE MOUNTAIN OF GOD

## PREVIEWING THE LESSON

**Lesson Scripture:** Isaiah 25:6-10a
**Background Scripture:** Isaiah 25
**Key Verse:** Isaiah 25:8

### Focus of the Lesson:
Oppressed people are always looking for relief from their injustices. Who will deliver them? Isaiah's prophecy reveals that the sovereign God will give deliverance from oppression.

### Goals for the Learners:
(1) to understand that God acts in the best interests of all peoples and nations.
(2) to appreciate that God removes barriers that cause people to feel separated from God and one another.
(3) to rejoice that God gives hope to all oppressed peoples.

### Supplies:
Bibles, newsprint and marker, paper and pencils, hymnals

## READING THE SCRIPTURE

| NRSV | CEB |
|---|---|
| Lesson Scripture: Isaiah 25:6-10a | Lesson Scripture: Isaiah 25:6-10a |
| <sup>6</sup>On this mountain the LORD of hosts will make for all peoples a feast of rich food, a feast of well-aged wines, of rich food filled with marrow, of well-aged wines strained clear. | <sup>6</sup>On this mountain, the LORD of heavenly forces will prepare for all peoples a rich feast, a feast of choice wines, of select foods rich in flavor, of choice wines well refined. |
| <sup>7</sup>And he will destroy on this mountain the shroud that is cast over all peoples, | <sup>7</sup>He will swallow up on this mountain the veil that is veiling all peoples, |

the sheet that is spread over
    all nations;
⁸he will swallow up death forever.
**Then the Lᴏʀᴅ God will wipe
    away the tears from all faces,
  and the disgrace of his people he
will take away from all the earth,
    for the Lᴏʀᴅ has spoken.**
⁹It will be said on that day,
  Lo, this is our God; we have
    waited for him, so that he
    might save us.
  This is the Lᴏʀᴅ for whom we
    have waited;
  let us be glad and rejoice in
    his salvation.
¹⁰For the hand of the Lᴏʀᴅ will rest
  on this mountain.

the shroud enshrouding all nations.
⁸He will swallow up death forever.
**The Lᴏʀᴅ God will wipe tears
    from every face;
he will remove his people's
    disgrace from off the
    whole earth,
for the Lᴏʀᴅ has spoken.**
⁹They will say on that day,
"Look! This is our God,
  for whom we have waited—
  and he has saved us!
This is the Lᴏʀᴅ, for whom we
  have waited;
  let's be glad and rejoice in
  his salvation!"
¹⁰The Lᴏʀᴅ's hand will indeed
  rest on this mountain.

---

## UNDERSTANDING THE SCRIPTURE

**Introduction.** Chapter 25 is part of what is known as the Isaiah Apocalypse. This section consists of chapters 24–27. These chapters were written later than the sections of Isaiah that are around them. They are called an Apocalypse because they are written in an early form of what we see in full bloom in the Book of Revelation (the name of which in Greek is The Apocalypse). This kind of writing uses dramatic imagery of worldwide or cosmic disasters to speak of God's judgment and idyllic language to speak of the blessings God gives to the faithful. Both of these elements characterize the Isaiah Apocalypse. Chapter 24 portrays the coming judgment of God, describing the condemnation of the wicked as a verdict that will put to shame even the gods who rule the sun and moon (24:21-23). Then at the beginning of chapter 25 Isaiah praises God for the salvation that comes to God's people.

**Isaiah 25:1-5.** Isaiah gives thanks that God is now expelling the oppressors and rescuing those who were oppressed. The oppressors in this passage are most likely the Babylonians who took Judah into exile. It seems their empire has now fallen. Isaiah can identify this as a cause for rejoicing because he sees it as a part of a divine plan to rescue God's people; it is a beginning of God's plan that was "formed of old, faithful and sure" (25:1). Even though Judah is still in exile, God has begun to act to free the people.

**Isaiah 25:6-8.** The extravagant banquet described here is sometimes understood as the feast that accompanied the enthronement of a new king. This most sumptuous meal has food fit for the celebration of a king's reign. The new king here is God who returns to reign in Jerusalem, that capital of Judah where his Temple had been.

When God takes the throne "on this mountain," that is, on Mount Zion (Jerusalem), it means the restoration of God's people.

This description of God's enthronement feast stands in some tension with the texts that surround it. In verses 1-5 the prophet celebrates the fall of a "fortified city" and in verses 10b-12 he chronicles the fall of Moab. But in this description of the feast all people are invited (25:6). When God reigns, all are welcome to come and be fed. There have been hints in other places in Isaiah that Israel's enemies could turn to God (19:16-25), and here all people join in the celebration of God's reign. At the same time, the celebration is held in Jerusalem. God remains the God of Abraham, Moses, and David, but now is recognized and honored by all peoples. The tension between this assertion of the universal invitation to come to God and the verses that describe the destruction of other nations indicates that the problem with those nations is not that they have been the enemies of Israel. Rather, the problem with them is that they are engaged in the same kinds of behaviors that brought judgment to Israel and Judah. They are destroyed or conquered because they refuse God's invitation to come to the feast. The celebration in verse 6, however, envisions them turning to God, coming to recognize God's power and rule. Perhaps Isaiah sees the way God has rescued Judah and been faithful to its people as the thing that has led the whole world to recognize God's sovereignty.

Isaiah sees the day of God's rule as a time when all that diminishes life is overcome. It is a time when even death is defeated. The shroud that is lifted in verse 7 is the shroud of mourning that was traditionally worn during the period of mourning for the dead (2 Samuel 15:30; 19:5; Esther 6:12). For all who come to God, death is "swallowed up." Some interpreters see this image as one that reverses a Canaanite image of death swallowing all people. Others think it uses the image of a myth in which a god named Death (Mot) swallows the god Baal and so begins the dry and unproductive season of the year. When the god Death is overcome in the spring, fertility returns. Whichever image Isaiah draws on, death seems to be more than just the inevitable end of life. It seems to be a power that overtakes all people. But in this time of the reign of God, it ceases to be a threat to those who turn to God. This is not a resurrection, but rather an eradication of death. Belief in a resurrection had not yet developed within Judaism when this poetic text is written. Still, Isaiah envisions a blessed time when all people are invited to live with God without the threat of death.

It is not just death that is overcome, but all that brings sadness is gone. At the same time, the disgrace of God's people the Israelites is removed. So once again, the particularity of Isaiah's vision contributes to his description of this blessed time. Even as all people come to God, God's faithfulness to the chosen people is highlighted. Again, perhaps it is this manifestation of God's faithfulness that brings all people to trust God.

**Isaiah 25:9-10a.** It is difficult to say who the prophet is referring to in verse 9. Who is it that will speak of "our God" and call God by the holy name? It may be the people of Judah or all those who have come to celebrate God's reign. Whoever the speakers are, the central point is about God:

God is the one who saves. God is the one with the power to rescue from enemies, and even from death. This salvation comes solely from God. It is God's power, not that of the people or their leaders. The task of the people here is to "wait," that is, to trust God to be faithful to God's promises. Now on the day of this banquet, the people who have trusted God can rejoice and praise God because the promises have been fulfilled. God has come bringing lasting salvation and blessing; God is resting (that is, living) with the people.

**Isaiah 25:10b-12.** This pronouncement of judgment and destruction against the people of Moab, who will "be trodden down," seems out of place after the celebratory mood of the previous verses.

---

# INTERPRETING THE SCRIPTURE

### The Lord's Feast

Isaiah begins our reading by describing a lavish feast. It is a meal that has all of the most expensive food and drink. It is a meal fit for a king—and it is for the King. Still, God sets it before God's people. Isaiah envisions a time when God will shower unprecedented blessing on God's people. In the surrounding verses Isaiah describes the end of oppression. This feast is set before those who have been oppressed. God's reign means that good things come to those who have been oppressed. As we read this description of an opulent feast we should remember that there was a great deal of food deprivation in that era. Many people often went hungry. Isaiah's image of the time of God's reign, then, solves one of the biggest problems that many of those he addresses know too well. Hunger is not replaced simply by sufficient food but by extravagant abundance. God's rescue of the people brings blessing that is nearly beyond imagination.

This feast is the precursor to the descriptions of the messianic banquet that will appear in later literature. These meals are a part of the writers' vision of the world when things work as God wants them to work. There is always abundant food and joy. The people live in security and peace under the rule of God's Messiah. In the New Testament this image of a feast is also used to describe the time of God's rule (for example, Revelation 19:9 where we find the marriage feast of the Lamb). This feast is the symbol for the life promised to those who turn to God.

### All Are Invited

Given where this description of God's reign appears in Isaiah, it is surprising to hear that "all peoples" are present (25:6). The verses that come before this celebrate the fall of Judah's oppressor Babylon, and the verses that follow it look forward to the punishment of Moab, a hostile neighbor. But in our reading, even those who have treated God's people badly are present. All who are willing to turn to God are present at God's banquet. Isaiah sees a time when all people turn to God and so receive God's blessings. When God takes the throne, the invitation to join the celebration will be issued to all people. The oppressors and their collaborators are there. So are the exiles, the poor, and the rejected. God invites all people to accept the abundance that can come only from God.

This is a jarring idea. We can understand how God rescues the oppressed and grants them relief. But here it is not just the poor or even the indifferent who receive God's mercy; even the enemies of God's people accept the invitation and so live in God's presence and receive God's blessings. God establishes a universal reign that takes in all the world. God's desire is to bless all nations and peoples. It is hard for us to think about God wanting to bless those who oppress the poor or who perpetrate violence against the innocent. It is especially hard to see God inviting our enemies. But Isaiah sees those who have destroyed God's capital city and killed its residents being invited to this banquet. These people are worse than terrorists; they have actually conquered and exiled God's people. Yet they are invited—and they accept. They are present at the banquet. No sin is so great that God cannot forgive and take in the sinner. No evil is beyond God's power to change and reconcile.

We struggle to reconcile this vision of all people being at God's banquet with God's needing to bring justice for the oppressed and injured. But Isaiah sees a time when God's mercy wins over even the enemies of God's people and God's purposes. When God's faithfulness and love are seen in the restoration of God's people, those whose hearts were filled with evil turn to God. Even those who formerly rejected God are brought into the feast. God's will for the world has all people turning from those things that keep them away from God and has God bringing all kinds of people and nations into the fullness of blessings that can come only by being in relationship with God.

New Testament writers take up this theme of a universal invitation. In Matthew (8:11) and Luke (13:29) people from all over the earth come to the feast. To do so, however, they must turn to God. In Isaiah that is symbolized by them coming to Jerusalem, the city in which God has promised to live and reign. In the New Testament passages this is seen by the comparison between those from afar who will be present and those close at hand who will not. Those excluded are those who refuse to acknowledge and obey God. Still, Isaiah's placement of this scene between two scenes of judgment shows that even those with great sin are welcome if they will come.

### Fullness of Life

A central characteristic of this ideal time of God's reign is that everything that brings sorrow or that diminishes life is absent. God removes all the things that distract us from enjoying God's presence and blessings. When Isaiah envisions this time of God's abundant provision for all people, nothing remains that might divert our attention from the richness that God offers. Even those things that bring us shame are gone. Isaiah says this to a people who have been defeated and sent into exile. All they hold dear has been subject to degradation. These people know the depth of the pain caused by collective and personal humiliation and shame. God promises that this disgrace and shame will be no more. All will live with dignity and have their worth recognized.

This is what God wants for the world and what God wants God's people to work for in the world.

The high point of this description of God taking away all that diminishes life is the absence of death. Death or the fear of death often casts a shadow over things that make life good. Worries about it coming on us or those we love can distract us from the richness of the creation around us and so diminish our enjoyment of God's presence and blessings. And so Isaiah sees life in God's kingdom to be so wonderful that even this most fearful nemesis is gone. The fullness of life here will be such that no one will be so ill or weighed down with illness or grief that they will desire death. Its absence will be one more sign and source of the goodness of God's reign.

As Isaiah looks to this ideal time of God's presence with and blessing of the world, he notes that it will be a time when God's people recognize that these blessings come from God alone. We can be sure that God will bring God's people joy and fullness of life because those blessings are not dependent on our doing. It is those who rely on God who will experience the gladness that comes from this salvation.

---

# SHARING THE SCRIPTURE

## PREPARING TO LEAD

### Preparing Our Hearts

Ponder this week's devotional reading from 1 Corinthians 15:1-11. How do Paul's teachings in these verses seem to be foundational for his teachings about the resurrection not only of Jesus but also of all believers? Can you say "amen" to his teachings? If not, what holds you back? How have you experienced God's grace in your own life?

Pray that you and the students will be empowered to proclaim to others the good news about Jesus' resurrection.

### Preparing Our Minds

Study the background Scripture from Isaiah 25 and the lesson Scripture from Isaiah 25:6-10a.

Consider this question: *Who will deliver oppressed people from injustice?*

Write on newsprint:
❏ questions for group discussion under Goal 3 in Sharing the Scripture.
❏ information for next week's lesson, found under Continue the Journey.
❏ activities for further spiritual growth in Continue the Journey.

Determine how you might use any of the features that precede the first lesson of this quarter in today's session.

## LEADING THE CLASS

### (1) Gather to Learn

❖ Welcome everyone and pray that those who have come today will praise God for all that God has done and will do.

❖ Invite the adults to work with a partner or small team to plan a very special dinner feast. They should discuss the menu, the venue (such as a restaurant, banquet facility, church fellowship hall, a home), and the guest list (naming groups of people such as coworkers or family members, but not using specific names).

❖ Encourage volunteers to briefly tell their plans for this celebration to the class. Conclude by noting that according to Isaiah God plans to throw a very special feast for all people, including those we would not normally think of as being invited to such a gala affair.

❖ Read aloud today's focus statement: **Oppressed people are always looking for relief from their injustices. Who will deliver them? Isaiah's prophecy reveals that the sovereign God will give deliverance from oppression.**

*(2) Goal 1: Understand that God Acts in the Best Interests of All Peoples and Nations*

❖ Introduce today's lesson by reading or retelling the Introduction and Isaiah 25:1-5 in Understanding the Scripture.

❖ Select a volunteer to read Isaiah 25:6-10a.

❖ Discuss these questions referring to the Understanding the Scripture portions.

1. **Where is the mountain mentioned in verse 6 located?**
2. **What is the significance of God coming to the Temple Mount in Jerusalem?**
3. **What is on the menu of this feast?**
4. **Who is invited to attend?**
5. **What is God said to be destroying on the mountain?** (See also Fullness of Life in Interpreting the Scripture).

6. **Why have the people waited for God?**

*(3) Goal 2: Appreciate that God Removes Barriers that Cause People to Feel Separated from God and One Another*

❖ Set up some kind of barrier where everyone can see it. You might use a table, several chairs, a portable bulletin board, or whatever is handy that can be easily moved. Solicit two volunteers to each stand on one side of the barrier. Ask them to comment on how it feels to be separated. Then remove (or ask someone else to remove) the barrier. Ask the two volunteers to comment again, this time on how it feels to be united with the other person.

❖ Use this visual demonstration to help the adults recognize barriers that separate people from God and/or other people. Make a list of such barriers on newsprint.

❖ Post another sheet of newsprint and draw a vertical line to create two columns. On the left write "Separated" and on the right write "Reunited." Prompt the students to call out words that describe how one might feel or act, depending on whether one is separated from God or reunited with God. List these ideas.

❖ Point out that in today's reading people who had been separated from God were all invited to God's banquet. Everyone was invited, including those who had been enemies of God and of one another.

❖ Read All Are Invited in Interpreting the Scripture and provide a few moments for participants to appreciate that God removes whatever hinders us from being reconciled to one another and to God.

*(4) Goal 3: Rejoice that God Gives Hope to All Oppressed Peoples*

❖ Look again at Isaiah 25:7 and 8 (today's key verse).

❖ Ask these two questions. Use Fullness of Life in Interpreting the Scripture to round out the discussion.

　1. What kinds of situations cast a shroud of sadness over people? (Be sure to include death itself.)

　2. What changes does Isaiah envision in the kingdom to come? In other words, why will all of our tears be dried?

❖ Distribute hymnals and form groups of three or four. Encourage the groups to page through their hymnals to find songs of hope. (Note that these may be grouped together, as in pages 451-508 in *The United Methodist Hymnal*. They may also be listed separately under the heading of "hope.") Post these questions on newsprint for the groups to discuss:

　1. What is the source or basis of hope according to this hymn?

　2. Who has access to this hope?

　3. How might this hope cause one to draw closer to God?

　4. How might this hope help to lift one out of sorrow or oppression?

❖ Invite volunteers to comment on the songs that they found most meaningful in terms of building hopefulness with them. If time permits, sing a verse of each hymn that is named.

*(5) Continue the Journey*

❖ Pray that as the learners depart, they will be aware of oppression even in their own community and do whatever possible to end that oppression and bring hope to people.

❖ Post information for next week's session on newsprint for the students to copy:

■ **Title: Foundations of the Earth**

■ **Background Scripture: Isaiah 40**

■ **Lesson Scripture: Isaiah 40:21-31**

■ **Focus of the Lesson: We often place loyalty in people or systems to sustain and guide our lives. Are these systems able to sustain us? Isaiah declares that God is the absolute power in whom we should depend.**

❖ Challenge the adults to grow spiritually by completing one or more of these activities related to this week's session.

**(1) Look at the country of origin of some products that you have recently purchased. Research the employment practices, average wages, and working conditions in the countries of origin. Do you have reason to believe that workers there are being exploited? What effect will your research have on future purchases?**

**(2) Be alert for people in your community who may be oppressed. For example, are there migrant workers or other seasonal laborers who may not be treated fairly? Are there people whose language skills are hampering them? What can you do to help such people? How can you get your church involved?**

**(3) Identify at least one missionary who ministers to people**

**living under oppression. Pray daily for this person and those that he or she serves. If possible, make a contribution to support the work of this missionary.**

❖ Sing or read aloud "Marching to Zion."

❖ Conclude today's session by leading the class in this benediction, which is adapted from Hebrews 12:1b-2a, the key verses for October 30: **May we go forth empowered to run with perseverance the race that is set before us, looking to Jesus the pioneer and perfecter of our faith. Amen.**

## UNIT 1: THE SOVEREIGNTY OF GOD
# FOUNDATIONS OF THE EARTH

### PREVIEWING THE LESSON

**Lesson Scripture:** Isaiah 40:21-31
**Background Scripture:** Isaiah 40
**Key Verse:** Isaiah 40:28

### Focus of the Lesson:

We often place loyalty in people or systems to sustain and guide our lives. Are these systems able to sustain us? Isaiah declares that God is the absolute power in whom we should depend.

### Goals for the Learners:

(1) to contrast God's power to control and effect change with human inability to do the same.
(2) to reflect on God's sovereign power and personal presence with people.
(3) to embrace God's sovereignty and ability to address situations and needs that humans face.

### Supplies:

Bibles, newsprint and marker, paper and pencils, hymnals

### READING THE SCRIPTURE

NRSV

Lesson Scripture: Isaiah 40:21-31

²¹Have you not known? Have you
  not heard?
Has it not been told you from
  the beginning?
Have you not understood from
  the foundations of the earth?
²²It is he who sits above the circle
  of the earth,

CEB

Lesson Scripture: Isaiah 40:21-31

²¹Don't you know? Haven't
  you heard?
Wasn't it announced to you
  from the beginning?
Haven't you understood since
  the earth was founded?
²²God inhabits the earth's horizon—
  its inhabitants are like locusts—
  stretches out the skies like a curtain

and its inhabitants are
  like grasshoppers;
who stretches out the heavens like
  a curtain,
  and spreads them like a tent to
  live in;
²³who brings princes to naught,
  and makes the rulers of the earth
  as nothing.
²⁴Scarcely are they planted, scarcely
  sown,
  scarcely has their stem taken root
  in the earth,
when he blows upon them, and
  they wither,
  and the tempest carries them
  off like stubble.
²⁵To whom then will you compare me,
  or who is my equal? says the
  Holy One.
²⁶Lift up your eyes on high and see:
  Who created these?
He who brings out their host
  and numbers them,
  calling them all by name;
because he is great in strength,
  mighty in power,
  not one is missing.
²⁷Why do you say, O Jacob,
  and speak, O Israel,
"My way is hidden from the LORD,
  and my right is disregarded by
  my God"?
**²⁸Have you not known? Have
  you not heard?
The LORD is the everlasting God,
  the Creator of the ends of the earth.
He does not faint or grow weary;
  his understanding is unsearchable.**
²⁹He gives power to the faint,
  and strengthens the powerless.
³⁰Even youths will faint and be weary,
  and the young will fall exhausted;
³¹but those who wait for the LORD
  shall renew their strength,
  they shall mount up with
  wings like eagles,
they shall run and not be weary,
  they shall walk and not faint.

and spreads it out like a tent for
dwelling.
²³God makes dignitaries useless
  and the earth's judges into nothing.
²⁴Scarcely are they planted,
  scarcely sown,
  scarcely is their shoot rooted in
  the earth
when God breathes on them,
  and they dry up;
  the windstorm carries them off
  like straw.
²⁵So to whom will you compare me,
  and who is my equal? says the
  holy one.
²⁶Look up at the sky and consider:
  Who created these?
  The one who brings out their
  attendants one by one,
  summoning each of them by name.
Because of God's great strength
  and mighty power, not one
  is missing.
²⁷Why do you say, Jacob,
  and declare, Israel,
  "My way is hidden from the LORD
  my God ignores my predicament"?
**²⁸Don't you know? Haven't
  you heard?
The LORD is the everlasting God,
  the creator of the ends of the earth.
He doesn't grow tired or weary.
His understanding is beyond
  human reach,**
²⁹giving power to the tired
  and reviving the exhausted.
³⁰Youths will become tired and weary,
  young men will certainly stumble;
³¹but those who hope in the LORD
  will renew their strength;
  they will fly up on wings
  like eagles;
  they will run and not be tired;
  they will walk and not be weary.

## UNDERSTANDING THE SCRIPTURE

**Introduction.** When this Isaiah writes, disaster has befallen Judah. The Babylonian Empire has conquered the nation and sacked Jerusalem. All the people of any note have been exiled to Babylon (the area of today's Iraq). The people have now been in exile for decades and they wonder whether God is able to hear their prayers. They call on God, but they are still in exile. Some interpret that circumstance as evidence that the gods of the Babylonians are stronger than God. Others think God may have abandoned them. In the face of these worries, Isaiah speaks a word of hope and promise.

**Isaiah 40:1-5.** Isaiah begins this poetic section with God's granting the people forgiveness and promising to return to Jerusalem with them. They have served out their punishment for abandoning God and abusing the helpless. Now they can prepare for God's return. Isaiah moves from having the people prepare for God to having God make the preparations. In the end, God returns because God has promised to do it: "the mouth of the Lord has spoken" (40:5).

**Isaiah 40:6-11.** Isaiah moves from promises of restoration to examination of the fickle will of humanity. Their faithfulness is as fleeting as the bud of a flower. But the word of God never fails. God recognizes the weakness of the people, but promises to be with them, to be gentle, and to care for them. So the restoration of the nation is not based on the faithfulness of the people, but on God's faithfulness to them and love for them. This is wonderful news to those who have faced judgment. Isaiah says that God's mercy and love will govern God's relationship with them from now on.

**Isaiah 40:12-20.** Isaiah tells people living under the mightiest empire of the world that their God is about to rescue them, about to lead them home in glorious fashion and live in their midst. This is good news, but hard to believe. Where was the power of this God when the nation fell? Where has it been all these many years in exile? Verses 12-20 declare that God is indeed powerful enough to accomplish the promises made in verses 1-11. In verses 12-17 Isaiah identifies God as the one who created all things. Most people who had believed in God before the exile had seen God as a local and national god. Few had envisioned God as standing over all of creation or as the creator of all things. But the early prophets of the exile (especially Ezekiel) had declared that the God of Jerusalem could and would be with the people in Babylon; that the God of Jerusalem was different from all other gods. Only this God had made the world and exercised rule over it all. Isaiah returns to this theme here. God is not only creator of the cosmos but God also possesses all knowledge. God is also the source of justice so that punishment will not be more than is deserved and the wicked will not escape. The power of God is such that powerful empires are just a drop in the bucket, dust on the scale that weighs out produce. They are tiny and inconsequential in comparison. God is so great that no worship is sufficient. It is this God whose power guarantees the promises of restoration and life.

The final part of this section, verses 18-20, compares God to other gods.

Here Isaiah draws on a common body of ridicule of other gods that we hear from the prophets. He says that those other gods are things that humans make (rather than being the God who made all things). Humans go cut down a tree, carve it, make sure it is shaped so it won't fall over, decorate it with expensive things, and then bow down to worship it. This ridicule intends to turn people from those gods and even makes them smirk at the foolishness of those who do worship them. Of course, had you talked to those people who worshiped before such images, they would have told you that the image was not the god. But the Hebrew prophets delight in making fun of them with this characterization. After all, Israelites are the only people without an image of their god. So their neighbors constantly chide them for being without an image. The prophets respond with this portrait of those who have them. So the choice is clear: Either worship and trust in a stick decorated with some gold and silver, or rely on the one who created the world and rules over all nations.

**Isaiah 40:21-26.** Isaiah here resumes his description of the might and majesty of God. God is the one who created and rules the whole earth. God is sovereign over the forces of nature. But more than that, God is also ruler of all other rulers. By comparison, the rulers of the great empires are mere seedlings that God can defeat simply by breathing on them. God's power over the nations is confirmed by recognizing God as the creator. This God is not raw power, however; God's power is combined with love: God knows each member of creation by name and continues to care for them.

**Isaiah 40:27-31.** The exile had made it seem that God has not seen the pain the people have endured in Babylon. They felt as though God was absent or unable to respond. "Not so!" says Isaiah. What God does may be hard to understand, but the creator of the earth has seen and knows that the people are exhausted. Now the great power that created the world is shared with God's people. Those who "wait for the LORD" (that is, those who trust in God) will be strengthened so that they will see the great blessings of restoration and blessing mentioned in the opening verses of the chapter. Both the courage to endure the difficult times and the blessings to come are guaranteed by the power, love, and sovereignty of God.

---

## INTERPRETING THE SCRIPTURE

*God's Faithfulness and Human Failings*

The first readers of Isaiah 40 had accepted the notion their grandparents had been sent into exile because of their sins, particularly because they had worshiped other gods and had mistreated the vulnerable. The covenant with God stipulated that the nation would be blessed if they were faithful, but God would allow others to destroy them if they were unfaithful. That is just what had happened; they were unfaithful, so the nation fell. Many of those in exile had turned to God and were struggling to be faithful under difficult circumstances. Now Isaiah says that God is ready to reestablish the nation and bless it, but the people know their weaknesses. If God's blessing comes to them only if they are faithful, then the restoration will be small and temporary. So Isaiah begins this proclamation of great promise by acknowledging human weakness and failing: "All people are grass, their consistency is like the flower of the field" (Isaiah 40:6). This long section on human weakness stands beside the promise of blessing to show that God is determined to bless God's people even if they are unfaithful. God's goodness, God's determination to bless, is greater than the need to punish every misstep.

Just as the early readers of Isaiah knew their tendency to fail God, we know ours. They were in a covenant relationship that called them to faithfulness, just as we are. And the conditions have not gotten easier for us. We may not be tempted to worship another god literally, but we often put other things before our relationship with God and we are constantly pulled into putting our own economic good ahead of the more vulnerable. This passage declares the good news that God's grace is indomitable. God knows how unfaithful we often are, and yet is determined to be in relationship with us. Even when our faithfulness is as fleeting as a flower in the field, God is committed to being with us. The blessings of God are not dependent upon our consistency or goodness. Isaiah says that despite our failing, God's great power will be used to nurture and bless God's people.

### When God Seems Absent

Isaiah spoke these words of promise to a discouraged audience. They had acknowledged that they were in exile because their nation had sinned. But those who had done the wrong were gone. It is their children and grandchildren who now live in exile. They have turned to God and have tried to be faithful, but they are still suffering. So they wonder if God sees their distress or cares about it (40:27). It is fine to talk about the power and forgiveness of God, but these people want to know why God's people continue to suffer. Why does God seem to disregard them?

This question is not foreign to us. We often wonder why God's people suffer unjustly, why their faithfulness is not rewarded by obvious and immediate blessing. Isaiah proclaims that blessing is coming, but his audience thinks it is coming too slowly. Isaiah's response gives one promise about the present and one about the future. Isaiah says that God does know and does care. When the faithful suffer it is not a sign that God has abandoned them. God does not immediately alleviate the difficulty, but divine power strengthens those who are suffering. Those who trust in God are given strength to endure. This is not a promise about health and wealth. Promises of that sort confuse money with fullness of life. Rather, this is a promise that those who are suffering may know that God is present with them and will give them the strength to endure with faith. It is the promise that we are not alone and that we are loved. Whatever happens, God remains present with us, strengthening us and holding us in a loving embrace. While this strengthening does not provide immediate relief, it does include the promise that such suffering will not be the last word. God promises blessing and restoration to those who trust in God's faithfulness and power. For Isaiah's hearers, that meant the restoration of the nation. For Christians, that promise includes the promise of life with God beyond the troubles of this world.

### The Power of God in a Troubled World

In our passage, Isaiah peers into an idealized time in which God reigns and all the enemies of God's people are subdued. Here God not only rules but also provides for and nurtures God's people. It is a time of peace and comfort. But that is not the way the world is in our experience. There is pain, loss, need, injustice, and oppression of the vulnerable. We have seen churches and saints work to bring about the world Isaiah dreams of. We may think of Mother Teresa or Dr. Martin Luther King Jr. as people who have dedicated their lives to bringing comfort or justice to the world.

But we do not need to look so far away. There are likely people in your church who are deeply committed to social justice outreach or to activities such as feeding the homeless. Perhaps your church participates in Room In the Inn to house the homeless on winter nights. Maybe your church has or supports a food bank. Many good, faithful people dedicate many hours over the course of many years to help the vulnerable and to change systems that perpetrate injustice. Such work is just what the church should be doing. The community that worships the God of justice and love should reflect those characteristics in its life. We sometimes see wonderful results of this work. People's lives are transformed, dangerous neighborhoods become safe places, and laws are passed that outlaw unjust practices. But injustice and violence do not seem to stay down. The forces of evil find a new place to make their home and our work must begin again. It is discouraging to see the unyielding power of evil resurface, and do so with a vengeance.

Isaiah has a word to say to us as we work to make the world the kind of place that God wants. His good news is that God is the ultimate ruler of the cosmos. Establishing justice and overcoming unjust or oppressive governments is not a lost cause. God has the power to set things right. Indeed, the task is so large that only God has the power to accomplish it. The grip of the powers that support unjust structures is too strong for us to defeat by ourselves. But this is not cause to be discouraged because God is powerful enough to defeat them. And Isaiah declares that God will establish justice and security. While Isaiah presents an idealized vision that we cannot actualize, he declares that this is the kind of existence God's power will give to the faithful. This is the work of God, work in which we are privileged to participate. When evil does not disappear, we have not failed because we have declared what God wants and given the world a glimpse of things as they should be. We have lived up to being God's people, even as we look forward to that sure exercise of God's power that will right all wrongs and establish justice and peace.

# SHARING THE SCRIPTURE

## PREPARING TO LEAD

### Preparing Our Hearts

Ponder this week's devotional reading from Isaiah 40:1-8, which is part of today's background Scripture. Imagine yourself as one of the captives in Babylon to whom Isaiah's message is addressed. As years turned into decades and new generations were born, you have felt abandoned by God. What hope does the message offer to you? What evidence might your life give that you believe—or disbelieve—the prophet's words?

Pray that you and the students will be consoled, especially in the midst of difficult circumstances, by knowing that God loves you and wants the best for you.

### Preparing Our Minds

Study the background Scripture from Isaiah 40 and the lesson Scripture from Isaiah 40:21-31.

Consider this question: *Are there systems that you rely on to guide your life that truly are able to sustain you?*

Write on newsprint:

❏ information for next week's lesson, found under Continue the Journey.

❏ activities for further spiritual growth in Continue the Journey.

Determine how you might use any of the features that precede the first lesson of this quarter in today's session.

## LEADING THE CLASS

### (1) Gather to Learn

❖ Welcome everyone and pray that those who have come today will recognize that they can depend completely on God for all their needs.

❖ Post several markers and sheets of newsprint on a wall or tabletop. As the students enter, invite them to write the name of something or someone they depend on to guide and sustain their lives. Answers will likely include things that are thought to bring financial or personal security, people who will care for them, and places where they can go to feel safe and secure.

❖ Call the class together and read aloud as many answers as possible. Ask: **Why do we depend on these people or things to guard and guide our lives?**

❖ Read aloud today's focus statement: **We often place loyalty in people or systems to sustain and guide our lives. Are these systems able to sustain us? Isaiah declares that God is the absolute power in whom we should depend.**

### (2) Goal 1: Contrast God's Power to Control and Effect Change with Human Inability to Do the Same

❖ Set the stage for today's lesson by reading or retelling information from Understanding the Scripture, beginning with Introduction and ending with Isaiah 40:12-20.

❖ Choose a volunteer to read Isaiah 40:21-31 and then discuss the following questions. Add information from Understanding the Scripture for these verses as you find it helpful.

1. **If all that you knew about God was what is contained in these verses, what would you know about God?**

2. **How would you describe God's power in relation to earthly rulers?**

3. **Verse 25 asks to whom God could be compared. What is the implied answer?** (no one) **Based on verse 26, why does God have no equal?** (God is the creator and sustainer of all that exists. God's power is unrivaled.)

4. **Isaiah claims that God is both the creator and the one who can intervene in human history. Why did the exiles believe— or fail to believe—this claim was true?** (They felt that God had abandoned them. They also believed that their military defeat demonstrated that the gods of Babylon were stronger than God.)

5. **Where might the exiles, who felt God had abandoned them, have heard good news in this passage? Where do you hear good news?** (Use God's Faithfulness and Human Failings in Interpreting the Scripture to explain that God's commitment to us is not dependent on our strength and faithfulness but on God's grace and power to keep us in relationship.)

*3) Goal 2: Reflect on God's Sovereign Power and Personal Presence with the People*

❖ Invite the students to close their eyes and focus on Isaiah 40:28-31, which you will read aloud.

❖ Read aloud these questions for silent reflection:

1. **How does the knowledge of the everlasting God's power and endurance influence the way that you live?** (pause)

2. **How does your body need to experience God's healing power? Ask God for that power.** (pause)

3. **In what ways do you feel powerless? Ask God to strengthen you.** (pause)

4. **Imagine yourself soaring with the eagles or running a marathon. Feel the joy of this power. Give thanks to God for strengthening and empowering you.** (pause)

❖ **Option:** Distribute paper (preferably unlined) and pencils. Invite the adults to draw a picture or symbol to illustrate the newly found strength they feel God has given them. Suggest that they display this picture where they can see it when they feel weak or that God is somehow absent from them.

*(4) Goal 3: Embrace God's Sovereignty and Ability to Address Situations and Needs that Humans Face*

❖ Read or retell The Power of God in a Troubled World in Interpreting the Scripture.

❖ Look again at the activities in the second paragraph that Christians may engage in "to help the vulnerable and to change systems that perpetrate injustice." Brainstorm a list of activities that your church supports to bring about such help and change.

❖ Use this list to address two questions:

1. **If we are not doing much to combat injustice in the short-term by providing needed services or in the long-term by advocating for justice, why are we failing to do so?** List reasons on newsprint. Try to discern

which of these reasons has merit and which represents a failure on the part of the congregation to be engaged. Ask: **How can we help our congregation to commit to such work?**

2. **What else could we be doing?** Brainstorm groups of people who need to be served and think about what their needs might be. If the congregation is small, which other churches or nonprofit organizations might you be able to partner with to make a difference?

*(5) Continue the Journey*

❖ Pray that as the learners depart, they will make a commitment to depend on the power of God to guide and sustain them, especially as they bring hope for justice to others.

❖ Post information for next week's session on newsprint for the students to copy:

- **Title: Everlasting Covenant**
- **Background Scripture: Isaiah 61**
- **Lesson Scripture: Isaiah 61:1-4, 8-11**
- **Focus of the Lesson: People make agreements, which they desire to last, but are too often broken, causing stress and dismay. Can anyone make an agreement that will not be broken? In Isaiah God promises an everlasting covenant, which can never be broken.**

❖ Challenge the adults to grow spiritually by completing one or more of these activities related to this week's session.

(1) **Recall the people and things identified in the Gather to Learn portion as being able to sustain and guide you. Which of these have you become overly reliant on? How can you wean yourself from this dependence and begin to trust more fully in God?**

(2) **Write in your spiritual journal about why you may find it difficult to believe that God is in complete control. What kinds of situations cause you to doubt? Take your doubts and questions to God in prayer.**

(3) **Read Isaiah 40:28-31 devotionally. Linger over words or phrases that help you to get to know God better. What power do you need from God?**

❖ Sing or read aloud "Immortal, Invisible, God Only Wise."

❖ Conclude today's session by leading the class in this benediction, which is adapted from Hebrews 12:1b-2a, the key verses for October 30: **May we go forth empowered to run with perseverance the race that is set before us, looking to Jesus the pioneer and perfecter of our faith. Amen.**

# UNIT 1: THE SOVEREIGNTY OF GOD
# EVERLASTING COVENANT

---

## PREVIEWING THE LESSON

**Lesson Scripture:** Isaiah 61:1-4, 8-11
**Background Scripture:** Isaiah 61
**Key Verse:** Isaiah 61:8

### Focus of the Lesson:
People make agreements, which they desire to last, but are too often broken, causing stress and dismay. Can anyone make an agreement that will not be broken? In Isaiah God promises an everlasting covenant, which can never be broken.

### Goals for the Learners:
(1) to know that God has high ethical standards and enters into secure and enduring covenants with people.
(2) to appreciate what it means to live justly and faithfully according to God's covenant expectations.
(3) to make a commitment to live as a promise-keeper.

### Supplies:
Bibles, newsprint and marker, paper and pencils, hymnals

---

## READING THE SCRIPTURE

**NRSV**

Lesson Scripture: Isaiah 61:1-4, 8-11

¹The spirit of the Lord God is
    upon me,
  because the Lord has anointed me;
he has sent me to bring good news
    to the oppressed,
  to bind up the brokenhearted,
to proclaim liberty to the captives,
  and release to the prisoners;

**CEB**

Lesson Scripture: Isaiah 61:1-4, 8-11

¹The Lord God's spirit is upon me,
  because the Lord has anointed me.
He has sent me
  to bring good news to the poor,
  to bind up the brokenhearted,
  to proclaim release for captives,
    and liberation for prisoners,

²to proclaim the year of the
    Lord's favor,
  and the day of vengeance of
    our God;
  to comfort all who mourn;
³to provide for those who mourn
    in Zion—
  to give them a garland instead
    of ashes,
the oil of gladness instead
    of mourning,
  the mantle of praise instead of
    a faint spirit.
They will be called oaks
    of righteousness,
  the planting of the Lord, to
    display his glory.
⁴They shall build up the ancient ruins,
  they shall raise up the
    former devastations;
they shall repair the ruined cities,
  the devastations of
    many generations.
**⁸For I the Lord love justice,**
  **I hate robbery and wrongdoing;**
**I will faithfully give them**
    **their recompense,**
  **and I will make an everlasting**
    **covenant with them.**
⁹Their descendants shall be known
    among the nations,
  and their offspring among the
    peoples;
all who see them shall acknowledge
  that they are a people whom
    the Lord has blessed.
¹⁰I will greatly rejoice in the Lord,
  my whole being shall exult in my
    God;
for he has clothed me with the
    garments of salvation,
  he has covered me with the robe
    of righteousness,
as a bridegroom decks himself with
    a garland,
  and as a bride adorns herself
    with her jewels.

²to proclaim the year of the
    Lord's favor
  and a day of vindication for
    our God,
  to comfort all who mourn,
³to provide for Zion's mourners,
  to give them a crown in place
    of ashes,
  oil of joy in place of mourning,
  a mantle of praise in place
    of discouragement.
They will be called Oaks
    of Righteousness,
  planted by the Lord to glorify
    himself.
⁴They will rebuild the ancient ruins;
  they will restore formerly deserted
    places;
  they will renew ruined cities,
  places deserted in generations past.
**⁸I, the Lord, love justice;**
  **I hate robbery and dishonesty.**
**I will faithfully give them their**
    **wage,**
  **and make with them an enduring**
    **covenant.**
⁹Their offspring will be known among
    the nations,
  and their descendants among
    the peoples.
All who see them will recognize
  that they are a people blessed
    by the Lord.
¹⁰I surely rejoice in the Lord;
  my heart is joyful because of
    my God,
  because he has clothed me with
    clothes of victory,
  wrapped me in a robe of
    righteousness
  like a bridegroom in a priestly
    crown,
  and like a bride adorned in jewelry.
¹¹As the earth puts out its growth,
  and as a garden grows its seeds,
  so the Lord God will grow righteousness and praise before all the
nations.

¹¹For as the earth brings forth
>    its shoots,
>  and as a garden causes what
>    is sown in it to spring up,
> so the LORD God will cause
>    righteousness and praise
>  to spring up before all the nations.

## UNDERSTANDING THE SCRIPTURE

**Introduction.** This section of Isaiah comes from the time after many have returned to Judah from exile. Perhaps those who returned had heard their grandparents tell of wonderful times in the homeland and so they expected life to be easy. But it was not. There was much rebuilding to do and the people who had been left behind were not that happy to see people coming in who had the backing of the empire to change things. The Isaiah of chapter 40 had spoken of how wonderful things would be when God led the people back to Judah. But this had not yet happened. Chapters 56–66 address the returnees. From these chapters we see that the difficult circumstances they faced had led some to turn to other gods and had led some to engage in unfair business practices. So chapters 56–66 alternate between calls to repentance and promises of restoration and glory when they are faithful. Isaiah 61 is one of the renewals of those promises.

**Isaiah 61:1-4.** This song of Isaiah begins with a familiar passage. It is a part of the material found in Luke that Jesus had quoted in his sermon at Nazareth as he begins his ministry (Luke 4:18-19). As we find it in Isaiah, it is the prophet who says that the Spirit of the Lord is on him. Isaiah recounts this experience to assure his readers that his message is true because God has directly and dramatically appointed him to proclaim this message of hope and promise. The time of God's blessing of Judah has come. The returnees were among the brokenhearted and the oppressed. They had come back dreaming of establishing a powerful and thriving nation. But they were still under the control of the Persian Empire, who had defeated the Babylonians, and economic conditions were still poor. They are becoming disillusioned and starting to doubt that God would restore the nation to its glory. Some who had been left behind were also among the oppressed. They were being treated unjustly by those who had returned. So the oppressed here represent the whole community of the faithful. Thus, Isaiah proclaims to the faithful that the time of rescue has arrived, the delay has finally ended. God is now ready to save; now is the time of God's favor. Isaiah says that their sorrow and difficulties will be replaced with joy. As verse 3 explains, the signs of grief and mourning (ashes on the head) will be replaced by signs of victory and rejoicing (garlands on the head and perfumed oil). Rather than seeming to be the grass that others can easily cut off or pull up, they will be mighty oaks (61:3).

Isaiah declares that the day has come when the cities will be rebuilt so that their glory is restored.

**Isaiah 61:5-7.** These verses shift our focus. Here it seems that Israel becomes a mediator of God's presence to the nations. Isaiah says the people will be priests and ministers to all nations. God's presence will be among them in a way that draws others to them and asks Judah to approach God for them. The judgment that Judah endured was the prelude to this role. They were shamed and dishonored, but now they will be granted dignity and honor. In this new time, the nations that once subdued them will serve them; the nations will tend the flocks of the people of Judah and farm their land and give the profit to them. (It may even be that the nations are the ones who rebuild the cities in verse 4.) Some interpreters see this service as a part of identifying the faithful of Judah as priests. The priests of the Israelites had theoretically been supported by the offerings of the other Israelites. When the whole nation is the priest, then the other nations bring them gifts.

It is important to note here that it is not just the faithful of Judah who are the recipients of blessings. Since those of Judah are priests, it is through them that the nations are brought into the presence of God. So when blessings come upon the faithful in Judah, they become a means through which the world is blessed. In this way, they fulfill the promise to Abraham that through him all nations would be blessed (Genesis 12:3). Later, the early church would see the imagery of the nations bringing gifts to Jerusalem as a sign that their mission should include Gentiles.

**Isaiah 61:8-11.** Isaiah has announced that the world is about to be reoriented. The oppressed faithful people will be comforted and blessed; they will even be a blessing to the world. In these verses Isaiah adds that this will be a time of justice and righteousness. It will be such a time because God hates injustice and sin, but loves justice. A central complaint of Isaiah 56–66 is that those who have returned to Judah have adopted unjust economic practices and have begun to oppress the poor (see Isaiah 58:6-14; 59:1-4, 14-16). Isaiah declares that in the time of the "LORD's favor" God will make the nation a place of justice. To do this, God will punish the perpetrators of injustice (61:2). Further, God will expect the faithful to live in justice and righteousness. When God gives them salvation, they also receive righteousness. Receiving salvation and beginning to live a righteous life are inseparable for Isaiah.

Perhaps Isaiah uses the metaphors of wedding clothes to emphasize the permanent nature of the relationship between God and Judah (61:10). He has said that this covenant is everlasting (61:8), so images of a wedding reinforce God's commitment to be with God's people. They will be famous for being blessed because they live in righteousness. Such a life is one of the blessings they receive from God. The final result of this giving of salvation and righteousness is not just that Judah will be recognized and served by those who oppressed her, but more important, this action brings forth praise that is offered to God (61:11).

# INTERPRETING THE SCRIPTURE

*The Spirit of the Lord Is upon Me*

This chapter of Isaiah begins with the prophet saying that God's Spirit has come to him with a message and has remained on him so that he can proclaim it. His message announces the availability and effectiveness of God's grace. In the midst of a world of despair and disbelief, Isaiah was sent to assure people of the presence of salvation from God. We previously noted that Luke has Jesus read this passage at the very beginning of his ministry (Luke 4:18-19). By reading it Jesus claims the task of proclaiming that the day of salvation has come. The earliest church, then, experienced the presence of God through the Spirit. In the first Christian sermon on the Day of Pentecost, the day the church is born, Peter declares that the time of God's salvation has come and the evidence is the presence of the Spirit in the church (Acts 2:16-21). So salvation is experienced as an intimate relationship with God, a relationship in which the Spirit lives in God's people. We should note that as salvation brings this assurance of the presence of God with us, it also brings mission. Isaiah is sent to proclaim that this salvation is coming. He calls people to be participants in this new thing God is doing.

Some who read Isaiah 61 and other places where the prophet speaks of his mission think that the prophet intends for his mission to be the mission of the whole community of the faithful. That is, the whole nation is to take on the task of the prophet. It is in this vein that the early church interpreted the coming of God's Spirit on all members. Now the whole church has the task of the prophet. They all must be those who proclaim the good news of God's grace to the world.

The church remains the place of the presence of God. God's Spirit dwells in each Christian. If we respond to this presence of God as Isaiah did, we see that it is our task to proclaim to the world that the time of God's presence and salvation is here. That presence brings grace and hope into a world full of despair. Isaiah's good news announces that God cares about the poor, the oppressed, the imprisoned, and all who suffer unjustly. His proclamation applies to those who have come back from exile and those who had been left desolate in the land. Those on both sides of the dispute, in trying to decide how to govern and build the nation, are included in this salvation.

The church's good news also proclaims that God cares about the oppressed, the poor, and the vulnerable. It says that God is present with those who mourn and wants to move them to gladness. Those who are the objects of this grace, and that is all of us, are made strong. Isaiah says that God makes us "oaks of righteousness" (61:3) that become demonstrations of the glory of God to the rest of the world. This rather grand task is not something we accomplish by our own efforts alone, God's Spirit is upon us to strengthen us to receive blessing and to be a blessing to the world.

*The Lord Loves Justice*

The restoration that Isaiah proclaims for Judah is not only the result of God's mercy and love but it is also an outworking of God's justice. It was an exercise of justice when God sent them into exile and once the proper chastisement for their sin was complete, justice would dictate their return. Isaiah thinks that time has come. These interpretations of Judah's history in terms of God's justice highlight that divine characteristic as one of the most important elements of the character of God. God's nature is to be just. Isaiah expresses that here by saying that God loves justice (61:8). God loves justice because the exercise of justice requires that the value and dignity of all of God's children are recognized. Justice makes sure that the injured are restored and the perpetrators of injustice are punished. They must not get away with abusing others because all are of equal value.

We sometimes fear the justice of God, wanting God to be merciful not just. But Isaiah sees salvation as something that includes both justice and mercy. We too often think of justice and mercy as opposites, but they are not. The opposite of justice is injustice, not mercy. We all need God to be just and to remain just at all times. That is the only way we can trust God. If God stops being just, then God may condemn people because of the color of their eyes or the month in which they were born. We depend on God to be just at all times. We also need God to be loving and merciful. But God does not stop being just to be merciful; rather, justice is informed by mercy and mercy is informed by justice. Even in Isaiah's proclamation of salvation and blessing we hear that it brings a day of "vindication" (61:2, CEB; the NRSV translates this as "vengeance," which is correct if we remember that it is not naked revenge; it is rather the just response to the evil inflicted on God's

children). For the exercise of mercy to be meaningful, it must result in the establishment of justice so that God's people can live in peace.

*Wearing the Robe of Righteousness*

One of the central guiding principles for determining how we are to live is the character of God. There are many places in Leviticus where there is a command followed by the phrase, "You shall be holy because I am holy" (for example Leviticus 11:44-45; 19:2). This way of determining how to live is taken up in 1 Peter 1:15-16, where this Leviticus phrase is quoted. It means that the lives of God's people are to reflect who God is. In Isaiah 61, this idea comes to expression in verse 3 where the prophet says that the people of God will be "called oaks of righteousness." The reputation of God's people will be that they live lives of justice and goodness, and thus they reflect the righteousness of the God who saves them.

Here and throughout the biblical witness, the gift of salvation includes the demand that God's people live in righteousness. Being in covenant relationship with God has always had its demands. Every relationship has demands, and this one is no exception. God's everlasting covenant (61:8) includes both God's saving of the people and the expectation that the people will be faithful to God's will. So, since God hates robbery and wrongdoing, God's people must rid themselves of such behavior. When we think of ethical demands, we often think of them as oppressive or limiting. But as Isaiah sees them, they are part of salvation. They are the guidelines that help us have the kinds of lives God means us to have. Accepting this covenant relationship with God, therefore, includes accepting the demand that we live as God commands. But as we do so we remember that those demands are saving graces as they lead us to have the rich and full lives God intends for us.

---

## SHARING THE SCRIPTURE

### PREPARING TO LEAD

#### *Preparing Our Hearts*

Ponder this week's devotional reading from Isaiah 42:5-9. What specific reasons do you see here for praising God as the creator? What reasons do you see here for praising God as the one who sustains Israel? What actions does God expect from Israel as it fulfills its role as "a covenant to the people" (42:6)? What reasons do you have to praise God today?

Pray that you and the students will live faithfully as God's covenant people.

#### *Preparing Our Minds*

Study the background Scripture from Isaiah 61 and the lesson Scripture from Isaiah 61:1-4, 8-11.

Consider this question: *Can you or anyone else make an agreement that will not be broken?*

Write on newsprint:

❏ information for next week's lesson, found under Continue the Journey.

❏ activities for further spiritual growth in Continue the Journey.

Determine how you might use any of the features that precede the first lesson of this quarter in today's session.

### LEADING THE CLASS

#### *(1) Gather to Learn*

❖ Welcome everyone and pray that those who have come today will recognize and give thanks for God's unbroken promises.

❖ Read: **Do you remember a time when a person's word and a firm handshake sealed a deal? John D. Rockefeller was quoted as saying, "I believe in the sacredness of a promise, that a man's word should be as good as his bond, that character— not wealth or power or position—is of supreme worth." In contrast, any major agreements these days require reams of paper to ensure that all parties understand what the expectations are on both sides of the table and that there are legal ways to hold both parties accountable. Still, deals are broken or borrowed money is not repaid. How do you decide whom you can trust to keep his or her word and follow through on an agreement?**

❖ Read aloud today's focus statement: **People make agreements, which they desire to last, but are too often broken, causing stress and dismay. Can anyone make an agreement that will not be broken? In Isaiah God promises an everlasting covenant, which can never be broken.**

*(2) Goal 1: Know that God Has High Ethical Standards and Enters into Secure and Enduring Covenants with People*

❖ Read The Spirit of the Lord Is upon Me in Interpreting the Scripture to set the context for today's lesson. Point out that in Christian understanding the Spirit is on all believers and, therefore, all are called to proclaim the good news that the prophet proclaims.

❖ Call on a volunteer to read Isaiah 61:1-4 and ask:

1. **What prophetic words are God's people called to declare?**
2. **How will their proclamation affect those who hear them?**
3. **How does the presence of the Spirit enable us to be "oaks of righteousness" (61:3) who display the glory of the Lord?**

❖ Invite the same volunteer to continue reading verses 8-11 and then ask:

1. **What is the relationship between God's justice and God's mercy?** (Add information from The Lord Loves Justice in Interpreting the Scripture.)
2. **How does God's everlasting covenant benefit the Israelites?**

*(3) Goal 2: Appreciate What It Means to Live Justly and Faithfully According to God's Covenant Expectations*

❖ Read Wearing the Robes of Righteousness in Interpreting the Scripture.

❖ Form small groups and give each group a marker and a sheet of newsprint on which they will write their answers to this question: **What actions and attitudes characterize those who live according to God's covenant expectations?**

❖ Bring everyone together and post the sheets of newsprint around the room. If possible, suggest that the adults walk around to read these responses and then return to their seats for a discussion of these questions:

- **As you reviewed each group's responses, what common themes did you notice?** (You may want to list these ideas on a separate sheet of newsprint.)
- **What other ideas do you think need to be added to the list?**
- **How could our church help its members do more to live up to God's expectations?** (Consider additional opportunities to learn what it means to live faithfully and justly. Think about tangible actions that the adults can take both individually as a body. Suggest ways that more mature Christians might be able to mentor younger and newer believers.)

❖ Conclude this portion of the lesson by reading in unison today's key verse, Isaiah 61:8, as a reminder that God loves justice and keeps promises.

*(4) Goal 3: Make a Commitment to Live as a Promise-keeper*

❖ Read: **Recall that the God of justice promised to make "an everlasting covenant" with the people (Isaiah 61:8). God is not only a promise-maker but also a promise-keeper. In the words of Friedrich W. Krummacher (1796–1868), "God's promises are, virtually, obligations that he imposes upon himself." And, as Colin Urquhart (1940– ) observed, "God is the God of promise.**

He keeps his word, even when that seems impossible; even when circumstances seem to point to the opposite." And what about you? Are you one who makes promises in the midst of crises but then forgets or refuses to honor them when things settle down? Or do you promise so much and deliver so little that you word really means nothing? Or are you one whose word is truly your bond such that people know they can rely on you to keep your promises?

❖ Distribute paper and pencils as you continue to read these directions:

- On a scale of one to ten, with one being Totally Unreliable and ten being Absolutely Reliable, rate yourself as a promise-keeper and write that number on your paper.
- Now think about what you can do to improve your score if you are not a 10.
- Write one sentence to indicate your commitment to living as a reliable promise-keeper.
- Refer to your paper whenever you make a promise.

*(5) Continue the Journey*

❖ Pray that as the learners depart, they will try to live as reliable promise-keepers.

❖ Post information for next week's session on newsprint for the students to copy:

- **Title: The Imprint of God**
- **Background Scripture: Hebrews 1**
- **Lesson Scripture: Hebrews 1:1-9**
- **Focus of the Lesson: People**

seek guidance for their lives but may question who the appropriate person is to give direction. Whom should they trust to provide direction in their quest for guidance? Christ, the reflection of God's glory, is the one who addresses life's questions with a powerful and sustaining word.

❖ Challenge the adults to grow spiritually by completing one or more of these activities related to this week's session.

(1) **Recall ideas discussed in class for living more justly and faithfully according to God's covenant expectations. Choose at least one idea that you will focus on this week.**

(2) **Identify an injustice in your community, school, or workplace. Bring the issue before people who have the authority to take action to correct this problem. Serve as an advocate for those who are being harmed by this injustice.**

(3) **Be aware of promises you have recently made. Which ones have you kept? Which ones have you not yet fulfilled but expect to keep? If you have broken any promises, what steps will you take to make up for this shortcoming?**

❖ Sing or read aloud "Standing on the Promises."

❖ Conclude today's session by leading the class in this benediction, which is adapted from Hebrews 12:1b-2a, the key verses for October 30: **May we go forth empowered to run with perseverance the race that is set before us, looking to Jesus the pioneer and perfecter of our faith. Amen.**

## UNIT 2: THE SOVEREIGNTY OF JESUS
# THE IMPRINT OF GOD

---

### PREVIEWING THE LESSON

**Lesson Scripture:** Hebrews 1:1-9
**Background Scripture:** Hebrews 1
**Key Verse:** Hebrews 1:3a

#### Focus of the Lesson:
People seek guidance for their lives but may question who the appropriate person is to give direction. Whom should they trust to provide direction in their quest for guidance? Christ, the reflection of God's glory, is the one who addresses life's questions with a powerful and sustaining word.

#### Goals for the Learners:
(1) to understand that Jesus expresses fully God's very being in the world.
(2) to appreciate Jesus' relationship with God.
(3) to create ways to seek Jesus' continued guidance in their lives.

#### Supplies:
Bibles, newsprint and marker, paper and pencils, hymnals

---

### READING THE SCRIPTURE

**NRSV**

Lesson Scripture: Hebrews 1:1-9

¹Long ago God spoke to our ancestors in many and various ways by the prophets, ²but in these last days he has spoken to us by a Son, whom he appointed heir of all things, through whom he also created the worlds. **³He is the reflection of God's glory and the exact imprint of God's very being, and he sustains all things by his powerful word.** When he had made purification for sins, he sat down at the right hand of the Majesty on high, ⁴having become as much

**CEB**

Lesson Scripture: Hebrews 1:1-9

¹In the past, God spoke through the prophets to our ancestors in many times and many ways. ²In these final days, though, he spoke to us through a Son. God made his Son the heir of everything and created the world through him. **³The Son is the light of God's glory and the imprint of God's being. He maintains everything with his powerful message.** After he carried out the cleansing of people from their sins, he sat down at the right side of the highest majesty. ⁴And the

superior to angels as the name he has inherited is more excellent than theirs. [5]For to which of the angels did God ever say,

"You are my Son;
    today I have begotten you"?
Or again,
"I will be his Father,
    and he will be my Son"?
[6]And again, when he brings the first-born into the world, he says,
"Let all God's angels worship him."
[7]Of the angels he says,
"He makes his angels winds,
    and his servants flames of fire."
[8]But of the Son he says,
"Your throne, O God, is forever
        and ever,
    and the righteous scepter is the
        scepter of your kingdom.
[9]You have loved righteousness and
        hated wickedness;
therefore God, your God, has
        anointed you
    with the oil of gladness beyond
        your companions."

Son became so much greater than the other messengers, such as angels, that he received a more important title than theirs.
[5]After all, when did God ever say to any of the angels:
*You are my Son.*
        *Today I have become your Father?*
Or, even,
*I will be his Father,*
        *and he will be my Son?*
[6]But then, when he brought his first-born into the world, he said,
*All of God's angels must worship him.*
[7]He talks about the angels:
*He's the one who uses the spirits for his*
        *messengers*
        *and who uses flames of fire*
        *as ministers.*
[8]But he says to his Son,
*God, your throne is forever*
        *and your kingdom's scepter is a*
        *rod of justice.*
[9]*You loved righteousness and hated*
        *lawless behavior.*
        *That is why God, your God,*
        *has anointed you with oil instead of*
*your companions.*

## UNDERSTANDING THE SCRIPTURE

**Introduction.** Hebrews begins with a rhetorical flourish. It affirms that God has spoken truly and often through Israel's prophets, and immediately asserts that God has now spoken in a new way. The author must acknowledge the greatness of the earlier revelations of God in order to celebrate the splendor of the new revelation of God in the "Son." The rest of the chapter gives scriptural support to the idea that Christ is not only higher than earlier prophets but also higher than all the angels. The point is to emphasize the value of the truth and salvation that come to the church through Christ.

**Hebrews 1:1-4.** This book opens with a series of exalted claims about Christ. Not only is he God's Son, he is God's agent of creation and the one who sustains the existence of the world; he is the reflection of God's glory and the one who purifies people of their sins; and he rules the cosmos from the place of power at God's throne. It will take the rest of this long and complicated book to explore and support those affirmations about who Christ is and what he has done for us. As these verses begin to tell of Christ's identity, Hebrews says that God has spoken to us through him "in these last days" (1:2). Like the rest of the New Testament, Hebrews sees the time of Christ and the church as the "last days." They do not always mean that they expect the world to end quickly, but rather that this is the time in history when God is most fully revealed and present with God's people. More clearly than in previous times, God is now known through Christ. As a child is more like the parent than a messenger is like a sender, so those who know God through the Son see God more clearly than those who have heard the messengers. To be certain we do not miss this point, Hebrews stresses how much like God Christ is: He is the "exact imprint" of God's being (1:3). We see precisely who God is in Christ. There can be no clearer revelation of God and God's will than this. Hebrews demonstrates how close Christ is to God by attributing to him things that only God can do, including creating and sustaining the world.

This most powerful being who reveals God to us also accomplishes another crucial task: He is the one who purifies believers of their sins so that they can live in right relationship with God. He takes away what separates people from God. Other parts of Hebrews will emphasize this part of Christ's work, seeing it as another way that he reveals God to us. This work shows us God's love and God's desire to be in relationship with us. But even that is not all. This same Son now wields God's power. This implies that he will be the one through whom God eventually reclaims the whole

world. So Christ is declared to be the one through whom God is known and through whom God acts from creation to the end of all things. All of this indicates that Christ is greater than any other beings in the cosmos, including angels. So Hebrews says God gives him a name higher than the angels. That name may be Son or as it is in Philippians (2:11) the name Lord. Both titles identify Christ very closely with God.

**Hebrews 1:5-9.** Hebrews supports the distinction between Christ and angels with a series of quotations from the Hebrew Bible. Some of these come from the royal psalms, that is, from the psalms that speak of the Davidic king. While they are clearly metaphorical when they apply to the king, Hebrews gives them a new meaning, applying them to Christ to show that Christ is higher than angels—something that was not true of the Davidic king. Quoting Psalm 2:7, Hebrews 1:5 uses the language of adoption so that God claims Christ as "my Son," something God does not do with angels. Then the author cites Deuteronomy 32:43, a passage originally about God, to assert that angels are to worship the Son. Such a demand requires a close identification of the Son with the Father. Then Hebrews reminds readers of what angels are: servants, even if they are powerful. The difference between angels and Christ is the difference between those who only serve and the one in line to inherit everything.

Verse 8 goes even further, addressing the Son as God. Here the Son is so closely identified with God that it is appropriate to address him as God. While the identity is close, God is still distinguishable from the Son. God is the one who appoints the Son to the position of power. The primary characteristic that the Son demonstrates and so reveals about God here is righteousness. God's righteous, and the demand that God's people be righteous, are prominent themes in Hebrews.

**Hebrews 1:10-14.** The acclamations about Christ momentarily shift back to his relationship to the creation in these verses. He again is the one through whom the world was created, and the world is transitory compared to him. This is one of those affirmations that observant Jews would have made only about God until the church began to make them about Christ. Such claims caused problems for the observant Jews in the church when they associated with those not in the church. One purpose of Hebrews is to offer these members evidence for such claims in their arguments with fellow Jews.

The final quotation in 1:13 again serves to compare Christ to angels, asserting God's commitment to uphold the reign of Christ until all evil is defeated. The last word (1:14) makes the divide between Christ and the angels even wider. Earlier in the passage angels were servants of God; now as servants of God they serve those who receive the salvation that comes through Christ.

---

## INTERPRETING THE SCRIPTURE

*Christ the Son and Image of God*

Hebrews contains some of the clearest and highest claims about Christ in all the New Testament. These claims are truly amazing when we remember that they are being made by people who are faithful Jews. Among all peoples of the ancient world, only Jews claimed that the world was made by only one God and that this one God was ruler of all creation. These two claims about God (sole creator and ruler) were what led Jews to claim that they should worship only God. Their covenant with God was secure because these aspects of God provide assurance that God's promises cannot be challenged by any force in the cosmos. In the opening paragraphs of this book, the author of Hebrews makes those very claims about Christ. He could hardly have said anything more exalted about Christ.

But Hebrews does not make a simplistic equation between God and Christ. Already in the first century some very careful thought had gone into how the church should understand the identity and work of Christ. Hebrews begins by saying that Christ is the clearest revelation of God the world has ever seen or can ever see. Yes, God has been seen truly by the prophets and others, including angels who had brought messages and shown God's glory. But Christ reveals God more clearly than any of these because of his relationship with God. Christ is not just appointed a task by God as the prophets and angels were; rather, he is God's Son, the one who bears the image of God in a way no one else does.

Other Jewish writers had spoken of God's Wisdom as an agent of creation. They personified this aspect of God's nature so that God worked through Wisdom to create and speak. In something of that same way,

Hebrews portrays the Son here as the revelation of the nature and character of God, so close to God that he is God's agent in creation and salvation. So close that Hebrews quotes one psalm to address the Son as God (1:8) and another as Lord (1:10). So close that angels (and by implication the church) are to worship him. The Son is the "exact imprint of God's very being" (1:3). Christ is the one who can reveal God most clearly because he is the image of God in an intimate and unique way. He is the best glimpse of God's character and glory humans can hope for.

The church continues to struggle with how to fit together the claims it makes about Christ and the claim that we worship only one God. We continue to wrestle with how to think of the God of the universe as being fully present and revealed in a seemingly normal person who lived in Palestine. But Hebrews insists early in this discussion that this one God was indeed present and visible in the human person Jesus and in the exalted Christ. These aspects of Christ's identity first come to expression in words of praise and thanksgiving.

### Christ the Revelation of the Power of God

In these verses, Hebrews speaks of two main aspects of God that Christ reveals. One of those is the power of God. As God's agent of creation, Christ reveals that God alone is powerful enough to design and create the world. It is through Christ that God continues to exercise this unequaled power as Christ sustains the world's existence (1:3). The act of creation was not a one-time event after which God simply withdrew. Rather, God remains present and active in sustaining the existence of the cosmos. Even in this constant sustaining that is done through Christ, the contrast between God and Christ on the one hand and the created order on the other is evident. While there is decay and change in the world, Christ, like God, remains the same forever (1:10-12). Hebrews proclaims that it is through Christ that God's power sustains the life and goodness of the world.

All of these displays of power provide assurance to believers when they face difficulties. If the readers of Hebrews were experiencing some hostility or rejection from those who did not have faith in Jesus, these assertions about the power of Christ are designed to give them hope. These declarations about Christ help them remember that the one in whom they believe has the power to sustain them. But even more, the writer declares that God exercises this power to defeat all the forces of evil. All who oppose the will of God in Christ will be deposed (1:13). So those who oppose them will not succeed in the end. The will of God will prevail in Christ. Thus, God reclaims the creation that has turned away and suffers in its alienation from God.

### Christ the Revelation of the Love of God

The second aspect of God that is revealed in Christ appears in the salvation God offers in him. As soon as Hebrews asserts that it is through Christ that God sustains the creation, the author maintains that this sustainer of creation is also the one who provides purification for sins. In other places in Hebrews, the writer will expound on this theme at length.

Here the writer introduces it as one of the central ways that the church understands Christ and he connects it directly to Christ's ascension to the place of power in heaven (1:3).

A central task of the one who sustains the cosmos is providing the means by which sinful people can approach the holy God. Christ not only sustains their existence but he also makes them pure. Just as people had to undergo purification to enter God's presence in the Jerusalem Temple, Christ makes believers pure so that they can enter the unmediated presence of God and live in right relationship with God. Part of the salvation that Christ reveals is the righteousness of God, that is, God's holiness and justice. Hebrews says Christ loves righteousness (1:9). Since God is righteous, God cannot simply pretend that people do not perpetrate injustice and evil. The revelation of Christ shows that God is both holy and the one who loves us enough to provide the means of renewing the relationships that are broken through sin. Since Christ loves righteousness, he is the one who shows us what God wants in the lives of God's people. He is the demonstration of the life that conforms to God's will.

Hebrews seldom points us to the teaching of Jesus or the ways that he interacted with those around him. The central element of the example Christ sets is his willingness to die for us. So the clearest pattern he provides is that of self-giving love offered in obedience to the will of God. Following this pattern of living enriches our lives so that they are fuller and richer; living such a life is a part of the salvation we receive in Christ. Both the fullness of life now and the promise of life with God are parts of the "oil of gladness" (1:9) that Christ brings us as the revelation of the power and love of God.

---

## SHARING THE SCRIPTURE

### PREPARING TO LEAD

*Preparing Our Hearts*

Ponder this week's devotional reading from John 1:1-5, 10-14, which are excerpts from the Prologue to John's Gospel, verses 1-18. What do you learn about the Word in relation to light and darkness in verses 1-5? How was the Word who came to live among humanity received according to verses 10-14? What relationship does John establish between the Word and God?

Pray that you and the students will recognize the Word—the light—who has come into the world and reflects the glory of the Father.

*Preparing Our Minds*

Study the background Scripture from Hebrews 1 and the lesson Scripture from Hebrews 1:1-9.

Consider this question: *When you need direction in life, whom do you trust to provide that guidance?*

Write on newsprint:
- ❑ categories for Gather to Learn.
- ❑ steps for seeking guidance under Goal 3.
- ❑ information for next week's lesson, found under Continue the Journey.

❏ activities for further spiritual growth in Continue the Journey.

Review the portion concerning Hebrews in The Big Picture: God in Isaiah, Hebrews, and Revelation, which precedes the first lesson of this quarter.

Be prepared to read or retell information in verses 1-4, 5-9 in Understanding the Scripture.

## LEADING THE CLASS

### (1) Gather to Learn

❖ Welcome everyone and pray that those who have come today will recognize the unique relationship between God the Father and God the Son.

❖ Post this list of categories, leaving space to write after or below each one:

| | |
|---|---|
| Financial advice | Medical care |
| Automotive help | Employment opportunities |
| Parenting | Restaurant recommendations |
| Travel arrangements | Personal problems |

❖ Read the categories one by one and invite participants to identify the kind of person or agency they would turn to for information. Note to conclude that we often have many choices when it comes to finding guidance in meeting particular needs.

❖ Read aloud today's focus statement: **People seek guidance for their lives but may question who the appropriate person is to give direction. Whom should they trust to provide direction in their quest for guidance? Christ, the reflection of God's glory, is the one who addresses life's questions with a powerful and sustaining word.**

### (2) Goal 1: Understand that Jesus Expresses Fully God's Very Being in the World

❖ Select a volunteer to read Hebrews 1:1-9.

❖ Unpack the meaning of the opening verses by retelling or reading Hebrews 1:1-4 in Understanding the Scripture.

❖ Discuss these questions:

1. **How would you describe the difference between the messages of the prophets and the revelation of God through the Son?**

2. **On what basis is the Son's revelation different from other ways that God has communicated with humanity?**

3. **How does the Son reveal the power of God?** (Add information from Christ the Revelation of the Power of God in Interpreting the Scripture.)

4. **How does the Son reveal the love of God?** (Add information from Christ the Revelation of the Love of God in Interpreting the Scripture.)

5. **What points does the writer of Hebrews make to show that the Son is superior to the angels?** (Refer to the quotations from the Old Testament found in verses 5-9 (and optionally, 10-14). Notice that in the CEB version these quotations are italicized for easy reference. If time permits, ask the students to turn to these verses.)

6. **Had you been an early Jewish-Christian reader of Hebrews, would the author's arguments about the Son have convinced you to**

remain strong in the face of persecution? Why or why not?

*(3) Goal 2: Appreciate Jesus' Relationship with God*

❖ Read Christ the Son and Image of God in Interpreting the Scripture.

❖ Form small groups and ask them to consider these questions: **What difference does the Son's relationship with God make to you in terms of your relationship with God? In other words, how would your relationship with God be different if you did not believe that Jesus was God's Son and that he was "the exact imprint of God's very being" (1:3)?**

❖ Bring the groups together and call for volunteers to name some ways their understanding of the Son's relationship with God affects their own relationship with God.

*(4) Goal 3: Create Ways to Seek Jesus' Continued Guidance in the Learners' Lives*

❖ Recall that in the Gather to Learn activity we identified sources for guidance to help us when we had various kinds of needs. Ask: **Why, or under what circumstances, would you go to Jesus for guidance?** (Note that you will likely get a wide variety of answers. Simply accept them; do not judge or challenge them.)

❖ Ask: **What are some of the ways that you can seek guidance from Jesus?** List responses on newsprint. Ideas may include: Bible study, devotional reading of the Bible, prayer, meditation, talking with a pastor or mature Christian friend whom I trust to advise me, hearing a sermon that

speaks to me, reading a book written from a Christian perspective, writing in a spiritual journal.

❖ Distribute paper and pencils and ask the students to follow these steps, which you will post on newsprint:

- Jot down a few words concerning a situation for which you need guidance from Jesus. You will not be asked to share this information, so be open and honest with God.
- Select one or more ways that the class has suggested that you could go about finding this guidance and write the way(s) on your paper.
- Determine your first steps. For example, will you look at a key word in a Bible concordance to find help? Will you make an appointment to see your pastor to discuss the matter? Will you set aside special prayer time?

❖ Reconvene the class and encourage volunteers to state the kinds of steps they will take to seek Jesus' guidance. (They are not to discuss the reason the guidance is needed.) Challenge them to follow through on their plan.

*(5) Continue the Journey*

❖ Pray that as the learners depart, they will seek guidance from the one who is the "exact imprint of God's very being" (1:3).

❖ Post information for next week's session on newsprint for the students to copy:

- **Title: Builder of the House**
- **Background Scripture: Hebrews 3:1-6; Matthew 7:19-29**

- Lesson Scripture: Hebrews 3:1-6; Matthew 7:24-29
- Focus of the Lesson: People often give credit for accomplishments to those who carry out the work rather than to the one who created the plan. Who is really responsible? The Scripture affirms that Jesus is the one who was faithful while accomplishing God's plan.

❖ Challenge the adults to grow spiritually by completing one or more of these activities related to this week's session.

(1) Read and reflect each day on Hebrews 1:1-4. What does it mean for all people—and for you in particular—to know that the Son is "the exact imprint of God's very being" (1:3)? How does that knowledge help to shape your relationship with God?

(2) Explore your relationship with angels. What role, if any, do they play in your life? What do you believe about them? How was your understanding of them informed by the Bible? How was it informed by popular movies, television shows, and books? How does your understanding square with the depiction of angels in Hebrews 1?

(3) Use a Bible concordance and commentaries to research the meaning of "purification for sins" (1:3). What do you learn about what the Son was able to do for you? Give thanks for this gracious action.

❖ Sing or read aloud "Word of God, Come Down on Earth."

❖ Conclude today's session by leading the class in this benediction, which is adapted from Hebrews 12:1b-2a, the key verses for October 30: **May we go forth empowered to run with perseverance the race that is set before us, looking to Jesus the pioneer and perfecter of our faith. Amen.**

## UNIT 2: THE SOVEREIGNTY OF JESUS
# BUILDER OF THE HOUSE

---

### PREVIEWING THE LESSON

**Lesson Scripture:** Hebrews 3:1-6; Matthew 7:24-29
**Background Scripture:** Hebrews 3:1-6; Matthew 7:19-29
**Key Verse:** Hebrews 3:3

#### Focus of the Lesson:
People often give credit for accomplishments to those who carry out the work rather than to the one who created the plan. Who is really responsible? The Scripture affirms that Jesus is the one who was faithful while accomplishing God's plan.

#### Goals for the Learners:
(1) to remember that Jesus, with divine authority, carried out God's intentions.
(2) to affirm that Jesus is the model for a life of dedication and service to the will of God.
(3) to dedicate one's life to Jesus with a commitment to engage in Christ-centered speech and actions.

#### Supplies:
Bibles, newsprint and marker, paper and pencils, hymnals

---

### READING THE SCRIPTURE

NRSV

Lesson Scripture: Hebrews 3:1-6

¹Therefore, brothers and sisters, holy partners in a heavenly calling, consider that Jesus, the apostle and high priest of our confession, ²was faithful to the one who appointed him, just as Moses also "was faithful in all God's house." **³Yet Jesus is worthy of more glory than Moses, just as the builder of a house has more**

CEB

Lesson Scripture: Hebrews 3:1-6

¹Therefore, brothers and sisters who are partners in the heavenly calling, think about Jesus, the apostle and high priest of our confession. ²Jesus was faithful to the one who appointed him just like Moses was faithful in God's house. **³But he deserves greater glory than Moses in the same way that the builder of**

honor than the house itself. ⁴(For every house is built by someone, but the builder of all things is God.) ⁵Now Moses was faithful in all God's house as a servant, to testify to the things that would be spoken later. ⁶Christ, however, was faithful over God's house as a son, and we are his house if we hold firm the confidence and the pride that belong to hope.

the house deserves more honor than the house itself. ⁴Every house is built by someone, but God is the builder of everything. ⁵Moses was faithful in all God's house as a servant in order to affirm the things that would be spoken later. ⁶But Jesus was faithful over God's house as a Son. We are his house if we hold on to the confidence and the pride that our hope gives us.

NRSV
Lesson Scripture: Matthew 7:24-29
²⁴"Everyone then who hears these words of mine and acts on them will be like a wise man who built his house on rock. ²⁵The rain fell, the floods came, and the winds blew and beat on that house, but it did not fall, because it had been founded on rock. ²⁶And everyone who hears these words of mine and does not act on them will be like a foolish man who built his house on sand. ²⁷The rain fell, and the floods came, and the winds blew and beat against that house, and it fell—and great was its fall!"
²⁸Now when Jesus had finished saying these things, the crowds were astounded at his teaching, ²⁹for he taught them as one having authority, and not as their scribes.

CEB
Lesson Scripture: Matthew 7:24-29
²⁴"Everybody who hears these words of mine and puts them into practice is like a wise builder who built a house on bedrock. ²⁵The rain fell, the floods came, and the wind blew and beat against that house. It didn't fall because it was firmly set on bedrock. ²⁶But everybody who hears these words of mine and doesn't put them into practice will be like a fool who built a house on sand. ²⁷The rain fell, the floods came, and the wind blew and beat against that house. It fell and was completely destroyed."
²⁸When Jesus finished these words, the crowds were amazed at his teaching ²⁹because he was teaching them like someone with authority and not like their legal experts.

## UNDERSTANDING THE SCRIPTURE

**Introduction.** The readings in Hebrews 3 and Matthew 7 are exhortations and warnings. The threatening nature of the warning is clear in our section of Matthew, but in Hebrews 3 it becomes clear only in the verses that immediately follow our reading. Both passages call for faithfulness to the will of God, with an eye toward what happens to those who are not faithful.

**Hebrews 3:1-6.** The tone of Hebrews 3:1-6 is quite different from the end of the Sermon on the Mount. Rather than a series of warnings, it focuses on who Christ is and what his life and work mean for believers. The author first identifies Jesus as "apostle and high priest" (3:1). This is the only place in the New Testament Jesus is called an apostle. An apostle is one who is sent; thus it usually refers to those sent by Christ to proclaim the gospel. But here in Hebrews, Jesus is the one sent by God. At the same time he is high priest, the one sent by the people to represent them to God. So Christ serves both parties as the mediator between them. As a human he is the appropriate one to represent the people to God, and as the one who is God's image (1:3) he is the best representative of God to the people. While this idea of being the mediator will be expanded later (8:6; 9:15; 12:24), the central emphasis in 3:1-6 is on Christ's faithfulness.

Hebrews often identifies Jesus or defines his work by making comparisons. In chapter 1 we saw that he is greater than the angels, but many of the comparisons of Hebrews are with things that are a part of the Mosaic covenant. While Hebrews claims superiority for what Christ has done, we should remember that this comparison is meaningful only if the thing Jesus is compared to is extremely valuable. In 3:1-6, Jesus is compared to Moses. Moses was God's faithful messenger. He served as both the one sent by God to the people and as the people's representative to God. He was the one who led the people out of Egypt, delivered the law, and led them in the wilderness. He was a faithful servant who obeyed God even when that was a demanding task. As great as Moses was, Hebrews says, Jesus is greater. The difference between them is not that Moses sometimes failed while Jesus was perfect, but that Moses was just a servant in God's household, whereas Jesus is the Son. This identity of Jesus makes him superior and allows him to offer more gifts from God than Moses could. Moses was a servant in the house. Jesus makes believers members of the household

(3:6). The faithfulness of Jesus that Hebrews has in mind is primarily that which is seen in his passion and death. When Hebrews makes precise the object of the example Jesus sets, the author always points to the Passion. It is the act of supreme faithfulness to God's will.

Just as Hebrews proclaims that the faithfulness of the Son allows him to bring believers into God's family, we begin to hear his exhortation and warning. The readers are assured that Christ makes them members of God's household *if* they maintain faithfulness. In verses 7-11 Hebrews quotes Psalm 95:7-11, which recounts the unfaithfulness of the people in the wilderness and the punishment that ensued. The faithfulness of Christ sets the example to be followed; the rebellion in the wilderness is the example of what happens when one is unfaithful. So in the midst of opposition from those outside the church (see the discussion in "The Big Picture: God in Isaiah, Hebrews, and Revelation"), Hebrews calls believers to costly faithfulness.

**Matthew 7:19-27.** Matthew 7 contains the conclusion of the Sermon on the Mount. While the Beatitudes and the Lord's Prayer come to mind when we think about this Sermon, it also contains numerous warnings and threats about coming judgment. The Sermon concludes with a series of such warnings. Matthew 7:19-20 is the conclusion of a warning about false teachers. Jesus threatens his listeners with being "thrown into the fire." But then the warning expands in 7:21-27 so that it addresses all who claim to be God's people. Jesus says that recognizing him as Lord is not sufficient; those who make this confession must live lives that conform to the will of God. Those who fail to live as though Jesus is their Lord will be rejected at judgment ("on that day," 7:22). The demand here is not for perfection but for a life that reflects the confession. If you call Jesus Lord, you must obey what that Lord tells you to do. In essence, Jesus says that professing that he is Lord is hollow and meaningless unless the one who says it accepts Jesus as the one who commands his or her life. The parable of the houses built on the rock and the sand supports this point. Jesus asserts that the person who puts his teaching into practice will build a strong life that can withstand the difficulties that come to it. But those who only hear his teaching and do not obey it will not be able to endure the problems that life brings. Perhaps the fall of the house on the sand again points us to final judgment. That final threat ends the Sermon on the Mount.

**Matthew 7:28-29.** These final two verses of Matthew 7 give us the reaction of the hearers. They say that Jesus teaches as one with authority. It is important to remember that this recognition comes on the heels of Jesus' claim that those who hear him must do as he commands or face condemnation. Matthew now has the people recognize the truth of the assertion that only those who obey the teaching of Jesus will stand at the judgment. They are all, then, responsible for obeying. These sound like harsh words, but they are not as uncommon in the Gospels as many of us think, and they are particularly present in Matthew (see especially chapters 23 and 25). Faith demands discipleship.

## INTERPRETING THE SCRIPTURE

### The Example of Jesus

One of the best ways to encourage someone to behave in a particular way is to set the example of doing so. First-century moralists knew this and advised people to imitate good people as the best way to begin to live a virtuous life. New Testament writers also point to various people that readers should imitate (for example, Philippians 3:17). But the primary exemplar for all believers is Christ. Hebrews 3 points to the faithfulness of Christ as the characteristic believers should imitate, saying that Christ is a better exemplar than even Moses.

In Judaism of this era, Moses was a prime example of faithfulness to God. He obeyed God by returning to Egypt;, he led the people who were not sure the struggle to freedom was worth it; he called them to repent when they worshiped other gods; he constantly fulfilled God's will. His faithfulness to God's will even extended to his pleading for mercy for the people when they sinned because he knew that salvation was the ultimate will of God. Hebrews 3:2 alludes to Numbers 12:7-8 where it says that God speaks to Moses face-to-face, a sign of Moses' faithfulness.

But even this faithfulness is eclipsed by that of Jesus. Jesus is not greater because there was something wrong with Moses, but because of the identity of Jesus. Jesus is the Son of God and so can show us who God is and what God wants in the clearest possible ways. The faithfulness of

Jesus does not come only from obligation or even gratitude; it comes from being related to God, to sharing by nature in the will of God. Perhaps this reminder of the oneness of the will of God and the Son calls readers to move toward shaping their will, not just their conduct, to conform to God's will.

## The Authority of the Son

This identity of Jesus also gives him the authority to define what faithful living is. His identity as the Son grants Christ the relationship with God that includes full knowledge of God and God's will. As the one who shares God's power as the "owner" of the household, he is authorized to determine what constitutes faithful living. This instruction about faithful living comes from the teaching of Jesus and from the teaching that comes from those who give us interpretations of his life in the New Testament. Hebrews assumes that its readers know of these teachings and about the church's teachings on how believers should live in light of the salvation they have received in Christ. Rather than reciting those teachings, this book provides encouragement and motivation for faithful living. It does so by noting that as the Son of the loving Father, Christ does not just issue commands. Instead, he participates in the world of the household and sets an example for those who would be members of the family. He is the example who truly lives up to the instructions he gives about ethical living. This consistency between demand and life increases the authority he wields to say what proper living is.

When Hebrews alludes to the faithfulness of Christ that believers are to imitate, it points to the Passion rather than to the broader ministry of Jesus. This is not because the ministry and teaching of Jesus were unimportant, but because the Passion is the exemplary moment of that ministry. As the supreme act of self-giving love it epitomizes the whole mission of Christ. This is the moment that embodies the teaching of Jesus and the commands he gives about how to live in relation to one another. The Passion is the supreme act of faithfulness that shows God's love for us and so the act that sets the pattern for Christian living. It is here that we see how far Christ's love extends to us and how he expects us to extend love to others. This definition of faithfulness sets a high, even radical, standard. It calls believers to put the good of others ahead of their own good, just as Christ did for us in the Passion (see Philippians 2:3-11). This demand is not just to make the good of others as important as our own good, but that their good is to be more important than ours. This runs counter to the normal ways that we evaluate things, but it is what the example of Christ calls for. The life of faithfulness to God turns out to be a life lived in service to others.

## We Are God's House

In the middle of praising Christ as God's Son and our exemplar of faithfulness, Hebrews identifies believers as God's house (3:6). Believers are in a special relationship with God: They are the place of the dwelling of God. Just as a temple is a house of God, a place where God is present, so the church is that center of the imminent presence of God. As the place where

God is present, the church must be holy, its members are "holy partners" (3:1). We must live as the people who have God in our midst. So, one purpose of the church's faithfulness is to live up to its identity as the house of God. Given that Christ has been identified as the Son here, this image probably has a second implication: Believers are members of God's family. As the Son who is over the estate, Christ brings believers into the family. This membership brings great privileges; it also brings responsibilities. Now believers must act in the ways that members of this family are expected to act. Of course, here that means they must imitate the faithfulness of Christ.

### The Demand of Obedience

Hebrews 3:6 ends with a warning: It says you are God's people *if* you remain faithful (that is, "if we hold firm"). This note of warning is much more pronounced in Matthew 7:19-23. The warning in Matthew is addressed to people who confess Jesus as Lord. They are even people who have given amazing demonstrations of the power of God (prophesied and exorcised demons). Yet they are ultimately rejected by Jesus because they failed to conform their lives to his demands. We may expect such threats to come to those outside the church, but Matthew directs them to people within the church. Genuine faith includes faithful living. While we are accustomed to separating faith from how we live or from ethical demands, Matthew makes no such separation. Jesus says here that how you live shows whether you really have faith. Faith is more than believing something. Jesus says that living in accord with his demands is an essential element of real faith. While all salvation comes to us through God's mercy, accepting that salvation includes accepting demands about how we live. Really, taking up the way of life God demands, the way of life shown us by Christ, is a part of receiving salvation. It gives us the most meaningful way to live in the midst of a culture that values things that do not bring true happiness and joy. This way of life gives us the depth of living that God wants for those God loves.

## SHARING THE SCRIPTURE

### PREPARING TO LEAD

#### Preparing Our Hearts

Ponder this week's devotional reading from Hebrews 10:19-25. Here the writer exhorts readers to remain faithful to Jesus and persevere in their faith. To do so he uses several images: blood, way, curtain, great priest over the house of God, hearts sprinkled clean, bodies washed with pure water. With what do you connect each of these images? What do they suggest about the relationship between Jesus and believers?

Pray that you and the students will strive constantly, with the help of God, to live lives worthy of the example and actions of Jesus.

#### Preparing Our Minds

Study the background Scripture from Hebrews 3:1-6; Matthew 7:19-29 and the lesson Scripture from Hebrews 3:1-6; Matthew 7:24-29.

Consider this question: *Do you give credit to the one who did the work or created the plan—or both?*

Write on newsprint:

❏ questions for Goal 2 under Sharing the Scripture.

❏ information for next week's lesson, found under Continue the Journey.

❏ activities for further spiritual growth in Continue the Journey.

Determine how you might use any of the features that precede the first lesson of this quarter in today's session. Look especially at the paragraphs related to Hebrews in The Big Picture: God in Isaiah, Hebrews, and Revelation. Be prepared to present a brief background lecture to help participants understand the persecution the church was facing from those who did not accept Christ.

## LEADING THE CLASS

### 1) Gather to Learn

❖ Welcome everyone and pray that those who have come today will be open to learning more about Jesus, whom they are called to imitate.

❖ Read: **Most people want to get credit for their accomplishments. The student wants an A; the athlete wants a medal; the worker wants a promotion; the musician wants a standing ovation. But according to Jeremiah 9:23, God has other ideas: "Thus says the Lord: Do not let the wise boast in their wisdom, do not let the mighty boast in their might, do not let the wealthy boast in their wealth." In other words, we are not to boast of our own accomplishments, but instead, as verse 24 states, God's people should boast in the Lord who acts with "steadfast love, justice, and righteousness."**

❖ Call on volunteers to identify actions of God in their lives for which they want to give God all the credit and glory.

❖ Read aloud today's focus statement: **People often give credit for accomplishments to those who carry out the work rather than to the one who created the plan. Who is really responsible? The Scripture affirms that Jesus is the one who was faithful while accomplishing God's plan.**

*(2) Goal 1: Remember that Jesus, with Divine Authority, Carried Out God's Intentions*

❖ Present the brief lecture that you have developed to remind class members of the perilous situation that confronted the readers of Hebrews.

❖ Choose a volunteer to read Hebrews 3:1-6.

❖ Discuss these questions. See Hebrews 3:1-6 in Understanding the Scripture for ideas to add to the discussion.

1. **In what ways does the writer compare Jesus to Moses?**

2. **Why is Jesus seen as greater than Moses?**

3. **How did Jesus show his faithfulness to God?**

4. **Under what conditions do we become members of the household of God and maintain our connection there?**

*(3) Goal 2: Affirm that Jesus Is the Model for a Life of Dedication and Service to the Will of God*

❖ Solicit a volunteer to read the first paragraph of The Authority of the Son in Interpreting the Scripture.

❖ Read or retell the information under The Demand of Obedience in Interpreting the Scripture.

❖ Ask: **Although we recognize that only Jesus is both the Son of God and a human being, what are some of the ways that we humans can follow his example of dedication and service to the will of God?** List these ideas on newsprint.

❖ Form several small groups. Encourage the groups to answer these two questions, which you will write on newsprint:

1. **Of the ways that we have identified, which ones do we tend to overlook, perhaps because we think there are too many barriers to acting as Jesus acted? For example, if we say that we are to love our enemies as Jesus taught us and lived, what barriers might we erect to keep us from loving?**
2. **Choose one of the ways listed that we can follow Jesus' example but seldom do so because we stumble over barriers. Brainstorm some ideas for overcoming these barriers.**

❖ Call everyone together to hear ideas. Take special note of recurring themes, since these may be especially helpful for the group as a whole.

❖ Affirm that we can each do more, with God's help, to follow Jesus' model.

*(4) Goal 3: Dedicate One's Life to Jesus with a Commitment to Engage in Christ-Centered Speech and Actions*

❖ Select a volunteer to read Matthew 7:24-29.

❖ Read or retell Matthew 7:19-27 and 7:28-29 in the Understanding the Scripture portion.

❖ Encourage the students to call out types of Christ-centered speech and actions that would enable them to follow Jesus more closely and draw others to him through their witness.

❖ Distribute paper and pencils. Tell participants that they are to write two or three actions that they could take to demonstrate more fully their commitment to live a Christ-centered life.

❖ Bring everyone together and lead them in repeating these words of commitment after you. Stop at each slash (/) so that the students can repeat your words: **With God's help/ I will commitment myself/ to engaging in the kind of Christ-centered speech and actions/ that I have felt led to list today.**

*(5) Continue the Journey*

❖ Pray that as the learners depart, they will go forth following the example of Jesus.

❖ Post information for next week's session on newsprint for the students to copy:

- **Title: The Great High Priest**
- **Background Scripture: Hebrews 4:14–5:10**
- **Lesson Scripture: Hebrews 4:14–5:10**
- **Focus of the Lesson: Gifted leaders carry out specific responsibilities on behalf of the communities they serve. How are such leaders chosen? Jesus was appointed by God to serve as a high priest for the people.**

❖ Challenge the adults to grow spiritually by completing one or more of these activities related to this week's session.

(1) Think of a hymn that encourages you to follow faithfully in the footsteps of Jesus. "Take My Life, and Let It Be," "Lord, I Want to Be a Christian," and "I Am Thine, O Lord" may be familiar examples. Ponder how the words of your selected hymn help you to live faithfully for Christ.

(2) Give credit to persons within your congregation who have planned and executed a program. A note or public acknowledgment (perhaps at a meeting or as a prayer request for joys) would be an appropriate way to thank these folks.

(3) Write a journal entry in which you identify ways that you see yourself as imitating Jesus. What areas in your life do you need to bring under his control? Ask God to help you become more conformed to the example of Jesus.

❖ Sing or read aloud "Ye Servants of God."

❖ Conclude today's session by leading the class in this benediction, which is adapted from Hebrews 12:1b-2a, the key verses for October 30: **May we go forth empowered to run with perseverance the race that is set before us, looking to Jesus the pioneer and perfecter of our faith. Amen.**

## UNIT 2: THE SOVEREIGNTY OF JESUS
# THE GREAT HIGH PRIEST

---

### PREVIEWING THE LESSON

**Lesson Scripture:** Hebrews 4:14–5:10
**Background Scripture:** Hebrews 4:14–5:10
**Key Verse:** Hebrews 4:14

**Focus of the Lesson:**
Gifted leaders carry out specific responsibilities on behalf of the communities they serve. How are such leaders chosen? Jesus was appointed by God to serve as a high priest for the people.

**Goals for the Learners:**
(1) to consider that God appointed Jesus as high priest for the people.
(2) to appreciate that Jesus, in his humanity, fully understands and identifies with the daily life of all peoples.
(3) to identify the kind of leaders who suffer, serve, and obey God's intentions in the spirit of Jesus.

**Supplies:**
Bibles, newsprint and marker, paper and pencils, hymnals

---

### READING THE SCRIPTURE

NRSV
Lesson Scripture: Hebrews 4:14–5:10

**14Since, then, we have a great high priest who has passed through the heavens, Jesus, the Son of God, let us hold fast to our confession.** 15For we do not have a high priest who is unable to sympathize with our weaknesses, but we have one who in every respect has been tested as we are, yet without sin. 16Let us therefore

CEB
Lesson Scripture: Hebrews 4:14–5:10

**14Also, let's hold on to the confession since we have a great high priest who passed through the heavens, who is Jesus, God's Son;** 15because we don't have a high priest who can't sympathize with our weaknesses but instead one who was tempted in every way that we are, except without sin.

approach the throne of grace with boldness, so that we may receive mercy and find grace to help in time of need.

[1]Every high priest chosen from among mortals is put in charge of things pertaining to God on their behalf, to offer gifts and sacrifices for sins. [2]He is able to deal gently with the ignorant and wayward, since he himself is subject to weakness; [3]and because of this he must offer sacrifice for his own sins as well as for those of the people. [4]And one does not presume to take this honor, but takes it only when called by God, just as Aaron was.

[5]So also Christ did not glorify himself in becoming a high priest, but was appointed by the one who said to him,
"You are my Son,
　today I have begotten you";
[6]as he says also in another place,
"You are a priest forever,
　according　to　the　order　of Melchizedek."

[7]In the days of his flesh, Jesus offered up prayers and supplications, with loud cries and tears, to the one who was able to save him from death, and he was heard because of his reverent submission. [8]Although he was a Son, he learned obedience through what he suffered; [9]and having been made perfect, he became the source of eternal salvation for all who obey him, [10]having been designated by God a high priest according to the order of Melchizedek.

[16]Finally, let's draw near to the throne of favor with confidence so that we can receive mercy and find grace when we need help.

[5:1]Every high priest is taken from the people and put in charge of things that relate to God for their sake, in order to offer gifts and sacrifices for sins. [2]The high priest is able to deal gently with the ignorant and those who are misled since he himself is prone to weakness. [3]Because of his weakness, he must offer sacrifices for his own sins as well as for the people. [4]No one takes this honor for themselves but takes it only when they are called by God, just like Aaron.

[5]In the same way Christ also didn't promote himself to become high priest. Instead, it was the one who said to him,
*You are my Son.*
　*Today I have become your Father,*
[6]as he also says in another place,
*You are a priest forever,*
　*according to the order of Melchizedek.*
[7]During his days on earth, Christ offered prayers and requests with loud cries and tears as his sacrifices to the one who was able to save him from death. He was heard because of his godly devotion. [8]Although he was a Son, he learned obedience from what he suffered. [9]After he had been made perfect, he became the source of eternal salvation for everyone who obeys him. [10]He was appointed by God to be a high priest according to the order of Melchizedek.

# UNDERSTANDING THE SCRIPTURE

**Introduction.** As a whole, Hebrews is a work that calls people to faithfulness and emphasizes the importance of faithfulness for the people who receive salvation. It has given us Christ as the exemplar of the faithfulness that all should try to attain. It has already recalled episodes of failure on the part of Israel and reminded readers of the judgment that followed that unfaithfulness. But Hebrews does not suggest that salvation comes from one's own efforts. As we saw earlier in chapter 1, the author identifies Christ as the image of God who has revealed God and brought us salvation. In our reading today, the emphasis is again on how Christ is the powerful agent through whom we receive salvation.

**Hebrews 4:14-16.** The author of Hebrews assumes that his readers are familiar with the Hebrew Bible and know a good deal about how worship was conducted at the Jerusalem Temple. So he assumes that everyone has a notion of what it means to call Jesus the "high priest" (4:14). All of his readers know that the high priest supervises the worship at the Temple and makes sure that the sacrifices are offered in the manner the law prescribes. Perhaps most important, he is the one priest who enters the Most Holy Place on the Day of Atonement to offer the sacrifice on the "mercy seat" once a year. This is the most holy of days and the most holy of rites. It is the ceremony that signals the commitment of the people to live in covenant with God because this is where they ask forgiveness for all the ways they have transgressed that covenant throughout the previous year. This day also assures them of

God's forgiveness and commitment to them.

As amazing as this office is, Jesus is no ordinary high priest; he has passed through the heavens and is the Son of God. His passage through the heavens is his exaltation following his death and resurrection. So this priest does not serve in the Jerusalem Temple (which may already have been destroyed), but in heaven in the very presence of God. No high priest could be more effective. In light of that position and status of Christ, Hebrews can reasonably assert that readers should faithfully maintain their confession of him. Hebrews is written to a church that is facing some kind of opposition from outsiders, probably from fellow members of their synagogues who are not church members. That opposition may be social or economic pressure or even consist of being expelled from their synagogue. This church needs assurance that their faith in Christ is correct and that God understands their sufferings. Hebrews assures them that Christ knows what they are going through because he experienced it himself. He was tested in every way they are now, with personal sin and with wanting to avoid problems and persecutions by compromising the faith. Yet he always endured without sinning. Still, he knows the power of the temptation and so can sympathize with the pain this church is experiencing. This common experience assures those who do sin that Christ is ready to provide forgiveness.

**Hebrews 5:1-6.** Jesus' empathy with a persecuted church is explicated further in 5:1-6. It is the job of every high priest to approach God for the people, to ask God for forgiveness for the people's sins. The high priest can do this with empathy for the failings of the people because he is also a sinner. Even the Day of Atonement ceremony recognizes that the high priest is a sinner. Before he can offer a sacrifice on behalf of the people, he must offer one for himself (see Leviticus 9:7-8). He must be forgiven so that he is in a position to ask for forgiveness for others. Placing oneself in the presence of a holy and just God in this intimate way is not something a person does lightly. And so Hebrews notes that the original high priest, Aaron, did not assume this position on his own; rather, God appointed him. It is assumed that those who follow him are likewise appointed by God and so are granted this access to God's presence.

While Hebrews sees Christ as the Son of God, the writer also wants it to be made clear that Christ does not assume the post of high priest by asserting prerogative. Instead, Christ is commissioned by God to fill the office. Indeed, God makes this priestly office a part of what it means to be the Son. When Hebrews says that Christ is a priest of the order of Melchizedek, it refers to a story from the life of Abraham (Genesis 14:17-20). We will explore this image in detail next week. Here we need only know that it means a priesthood that will have no end. Christ is installed in heaven as permanent high priest.

**Hebrews 5:7-10.** The prayers of Jesus for others begin during his earthly ministry, even before his exaltation to his priestly position in heaven. As Jesus believes in the power of God to raise him from the dead, he believes that God will forgive sinners through his intercession. Given that Hebrews has already said that Jesus was without sin, it is strange to hear in verse 8 that he learned from suffering. Unlike us, he did not learn the right way to live by suffering consequences of bad choices. What he learns through the submitting to the will of God and suffering as a human is our plight, how painful and difficult it can be to live faithfully in times of trouble. This knowledge makes him the perfect one to intercede for us (5:9). He has both the power of the Son with the office of high priest and the experience of knowing the difficulties of human life. This combination makes him the perfect one to plead our case before God. As Son and high priest he grants forgiveness and eternal salvation to all who "obey him" (5:9), that is, to all who live faithfully by his commands—or as 4:14 says it, those who "hold fast to our confession."

---

## INTERPRETING THE SCRIPTURE

### Jesus as High Priest

This passage assigns to Jesus the highest liturgical office in all of ancient Judaism. The high priest in Jerusalem was responsible for the worship activities at the one Temple to God. His most important task was his offering of the sacrifice on the Day of Atonement. This is the ceremonial wiping clean of the slate that acknowledged how the people had failed to live up to their covenant responsibilities. This priestly function of mediating forgiveness by God is the focus of Hebrews' identification of Jesus as high priest; he is the one who can mediate forgiveness for us. Hebrews provides even more assurance that those who believe in Christ are forgiven by locating his place of service in heaven. If the work of the high priest was effective in Jerusalem, think of how effective it must be in heaven in the immediate presence of God. Calling Jesus the high priest is clearly metaphorical. The author does not envision Jesus literally offering sacrifices of sheep and other things in heaven. This image assures believers that they have access to God and God's forgiveness in a way that is superior even to the sacrifices that were offered at the Temple. Everyone agreed that the Jerusalem Temple sacrifices had signaled forgiveness and renewed the relationship between God and the people. So to say that something is even more effective is high praise. Even more, this sacrifice is offered by a high priest who had no sin of his own to confess.

All high priests prior to Jesus had been sinners themselves. They had all failed to be fully faithful to God, and this sinning was something that continued while the priest was in office because he had to offer the sacrifice for his own sin, along with everyone else's, every year. Those asking for forgiveness in Christ have a much better qualified priest, one who is sinless. Even that qualification is not all that makes the forgiveness more secure. This high priest holds the office eternally; he has none of the weaknesses that plagued early occupants of the office. All of these factors demonstrate that the sacrifice offered by Christ is even more effective than the Jerusalem worship. We must remember that this is no denigration of the true and faithful worship of the Jerusalem Temple. If it were not powerful and effective, the claims about Jesus would mean little. As it stands, the claimed forgiveness and relationship with God are more secure than ever because the priest and the place of sacrifice are far better than ever before. This is all the more important because the church reading Hebrews was facing opposition from those who saw the worship in Jerusalem as the pinnacle of proper worship.

### Perfect but Empathetic

As we think of those who understand us best, it is usually those who have experiences we have been through, those who have endured the same difficulties. This is why so many support groups ask people with similar struggles to help one another. Even if these people are very understanding, we doubt that they really know how we feel unless they have found themselves in the same circumstances. Hebrews says high priests can be sympathetic with those who come asking for forgiveness because they know from personal experience the same weaknesses. In fact, they have succumbed to the same weaknesses. The priest knows how hard it is to live for God from personal experience and failure. Pleas for forgiveness are forwarded to God by a high priest who can plead the case from experience. It is reassuring to know that the one who approaches God for us knows just how we feel and just how hard it is to do what we are supposed to do. That kind of person can make a good case for us.

As Hebrews proclaims the exalted position of Jesus and his identity as the Son of God, we may wonder whether he could ever understand our struggles. Looking down from above, observing our pain is not the same as having it himself. The idea that a person must have common experiences to fully understand what the other person is going through guides the thought in our passage. One of the things that makes Jesus a perfect high priest and intercessor for us is that he has the experience of being human. Through the Incarnation he knows what it is like to be tempted, to try to avoid pain, or to want immediate pleasure rather than to remain faithful to that way of life that God wants for us (4:15). Hebrews probably does not have in mind the story of the temptations of Christ in the Gospels (Matthew 4:1-11; Mark 1:12-13; Luke 4:1-13), but a part of the reason the Gospel writers included those stories was to show that Jesus was subjected to powerful temptations. He resisted but he experienced the power of the deceptions that lead us to sin. Hebrews sums it up dramatically saying that he was tempted in all the ways we are (4:15). Since he has had these experiences Jesus, like other high priests, is sympathetic to our plight and in responding to our failures.

### Taking the Office with Humility

It is perhaps an unexpected turn when Hebrews notes that Jesus did not presume to take this office for himself but was appointed to the position by God. It is easy to see why a caveat about other high priests was necessary. It would take a lot of arrogance for any person to decide to be the representative of the people before God, to decide on one's own to walk into the place of the presence of God. So Hebrews notes that high priests are called by God, not self-appointed, to accept such a weighty responsibility. Similarly, even as the image of God, Christ does not appoint himself as high priest. God calls Christ to accept this task and with it to accept the demand to be obedient and submissive to God's will (5:7-8).

It may seem strange, but accepting the exalted position of high priest requires humility and submission. This is also the way Philippians 2:6-11 envisions the Incarnation; it is an act of intentional acceptance of a lower of status for the good others. This pattern of being humble and of accepting suffering for the good of others is the central way that Christ serves as an example of how we are to live. He is particularly the exemplar for the ways leaders are to act in the church. Leaders have public roles that automatically give them status and power. The way that Jesus becomes high priest by accepting the Incarnation with its requirements of being submissive and obedient is the example for Christian leaders. Christ does not exert his power to force others to accept what he wants; he does what God wants for the good of others. He offers himself in service to others rather than expecting them to serve him. All Christians are called to this manner of life, but the description of what was required of Jesus to be high priest points special attention to leaders. Leaders should be those who exemplify Christ's humility as seen in his willingness to obey God's will by suffering for others and putting the good of others above his own good.

## SHARING THE SCRIPTURE

### PREPARING TO LEAD

#### Preparing Our Hearts

Ponder this week's devotional reading from Ephesians 4:7-13. What do you learn about Jesus from these verses? What do you learn about the types of gifts and their roles in the life of the church? What examples can you give to show that your congregation works together in the unity of faith?

Pray that you and the students will give thanks for these gifts given to equip the body of Christ and promise to use whatever gift(s) you have been given to build up the church.

#### Preparing Our Minds

Study the background Scripture and the lesson Scripture, which are both from Hebrews 4:14–5:10.

Consider this question: *How are gifted leaders chosen to carry out specific responsibilities on behalf of the communities they serve?*

Write on newsprint:

❏ information for next week's lesson, found under Continue the Journey.

❏ activities for further spiritual growth in Continue the Journey.

Determine how you might use any of the features that precede the first lesson of this quarter in today's session. Look especially at Close-up: A Comparison of Priestly Types. Consider copying this chart onto newsprint for the class to see. Or create a brief lecture from these points to compare the priesthood of the Levites to that of Jesus.

### LEADING THE CLASS

#### (1) Gather to Learn

❖ Welcome everyone and pray that those who have come today will recognize and appreciate gifted leaders within the church.

❖ Read: **People in the United States go to the voting polls every four years to elect a new president and other leaders. Let's form two groups and ask Group 1 to consider how we choose our leaders and Group 2 to identify personal gifts and character traits we want to see in our leaders. We'll come back together in four minutes to hear the top three choices from each group.**

❖ Read aloud today's focus statement: **Gifted leaders carry out specific responsibilities on behalf of the communities they serve. How are such leaders chosen? Jesus was appointed by God to serve as a high priest for the people.**

#### (2) Goal 1: Consider that God Appointed Jesus as High Priest for the People

❖ Note that we have talked about how we elect leaders in a democracy. Now as we turn to Hebrews we are going to see how God appointed priests, particularly Jesus, our high priest.

❖ Retell Jesus as High Priest from Interpreting the Scripture. Add information from Hebrews 4:14-16 in Understanding the Scripture to help the students understand the office and role of the priest. Since most Protestants think of their clergy leaders as pastors, not priests, the idea of the priesthood may be unfamiliar to some of the class.

❖ Call on two volunteers, the first to read Hebrews 4:14–5:4 and the second to read Hebrews 5:5–5:10.

Compare the Levitical priests with Jesus by either posting the chart you have copied from Close-up: A Comparison of Priestly Types or presenting the lecture you have prepared based on this chart.

*(3) Goal 2: Appreciate that Jesus, in His Humanity, Fully Understands and Identifies with the Daily Life of All Peoples*

❖ Read Perfect but Empathetic from Interpreting the Scripture.

❖ Identify situations in your community where understanding and empathy are needed. Perhaps elders are in need of people to transport them to medical appointments and help with shopping. Maybe children need safe places to play. Possibly teens need businesses that will offer them jobs. Make a list on newsprint.

❖ Discuss how Jesus might identify with the kinds of people you have listed. What might he say to them or do for them to indicate his concern for them?

❖ Consider how the class members, individually and collectively, could offer help to at least one group on the list. Maybe this help could be offered through the church. If an agency or community program already exists to help meet the need, perhaps class members would be willing to volunteer to work with an established group.

*(4) Goal 3: Identify the Kind of Leaders Who Suffer, Serve, and Obey God's Intentions in the Spirit of Jesus*

❖ Recall that in the Gather to Learn portion we talked about how

leaders are chosen in a democracy, as well as the characteristics of persons whom we think can ably fill such leadership roles.

❖ Spend a few moments talking about how lay and clergy leaders are selected in your denomination. If you are unsure of this process, contact your pastor in advance to get a basic understanding.

❖ Post newsprint and invite participants to brainstorm answers to this question: **How would you describe the kinds of leaders we need in the church today?** List ideas on newsprint.

❖ Distribute paper and pencils. Invite the students to make some notes about how they may fit the description the group has just brainstormed. Emphasize that some may see themselves as having the gifts and graces for ordained ministry but others may see gifts that would make them effective Sunday school teachers or committee leaders or organizers of a volunteer mission project.

❖ Encourage volunteers to comment on what they have written about how they see themselves as leaders.

❖ **Option:** Instead of asking people to read what they have written, ask others in the group to name leadership roles that would fit individuals within the group. For example, Eileen may be a great organizer who could direct vacation Bible school. Tim may have the gifts to welcome newcomers and make them feel at home in the church.

*(5) Continue the Journey*

Pray that as the learners depart, they will recognize that just as God chose and appointed Jesus for the role as the great high priest, so too they have been chosen and equipped with gifts needed to build up the church.

Post information for next week's session on newsprint for the students to copy:

- **Title: The High Priest Forever**
- **Background Scripture: Hebrews 7**
- **Lesson Scripture: Hebrews 7:1-3, 19b-28**
- **Focus of the Lesson: Practices, traditions, and institutions begun in the past are expected to continue. Who will sustain them? Jesus was named to give the practices, traditions, and institutions their ultimate meaning and role for the people for all generations.**

❖ Challenge the adults to grow spiritually by completing one or more of these activities related to this week's session.

(1) **Identify a problem that is causing you pain. Take this problem to Jesus in prayer. Listen for guidance on how to handle this situation. If change is not possible (for example, you are dealing with the death of a loved one), seek Jesus' comfort and guidance as you seek to reorient your life.**

(2) **Do some research on the office of the priesthood. Write a job description in which you outline the type of person needed for this job, the work the person is to do, and the risks and rewards that may come with the job.**

(3) **Empathize with another person who is experiencing a challenge that you have faced and overcome. Encourage this person to find strength and help in Jesus.**

❖ Sing or read aloud "Lead Me, Lord."

❖ Conclude today's session by leading the class in this benediction, which is adapted from Hebrews 12:1b-2a, the key verses for October 30: **May we go forth empowered to run with perseverance the race that is set before us, looking to Jesus the pioneer and perfecter of our faith. Amen.**

UNIT 2: THE SOVEREIGNTY OF JESUS
# The High Priest Forever

---

## PREVIEWING THE LESSON

**Lesson Scripture:** Hebrews 7:1-3, 19b-28
**Background Scripture:** Hebrews 7
**Key Verse:** Hebrews 7:24

### Focus of the Lesson:
Practices, traditions, and institutions begun in the past are expected to continue. Who will sustain them? Jesus was named to give the practices, traditions, and institutions their ultimate meaning and role for the people for all generations.

### Goals for the Learners:
(1) to compare Melchizedek, "priest of the Most High God," with Jesus, the "priest forever."
(2) to appreciate that people have one who intercedes for them before God.
(3) to respond to the realization that Jesus will always be believers' ultimate spiritual leader.

### Supplies:
Bibles, newsprint and marker, paper and pencils, hymnals

---

## READING THE SCRIPTURE

NRSV

Lesson Scripture: Hebrews 7:1-3, 19b-28

¹This "King Melchizedek of Salem, priest of the Most High God, met Abraham as he was returning from defeating the kings and blessed him"; ²and to him Abraham apportioned "one-tenth of everything." His name,

CEB

Lesson Scripture: Hebrews 7:1-3, 19b-28

¹This Melchizedek, who was king of Salem and priest of the Most High God, met Abraham as he returned from the defeat of the kings, and Melchizedek blessed him. ²Abraham gave a tenth of everything to him. His

in the first place, means "king of righteousness"; next he is also king of Salem, that is, "king of peace." ³Without father, without mother, without genealogy, having neither beginning of days nor end of life, but resembling the Son of God, he remains a priest forever.

¹⁹ᵇ[T]here is, on the other hand, the introduction of a better hope, through which we approach God.

²⁰This was confirmed with an oath; for others who became priests took their office without an oath, ²¹but this one became a priest with an oath, because of the one who said to him,

"The Lord has sworn

and will not change his mind,

'You are a priest forever'"—

²²accordingly Jesus has also become the guarantee of a better covenant.

²³Furthermore, the former priests were many in number, because they were prevented by death from continuing in office; ²⁴but **he holds his priesthood permanently, because he continues forever.** ²⁵Consequently he is able for all time to save those who approach God through him, since he always lives to make intercession for them.

²⁶For it was fitting that we should have such a high priest, holy, blameless, undefiled, separated from sinners, and exalted above the heavens. ²⁷Unlike the other high priests, he has no need to offer sacrifices day after day, first for his own sins, and then for those of the people; this he did once for all when he offered himself. ²⁸For the law appoints as high priests those who are subject to weakness, but the word of the oath, which came later than the law, appoints a Son who has been made perfect forever.

name means first "king of righteousness," and then "king of Salem," that is, "king of peace." ³He is without father or mother or any family. He has no beginning or end of life, but he's like God's Son and remains a priest for all time.

¹⁹ᵇOn the other hand, a better hope is introduced, through which we draw near to God. ²⁰And this was not done without a solemn pledge! The others have become priests without a solemn pledge, ²¹but this priest was affirmed with a solemn pledge by the one who said,

*The Lord has made a solemn pledge*

*and will not change his mind:*

*You are a priest forever.*

²²As a result, Jesus has become the guarantee of a better covenant. ²³The others who became priests are numerous because death prevented them from continuing to serve. ²⁴In contrast, **he holds the office of priest permanently because he continues to serve forever.** ²⁵This is why he can completely save those who are approaching God through him, because he always lives to speak with God for them.

²⁶It's appropriate for us to have this kind of high priest: holy, innocent, incorrupt, separate from sinners, and raised high above the heavens. ²⁷He doesn't need to offer sacrifices every day like the other high priests, first for their own sins and then for the sins of the people. He did this once for all when he offered himself. ²⁸The Law appoints people who are prone to weakness as high priests, but the content of the solemn pledge, which came after the Law, appointed a Son who has been made perfect forever.

# UNDERSTANDING THE SCRIPTURE

**Introduction.** Two constant focal points of Hebrews are assuring readers of the salvation they have in Christ and encouraging them to remain faithful because they have such a great salvation. This exhortation is necessary because the only thing that can take away their salvation is their own unfaithfulness, their own turning away from it. Chapter 7 assures readers that salvation is secure because they receive it through the eternal priest.

**Hebrews 7:1-3.** Hebrews 6 ends by again asserting that Jesus is a priest like Melchizedek, a character in Genesis 14:18-20. Then chapter 7 opens with a description of Melchizedek that shows why the author wants to associate Jesus with him. In the Genesis story, Abraham's nephew Lot has been captured in a war. Abraham musters an army, defeats the kings who took Lot, and is returning home with spoils. On the return trip they meet Melchizedek, king of Salem and a priest of God. He blesses Abraham and praises God. In response Abraham gives him a tithe of the spoils of the war. Melchizedek then disappears and never reappears in the Genesis narrative. The writer of Hebrews seizes on the story and the absence of information about Melchizedek to describe the priesthood of Jesus.

Hebrews first interprets Melchizedek's names and titles, giving them meanings they did not have in their original usage, but that are important to the description of Jesus. Giving the meanings "king of righteousness" and "king of peace" (7:2-3) make Melchizedek a good pattern for who Jesus is because Christ is the one who brings righteousness and peace.

Beyond these titles, Hebrews uses the silence of Genesis to make astonishing claims about Melchizedek: He is without parents and without beginning or end of life. The Genesis text is silent on these points. The reference to Melchizedek is so brief that there is no mention of his ancestry, birth, or death. Hebrews interprets that silence to mean that he is like the Son of God and is eternally a priest. This author is not the only ancient author to be intrigued by this character and to interpret him for his own purposes. What Hebrews does with the Genesis story may seem strange to us, but it was a practice among at least some other interpreters of that era.

**Hebrews 7:4-14.** The author next draws an implication from Abraham giving Melchizedek a tithe of the spoils and from Melchizedek blessing Abraham. The gift and blessing show that Melchizedek is superior to Abraham because the inferior one receives the blessing. Since Abraham is the ancestor of all Levitical priests, Hebrews reasons that they must all also be inferior to Melchizedek. Hebrews adds that the Levitical priesthood did not bring perfection to the worshipers. This, he says, shows that another priesthood is needed, one like that of Melchizedek. A priesthood like that of Melchizedek will be held by one who remains priest forever because he is not mortal. The author extends this line of thought further asserting that a new priesthood demands a new set of laws. The point of this line of argument is that there needs to be a new set of laws so that the new priest does not have to come from the tribe of Levi. That is crucially important because Jesus is from the tribe of Judah and so would not be qualified to be a priest under the Mosaic regulations. The different laws allow Jesus to be the high priest who belongs to the order of Melchizedek rather than Levi. This is why the writer argued that the order of Melchizedek is superior to that of Levi.

**Hebrews 7:15-25.** Hebrews continues its argument for the legitimacy and superiority of the priesthood of Jesus by repeating the claim that Jesus is immortal while the Levitical priests die. Christ's immortal nature is a proof that there had to be both a new law and a new priesthood. Furthermore, new law was needed because the Mosaic covenant did not lead to perfection. Hebrews recognizes that the Levitical priesthood's work did accomplish its role of maintaining the covenant relationship between God and Israel. But from the perspective of one who now has the presence of the Spirit in his life through the salvation that comes in Christ, the author of Hebrews asserts that Jesus has brought a fuller, more "perfect" sharing in life with God. So the priesthood of Christ brings a greater salvation than what was available before his appointment to that position. Moreover, this salvation is more secure than the previous relationship with God because in the Mosaic system each priest took an oath to serve, but when Christ became high priest it was God who swore that Christ would be the priest forever. You cannot get a more secure promise

of salvation than that. Therefore, all who come to God through Christ are assured of eternal salvation.

**Hebrews 7:26-28.** The concluding verses of chapter 7 renew the comparison between Christ and Levitical priests, focusing on two elements. The first is that former priests were sinners, while Jesus is sinless and exalted. The phrase in verse 26, "it was fitting" that we have a high priest like Jesus, means that Jesus is the kind of high priest who meets the human need to be brought fully into life with God. We needed a priest who was sinless to provide this mediation for us. The second element the author mentions again is the oath of God that made Christ the new high priest. Since this oath is from God, its fulfillment is certain. Since the oath of God comes after the establishment of the Levitical priesthood, it endures past it and brings the new law. And finally, that oath means that the priesthood of Christ is eternal.

The whole argument of this chapter about the priesthood of Christ has as its goal giving its readers assurance about the salvation they possess through Christ. Whatever difficulties they face and whatever assessments are made about them by fellow members of the synagogue, the exalted position and work of Christ as high priest demonstrate that they really do possess the closest possible relationship with God, a relationship that is secure because Christ eternally intercedes for them.

## INTERPRETING THE SCRIPTURE

### The Comparisons in Hebrews

One of the central strategies the author of Hebrews uses to assure the

members of his church of the certainty of their salvation is comparisons. He most often compares what believers have in the church with what members of the Mosaic covenant have. These comparisons have sometimes led Christians to claim that there was no real value in the Mosaic covenant and have even led to anti-Semitism. These readings misunderstand the message of Hebrews. The original readers were not in danger of falling into the trap of thinking that the Mosaic covenant had no value because they were Jews. In fact, just the opposite was the case. They were being urged by others to value what is in the Mosaic covenant above what they have in Christ.

Such an argument was plausible because they already knew and had experienced the blessings of the Sinai covenant in their lives. The author of Hebrews makes these comparisons to try to keep members of his church who know those other blessings from leaving. His churches are facing persecution that has made them question their belief in Christ and so they are considering abandoning connection with the church. These members of the church had remained members of the synagogue. Most early Jewish believers in Christ remained in their synagogue while they were also members of the church. Hebrews is trying to convince these church members that they have more blessings and a greater relationship with God through Christ than they have without him. Everyone assumes that great blessings come from being members of the Mosaic covenant. Hebrews agrees, but contends that there is even fuller salvation through Christ. We, then, must not use these comparisons to denigrate the Mosaic covenant.

### A Priest Like Melchizedek

Hebrews 7 compares the priesthood of the Levites with that of Melchizedek, and compares both with the priesthood of Christ. These comparisons and classifications of priesthoods intend to assure us of the certainty of our salvation. The writer assumes that everyone agrees that the greater the high priest, the more effective his service for the people. Our author is not the first to use Melchizedek to help readers understand their salvation. In verse 21 he quotes Psalm 110:4. This psalm promises God's people victory and says God will establish their leader as king and priest forever. The psalmist read the silence of Genesis about the origins and death of Melchizedek as a way to promise everlasting life to the priest-king of this psalm. The psalmist says that through this person God will establish justice. Since the term of the priest-king is like that of Melchizedek, this peaceful existence in a just society is permanent. This great hope had not been fulfilled in the history of the Israelite nations. Now Hebrews declares that this yearned-for ruling priest has come in Jesus, who fulfills this hope and this mission.

Hebrews makes explicit the textual justification for saying Melchizedek is immortal by noting that there is no mention of his ancestry or death. Since Melchizedek is without beginning or end, he is an apt parallel for God's immortal Son. The writer returns to the unending nature of Christ's priesthood in verses 21-25 and 28. This repetition shows how important the point is to his argument. Having a high priest who is immortal and who holds his office eternally provides assurance that he can mediate an eternal salvation. And it is not only that Christ is eternal but also that God has sworn to make his priesthood eternal.

Like the readers of Hebrews, we face questions and situations in our lives that make us wonder about the presence of God with us. The problems that raise these questions for us may involve economic struggles or internal struggles with sin or the ends of relationships. We know there are times when God seems absent and when we question our value and doubt that even God would be willing to accept or forgive us. When we have such doubts about God's presence and our salvation, Hebrews would have us remember who secures our salvation for us. It is the eternal high priest to whom God has sworn to listen. Christ's nature and God's promise make it certain that Christ will always be there for us and with us to ensure our salvation and life with God.

### Christ Our Mediator

For many present-day readers, the image of having a high priest has little significance. Protestants have long argued that they do not need priests because they have access to God without them and have argued for the belief in the "priesthood of all believers." So we may wonder just what Hebrews is claiming with this image of Jesus. The first readers of Hebrews knew all about having a high priest and so giving Jesus that position had great significance. Both within Judaism and in all the religions around them, priests were the people authorized to come into the presence of God and offer gifts of thanks or petition. They were the mediators between the people and God (or the gods). A high priest is charged with these responsibilities and with being sure that other priests performed their tasks properly and effectively.

The image assumes that the worshipers need a mediator between them and God, that there is such a difference between God and the worshiper that they need a go-between.

As Hebrews uses this image, what separates God and humans is sin. There is something improper about entering the presence of a holy God when a person is contaminated by sin. Sin is here seen as something that alienates us from God, something that makes it improper for us to appear in God's presence. Once the offense has been committed, humans have nothing to give God to make amends because they already owe their entire being to God. We are sometimes offended if we are told that we need anyone's help. We really think that we are quite deserving of the things we receive. Hebrews would want us to look more deeply into our faults and acknowledge our need, even our helplessness, to live as God expects. But this author does not find that this helplessness leaves us in a completely desperate situation because he is equally certain that Christ serves as the sinless mediator between God and us. Christ intercedes for those who are genuinely guilty, and Hebrews says he can plead our case convincingly because he has experienced the struggles we have as we live in a world that draws us away from God. This image does not assume that God stands aloof and uncaring. Hebrews insists that Christ has this position because God placed him there. The initiative to repair and renew our relationship with God comes from God who swears that Christ will always be in the position to ask for forgiveness for us. Since God is the one who placed him there, it is certain that God will grant the request. But God has done even more,

Hebrews says. The appointment of Christ as mediator assures not only forgiveness but also a new covenant that brings greater blessing and life with God than had ever been available before. It brings us into the fullest possible life in relationship with God.

---

# SHARING THE SCRIPTURE

## PREPARING TO LEAD

### Preparing Our Hearts

Ponder this week's devotional reading from Psalm 110. This short psalm speaks of the installation or enthronement of a king who will rule over Zion. Who gives power to the king to rule? What expectations does God have for one who rules over the Holy City? Psalm 110 is quoted fourteen times in the New Testament, including in Hebrews 7:21. Why do you suppose that those writers found this psalm important enough to quote repeatedly?

Pray that you and the students will support leaders who rule justly on God's behalf.

### Preparing Our Minds

Study the background Scripture from Hebrews 7 and the lesson Scripture from Hebrews 7:1-3, 19b-28.

Consider this question: *Who will sustain the traditions and institutions begun in the past?*

Write on newsprint:
❏ information for next week's lesson, found under Continue the Journey.
❏ activities for further spiritual growth in Continue the Journey.

Determine how you might use any of the features that precede the first lesson of this quarter in today's session. Look especially at Close-up: Comparison of Priestly Types, which also gives references to Melchizedek.

Familiarize yourself with information in any of the segments of the lesson that you are being asked to refer to, read, or retell.

## LEADING THE CLASS

### (1) Gather to Learn

❖ Welcome everyone and pray that those who have come today will be aware of institutional practices in their own denominations.

❖ Discuss these questions with the class:

1. **What traditions in our church are especially meaningful to you? Why?**

2. **Are there any traditions that have been discontinued that you particularly enjoyed? If so, what are they? Why were they discontinued?**

3. **How can we maintain continuity throughout the years as a congregation even as we experience change?**

❖ Read aloud today's focus statement: **Practices, traditions, and institutions begun in the past are expected to continue. Who will sustain them? Jesus was named to give the practices, traditions, and institutions their ultimate meaning and role for the people for all generations.**

*(2) Goal 1: Compare Melchizedek, "the Priest of the Most High God" with Jesus, "the Priest Forever"*

❖ Read or retell The Comparisons in Hebrews in Interpreting the Scripture to help the class understand that the comparisons the writer of Hebrews makes are not intended to denigrate the Mosaic law but rather to show that a fuller salvation is available through Christ.

❖ Select a volunteer to read Hebrews 7:1-3 and 19b-28.

❖ Post a sheet of newsprint. Invite participants to call out any information they learn about Melchizedek and list that on the paper. Use the information concerning Melchizedek from Close-up: Comparison of Priestly Types to enlarge your list.

❖ Form several small groups and ask each one to answer these questions: **What similarities do you discover between Jesus and Melchizedek? What differences do you see?**

❖ Call the groups together and encourage a spokesperson for each to state one point the group discussed.

❖ Wrap up by using any information from A Priest Like Melchizedek in Interpreting the Scripture that may help participants understand the relationship between Jesus and this mysterious priest who met Abram.

*(3) Goal 2: Appreciate that People Have One Who Intercedes for Them Before God*

❖ Ask these questions:
  **1. What is a mediator?** (Students may offer answers such as a go-between or someone who tries to help people involved in a dispute come to some sort of agreement.)

  **2. How do you envision Christ as a mediator for you—or do you see him acting in that capacity? Explain your answer.** (Use information from Christ Our Mediator in Interpreting the Scripture for additional ideas.)

❖ Remind the adults that they, too, can intercede on behalf of others before God. Post a sheet of newsprint. Invite participants to call out first names of person who stand in need of prayer. To protect confidentiality, do not let the students go into detail about the need. Saying "I lift up my friend Mary who seeks healing" is usually acceptable—unless there is a question as to whether Mary wants anyone to know about her illness. Giving specifics such as "seeks healing following surgery for colon cancer" is too much information.

❖ Call out each name on the list in turn and allow a few moments for silent prayers to be offered. As you close the prayer, give thanks that we have a trustworthy intercessor.

*(4) Goal 3: Respond to the Realization that Jesus Will Always Be Believers' Ultimate Spiritual Leader*

❖ Observe that leaders, no matter how qualified or effective they are, only hold their posts for so many years. Politicians have to run for re-election on a regular schedule. Business and educational leaders may be under contract for a certain number of years. Even if they are not, they still have to perform to standards to retain their positions. Ordained clergy may serve for decades, but in some denominations, such as The United Methodist Church, they will be appointed to a particular congregation for only so long.

❖ Ask:

1. **How is the tenure of Jesus' leadership different from that of other leaders we know?**

2. **What difference does it make to you that Jesus will always be your spiritual leader?**

❖ Distribute paper and pencils. Provide a few moments for silent reflection by encouraging the students to write a sentence or two in which they express their commitment and loyalty to Jesus as their leader.

### (5) Continue the Journey

❖ Pray that as the learners depart, they will give thanks for the continuity and permanence of Jesus as their mediator with God and their spiritual leader.

❖ Post information for next week's session on newsprint for the students to copy:

- **Title: Pioneer and Perfecter of Our Faith**
- **Background Scripture: Hebrews 12:1-13**
- **Lesson Scripture: Hebrews 12:1-13**
- **Focus of the Lesson: People are looking for someone to help them endure life's trials and temptations. Is there anyone who can show them how to endure? Because Jesus endured suffering and death, he is the model for disciples who choose to follow him faithfully.**

❖ Challenge the adults to grow spiritually by completing one or more of these activities related to this week's session.

(1) **Make a list of customs or traditions that are important to you. Are any of your favorites disappearing or being greatly modified? If so, how do these changes make you feel? How are you adjusting to these changes?**

(2) **Recall that Hebrews affirmed the permanent nature of Jesus' priesthood. How might you help people who have no religious affiliation to recognize that whereas things on earth are fleeting, one's relationship with Jesus lasts forever?**

(3) **Research the biblical understanding of a tithe, which is what Abram gave to Melchizedek. What role does (or might) tithing play in your own life? If you are not currently giving 10 percent, consider giving proportionately, that is, a specific percentage, even if it less or more than 10 percent.**

❖ Sing or read aloud "Jesus, My Great High Priest." (This Isaac Watts hymn, sung to the tune of BEVAN, can be found on Internet sites, including http://www.hymnary.org/hymn/TH1990/306.)

❖ Conclude today's session by leading the class in this benediction, which is adapted from Hebrews 12:1b-2a, the key verses for October 30: **May we go forth empowered to run with perseverance the race that is set before us, looking to Jesus the pioneer and perfecter of our faith. Amen.**

UNIT 2: THE SOVEREIGNTY OF JESUS

# PIONEER AND PERFECTER OF OUR FAITH

---

## PREVIEWING THE LESSON/

**Lesson Scripture:** Hebrews 12:1-13
**Background Scripture:** Hebrews 12:1-13
**Key Verses:** Hebrews 12:1b-2a

### Focus of the Lesson:

People are looking for someone to help them endure life's trials and temptations. Is there anyone who can show them how to endure? Because Jesus endured suffering and death, he is the model for disciples who choose to follow him faithfully.

### Goals for the Learners:

(1) to know the value of discipline in the family, congregation, and other human settings.
(2) to appreciate the help provided by others who have experienced discipline.
(3) to share personal struggles that resulted in victorious and growing faith.

### Supplies:

Bibles, newsprint and marker, paper and pencils, hymnals

---

## READING THE SCRIPTURE

NRSV
Lesson Scripture: Hebrews 12:1-13

¹Therefore, since we are surrounded by so great a cloud of witnesses, **let us also lay aside every weight and the sin that clings so closely, and let us run with perseverance the race that is set before us,** ²looking

CEB
Lesson Scripture: Hebrews 12:1-13

¹So then let's also run the race that is laid out in front of us, since we have such a great cloud of witnesses surrounding us. **Let's throw off any extra baggage, get rid of the sin that trips us up,** ²and fix our eyes on

**to Jesus the pioneer and perfecter of our faith,** who for the sake of the joy that was set before him endured the cross, disregarding its shame, and has taken his seat at the right hand of the throne of God.

³Consider him who endured such hostility against himself from sinners, so that you may not grow weary or lose heart. ⁴In your struggle against sin you have not yet resisted to the point of shedding your blood. ⁵And you have forgotten the exhortation that addresses you as children—

"My child, do not regard lightly the discipline of the Lord,

or lose heart when you are punished by him;

⁶for the Lord disciplines those whom he loves,

and chastises every child whom he accepts."

⁷Endure trials for the sake of discipline. God is treating you as children; for what child is there whom a parent does not discipline? ⁸If you do not have that discipline in which all children share, then you are illegitimate and not his children. ⁹Moreover, we had human parents to discipline us, and we respected them. Should we not be even more willing to be subject to the Father of spirits and live? ¹⁰For they disciplined us for a short time as seemed best to them, but he disciplines us for our good, in order that we may share his holiness. ¹¹Now, discipline always seems painful rather than pleasant at the time, but later it yields the peaceful fruit of righteousness to those who have been trained by it.

¹²Therefore lift your drooping hands and strengthen your weak knees, ¹³and make straight paths for your feet, so that what is lame may not be put out of joint, but rather be healed.

**Jesus, faith's pioneer and perfecter.** He endured the cross, ignoring the shame, for the sake of the joy that was laid out in front of him, and sat down at the right side of God's throne.

³Think about the one who endured such opposition from sinners so that you won't be discouraged and you won't give up. ⁴In your struggle against sin, you haven't resisted yet to the point of shedding blood, ⁵and you have forgotten the encouragement that addresses you as sons and daughters:

*My child, don't make light of the Lord's discipline*

*or give up when you are corrected by him,*

⁶*because the Lord disciplines whomever he loves,*

*and he punishes every son or daughter whom he accepts.*

⁷Bear hardship for the sake of discipline. God is treating you like sons and daughters! What child isn't disciplined by his or her father? ⁸But if you don't experience discipline, which happens to all children, then you are illegitimate and not real sons and daughters. ⁹What's more, we had human parents who disciplined us, and we respected them for it. How much more should we submit to the Father of spirits and live? ¹⁰Our human parents disciplined us for a little while, as it seemed best to them, but God does it for our benefit so that we can share his holiness. ¹¹No discipline is fun while it lasts, but it seems painful at the time. Later, however, it yields the peaceful fruit of righteousness for those who have been trained by it.

¹²So strengthen your drooping hands and weak knees! ¹³Make straight paths for your feet so that if any part is lame, it will be healed rather than injured more seriously.

# UNDERSTANDING THE SCRIPTURE

**Introduction.** Hebrews addresses a church that is enduring some kind of ongoing persecution. One of the main tasks of the book is to encourage the people to retain their faith despite the bad treatment they are experiencing. One way it does this is to give interpretations of their experience that assure them of God's care for them. The immediately previous chapter (11) does this by recounting the difficulties that the faithful of Israel endured because they were faithful. In Hebrews 12:1-13, the writer brings the exhortation based on their example to a powerful conclusion.

**Hebrews 12:1-3.** Chapter 12 begins with an athletic metaphor. It envisions the readers as runners in a stadium who are surrounded by the crowds, the "great . . . cloud of witnesses." The witnesses are those heroes of faith from chapter 11. So these are not disinterested observers, but runners themselves who are cheering on these readers. Not only have they experienced the pain and difficulties that the present runners know, but they await the completion of the race by this later group so that their own reward can be brought to completeness (11:40). Hebrews tells those suffering in this church that they are engaged in the same struggle as those who have gone on before. Those who suffered persecution before and were able to endure can assure the readers that they can also endure. The comparison is drawn directly in 12:3-4.

These "runners" are advised to get rid of anything that could slow them down, just as runners today wear the lightest possible uniforms. The nature of the race becomes clearer when we hear that what holds them back is sin. So this race is not just to get through persecution but also a striving to live a moral life. A central element of a life of faith is living as God calls people to live. The exemplar of this life of faith is Jesus.

Hebrews calls Jesus the "pioneer and perfecter of our faith" (12:2). Jesus is the leader and trailblazer for those who are in the race to live a faithful life. He has completed the race. So when he stands at the finish line urging the runners to finish, he knows what he is asking. He has set the pattern for what they should do and be. But the term "pioneer" captures only part of this description of Jesus. The term Hebrews uses (*archēgos*) presents Jesus as more than the leader and predecessor. It means he is the one who is the source of faith. He is the first to attain faith's goal, life with God, and he opens that possibility to others. He is, then, the one in whom they are to place their faith. Jesus is the "perfecter" of the faith in the sense that he is the one who brought salvation to its fullness. It is through him that the new covenant is established and that the new and fuller access to God is given. Additionally, he is the one who provides the perfect exemplar of that life of faith. He is the model for those who come after him. The play on words in the Greek text gives a sense of what Hebrews wants to say about Jesus. The word "pioneer" is derived from the word that means beginning or source; the word "perfecter" from a word that means end or completion. So Jesus is the source and the completer of our salvation.

The example Jesus sets is his willingness to endure the most shameful of deaths to attain something of great value, "the joy that was set before him" (12:2). This idea continues the athletic image, asking the readers to imagine the prize that awaited the winner of a race. The joy that was set before Jesus is not only his attainment of glory and exaltation to the place of power in heaven but also his opening of the way of salvation for others. From that place of power Christ can grant the faithful a joyful life with God. So these verses present Christ as the example of enduring persecution and of how God responds to that faithfulness. Furthermore, he is the one through whom believers receive salvation.

The writer tells these suffering Christians to keep Jesus and his suffering, and God's response to that suffering, in view as they try to endure. Jesus provides not just an example but also hope, because God does not allow the suffering of Jesus to be the final verdict. God responds by raising and exalting him. The faithful can also expect that God will not allow their suffering to be the final word; God will raise them as well. This assurance comes even as the readers hear that things could be worse.

**Hebrews 12:4-11.** The readers have not yet endured the worst possible persecution, though that may come. But even a death threat pales in comparison with the assurance of a blessed life with God beyond that momentary difficulty. In verses 5-11 Hebrews interprets the persecution they are enduring as discipline from God. This may suggest that previous unfaithfulness is the cause of their suffering, though this is less explicit than the purpose of the discipline: to engender greater faith. Hebrews offers this interpretation of persecution rather than allowing them to think that it means God has deserted them. Rather, this is a sign of God's desire to help them live more faithfully. Just as parents discipline children to teach them how to live, so God is helping them learn how to live. The whole passage assumes that people learn through suffering—a view that was common in the first century.

**Hebrews 12:12-13.** Interpreting persecution as discipline is supposed to be encouraging! Readers of Hebrews must not let the troubles they face discourage them or cause them to turn from the faith. Since such difficulties are evidence that God loves them and wants them to grow in faith, they should take courage and resolve to stand firm whatever comes. They can do this because they can know that God's ultimate purpose is healing and salvation.

## INTERPRETING THE SCRIPTURE

*Jesus the Pioneer and Perfecter*

This chapter of Hebrews celebrates Jesus as the source and provider of our salvation. It is because of what Jesus has done that we have access to God's saving presence. In addition to this role as savior, Hebrews presents Jesus as our exemplar in times of difficulty. Jesus went through troubles worse than ours and managed to retain his faith. The figures from the

Israelites' past mentioned in chapter 11 also held on to their faith in the midst of fierce persecution, but the example of Jesus is the pinnacle of these examples. Importantly, he is the demonstration of God's response to such faithfulness. Even though his difficulties went so far that they caused his death, he was not beyond God's saving acts. The experience of Christ is the evidence that demonstrates that the power of God to bless reaches beyond any pain or distress in this life. The exaltation of Christ shows that God will not allow evil and suffering to ultimately win out over faithfulness. The faithful who follow Christ will not, of course, be saviors themselves. They are following the example and being brought into the life with God that was initiated by that Pioneer and Originator of our salvation. Still, Christ serves as the example of both the possibility of endurance and of why faithful persistence in living for God is worth the pain it may bring. The blessing from God that follows a life of faithfulness outweighs the trouble inflicted by those who oppose God's will. Even as Christ's example sets a high standard of faithfulness, it also provides a glorious guarantee of God's love and care for the faithful.

## Discipline as a Teacher

We all know people (perhaps ourselves) who can learn only through the "School of Hard Knocks." Many of us don't seem to be able to take the advice of those who have gone before. We have to make those mistakes for ourselves. When those who act this way are our children, we may step in to dissuade them from certain behaviors by imposing some punishment that is less painful than the consequences of continuing to act in that way. Children often do not see or refuse to believe that certain behaviors have bad outcomes in the long run, so loving parents intervene and impose quicker and less severe consequences. We see such interventions as acts of love because these impositions of discipline not only stop an immediate behavior but also intend to help mold character. We want the rewards that follow some behaviors along with the unhappy results of others to instill habits of life that will lead to better and fuller lives. This way of understanding discipline was common in the ancient world as well. Ancient philosophers thought it was true, as did teachers of morality in the first century. Proverbs speaks of the importance of discipline in teaching children (13:24; 29:15). Hebrews also assumes that receiving discipline is a sign of love. In fact, this writer goes so far as to say that a lack of discipline shows a lack of love. So he interprets the persecution this church is enduring as discipline. In this case, the discipline is not imposed because of something done wrong but as a means of teaching, as a way of molding character. He contends that the difficulties they endure can help them conform to God's will. While this may not sound like an interpretation of their suffering that would encourage them, if they understand discipline as a show of love they can at least be assured that God has their best interests at heart.

## Discipline as a Danger

While it seems odd to us that Hebrews interprets persecution as discipline, it is also dangerous for us to interpret the suffering of others or of ourselves as discipline for wrong-doing. It is far too easy to fall into a judgmental attitude about what others may have done if this is the way we understand why someone is going through some hard times. The friends in the story of Job are an important object lesson. You will remember that Job lost his children, his wealth, his health, nearly everything. His friends are convinced that he must have sinned grievously and so is reaping the consequences. A central point of the book of Job is to warn us that seeing people suffering is not a sure indicator that they have done wrong.

At the same time, we know that some kinds of behaviors bring bad consequences. Jumping out of a third-floor window will cause significant injury to a person. This is not because God is punishing this person, but because that is the way the world works. We can think of immoral conduct that similarly almost always leads to pain and suffering. For example, unfaithfulness in a relationship always leads to hurt, often to the painful end of what was earlier a very loving relationship. This is not punishment in the sense that God is doing something out of the ordinary to inflict pain. Rather, given the nature of human existence and of the world, these are the expected consequences of those kinds of behaviors. So we should issue warnings about the results of acting in some ways, reminders of how those actions inflict pain on others and on the ones who do them, but we cannot assume that suffering is a sure sign that a person has done something wrong.

## Discipline as Training

It is important to note that Hebrews 12 does not say that the church is being punished for doing wrong. The persecution is discipline, but not necessarily punishment. Some types of discipline are undertaken intentionally in order to gain some level of competence or expertise at a skill. All sorts of athletes discipline themselves in many ways in order to be able to perform their best. This is the best way to think about the discipline that Hebrews 12 talks about; it is discipline undertaken to produce something rather than discipline inflicted as punishment. The discipline experienced by the recipients of Hebrews is to lead to holiness and righteousness (12:10-11). The writer does not want them to seek out such experiences, but there are occasions when we may take up a discipline to enhance our walk with God. That might be extra time set aside for prayer or even fasting at lunch to give time for reflection or for helping others. These kinds of disciplines can draw us near to God and begin to mold our character. Even imposed troubles that we face through faith can help us draw near to God as they remind us of just how dependent we are on God for our lives and well-being. As the writer of Hebrews thought about it, understanding some troubles as opportunities to see things through the eyes of faith can encourage us because we become aware that God is always with us, especially in difficult times. The writer saw even persecution as an experience in which we can be healed as we remember that the ultimate will of God for us is salvation, that full life in the very presence of God.

# SHARING THE SCRIPTURE

## PREPARING TO LEAD

### Preparing Our Hearts

Ponder this week's devotional reading from Isaiah 53:1-6, which is part of the fourth and final Servant Song in Isaiah. What do you learn about this servant? Early Christians connected this suffering servant with Jesus. What do you find in these verses to affirm or challenge this connection?

Pray that you and the students will remember the sufferings of Isaiah's servant and of Jesus when you face trials and tribulations of your own.

### Preparing Our Minds

Study the background Scripture and the lesson Scripture, which are both from Hebrews 12:1-13.

Consider this question: *Who can help you to endure life's trials and temptations?*

Write on newsprint:

❏ information for next week's lesson, found under Continue the Journey.

❏ activities for further spiritual growth in Continue the Journey.

Determine how you might use any of the features that precede the first lesson of this quarter in today's session.

## LEADING THE CLASS

### (1) Gather to Learn

❖ Welcome everyone and pray that those who have come today will give thanks for Jesus, the pioneer and perfecter of our faith.

❖ Read: **In May 2015, ninety-two-year-old Harriette Thompson became the oldest woman to run a 26.2 mile marathon. A former concert pianist and cancer survivor, this mother of five entered her first marathon at the age of seventy-six. Over the years, she has raised $100,000 for the Leukemia and Lymphoma Society, missing only one race during her own cancer treatments. Although she had doubts, she not only ran this race in San Diego but also set a world record for women in her age group. Her fifty-six-year-old son Brenny ran with her, snapping pictures to record the event. Running a marathon is a test of endurance. Mrs. Thompson's perseverance and determination can inspire and motivate others to press on toward the finish line.**

❖ Ask these questions:

1. **What enables a person to endure what for most of us would seem to be an insurmountable challenge?**

2. **How could Mrs. Thompson be a role model for you?**

❖ Read aloud today's focus statement: **People are looking for someone to help them endure life's trials and temptations. Is there anyone who can show them how to endure? Because Jesus endured suffering and death, he is the model for disciples who choose to follow him faithfully.**

### (2) Goal 1: Know the Value of Discipline in the Family, Congregation, and Other Human Settings

❖ Read Introduction in Understanding the Scripture to set the stage for the lesson.

❖ Call on a volunteer to read Hebrews 12:1-13. Invite the listeners to imagine that these words are being written especially for them.

❖ Discuss the following questions. Use information from Understanding the Scripture as noted below to augment the discussion:

1. **Who are the "cloud of witnesses"?** (See Hebrews 12:1-3.)

2. **How does the use of the image of the runner help to make the writer's point?** (See Hebrews 12:1-3.)

3. **What does it mean to say that Jesus is "the pioneer and perfecter of our faith"?** (See Hebrews 12:1-3 and Jesus the Pioneer and Perfecter in Interpreting the Scripture.)

4. **What is God's purpose in disciplining us?** (See Hebrews 12:4-11.)

5. **How does Jesus' suffering provide hope for you?** (See Hebrews 12:4-11.)

6. **How might you interpret discipline?** (See Hebrews 12:12-13 and Discipline as a Teacher in Interpreting the Scripture.)

7. **What lessons did you glean from the writer of Hebrews as you listened to today's verses?**

*(3) Goal 2: Appreciate the Help Provided by Others Who Have Experienced Discipline*

❖ Recall that the cloud of witnesses to which the writer of Hebrews refers in verse 1 are those who have already persevered to the end and finished the race.

❖ Invite the students to sit quietly as you lead them through this guided imagery activity.

- **Imagine yourself in a marathon. You have 26.2 miles to run but have only made it to mile 16. You know the finish line is ahead—somewhere— but you can't begin to see it. What images might you see in your mind's eye to help you persevere?** (pause)

- **Friends along the race route are calling your name and yelling words of encouragement. How does their support make you feel? What does the support prompt you to do?** (pause)

- **At last, you can see the finish line. You are exhausted and your legs ache terribly. Still, people are cheering you home. You've made it! As you cross the line, friends surround you. What do they say to you? What do you say to them?** (pause)

- **Jesus rushes up to you. Hear what he says about the race you have run**. (pause)

❖ Call everyone back together. Invite volunteers to say briefly how the support of their friends, their cloud of witnesses, along with the approval of Jesus, empowers them to run the race of life faithfully.

*(4) Goal 3: Share Personal Struggles that Resulted in Victorious and Growing Faith*

❖ Form small groups. Invite each person who feels comfortable doing so to recount an instance of a personal struggle that helped him or her to grow in faith. Perhaps an illness, financial reversal, family crisis, or change in life status (such as a marriage or divorce, new job or retirement) caused this struggle. Some students may be willing to share more details than others, but set a two-minute time limit for each person so that one person does not monopolize the conversation.

❖ Bring everyone together and ask: **How did these stories serve as examples to you for how you can meet trials head-on?** Ask that the students not share details of other people's stories, but rather say, "I saw how an illness empowered my classmate to trust God more fully."

❖ Conclude by reading or retelling Discipline as Training from Interpreting the Scripture.

*(5) Continue the Journey*

❖ Pray that as the learners depart, they will be aware not only of their own trials but also do whatever they can to help others who are facing trials.

❖ Post information for next week's session on newsprint for the students to copy:
- **Title: Everything Is Brand New**
- **Background Scripture: Revelation 21:1-8**
- **Lesson Scripture: Revelation 21:1-8**
- **Focus of the Lesson: People look for a place and time when life's stresses will not exist. Is such a time and place**

**possible? John, the writer of the Book of Revelation, suggests that God will create a new heaven and earth where life's challenges and stresses will be banished forever.**

Challenge the adults to grow spiritually by completing one or more of these activities related to this week's session.

(1) **Think about your own gifts and talents. Which one(s) of these could you showcase in order to be a role model for someone else who would like to be able to do what you do?**

(2) **Identify areas in your life where you need more self-discipline to grow in your faith or meet another goal. What steps can you take to act with greater patience, endurance, and discipline?**

(3) **Think about trials and tribulations you may be enduring right now. If you begin to think about them as discipline from God that is for your benefit, how can you reinterpret your situation?**

❖ Sing or read aloud "For All the Saints."

❖ Conclude today's session by leading the class in this benediction, which is adapted from Hebrews 12:1b-2a, the key verses for today: **May we go forth empowered to run with perseverance the race that is set before us, looking to Jesus the pioneer and perfecter of our faith. Amen.**

UNIT 3: ALPHA AND OMEGA
# EVERYTHING IS
# BRAND NEW

---

## PREVIEWING THE LESSON

**Lesson Scripture:** Revelation 21:1-8
**Background Scripture:** Revelation 21:1-8
**Key Verse:** Revelation 21:4

### Focus of the Lesson:
People look for a place and time when life's stresses will not exist. Is such a time and place possible? John, the writer of the Book of Revelation, suggests that God will create a new heaven and earth where life's challenges and stresses will be banished forever.

### Goals for the Learners:
(1) to examine the unique genre "apocalypse" that characterizes the Book of Revelation to understand and apply its message to daily life.
(2) to contemplate the coming of "a new heaven and a new earth" for the hope that this vision engenders among the faithful.
(3) to embrace the peace of God that begins in this life with Jesus and continues throughout eternal life.

### Supplies:
Bibles, newsprint and marker, paper and pencils, hymnals

---

## READING THE SCRIPTURE

NRSV

Lesson Scripture: Revelation 21:1-8

¹Then I saw a new heaven and a new earth; for the first heaven and the first earth had passed away, and the sea was no more. ²And I saw the holy city, the new Jerusalem, coming down out of heaven from God, prepared as a bride adorned for her husband. ³And I heard a loud voice from the throne saying,

CEB

Lesson Scripture: Revelation 21:1-8

¹Then I saw a new heaven and a new earth, for the former heaven and the former earth had passed away, and the sea was no more. ²I saw the holy city, New Jerusalem, coming down out of heaven from God, made ready as a bride beautifully dressed for her husband. ³I heard a loud voice from the throne say, "Look! God's

"See, the home of God is among mortals.
He will dwell with them;
they will be his peoples,
and God himself will be with them;
**⁴he will wipe every tear from their eyes.**
**Death will be no more;**
**mourning and crying and pain will be no more,**
**for the first things have passed away."**

⁵And the one who was seated on the throne said, "See, I am making all things new." Also he said, "Write this, for these words are trustworthy and true." ⁶Then he said to me, "It is done! I am the Alpha and the Omega, the beginning and the end. To the thirsty I will give water as a gift from the spring of the water of life. ⁷Those who conquer will inherit these things, and I will be their God and they will be my children. ⁸But as for the cowardly, the faithless, the polluted, the murderers, the fornicators, the sorcerers, the idolaters, and all liars, their place will be in the lake that burns with fire and sulfur, which is the second death."

dwelling is here with humankind. He will dwell with them, and they will be his peoples. God himself will be with them as their God. **⁴He will wipe away every tear from their eyes. Death will be no more. There will be no mourning, crying, or pain anymore, for the former things have passed away."** ⁵Then the one seated on the throne said, "Look! I'm making all things new." He also said, "Write this down, for these words are trustworthy and true." ⁶Then he said to me, "All is done. I am the Alpha and the Omega, the beginning and the end. To the thirsty I will freely give water from the life-giving spring. ⁷Those who emerge victorious will inherit these things. I will be their God, and they will be my sons and daughters. ⁸But for the cowardly, the faithless, the vile, the murderers, those who commit sexual immorality, those who use drugs and cast spells, the idolaters and all liars—their share will be in the lake that burns with fire and sulfur. This is the second death."

## UNDERSTANDING THE SCRIPTURE

**Introduction.** Revelation is a difficult book for us. That is the case largely because this is the only book that many of us know that is written in this style. Just as we had to learn to read poetry and know how it is different from prose, so we have to think about how to read this kind of book. The style of Revelation is known as apocalyptic. This type of literature emerged about two hundred years before Revelation was written. So when John pens Revelation, he is writing in an established tradition with

which his readers are familiar. Many of those earlier apocalyptic writings are still available today. For example, 2 Esdras, a book in the Apocrypha, is written in this style.

The first thing to note is that these books were written to communities in crisis. They face such opposition and persecution that they see the world as so profoundly controlled by the power of evil that only a cataclysmic act of God can make things right. This literature uses dramatic imagery to assure the faithful that God will act to reward their faith and punish those who persecute and take advantage of them. All the imagery in these books is figurative; none of it is meant to be taken literally. Each time we see an image, we must ask what the writer is trying to convey with it. For example, Revelation 17:1-6 tells of a grotesque giant prostitute drinking blood. From hints that come later in the chapter, we see that she represents the Roman Empire that is persecuting the church. We must read all of Revelation as we read this image; all of its images are symbolic. These shocking images intend to help its original readers believe that God has more power than those overwhelming forces that now control and harm their lives. The purpose of apocalyptic literature is to assure the readers of the power and victory of God and through that assurance to encourage them to remain faithful even when those against them seem to be winning. Apocalyptic works also always say that the end is coming soon, that God is ready to act to rescue God's people. So they only have to hold on for a little while. This literature promises that in the end, God will defeat evil and bring the faithful salvation and a blessed existence in God's presence. This is, then, literature of hope. Even as its writers and readers see the present world as captured by evil, they trust in the power, love, and justice of God to make all things right.

**Revelation 21:1-4.** Chapter 21 is part of the conclusion of the whole of Revelation. The previous chapter sketched scenes of the overthrow of the evil powers and their source, Satan. At the end of that chapter, John briefly mentions the end time judgment of humans. It is on the heels of the reference to judgment that this scene of great blessing appears at the beginning of chapter 21. John sees the earth and heavens disappear and then replaced by the New Jerusalem. Jerusalem had been the center of God's presence since the time of King David. It is the "holy city" because it is the place where the Temple is and so access to the focused presence of God in the world. Now God provides a New Jerusalem that is so ornately appointed that it is like a bride on her wedding day.

The end of the old creation includes the disappearance of the sea. The sea was a menacing image in ancient literature. Its disappearance means that a chaotic power that threatens life has been overcome. The new life that is appearing is not threatened even by this primordial nemesis.

In verse 3 a voice from God's throne, and so from one who knows God's will, interprets the image of the New Jerusalem coming down from heaven. It means that the dwelling place of God is now with God's people. If it seemed as though God had been distant or removed from the world as God's people suffered and as evil reigned, now is the time when God moves God's house to be with the faithful. Now God is even more directly present than God had been in the Jerusalem Temple. At this point it will be clear to all who God's people are and that God is their God. The covenant relationship that binds God and the people will now be more evident. When God is present in this intimate way, all things that cause sorrow and hardship will be gone because the "first things," that is the structures of the world as we know them now, no longer exist.

**Revelation 21:5-8.** In verse 6, God speaks. This word from God adds assurance to the coming rescue and salvation of God's people. God promises to make all things new and tells John to write that this coming act is a certainty because God is the one with the power to make things new (21:6). God is the beginning and end of all things; as the one who initiated the first creation, God is the one who can create again. When God does that, God claims the faithful as heirs and gives them life in God's presence by the water that gives life. Verse 8 demonstrates that an important function of this description of God's blessings is to encourage faithfulness.

This final verse of our reading tells what happens to those who turn from God's will. Those who fail in persecution or lead a life of sin are destined for "the second death." They are permanently sent away from the presence of God. John expresses the pain of this exclusion by describing their fate as being sent into a burning lake. The CEB includes "those who use drugs" in the list of those excluded. The term used here refers to sorcerers or magicians who did use elixirs such as love potions or poisons, but does not point to what we today think of as using drugs.

## INTERPRETING THE SCRIPTURE

### Help in Difficult Times

The first readers of Revelation endured persecution precisely because they were believers in Christ. The persecution most of them faced consisted of economic and social ostracizing. They might have their neighbors refuse to do business with them or their children might be subject to violence because of their faith. Neighbors would be inclined to react this way because the believers had withdrawn from some important relationships and events. Those in the church no longer worshiped the gods of the city or of their profession. Their absence from public events that honored these gods would lead others to think they cared nothing for the general good and to worry that the gods would retaliate, especially if the numbers of these people grew. The effect of this shunning might be more dramatic than it sounds because some of these people were just able to feed themselves. Having others refuse to do business with them might mean their children went to bed hungry on a regular basis. That is painful and ongoing persecution that is at least as bad as facing the lions once. This persecution led some to wonder whether God was really with them or if they had made a mistake in deciding to worship only this god. Revelation wants to assure them that they are on the right side. The God they have chosen is the most powerful and is faithful to those who honor God. So God will make it more than worth the suffering they endure.

Most of us never face circumstances like those the first readers of Revelation faced. Yet we know the pain of thinking that God is absent or does not care. Those feelings come when we see bad things happening to the faithful who do not deserve them. Our sense of desertion and rejection is worse in times of illness or loneliness or perhaps in times when relationships fail or we lose someone. When we are enduring such circumstances we want to know why God doesn't do something about them. When this happens, we are asking the same question the readers of Revelation are asking. This whole book is written to respond to those kinds of experiences. It is written to assure those suffering that God knows, cares, will make all things right. God will not allow the injustice inflicted on the faithful to have the last word. While we might not see God stepping in to fix things now, seen in the fullest perspective, the love and justice of God prevail for all of God's people. Revelation promises this to us in the most desperate of times. In chapter 21, this promise is a vision of a new world. This world has no sea, none of the threatening elements that diminish and threaten life. God's new creative act, John says, will rid the world of such experiences so that God's people can live full lives.

### God Has the Power

John claims that God can do amazing things. He claims that God can overcome all evil and create an existence for the faithful that is rich and fully in the presence of God. This life more than makes up for all the difficulties believers endure during their mortal lives. For that promise to be believable, God has to be powerful enough to accomplish all those tasks. John shows God is that strong by describing the powers that injure God's people and God's response to evil in dramatic terms. The readers already know the oppressive power of the structures that harm them. They know how the empire turns its power against them in ways they cannot resist. So when John describes those powers as dragons or giant beasts, those images fit the readers' experience. To show God's power, John describes their defeat in dramatic, at times gruesome, imagery. Sometimes Christ is a powerful warrior who easily defeats so many enemies that vultures from all over the world are gorged on the fallen (19:11-21). Other times angels just pour bowls on the earth and the evil people are consumed (16:1-16).

Declaring this power of God is difficult when God's people are suffering. But John can point us to one event of the past that assures us that God is more powerful than the worst that anyone can do to harm us. That event is the resurrection of Christ. In a wonderful image that catches the dilemma of God's people in a world that opposes them and shows the overwhelming power of God, John talks of Jesus as the lamb who appears to have been slaughtered but who now lives in glory (5:6-10). The world did its worst: It killed Jesus. God responded by raising him from the dead. Christ's resurrection is the demonstration that God has the power to defeat evil and bring those who suffer into a full and blessed life.

### The New Jerusalem

John's sense of the brokenness of the world is deeper than it is for most of us. Our experience of the world leads us to see good and bad in it. John's experience has convinced him that God's good creation has been permeated with evil so deeply there must be a new act of creation. He calls that new creation the New Jerusalem. A central aspect of the New Jerusalem is that God will be obviously and immanently present with God's people. Even when we feel that God is absent, we already have the promise that the Spirit is always with us. This presence of God that we can at times fail to sense will be replaced in the New Jerusalem with the unmistakable and loving immediate presence of God. The promise of this new act of God and new life God gives is that there will be no more trouble or sorrow. This will be an existence in which the faithful are given joy and fullness of life that is beyond anything that can be experienced in the present. The New Jerusalem is God's promise for all God's people who suffer and are aggrieved now. It is God's gracious response to their faithfulness when the pain in their lives leads them to question God's care for them.

### Encouragement and Exhortation

While John describes the New Jerusalem in glowing terms and promises blessings that are almost beyond imagination, he also talks about those who will be excluded. To hear John clearly we must remember that he is addressing people who suffer for their faith. The promise of blessing becomes a threat to those who turn away from God. John asserts that those who fail to maintain faithfulness in the midst of these troubles and finally turn from God will not share in these wonderful blessings.

These are not threats to outsiders that we might use to coerce them to come to faith. No, these are warnings to those who already have faith. The point is not so much to frighten as it is to encourage faithfulness by contrasting the fate of those who remain faithful with those who turn from their faith. John encourages us to remain faithful by telling of the blessings those who trust God receive and by reminding us of how painful it is not to have the promise of those blessings.

## SHARING THE SCRIPTURE

### PREPARING TO LEAD

#### Preparing Our Hearts

Ponder this week's devotional reading from Revelation 7:13-17, which describes "a great multitude" (7:9) from all over the earth worshiping God and the Lamb in heaven. What familiar images do you encounter in these verses? Which aspect of this heavenly scene sparks your imagination the most or prompts you to want to be with the worshipers?

Pray that you and the students will live now so as to be prepared to join this great throng of people.

#### Preparing Our Minds

Study the background Scripture and the lesson Scripture, which are both from Revelation 21:1-8.

Consider this question: *Do you foresee a time and place when life's stresses will not exist?*

Write on newsprint:
❏ questions for Goal 1 in Sharing the Scripture.
❏ information for next week's lesson, found under Continue the Journey.
❏ activities for further spiritual growth in Continue the Journey.

Prepare a brief lecture using The Big Picture: God in Isaiah, Hebrews, and Revelation (beginning with the words "The third book that a major portion. . .") and Introduction in Understanding the Scripture to help participants understand the purpose of the Book of Revelation, its images, and its audience.

## LEADING THE CLASS

### (1) Gather to Learn

❖ Welcome everyone and pray that those who have come today will each be transformed so as to become new creatures in Christ.

❖ Read these top ten life stresses from a list of forty-three developed in 1967 by psychiatrists Thomas Holmes and Richard Rahe. If you prefer, download a printable list from a site such as http://www.stress.org /holmes-rahe-stress-inventory and distribute it to the class. Invite class members to identify stresses in their own lives.
- Death of a spouse
- Divorce
- Marital separation from mate
- Detention in jail or other institution
- Death of a close family member
- Major personal injury or illness
- Marriage
- Being fired at work
- Marital reconciliation with mate
- Retirement from work

❖ Read or retell Help in Difficult Times from Interpreting the Scripture to create a link between the class members and the early readers of John's Revelation, all of whom were facing stress just as contemporary Christians do.

❖ Read aloud today's focus statement: **People look for a place and time when life's stresses will not exist. Is such a time and place possible? John, the writer of the Book of Revelation, suggests that God will create a new heaven and earth where life's challenges and stresses will be banished forever.**

### (2) Goal 1: Analyze the Unique Genre "Apocalypse" that Characterizes the Book of Revelation to Understand and Apply Its Message to Daily Life

❖ Introduce the Book of Revelation and apocalyptic literature by presenting the lecture as suggested under Preparing Our Minds.

❖ Recruit a volunteer to read Revelation 21:1-8. Invite participants to be aware of anything in this reading that they can see, hear, taste, touch, or smell.

❖ Discuss these questions:
1. **What sensual images did you notice?** (For example, students may have envisioned a bride, heard the voice of God, felt the wetness of tears and tasted their saltiness, touched pen and paper as they wrote God's words, tasted spring water, smelled the sulfur of the burning lake.)
2. **How did recognition of these sensual images help you enter into the story, rather than just hear words?**

❖ Encourage the students to think of themselves as reporters on the scene with John. Form small groups and assign one or more questions to each group:
1. **Who is involved in this vision? What role does each play?**

2. **What announcement does God make about divine intentions?**

3. **Given what will happen, would you want to be present when God makes all things new—or not? Why?**

❖ Call on a spokesperson for each group to summarize their discussion.

❖ Close by asking: **How do you know that God will be able to do all that God has said?** (See God Has the Power in Interpreting the Scripture.)

*(3) Goal 2: Contemplate the Coming of "a New Heaven and a New Earth" for the Hope that This Vision Engenders Among the Faithful*

❖ Note that although the Book of Revelation seems to be filled with catastrophe upon catastrophe, it is really a book of hope for those who are faithful to God.

❖ Read or retell The New Jerusalem in Interpreting the Scripture.

❖ Discuss these questions:

1. What hope does John's vision give you?

2. What groups of people in the world or in your community need to hear this message of hope? Why?

3. **What steps can you take, both as an individual believer and as part of the body of Christ, to give these people God's hope for a brighter future?** (Suggest that those who are willing to take action get together after class to begin to devise a plan for helping those who need hope.)

4. **What steps might you take to reconnect those who have fallen away from the faith?** (See Encouragement and Exhortation in Interpreting the Scripture.)

*(4) Goal 3: Embrace the Peace of God that Begins in This Life with Jesus and Continues Throughout Life Eternal*

❖ Distribute paper and pencils. Encourage the adults to write a short description of what paradise would be like for them. What will it look like? What sounds will they hear? What will they be able to taste? What might they touch? What aromas will fill the air?

❖ Bring everyone together. Call on volunteers to select two or three items from their descriptions to share with the group.

❖ Conclude this activity by asking:

1. **How will life in paradise be different from the life you experience here and now?**

2. **What can you do now to begin to embrace the peace of God that is yours through Jesus Christ, eternally and in the present?**

*(5) Continue the Journey*

❖ Pray that as the learners depart, they will live as though God will soon make heaven and earth new.

❖ Post information for next week's session on newsprint for the students to copy:

■ **Title: I See a New Jerusalem**

■ **Background Scripture: Revelation 21:9-27**

■ **Lesson Scripture: Revelation 21:9-14, 22-27**

■ **Focus of the Lesson: It is difficult for people to imagine living in a place that is different from the one in which they presently live. What** will the new place be like? John uses figurative non-literal language to describe the new place that God will create.

❖ Challenge the adults to grow spiritually by completing one or more of these activities related to this week's session.

(1) Use a concordance or Bible dictionary or check the Internet to discover how the sea was perceived, literally and figuratively, by ancient peoples. Can you think of any modern images that may convey similar meanings?

(2) Page through a hymnal to locate songs about the peace that God provides. Choose one or two favorites and sing or recite at least one verse every day this week to remind you of this peace that passes all understanding.

(3) Remember that apocalyptic literature, such as Revelation, uses poetry and symbolism to proclaim truth. We need not take these symbols literally, just as we do not associate literal elephants and donkeys with the Republican and Democrat parties, respectively. Identify some symbols (perhaps from political cartoons) that somehow represent the truth for you.

❖ Sing or read aloud "Soon and Very Soon."

❖ Conclude today's session by leading the class in this benediction, which is adapted from Hebrews 12:1b-2a, the key verses for October 30: **May we go forth empowered to run with perseverance the race that is set before us, looking to Jesus the pioneer and perfecter of our faith. Amen.**

# UNIT 3: ALPHA AND OMEGA
# I SEE A NEW JERUSALEM

---

## PREVIEWING THE LESSON

**Lesson Scripture:** Revelation 21:9-14, 22-27
**Background Scripture:** Revelation 21:9-27
**Key Verses:** Revelation 21:22-23

### Focus of the Lesson:
It is difficult for people to imagine living in a place that is different from the one in which they presently live. What will the new place be like? John uses figurative nonliteral language to describe the new place that God will create.

### Goals for the Learners:
(1) to explore the possibility of living in a new place, even in another dimension of life.
(2) to imagine the richness and serenity of living in the New Jerusalem.
(3) to celebrate God's provision of a new place for believers at the end of all things temporal and throughout eternity.

### Supplies:
Bibles, newsprint and marker, paper and pencils, hymnals

---

## READING THE SCRIPTURE

NRSV
Lesson Scripture: Revelation 21:9-14, 22-27

⁹Then one of the seven angels who had the seven bowls full of the seven last plagues came and said to me, "Come, I will show you the bride, the wife of the Lamb." ¹⁰And in the spirit he carried me away to a great, high mountain and showed me the

CEB
Lesson Scripture: Revelation 21:9-14, 22-27

⁹Then one of the seven angels who had the seven bowls full of the seven last plagues spoke with me. "Come," he said, "I will show you the bride, the Lamb's wife." ¹⁰He took me in a Spirit-inspired trance to a great, high mountain, and he showed me the

holy city Jerusalem coming down out of heaven from God. [11]It has the glory of God and a radiance like a very rare jewel, like jasper, clear as crystal. [12]It has a great, high wall with twelve gates, and at the gates twelve angels, and on the gates are inscribed the names of the twelve tribes of the Israelites; [13]on the east three gates, on the north three gates, on the south three gates, and on the west three gates. [14]And the wall of the city has twelve foundations, and on them are the twelve names of the twelve apostles of the Lamb.

[22]**I saw no temple in the city, for its temple is the Lord God the Almighty and the Lamb. [23]And the city has no need of sun or moon to shine on it, for the glory of God is its light, and its lamp is the Lamb.** [24]The nations will walk by its light, and the kings of the earth will bring their glory into it. [25]Its gates will never be shut by day— and there will be no night there. [26]People will bring into it the glory and honor of the nations. [27]But nothing unclean will enter it, nor anyone who practices abomination or falsehood, but only those who are written in the Lamb's book of life.

holy city, Jerusalem, coming down out of heaven from God. [11]The city had God's glory. Its brilliance was like a priceless jewel, like jasper that was as clear as crystal. [12]It had a great high wall with twelve gates. By the gates were twelve angels, and on the gates were written the names of the twelve tribes of Israel's sons. [13]There were three gates on the east, three gates on the north, three gates on the south, and three gates on the west. [14]The city wall had twelve foundations, and on them were the twelve names of the Lamb's twelve apostles.

[22]**I didn't see a temple in the city, because its temple is the Lord God Almighty and the Lamb. [23]The city doesn't need the sun or the moon to shine on it, because God's glory is its light, and its lamp is the Lamb.** [24]The nations will walk by its light, and the kings of the earth will bring their glory into it. [25]Its gates will never be shut by day, and there will be no night there. [26]They will bring the glory and honor of the nations into it. [27]Nothing unclean will ever enter it, nor anyone who does what is vile and deceitful, but only those who are registered in the Lamb's scroll of life.

---

## UNDERSTANDING THE SCRIPTURE

**Introduction.** John starts a second description of the New Jerusalem in 21:9. This description of the New Jerusalem stands in deliberate contrast to the giant prostitute of chapter 17. An angel calls John in the same way at the beginning of the two episodes, the prostitute is in the wilderness (the place of temptation and sin), whereas the New Jerusalem is brought to a mountain (a place of meeting God and of revelation). The former is dressed as a prostitute, but the New Jerusalem is dressed as a bride. Both are adorned with jewels. The prostitute is a dwelling place of demons, but the New Jerusalem is the dwelling place of God. The kings of the earth commit fornication with the prostitute; in contrast, they bring their most valuable possessions to the New Jerusalem. The grotesque figure in chapter 17 represents Rome and its imperial power that defies God's will; the New

Jerusalem is the result of God's victory over that power. John's description of this city also draws on the vision of the new temple in Ezekiel 40–46, where Ezekiel points to a time when the presence of God would live with the people of God.

**Revelation 21:9-14.** The angel summons John and whisks him to a mountain, saying that John will see the bride of the Lamb, but when he gets there he sees a city. It seems that this New Jerusalem is both the people of God and the place God has prepared for them to live. From the beginning John emphasizes the holiness of this place/people: She is a pure bride and a holy city. But the real focus is on how God is present. Not only does the city come from God but it also has the glory of God in it. This glory bathes the city with the glow of precious jewels. The city has a huge wall that symbolizes how safe the people of God are inside. Even as it has enormous walls, it also has a lot of gates: twelve. These gates may suggest openness, but they do not create any worries because they are each attended by an angel. These gates face all directions and each one has a name of a tribe of Israel inscribed on it. They symbolize the full restoration of all of Israel, including the ten tribes that had been lost since the fall of the Northern Kingdom in 722 B.C. Now the promises of restoration are fulfilled. But the New Jerusalem also includes a broader people of God. Just as there are twelve gates, so also there are twelve foundations for the walls. Written on each foundation stone is the name of one of the twelve apostles. They represent the church. These architectural details show that the fully formed people of God in this new creation include the faithful of Israel and of the church. All of God's people are gathered together in God's presence.

**Revelation 21:15-21.** John now gives a more detailed and highly symbolic description of the New Jerusalem. The angel who brought him to the city now has a golden yardstick to measure the city. It is a perfect cube that is twelve thousand stadia in all directions. It is a cube because that was seen as a perfect geometric shape. The NRSV translates the size of each side of the cube as fifteen hundred miles. This is correct, but it obscures the meaning. John says the sides of the cube are twelve thousand stadia. Twelve was a number of perfection, a number with even more powerful meaning for Jews. The measurement of this city indicates that it is perfect, times a thousand! It may also suggest that it comprises all of the people of God, which includes a greater number than had been imagined. Next we hear about the wall of the city. It is a mere 144 (a multiple of 12) cubits (almost 75 yards) high. But that is plenty to do the job because the enemies of God have all been defeated, so there is no threat from outside. The wall and its foundation are made from and decorated with precious gems and gold. Further, each of the twelve gates is made of a single pearl. While we are not sure about the identification of each rare jewel in the list, that does not keep us from getting the point. This is the most impressive, really unimaginably beautiful, city that could ever be. The awe-inspiring size and appearance of the city suggests that it is the complete and perfect kingdom of God.

**Revelation 21:22-27.** Verse 22 begins with a surprise: There is no temple in the city that is known for having the Temple. It has no temple because the all-powerful God and the Lamb are directly present and so they are its temple. Their radiance also makes it unnecessary to have any other light. Both Israel and the nations, again all the people of God, live in this light of God's glory and in gratitude bring their most precious things to give to God. The brilliance of God's glory is so overwhelming that there is no night in this city. So even though it has an impressive wall with stunning gates, those gates are never closed. Both the enemies of God and the night, the time when evil has the advantage, are overcome.

While this city is open and welcomes Gentiles who wish to honor God, as well as the earlier covenant people, the wicked are not allowed in. Only those whose names are in "the Lamb's book of life" enjoy the magnificent gifts of the New Jerusalem (21:27). This way of identifying the saved reminds readers of the importance of Christ's work in mediating these blessings to God's people. The Lamb and God are closely identified in this section of Revelation, even as their identities are kept distinct. It is through Christ that God's enemies are defeated and through him that believers share in God's blessings and presence. John again reminds his readers that proper living is a necessary part of faith.

## INTERPRETING THE SCRIPTURE

### A Home for All of God's People

John's description of this beautiful city represents the salvation of the faithful and the exercise of God's power to make all things right. Importantly, the inhabitants of this city include both Jews and Gentiles. As John envisions who belongs among the saved, he includes the faithful of Israel as well as the Gentiles who are members of the church. This is an important element in his thought about God and God's ultimate purposes. The inclusion of all the tribes of Israel demonstrates God's faithfulness and trustworthiness. Israel's prophets had often predicted the restoration of the whole of Israel, meaning all twelve tribes. But the ten tribes of the Northern Kingdom were lost after falling to the Assyrians; they had been assimilated into the surrounding nations. God's restoration of all the tribes illustrates the magnitude of this salvation. God saves not just individuals, but the whole people. This restoration also demonstrates God's faithfulness by showing that the salvation Christ brought does not mean that God has forgotten or forsaken the earlier covenant. God draws the covenant people into the new salvation that is given in Christ. They are an integral part of the New Jerusalem. What some early believers might have found surprising is not that Israel is restored, but that Gentiles are in the holy city. Gentiles are now among the holy people and are recipients of God's salvation. God's commitment to save is so powerful that it brings in both Jews and Gentiles and makes them one people.

This is good news for John's first readers and for us. Those earlier readers needed reassurance that God had not forsaken them as they endured persecution. We also need assurance of God's love and commitment to us when we wonder about our own relationship with God. We sometimes wonder whether God can forgive some things or feel that we have done things that cannot be overcome. This image of salvation is assurance that God is determined to save all who are willing to accept it. God's promises of love and commitment are eternal. We can trust the God who restores even the hopelessly lost tribes of Israel and Gentiles to love, forgive, and save us.

### A Secure Home

John describes the New Jerusalem as a completely secure city. It has a formidable wall and all its gates have an angel attending them. Beyond that, there is no night, so no time for wicked characters to hide their threatening machinations. No harm can invade or creep up on the inhabitants of this city. The insecurities of life can be paralyzing as we recognize the fragility of life and even when we recognize the goodness of life that we possess. We know the fear of death or of extended illness. We feel anxious about the loneliness that follows emotional betrayals or the loss of one we love. We worry about our financial security in the present and as we look to later years. We have seen difficulties come upon even the most careful. Even in calm and secure circumstances such thoughts and other, even nameless, trepidations sometimes nag at us.

By referring to Christ as the Lamb five times in this passage (21:9, 14, 22, 23, and 27), John reminds us that Jesus can empathize with our fears and weaknesses. Jesus is the Lamb who was killed by those powers that threaten and diminish our lives. But

he is also the one who was raised by God and so reminds us that even in those darkest of times, God does not abandon us. John's description of the New Jerusalem more explicitly promises a salvation that frees us from all anxieties. In this city there is no reason to fear anything. John says that all things that deceive or threaten us are excluded from this city. Only the people of God live in it and there is no possibility that anyone who can do us harm can get in since angels are the sentries at its gates. God's people live here in complete security, sheltered from any possible threat.

God's determination to give us secure and full lives is evident in the angel's opening remark to John. The angel says he is taking John to see the bride of the Lamb. In the first century this would mean that the bride came to the groom's home and came under his protection. So this new city and its inhabitants have a loving relationship with Christ that assures them of his protection. The secure life God's people are given in this city does not come at the cost of surrendering to a dull and confining way of living. This is a magnificent city; even its security features are exquisite. The walls are constructed of gold and jewels and its gates are pearl. This is a perfect existence with complete security and stunning beauty.

### Life in the Presence of God

The feature of the New Jerusalem that gets the most attention in this reading is that God will be directly present. We first hear that the brilliance of God's glory shines on it (21:11). This is comforting, but the description takes a dramatic and surprising turn when John says that there is no temple in the New Jerusalem. There is no temple because there is no need for one; there is no need to have a place people can go to feel the presence of God because God is directly present everywhere in the city. The all-powerful Lord and Christ are present in such an immediate and direct way that no other light is needed. The glory of God seen in the Lamb illumines everything and everyone in this new existence.

Life in the very presence of God is the best of all blessings, even the source of all the other blessings. It assures us of more than security from harm or death. The presence of God gives life that is as full and rich as humans can experience. All difficulties, regrets, and sorrows dissipate in the light of God's radiant love. All who are here are immersed in the light of God's love, lacking nothing that could make life deeper or more meaningful. When all of God's people come together in this resplendent

light, they are full of joy. That joy overflows in the bringing to God the best of everything we are and have. Even those with power and wealth willingly cede them to God in this experience of the divine.

This unending life of joy and fulfillment in God's presence is the culmination of the saving work of the Lamb. John's references to "the Lamb" show that the giving of this life and the desire to draw us into this presence of God are the reasons for Christ's coming to earth; God was so determined to bring us into this blessed life that God gave Christ to come and to die for us. Consequently, we can be sure that God intends to extend the grace to us that brings us into this existence in fellowship with God and Christ. This blissful life is what God wants for God's people, and because of God's determined love and power, it is what God will give us.

## SHARING THE SCRIPTURE

### PREPARING TO LEAD

#### Preparing Our Hearts

Ponder this week's devotional reading from Genesis 1:28–2:3, which is the familiar story of God creating humankind. Recall that God had a close relationship with both Adam and Eve in the garden of Eden. How does this first paradise compare with and contrast to John's visions of the new heaven and earth? What would you expect the relationship between God and humanity to be in this new place?

Pray that you and the students will live now in the presence of God.

#### Preparing Our Minds

Study the background Scripture from Revelation 21:9-27 and the lesson Scripture from Revelation 21:9-14, 22-27.

Consider this question: *What do you imagine living in a new place would be like?*

Write on newsprint:
❑ information for next week's lesson, found under Continue the Journey.
❑ activities for further spiritual

growth in Continue the Journey. Determine how you might use any of the features that precede the first lesson of this quarter in today's session.

**Option:** Locate a recording of "The Holy City" by Frederic Weatherly and Michael Maybrick (using the alias Stephen Adams). This music is often sung around Easter, so your music director may have a copy. Numerous performances are available on YouTube (for example: https://www.youtube.com/watch?v=42cKKPPmDT8).

**Option:** Locate some meditative instrumental music and bring whatever device you need to play this.

## LEADING THE CLASS

### (1) Gather to Learn

❖ Welcome everyone and pray that those who have come today will try to imagine the new life that awaits the faithful with God.

❖ Read: **Perhaps you watch the popular Home and Garden Television (HGTV) show "House Hunters International." Viewers accompany people looking to buy or rent a home in a country different from their own. Often these moves are made due to job transfers, but sometimes people are just seeking a new adventure in a place foreign to them, or parents want their children to have experiences with different cultures to broaden their horizons. A local real estate agent takes the house hunters on a tour of three residences that have the location and amenities that most closely match the client's wish list and budget. Then the family must choose which house they want. As the show ends,** **the selected home is shown, usually several months later, after the family has decorated it and become acclimated. Often there is comment about how the family is adjusting to life in their adopted country.**

❖ Invite class members to imagine what it must be like to live in a place that is entirely new to them.

❖ **Option:** As time permits, invite participants who have made a major move to comment on how it feels to live in a place that is different from the one they have known.

❖ Read aloud today's focus statement: **It is difficult for people to imagine living in a place that is different from the one in which they presently live. What will the new place be like? John uses figurative nonliteral language to describe the new place that God will create.**

### (2) Goal 1: Explore the Possibility of Living in a New Place, Even in Another Dimension of Life

❖ Read or retell A Home for All of God's People in Interpreting the Scripture. Point out the inclusive nature of the New Jerusalem.

❖ Solicit a volunteer to read a description of the New Jerusalem as recorded by John in Revelation 21:9-14, 22-27.

❖ Discuss these questions:
1. **The holy city has twelve gates and a high city wall, but the gates are never shut. What makes this dwelling secure?** (See A Secure Home in Interpreting the Scripture.)
2. **Why is there no temple in this city?** (See Revelation 21:22-27 in Understanding the Scripture.)

3. **Who will be able to enter the city?** (See verses 23-27 and the second paragraph of Revelation 21:22-27 in Understanding the Scripture.)

4. **What might it be like to live in the constant presence of God?** (See Life in the Presence of God in Interpreting the Scripture.)

*(3) Goal 2: Imagine the Richness and Serenity of Living in the New Jerusalem*

❖ **Option:** Play, if possible, "The Holy City." Note the third verse that begins "And once again the scene was changed, new earth there seemed to be." Invite the class to discuss how this music helps them to better envision the city about which John wrote.

❖ Encourage the adults to imagine themselves walking around the New Jerusalem as you read again Revelation 21:11-14 and 25-26. As an option, play some meditative instrumental music in the background as you read. Keep silence (or allow the music to play on) as the students continue to imagine the scene.

❖ Break the silence (or end the music) and invite the students to call out words to describe this place. Jot down their ideas on newsprint.

*(4) Goal 3: Celebrate God's Provision of a New Place for Believers at the End of All Things Temporal and Throughout Eternity*

❖ Look again at the words the students have identified. Note any negative descriptors, but most likely the words will be positive.

❖ Recall that in the Gather to Learn portion we considered what it would be like to move to a different country—a place where we may have to learn a new language, become acquainted with new customs, and learn to cook and eat local food.

❖ Discuss these questions:
- **What about the New Jerusalem do you expect to feel foreign to you?**
- **What about the New Jerusalem do you expect to feel familiar?**
- **What would you expect to do in this new place that will be pleasing unto God?**
- **If you were going to throw a housewarming party in this new place that you will one day call home, how would you celebrate?** (Assume that you can choose food, music, and decorations. Think about the kinds of people who would be on your guest list.)

*(5) Continue the Journey*

❖ Pray that as the learners depart, they will keep the eternal beauty of the New Jerusalem ever before them as they continue to do the work that needs to be done here on earth.

❖ Post information for next week's session on newsprint for the students to copy:
- **Title: Living Water**
- **Background Scripture: Revelation 22:1-7**
- **Lesson Scripture: Revelation 22:1-7**
- **Focus of the Lesson: People are aware that rivers give life and nourishment to the things that exist around them. How do rivers nourish our lives? According to John, in the new world, God's**

power will be in the river and will nourish and heal everything in the city.

■ Challenge the adults to grow spiritually by completing one or more of these activities related to this week's session.

(1) Do a Google search for images of the New Jerusalem. Study several images that appeal to you. Which one(s) most closely represents the way you envision the city? Why?

(2) Relate the description of the heavenly city in Revelation 21 to Jesus' prayer in Matthew 6:10. How can you help God's kingdom to come and God's will to be done on earth as it is in the heaven that John describes?

(3) Read Ezekiel 40. What similarities do you note between Ezekiel's prophecy and John's vision?

❖ Sing or read aloud "O Holy City, Seen of John."

❖ Conclude today's session by leading the class in this benediction, which is adapted from Hebrews 12:1b-2a, the key verses for October 30: May we go forth empowered to run with perseverance the race that is set before us, looking to Jesus the pioneer and perfecter of our faith. Amen.

# UNIT 3: ALPHA AND OMEGA
# LIVING WATERS

---

## PREVIEWING THE LESSON

**Lesson Scripture:** Revelation 22:1-7
**Background Scripture:** Revelation 22:1-7
**Key Verse:** Revelation 22:1

### Focus of the Lesson:
People are aware that rivers give life and nourishment to the things that exist around them. How do rivers nourish our lives? According to John, in the new world, God's power will be in the river and will nourish and heal everything in the city.

### Goals for the Learners:
(1) to explore the image of "the river of the water of life."
(2) to appreciate that in the "river of the water of life" is God's continual provision for sustaining a full and rich life.
(3) to respond to the "river of the water of life" through acceptance, faith, and entrance into the fullness of the Kingdom.

### Supplies:
Bibles, newsprint and marker, paper and pencils, hymnals, three glass containers of water, optional bowl

---

## READING THE SCRIPTURE

**NRSV**
Lesson Scripture: Revelation 22:1-7

**¹Then the angel showed me the river of the water of life, bright as crystal, flowing from the throne of God and of the Lamb** ²through the middle of the street of the city. On either side of the river, is the tree of life, with its twelve kinds of fruit, producing its fruit each month; and

**CEB**
Lesson Scripture: Revelation 22:1-7

**¹Then the angel showed me the river of life-giving water, shining like crystal, flowing from the throne of God and the Lamb** ²through the middle of the city's main street. On each side of the river is the tree of life, which produces twelve crops of fruit, bearing its fruit each month.

the leaves of the tree are for the healing of the nations. ³Nothing accursed with be found there anymore. But the throne of God and of the Lamb will be in it, and his servants will worship him; ⁴they will see his face, and his name will be on their foreheads. ⁵And there will be no more night; they need no light of lamp or sun, for the Lord God will be their light, and they will reign forever and ever.

⁶And he said to me, "These words are trustworthy and true, for the Lord, the God of the spirits of the prophets, sent his angel to show his servants what must soon take place."

⁷"See, I am coming soon. Blessed is the one who keeps the words of the prophecy of this book."

The tree's leaves are for the healing of the nations. ³There will no longer be any curse. The throne of God and the Lamb will be in it, and his servants will worship him. ⁴They will see his face, and his name will be on their foreheads. ⁵Night will be no more. They won't need the light of a lamp or the light of the sun, for the Lord God will shine on them, and they will rule forever and always.

⁶Then he said to me, "These words are trustworthy and true. The Lord, the God of the spirits of the prophets, sent his angel to show his servants what must soon take place.

⁷"Look! I'm coming soon. Favored is the one who keeps the words of the prophecy contained in this scroll."

## UNDERSTANDING THE SCRIPTURE

**Introduction.** Today's reading draws on well-known imagery as John continues his description of the New Jerusalem and exhorts his readers to remain faithful. He reaches all the way back to the creation story to show how far-reaching the saving acts of God truly are. The blessed time to come regains, and even surpasses, the goodness of the original creation before the Fall.

**Revelation 22:1-5.** The angel who has been showing John various images of the salvation that awaits the faithful now provides another portrait of what is in the New Jerusalem. The description starts with a pun. The term for "running water" in ancient Greek was "living water." John says there is a river of running/living water in the new creation. This river is not just running water; it is life-giving water, as the following description shows. The mention of this river

may point us back to Eden, which had four rivers and thus abundant water to sustain and enrich life. Ezekiel had envisioned a river flowing from the new ideal temple in the time of God's restoration of the people from exile (47:1-6).

John picks up this image so that this river in the New Jerusalem shows that God's good intentions for the creation and for humans are now being fulfilled. Its source assures us of its life-giving power; it flows from the throne of God and of the Lamb. Thus, its place of origin is the source of all life. Once again the Lamb is identified closely with God as he shares God's throne. So the Lamb and God are distinguishable, but both have divine status. This is important for John because he demands that people worship only God and he has various heavenly and human beings worship Christ. Since he seems to feel no tension between these demands, he must accord Christ some identity with God.

This river that gives life flows right between the lanes of the main street of the New Jerusalem. There it sustains the tree of life. An indication of the abundance of the blessings of this city is that this tree bears fruit every month of the year (another image drawn from Ezekiel; see 47:12). The symbolic designation of the single tree of life really stands for a grove of trees since they stand on each side of the street. Since these trees take turns bearing fruit, such that one of them has ripe fruit available each month of the year, there is never a need to store up food to prepare for a season of scarcity. It is always a time of abundance; it is always harvest time. Even better than the daily provision of manna God gave in the wilderness, this food has variety and comes from trees whose nutrients come from the river that gives life. This is a sign of God's gift of a full life without anxiety. All the needs of God's people are always met in this city.

John refers to this grove as the singular tree of life to again send us to Eden. After Adam and Eve sin, God expels them from the garden so they will not eat of the tree of life and live forever (Genesis 3:22-23). Now John says that the tree that gives eternal life is the food source for all who live in the New Jerusalem. All who are admitted to this city live forever. And this salvation is not just for individuals because the leaves of the tree heal the nations. The life God gives does not just give us a good relationship with God; it also heals the rifts between us and our neighbors, even between us and our enemies. God intends our lives to have the fullness of healthy and nurturing relationships with fellow human beings, as well as with God. Just as Adam needed a companion to have full life, so those in the New Jerusalem will have life-enriching relationships with those who are saved with them. John again points us to Eden at the beginning of verse 3. The NRSV translates this sentence to mean that there are no accursed things there, while the CEB says there is no longer any curse. Both are legitimate translations of the words of the verse. But given how many times John has picked up images from Eden in the first two verses of this chapter, it seems likely that the CEB is on target here. John intends to say that the curse of Eden is no longer in effect. All that has gone wrong because of human sin is now repaired. Indeed much is even better than its original state.

Things are better in the New Jerusalem than in Eden because the throne of God and the Lamb, and so God's presence, are now directly among God's people. God's throne was not in Eden. And while God interacted directly with those first humans, God's dwelling place was apart from them. Now God is immediately present always. As before, the indication of the nearness of God is the absence of night. While no one could look directly at God before (Exodus 33:20; Deuteronomy 4:12), now those who are saved see God's face constantly. They are empowered to be in the immediate presence of God. The name on their forehead protects them from any harm and marks them as the people of God. They are so close to God that they are said to reign, just as God is reigning.

**Revelation 22:6-7.** The angel now assures John that what he has seen is certain to happen because the vision comes from the Lord God who inspired all the prophets, the God who is faithful to keep promises. He promises further that these things will happen soon. These things have been revealed so that the persecuted and discouraged hear that they do not have to wait much longer, their Savior is coming soon. Interestingly, those who have just been told they will reign are called Christ's slaves (also translated as servants). They must still be obedient to their Lord. Christ then speaks directly, saying he is coming quickly, adding that only those who remain faithful will experience the blessings John has described.

---

## INTERPRETING THE SCRIPTURE

### River of Life

John creates a beautiful image of downtown New Jerusalem that has the river of life as its focal point. Ancient people knew the importance of rivers as centers of civilizations, as boundary markers, and as sources of food and comfort. Most of the great cities of the ancient world were built on rivers. Beyond the need of water for existence, it provided means of transportation and enabled farmers to irrigate their fields. Some cities even had water systems that brought running water into the downtown district where there were public fountains for people to get water. Having running water in your house was a sign of wealth. Many wealthy people piped in enough water for elaborate fountains and pools. Abundant water means abundant life.

The New Jerusalem supplies abundance for all needs and comforts. The life that God wants for God's people is one with no anxiety and complete security. Such a life is elusive, even impossible in this world. John's readers knew this all too well. They faced not only the usual uncertainties of life but also the burden of persecution. They needed assurance of God's love for them, and they needed to know what God has in store for those who remain faithful. The life John describes and promises is more than an adequate response to the mistreatment they are receiving from their neighbors or the Roman Empire. The marks on their foreheads assure them that they really are God's people; they belong to God, so God will not abandon them. This new life they are promised is eternal. This promise is the flipside of the temporary, even fleeting, nature of their present difficulties. Christ says he is coming soon to relieve their pain and give them this new life.

Like John's first readers, we seem to be in a constant search for security and comfort. We take that more difficult but better-paying job or we save for retirement or we get that bigger house in a better part of town. We hear the world around us promising that just a bit more money, position, or power will bring us security and assurance against the troubles of life. But in our hearts we know that these things are not what really give us good lives that are filled with joy. Even when we look to relationships for this full life, we know the possibility of disappointment or of separation at the end. We yearn for the peace and well-being that gives us certainty of our value and of God's love. John's vision assures us that God knows our circumstances and loves us, even when we seem to be enduring things that are unfair and that push us to the edge of losing our faith. When we do not feel God's presence, power, or love, when we face pain, injury, or loneliness, this vision of the New Jerusalem is the promise that God does love us and will not allow those difficulties to have the last word. Even when those experiences bring us to the end of life, God promises that a glorious life in God's presence will be our ultimate destiny. We will have that fullness with comfort, security, and joy that can never be taken from us.

### God's Gift of a Full Life

John's vision intends to bring us comfort and joy in the midst of the uncertainties of existence in this world. It promises that the love and goodness of God prevails over all things that would diminish life. When we think of this wonderful existence in the presence of God and in loving relationship with God, we usually think of our personal salvation. This is an essential element of salvation, but God has even more in mind. John says that the leaves of the tree of life are for the "healing of the nations" (22:2). The salvation of God includes resolving the conflicts that make people of various nations turn against one another. The uncertainty and need that drive people to war are gone; so is the greed that makes people want to take what others have. God's peace is established everywhere. Relations among nations are healed so that there is no threat of war that might interrupt the bliss of the New Jerusalem. God's salvation is so broad that it extends to all places. This new peace may be another aspect of the return of creation to what God originally wanted for it.

Beyond the abstract peace that John sees for all nations, he also sees the salvation of each person in the context of a saved people. God claims us in community. Just as Adam needed companionship in the beginning, so God's people are given the fullness of life that includes life in community, life in harmonious relationship with all others who love God and love to be in God's presence. Loneliness or the threat of loneliness is often one of our greatest fears. We need people with whom to share our joys. Without that fellowship our joy is more fleeting and less complete. Knowing that we are created to live in community, God provides it. While reveling in God's presence we have the great pleasure of sharing in community with our brothers and sisters who love God and one another.

Another aspect of this full life is that it is spent in offering worship to God. While some of the evil powers that Revelation envisions are forced into submission, that kind of honoring of God is far from John's mind in this scene. Here those who love God and have been given new and eternal life express their love and gratitude through worship. We know the feeling of needing to say thank you when we have been given an overwhelming gift or received a kindness that we could not have expected. That is the worship John has in mind here: a spontaneous and continuous outpouring of thanks, gratitude, and love for God. This response to God and God's blessings is at the heart of all worship.

### The Promise and the Demand

The pattern we have seen in other passages of Revelation continues here. God or Christ makes great promises that are followed by exhortations to faithfulness. The difficult circumstances that the original readers faced made both the promise and the encouragement necessary. Persecution seems to suggest that God does not care and so tempts those who are suffering to turn from faith. Like them, we need both assurance and exhortation. In our reading today, John assures readers that these promises come from God and so are "trustworthy and true" (22:6).

When Christ speaks in the next verse he says he is coming soon. This news is both comforting and threatening. Christ assures readers that their suffering will not last much longer, even as his imminence means that his judgment is also close at hand. Thus they must obey what he commands. We may not be expecting a quick return of Christ, but these words also encourage us to know that our pain and anguishes will not last long in comparison to that which God has in store for the faithful. They also encourage us to remain faithful when those feelings of God's absence tempt us to turn from God. John tells us that the promise of God will bring wholeness and joy. Moreover, that promise is unbreakable.

---

## SHARING THE SCRIPTURE

### PREPARING TO LEAD

#### Preparing Our Hearts

Ponder this week's devotional reading from Psalm 46. What do you learn about the river in the city of God? What images does the psalmist use to express his understandings of who God is and how God is related to him? The writer says, "Be still, and know that I am God!" (46:10). Take some time to sit quietly to listen for God.

Pray that you and the students will rely on God, who is our refuge and strength.

#### Preparing Our Minds

Study the background Scripture and the lesson Scripture, which are both from Revelation 22:1-7.

Consider this question: *How do rivers nourish life?*

Write on newsprint:
- ❏ information for next week's lesson, found under Continue the Journey.
- ❏ activities for further spiritual growth in Continue the Journey.

Determine how you might use any of the features that precede the first lesson of this quarter in today's session.

Bring to class several jars of water, each in a separate glass (transparent) container: one that is clear; one that is muddy; and one containing sand, stone, or other foreign objects. You may want to enlist class members to assist you in collecting water if you cannot easily do this yourself.

## LEADING THE CLASS

### (1) Gather to Learn

❖ Welcome everyone and pray that those who have come today will find life and nourishment in the literal and figurative water of life.

❖ Set the three containers of water you have brought on a table where all can see them. Hold up the containers, one at a time (or pour each one into a separate bowl to ensure that everyone can see), and then ask the class which one they would like to drink from—and why they chose that one.

❖ Talk about the importance of safe, clean drinking water by mentioning these statistics (as of 2015) and then add that water is essential for life.

- One in nine people around the world lacks access to safe water.
- Worldwide, 750 million people lack access to clean water, which is almost two and a half times the population of the United States.
- Every minute a child dies of a water-borne illness.

❖ Read aloud today's focus statement: **People are aware that rivers give life and nourishment to the things that exist around them. How do rivers nourish our lives? According to John, in the new world, God's power will be in the river and will nourish and heal everything in the city.**

### (2) Goal 1: Explore the Image of the "River of the Water of Life"

❖ Choose a volunteer to read Revelation 22:1-7.

❖ Read or retell Revelation 22:1-5 from Understanding the Scripture. You may want to add information

from the first paragraph of River of Life in Interpreting the Scripture.

❖ Do an in-depth Bible study by enlisting three volunteers to read Genesis 2:9-14; Genesis 3:22-23; Ezekiel 47:1-12. Then discuss these questions using these Scriptures, as well as Revelation 22:1-2.

1. **What do you learn about the river of life and its source?** (Be sure to note that in Ezekiel 47:1 the water flows "from below the threshold of the temple," whereas in Revelation 22:1 it flows "from the throne of God and of the Lamb.")

2. **Describe what is on either side of the river.**

3. **What do you know about the fruit, according to Revelation and Genesis?**

4. **What do you know about the leaves?**

❖ Look now at Revelation 22:3-7 and discuss these questions. Add information from Understanding the Scripture as appropriate.

1. **What else is—or is not—found near the river?**

2. **How will the relationship with the worshipers here be different from earthly worship?** (Worshipers will be able to see the face of God, which was not previously permitted.)

3. **What does the fact that there will be no more night—only light—suggest to you?**

4. **What guarantee do we have that these words are true?** (See Revelation 22:6-7 in Understanding the Scripture.)

❖ Summarize this portion of the lesson by asking: **How do the images we have explored that stretch from Genesis through Revelation help you to better understand the importance**

**of the river of life and the trees that grow along its banks?**

*(3) Goal 2: Appreciate that in the "River of the Water of Life" Is God's Continual Provision for Sustaining a Full and Rich Life*

❖ Read or retell God's Gift of a Full Life in Interpreting the Scripture.

❖ Form several groups and give each one a sheet of newsprint and several markers. Invite the students to sketch a river with trees on its banks. (Artistic ability is not important! Stick trees will work quite well.) Then, on the leaves or limbs or bark of the trees they are to write or draw something for which they give thanks to God. This "something" may be a thing, an emotion, or a person, so long as it helps the adults to live a full life. Suggest that as the students work, they talk with one another about why they are choosing their specific items. Encourage each person to put as many items on an individual tree as he or she wants.

❖ Post the newsprint. Allow time for participants to circulate around the room to see what provisions for a full life their classmates have identified.

*(4) Goal 3: Respond to the "River of the Water of Life" Through Acceptance, Faith, and Entrance into the Fullness of the Kingdom*

❖ Read Psalm 46:4-5 aloud.

❖ Provide a few moments for reflection. Invite the students to envision the city with God in the midst of it as the river flows through it. Suggest that they make a silent commitment to enter into these life-giving waters that God has so graciously provided.

*(5) Continue the Journey*

❖ Break the silence by praying that as the learners depart, they will seek the life and healing that God's life-giving water provides.

❖ Post information for next week's session on newsprint for the students to copy:

- **Title: Alpha and Omega**
- **Background Scripture: Revelation 22:8-21**
- **Lesson Scripture: Revelation 22:12-21**
- **Focus of the Lesson: People are aware that things have a beginning and an end. What is the source and final purpose of human life? Revelation affirms that God, who is the Alpha and Omega, controls all things.**

❖ Challenge the adults to grow spiritually by completing one or more of these activities related to this week's session.

(1) **Locate and support a project that is devoted to providing safe, clean drinking water. One such project, sponsored by The United Methodist Church, is Water for Life (see http://www. umcmission.org/Give-to-Mission/Search-for-Projects/ Projects/3020811).**

(2) **Recall your baptism as you take a bath or shower this week. How do the waters of life cleanse you, both literally and figuratively? Give thanks to God as you remember your baptism.**

(3) **Visit, if possible, a body of water. How do you feel when you are at an ocean, river, canal, or lake, as opposed to**

when you are surrounded by land? Why do you suppose you feel differently? What affect does the water have on your spirit?

❖ Sing or read aloud "Shall We Gather at the River."

❖ Conclude today's session by leading the class in this benediction, which is adapted from Hebrews 12:1b-2a, the key verses for October 30: **May we go forth empowered to run with perseverance the race that is set before us, looking to Jesus the pioneer and perfecter of our faith. Amen.**

## UNIT 3: ALPHA AND OMEGA
# ALPHA AND OMEGA

---

### PREVIEWING THE LESSON

**Lesson Scripture:** Revelation 22:12-21
**Background Scripture:** Revelation 22:8-21
**Key Verse:** Revelation 22:13

#### Focus of the Lesson:
People are aware that things have a beginning and an end. What is the source and final purpose of human life? Revelation affirms that God, who is the Alpha and Omega, controls all things.

#### Goals for the Learners:
(1) to explore the meaning of the Second Coming to see the importance of this hoped-for reality.
(2) to rejoice that the invitation from Jesus to join the new community continues through the end of all things.
(3) to embrace the call to become part of God's kingdom.

#### Supplies:
Bibles, newsprint and marker, paper and pencils, hymnals; pitcher of water, paper cups; optional Advent wreath, candles, matches

---

### READING THE SCRIPTURE

**NRSV**

Lesson Scripture: Revelation 22:12-21

<sup>12</sup>"See, I am coming soon; my reward is with me, to repay according to everyone's work. **<sup>13</sup>I am the Alpha and the Omega, the first and the last, the beginning and the end."** <sup>14</sup>Blessed are those who wash their robes so that they will have the right to the tree of life and may enter the city by the gates. <sup>15</sup>Outside are the

**CEB**

Lesson Scripture: Revelation 22:12-21

<sup>12</sup>"Look! I'm coming soon. My reward is with me, to repay all people as their actions deserve. **<sup>13</sup>I am the alpha and the omega, the first and the last, the beginning and the end.** <sup>14</sup>Favored are those who wash their robes so that they may have the right of access to the tree of life and may enter the city by the gates.

dogs and sorcerers and fornicators and murderers and idolaters, and everyone who loves and practices falsehood.

[16]"It is I, Jesus, who sent my angel to you with this testimony for the churches. I am the root and the descendant of David, the bright morning star."

[17]The Spirit and the bride say, "Come." And let everyone who hears
　　say, "Come."
And let everyone who is thirsty come.
Let anyone who wishes take the water
　　of life as a gift.

[18]I warn everyone who hears the words of the prophecy of this book: if anyone adds to them, God will add to that person the plagues described in this book; [19]if anyone takes away from the words of the book of this prophecy, God will take away that person's share in the tree of life and in the holy city, which are described in this book. [20]The one who testifies to these things says, "Surely I am coming soon."

　　Amen. Come, Lord Jesus!

[21]The grace of the Lord Jesus be with all the saints. Amen.

[15]Outside are the dogs, the drug users and spell-casters, those who commit sexual immorality, the murderers, the idolaters, and all who love and practice deception.

[16]"I, Jesus, have sent my angel to bear witness to all of you about these things for the churches. I'm the root and descendant of David, the bright morning star. [17]The Spirit and the bride say, 'Come!' Let the one who hears say, 'Come!' And let the one who is thirsty come! Let the one who wishes receive life-giving water as a gift."

[18]Now I bear witness to everyone who hears the words of the prophecy contained in this scroll: If anyone adds to them, God will add to that person the plagues that are written in this scroll. [19]If anyone takes away from the words of this scroll of prophecy, God will take away that person's share in the tree of life and the holy city, which are described in this scroll.

[20]The one who bears witness to these things says, "Yes, I'm coming soon." Amen. Come, Lord Jesus!

[21]The grace of the Lord Jesus be with all.

## UNDERSTANDING THE SCRIPTURE

**Introduction.** Today we read the conclusion of the Book of Revelation. John has acknowledged the enormous evil that threatens and harms God's people and he has dramatically depicted its defeat by Christ. He has sympathetically depicted the suffering of the faithful and promised a glorious salvation. Interspersed in these visions he has given exhortations and issued warnings about the importance of maintaining faithfulness. This conclusion reiterates and strengthens the

promises and the exhortations.

**Revelation 22:8-11.** John makes a mistake as the book draws to a close. Naming himself as the recipient of the visions, for the second time he bows to worship the angel who mediated them (19:10). The repetition of this same mistake suggests that John thinks it is necessary to remind his readers that no being is worthy of worship other than God. Some in the early church may have been inclined to worship angels or other beings who might offer them favors. There is clear evidence that many people, including some Jews, prayed to angels for protection, healing, or help. John sees that as unfaithfulness to God and rejects it. Unlike nearly all books written in the style of Revelation, John is told to share immediately what he has been shown with everyone who would listen. The time left is so short that the message needs to be spread as immediately as possible. The angel suggests that the contents are not likely to sway unbelievers, but it can strengthen the faithful as they strive to be holy and righteous (22:10-11). This strengthening of the resolve of those being persecuted is a central purpose of Revelation. One way John accomplishes that is by assuring them that their suffering will not last long.

**Revelation 22:12-16.** It is difficult to keep up with who is speaking in this section of Revelation. In verses 8-11 we have a conversation between John and the angel. Without any indication other than the content, Jesus begins speaking in verse 12 and continues through verse 17 and perhaps through verse 19. Christ first repeats the assurance that he is coming soon. This is a common assurance in Revelation, but earlier in the book John acknowledges that Christ's return has taken longer than anyone thought it would. He signals this with unexplained pauses at the climax of the action in his visions (for example, 8:1) or with an unexpected interlude near the end of a cycle of action (for example, 10:1–11:14). He balances promises of imminence with recognition that it has taken longer than they think it should. But if the delay has sparked a doubt, Christ identifies himself in verse 13 as the Alpha and Omega, the first and last letters of the Greek alphabet. Thus, Christ identifies himself as the origin and completion of all things, of creation and salvation. All will be summed up by and in him. Nothing will be out of his control when he brings about that conclusion. So the delay does not suggest a lack of power or concern.

Jesus makes judgment a primary element of his return. As he speaks in verse 12, he says that everyone will be judged according to their deeds. This sounds unusual because we often say that Christians are freed from judgment because of their faith. That way of expressing the certainty of our salvation rests on later developments in the history of the church. New Testament writers regularly say that all people are answerable to God for their deeds. While this may seem like a threat, it is also great assurance because it means that those who abuse believers will not get away with it. Those who oppose the purposes of God will receive due recompense. The reminder that Christ will evaluate the lives of all people does not place the salvation of believers at risk. Verse 14 immediately reminds readers that those who have faith, those who wash their robes, receive salvation; they have access to the tree of life and are made residents of the New Jerusalem.

Verse 16 reminds readers that the promises and demands of this book come from the One who has power in heaven and who is the fulfillment of God's promises. Jesus is the One who can command angels. Since the commands come from him, the churches must obey. As the descendant of David, he is also the reigning fulfillment of the hopes of Israel. Identifying Jesus as the "bright morning star" is another way of identifying him as the Messiah of Israel. He is the brightest star and so the hope of good things to come.

**Revelation 22:17-21.** Christ issues the invitation of salvation to all. The bride of verse 17 is the church. So the Spirit and the church offer the invitation of salvation to all who will accept. Everyone who yearns for the good life that salvation brings is invited into the realm of salvation. Those who accept this invitation also accept some demands. Verse 18 warns readers that they must be faithful to God in the ways described in Revelation if they are to receive the glorious life it describes. Those who fail to live faithfully will be excluded from salvation. This gives the instructions in this book ultimate authority. God's judgment and the determination of people's salvation will be determined by whether they accept the commands found here. This threat comes to people who are being persecuted, but it is tempered by the promises of strengthening and salvation that have come before it. Revelation has worked hard to convince readers that the hardships of this life pale in comparison to the salvation the faithful will receive.

The book concludes with Jesus again promising to come quickly. John's response is to ask for the end to come. Given the treatment that believers endure, he is ready for Christ to return to punish those who abuse them and to give salvation to the faithful. He uses one of the earliest expressions of the church (*maranatha*; the Aramaic expression for "come Lord") to ask Jesus to return. He concludes the book with a benediction that assures all believers ("all the saints") of the grace of Christ.

---

## INTERPRETING THE SCRIPTURE

### The Second Coming

The early church and the New Testament gave a great deal of attention to the topic of the Second Coming of Christ. It was a central hope and a pervasive piece of the church's exhortation and encouragement. Since the resurrection of the dead was seen as an event of the end, they interpreted the resurrection of Christ as the beginning of that end, the signal that the resurrection of all people was near. They looked forward to that day as a time of freedom from the oppression they faced in this world and as the time they would live in bliss with God and Christ. As the decades passed and Christ did not return to bring the end, the church had to think about what the delay meant. Their experience of the Spirit was a clear sign that they were living in "the last days" (see Acts 2:16-18), so they maintained the belief that the resurrection of Christ had begun those last days. But they adjusted their thinking about how many last days there would be. Rather than saying Christ would return soon, they start to say he would come suddenly—"like a thief in the night" (see, for example, Matthew 24:42-44; Luke 12:39-40; 1 Thessalonians 5:2). Even the Book of Revelation reminds readers of the delay. It often says Jesus is coming soon, but its visions have unexpected delays (see the examples in Understanding the Scripture under Revelation 22:12-16).

While the Second Coming was delayed, its importance remained crucial. The emphasis of the discussion turns so that its certainty is the central point rather than its nearness. Its nearness was emphasized when the church was facing persecution and needed to know that their pain would come to an end. The Second Coming is important because that is the time when God's love and justice are fully known. Until then, God does not fully reign. The promise of the Second Coming is our assurance that God really does care about us and the world. It is the promise that God will not allow injustice, greed, and all that harms God's people and world to prevail. It is how God's salvation eventually and fully comes to the faithful. At his Second Coming, Christ comes as ruler and judge. He comes to eradicate evil, establish justice, and give the promised blessings to God's people. It is the time when we see all things conform to who God is and what God wants, and so it is the moment that vindicates our faith.

Most Christians today do not hope for the swift return of Christ. We are more comfortable with the world than were the earliest Christians. Still, the suffering and injustice in the world points us to the importance of the promises that all things will ultimately conform to God's will and that salvation will come to God's people. Our own persistence in working for justice in the world is strengthened by knowing that we are working for the will of God, which will finally prevail over evil. Even if we do not want it to happen tomorrow, we need the assurance of salvation that the Second Coming promises.

## An Open Invitation

Revelation draws a clear line between the saved and the lost. In 22:14-15 the saved are washed and given eternal life, while those not saved are referred to as dogs and evil workers. But as stark as these distinctions are, those outside are invited in. In verse 17, the Holy Spirit and the church (the "bride") invite all people into the blessings of salvation. Everyone is invited into this bliss and anyone who knows the thirst for God and for a life with meaning is invited to accept the full life God offers. The church is not to be the smug receiver of salvation that it keeps to itself. When we experience the life God gives, the proper response is to want to share it with others. If we remember all that this gift of salvation means for our present life and our life to come, we should be bursting to invite others to join us.

We may grow accustomed to having lives enriched by God's presence and forget what joys we have as God's people. But if we awaken ourselves to the amazing ways we are blessed by God, we will have an almost unstoppable impulse to invite others to accept those gifts. It is not the job of the church alone to offer this invitation; the Spirit also invites people in. The God who offers these gifts sends the Spirit to move people to recognize and accept them. God continually reaches out to those who do not know God or who oppose God's will. Their rejection does not deter God's desire and effort to reclaim them and give them salvation. Together the church and the Spirit offer God's invitation to all; everyone is eligible to receive life, but acceptance of that life requires the recipients to accept the demands of living for God.

### Christ Brings the Kingdom

We often pray, "Thy Kingdom come." This prayer asks God to bring the Kingdom, but in much of what we say in other contexts we talk as though it is our job to bring the Kingdom into existence. If we think this, we take on an impossible task. The work of bringing the Kingdom to fullness is God's. Through Christ, God promises to establish God's rule over all things. As Revelation (and all the New Testament) sees it, the Kingdom (in the church) has been established, but has not come in its fullness. Only the Second Coming will bring the Kingdom in its fullness. Meanwhile, the church is blessed to live in the first phase of the fullness that is to come.

At the Second Coming we will be in the full presence of God, while now we have the Spirit as the foretaste and promise of that glorious existence. This presence of the Spirit enables us to live more nearly as God wants and so to live fuller and more meaningful lives. In the time to come our wills will conform fully to God's will. As the church now enjoys a portion of the gifts God has in store for us, we can look forward to their fullness in the time to come.

### The Foundation of All Hope

All of the promises of Revelation are dependent upon the power and sovereignty of God. Its dramatic imagery and victories over evil are designed to assure us that God has more power than all things that would separate us from God or that would diminish the life that God wants for us. In many ways, the book is a celebration of the power of God to overcome evil and those things that bring us sorrow. Even more, it promises us that this most powerful God will use that potency to draw us close and to give us blessing beyond description. This God that demands faithfulness uses that power to enable faithfulness in us so that we begin to experience fullness of life even now. It is this God who promises us the tree of life and life before the throne of God and the Lamb.

---

## SHARING THE SCRIPTURE

### PREPARING TO LEAD

#### Preparing Our Hearts

Ponder this week's devotional reading from Revelation 1:4b-8. What is said to the seven churches in Asia concerning the Second Coming of the Lord? What does it mean to you to believe that the Lord God is the Alpha and Omega, the beginning and the end? Verse 8 makes reference to the One "who is and who was and who is to come." Some services of Holy Communion express this same idea when the congregation says, "Christ has died; Christ is risen; Christ will come again." Are you awaiting his return? Why or why not?

Pray that you and the students will give thanks to the One who is the first and the last.

#### Preparing Our Minds

Study the background Scripture from Revelation 22:8-21 and the lesson Scripture from Revelation 22:12-21.

Consider this question: *What is the source and final purpose of human life?*

Write on newsprint:

❏ information for next week's lesson, found under Continue the Journey.

❏ activities for further spiritual growth in Continue the Journey.

Determine how you might use any of the features that precede the first lesson of this quarter in today's session.

Gather supplies you will need to light an Advent wreath if you choose this option in the Gather to Learn portion.

## LEADING THE CLASS

### (1) Gather to Learn

❖ Welcome everyone and pray that those who have come today will feel welcomed and extend an invitation to others to "come," especially as we begin this Advent season.

❖ **Option:** Provide time to light the first candle of an Advent wreath. You will need a wreath of greens, four candles, and matches or lighter. You can tie this activity in with today's Scripture, which focuses on the beginning and end, since this is the beginning of the season of Advent. During Advent we look back to the coming of Jesus as God-with-us; we also look ahead to his Second Coming. If you choose this option, plan to light the Advent wreath on each of the succeeding three Sundays.

❖ Read: **Have you ever read a good detective novel and quickly realized that although you are on page 3, the story has been in progress for some time? Perhaps the novel has started just a few pages before the chief inspector appears at a crime scene to gather evidence. Toward the middle of the book, you learn that the animosity causing a murder has roots that stretch back over time. As you come to the end of the book and learn "whodunit," you can look back and see how the clues, which were planted throughout the story, now fit together as jigsaw puzzle pieces to reveal the perpetrator of the crime. Without a beginning, middle, and an end to the story you could not understand what happened or why.**

❖ Ask: **In addition to stories, what else in life has a beginning and end?**

❖ Read aloud today's focus statement: **People are aware that things have a beginning and an end. What is the source and final purpose of human life? Revelation affirms that God, who is the Alpha and Omega, controls all things.**

### (2) Goal 1: Explore the Meaning of the "Second Coming" to See the Importance of This Hoped-for Reality

❖ Choose a volunteer to read Revelation 22:12-21.

❖ Point out that although the term "Second Coming" is not found in the Bible, other terms such as *Parousia* or Day of the Lord are used. In Revelation 22:20 Jesus says, "I am coming soon." The concept is deeply embedded in the Scriptures even if the term "Second Coming" is not.

❖ Read or retell The Second Coming in Interpreting the Scripture to help students understand what this end-time term refers to and discuss these questions:

1. **What connections were drawn between Christ's return and the persecution the early Christians faced?**

2. **How did the early church handle the delay of Christ's return?**

3. **Christ referred to himself as the Alpha and Omega, the beginning and end. How might that understanding of who he is ease the church's concern about his delay?** (See the first paragraph of Revelation 12:12-16 in Understanding the Scripture.)

4. **What role will judgment play in Christ's return?** (See the second paragraph of Revelation 12:12-16 in Understanding the Scripture.)

5. **How do you respond to the statement, "Most Christians today do not hope for the swift return of Christ"?**

*(3) Goal 2: Rejoice that the Invitation from Jesus to Join the New Community Continues Through the End of All Things*

❖ Reread verses 14-17 and ask:

1. **Who will be admitted to the Kingdom?** (See An Open Invitation in Interpreting the Scripture and Revelation 22:17-21 in Understanding the Scripture.)

2. **Who issues the invitation to "come" and to whom is this invitation addressed?** (See verse 17. Note that "bride" refers to the church.)

3. **What is your church doing right now to invite outsiders in?**

4. **What difference can it make for the church to issue an open invitation for all to come?**

❖ Conclude this portion by reading Isaiah 55:1-9 and encouraging the students to be as enthusiastic and inclusive in issuing invitations to come to their church as Isaiah was in inviting people to God's abundant life.

*(4) Goal 3: Embrace the Call to Become Part of God's Kingdom*

❖ Pour a cup of water for each participant and distribute the cups.

❖ Call on four volunteers to each read one line of invitation from Revelation 22:17.

❖ Invite any who want to commit themselves to being part of God's kingdom "to take the water of life as a gift" (22:17) and drink it.

*(5) Continue the Journey*

❖ Pray that as the learners depart they will accept the gift of life that Christ offers and help others become aware that they too are invited to accept the gift of salvation.

❖ Post information for next week's session on newsprint for the students to copy:

- **Title: God Promises a Savior**
- **Background Scripture: Luke 1:26-38**
- **Lesson Scripture: Luke 1:26-38**
- **Focus of the Lesson: Our actions, decisions, and even well-being are often based on our trust in the promises made by others. On whose promises can we ultimately depend? Luke recounts the angel's announcement of the coming birth of Jesus, God's promised Savior.**

❖ Challenge the adults to grow spiritually by completing one or more of these activities related to this week's session.

(1) **Take stock of your life. If Jesus were to come today—to**

find you doing whatever you normally do—would he be pleased to welcome you into the kingdom of God? If there are facets of your life that need improvement, what changes will you make with the help of God?

(2) Note in Revelation 22:12 that Jesus plans to reward everyone's work. Although salvation does not depend on our actions, Jesus does plan to reward those who have worked for the kingdom of God. What are you doing that he may choose to reward? What might you begin to do, not so much to get a reward but rather to respond to the love you have experienced because of the Savior's saving grace?

(3) Recall the invitation to "come" that Christ issued in verse 17. Who will you invite this week to worship or a small group where he or she can get to know Christ? What steps can you take to help your congregation become more opening and welcoming?

❖ Sing the response and read aloud "Canticle of Hope," number 734 of *The United Methodist Hymnal*. Or sing "Just as I Am, Without One Plea."

❖ Conclude today's session by leading the class in this benediction, which is adapted from Hebrews 12:1b-2a, the key verses for October 30: **May we go forth empowered to run with perseverance the race that is set before us, looking to Jesus the pioneer and perfecter of our faith. Amen.**

# SECOND QUARTER
## Creation: A Divine Cycle
### DECEMBER 4, 2016–FEBRUARY 26, 2017

The thirteen sessions of this winter's quarter focus on the theme of creation as viewed from perspectives in Luke's Gospel, selected psalms, and Galatians. We will be exploring God's ongoing actions in blessing and reconciling the whole creation.

Four lessons from Luke's Gospel focus on the events leading to the nativity of Jesus in Unit 1, The Savior Has Been Born. We begin on the Second Sunday of Advent, December 4, by studying the angel Gabriel's visit to Mary, recorded in Luke 1:26-38, where she learns that God Promises a Savior. On December 11 we hear the soaring words of The Affirmation of the Promise as Mary sings a hymn of praise in Luke 1:39-56. God Promised Zechariah a Son, the lesson for December 18 that is rooted in Luke 1:1-23, 57-66, considers the angel's message to the elderly priest Zechariah that he and his wife Elizabeth will have a son who is to be named John. The pinnacle of good news—God's Promised Savior Is Born—is highlighted in our lesson for Christmas Day from Luke 2:1-21.

Five psalms that emphasize creation's praise of God or call humanity to praise God form the basis for the lessons for Unit 2, Praise from and for God's Creation. This unit begins on New Year's Day by Praising God the Creator along with the writer in Psalm 33:1-9. The message of Psalm 96, All Creation Overflows with Praise, prompts us to sing a new song on January 8. On January 15 we turn to Psalms 65 and 67:6-7 as we Praise God the Provider. Psalm 104, which we will encounter on January 22, encourages us to Praise God the Creator. Our final lesson of this unit, which we will study on January 29, is based in the resounding Psalm 148, which testifies that All Creation Praises God.

Unit 3, The Birthing of a New Community, looks at four excerpts from Galatians to examine how God's creative process can be seen through the birthing of a new faith community with Jesus as its foundation. On February 5, Re-created to Live in Harmony investigates Paul's message in Galatians 3:26–4:7 concerning what it means to be one in Christ. On February 12 we learn from Galatians 4 that New Birth Brings Freedom. Paul continues with the concept of Freedom in Christ in the lesson for February 19, which is based on Galatians 5:1-17. The quarter concludes on February 26 with Christ Creates Holy Living, a lesson on fruitful living from Galatians 5:18–6:10.

# MEET OUR WRITER

## REV. JOHN INDERMARK

John Indermark is a retired United Church of Christ minister. He and his wife, Judy, a retired 911 dispatcher, now split their time between their long-time home in southwest Washington State and their newfound home in Tucson, Arizona.

John was born and reared in St. Louis, Missouri. He graduated from Northwest High School, St. Louis University, and Eden Theological Seminary. Ordained in the United Church of Christ, John served as a full-time parish pastor for sixteen years before shifting to a ministry of the written word. He has also served in a variety of interim and extended pulpit supply positions for Presbyterian, Methodist, and Lutheran congregations in southwest Washington and northwest Oregon along with his writing ministry. His most recent parish experience was in the spring of 2013 as visiting associate pastor of the Church of the Holy Cross (U.C.C.) in Hilo, Hawaii.

John's ministry of writing focuses on biblical faith formation books and Christian education curricula. Most recently, John and Sharon Harding coauthored *Advent: A to Z*, a "prayerful and playful" resource for adults and families with children. John is currently working on a book tentatively titled *Cruciform Worship: A Daily Lenten Pilgrimage* scheduled for publication in the fall of 2016 by Upper Room Books. His ongoing curricula work, besides *The New International Lesson Annual*, includes *Feasting on the Word* and *The Present Word*. He wrote the New Testament materials for youth and leaders in *Crossings: God's Journey with Us*, a confirmation resource published by Logos Productions, Inc., and later revised that resource for use with adults.

John and Judy enjoy walking the logging roads of the lower Columbia region and the desert trails of the greater Tucson area and in particular Saguaro National Park. With retirement, Judy is finding more time for painting, while John has taken up outdoor photography.

# THE BIG PICTURE: CREATION AND NEW CREATION

This quarter explores the theme of creation from three perspectives. The first perspective is that of Advent, where Luke's stories of annunciation and preparation and birth invite us to see God's redemptive plan for creation unfold in the coming of Jesus. The second perspective, arising anywhere from six to ten centuries prior to the first, is provided by a quintet of psalms that praise God for and with creation. The third perspective vaults forward to the generation following Jesus, as Paul's Letter to the Galatians leads us to consider God's ongoing creative process in birthing (and rebirthing!) the church.

The theme of creation and new creation, however, stretches far broader on the biblical canvas than these sets of readings. Whether we are speaking of Luke or the psalmists or Paul, all drew on long-standing traditions that thread through the biblical witness from the opening chapters of Genesis to the closing chapters of Revelation.

This article will offer an introductory sketch of that wider biblical context by exploring theologies of creation and new creation from the following sources: Genesis 1–2, Psalms, Second Isaiah, and Revelation. The article does not attempt to be exhaustive of every possible nuance of creation theology in Scripture, but rather illustrative of some of its main elements for the purpose of deepening your encounter with this quarter's texts.

## Creation and New Creation: Genesis 1 and 2

These chapters relate two creation narratives. Genesis 1:1–2:4a takes a wide-angle view of the entire universe coming into being. Genesis 2:4b-25 focuses first on the fashioning and then the vocation of humanity.

In the first narrative, two powerful assertions mark the whole of creation. First is the power of God's word to fashion all things. "And God said" initiates each day's creation. The sufficiency of God's word to create offers a prelude to the central role God's word will play in the ensuing biblical witness, whether that word is linked with the declaration of prophets (Jeremiah 1:4; Ezekiel 37:7 and following) or embodied in the word "incarnate" (John 1:1, 14). An intriguing implication of God's word speaking creation into being is that speaking presumes hearing or giving response. In one sense, Genesis 1 testifies to the response-ability of creation to spring into life at the hearing of God's word. This is not a limitation upon God's word to create unilaterally. Rather, it is an insight into the significance of response to God's word. That insight is hinted at in the Hebrew language, where the word for "hear" or "listen" also means "obey." To truly hear the word of God is to respond in obedience to that word. In Genesis

1, God speaks—and creation responds by coming into life. In Genesis 2, God speaks limitations on what may or may not be eaten—and humanity's story from that point forward hinges on whether God's speaking will evoke faithful response.

This last point leads to a second key assertion about creation in Genesis 1. Too often, Christian theology begins with Genesis 3 and the Fall. If that is taken as creation's starting point, then sin and separation from God become the primal condition of all things. But Genesis 1 posits a starting point with a much different proclamation. Each day ends with God's observation that "it was good." At the end of the sixth day, the day of humanity's fashioning, the declaration is even stronger: "it was *very* good" (1:31, emphasis added). To take Genesis 1 seriously is to understand that creation begins not in utter depravity but in original goodness. Consider how God's primal deeming of creation as good might shape our understanding of what salvation entails in the Bible's ensuing narratives: the "re-deeming" of creation's original goodness. Grace did not originate with Jesus. Grace originated in the evangelical proclamation of Genesis 1 bestowed on all creation: "and God saw that it was good."

## Creation and New Creation: Psalms

The Book of Psalms collects 150 works of ancient Israelite worship and spiritual reflection. All are poetic; many have their origins in song or chant. Some are individual and personal in nature. Others are corporate. Some praise, some lament, some pray, some complain—but all embody expressions to and about God. In terms of the previous section's emphasis on speech presuming hearing: The Psalms presume the words of Israel, in whatever form they take, will be heard by God. And the hope of the Psalms and biblical faith is that God will hear and respond (see, for example, Exodus 2:23-24).

In our time, the Psalms tend to be some of the most used yet least interpreted of biblical materials. Many liturgical traditions employ one of the psalms either in adaptations for weekly calls to worship or outright as one of the lections read each Sunday. But how often does a psalm serve as a sermon text, as gist for the church's proclamation? The theme of creation looms large in a number of the psalms. Five of these compose the focus texts of this quarter's second unit (Praise from and for God's Creation). But they are by no means the only such psalms. Taken together with others—in particular Psalms 8, 29, and 145—the psalmists bring several points of emphasis to the theme of creation and new creation.

Similar to the highly structured sequencing of Genesis 1, the Psalms portray creation first of all as a God-ordered universe whose diverse elements reflect God's reliable and generous providing for life. The depiction of God in terms that suggest the workings of a gardener (Psalm 65:9-11) underscores God's providential care, not just for humanity but for all creation (Psalm 104:27-28). Psalm 145 employs a distinctive literary form to convey God's beneficial ordering of creation: an acrostic poem. Though not visible in English translation, each line begins with a letter of the Hebrew alphabet in sequence (line 1 starts with an "a," line 2 starts with a "b," and so on). In other words, the psalm's structure witnesses to God's sustaining the life of all creation—quite literally, from A to Z.

The Psalms invoke another important facet to worship evoked by creation's God-given beauty and harmony: wonder. In Psalm 8, wonder expresses the psalmist's response to the lofty place of humanity in contemplation of all that God has made. Psalm 29 summons wonder at the raw power of God in creation. Some of Israel's neighbors (and on occasion Israel herself) practiced idolatry, whose premise is that deities can be fashioned and manipulated by our power to do our bidding. The God of Psalm 29 brooks no rival, exercising power freely without constraint like a storm sweeping over the landscape. Yet, remarkably, the God in Psalm 29 is also no omnipotent despot indifferent to creation's needs. Verse 10 testifies to God keeping the chaotic and life-threatening waters controlled (see Genesis 1:1 and 7:11). And Psalm 29:11 further declares God to be the source of peace, *shalom*, a word that entails not simply an absence of war, but more broadly an abundance of all that makes for safety and health and prosperity. The irrepressible power of God is the power that makes, and makes for, life.

## Creation and New Creation: Second Isaiah

In the sixth century B.C., Judaism endured the crisis of exile. Most Israelites not scattered in Diaspora or killed were taken as captives to Babylon. Jerusalem and its Temple were destroyed. The resulting sociopolitical crisis was also a religious one. Had God given up on the people and forgotten the promises of old? Had Babylon's gods proved too strong even for Israel's God?

The writings that have come to be known as Second Isaiah (found mainly, though not exclusively, in Isaiah 40–55) confront this crisis with an extraordinary word of hope. What connects this prophetic anticipation of return to the theme of creation and new creation comes in where Isaiah locates the power of God to make this possible. "Has it not been told you from the beginning" (Isaiah 40:21b) recalls God as the Creator who makes, among other things, the "rulers of the earth as nothing" (40:23). In other words, the God who created all things will initiate the "new creation" of return from exile to the land. Time and again, Second Isaiah links the power of God as Creator with the power of God as Deliverer (43:15; 44:24-28) and the power of the Holy One who will turn Babylon's vaunted empire on its head (43:14; 48:14).

The writings of Second Isaiah make clear that the theme of creation is by no means a purely historical artifact that considers only what God once did at the beginning. Rather, Second Isaiah's theology of creation is a present- and future-oriented dynamic the purpose of which is to prepare us for and engage us in God's ongoing work of new creation. This emphasis is of particular importance in our day. Too often, the church gets caught in the web of incessant arguments about the mechanics of creation (*Did it really take only six days? Was a day then like a day is now?*). Two consequences often follow. First, creation faith is frequently ridiculed, and with justification, for being in denial about all manner of scientific evidence ranging from the age of the earth and evolutionary adaptations and fossil remains of dinosaurs. But second, and perhaps worse, we lose sight of what Second Isaiah saw so clearly: the implications of God as Creator for our present vocation and future hope. Creation faith is not an alternative scientific model. Creation faith is a defiant witness to any and all powers that claim authority over creation and those whom God has fashioned in the divine image. "See, the former things have come to pass, and new things I now declare" (Isaiah 42:9). Second Isaiah's theology of creation orients us to the new creation God would work through us.

## Creation and New Creation: Revelation

Many biblical scholars date the Book of Revelation among the latest of New Testament materials. One might then ask why this book should be considered among the traditions that shaped the church's theologies of creation and new creation. The reason is this: No other New Testament writing addresses the theme of new creation more clearly than Revelation 21–22.

"Then I saw a new heaven and new earth," which may be Revelation's most familiar use of creation imagery, comes in the opening verse of chapter 21.What constitutes the newness of this creation is revealed in two ensuing promises. The first promise is "God will be with them" (Revelation 21:3). The phrasing recalls Isaiah 40:9's declaration to the exiles :"Here is your God," as well as the even older promise of Isaiah 7:14 (a promise later incorporated into Matthew 1:23's anticipation of Jesus' birth) of Emmanuel, whose meaning is "God with us." The second promise is "death will be no more" (Revelation 21:4), echoing the gist of an earlier anticipation of the new creation in Isaiah 25:7-8a. The newness is thus focused not on geographical relocation of one "creation" for another, but rather on the spiritual change wrought by God's immanence and death's absence.

The remaining verses in chapter 21 and the opening seven verses in chapter 22 constitute a vision of the New Jerusalem that, in important ways, presents a transformed version of Genesis 2. One central element of the change can be expressed as follows: Creation began in a garden, and ends (or more to the point, begins anew) in a city. The new creation is envisioned no longer as the pastoral scene of an idyllic garden, but rather in the safe and hospitable setting of the city of God. And where the first of God's creative acts in Genesis 1 had been the fashioning of light—now, in the new creation of Revelation 21–22, light will radiate from the presence of God (22:5). Gates always open (21:25) proclaim the hospitality of grace. And the river of the water of life flows to irrigate trees whose leaves are "for the healing of the nations" (22:2).

In sum, the theologies of creation and new creation aim to water and nurture our faith and service for the sake of the Creator and hope of all.

# CLOSE-UP: THE PSALMS

The 150 psalms have served not only as Israel's hymnbook but also as the songs of many seasons of life for Christians. The writers of the various psalms pour out their hearts, expressing a range of emotions from praise and thanksgiving to pleas for protection from enemies to expressions of trust in God to cries of help in times of illness to recitations of major events in Israelite history to portraits of happiness. Each psalm spoke on behalf of an individual or the entire community of faith who had a pressing reason for addressing God. The psalms are categorized in various ways, and some can easily fit into more than one category. Here are possible categories for the background psalms selected for Unit 2:

Psalm 33 is a communal hymn of praise.

Psalm 65 is usually referred to as a communal song of praise or as a communal song of thanksgiving.

Psalm 67 is classified as a communal prayer for God's blessing and also as a song of thanksgiving.

Psalm 96 is an enthronement hymn, which would be sung to celebrate the enthronement of a king, which in this psalm is God. Sometimes similar types of psalms are placed together, as is the case here where Psalms 93, 95–99 all celebrate enthronement.

Psalm 104 is a song of praise that focuses on creation.

Psalm 148 is part of a final collection of hymns of praise (Psalms 146–150). These five psalms all begin and end with "Praise the LORD!"

All of the Psalms are written as poetry, but this poetry is structured differently than most poetry originally written in English. Whereas English poetry may focus on rhythm, rhyme, and the sounds of the words, Hebrew poetry relies on "parallelism." "Synonymous parallelism" occurs when two lines say essentially the same thing by using words that have similar meanings. (See, for example, Psalm 146:2.) In contrast "antithetic parallelism" expresses an opposite meaning. (See, for example, Psalm 146:9.)

As you look at the beginning of a psalm, in many translations you will notice that often words of instruction or information are given. These introductory words are known as "superscriptions." For example, in Psalm 67, part of our background Scripture for January 15, we read in the NRSV: "To the leader: with stringed instruments. A Psalm. A Song." Thus, the director of the instrumental choir is told what the musical accompaniment is to be. Although we have no musical scores, we do know that a variety of stringed instruments—harp, psaltery, viol, for example—were played.

In addition to these initial instructions, some psalms include the word "Selah," as is true in Psalm 67. In fact, the word is found seventy-four times in the Old Testament, only three occurrences of which are not in the Psalms. "Selah" often occurs where there is a reference to the choirmaster or leader. This association prompts some scholars to believe that the "Selah" is a musical notation, perhaps a pause or interlude. By including the words "pause, and calmly think of that" after Selah, the Amplified Bible points in the direction of an interlude.

# FAITH IN ACTION: ACTING AS A COCREATOR WITH GOD

During the winter quarter we are exploring Creation: A Divine Cycle. We start in Advent with the birth of the Savior who has come to fulfill God's divine plan of salvation for all of creation. Then we investigate several psalms that emphasize praise for God that emanates from creation itself and others that invite us to praise God for creation. In the final unit we examine the birth of a new faith community, created with Jesus Christ as its foundation. As we consider these different facets of God's creative nature and work, we have the opportunity to envision ourselves as cocreators with God. We can participate in creation as we care for creation itself and as we work creatively to develop and maintain the community of faith. Here are suggestions for activities that you can recommend to the class members to work on at home. Either post this entire list at the beginning of the quarter, or select activities that you will recommend on certain weeks.

1.  Provide for God's creation during these winter months by setting out food and water and providing shelter for wildlife that may inhabit your area.
2.  Be aware of the ingredients used in any products you use to remove snow and ice. Some products are labeled eco and pet friendly. Others contain harmful ingredients that you will want to avoid.
3.  Begin to plan for a garden that will provide food for people and animals. Even if you do not have much space, it is possible to grow some foods, such as tomatoes, in a container that can set on a patio or balcony.
4.  Consider redoing sections of your lawn so that you no longer need to add fertilizer and use water to care for it. Xeriscaping uses very little water. Adding native plants can add not only beauty but also food and shelter for birds, bees, butterflies, and other wildlife. Talk to master gardeners in your area; most are very willing to help you.
5.  Practice good stewardship in your home and church by being mindful of your use of electricity, water, and disposable supplies such as paper. Keep this slogan in mind: *Reduce, reuse, recycle*. Also practice precycling by buying, for example, a whole fruit rather than one that has been sliced and packaged. That way you do not need to dispose of the packaging.
6.  Act as a cocreator with God by caring for those for whom God cares. God loves all people but has a special concern for the stranger, the widow, the orphan—in other words, those who live on the margins of society.

Take action to help someone (or a group) in the short term; for example, provide food for a pantry or soup kitchen. Also do something to help a group in the long term by acting as an advocate. Contact elected officials, for example, to try to change a public policy that has an adverse effect on low-income people.

# PRONUNCIATION GUIDE

Abijah (uh bi' juh)
*adam* (aw dawm')
*adamah* (ad aw maw')
*agape* (ag ah' pay)
*agora* (ag or ah')
antiphon (an tuh' fon)
Diaspora (di as' puh ruh)
Docetism (doh' suh tiz' uhm)
*elohiym* (el o heem')
*energeo* (en erg eh' o)
*euaggelizo* (yoo ang ghel id' zo)
*Iesous* (ee ay sooce')
Jezreel (jez' ree uhl)
Loammi (loh am' i)
Lo-ruhamah (loh roo hah' muh)
Magnificat (mag nif' uh kat)

Nazarite (na' uh rite)
*nephesh* (neh' fesh)
*parthenos* (par then' os)
*pharmakeia* (far mak i' ah)
Quirinius (kwi rin' ee uhs)
Selah (see' luh)
Sepphoris (sef' uh ris)
*shalam* (shaw lam')
*skandalon* (skan' dal on)
*soter* (so tare')
theophany (thee' of uh nee)
Theophilus (thee of' uh luhs)
*tsedeq* (tseh' dek)
*yare* (yaw ray')
*Yehoshua* (yeh ho shoo' ah)

UNIT 1: THE SAVIOR HAS BEEN BORN
# GOD PROMISES A SAVIOR

---

## PREVIEWING THE LESSON

**Lesson Scripture:** Luke 1:26-38
**Background Scripture:** Luke 1:26-38
**Key Verse:** Luke 1:31

### Focus of the Lesson:
Our actions, decisions, and even well-being are often based on our trust in the promises made by others. On whose promises can we ultimately depend? Luke recounts the angel's announcement of the coming birth of Jesus, God's promised Savior.

### Goals for the Learners:
(1) to acknowledge God's faithfulness to Mary and ultimately to all God's people.
(2) to experience the joy of worshiping Jesus as God's promised Savior.
(3) to express trust in God's promises by affirming God's will for their lives.

### Supplies:
Bibles, newsprint and marker, paper and pencils, hymnals; optional Advent wreath, matches

---

## READING THE SCRIPTURE

NRSV
Lesson Scripture: Luke 1:26-38
26 In the sixth month the angel Gabriel was sent by God to a town in Galilee called Nazareth, 27to a virgin engaged to a man whose name was Joseph, of the house of David. The virgin's name was Mary. 28And he came to her and said, "Greetings,

CEB
Lesson Scripture: Luke 1:26-38
26When Elizabeth was six months pregnant, God sent the angel Gabriel to Nazareth, a city in Galilee, 27to a virgin who was engaged to a man named Joseph, a descendant of David's house. The virgin's name was Mary. 28When the angel came to

favored one! The Lord is with you." 29But she was much perplexed by his words and pondered what sort of greeting this might be. 30The angel said to her, "Do not be afraid, Mary, for you have found favor with God. 31And now, **you will conceive in your womb and bear a son, and you will name him Jesus.** 32He will be great, and will be called the Son of the Most High, and the Lord God will give to him the throne of his ancestor David. 33He will reign over the house of Jacob forever, and of his kingdom there will be no end." 34Mary said to the angel, "How can this be, since I am a virgin?" 35The angel said to her, "The Holy Spirit will come upon you, and the power of the Most High will overshadow you; therefore the child to be born will be holy; he will be called Son of God. 36And now, your relative Elizabeth in her old age has also conceived a son; and this is the sixth month for her who was said to be barren. 37For nothing will be impossible with God." 38Then Mary said, "Here am I, the servant of the Lord; let it be with me according to your word." Then the angel departed from her.

her, he said, "Rejoice, favored one! The Lord is with you!" 29She was confused by these words and wondered what kind of greeting this might be. 30The angel said, "Don't be afraid, Mary. God is honoring you. 31Look! **You will conceive and give birth to a son, and you will name him Jesus.** 32He will be great and he will be called the Son of the Most High. The Lord God will give him the throne of David his father. 33He will rule over Jacob's house forever, and there will be no end to his kingdom." 34Then Mary said to the angel, "How will this happen since I haven't had sexual relations with a man?" 35The angel replied, "The Holy Spirit will come over you and the power of the Most High will overshadow you. Therefore, the one who is to be born will be holy. He will be called God's Son. 36Look, even in her old age, your relative Elizabeth has conceived a son. This woman who was labeled 'unable to conceive' is now six months pregnant. 37Nothing is impossible for God." 38Then Mary said, "I am the Lord's servant. Let it be with me just as you have said." Then the angel left her.

---

## UNDERSTANDING THE SCRIPTURE

**Luke 1:26-27.** "In the sixth month" refers to the promise of a child to the barren couple Zechariah and Elizabeth (see also 1:24 and 1:56-57). The other key link to that earlier passage is the identification of Gabriel as the one who brings news to both Zechariah (1:19) and Mary (1:26). Gabriel appears only in the announcement story of Luke in the New Testament. (An angel also appears to Joseph in Matthew 1:20, but

that messenger is unnamed.) Gabriel's only Old Testament appearance is in Daniel 8:16 and 9:21, where he is tasked with making Daniel understand the vision announced to him. The reception to Gabriel's messages finds contrasting examples in Luke, where acceptance escapes Zechariah but not Mary. Battle lines frequently form in the church over the interpretation of Mary as "virgin." The Greek word is *parthenos* (as in the Greek temple known as the Parthenon). The word can refer to a woman who has not had sexual relations. However, it can also refer to a young woman of marriageable age. Nazareth was a small village in Galilee nearly midway between the Sea of Galilee and the Mediterranean. It was dwarfed in importance by Sepphoris, the political and economic center of lower Galilee about four miles to the northwest.

**Luke 1:28-29.** The opening two words of Gabriel's greeting to Mary are freighted with meaning, not just for Mary but for the whole of Luke's Gospel. "Greetings" renders a word used frequently in Luke, often translated as "rejoice" (as when the father rejoices at the return of the prodigal in 15:32). "Favored" translates a word whose root in Greek means "grace," a theme as fundamental in Luke as it is for Paul. While it is shown only in a textual footnote in the NRSV, other ancient manuscripts add yet another line to Gabriel's greeting: "Blessed are you among women." Elizabeth included these same words as she greeted Mary (1:42). Initially, Mary's response to Gabriel reflects that of Zechariah. The use of "perplexed" to describe her reaction should not be minimized— Luke employs a word here that is used nowhere else in the New Testament to describe her reaction.

**Luke 1:30-31.** "Do not be afraid," and its variant "do not fear" often occur in the Old and New Testaments when an encounter with God, or the one(s) God sends, proves unsettling. This phrase is found frequently in Luke: Gabriel to Zechariah (1:13), the angel to the Bethlehem shepherds (2:10), and Jesus to the fisherman he had just called to follow him (5:10). The reason Gabriel offers Mary as to

why she should not be afraid returns to his initial greeting, as he assures Mary that she has found "favor" (literally, "grace") with God. Consequently, Gabriel's "and now" introduces the message that has brought him to her: the conception, birth, and naming of Jesus. "Jesus" is an Anglicization of the Greek *Iesous*, which in turn renders the Hebrew *Yehoshua* or "Joshua"—meaning "God saves." That Luke has Mary naming Jesus, and not Joseph as tradition would have dictated (and as seen in Matthew 1:21), anticipates the reversals Luke highlights in Jesus' ministry, including the elevation of the role of women in this Gospel's narrative.

**Luke 1:32-33.** In one sense, verses 32-33 list a number of affirmations that reveal why the child Mary will bear merits the name of "Jesus" or "God saves." The term "Son of the Most High" appears only here and in the story of the Gerasene demoniac (Luke 8:28 and Mark 5:7). "Most High" referenced the God of Israel. Verse 32 is then linked with the messianic promise of this child's receiving the "throne of his ancestor David." In the blessing of Zechariah after the birth of his son, Luke 1:69 records another Davidic reference in God's raising up of a savior in the house of David. The messianic theme continues in verse 33 when Gabriel speaks of this child's "reign" and "kingdom." Both words derive from the same Greek root, which is the common designation for king or leader. These promises of reign and kingdom having no end echo a much earlier messianic passage (Isaiah 9:6-7) where again a child's birth portended such hope.

**Luke 1:34-35.** Mary frames her question of "how this can be" out of her experience of not having known a man (the literal meaning of her words; the Greek word for "virgin" is not used here). "Knowing" is a frequent euphemism in the Old Testament for intercourse (for example, Genesis 4:1; 19:8). Gabriel's answer to Mary's query has two elements. First is the action of God's Spirit. The role of Spirit in creative acts traces back to Genesis 1:2. The introduction of the Spirit by Luke at this early juncture also serves notice of the Spirit's importance throughout this Gospel. The second part of Gabriel's answer asserts the power of God that will "overshadow" Mary. This peculiar verb carries the meaning of being enveloped in a shadow. Its only other Gospel use comes in the Transfiguration accounts where Jesus and the disciples are overshadowed by a cloud. Clouds often accompanied a theophany (revealing of God) in the Old Testament (for example, Exodus 13:21-22; Numbers 9:15-16). This verb and its symbolism convey a sense of deep mystery, continued in Gabriel's revealing that this child will not only be holy but also "Son of God."

**Luke 1:36-38.** Once more, the passage returns to the earlier story of Zechariah and Elizabeth. Only now, Luke reveals that Elizabeth and Mary (and thus John and Jesus) are kin. The gift of God giving life to the barren has roots in Old Testament stories (for example, Sarah, Hannah). Here, Gabriel asserts such reversals derive from nothing being "impossible" for God. "Impossible" translates a Greek word that literally means "without power." What is at stake here is not abstract philosophical possibility, but whether God has the power (see also 1:35). Mary's accepting response to this word, and to her being a servant of God, conclude the passage and Gabriel departs.

---

## INTERPRETING THE SCRIPTURE

*"Of All the People . . ."*

Theodosia Garrison began her poem "The Annunciation" with these two lines:

"God whispered and a silence fell; the world
Poised one expectant moment . . ."

That beginning captures beautifully several senses of today's story of the annunciation to Mary. First is the notion of God's whispering. When God confronted Elijah in the cave, the means of God's revealing came not in wind or earthquake or fire—but in "sheer silence" (1 Kings 19:11-12). There is a sense of extraordinary silence in the midst of Gabriel's words to Mary, not the least of which would be the silence evoked by wondering why such words would come to such a one. Luke provides no résumé for Mary to explain why she of all people is to be entrusted so. Then again, the point in Luke—here and later—will not be the résumés we bring to God, but the grace God bears to us. Of all the people God could choose, Mary is the one. But if we linger on "why," we may find ourselves having the question turned on us: Of all the people God could choose, why me? But that is where gospel is headed.

The second sense in which this poem's opening sheds light on Luke's story of annunciation is its notion of the world "poised expectant." Surely that would be true of Mary. She finds herself poised at the edge of an enormous precipice. What will her decision be? And with her, the world—and the church—stand poised as well. The expectation, the hope, is assent . . . but that is getting ahead of the story just a bit. For now, sit with Mary, listen with Mary, as Gabriel addresses her . . . and you.

That word is first one of rejoicing, the more literal meaning of the word translated as "greetings." What is it today, what is it in this season, that brings joy to you—and that might bring joy to the world through you?

"Favored one." Do you consider yourself graced of God—and if so graced, for what? The announcement of Mary's favor is not "aren't you lucky!" The announcement of Mary's favor, and ours, is "I have need of you."

"The Lord is with you." Do you sense God's presence with you in this day, in its possibilities and its seeming dead-ends? Does the season of Advent bear to you a heightened awareness of God's power to act, or a depressing "when is God going to do something about this mess?" There is often good reason to slip into the latter way of thinking. But even then, God's message of the annunciation has the potential to become: "I am going to do something, and you are one through whom I am going to work."

God still whispers . . . will we be poised expectantly, and in so doing, open ourselves to enter the story as did Mary?

### What in Jesus' Name Are You Waiting For?

The naming of children among the peoples of the ancient Middle East often was seen as prefiguring what this child was to do in life, or to illustrate what this child represented in the family or even community. For example, Hosea named his three children to reveal how Israel stood in relationship with God. He named his eldest son Jezreel (Hosea 1:4), which means "God sows." "God sows" served as the prophet's warning about the judgment God prepared to sow in the land. The prophet named his next child Lo-ruhamah (1:6), "not pitied." The tiny bundle "Not Pitied" revealed that God would no longer pity the people who had broken covenant. Hosea named his third child Loammi (1:8), the most devastating name of all: "not my people." The son who bore this name became the symbol of God's momentary rejection of a people.

So consider the name Gabriel passes on to Mary for the promised child: Jesus. Similar to its use as a common name in Hispanic cultures, "Jesus" was actually a common name in that day. The reason? In a time of ferment, when chafing against Roman occupation was widespread, why not choose the name of a great warrior? And who had been the warrior who had led Israel into the land and conquered it in the first place? Joshua. And Jesus is simply Joshua or "Yehoshua" rendered in English.

That such nationalistic hopes rang true to the bestowing of this name on this child is reflected in Gabriel's language of "reign" and "kingdom," "house of Jacob" and "throne of his ancestor David."

This naming of Jesus is thus no innocuous act. Indeed, as Luke's Gospel progresses, what becomes intriguing will be how the common expectations for such "reign" and "kingdom" play out—and indeed, come into conflict with—the nature of the kingdom Jesus proclaims and embodies. The crowd that later cries for his crucifixion does so because in their view Jesus did not live up to his name. He was not "God saves" when it came to Rome. Then again, that is the task the yet-to-be-born Joshua has before him: to reveal "God saves" not by the point of a sword but by the grace of love and forgiveness extended to sinners and outcasts and prodigals.

As much as things change, things stay the same. Does Jesus live up to his name in our day—or perhaps more aptly put, do we *allow* Jesus to live up to his name, or burden him with the task of saving those we want and discarding the rest?

What in Jesus' name are we waiting for? How we answer is important, because the answer will reveal in whose service we are engaged.

### *"Letting It Be" as "Taking It On"*

In the end, Mary has to act on trust. Gabriel can talk all he wants about favor and grace, about a reign and a kingdom without end. All those things are a long way off. They are, Gabriel would have to admit, cloaked in mystery. "Overshadowing" is an apt description. The promises remain in shadows.

Mary will have to decide.

"Here am I . . . let it be with me according to your word" (1:38). Some might hear resignation in Mary's phrasing. *Go ahead, God, do whatever you want.* In truth, however, Mary's words are assertive. She is not letting go of anything. Mary is taking on the responsibility, the possibility, the mystery, of the promises cut to the core of Advent's hopes.

The question is this: Will we join Mary? To do so requires remarkable trust in promises made—and in the One who makes them. When all is said and done, what Mary is about is not "wait and see." What Mary is about now is "wait and do." She becomes an active participant in the drama of salvation, all because she trusts in God's promises that begin to transform her life from that moment on.

Sometimes, we might prefer to hold on to God's promises at arm's length, at a distance. I believe that is why Christian hope too often dissolves into what happens in the future, way off when. Mary would understand none of that. The promises of God for the future are all about life in this moment: how we live, why we live, for whom we live.

Like Mary, may our "let it be" become the promises we take on. In this moment. For the living of this day.

---

## SHARING THE SCRIPTURE

### PREPARING TO LEAD

#### *Preparing Our Hearts*

Ponder this week's devotional reading from Isaiah 6:1-8. As you read, notice whatever can you see, hear, taste, touch, or smell. How do these sensory images help the story of Isaiah's call come alive for you? What connections can you draw between Isaiah's vision and Luke's account of Gabriel's announcement to Mary?

Pray that you and the students will

be sensitive to God's call on your own lives.

### Preparing Our Minds

Study the background Scripture and the lesson Scripture, which are both from Luke 1:26-38.

Consider this question: *On whose promises can we ultimately depend?*

Write on newsprint:

❏ information for next week's lesson, found under "Continue the Journey."
❏ activities for further spiritual growth in "Continue the Journey."

Determine how you might use any of the features that precede the first lesson of this quarter in today's session.

**Option:** If you chose to light an Advent wreath last week, be prepared to light it again on this Second Sunday of Advent.

### LEADING THE CLASS

### (1) Gather to Learn

❖ Welcome everyone and pray that those who have come today will eagerly hear the announcement of the coming of Jesus.

❖ **Option:** Light the first and second candles of the Advent wreath, if you choose to mark the Sundays of Advent. Check with your pastor for an appropriate reading or Scripture for this activity.

❖ Encourage the adults to recall silently promises made to them, perhaps as children or teens, which went unfulfilled. Invite them to call out words to express how they felt when they realized that a promise was not going to be fulfilled. Now ask them to comment on their responses to unfulfilled promises and the effect that had on their ability to trust certain unnamed individuals.

❖ Read aloud today's focus statement: **Our actions, decisions, and even well-being are often based on our trust in the promises made by others. On whose promises can we ultimately depend? Luke recounts the angel's announcement of the coming birth of Jesus, God's promised Savior.**

### (2) Goal 1: Acknowledge God's Faithfulness to Mary and Ultimately to All God's People

❖ Enlist a volunteer to read Luke 1:26-38. Encourage the adults to listen as if they were Mary hearing these words for the first time.

❖ Discuss these questions:

1. **What would have been your reaction to Gabriel's salutation in verse 28, "Greetings, favored one! The Lord is with you"?** (Delve into the meaning of these words by using information for Luke 1:28-29 in Understanding the Scripture. Note that Mary was "perplexed.")

2. **What is the content of Gabriel's announcement?** (See verse 31.)

3. **What does Jesus' name tell you about him?** (See Luke 1:30-31 in Understanding the Scripture.)

4. **What else do you learn about the child who will be born?** (See What in Jesus' Name Are You Waiting For? in Interpreting the Scripture.)

5. **Mary responded to Gabriel in verse 38. What would your response have been? Why?** (Before people get too confident of their answers, remind them that Mary is young and betrothed but not yet married.)

6. **How has Mary's trust and faithfulness affected history?**

*(3) Goal 2: Experience the Joy of Worshiping Jesus as God's Promised Savior*

❖ Use music to worship Jesus as God's promised Savior. Distribute hymnals. Invite participants to page through the portion concerning Jesus and call out some favorite hymns that speak of his promised coming.

❖ Focus on one hymn that all will likely know, "O Come, O Come, Emmanuel." The class may choose to sing or say this hymn. If possible, use the antiphons that go with it. (Antiphons are short sentences recited before or after each stanza of a psalm or canticle.) If you have access to *The United Methodist Hymnal*, you will find the hymn, which includes seven verses, and the seven accompanying antiphons on page 211. Assign one person to read the antiphon (in regular type), to which the class will respond (in bold type).

❖ Review the hymn and its antiphons to see what images or ideas you find in this hymn, most of which come from the Old Testament. Draw connections where possible between the hymn and Gabriel's announcement in Luke.

❖ Ask: **In what ways do these images bring you joy as you worship Jesus?**

❖ **Option:** If you do not have access to this hymn, find images for Jesus in hymns that concern his coming, using whatever songs are in the hymnal the class uses.

*(4) Goal 3: Express Trust in God's Promises by Affirming God's Will for the Learner's Lives*

❖ Read "Letting It Be" as "Taking It On" from Interpreting the Scripture. Note that Mary could have said no, and there were reasons for her to do so, but she chose to say yes to God because she saw herself as an obedient servant of the Lord.

❖ Distribute paper and pencils. Tell the students to fold the paper in half vertically and label the left side "Pros" and the right side "Cons." Encourage participants to reflect quietly on this question: **Will you join Mary in affirming God's will for your life?** Suggest that they think of reasons why they would not want to follow God's will and list those under "Cons." Under "Pros" they are to write reasons why they would agree to follow God's will.

❖ Call everyone together. Invite the adults to talk with a partner or small group about the insights they gleaned concerning themselves and their commitment to doing God's will.

*(5) Continue the Journey*

❖ Pray that as the learners depart, they will seek and affirm God's will for their own lives.

❖ Post information for next week's session on newsprint for the students to copy:

   ■ **Title: The Affirmation of the Promise**

- Background Scripture: Luke 1:39-56
- Lesson Scripture: Luke 1:39-56
- Focus of the Lesson: Receiving confirmation of pending good fortune is a joyful event. In such moments, how can we respond? Luke tells of Elizabeth's affirmation of God's promise of the Savior and Mary's joyful praise to God for being chosen as the bearer of that divine promise.

❖ Challenge the adults to grow spiritually by completing one or more of these activities related to this week's session.

(1) Plan to help a family who needs assistance with food, clothing, toys, or all of these for Christmas. If your church does not do such a project, check with your local Salvation Army or Department of Social Services to learn how you can help.

(2) Compare Matthew's account of events leading up to Jesus' birth, found in 1:18-25, with Luke's account. How are these stories similar? How are they different? Speculate on why these stories may seem so very different.

(3) Recall promises that you have made to family, friends, your church, or work colleagues over the past month or so. Which ones have you fulfilled? Which ones remain to be fulfilled? If you have broken any promises, why did that happen? What will you do to restore people's trust in your word?

❖ Sing or read aloud "My Soul Gives Glory to My God."

❖ Conclude today's session by leading the class in this benediction, which is adapted from Galatians 5:22-23, the key verses for February 26: Empower us to go forth to bear the fruit of the Spirit, which is love, joy, peace, patience, kindness, generosity, faithfulness, gentleness, and self-control. Amen.

# UNIT 1: THE SAVIOR HAS BEEN BORN
# THE AFFIRMATION OF THE PROMISE

---

## PREVIEWING THE LESSON

**Lesson Scripture:** Luke 1:39-56
**Background Scripture:** Luke 1:39-56
**Key Verses:** Luke 1:46-47

### Focus of the Lesson:
Receiving confirmation of pending good fortune is a joyful event. In such moments, how can we respond? Luke tells of Elizabeth's affirmation of God's promise of the Savior and Mary's joyful praise to God for being chosen as the bearer of that divine promise.

### Goals for the Learners:
(1) to explore the ways Elizabeth and Mary celebrated God's promise of a Savior.
(2) to feel thankful the ways God is at work in the world.
(3) to creatively express their confidence in God's promises.

## Supplies:
Bibles, newsprint and marker, paper and pencils, hymnals, sandwich-sized plastic bags; optional Advent wreath, candles, matches

---

## READING THE SCRIPTURE

**NRSV**
Lesson Scripture: Luke 1:39-56

<sup></sup>³⁹In those days Mary set out and went with haste to a Judean town in the hill country, ⁴⁰where she entered the house of Zechariah and greeted Elizabeth. ⁴¹When Elizabeth heard Mary's greeting, the child leaped in her womb. And Elizabeth was filled with the Holy Spirit ⁴²and exclaimed

**CEB**
Lesson Scripture: Luke 1:39-56

³⁹Mary got up and hurried to a city in the Judean highlands. ⁴⁰She entered Zechariah's home and greeted Elizabeth. ⁴¹When Elizabeth heard Mary's greeting, the child leaped in her womb, and Elizabeth was filled with the Holy Spirit. ⁴²With a loud voice she blurted out, "God has blessed you

with a loud cry, "Blessed are you among women, and blessed is the fruit of your womb. [43]And why has this happened to me, that the mother of my Lord comes to me? [44]For as soon as I heard the sound of your greeting, the child in my womb leaped for joy. [45]And blessed is she who believed that there would be a fulfillment of what was spoken to her by the Lord."

[46]And Mary said,

"My soul magnifies the Lord,
　[47]and my spirit rejoices in God
　　my Savior,
[48]for he has looked with favor on
　　the lowliness of his servant.
　Surely, from now on all
　　generations will call me blessed;
[49]for the Mighty One has done great
　　things for me,
　and holy is his name.
[50]His mercy is for those who fear him
　from generation to generation.
[51]He has shown strength with his
　　arm;
　he has scattered the proud in the
　　thoughts of their hearts.
[52]He has brought down the powerful
　　from their thrones,
　and lifted up the lowly;
[53]he has filled the hungry with good
　　things,
　and sent the rich away empty.
[54]He has helped his servant Israel,
　in remembrance of his mercy,
[55]according to the promise he made
　　to our ancestors,
　to Abraham and to his descendants
　　forever."
[56]And Mary remained with her about three months and then returned to her home.

above all women, and he has blessed the child you carry. [43]Why do I have this honor, that the mother of my Lord should come to me? [44]As soon as I heard your greeting, the baby in my womb jumped for joy. [45]Happy is she who believed that the Lord would fulfill the promises he made to her."

[46]Mary said,

"With all my heart I glorify the
　　Lord!
[47]In the depths of who I am I
　　rejoice in God my savior.
[48]He has looked with favor on the
　　low status of his servant.
　Look! From now on, everyone will
　　consider me highly favored
[49]because the mighty one has
　　done great things for me.
Holy is his name.
[50]He shows mercy to everyone,
　from one generation to the next,
　who honors him as God.
[51]He has shown strength with his
　　arm.
　He has scattered those with arrogant thoughts and proud
　　inclinations.
[52]He has pulled the powerful down
　　from their thrones
　and lifted up the lowly.
[53]He has filled the hungry with good
　　things
　and sent the rich away
　　empty-handed.
[54]He has come to the aid of his
　　servant Israel,
　remembering his mercy,
[55]just as he promised to our
　　ancestors,
　to Abraham and to Abraham's
　　descendants forever."
[56]Mary stayed with Elizabeth about three months, and then returned to her home.

## UNDERSTANDING THE SCRIPTURE

**Luke 1:39-40.** The "hill country" in Judea and its counterpart in Galilee separate the coastal plains from the wilderness that begins on the east slope of these highlands and becomes pronounced in the Jordan rift. The hill country of Judea is situated well south of Nazareth, a minor agricultural community in south-central Galilee. The journey from Nazareth to the Judean hill country (Luke does not tell us what particular town is the end point) was a significant one that would have required several days. Beyond the topographical challenges, Samaria lay directly between the two regions. Samaria and Samaritans were to be avoided by pious Jews, a key dynamic in Jesus' later parable in Luke of the good Samaritan. Luke does not say how Mary would have known where to find the house of Zechariah or her cousin Elizabeth. Given the distance involved, it cannot be assumed she had been to this place before—and even if she had, given the tradition of Mary being a young woman, if she would have remembered the way from a childhood visit.

**Luke 1:41-45.** Luke's description of Elizabeth as "filled with the Holy Spirit" (1:41) has layers of meanings. Luke 4:14 depicts Jesus as "filled with the power of the Spirit" at the beginning of his public ministry. In the Old Testament, a prophet is one who primarily speaks (Isaiah 61:1; Ezekiel 11:5) or is driven (1 Samuel 19:20; Ezekiel 11:1) by the Spirit of God. "Filled with the Holy Spirit" occurs again in Luke 1:67, where it introduces the prophetic blessing pronounced by Elizabeth's husband, Zechariah. Elizabeth's filling with the Holy Spirit is likewise a testimony that she, too, speaks as a prophet. The core of her prophecy to Mary comes in three blessings Elizabeth bestows upon seeing her kinswoman. The first, Mary's blessedness among women, repeats a portion of Gabriel's initial greeting of Mary (1:28) contained in some ancient manuscripts of Luke but not reflected in the NRSV and other translations including the CEB and NIV. The second blessing Elizabeth bestows is upon Mary's unborn child. Woven into the cause for this blessing is Elizabeth's testifying to what Luke had previously described as the leaping for joy of the child Elizabeth still carried when Mary entered. Luke adds to Elizabeth's witness a question that is both rhetorical and evangelical (witnessing to the gospel Luke will proclaim) in asking why the mother of my Lord has come. "Lord" in Luke is used interchangeably as a reference to both Jesus and God (see 2:22 and 7:18 for examples of both uses). Elizabeth's third blessing is again of Mary, and the cause is linked to Mary's faith that trusts God to bring promise into fulfillment. Thus, the Spirit of God speaking through Elizabeth declares Mary to be the first person of faith—one might even say, disciple—in the New Testament.

**Luke 1:46-49.** The traditional name of Mary's response is Magnificat, the Latin word for the passage's opening verb of "magnify." Mary's words or "song," as this passage is also described, strongly parallel the "song" of Hannah in 1 Samuel 2:1-10. Hannah, like Elizabeth, was a woman previously barren. Her child Samuel was a prophet, just as Elizabeth's son John would become. Hannah and Mary both celebrate a God who overturns the normal social, economic, and political orders. These particular four verses of Mary's song lift up personal reasons for her thanksgiving: God has looked with favor upon her lowliness (1:48) and has done "great things" for her (1:49). (Luke leaves it to the reader to deduce from Gabriel's message and Elizabeth's greeting what exactly those great things might be.) Mary rejoices in God my "Savior." The only other time "savior" is used in Luke is in the promissory word of the angels to the shepherds (2:11). The word occurs far more frequently in later epistles of the New Testament (Timothy, Titus, and Peter). It should be noted that this word in Greek, *soter*, was a designation claimed by Roman emperors. Mary's declaration of God as Savior is thus not simply religious confession but political dissent—even as the next stanza of her song lifts up the reversals inherent with a Savior who is not bound by the power structures of Caesar.

**Luke 1:50-53**. Mary's praise of God continues, though her litany now shifts to the unexpected ways (and ones) involved in God's working. A daughter of Israel, she confesses with her ancestors that God's mercy extends toward those who fear God. The "generation to generation" phrase hearkens back to God's covenant with Israel (Exodus 20:6). Mary's assertion of God's mercy takes on a decided bent toward prophetic justice as she relates how and toward whom that mercy has been exercised. The word translated as "scattering" the proud is the verb used in Luke 15:13 to describe the prodigal's "wasting" of his inheritance. Another insight comes in the word translated as "powerful," as those whom God will bring down from their places of power. That Greek word used here shares the same root of the reference to God in verse 49 as "Mighty One." The imagery suggests God taking down those who would claim god-like power, particularly when it preys on those whom Mary declares that God has "lifted up" and "filled." Mary's words of such reversals anticipate Jesus' own teaching in Luke 6:20-26.

**Luke 1:54-56**. Mary's closing words of praise are grounded in God's promissory history of covenant. But they also possibly contain Mary's own perception of such hope and promise in the imagery of children. While that word translated here in reference to Israel as "servant" can mean just that, it is also the Greek word for "child." Does Mary see in God's helping the "child" Israel a metaphor for God's helping her own child and herself? Verse 56 brings not only an end to Mary's visit of Elizabeth but also, remembering that this visit came six months after Elizabeth's conceiving, Mary's leaving sets the stage for the birth of John, the one who will be called "baptizer."

---

## INTERPRETING THE SCRIPTURE

*Responding to Good News*

How do you react when confronted with good news? Do you try and dampen enthusiasm, knowing every silver lining has a cloud? Do you congratulate yourself for being so deserving of such a just reward? Do you race around and tell everyone in earshot how fortunate you are, not always attentive to what may be uplifting or down-pulling in others' lives? Do you accept the news wholeheartedly, perhaps wondering why this has come to you—or what transformation this news might hold in store?

The encounter between Elizabeth and Mary, in one sense, is a study on how these two women respond to good news.

Elizabeth has, for all practical purposes, been living with good news for six months. Previously barren, a condition in this era that often evoked blame by others (*what have you done to deserve this?*) or self-recrimination (*what have I done to deserve this?*), Elizabeth now carries a remarkable child of promise within her. Yet when Mary comes calling, Elizabeth does not engage in the equivalent of *hey, look at me!* Rather, Elizabeth's living with good news for more than six months spills into testimony of the good news she now sees before her—a reaction, Luke discloses, that stirs deep within as her unborn child "leaped for joy" (1:44). Elizabeth's bestowal of blessings upon Mary and the child she carries serves as a reminder that joy cannot be contained—and that the best expression of one's own good news can be the joyful graciousness with which one responds to others. Put another way, Elizabeth demonstrates that one's own good fortune is not diminished by nor does it need to undercut the good fortune of others.

The response of Mary, expressed in her words of Magnificat, likewise celebrates the good news entrusted, but not limited, to her. That Mary personally "owns" the news is clear in her affirmation of God's gracious choice of such a lowly one as her to birth the One who will embody God's promised Savior. But for Mary the good news is not simply what God has done for her. The core of her praise celebrates what God is doing for other lowly ones like her, in keeping with the promises God made in covenant with Israel.

As Elizabeth and Mary both exemplify, our celebration of the good news of God's saving actions bids us integrate personal wonder at the grace extended our way with faithful vocation as those who actively and joyfully bear grace toward others.

### What in the World Is God Doing?

Sometimes, the church needs a history lesson. Or to put it another way: If you want the old-time religion, make sure you get it old enough.

To a disinterested outside observer, it might seem as if the church understands the answer to the question of "what in the world is God doing?" to be some variation on institutional maintenance. Buildings can provide marvelous settings for liturgy and fellowship and service. But buildings, and the budgets they require, can sometimes become idols, ends rather than means to the gospel. Committee structures can expediently engage folks in worthy activities—or they can suck the joy out of life and the possibilities out of service when established ways of doing things become fossilized rather than living. Confessions of faith can give common witness to our experience of the movement of God among us, or they can become doctrinal measuring sticks used less to announce good news and more to test the orthodoxy of others against our particular interpretations.

So if the church's most basic business is to be participants in and witnesses to what God is doing in the world, what wisdom does the "old-time" religion shed on that?

The Magnificat of Mary testifies to what God is doing in the world. Mary first testifies to her own experience of what God is doing in her life, looking with favor upon her and lifting up such a lowly one for such a lofty task. How good are we at looking with favor, much less entrusting significant vocation, upon the ones among us we normally overlook?

Mary also testifies to the wider working of God in the world. That world in Mary's time was in many ways not all that different from ours. The Roman Empire vigorously enforced and maintained a top-down hierarchy of power. But Mary sang that God is at work toppling those thrones and lifting up the ones otherwise kept underfoot. Those same imperial attitudes applied to wealth and class resulted in a few at the top who thought they were entitled to that position and all with which it filled their lives. But Mary sang that such pride goes scattered and emptied, and the hungry ones are the ones God fills. If you read this portion of Mary's song alongside of her son's later teaching in Luke 6:20-26, you might wonder if she used this as a lullaby, as her words of Magnificat resonate with Jesus' later own vision of what God is doing the world.

What is God doing in the world? This question prompts another: What is the church doing in the world? Let us hope that the answer to the latter is formed by the answer to the former . . . an answer we hear sounded in Mary's Magnificat. Gimme *that* old-time religion!

*Taking Our Place with
Elizabeth and Mary*

Two women meet and share joyful news of promised births. On the surface, it does not sound like an unusual event. Coupled with the fact that this encounter involving Elizabeth and Mary is more than two thousand years distant from us, we might ask, So what?

This is always the question that faith raises, "So what?" What difference do the words we confess, the hymns we sing, the faith we claim, make in the conduct of our lives?

Two women, Elizabeth and Mary, beckon us to join their circle. They invite us to listen in on what they have to say, and the joy that flows from each—and in listening, to join not only their circle but also to join them in living the faith and owning the joy as our own.

Elizabeth and Mary celebrated God's promise of a Savior. How are our lives changed by the confession that God is at work in saving ways among us? How do we affirm that God is still about choosing lowly ones, even ones such as ourselves, for bearing grace in and to this world? Think about the day ahead of you for a moment. If Elizabeth or Mary were in your shoes, what might she do when faced with the choices that will come to you this day and to the ones you encounter? How would her actions stem from trust in God's promises? What might she reveal about the unexpected ones God chooses—including you?

Advent bids us to make preparations for the birth of Jesus Christ in anticipation of Christ's return at history's end. We have the good news that God remains on the move among us. We have the good news that God seeks us as partners in manifesting God's sovereign realm in this day and through our lives. We have the good news that God keeps promises, and that we can stake our hopes on God's trustworthiness.

We have all this good news set out before us. The only question that remains is, So what? How will we respond with joy and faithfulness in our time, as Elizabeth and Mary did in theirs?

## SHARING THE SCRIPTURE

### PREPARING TO LEAD

#### Preparing Our Hearts

Ponder this week's devotional reading from Psalm 111. What do you learn from this hymn of praise that teaches lessons from Israel's wisdom tradition? What, specifically, do you learn about the virtues of God? For what reasons does the psalmist sing praise? What other reasons do you have to praise God today?

Pray that you and the students will be always ready to sing God's praises.

#### Preparing Our Minds

Study the background Scripture and the lesson Scripture, which are both from Luke 1:39-56.

Consider this question: *How can we respond when we hear confirmation of pending good fortune?*

Write on newsprint:

❏ information for next week's lesson, found under Continue the Journey.

❏ activities for further spiritual growth in Continue the Journey.

Determine how you might use any of the features that precede the first lesson of this quarter in today's session.

**Option:** If you chose to light an Advent wreath last week, be prepared to light it again on this Third Sunday of Advent.

### LEADING THE CLASS

#### (1) Gather to Learn

❖ Welcome everyone and pray that those who have come today will celebrate God's promise of a Savior.

❖ **Option:** Light the first, second, and third candles of the Advent wreath, if you choose to mark the Sundays of Advent. Check with your pastor for an appropriate reading or Scripture for this activity.

❖ Go around the room and give everyone a chance to complete this sentence: **With Christmas just around the corner, the news I'm most eager to hear right now is . . .** (Suggest that some people may want to hear that an adult child is home from college, the military, or another state; others are excited to meet a new grandchild; perhaps others are retiring at the end of the year and looking forward to a new way of life. Be sure to allow those who do not want to give an answer to say "pass," though note that there are no right or wrong answers.)

❖ Read aloud today's focus statement: **Receiving confirmation of pending good fortune is a joyful event. In such moments, how can we respond? Luke tells of Elizabeth's**

**affirmation of God's promise of the Savior and Mary's joyful praise to God for being chosen as the bearer of that divine promise.**

*(2) Goal 1: Explore the Ways Elizabeth and Mary Celebrated God's Promise of a Savior*

❖ Choose a volunteer to read Luke 1:39-45.

❖ Discuss these questions, using information from Understanding the Scripture to augment answers.

1. **What does Mary's journey to the hill country of Judea to see Elizabeth suggest to you about her reaction to Gabriel's visit?** (See Luke 1:39-40.)
2. **What blessings does Elizabeth pronounce upon Mary? What do these blessings suggest about Elizabeth's way of celebrating the fulfillment of God's promise of a Savior?** (See Luke 1:41-45.)
3. **What connections do you see between Elizabeth and God's prophets?** (See Luke 1:41-45.)

❖ Conclude this portion by reading Responding to Good News in Interpreting the Scripture.

*(3) Goal 2: Feel Thankful for the Ways God Is at Work in the World*

❖ Recruit a volunteer to read Mary's Magnificat from Luke 1:46-56. Listen for Mary's understanding of what God has promised to her and to all people.

❖ Ask: **What indications do these words give about what God is doing in the world?** (Add information from What in the World Is God Doing? in Interpreting the Scripture.)

❖ Write a corporate litany of thanksgiving for God's work in the world by following these steps.

1. **Step 1:** Began by posting a refrain that will be used throughout the litany. These words from Psalm 111:1 would be appropriate, but the class may want to choose to write other words: **I will give thanks to the Lord with my whole heart.**
2. **Step 2:** Distribute paper and pencils to each person. Suggest that each student work with a partner to write one line of thanksgiving. Here is an example: **I give thanks, O God, that you chose to become enfleshed as a tiny babe so that we might be reconciled to you.**
3. **Step 3:** Call time and read this litany. One person from each team will read their words, and the class will read the selected response in unison. Point to each team as it is its turn to read.

*(4) Goal 3: Creatively Express the Learners' Confidence in God's Promises*

❖ Distribute sandwich bags (or paper bags, if you prefer), pencils, and paper. Tell the group that the purpose of this activity is to express their confidence in God's promises by recalling how prior promises have been fulfilled. Tell the group that you will read directions and then pause so that they can follow them.

1. **Fold your paper from top to bottom and tear along the fold so that you have two sheets of paper.** (pause)

2. **Recall a situation that made you very anxious and uncertain about the outcome. Write a few words about that on the front of one sheet of paper.** (pause)

3. **Turn the paper over and write about how this situation was resolved in a way that prompted you to believe that God was present in this situation.** (pause)

4. **Option:** If time permits, repeat this process.

5. **Place your paper(s) inside your bag, which you need to think of as your memory purse. Add more sheets as you are able. Whenever a situation arises that threatens your peace of mind, take a sheet from your memory purse, read it, and express confidence that if God was able to take care of things in the past, God can be relied on to help in the current situation.**

❖ Encourage the adults to report on experiences with their memory purses at future sessions as testimonies to the ways in which God is a promise-keeper.

*(5) Continue the Journey*

❖ Pray that as the learners depart, they will tell others of their confidence in God's promises.

❖ Post information for next week's session on newsprint for the students to copy:

- **Title: God Promised Zechariah a Son**
- **Background Scripture: Luke 1:1-23, 57-66**
- **Lesson Scripture: Luke 1:8-20**

■ **Focus of the Lesson: At times we are entrusted with incredible responsibilities that are beyond anything we might have imagined for ourselves. How might we respond? Luke tells of Zechariah's growing acceptance of his role as father to John, the one called to be the forerunner of the Savior.**

❖ Challenge the adults to grow spiritually by completing one or more of these activities related to this week's session.

(1) **Talk with someone this week who may not understand the real reason for Christmas. Explain why you celebrate the coming of the incarnate Jesus, God with us.**

(2) **Share someone else's joy by visiting, sending a gift, or doing whatever seems appropriate to mark a special occasion.**

(3) **Read Luke 1:46-55 each day this week. Ask God to help you become keenly aware of the changes that are promised in Mary's Magnificat. What can you do now to help those people on the margins experience God's justice?**

❖ Sing or read aloud "Tell Out, My Soul."

❖ Conclude today's session by leading the class in this benediction, which is adapted from Galatians 5:22-23, the key verses for February 26: **Empower us to go forth to bear the fruit of the Spirit, which is love, joy, peace, patience, kindness, generosity, faithfulness, gentleness, and self-control. Amen.**

## UNIT 1: THE SAVIOR HAS BEEN BORN
# GOD PROMISED ZECHARIAH A SON

---

### PREVIEWING THE LESSON

**Lesson Scripture:** Luke 1:8-20
**Background Scripture:** Luke 1:1-23, 57-66
**Key Verses:** Luke 1:13-14

**Focus of the Lesson:**
At times we are entrusted with incredible responsibilities that are beyond anything we might have imagined for ourselves. How might we respond? Luke tells of Zechariah's growing acceptance of his role as father to John, the one called to be the forerunner of the Savior.

**Goals for the Learners:**
(1) to understand Zechariah's role in the story of the birth of John.
(2) to identify with Zechariah's feelings of doubt and apprehension.
(3) to accept and fulfill the tasks to which God has called them.

**Supplies:**
Bibles, newsprint and marker, paper and pencils, hymnals

---

### READING THE SCRIPTURE

NRSV
Lesson Scripture: Luke 1:8-20

⁸Once when he [Zechariah] was serving as priest before God and his section was on duty, ⁹he was chosen by lot, according to the custom of the priesthood, to enter the sanctuary of the Lord and offer incense. ¹⁰Now at the time of the incense offering, the whole assembly of the people was praying outside. ¹¹Then there appeared to him an angel of the Lord,

CEB
Lesson Scripture: Luke 1:8-20

⁸One day Zechariah was serving as a priest before God because his priestly division was on duty. ⁹Following the customs of priestly service, he was chosen by lottery to go into the Lord's sanctuary and burn incense. ¹⁰All the people who gathered to worship were praying outside during this hour of incense offering. ¹¹An angel from the Lord appeared to

standing at the right side of the altar of incense. ¹²When Zechariah saw him, he was terrified; and fear overwhelmed him. ¹³But the angel said to him, "Do not be afraid, Zechariah, for your prayer has been heard. **Your wife Elizabeth will bear you a son, and you will name him John. ¹⁴You will have joy and gladness, and many will rejoice at his birth,** ¹⁵for he will be great in the sight of the Lord. He must never drink wine or strong drink; even before his birth he will be filled with the Holy Spirit. ¹⁶He will turn many of the people of Israel to the Lord their God. ¹⁷With the spirit and power of Elijah he will go before him, to turn the hearts of parents to their children, and the disobedient to the wisdom of the righteous, to make ready a people prepared for the Lord." ¹⁸Zechariah said to the angel, "How will I know that this is so? For I am an old man, and my wife is getting on in years." ¹⁹The angel replied, "I am Gabriel. I stand in the presence of God, and I have been sent to speak to you and to bring you this good news. ²⁰But now, because you did not believe my words, which will be fulfilled in their time, you will become mute, unable to speak, until the day these things occur."

him, standing to the right of the altar of incense. ¹²When Zechariah saw the angel, he was startled and overcome with fear.

¹³The angel said, "Don't be afraid, Zechariah. Your prayers have been heard. **Your wife Elizabeth will give birth to your son and you must name him John. ¹⁴He will be a joy and delight to you, and many people will rejoice at his birth,** ¹⁵for he will be great in the Lord's eyes. He must not drink wine and liquor. He will be filled with the Holy Spirit even before his birth. ¹⁶He will bring many Israelites back to the Lord their God. ¹⁷He will go forth before the Lord, equipped with the spirit and power of Elijah. He will turn the hearts of fathers back to their children, and he will turn the disobedient to righteous patterns of thinking. He will make ready a people prepared for the Lord."

¹⁸Zechariah said to the angel, "How can I be sure of this? My wife and I are very old."

¹⁹The angel replied, "I am Gabriel. I stand in God's presence. I was sent to speak to you and to bring this good news to you. ²⁰Know this: What I have spoken will come true at the proper time. But because you didn't believe, you will remain silent, unable to speak until the day when these things happen."

## UNDERSTANDING THE SCRIPTURE

**Luke 1:1-4.** Luke introduces his Gospel with an acknowledgment that his is but one of many accounts of Jesus' life and ministry. The second verse reveals that the author of Luke belongs to the second generation of the church, relying on the eyewitness accounts of Jesus' original followers to frame his narrative. Interpreters have long debated the precise identity of Theophilus, the one for whom Luke writes this work. Other writings of this era identify patrons who sponsored writers in their work. Some suggest Theophilus is such a benefactor. Other interpreters see Theophilus as a symbolic figure for the whole Christian community to whom Luke addressed his Gospel (and Acts as well, where Acts 1:1 begins with "In the first book, Theophilus"). Part of the argument for the symbolic character of Theophilus comes in the literal meaning of this name: "friend or lover of God." Such a connection with the broader community might also be alluded to in verse 3's reference to what Theophilus has been "instructed." The Greek word used here is the root of the English *catechism*, the teaching of faith that came to be later associated with a particular question-and-answer format for instructing confirmands and new believers.

**Luke 1:5-10.** The priests who served the Temple in Jerusalem did so in the equivalent of shifts, spending a designated period of time in such service before returning to their homes. King David is credited with dividing the Aaronic priesthood into twenty-four divisions to take turns in such service (1 Chronicles 24, especially verses 3-4). Luke identifies Zechariah as a priest of the "order" (division) of Abijah (1:5; see also 1 Chronicles 24:10). Intriguingly, Luke also identifies Elizabeth not only as a member of a priestly family but also as a descendant of Aaron. This may be a subtle hint by Luke suggestive of an equal standing between the two, a dynamic that may be seen in how the child promised comes to be named. Likewise, Luke asserts both Elizabeth and Zechariah are "righteous" and "blameless." Such standing removes any culpability from Elizabeth for

Luke's ensuing declaration that she was barren. Incense could be one of a number of fragrant substances burned, in association with prayer or sacrifice. Exodus 30:7-8 depicts the use of incense as a twice-daily routine.

**Luke 1:11-17.** Zechariah's fear at the appearance of the angel receives the same personal assurance of "Do not be afraid" as will Mary in 1:30. The word that Zechariah's "prayer has been heard" apparently is not connected with the daily office he carries out as a priest, but rather a previously unstated prayer for a child. The son God promises Zechariah, like the child later promised to Mary, will be a cause of joy not simply for the parents but also for the wider community. The command in verse 15 that this child "must never drink wine or strong drink" recalls the ancient tradition of Nazarites (literally, "consecrated") who abstain from strong drink (Numbers 6:1-3; 1 Samuel 1:11). Declaring the promised child will be "filled with the Holy Spirit" from before birth is not without precedent in Scripture. Jeremiah 1:5 asserts God "consecrated" Jeremiah before he was born—and like John, he is set apart to be a prophet. Luke's twofold use of "turn" in verses 16-17 anticipates John's calling of people to repentance. The association of John with Elijah is rich in symbolism, as Jewish tradition viewed Elijah not only as one of the greatest of Israel's prophets but also anticipated that Elijah would return to usher in the promised Messiah. "Make ready" and "prepare" recall the work of the wilderness prophet in Isaiah 40:3, a theme Luke returns to in describing the later ministry of John (Luke 3:3-4).

**Luke 1:18-20.** The incredulous

words of Zechariah to the angel in response to the promise of a child are not only understandable, given his and Elizabeth's ages, but they are in keeping with the responses of none other than Abraham (Genesis 17:17) and later Sarah (Genesis 18:12) who both laugh at the promise of a child to ones as old as themselves. Gabriel's identifying himself in verse 19 provides a link to his later appearance to Mary (1:26). Perhaps most telling in that verse, however, is Gabriel's declaration of his mission in this encounter: "to bring you good news." That phrase translates a single Greek verb: *euaggelizo*, from which comes the English "evangel" or "evangelize." That verb occurs frequently in both Luke, related to the mission of Jesus, and Acts, related to the mission of the church (for example, Luke 4:18 and Acts 5:42). The contrast between Zechariah's unbelief (1:20) and Mary's belief (1:38, 45) is drawn in the judgment of his speech being taken away "until the day these things occur" (1:20).

**Luke 1:21-23.** It is unclear what constituted a normal amount of time that a priest with Zechariah's duties that day would have taken, and thus what length of time would have seemed a "delay." Some commentators suggest half an hour, perhaps on the basis of Revelation 8:1-5, where an angel offers incense to accompany the prayers of the saints for that length of time. Luke asserts, without explanation of how, that the people understood his inability to speak as the result of a vision. Zechariah's motioning may have sought to communicate that, but the phrasing in verse 22 that he "kept motioning to them" suggests that his purpose in doing so was not initially understood.

**Luke 1:57-66.** The rejoicing of family and neighbors at the child's birth (and the end to Elizabeth's barrenness) suggests an initial fulfillment of the angel's promise in 1:14 that the child would be a source of joy for many. Children were traditionally named by the father. Elizabeth's naming of the child (Zechariah simply affirms the name in 1:63) is evocative of Ruth 4:13-17, where it is not the father but "the women of the neighborhood" who name the son of Ruth and Boaz (a child who will go on to be the grandfather of David). Similarly, Luke 1:31 records Gabriel instructing Mary (not Joseph as in Matthew 1:21) to name the child Jesus. This elevation of the role and status of women is a consistent theme throughout Luke's Gospel (see, for example, Luke 8:1-3).

The passage ends with the restoration of Zechariah's speech, and the wider community's wonderment at what this promised child will become.

---

## INTERPRETING THE SCRIPTURE

### Overlooked

When was the last time you heard an Advent or Christmas sermon on Zechariah? We all know Mary and Joseph. We might even have some familiarity with Elizabeth, at least in connection with Mary's visit. But Zechariah? Of all the characters in this season's narrative, none is perhaps more overlooked than Zechariah. That is a puzzle, as Zechariah is the first character to take the stage in Luke's Gospel. Before there is any mention of a holy family, before there is any reference to Emperor Augustus or Governor Quirinius, the movers and shakers of their day, there is Zechariah.

Zechariah's relative anonymity might suggest that Luke made a strategic blunder in opening his Gospel. Surely the better introduction would have involved an unforgettable character whose imprint on the unfolding narrative would secure his or her remembrance. So why might Luke have placed Zechariah in this crucial opening position?

First, Zechariah was a priest engaged in service at the Jerusalem Temple. If that seems a minor point, consider this: The Gospel of Luke not only begins at the Temple, it ends there (24:53) as well. The Temple served in the Judaism of this era as the place of most intimate encounter between God and people. Thus, the ministry of Jesus is bracketed between Zechariah's prayers and the disciples' rejoicing. Through Zechariah, Luke grounds this Gospel in the encounter with holy presence, the fundamental purpose of the Temple, and the theme of Luke's Gospel for what it means to encounter Jesus.

Second, Luke identifies both Zechariah and his wife, Elizabeth, as righteous. "Righteous," translated elsewhere as "just," is also used in reference to Joseph (Matthew 1:19), Simeon (Luke 2:25), and Jesus (Luke 23:47; translated as "innocent" in NRSV with alternate as "righteous"). Righteousness and justice in the Hebrew Scriptures often are associated with matters of societal equity and the treatment of the vulnerable. Zechariah the "just" initiates a theme that will be consistent in Luke's depiction of the ministry of Jesus.

Third, God promises a son to Zechariah, which is to say, Zechariah is the recipient of a gracious promise that invites trust. Not everyone in Luke's Gospel will be promised a child. But the narrative of Luke consists of recurring episodes where God's promises are presented to people, who are then invited to respond. In a few short verses, Mary will be confronted with such a promise, as later will the shepherds, who receive the promise of a Savior. And so the narrative will continue as Jesus' ministry brings promissory words and actions that present opportunities for faithful response.

All this begins in Luke with the patron saint of the overlooked, Zechariah.

### Overwhelmed

Overlooked is not the only adjective to describe Zechariah. When the angel extends God's promise of a son to Zechariah and announces what this child will be and accomplish, Zechariah is overwhelmed.

In the text, Zechariah's sense of being overwhelmed is met with judgment. Gabriel upbraids Zechariah for unbelief. Are you familiar with the saying "be careful what you ask for, because you might get it"? In answer to Zechariah's "How will I know that this is so" (1:18), Gabriel declares Zechariah shall have his ability to speak withheld "until the day these things occur" (1:20). Luke's narrative implicitly draws a distinction between Zechariah's "unbelief" and the trust Mary confesses (1:38) and is celebrated for (1:45).

But is this fair? Was not Mary's initial response to the appearance and greeting of Gabriel in 1:29 one of being "perplexed" (CEB: "confused")?

Place yourselves in Zechariah's position. In the midst of your priestly duties, you are interrupted and startled by the appearance of an angel. You are alone in that place, with no one to verify whether this is a genuine vision or an illusion. Childless and elderly, you are now promised a child. And not just any child. Your child will accomplish what generations of prophets (and priests like yourself) have often been unable to do: turn many to God, turn parents to children, and turn the disobedient to righteousness. So truthfully now, what would your first response be? Would it be unquestioning acceptance of all that has been revealed? Or would you not wonder, *Can this be true? And even if it could be true, why me, and why my child?*

In truth, Zechariah serves as a worthy exemplar for those on the journey of faith. He reminds us that faith (and life in a broader sense) is not always or even often experienced with certainty intact and complete understanding. When the unexpected confronts us, for good or ill, we too can be overwhelmed, wondering how this can be—and especially, what change this will bring to our lives. We might even, like Zechariah, find that words fail us in such moments. But what remains trustworthy, when all around seems in a state of upheaval and beyond comprehension, are the good purposes of God's promises for our lives. Even when it is difficult to grasp them, faith bids us to trust in the One who makes and keeps those promises. Such trust, as we will come to see in the next section, takes hold and emerges in Zechariah.

## Emerging Acceptance

I once had a Sunday school teacher who told us with absolute clarity and sincerity the day, time, and what bridge over the Mississippi River while he was stuck in traffic, marked his accepting of Christ. I also know of folks, myself included, who have no such singular moment. For us, faith emerged over time, in a growing understanding of God's gracious purposes. In such circumstances, faith is not the lifting of a blackout shade so light suddenly blinds eyes accustomed to dark. Rather, faith is like the slow turning of night into the faintly glowing light that gradually but steadily issues in sunrise.

Zechariah's is such a faith. The one lambasted for unbelief by Gabriel does not remain in that status. The eventual emergence of Zechariah's faith lies beyond the verses designated as today's lesson Scripture (1:8-20). The gradual appearance of trust begins in the final portion of today's background Scripture. With Zechariah still unable to speak, and the day of circumcision at hand when a child was to be named, Elizabeth declares that the child is to be called John. The gathered kin object, ostensibly to the fact that there is no such name in the family—and perhaps more subtly, that the mother rather than the father proposes to name the child. But when they bring their objections to Zechariah, he writes to affirm her decision. In doing so, Zechariah affirms what Gabriel had directed him to do in naming the child "John." It has taken nine months, but Zechariah has accepted what had been told him. And in that acceptance, he finds his ability to speak restored.

The full substance of Zechariah's

faith goes beyond the bounds of even the background Scripture, into the closing of Luke's first chapter. For there, in the last time Zechariah appears in this Gospel, he utters words of blessing upon the coming Messiah whose way his child will prepare (1:68-79). It is a fitting end to Zechariah's role in Luke, for one of the chief duties of a priest is to pronounce blessing upon God's people. Zechariah, who did not believe, proves to be Zechariah who not only believes but also testifies.

May we go and do likewise! In the example of Zechariah, may we grow to accept the promises God entrusts to us—and in accepting, may we set about faithful keeping of the responsibilities those promises bestow upon us.

---

# SHARING THE SCRIPTURE

## PREPARING TO LEAD

### Preparing Our Hearts

Ponder this week's devotional reading from John 1:19-23, where we hear the testimony of John the Baptist concerning his identity. Who do some priests and Levites suggest that John is? What do you make of what John said about himself in verse 23, where he quotes from Isaiah 40:3? As you read today's Scripture lesson, what connections can you make between what John said and what his father, Zechariah, was told prior to John's birth?

Pray that you and the students will expect the very best that God has to offer.

### Preparing Our Minds

Study the background Scripture from Luke 1:1-23, 57-66 and the lesson Scripture from Luke 1:8-20.

Consider this question: *How might you respond when you are entrusted with responsibilities beyond anything you might have imagined for yourself?*

Write on newsprint:
❏ information for next week's lesson, found under Continue the Journey.
❏ activities for further spiritual growth in Continue the Journey.

Determine how you might use any of the features that precede the first lesson of this quarter in today's session.

**Option:** If you have chosen to light an Advent wreath, be prepared to light it again on this Fourth and final Sunday of Advent.

## LEADING THE CLASS

### (1) Gather to Learn

❖ Welcome everyone and pray that those who have come today will be open to God's gracious and unexpected activity.

❖ **Option:** Light all of the candles of the Advent wreath, if you have chosen to mark the Sundays of Advent. Check with your pastor for an appropriate reading or Scripture for this activity.

❖ Read: **Think back to your childhood and teen years. Can you recall being entrusted with a responsibility that at the time seemed too much for you to handle? Perhaps you were asked to babysit a younger sibling for the first time. Or maybe you were cast in the starring** role of a school play. You may have been asked to keep an ill grandparent company. A team may have been depending on you to score a tie-breaking run. How did you respond to this responsibility? Do you feel you lived up to your own expectations—and those of other people? (Call on several volunteers to give brief answers.)

❖ Read aloud today's focus statement: **At times we are entrusted with incredible responsibilities that are beyond anything we might have imagined for ourselves. How might we respond? Luke tells of Zechariah's growing acceptance of his role as father to John, the one called to be the forerunner of the Savior.**

*(2) Goal 1: Understand Zechariah's Role in the Story of the Birth of John*

❖ Select a volunteer to read Luke 1:8-20.

❖ Discuss these questions, referring as needed to Understanding the Scripture.

1. **What do you learn about Zechariah?** (See also Overlooked in Interpreting the Scripture.)
2. **What do you learn about the son promised to Zechariah and Elizabeth?**
3. **How would you describe Zechariah's response to the angel Gabriel?**
4. **Do you think that Zechariah's muteness was fair or unfair? Why?**
5. **As you think over Zechariah's experience, what about it surprises you or especially piques your interest?**

*(3) Goal 2: Identify with Zechariah's Feelings of Doubt and Apprehension*

❖ Read or retell Overwhelmed in Interpreting the Scripture.

❖ Help the class members relate to Zechariah's feelings by leading them through this guided imagery activity:

- **Envision yourself doing something that you normally do. How do you feel as you go about this very familiar work?** (pause)
- **Imagine that Jesus walks over to you and engages you in conversation in which he offers you the opportunity to do something you have wanted to do for a long time. What, exactly, is he offering you?** (pause)
- **Even though he is offering to fulfill a dream you've had for years, you suddenly feel fearful. You worry that you will fail, that you can't handle such a big responsibility. Listen to your own negative voice.** (pause)
- **Now see yourself being congratulated on accomplishing whatever you wanted to do but did not think possible. Describe how you are feeling at this moment.** (pause)

❖ Call everyone back together. Invite volunteers to talk about how they could identify with Zechariah and also how they worked through their fear and apprehension.

*(4) Goal 3: Accept and Fulfill the Tasks to which God Has Called the Learners*

❖ Distribute paper and pencils. Encourage the adults to each write one tangible task that they believe

God is calling them to undertake. The task need not change the entire world, but it may change the world for one person. (For example, "witness to Uncle Jim during the holidays" could open new doors for him.) Underneath this task, the learners are to write words or phrases that play in their heads suggesting that they cannot possibly complete this task. (For example, "Uncle Jim would never listen to anything anyone has to say about Jesus.") Then ask them to write several reasons why they think they can accomplish what God has called them to do.

❖ Read these words of encouragement: **Hear the good news: Just as John was filled with the Holy Spirit before his birth and the pregnant Elizabeth was also Spirit-filled, you too have not only been called but also equipped to be a servant of the Lord. Accept God's will for your life and do not be afraid.**

❖ Conclude this activity by distributing paper and pencils and suggesting that the class members write one or two steps they will take this week to begin to fulfill a task to which God has called them.

*(5) Continue the Journey*

❖ Pray that as the learners depart, they will eagerly assume whatever tasks God has called them to do this week.

❖ Post information for next week's session on newsprint for the students to copy:

■ **Title: God's Promised Savior Is Born**

■ **Background Scripture: Luke 2:1-21**
■ **Lesson Scripture: Luke 2:8-20**
■ **Focus of the Lesson: People wait with great anticipation for the birth of a new baby. How do they react when at last the child is safely delivered? Luke tells the good news of the promised Savior's birth and the reactions of the angels, shepherds, and Mary to this miraculous event.**

❖ Challenge the adults to grow spiritually by completing one or more of these activities related to this week's session.

(1) **Offer support to someone who is skeptical or apprehensive about an impending life change or challenge. Encourage this person to "be not afraid."**

(2) **Do whatever you can to help an older parent or grandparent who is raising a child.**

(3) **Spend extra time in prayer and meditation during this week leading to the celebration of the Savior's birth. What does Jesus' coming as God-in-the-flesh mean for your life?**

❖ Sing or read aloud "Come, Thou Long-Expected Jesus."

❖ Conclude today's session by leading the class in this benediction, which is adapted from Galatians 5:22-23, the key verses for February 26: **Empower us to go forth to bear the fruit of the Spirit, which is love, joy, peace, patience, kindness, generosity, faithfulness, gentleness, and self-control. Amen.**

## UNIT 1: THE SAVIOR HAS BEEN BORN
# GOD'S PROMISED SAVIOR IS BORN

---

### PREVIEWING THE LESSON

**Lesson Scripture:** Luke 2:8-20
**Background Scripture:** Luke 2:1-21
**Key Verse:** Luke 2:11

#### Focus of the Lesson:
People wait with great anticipation for the birth of a new baby. How do they react when at last the child is safely delivered? Luke tells the good news of the promised Savior's birth and the reactions of the angels, shepherds, and Mary to this miraculous event.

#### Goals for the Learners:
(1) to remember the responses of the angels, shepherds, and Mary to the birth of Christ.
(2) to feel gratitude for God's gift of a Savior.
(3) to follow the shepherds' example in sharing the good news of Christ's birth with others.

#### Supplies:
Bibles, newsprint and marker, paper and pencils, hymnals, crèche or other visual representation of the manger

---

### READING THE SCRIPTURE

NRSV
Lesson Scripture: Luke 2:8-20

⁸In that region there were shepherds living in the fields, keeping watch over their flock by night. ⁹Then an angel of the Lord stood before them, and the glory of the Lord shone

CEB
Lesson Scripture: Luke 2:8-20

⁸Nearby shepherds were living in the fields, guarding their sheep at night. ⁹The Lord's angel stood before them, the Lord's glory shone around them, and they were terrified.

around them, and they were terrified. ¹⁰But the angel said to them, "Do not be afraid; for see—I am bringing you good news of great joy for all the people: ¹¹**to you is born this day in the city of David a Savior, who is the Messiah, the Lord.** ¹²This will be a sign for you: you will find a child wrapped in bands of cloth and lying in a manger." ¹³And suddenly there was with the angel a multitude of the heavenly host, praising God and saying,

¹⁴"Glory to God in the highest heaven, and on earth peace among those whom he favors!"

¹⁵When the angels had left them and gone into heaven, the shepherds said to one another, "Let us go now to Bethlehem and see this thing that has taken place, which the Lord has made known to us." ¹⁶So they went with haste and found Mary and Joseph, and the child lying in the manger. ¹⁷When they saw this, they made known what had been told them about this child; ¹⁸and all who heard it were amazed at what the shepherds told them. ¹⁹But Mary treasured all these words and pondered them in her heart. ²⁰The shepherds returned, glorifying and praising God for all they had heard and seen, as it had been told them.

¹⁰The angel said, "Don't be afraid! Look! I bring good news to you—wonderful, joyous news for all people. ¹¹**Your savior is born today in David's city. He is Christ the Lord.** ¹²This is a sign for you: you will find a newborn baby wrapped snugly and lying in a manger." ¹³Suddenly a great assembly of the heavenly forces was with the angel praising God. They said, ¹⁴"Glory to God in heaven, and on earth peace among those whom he favors."

¹⁵When the angels returned to heaven, the shepherds said to each other, "Let's go right now to Bethlehem and see what's happened. Let's confirm what the Lord has revealed to us." ¹⁶They went quickly and found Mary and Joseph, and the baby lying in the manger. ¹⁷When they saw this, they reported what they had been told about this child. ¹⁸Everyone who heard it was amazed at what the shepherds told them. ¹⁹Mary committed these things to memory and considered them carefully. ²⁰The shepherds returned home, glorifying and praising God for all they had heard and seen. Everything happened just as they had been told.

## UNDERSTANDING THE SCRIPTURE

**Introduction.** Of the four Gospels, only Luke and Matthew have accounts of the birth of Jesus. Some traditions associated with this season, such as the birth taking place in a cave or the number of magi, come from other early writings the church eventually excluded from the canon of Scripture.

**Luke 2:1-3.** In Matthew, Herod is the political figure who plays a prominent role in the birth narrative. Luke expands the scope of his birth narrative by naming Emperor Augustus (Octavian) at the start. Considerable debate surrounds the "census" Luke says Augustus ordered that was carried out by the Syrian governor Quirinius. No outside testimony exists as to any worldwide census ordered by

Augustus. But even if the point that there was a census might be granted, Quirinius did not receive appointment as governor until A.D. 6. That timing conflicts with Herod's role in the birth narrative of Matthew, since Herod died in 4 B.C. One possible explanation for asserting the census in the time of Quirinius is that the census he did oversee at the outset of his term resulted in a failed rebellion led by Judas of Galilee, whom Josephus credits with helping to form the group that became known as the Zealots. This interpretation of the census' detail would be that Luke deliberately sets up a contrast between the way power is executed by Judas (and Augustus) and the realm that Jesus' birth portends.

**Luke 2:4-7.** Luke references none of Matthew's story about the dilemma faced by Joseph because his betrothed Mary is pregnant, and his subsequent dream where he is instructed to take Mary as his wife (compare Matthew 1:18-25). Joseph's chief role in Luke's birth narrative is to account for why this Galilean couple from Nazareth came to be in Bethlehem for the birth. The most important detail that Luke reveals about Joseph is that he is a descendant of David. Thus, not only is Jesus born in the town associated with David (1 Samuel 17:12) but he can also claim royal lineage. It should be pointed out in this regard, however, that Luke writes in his genealogy that Jesus was "the son (as was thought) of Joseph" (3:23). The line suggests that even Davidic descent, in Luke, becomes secondary to Gabriel's promise in 1:35 that the child would be called "Son of God." What Luke has in mind by "inn" is unclear. Later in this Gospel, the

same word references a guest room sought for the Last Supper (22:11). Places called "caravansaries" did provide lodging along trade routes for caravans and perhaps other travelers. The presence of animals, presumed by Jesus being laid in what was literally a feeding trough, may suggest such a place. However, it is also true that in towns, families kept animals inside their homes in a room that might also be used for guests.

**Luke 2:8-12.** "Shepherds" brings several layers of meaning to the text. Bethlehem had strong associations with David. The story of his ascension to king begins with David's vocation as a shepherd (1 Samuel 16:11-13). "Shepherd" later served as a metaphor in Hebrew Scripture for rulers or kings (as in Isaiah 56:11; Jeremiah 3:15). By the time of Jesus' birth, shepherds had come to be viewed with suspicion and often treated as outcasts. Their presence in the birth narrative serves as precursor not only to Jesus as Davidic leader but also as one whose ministry will embrace outcasts. God's "glory" in the Hebrew Scriptures has associations ranging from awe-inducing acts of power (Exodus 14:16-18) to fire and light (Exodus 24:17) to the very presence of God (Ezekiel 10:18-19). Similar to Zechariah and Mary's initial response, Luke summarizes the reaction of the shepherds to the angel and "glory" by saying they were "terrified." That may be a weak translation, as "terrified" translates a phrase in Greek that literally means "feared [with] great fear." "Bringing you good news" (2:10) restates the reassuring promise of Gabriel to Zechariah (1:19). And, as in Mary's praise of God in 1:47, the angel declares to the shepherds that this child is to be a Savior. (Refer to Understanding the Scripture on December 11 to Luke 1:46-49 for the meanings of "Savior" here.)

**Luke 2:13-16.** "Host" translates a Greek word, which literally means an army or group of soldiers. As in Old Testament references to the "hosts of heaven" or "Lord of hosts," the phrase here alludes to the powers under God's command, perhaps in subtle contrast or defiance to the powers of the Roman Empire into whose dominion this child has been born. Luke's later emphasis upon the grace of God evidenced in Jesus' ministry finds announcement here in the "favor" God has toward creation. The added assertion of "on earth peace" (2:14) may serve as a further positioning of Jesus' realm versus that of Augustus, who was often hailed for establishing the Pax Romana (peace of Rome). The hasty departure of the shepherds underscores the spontaneity of their response, as does Luke's omission of any arrangements being made for the flocks now left alone at night, the most dangerous time for attack by predators.

**Luke 2:17-21.** Similar to the women returned from the tomb (Luke 24:1-11) in an era when the testimony of women would not be acceptable in court, outcast shepherds at the manger make them unlikely witnesses to God's extraordinary workings. The "amazement" at the shepherds' testimony translates a Greek verb that sometimes accompanies disbelief (24:41). Trust, not amazement, is the desired outcome of encounter with Jesus and the Gospel in Luke. Mary's internalizing of these things will be repeated later after the episode of the child Jesus at the Temple (2:51). Such reflection may be indicative not only of her posture at the end of the annunciation (1:38, "let it be with me")—but if Acts is held as the "second half" of Luke's work, her treasuring these things may explain her being numbered among the followers of Jesus (Acts 1:14). The narrative ends with the return of the shepherds to their flocks. Beyond simply getting them off the stage and allowing the story to continue, this detail serves as a reminder that in Luke, life and gospel unfold in the ordinary places and persons of life. Jesus' life goes on in typical Jewish fashion as he is circumcised and named "after eight days had passed" (2:21).

## INTERPRETING THE SCRIPTURE

### Birth Stories

Everyone has a birth story. It may take the form of anecdotes passed down to us about the stories of our own births. My favorite is that my parents told me I was born on a Sunday afternoon of a St. Louis Cardinals doubleheader—and that I couldn't wait until the outcome of the second game to make my appearance. Such stories may take the form of remembrances of what that day was like from the perspective of the mother- or father-to-be. There are also the recollections of family and friends who were there, lending support and encouragement, and finally sharing the joy of new life. It is also true that a single birth will generate a variety of stories, whose differences arise from the diverse perspectives and responses, depending upon where we found our place in that experience.

Consider the characters involved in Luke's account of Jesus' birth. For the shepherds, the birth of Jesus interrupted normal—and import-ant—routine with an extraordinary experience. It is not that they ceased being shepherds, or having flocks entrusted into their care, when they rushed down the hillside to see this thing that had been told them. They allowed the gift of that moment to overflow with joy, and then convey that joy to others. Having done so, they returned to their flocks. And if their haste and ensuing witness are to be trusted, it is likely they returned to those flocks *changed*.

For the angels, the birth of Jesus provided an opportunity to live out what their name literally means in Greek and Hebrew: *messenger*. It goes beyond the bounds of Luke's interest to speculate on what the angels were doing before this happened. But at the time of birth, Luke asserts that those whose identity and vocation hinged on messages exercised that calling—and they did so in words (2:14) that have often been associated less with prosaic statement and more with joyous song.

For Mary, the birth of Jesus brought an end to the long journey of pregnancy—and began the even lon-ger journey of motherhood. But not motherhood alone. Mary had been told wondrous things about this child long before his birth. And now, what with shepherds interrupting her time with her newborn with marvel-filled stories of their own, Mary pondered these things in her heart—not the first and certainly not the last such experi-ence of reflecting on what all of this would mean for her child . . . and for her.

And then there is Joseph. Luke does not say anything about Joseph here, apart from his betrothal to Mary and the journey to Bethlehem necessi-tated by his family lineage. One is left to wonder what is running through Joseph's mind and heart at the sights and sounds of birth and its aftermath. But if we wish Luke had said more, it may be that this silence about Joseph bids us to enter this story through him more than anyone else in this story. For as we wonder about what his response may have been, that ques-tion naturally leads to the question of what *our* response may have been had we been there. Would we have rushed headlong in the night? Would we have treasured in our hearts what had just taken place? Would we have had a message to carry in and out of the story?

The stories surrounding Jesus' birth are not artifacts, meant to be dusted and brought out once a year for sentimental reasons. The sto-ries, ancient as they are, beckon us to ask not simply, what would we have done, but more to the point, to ask what we are to do now to live in response to the birth of God's prom-ised Savior.

### Joy and Gratitude

What does it feel like to experience someone's favor for you? I don't mean by that the kind of favor that lifts you up by relegating others to lesser posi-tions. Such "favor" can be seen in the unfortunate examples of parents or teachers who favor one child at the expense of others. One could argue that is really not favor so much as it is prejudice. Rather, I mean by favor the assurance of knowing someone you value and trust truly has your back. How does that assurance affect your relationship with that other? How does that assurance play out in the way you treat others, especially if you understand them to be so favored by that other as well?

In the wake of announcing the extraordinary news to the shepherds, the angel declares they will be given a sign as if to "verify" that what they have been told is true. The first part of the sign will be the sight of a child swaddled in cloths. This by itself would not have set this child apart from any other that might have been born in Bethlehem that night. Wrapping an infant in cloths was a customary practice of the time. The second part of the sign would have been more unusual: the child in a feeding trough. In a sense, though, this too asserts the ordinariness of this child. The Savior of the world wrapped up like every other infant, and then laid in all places in a trough. For shepherds, this sign brings connection with their own very ordinary lives. The Savior is for folks like them.

Beyond that, however, the joy and gratitude surrounding this birth come to fruition in the angel's praise, evoked by the birth, of God's favor. To shepherds held in disrepute and ill favor that word as much as the sight of angels may have caught them off guard. Favor? For us? Then again, that will be the consistent theme of the ministry of this child in later years: God's favor, God's grace. Favor for a Samaritan? For a runaway child?

For a crucified thief? Luke's Gospel announces God's favor (4:19).

And make no mistake: The favor of God extends far beyond the bounds of Luke's words. The announcement of God's favor takes aim at you and everyone you will ever encounter. The announcement of God's favor sung by the angels reflects the consistent assessment of God in Genesis 1 as God looks upon each day's creation and "saw that is was good." With such favor, spoken at creation and heralded at Jesus' birth, God sees you, and your neighbor, and all creation fashioned by God's hand.

Such favor evokes our joy and gratitude, as it did from those shepherds long ago.

### Go and Tell

The old spiritual "Go, Tell It on the Mountain" has it right. The news of Jesus' birth is a go-and-tell event. It was for the shepherds. It is for us. It is good to have church services and ceremonies rich with symbolism on Christmas Eve and Christmas Day where we gather to celebrate the glad news. But in one sense, the services and ceremonies that bring us in have as their most important purpose sending us out. God sends us out to *tell* good news. God sends us out to *live* good news.

The news of Jesus' birth, the favor of God, the kept promise of a Savior: All these things, and more, Christmas beckons us through the shepherd's example to go and tell. And all these things, and more, Christ bids us in the example of his life to go and live.

So graced, so favored, so saved: Go and tell, go and live!

# SHARING THE SCRIPTURE

## PREPARING TO LEAD

### Preparing Our Hearts

Ponder this week's devotional reading from Luke 2:1-7, which is also part of our background Scripture. Why do you think Luke spent time explaining the political situation at the time of Jesus' birth? Why is it important for Joseph and Mary to be in Bethlehem when Jesus is born? How does the kingdom that ushered in Jesus contrast with the kingdom that he will usher in?

Pray that you and the students will be open to the wonder and joy of this day of celebration.

### Preparing Our Minds

Study the background Scripture from Luke 2:1-21 and the lesson Scripture from Luke 2:8-20.

Consider this question: *How do people react when an eagerly anticipated child is born?*

Write on newsprint:
❑ questions for Goal 1 in Sharing the Scripture.
❑ information for next week's lesson, found under "Continue the Journey."
❑ activities for further spiritual growth in "Continue the Journey."

Determine how you might use any of the features that precede the first lesson of this quarter in today's session.

Bring a crèche, picture of Jesus' Nativity, or other visual representation of the scene.

Recognize that attendance may be low today as families are out of town, are hosting guests, or have small children in the home. Perhaps some guests will join you today, so be sure they are introduced and made to feel welcome.

## LEADING THE CLASS

### (1) Gather to Learn

❖ Welcome everyone and pray that those who have come today will rejoice at the good news that a Savior has been born for us.

❖ Encourage participants to recall childhood memories of the birth of a sibling, cousin, or child of a close friend of their family by addressing these questions:

1. **How old was the class member when this new child came along?**
2. **What can he or she remember about the excitement leading up to the birth?**
3. **How did he or she respond (if old enough to remember or had been told later) upon first meeting this baby?**
4. **Why was the birth of this child good news for the class member—or was it?**

❖ Read aloud today's focus statement: **People wait with great anticipation for the birth of a new baby. How do they react when at last the child is safely delivered? Luke tells the good news of the promised Savior's birth and the reactions of the angels, shepherds, and Mary to this miraculous event.**

*(2) Goal 1: Remember the Responses of the Angels, Shepherds, and Mary to the Birth of Christ*

❖ Select a volunteer to read Luke 2:8-20. Ask two or three people who have the same Bible translation as the volunteer to read the words of the heavenly host in verse 14.

❖ Form three groups to view the story from the perspective of one of these groups of characters: the shepherds, the angels, Mary and Joseph. Provide time for the groups to look at the story through the eyes of their assigned characters and answer these questions, which you will post on newsprint.

    1. **What were you told about this child?**

    2. **How did you react to the news you heard?**

    3. **How could you be a role model to help others hear and respond to the news that God's promised Savior has been born?**

❖ Call the groups together and hear a summary of their responses. (Add information from the second through fifth paragraphs of Birth Stories in Interpreting the Scripture.)

❖ Conclude by reading in unison the good news of great joy as found in today's key verse, Luke 2:11.

*(3) Goal 2: Feel Gratitude for God's Gift of a Savior*

❖ Read or retell the first paragraph of Birth Stories in Interpreting the Scripture.

❖ Invite class members to recall stories told of their own births, or the births of their children or grandchildren. Guide the discussion so that the adults identify the gratitude and joy others felt when they were born, or that they felt when a special child came into their lives.

❖ Connect these personal experiences, which were likely filled with joy and gratitude, with the gratitude that believers feel for God's gift of Jesus. Ask: **What are some ways that people express their gratitude to God for Jesus?** You may begin the discussion with the small but very poignant gift of the drummer boy of song who played his drum for baby Jesus, which was the best gift he had to offer. Hear ways that participants give of themselves, their time, and their treasure to give thanks for Jesus. You may wish to list ideas on newsprint.

❖ Conclude with quiet time in which the learners may express their gratitude. End with "amen."

*(4) Goal 3: Follow the Shepherds' Example in Sharing the Good News of Jesus' Birth with Others*

❖ Read Go and Tell in Interpreting the Scripture.

❖ Set up a crèche, post a picture, or show whatever visual representation you have brought of the Nativity scene. Encourage the students to take turns showing and telling the story (or segments of it) by using whatever props are available. Suggest that they think about how they would tell this story so that a preschooler or elementary school–aged child could easily understand. After introducing the characters and plot, be sure the storyteller(s) add what this very special event means to them and to those who hear the story.

❖ **Option:** Some adults may want to tell the story as if they are talking with teens or with adults who are new Christians.

*(5) Continue the Journey*

❖ Pray that as the learners depart, they will tell the good news of the Savior to everyone they meet.

❖ Post information for next week's session on newsprint for the students to copy:

- Title: Praising God the Creator
- Background Scripture: Psalm 33:1-9
- Lesson Scripture: Psalm 33:1-9
- Focus of the Lesson: People praise the achievements of others. What should be the subject of our praise? The psalmist teaches that the word and work of God the Creator are worthy of our praise.

❖ Challenge the adults to grow spiritually by completing one or more of these activities related to this week's session.

(1) Be prepared to tell the story of Jesus' birth as you gather with friends and family over the holidays. Read the story from the Bible or use a crèche to introduce the characters, or both. Encourage children who know the story to retell it using pictures or puppets.

(2) Take time to reflect on how the story of the Savior's birth is good news not only for all humanity but also for you personally. Give thanks for the love and grace that God has shown in sending the Beloved Son.

(3) Read the stories of Jesus' birth and early life as they are found in Luke 2:1-40 and Matthew 1:18–2:23. What can you learn from these very different accounts?

❖ Sing or read aloud "Go, Tell It on the Mountain."

❖ Conclude today's session by leading the class in this benediction, which is adapted from Galatians 5:22-23, the key verses for February 26: **Empower us to go forth to bear the fruit of the Spirit, which is love, joy, peace, patience, kindness, generosity, faithfulness, gentleness, and self-control. Amen.**

UNIT 2: PRAISE FROM AND FOR GOD'S CREATION

# PRAISING GOD THE CREATOR

---

## PREVIEWING THE LESSON

**Lesson Scripture:** Psalm 33:1-9
**Background Scripture:** Psalm 33:1-9
**Key Verse:** Psalm 33:6

### Focus of the Lesson:
People praise the achievements of others. What should be the subject of our praise? The psalmist teaches that the word and work of God the Creator are worthy of our praise.

### Goals for the Learners:
(1) to acknowledge God as the just and loving Creator of heaven and earth.
(2) to rejoice in God's word and work in creation.
(3) to strategize ways to make praising God their highest priority.

### Supplies:
Bibles, newsprint and marker, paper and pencils, hymnals

---

## READING THE SCRIPTURE

NRSV
Lesson Scripture: Psalm 33:1-9
[1]Rejoice in the LORD, O you
    righteous.
  Praise befits the upright.
[2]Praise the LORD with the lyre;
  make melody to him with the
    harp of ten strings.
[3]Sing to him a new song;
  play skillfully on the strings,
    with loud shouts.
[4]For the word of the LORD is upright,
  and all his work is done

CEB
Lesson Scripture: Psalm 33:1-9
[1]All you who are righteous,
    shout joyfully to the LORD!
  It's right for those who do right
    to praise God.
[2]Give thanks to the LORD with the
    lyre!
  Sing praises to him with the
    ten-stringed harp!
[3]Sing to him a new song!
  Play your best with joyful shouts!
[4]Because the LORD's word is right,

in faithfulness.

⁵He loves righteousness and justice;
  the earth is full of the steadfast
  love of the LORD.

**⁶By the word of the LORD the
  heavens were made,
  and all their host by the breath
  of his mouth.**

⁷He gathered the waters of the sea
  as in a bottle;
  he put the deeps in storehouses.

⁸Let all the earth fear the LORD;
  let all the inhabitants of the world
  stand in awe of him.

⁹For he spoke, and it came to be;
  he commanded, and it stood firm.

his every act is done in good faith.

⁵He loves righteousness and justice;
  the LORD's faithful love fills the
  whole earth.

**⁶The skies were made by the
  LORD's word,
  all their starry multitude by the
  breath of his mouth.**

⁷He gathered the ocean waters into
  a heap;
  he put the deep seas into
  storerooms.

⁸All the earth honors the LORD;
  all the earth's inhabitants stand in
  awe of him.

⁹Because when he spoke, it
  happened!
  When he commanded, there
  it was!

---

## UNDERSTANDING THE SCRIPTURE

**Introduction.** The Book of Psalms as a whole contains a diverse collection of poetry, songs, and prayers. Among the 150 psalms that have come to us in the canon of Scripture are a number that celebrate Creator and creation. The five sessions of this quarter's second unit will explore several psalms that emphasize praise for God grounded in the manifold gifts of creation. Throughout today's psalm and others in this unit, you will encounter "Lord" spelled with capital letters. This is to denote the use of "YHWH" ("Yahweh") in the text, the name of God announced to Moses in Exodus 3:14. Tradition holds that YHWH is not to be pronounced aloud.

**Psalm 33:1-3.** Two of the most frequently encountered elements of literary structure in the Psalms are parallelism and repetition. Both those elements are blended in the verbs that

dominate these opening three verses. Listen to what the psalm bids Israel to do in response to God: rejoice, praise, make melody, sing, play. Every word is a distinct Hebrew verb. Together they serve as a multifaceted call to worship. Even the verb translated "praise" in verse 2 and the noun translated "praise" in verse 1 are entirely different Hebrew words, signaling the diverse ways in which God may be praised. This psalm, and in particular its opening verses, suggests a formal setting of worship, likely at the Temple. This liturgical setting is further underscored by the repeated references to musical instruments (lyre, harp, and then the command to "play skillfully on the strings") typically used in such ancient Jewish religious ceremonies. Verse 1 also introduces a parallel twinning of "righteous" and "upright" to describe those who are summoned to worshipful actions. These words in verse 1 are repeated in verses 4-5. One intriguing detail in verse 3 comes in the words "sing" and "new song." The literal meaning of the root for the Hebrew word rendered here as "sing" (and in noun form as "song") is "to journey or travel." That meaning is suggestive of the way such songs were used not only in processions within the Temple but also on religious pilgrimages made to Jerusalem.

**Psalm 33:4-5.** These next two verses shift the emphasis from the response of the worshiper to the character of the One who is to be worshiped. The "word" of God, along with God's "work," introduces a creation theme that will be made more explicit later in the psalm in another set of repetitions. Parallel to the list of five responses of praise in verses 1-3, verses 4-5 lift up five particular qualities in witness to God's character: upright, faithfulness, righteousness, justice, and steadfast love. Note that two of the characteristics attributed to God are likewise used in references to the worshipers in verse 1 (righteous, upright). Both Creator and human creations share commonalities. But Creator and creature are not synonymous. The nature and character of God exceed even those fashioned in God's image. In these verses, that differentiation is signified by the addition of faithfulness, justice, and steadfast love to the descriptors of God. It would be incorrect, however, to conclude that these qualities are reserved for God alone. Other passages make clear that each of these qualities is to be sought in human life and conduct: faithfulness (Habakkuk 2:4), justice (Amos 5:24), and steadfast love (Micah 6:8, where this word is translated in the NRSV as "love kindness").

**Psalm 33:6-7.** These verses open (even as verses 8-9 close) with a foundational theme in creation theology: the creation of all things by the speaking of God's word. Genesis 1 is an extended litany of that theme, where each day's creation is initiated in the narrative's repeated refrain: "And God said, 'Let there be . . .'" Psalm 33:6 echoes that in parallel statements about the heavens being made by God's word and their "host" by the breath of his mouth. "Breath" subtly alludes to several elements of Jewish creation theology. First, the Hebrew word translated here as "breath" interchangeably means "breath," "wind," and "spirit." In Genesis 1:2, this same word appears to describe the wind/breath/spirit of God moving over the waters immediately prior to God's speaking creation into being. Second, Genesis 2:7 employs "breath" imagery as the means by which God brings life to the human formed of dust. Psalm 33:7 speaks almost playfully about the sovereignty of God in the image of God's gathering all the waters of the sea in a single bottle. Beneath the lightness of this metaphor, however, are far more serious themes. In other creation stories in the Near East, creation results from a battle wherein the forces of chaos, symbolized by the sea, are subdued and defeated. One may hear a remnant of that in God's control over the "deeps," a Hebrew word that also references the waters that flooded the earth in Noah's time (Genesis 7:11), swallowed up the Egyptian army (Exodus 15:5), and engulfed Jonah (Jonah 2:5).

**Psalm 33:8-9.** In light of God's power revealed in the speaking of creation into being and in the subduing of the primal deep, the psalm summons not just the gathered congregation but

194

the "earth" and "all the inhabitants of the world" to an attitude of awe and fear. It is natural to "tone down" the note of fear into something more of reverence. But even so, the witness to God's power in and over creation just recited cannot help inspiring a degree of fear—tempered by the earlier affirmations of God's righteousness and steadfast love. Verse 9 completes this portion of the psalm not only with another pair of parallel statements (God spoke, it came to be/God commanded, it stood firm) but by this paired statement's repetition of verse 6's affirmation of creation brought into being by the word of God. Keeping in mind the likely setting of this psalm in worship, this witness to the efficacy of God's word is not simply a recollection of what God has done. Worship attends to God's word, which thus opens worship—and worshipers—to God's ongoing creative and life-forming word.

---

## INTERPRETING THE SCRIPTURE

### Creationism, Intelligent Design, and Biblical Faith

Ever since the days of the Scopes trial in Tennessee, science and religion have often been posed as sparring partners. More recently, proponents of creationism have sought to strengthen their side of the argument with alleged scientific "proof" of their theories, most notably with "intelligent design" assertions about the universe.

But there is a fatal flaw with modern-day creationism and even the doctrine of intelligent design. That flaw is this: They miss the point of the biblical witness to God as Creator. Neither the opening chapters of Genesis nor the psalms of creation (including this session's Psalm 33) detail the mechanics of creation. Biblical faith is not about some scientific method that can "prove" what has come to be and how. Biblical faith is the evangelical (in its foundational meaning as "good news") proclamation of the inherent nature of Creator and creation that relies on trust.

The biblical writers were not interested in arguing whether "intelligence" undergirds the created order. "Intelligence" is a morally neutral term. To say that the world traces back to "Intelligent Design" is simply a knee-jerk reaction to Darwinian evolution that brings no good news. After all, the best criminals are not stupid, but highly intelligent in their scheming. So what if the intelligence behind all things had evil as its intent, so that creation might then be a testing ground for malevolent purposes? Intelligent design proves nothing, at least in terms of what Scripture holds as primary.

Psalm 33 takes us to the core of the biblical witness's affirmations about God as Creator: that God is just and loving. Taken together, those two assertions form the truly evangelical witness to Creator and creation. To assert God as loving in the context of creation is to affirm that the world has been formed out of love. In other words, God as loving Creator testifies that this universe into which we have come is not indifferent or hostile to us. The One who fashioned Creation holds us in love. We are not alone. We are loved.

Second, to assert God as just in the context of creation is to affirm that the world is not ultimately nihilistic, abandoned of any ethic or higher purpose other than getting whatever you or I can out of life. God's justice is woven into the fabric of creation, which means among other things that that which is just and right will triumph in the end. Living just lives in response is not whistling in the dark, but aligning ourselves with the God whom we confess is the just Creator of all.

In the end, creationism and intelligent design come up short because they obsess on minor issues. Evangelical faith is not determined by whether one believes all things came into being in seven calendar days as we know them. Evangelical faith seeks the more demanding act of trust in a Creator who is just and loving—and the ensuing discipleship of living just and loving lives in faithful response.

*Rejoicing in God and Creation*

What we say about God as Creator has implications for how we live in creation. And what Psalm 33 makes clear, particularly in verses 1-3, is our grounding in praise and rejoicing in God and God's work that is creation. One of the more memorable expressions of this truth comes in the very first question and answer of the *Westminster Shorter Catechism*, written between 1646 and 1647 by English and Scottish Protestants as an educational tool for the church:

"Q. 1. What is the chief end of man?

A. Man's chief end is to glorify God, and enjoy him forever."

On the surface, this might seem rather simplistic and even absent of discipleship. For if all we need to do is praise and enjoy God, does that mean our only calling is to sit in worship with smiles on our faces as we sing?

That caricature relies on a poor and weak understanding of praise, and its implications for faithful living. To rejoice, to praise, is above all else to put "first things first." Worship is at heart an act of allegiance, a pledge of fidelity to the One who is above all else. Worship and praise and rejoicing, whose confessions and allegiances are limited to the sanctuary, are poor imitations of the real thing. To rejoice in God, and in the creation God has fashioned, evokes from us not only words of devotion but also acts of discipleship. To rejoice in God is, among other things, to assert that no other power holds the place of God in our lives. To rejoice in God's work of creation means, among other things, that any abuses of creation's goodness and bounties runs contrary to our faith and demands faithful protest.

So as we hear this psalm bidding us to sing and rejoice, praise and make melody, do not hear this as an excuse to detach ourselves from the world around us in sanctuaried retreat. God is Creator of all. Sometimes our praise and rejoicing will be pure celebration, delighting in God and the manifold gifts of creations. Sometimes our praise and rejoicing will be defiant witness, contradicting claims that would usurp the place of God or abuse God's creation for selfish purposes.

In times of celebration, in times of defiance, we are called to rejoice in God, to praise the One whom we serve.

### On Our Way Rejoicing

I first encountered and sung the hymn, whose title serves as the heading for this segment, in a small Lutheran church we attend. It often served as the commissioning song after Communion. Fed by sacrament, inspired by Word, the hymn sent us out the doors to live with the same praise we had engaged in during the service.

So here is the question: How will you go on your way rejoicing today? With what words, and through what actions, will your rejoicing in God be reflected in the choices you face and the opportunities presented to you. How will you go on your way rejoicing if that way in this moment involves estrangement or suffering? Another of the psalms sounds the question once raised by the Jewish exiles in Babylon: "How shall we sing the LORD's song in a strange land?" (Psalm 137:4 KJV). Their question lingers, and perhaps is close to you this day. How can we do on our rejoicing when the way does not seem all that joy-filled?

That is precisely when Psalm 33 invites us to consider its core affirmations about the Creator: Just. Steadfast love. Our anchor point is not in each circumstance that befalls us, but in the God who stands above all. It is not that we need to take joy in all that comes our way, but rather in all that comes, faith bids us to rejoice in God whose justice and love are steadfast, and will in the end bear us up.

On our way rejoicing is not a blithe ignoring of circumstances in our lives and in the broader life of society that are not praiseworthy in the least. Rather, on our way rejoicing, as the psalmist bids us do, is celebrating the just and loving God who is not simply our companion but our hope on life's journey. Remember the verse 3 detail noted in Understanding the Scripture: The root for the Hebrew word translated there as "sing" and "song" more literally means "to journey." To praise God is, at its heart, best expressed not in bolted-down pews, but in faithful movement on the ways that come to trust. Thanks be to God, the Creator and hope of all!

---

## SHARING THE SCRIPTURE

### PREPARING TO LEAD

#### Preparing Our Hearts

Ponder this week's devotional reading from Psalm 146 in which an individual sings praise to God. Why does the psalmist warn against putting trust in princes? What does the psalmist say about who God is and what God does? Do you share the psalmist's commitment to praise God throughout your life? How do your actions reflect that commitment?

Pray that you and the students will praise the Creator God who cares for all.

#### Preparing Our Minds

Study the background Scripture from and the lesson Scripture, which are both from Psalm 33:1-9.

Consider this question: *Who or what should be the subject of our praise?*

Write on newsprint:

❏ information for next week's lesson, found under "Continue the Journey."

❏ activities for further spiritual growth in "Continue the Journey."

Be prepared to use Close-up: The Psalms, which precedes the first lesson of this quarter in today's session.

## LEADING THE CLASS

### (1) Gather to Learn

❖ Welcome everyone and pray that those who have come today will be eager to praise God the Creator.

❖ Invite the class members to identify publicly known individuals or groups who are (or deserve to be) praised for their achievements. List names on newsprint. Talk about why these names were mentioned. What criteria were used to determine whether particular names should be included? Did their achievements bring them personal glory as individuals or a group? Did they also in some way help humanity?

❖ Read aloud today's focus statement: **People praise the achievements of others. What should be the subject of our praise? The psalmist teaches that the word and work of God the Creator are worthy of our praise.**

### (2) Goal 1: Acknowledge God as the Just and Loving Creator of Heaven and Earth

❖ Inform the class that the Book of Psalms will be the focus of our five sessions in Unit 2. Briefly introduce the psalms by reading or retelling information from Close-up: The Psalms. Be sure to note that Psalm 33 is a communal hymn of praise. We will refer to this information as we continue with Goal 1.

❖ Select, if possible, nine different readers to each read one verse. (If that many people are not available, alternate readers between verses.)

❖ Use information from Understanding the Scripture to add to the group's discussion of these questions:

1. **Who does the psalmist call to praise or rejoice in God?** (verse 1)
2. **How does the psalmist suggest that we are to praise God?** (verses 2-3)
3. **What are the characteristics of God as seen in verses 4-5?**
4. **In what ways are those who are called to worship in verse 1 similar to God as described in verses 4-5?**
5. **What does the psalmist say about God as Creator?** (verses 6-9)
6. **What role does the word of the Lord play in these verses?**

❖ Return to Close-up: The Psalms to consider parallelism. Look for instances of parallelism in Psalm 33:1-9. Your purpose here is to demonstrate how this important facet of Hebrew poetry—parallelism, in this case, synonymous parallelism—works. For example, in the first line of verse 1, the righteous are called to rejoice in the Lord. Notice that in the second line we find a similar idea, though here the upright are told that praise "befits" them. Similarly, in verse 2, the first line calls participants to praise the Lord with the lyre (a stringed instrument). Likewise, the second line calls for making melody to the Lord "with the harp of ten strings." Verse 9 is another example of synonymous parallelism concerning the effectiveness of God's word, where God's speaking calls something into being.

### (3) Goal 2: Rejoice in God's Word and Work in Creation

❖ Read or retell Rejoicing in God and Creation from Interpreting the Scripture.

❖ Form several small groups. Distribute hymnals, newsprint, and markers to each group. Direct the groups to turn to sections in the hymnal where they will find hymns of praise. For example, in *The United Methodist Hymnal* there are three sections of praise, one for each person in the Trinity: "Praise and Thanksgiving," "In Praise of Christ," and "In Praise of the Holy Spirit." Ask each group to choose at least one hymn and list the reasons this hymn praises one or more members of the Trinity.

❖ Bring the groups together and ask them to review what they have written. If time permits after each group has reported, ask: **What prompted you to choose this particular hymn?** It will be interesting to note if the same hymn was chosen by multiple groups—and why.

### (4) Goal 3: Strategize Ways to Make Praising God the Learners' Highest Priority

❖ Read On Our Way Rejoicing in Interpreting the Scripture.

❖ Ask: **How will you go on your way rejoicing today? Think of a troubadour, a traveling musician, who went about singing. How can you joyously praise God as you go about your daily life?** List ideas on newsprint. Some ideas may entail private times of praise, such as when

one takes a walk and silently praises God along the way. Other ideas may be more public, such as when one lifts a word of praise during a time of prayer as part of worship.

❖ Distribute paper and pencils. Invite the learners to commit themselves to praising God by completing this sentence: *I will make praising God a high priority in my life by. . . .* Suggest that they list two to five ideas from the newsprint and then sign their names to seal their commitments.

### (5) Continue the Journey

❖ Pray that as the learners depart, they will continue to praise God always.

❖ Post information for next week's session on newsprint for the students to copy:

- **Title: All Creation Overflows with Praise**
- **Background Scripture: Psalm 96**
- **Lesson Scripture: Psalm 96:1-6, 10-13**
- **Focus of the Lesson: We are awed by the beauty and grandeur of creation. How can we give appropriate expression to these feelings of awe? The psalmist calls all creation to declare the glory of God and God's marvelous works.**

❖ Challenge the adults to grow spiritually by completing one or more of these activities related to this week's session.

(1) Write a hymn of praise to the Creator. You may do this as a poem. Or you may choose a favorite hymn tune and write words of praise to that tune.
(2) Note in Psalm 146:9 God's care for strangers, orphans,

and widows. Identify ways that you can help such people who live on the margins. Do whatever you can to make them feel welcomed, mentor them, or ease their loneliness.

(3) Discern ways that you can be a better steward of the world that God created. Can you grow more native plants, or recycle more, or conserve more water, for example?

Take whatever action you can.

❖ Sing or read aloud "God of the Sparrow, God of the Whale."

❖ Conclude today's session by leading the class in this benediction, which is adapted from Galatians 5:22-23, the key verses for February 26: **Empower us to go forth to bear the fruit of the Spirit, which is love, joy, peace, patience, kindness, generosity, faithfulness, gentleness, and self-control. Amen.**

UNIT 2: PRAISE FROM AND FOR GOD'S CREATION

# All Creation Overflows with Praise

---

## PREVIEWING THE LESSON

**Lesson Scripture:** Psalm 96:1-6, 10-13
**Background Scripture:** Psalm 96
**Key Verse:** Psalm 96:1

**Focus of the Lesson:**
We are awed by the beauty and grandeur of creation. How can we give appropriate expression to these feelings of awe? The psalmist calls all creation to declare the glory of God and God's marvelous works.

**Goals for the Learners:**
(1) to contemplate creation's testimony to the majesty of God.
(2) to experience awe in the presence of God's creation.
(3) to praise God wholeheartedly in corporate and individual acts of worship.

**Supplies:**
Bibles, newsprint and marker, paper and pencils, hymnals, examples or pictures of creation, worship service bulletins (any week)

---

## READING THE SCRIPTURE

NRSV

Lesson Scripture: Psalm 96:1-6, 10-13

¹**O sing to the LORD a new song;**
　**sing to the LORD, all the earth.**
²Sing to the LORD, bless his name;
　tell of his salvation from day
　　to day.
³Declare his glory among the nations,

CEB

Lesson Scripture: Psalm 96:1-6, 10-13

¹**Sing to the LORD a new song!**
　**Sing to the LORD, all the earth!**
²Sing to the LORD! Bless his name!
　Share the news of his saving
　work every single day!

his marvelous works among all
the peoples.
⁴For great is the LORD, and greatly
to be praised;
he is to be revered above all gods.
⁵For all the gods of the peoples
are idols,
but the LORD made the heavens.
⁶Honor and majesty are before him;
strength and beauty are in his
sanctuary.
¹⁰Say among the nations, "The
LORD is king!
The world is firmly established;
it shall never be moved.
He will judge the peoples with
equity."
¹¹Let the heavens be glad, and let
the earth rejoice;
let the sea roar, and all that fills it;
¹²let the field exult, and everything
in it.
Then shall all the trees of the forest
sing for joy
¹³before the LORD; for he is coming,
for he is coming to judge the earth.
He will judge the world with
righteousness,
and the peoples with his truth.

³Declare God's glory among the
nations;
declare his wondrous works
among all people
⁴because the LORD is great and so
worthy of praise.
He is awesome beyond all other gods
⁵because all the gods of the nations
are just idols,
but it is the LORD who created
heaven!
⁶Greatness and grandeur are in front
of him;
strength and beauty are in his
sanctuary.
¹⁰Tell the nations, "The LORD rules!
Yes, he set the world firmly
in place;
it won't be shaken.
He will judge all people fairly."
¹¹Let heaven celebrate! Let the
earth rejoice!
Let the sea and everything
in it roar!
¹²Let the countryside and
everything in it celebrate!
Then all the trees of the forest too
will shout out joyfully
¹³before the LORD because he
is coming!
He is coming to establish justice
on the earth!
He will establish justice in
the world rightly.
He will establish justice among
all people fairly.

## UNDERSTANDING THE SCRIPTURE

**Introduction.** In *The Message of the Psalms*, Walter Brueggemann categorizes this psalm among the "victory-enthronement" songs in the Psalter that not only celebrate the sovereignty of God but also hearken back to Israel's ancient traditions of deliverance (especially from Egypt, as in Miriam's song in Exodus 15). It is also important to note that, with some very minor variations, the entire text of Psalm 96 is repeated in 1 Chronicles 16:23-33. First Chronicles 16:1-7 identifies the context of Psalm 96's counterpart as when David brought the ark into Jerusalem and placed it in a tent (there was as yet no Temple in Jerusalem, as the first Temple was built by David's son Solomon). However, the dating of 1 Chronicles' final composition is generally held to be in the postexilic era. One piece of evidence for this late dating is that 1 Chronicles 3:17-24 contains a list of Davidic descendants that extends to the time of exile. The importance for that in interpreting Psalm 96 comes in seeing this appeal to God's sovereignty over all creation set against the claims of sovereignty made by the Babylonian and then Persian empires. Similar to Second Isaiah's use of creation theology to critique the Babylonian imperial claims in proclaiming hope to the exiles, Psalm 96 can be heard as a defiant celebration of the God to whom all nations truly belong, above and beyond all earthly powers—empires included.

**Psalm 96:1-3.** This summons for Israel to sing a "new song" occurs in several other psalms, including Psalm 98, which bears close thematic resemblance to Psalm 96. More important, Isaiah 42:10 also bids the exiles in Babylon to "sing to the Lord a new song." What makes this parallel even closer is that the preceding and following verses in Isaiah assert God as Creator (42:5) and invoke God's praise from all creation (42:10-11). The threefold summons to "sing" in Psalm 96:1-2a is followed by a twofold call for Israel to "tell" and "declare"—that is, bear witness. The substance of that witness is threefold: God's salvation, God's glory, and God's marvelous works. Salvation appears in the song of Moses (Exodus 15:2), celebrating Israel's deliverance from Egypt as well as recounting the Egyptian

army's catastrophe in the closing of the once-parted waters over them. God's glory hearkens back to Israel's deliverance from Egypt, where the cloud and fire on Mount Sinai were referenced as God's "glory" (Exodus 24:15-17). God's "marvelous works" likewise summons remembrances of deliverance from exile (Exodus 3:20) and return to the land (Joshua 3:5). Psalm 96's theme of God's universal sovereignty finds the first in verse 3 of what will be repeated references to inclusiveness.

**Psalm 96:4-6.** The monotheism (belief in one God) of Judaism did not deny the polytheism (belief in multiple gods) of its neighbors. Rather, Judaism confessed its God to be above all others gods. The Hebrew language both complicates and clarifies this. As highlighted in the previous session, "Lord" in English translations represents the name God reveals to Moses. It is frequently used in the Psalms (as in this psalm in verses 1, 2, 4, and others) and throughout the Hebrew Scriptures. However, when "God" is encountered in English translations, it most often translates the Hebrew *elohiym*. That word, however, is a plural form of its root *el*. Complicating matters further: Whereas *elohiym* in Genesis 1 is translated "God," the very same word is translated in Psalm 96:5 as "gods." So how does Psalm 96 distinguish the difference between "gods" and "God"? By the power to create. Or as verse 5 renders that distinction: "the gods of the peoples are idols, but the Lord made the heavens." God as Creator separates true deity from idols. Again, the Hebrew language points us in this direction. The word translated as "idols" in 96:5 more literally means "worthless."

**Psalm 96:7-9.** The introduction

noted the parallel version of this psalm in 1 Chronicles. Psalm 96:7-9 also appears as the opening two verses of Psalm 29—with one notable difference that reflects a theme similar to those in verses 4-6. Psalm 96:7 begins: "Ascribe to the Lord, O families of the peoples." Psalm 29:1 begins: "Ascribe to the Lord, O *heavenly beings*" (emphasis added). "Heavenly beings" expands the vision of those summoned to God's praise, a theme that will be given expression near the end of Psalm 96 in other ways. Psalm 96:8b-9 evokes a setting of formal worship, most likely the Temple in Jerusalem.

**Psalm 96:10.** This verse bids Israel into the role of something like a royal herald announcing a royal coronation. The news, however, is not just to the particular subjects of a limited realm. The message is for the "nations," a word whose meaning is not so much the modern understanding of "nation states" but a more ancient one of "peoples"—and often in reference to anyone outside of Judaism (the New Testament parallel to this word would be "Gentiles"). The message of God's kingship has consequences. The "world" is established,

with the psalmist employing yet another term to make the breadth of this reign inclusive of all. Its stability finds expression in a phrase ("it shall never be moved") that is employed in Psalm 46:5 to convey the stability of God's holy city. Beyond the assurance of the steadiness of God's realm and reign, however, the psalm witnesses to the good news of the underlying nature of that reign in God's justice and equity.

**Psalm 96:11-13.** The psalm closes with an even more expansive summons to God's praise. Heavens and earth are bid to rejoice. All that fills the sea, everything in the fields, all the trees of the forest: the dominant image is "all," and the predominant action is praise. The psalmist's reason for doing so is simple: God is coming. Like Second Isaiah's herald getting up on a high mountain to announce "Here is your God!" to the exiles (Isaiah 40:9), the psalmist bids Israel and all creation to line up for the procession of the Sovereign. And the news brought by the psalmist, like Isaiah's "herald of good tidings," is good indeed: This Sovereign's reign will be marked by righteousness (justice) and truth (fidelity).

---

## INTERPRETING THE SCRIPTURE

*Listening to Creation*

Creation is God's primal witness. Before there were stories to be told, mountains and seas, valleys and rivers, and all the range of living things bore the spark of life that did not self-originate. Before there was Scripture, the beauties of sunsets and the intricacies of life evolving and the sheer power of storms bore witness

to the power of God. Those with eyes and ears and minds open to the mysteries of the created order may listen and hear the soundings of God.

Two early theologians, Augustine and Thomas Aquinas, both argued for such an understanding in their development of what came to be known as "natural theology." The theological basis for "listening to creation" can even by discerned in Paul, when he writes: "Ever since the creation of the world, [God's] eternal power and divine nature, invisible though they are, have been understood and seen through the things he has made" (Romans 1:20).

So when we encounter Psalm 96's invitation to contemplate creation's testimony to God as Creator, we are not denigrating the role of Scripture or daydreaming in pretty places. If we take the assertion of God as Creator seriously, then we of all people should be attentive to the ways in which creation's diversity and complexity, its utter simplicities as well as its baffling mysteries, point us Godward.

Unfortunately, there is a strain in Christian theology that takes the matter of sin to such an extreme that creation, human and otherwise, is obliterated in the cloud of utter depravity. In its earliest forms, this view took shape in something called Docetism. From a Greek word meaning "to seem," adherents of this philosophy held that only "spirit" reflected God, and the body and the material world were to be rejected because of its utter sinfulness. Some took this position so far as to argue that Jesus only "seemed" to have a human body, and thus that he never really died.

There may not be many card-carrying Docetists around these days who hold those extreme views. Even so, there are more than enough folks who still adhere to Docetism's fundamental rejection of the value of creation—other than creation subjugated to human exploitation. Out of such theologies, and they are theologies, comes the willingness to exploit creation for whatever short-term benefits are available. Why? Because creation is viewed purely as a resource for humans to consume, rather than a God-given gift that itself brings testimony to God as Creator.

Psalm 96 offers a different view. Psalm 96:11-12 speaks of heavens that are glad and an earth that rejoices, seas that roar and fields that exult, all in praise of God. Creation does so, not in some ancient snapshot of how things were at the dawn of time. No, Psalm 96 testifies to the witness of creation that sounds around and ahead of us. If only we would open our minds and hearts to listen, if only we would value creation as God values creation.

*Awe as a Prelude to Hope*

Psalm 96 solicits awe on our part for several reasons. One of those has been the focus of the previous paragraphs: the chorus of God's praise provided by creation. It is hard not to be struck by awe in the face of storm waves crashing against rocks on the shores of the Pacific Northwest or the coast of Maine. It is hard not to be struck by awe when immersed in colors of a desert sunset, or a sunrise over a mirror-surfaced lake. It is hard not to be struck with awe when peering down the cliffs of canyons cut narrow and deep by water and wind. It is hard not to be struck by awe in cathedral-like groves of trees whose canopies seem to reach the sky, or in twisted and weathered trunks of bristlecone pine in the Sierras that were growing before Jesus or Moses lived. In the presence of such witnesses of what God has done in creation, awe is the proper response.

But Psalm 96 lifts up another reason for awe, and it is not what God *has* done—it is what God *will* do. Such awe begins in the announcement made twice in verse 13 just to make sure we don't miss it: "God is coming." God has not withdrawn from the world, letting things run their course helter-skelter. God is not the grand Watchmaker, who designed the clockwork and then left the stage. God is coming. The One who fashioned the universe is on the way.

Given the extraordinary power attested to in and by creation, such a coming might well be accompanied by awe swallowed up in fear. Does God come as Destroyer? Does God come as One indifferent to all but God's own Self? Listen to the psalmist as to the nature of God's coming: "[God] will judge the earth with righteousness, and the peoples with his truth" (96:13).

Righteousness: the Hebrew word, as noted in the Understanding the Scripture commentary above on this verse, means "justice." In a world too often rent apart by injustice, justice will come. Equity, right relationships, will be restored. Truth: again, the Hebrew word, as noted in the commentary above, means "fidelity" or "steadiness." It is the word used of the arms of Moses in Exodus 17:12, held up in blessing throughout the day until those who attacked the exiles were defeated. In a world too often disappointed by words or actions that give up on us or fail us, God will prove dependable.

The awe generated by such righteousness and truth, such justice and fidelity, serves as prelude to our hope. For if the One who comes truly is just and faithful, we can live with hope—and we can sing with joy the new song of God's coming re-creation.

### Singers of a New Song

In Bible study, a leader will sometimes invite learners to imagine themselves as one of the characters in the story. What do you hear and see? Why do you act the way you do? What will you come away with from this encounter? Psalm 96 is not a narrative. But the psalmist does bid us to enter into its story. It invites us to become one of the singers of the new song.

So as you today hear "sing to the Lord a new song," what would your contribution to that song be? That is, what in your experience of God would cause you to lift up your voice in praise?

Or consider this: The psalm in its recitation of God's authority over all other gods, and in its description of all creation taking up the chorus of God's praise, evokes a sense of awe from us. When, and how, have you experienced such awe in the presence of God: whether in private devotion, or corporate worship, or in the natural creation?

And finally, the psalm ends by sounding the hope of God's coming grounded in God's justice and fidelity. Where in your life might that hope stir new faith and action on your part? And how might you bear witness to this God in praise—and in service?

"Sing to the Lord a new song"—for you are, with all creation, a member of the choir!

## SHARING THE SCRIPTURE

### PREPARING TO LEAD

#### Preparing Our Hearts

Ponder this week's devotional reading from 1 Chronicles 16:23-34. As you read, set two Bibles together, one opened to 1 Chronicles and the other opened to Psalm 96. How do you hear God's sovereign glory expressed in both of these passages? What ideas do you glean about how to praise God?

Pray that you and the students will give praise and glory to God today and always, for the steadfast love of our good God endures forever.

#### Preparing Our Minds

Study the background Scripture from Psalm 96 and the lesson Scripture from Psalm 96:1-6, 10-13.

Consider this question: *How can you give appropriate expression to the feelings of awe you experience in the presence of the grandeur of creation?*

Write on newsprint:
- ❏ information for next week's lesson, found under Continue the Journey.
- ❏ activities for further spiritual growth in Continue the Journey.

Determine how you might use any of the features that precede the first lesson of this quarter in today's session. Note under Goal 1 an option to refer to the section titled Creation and New Creation: The Psalms, found in The Big Picture: Creation and New Creation. If you decide to use this information, either be ready to read it or prepare a brief lecture.

Collect examples of nature, such as shells, leaves, pinecones, stones, or green plants. You may wish to enlist class members to bring items as well. If you cannot bring such items, use pictures of natural items.

Collect enough copies of your church's current (or previous) worship services so each person (or a pair) can have one. The bulletins need not be for the same week.

### LEADING THE CLASS

#### (1) Gather to Learn

Welcome everyone and pray that those who have come today will experience wonder and awe in the presence of God's creation.

Invite participants to talk with a small group about where and why they experience wonder in God's creation. The adults may find that some are awed by ocean waves crashing on the beach; others prefer the glassy stillness of a lake; others find peace in a wooded mountain retreat. Some people may know why a certain aspect of nature thrills them (for example, they may have fond memories of going to the beach with a beloved family member), but others may simply say that why they are drawn to a certain place or natural feature is a mystery.

Read aloud today's focus statement: **We are awed by the beauty and grandeur of creation. How can we give appropriate expression to these feelings of awe? The psalmist calls all creation to declare the glory of God and God's marvelous works.**

#### (2) Goal 1: Contemplate Creation's Testimony to the Majesty of God

❖ **Option:** Refer to information in the section of The Big Picture: Creation and New Creation, which is titled Creation and New Creation: The Psalms. Read or retell this to add to the information from last week's lesson that we considered from Close-up: The Psalms.

❖ Distribute hymnals that include a Psalter and invite the group to read Psalm 96 responsively, with half of the class reading the regular type and the other half reading the boldfaced type. If there is a sung response, use this as well. (If you have access to *The United Methodist Hymnal*, you will find this psalm on pages 815–816.)

❖ **Option:** If you do not have a Psalter, ask one volunteer to read verses 1-6 and a second to read verses 10-13.

❖ Form two groups. The first will look at verses 1-6 to determine who/what is being called to praise and the reason for this praise. The second group will examine verses 10-13 to discover who/what is being asked to praise and how they respond to the Lord.

❖ Call the groups together to report their findings. Wrap up by asking: **Where in this poem do you see the created order bear witness in its praise to the majesty of God?**

*(3) Goal 2: Experience Awe in the Presence of God's Creation*

❖ Show the items of nature (or pictures of such items) that you have collected.

❖ Invite each participant to select one of these items to focus on. Encourage them to meditate on these questions silently as you read them aloud:

1. **Why does this natural**

**item draw your attention?** (pause)

2. **Does such an object prompt any special memories for you, such as a trip to the beach with grandparents?** (pause)

3. **What song will you sing to God in your heart as an act of praise for such an object?** (pause)

❖ Call everyone together to read in unison today's key verse, Psalm 96:1.

*(4) Goal 3: Praise God Wholeheartedly in Corporate and Individual Acts of Worship*

❖ Distribute the worship bulletins you have collected. Encourage participants to call out portions of the service that for them focus on praise. These may be generic names, such as "hymn of praise," or specific, such as the name of a particular hymn. (Let the students know if the bulletins are for different weeks, since specific answers will vary if that is the case.)

❖ Discuss these questions:

1. **What portions of the service are mostly likely to prompt you to offer praise?**

2. **How do you experience God in the midst of your praise with the congregation?**

3. **How might your experience of God in individual acts of worship be different from that during corporate worship?**

❖ Encourage the adults to suggest ways of offering praise (perhaps a certain hymn or psalm or act of worship) that they can participate in right now.

*(5) Continue the Journey*

❖ Pray that as the learners depart they will seek opportunities to whole-heartedly worship God with praise.

❖ Post information for next week's session on newsprint for the students to copy:

- **Title: Praise God the Provider**
- **Background Scripture: Psalm 65; 67:6-7**
- **Lesson Scripture: Psalm 65:1-2, 9-13**
- **Focus of the Lesson: We often take for granted how we get the good things we enjoy. What is the source of our material bounty? The psalmist calls us to praise God for the bounty God provides.**

❖ Challenge the adults to grow spiritually by completing one or more of these activities related to this week's session.

(1) **Take a walk and enjoy the beauty of creation in your community. What fills you with awe? How does the weather, which for many of us in North America is cold and even snowy at this time of the year, affect your appreciation of creation?**

(2) **Talk with someone who may be feeling blue due to a personal issue or simply because it is winter. Offer your own reasons for praising the God of creation and encourage your friend to consider reasons he or she has for praising God.**

(3) **Compare Psalm 96 with other psalms celebrating the enthronement of a king, including 47, 93, 97, 98, 99. How is Psalm 96 similar to these other psalms? In what ways is it unique?**

❖ Sing or read aloud "All Creatures of Our God and King."

❖ Conclude today's session by leading the class in this benediction, which is adapted from Galatians 5:22-23, the key verses for February 26: **Empower us to go forth to bear the fruit of the Spirit, which is love, joy, peace, patience, kindness, generosity, faithfulness, gentleness, and self-control. Amen.**

UNIT 2: PRAISE FROM AND FOR GOD'S CREATION

# PRAISE GOD
# THE PROVIDER

---

## PREVIEWING THE LESSON

**Lesson Scripture:** Psalm 65:1-2, 9-13
**Background Scripture:** Psalm 65; 67:6-7
**Key Verse:** Psalm 65:5

### Focus of the Lesson:
We often take for granted how we get the good things we enjoy. What is the source of our material bounty? The psalmist calls us to praise God for the bounty God provides.

### Goals for the Learners:
(1) to become aware of the natural and human factors responsible for our material well-being.
(2) to feel gratitude for the ways God meets our physical needs.
(3) to praise the Creator through good stewardship of our material blessings.

### Supplies:
Bibles, newsprint and marker, paper and pencils, hymnals

---

## READING THE SCRIPTURE

NRSV
Lesson Scripture: Psalm 65:1-2, 5, 9-13

[1]Praise is due to you,
  O God, in Zion;
and to you shall vows be performed,
  [2]O you who answer prayer!
To you all flesh shall come.
[5]**By awesome deeds you answer us
  with deliverance,**

CEB
Lesson Scripture: Psalm 65:1-2, 5, 9-13

[1]God of Zion, to you even silence
  is praise.
  Promises made to you are kept—
[2]you listen to prayer—
  and all living things come to you.
[5]**In righteousness you answer us,
  by your awesome deeds,**

O God of our salvation;
you are the hope of all the ends of
    the earth
and of the farthest seas.
⁹You visit the earth and water it,
    you greatly enrich it;
the river of God is full of water;
    you provide the people with grain,
    for so you have prepared it.
¹⁰You water its furrows abundantly,
    settling its ridges,
softening it with showers,
    and blessing its growth.
¹¹You crown the year with your
    bounty;
    your wagon tracks overflow with
    richness.
¹²The pastures of the wilderness
    overflow,
    the hills gird themselves with joy,
¹³the meadows clothe themselves
    with flocks,
    the valleys deck themselves with
    grain,
    they shout and sing together for
    joy.

God of our salvation—
you, who are the security
    of all the far edges of the earth,
    even the distant seas.
⁹You visit the earth and make it
    abundant,
    enriching it greatly
    by God's stream, full of water.
You provide people with grain
    because that is what you've
    decided.
¹⁰Drenching the earth's furrows,
    leveling its ridges,
    you soften it with rain showers;
    you bless its growth.
¹¹You crown the year with your
    goodness;
    your paths overflow with rich
    food.
¹²Even the desert pastures drip
    with it,
    and the hills are dressed in
    pure joy.
¹³The meadowlands are covered
    with flocks,
    the valleys decked out in grain—
    they shout for joy;
    they break out in song!

---

## UNDERSTANDING THE SCRIPTURE

**Psalm 65:1-2.** These verses open the psalm with a strong sense of praise exclusively due to God. The three-fold refrain "to you" leaves unquestioned to whom Israel's praise is to be directed. This may suggest a subtle rejection of other claimants to praise, whether imperial authorities or neighboring "gods" or even the seductive idea that we are self-made men and women (thus, the second half of the psalm asserting God as Creator). Zion is the mountain upon which Jerusalem, and in particular the Temple, was erected. The performing of vows there points to the setting of worship in the Temple. The word translated as "performed" is *shalam*. It is the verb form of the Hebrew *shalom*. The word, while often associated with "peace," also has the sense of "completeness" or "wholeness." Its use in this verse evokes a sense of religious duties being fulfilled on Zion. Its use also may be a wordplay, as *shalam* serves as one of the roots for the name of this city: Jeru-*salem*. "*All* flesh shall come" (emphasis added) underscores the universality of this psalm, not only in its witness to the cause of our thanksgiving for the whole of creation but also to the inclusion of all peoples in those who are summoned to such grateful praise. The linkage in verse 2 of "all flesh" to "you who answer prayer" also calls to mind an often-overlooked petition in Solomon's prayer of dedication for this very Temple. In 1 Kings 8:41-43, Solomon speaks of the Temple as a house of prayer where those *not* of Israel may come for prayer. Beyond that, Solomon pleads in verse 43 that God will hear and "do according to all that the foreigner calls to you, so that all the peoples of the earth may know your name and fear you." Praise for, and prayer to, God the provider knows no bounds for those moved to do either or both.

**Psalm 65:3-4.** The praise of God elicited in verses 1-2 is given particular reason in verse 3 by virtue of God's forgiveness of sin. The necessity of God's forgiving, rather than our handling sin all on our own, is alluded to in the verse's identifying the power of sin as "overwhelming" us. The Hebrew word translated as "forgiveness" occurs most frequently in Leviticus and Numbers, in reference to cultic prescriptions related to sin offerings. But the word's more literal meaning of "cover over" can be seen in its use in Genesis 6:14, where God instructs Noah to "cover" the ark with pitch. That ancient relationship between "covering" and forgiveness may be heard in the way we today sometimes speak of our "covering" other persons when they are in danger (in the psalm's term, "overwhelmed" by something for which they need help). Verse 4 adds the gratitude for being "chosen" by God,

a choice signified in this verse by the opportunity and gift of rendering worship in the Temple, the place in ancient Judaism most identified with God's presence among the people. The closing affirmation of being "satisfied" with the goodness of God's house is suggestive of the imagery in Psalm 23:1 of not "wanting" in God's shepherding presence.

**Psalm 65:5.** Today's key verse stands at the core of the psalm structurally and thematically. The call to and cause for praise in the psalm's opening four verses, and its celebration of God's providence in verses 6-13, hinges on verse 5's confession of God's saving power that extends across creation. Two of the words in this verse, and their translations, merit a closer look. Where the NRSV has "deliverance," the CEB has "righteousness." The Hebrew word is *tsedeq*, and its connotation is "justice" or "righteousness." Consider how that might influence the way we hear this verse ("you answer us with *justice*"). What might that affirm not only about the way God works in the world but also in the priorities of those who would be about that work in word and deed? For the second word in question, both the NRSV and the CEB have "awesome deeds," whereas the KJV has "terrible things." That latter translation may convey more closely the sense of the Hebrew word *yare*, most commonly rendered as "fear." *Yare* invokes a deeper sense of mystery and awe than even "awesome deeds" conveys about the One confessed in this same verse as our salvation ("safety") and hope ("trust").

**Psalm 65:6-13.** The psalm concludes in this extended confession of wonder at all that God has done in fashioning and supplying the created order with life. What is immediately apparent in these verses is the psalmist's direct address of God in a litany that celebrates God's working in creation. Listen to the steady wave of verbs by which the psalmist unpacks the diversity of God's providential activity for all creation: "you established . . . you silence . . . you make . . . you visit . . . you greatly enrich . . . you provide . . . you have prepared . . . you water . . . you crown." Only in the psalm's final two verses does the psalmist shift from confession of God's actions to creation's response in fitting praise, where "joy" is used in both verses to ensure the nature of praise is clear.

**Psalm 67:6-7.** Verse 6 sounds the theme of the God of harvest, where earth's produce and fruit serve as a metaphor for God's providential blessing of creation. It is an abbreviation of the same theme developed in more detail in Psalm 65:9-12. The closing verse of Psalm 67 hearkens back to its opening verse: the invocation of God's blessing upon Israel, where that blessing is linked to the revelation of God's saving power among all nations. The recognition by Israel that this blessing is not theirs alone is reiterated in the final phrase of verse 7, where all creation is bid to "revere" (*yare*, see comments on Psalm 65:5) God.

## INTERPRETING THE SCRIPTURE

### For the Beauty of the Earth

According to *The Hymns of the United Methodist Hymnal*, the inspiration for this familiar hymn was the "beauty of the English countryside." Two things are important to be said, particularly as the words of this hymn relate to Psalm 65.

First, one does not need to have traveled to the Avon River near Bath to grasp the beauty of creation celebrated in Folliot Pierpoint's song. As with Psalm 65, written in a natural setting far different than most of ours, the hymn touches universal nerves, helping us see the beauties of creation in our particular settings as well as encouraging us to take notice of all the ways our lives are enriched and sustained by such natural gifts.

The second element of this hymn that ties it to the psalm's affirmation

is this: The song does not simply celebrate the gifts of the natural order. The phrases in the hymn expand our horizons on what brings value and beauty to our lives: love that surrounds us, a celebration of the human senses that allows us to take in creation and to give response, for relationships of friend and family. All these testimonies of the way we have been created and fashioned resonate with the psalm's witness to the manifold aspects of God's creative workings in our lives and the whole of creation.

It would be difficult to faithfully sing this hymn or this psalm without a sense of wonder. Perhaps that is why sprinkled inside of the psalm are references to "awesome deeds" and "revere," both of which translate a Hebrew word (*yare*) that literally means "fear." Like the questions posed to Job out of the whirlwind

(Job 38–41), the created order—and the Creator—can pose mysteries that exceed our understanding and generate sheer awe. Unfortunately, some mistake the reverence generated by awe with a closed mind when it comes to our ponderings of creation and Creator. I once heard a friend who worked at an aerospace company in St. Louis describe how an engineer she worked with spoke of leaving his mind at the door when he entered his church for worship. Someone misled that man severely. And he is not alone by any means, given the church's track record, past and present, when it comes to reactionary positions toward science and knowledge. Our head has been fashioned by God to be more than a hat rack. Like our senses, our minds *and* our hearts help us to more fully experience God's handiwork—and in doing so, to return thanks to God for the wholeness of our creation as individuals of heart and mind, and communities who value and nurture all those gifts with which God has blessed us. Such providential blessings move us, as the hymn repeats after each verse, to grateful praise.

### Providence and Gratitude

A family gathers at a table. It may be a festive holiday banquet, with grandparents and cousins crowding around tables covered by heaping platters. It may be an ordinary meal eaten in solitude, sometimes in the eye of the storm that comes between a day's business or school and an evening's rushed activities. What often forms the common thread linking such disparate experiences of breaking bread? Someone says grace.

*Saying grace.* It's an odd sort of expression, when you think about it. Set in the context of sanctuary or pulpit, grace may carry the aura of weighty theological doctrine. The grace of God as the great mystery of our salvation. The grace of God as the unfathomable decision to choose love rather than judgment. But such imposing understandings retreat when we simply say grace, or teach a child to do so. "Come Lord Jesus, be our guest, and let this food to us be blest."

There are any number of table graces that have been and continue to be spoken. Two traits belong to many: they are simple, easily remembered over time. And they are grounded in gratitude. They are thankful for the gift of food, a gift that the "grace" reinforces is a tangible sign of God's providential care. Gratitude and providence are natural tablemates. Beyond that, gratitude and providence are natural partners. For when we consider the blessings in the created order as enumerated in Psalm 65:5-13, gratitude ought to be our constant companion.

But is it? Gratitude grounded solely in the material blessings bestowed upon us can lead us into trouble. For what happens when material blessings dry up? What happens when harvests fail or recession strikes? What happens when the joy of ear and eye succumb, by age or illness, to deafness and blindness? What happens when the delight of the human mind is swallowed up in dementia? If we are grateful to God only for the good that comes to us, does gratitude depart when mortality shows up in unwanted ways?

Gratitude in such times may perhaps be best expressed in the opening line of that table grace cited before: "come, Lord Jesus, be our guest." In the end, providence is most simply—and most enduringly—the promise and hope of God's presence in our lives, even when that presence appears at risk or hidden. We are reminded in such times that God's providence and presence are matters that ultimately rest on trust.

*Come, Lord Jesus, be our guest.* For such providential companionship, we can be eternally grateful.

### How Does the Creature Say Praise?

It is not unintentional that two of this session's three headings come from hymns of the church. After all, Psalms was the songbook of ancient Judaism. They sang the theology of Judaism, as do our songs today. Through music, in ways that defy clear explanation, words of faith sometimes penetrate deeper and resonate longer than words read or spoken.

Jaroslav Vadja wrote "God of the Sparrow, God of the Whale" only thirty-four years ago, compared with the more than twenty-five hundred years that have passed since Psalm 65 took form. Yet the refrains of Vadja's song verses, each a series of questions as to how the creatures/creations of God might express praise or awe of thanks, form a fitting companion to the psalm's assertions of God as Creator. The psalm thus beckons those who sing or speak its words to consider: What then shall we do?

If we are called to praise God, how shall that praise be rendered? Praise in acts of worship is certainly evoked by this psalm. But how else might we rightly praise God as Creator? Such praise might take the form of assuring that creation's beauties and gifts are created, not destroyed. Similarly, if the psalm beckons our gratitude for God's providential care and presence, how might our lives express such gratitude in faithful action as well as in word? Such gratitude might take the form of bearing the gift of loving and caring presence to those who may be in want of it—or even denied it by others. Who are the ones in your community, and in wider society, who fit that bill? For whom might you serve as an instrument of God's care and love and justice?

The psalm bids us to be, if you will, *stewards* of God's good purposes in creation. The praise we sing, the gratitude we offer, is not only meant for expression in liturgy. It intends to spark service lived out in and on behalf of creation. For God's providence entails not only what God provides *for* us but also what God provides for creation's good *through* us.

Thanks be to God!

---

## SHARING THE SCRIPTURE

### PREPARING TO LEAD

#### Preparing Our Hearts

Ponder this week's devotional reading from Psalm 66:1-5. Why is "all the earth" called to sing glory to God's name? What awesome deeds do you want to give God praise and thanks for today? If you were to call someone to "come and see what God has done," what would you want to show this person?

Pray that you and the students will

not only recognize God's awesome deeds but also give thanks for them and share the good news of these deeds with others.

*Preparing Our Minds*

Study the background Scripture from Psalm 65 and 67:6-7 and the lesson Scripture from Psalm 65:1-2, 5 (key verse), 9-13.

Consider this question: *What is the source of our material bounty?*

Write on newsprint:

❏ questions for Goal 3 in Sharing the Scripture if you plan to work in small groups.
❏ information for next week's lesson, found under Continue the Journey.
❏ activities for further spiritual growth in Continue the Journey.

Determine how you might use any of the features that precede the first lesson of this quarter in today's session.

LEADING THE CLASS

*(1) Gather to Learn*

❖ Welcome everyone and pray that those who have come today will give thanks to God for their blessings.

❖ Read: **People who did not grow up in elite families but have had to overcome disadvantages and work hard for everything they have may refer to themselves as "self-made." They take credit for all that they have and all that they are, especially if they have amassed considerable material goods. The notion that people can create themselves and their fortunes has been deeply ingrained in the culture of the United States. While it is certainly true that some people have had to surmount greater obstacles than others, is it really true that anyone can be "self-made"? Certainly some of our success is due to our own efforts, but what role does the society around us play? What is the deepest source of our good fortune?**

❖ Read aloud today's focus statement: **We often take for granted how we get the good things we enjoy. What is the source of our material bounty? The psalmist calls us to praise God for the bounty God provides.**

*(2) Goal 1: Become Aware of the Natural and Human Factors Responsible for Our Material Well-being*

❖ Choose six volunteers to read Psalm 65:1-2, 5, 9, 10, 11, 12-13.

❖ Distribute hymnals that include "For the Beauty of the Earth." Invite the learners to sing or read this hymn and then ask:

1. **What connections do you see between this hymn and Psalm 65?**
2. **How do this hymn and Psalm 65 help you to see the beauties of creation?**
3. **How do this hymn and Psalm 65 encourage you to take notice of all the ways your life is enriched and sustained by such natural gifts?**

❖ Read or retell For the Beauty of the Earth in Interpreting the Scripture so as to include ideas that may have been omitted from the discussion.

*(3) Goal 2: Feel Gratitude for the Ways God Meets the Learners' Physical Needs*

❖ Read this statement by Gotthold E. Lessing (1729–1781) and invite students to agree, modify, or disagree with it: **"A grateful thought toward heaven is of itself a prayer."**

❖ Distribute paper and pencils. Encourage the adults to take these steps, which you will read aloud, pausing after each one:

Step 1: **List three to five blessings that meet your physical needs.** (Ideas might include nutritious food, adequate shelter, clean water, breathable air, a job that pays well enough to live with some degree of comfort.)

Step 2: **Write a sentence or two in which you prayerfully express gratitude to God for each of these blessings.**

Step 3: **Read your words of thanks to at least one other member of the class.**

❖ Conclude by reading or retelling How Does the Creature Say Praise? in Interpreting the Scripture.

*(4) Goal 3: Praise God the Creator Through Good Stewardship of Our Material Blessings*

❖ Remind participants that in Matthew 6:21 Jesus taught that where our treasures are our hearts will also be. Thus, we are called to be good stewards of our possessions.

❖ Discuss these questions either with the entire class or in small groups:

1. **Do you see yourself as the owner of what you have—or as a steward/manager/trustee entrusted by God to take care of what belongs to God? Explain your answer.**

2. **Why would God think you are—or are not—doing a good job as a steward of your material blessings?**

3. **What improvements would God want to see in your stewardship of your material goods?**

4. **Who might be role models for you in handling your material goods in a Christlike way?** (Students may mention some people they know, but don't forget biblical characters, such as the boy whose lunch was used by Jesus to feed the multitude or the woman who had only a small coin to offer but gave it willingly.)

5. **What evidence do you have that your congregation is acting as good stewards of whatever property and material goods God has entrusted to this faith community?**

❖ Bring everyone together and ask this question: **How might the way that one spends money or uses possessions be a way to offer praise to God?**

*(5) Continue the Journey*

❖ Pray that as the learners depart, they will look for ways to become better stewards of all that they have and all of creation.

❖ Post information for next week's session on newsprint for the students to copy:

- **Title: Praise God the Creator**
- **Background Scripture: Psalm 104**
- **Lesson Scripture: Psalm 104:1-4, 24-30**
- **Focus of the Lesson: When we experience the vast diversity of creation we wonder how it is all held together. What does this complexity tell us about the world in which we live? The psalmist praises God for sustaining creation.**

❖ Challenge the adults to grow spiritually by completing one or more of these activities related to this week's session.

(1) **Review your checkbook, receipts for purchases, and receipts for charitable contributions. Do you believe you are being a good steward of the financial bounty God has entrusted to you? If not, what changes will you make to improve your stewardship?**

(2) **Be aware of the natural resources that God has provided for your community. How do you think God would rate the community's stewardship of these natural treasures? Can you identify any particular threats to God's creation, such as polluted water, contaminated soil, or poor air quality? What can you do to help the community take better care of God's created world?**

(3) **Research the meanings of these Greek words that are related to stewardship: *oikos* (household), *oikonomos* (steward, household manager), *oikonomia* (administration of a household), *oikoumene* (the whole world; God's entire household). These are the root words for the English words ecology, economy, and ecumenical. How does this word study help you to expand your understanding of your role as a steward? How will you act on this knowledge?**

❖ Sing or read aloud "Mountains Are All Aglow."

❖ Conclude today's session by leading the class in this benediction, which is adapted from Galatians 5:22-23, the key verses for February 26: **Empower us to go forth to bear the fruit of the Spirit, which is love, joy, peace, patience, kindness, generosity, faithfulness, gentleness, and self-control. Amen.**

UNIT 2: PRAISE FROM AND FOR GOD'S CREATION

# PRAISE GOD
# THE CREATOR

---

## PREVIEWING THE LESSON

**Lesson Scripture:** Psalm 104:1-4, 24-30
**Background Scripture:** Psalm 104
**Key Verse:** Psalm 104:24

### Focus of the Lesson:
When we experience the vast diversity of creation we wonder how it is all held together. What does this complexity tell us about the world in which we live? The psalmist praises God for sustaining creation.

### Goals for the Learners:
(1) to ponder the diversity and complexity of God's creation.
(2) to affirm God's wisdom in ordering the world.
(3) to honor God by working to preserve the world's magnificent natural diversity.

### Supplies:
Bibles, newsprint and marker, paper and pencils, hymnals

---

## READING THE SCRIPTURE

NRSV
Lesson Scripture: Psalm 104:1-4, 24-30
[1]Bless the LORD, O my soul.
    O LORD my God, you are very great.
You are clothed with honor and majesty,
    [2]wrapped in light as with a garment.

CEB
Lesson Scripture: Psalm 104:1-4, 24-30
[1]Let my whole being bless the LORD!
    LORD my God, how fantastic you are!
You are clothed in glory and grandeur!
    [2]You wear light like a robe;
    you open the skies like a curtain

You stretch out the heavens like
　　a tent,
　　[3]you set the beams of your
　　　chambers on the waters,
you make the clouds your chariot,
　　you ride on the wings of the wind,
[4]you make the winds your
　　messengers,
　　fire and flame your ministers.
[24]O LORD, **how manifold are your
　　works!**
　　**In wisdom you have made them
　　all;**
　　**the earth is full of your creatures.**
[25]Yonder is the sea, great and wide,
　　creeping things innumerable are
　　　there,
　　living things both small and great.
[26]There go the ships,
　　and Leviathan that you formed
　　　to sport in it.
[27]These all look to you
　　to give them their food in due
　　　season;
[28]when you give to them, they gather
　　it up;
　　when you open your hand, they
　　　are filled with good things.
[29]When you hide your face, they are
　　dismayed;
　　when you take away their breath,
　　　they die
　　and return to their dust.
[30]When you send forth your spirit,
　　they are created;
　　and you renew the face of the
　　　ground.

[3]You build your lofty house on the
　　waters;
　　you make the clouds your chariot,
　　going around on the wings of
　　　the wind.
[4]You make the winds your
　　messengers;
　　you make fire and flame your
　　ministers.
[24]LORD, **you have done so many
　　things!**
　　**You made them all so wisely!**
**The earth is full of your creations!**
[25]And then there's the sea, wide
　　and deep,
　　with its countless creatures—
　　living things both small and large.
[26]There go the ships on it,
　　and Leviathan, which you made,
　　　plays in it!
[27]All your creations wait for you
　　to give them their food on time.
[28]When you give it to them, they
　　gather it up;
　　when you open your hand, they
　　　are filled completely full!
[29]But when you hide your face,
　　they are terrified;
　　when you take away their breath,
　　they die and return to dust.
[30]When you let loose your breath,
　　they are created,
　　and you make the surface of the
　　　ground brand-new again.

---

## UNDERSTANDING THE SCRIPTURE

**Psalm 104:1-2a.** "Bless the LORD, O my soul" serves as the framework of this psalm by appearing in both its opening and closing verses. It also serves that same function for Psalm 103. "Soul" translates the Hebrew word *nephesh*. *Nephesh* carries the sense of "self" or "living being." Only in later Greek thought and philosophy did "soul" become identified with a separate aspect of being apart from body. According to Joel

Green, "Throughout the OT [Old Testament], *nefesh* is used in reference to the whole person as the seat of desire and emotion, not to the `inner self' as though this were something separate from one's being." Another important detail about this Hebrew word: In the Old Testament, it is not used exclusively of human beings. In Genesis 1:21 and 24, *nephesh* is translated by "creatures" in reference to the entirety of the animal kingdom. The remainder of Psalm 104:1b-2a uses the imagery of clothing to affirm God's vesting with honor and majesty. The assertion of God garbed in "light" is the first of many clear allusions in this psalm to the creation stories in Genesis 1 and 2, as light recalls the first of God's acts of creation by word (Genesis 1:3).

**Psalm 104:2b-13.** This portion of the psalm is dominated by a series of second-person ("you") declarations regarding the varied actions of God in establishing creation's diverse order: "You stretch out . . . you set . . . you make . . . you ride . . ." and so on. These declarations directly address God, setting the psalm's tone as a relational litany rather than a detached observation of the created order by the community. There is also a progression evident in these declarations. The workings of God begin in things seen above in verses 2b-4 (heavens, clouds, winds), then to the "foundations" below (104:5), then to the waters whose rising and falling respond to God's command (104:6-10), and finally to the living things that have their being in this structured creation (104:11-12). Both "wind" (same word in Hebrew for "spirit" and "breath") and "waters" summon remembrance of the primal setting for God's acts of creation in Genesis 1:1-2. Psalm 104:13b provides a summary

statement of God's providential care in sustaining life. Two words in this verse evoke remembrances of God's work in creation ("fruit" is the same word that appears in Genesis 1:11, 12, 29) and God's work in deliverance ("satisfy" is the same Hebrew word that describes the consequence of the gift of manna in Exodus 16:8, 12).

**Psalm 104:14-23.** While the focus remains on what God has done in all creation, the emphasis shifts slightly to how those works have particular connection to human existence. Opening these verses is a reference to plants "for people to use." This parallels Genesis 1:29, where the text declares how God created seeds of plants and fruit of trees for human consumption. Closing these verses in the psalm is the image of people going out to work and laboring until evening. This image recalls the "second" creation story of Genesis where "Adam" (see comments on verse 29) is given the vocation of tilling and keeping the garden (Genesis 2:15). Another key disclosure regarding human creation in these verses of the psalm comes in verses 14b-15, where the nourishing and nurturing gifts of creation have for their purpose not simply "strengthening" human life but "gladdening" it.

**Psalm 104:24.** If "bless the LORD, O my soul" frames this psalm at beginning and end, then verse 24 gives specific expression for what evokes our praise and blessing of God: the wisdom of God revealed in the astonishing breadth of all creation. The earth being filled with its creatures hearkens back to the primal story of creation in Genesis 1. It also serves as a subtle reminder that God's blessing and command to "be fruitful and multiply" to humanity (Genesis 1:28) was *preceded* by that same blessing and command to the "swarms" of sea creatures and birds (1:22). The psalm's reference in verse 24 to "wisdom" in God's making of all things resonates with Proverbs 8:22-36. There, wisdom is personified as the first act of God's creations, picturing wisdom standing beside God when all things were fashioned by God.

**Psalm 104:25-30.** The sea, often a symbol of chaos in Near Eastern creation stories, is pictured in verse 25 simply as part of God's created order. Even the sea monster called Leviathan (referenced six times in the Old Testament) is reduced to playing in the waters. The dependency of all creation on God's providential care is recounted in verses 27-30. The food "gathered" by the creatures employs the same verb used nine times in Exodus 16 to describe the gathering of life-giving manna in the wilderness. The Genesis 2 account of human creation can be seen in the background of verse 29 of the psalm. The removal of "breath" brings a return to the "dust," a reversal of Genesis 2:7 where God breathes life into the "man" (Hebrew *adam*) formed of the dust of the "ground" (Hebrew *adamah*). Likewise, verse 30's linkage of the sending of God's spirit with the act of creation recalls Genesis 1:2 ("wind" and "spirit" in Hebrew are the same word).

**Psalm 104:31-35.** Verse 31 binds together two hopes of the psalmist: for the enduring of God's glory, and for God's taking joy in creation. The imagery in verse 32 of earthquake (trembling) and mountains and smoke is reminiscent of the theophany (God's revealing of self) on Mount Sinai in Israel's wilderness sojourn (Exodus 19:18). The psalm moves in verses 33-34 to personal testimony of the response summoned by God's acts in creation ("I will sing . . . I will sing praise . . . I rejoice."). The psalm's concluding verse pauses to invoke a purging of wickedness from God's good creation before its final blessing and praising of God.

---

## INTERPRETING THE SCRIPTURE

### The Weave of Creation

At one church I pastored, women gathered two mornings a week to weave rugs. At the back of the loom were a series of pegs that held the spools of thread ("weft") that would be drawn through the material ("warp") to create the rugs. What distinguished these rugs was that the rolls of warp used were not new balls of yarn, but rags. Looking at the multicolored mounds of used clothing that would be donated, one could easily be skeptical about their potential for rug material. But after the women cut the rags into strips, rolled them into balls, and ran them through the loom, the rugs so created became highly valued in our community—as evidenced by the yearly rush on the tables where they were sold at the annual Christmas bazaar.

Those rugs come to mind when contemplating Psalm 104's witness to the diversity and complexity God has woven into creation. Each element fashioned by God and enumerated in the psalm—clouds and winds, mountains and waters, birds and animals, food to strengthen and wine to gladden human life—reflects the individual threads and "yarns" of matter that God has formed into the richness of creation. Make no mistake: Just as with the rugs woven in that church basement, God's weaving of creation results in a life-giving interdependence. Pull out one of the threads or pieces of rag, and the whole begins to unravel. Without the protective atmosphere above, the sun's radiation would quickly threaten all life that did not live underground. Without the right balance of waters, the earth and its life would either shrivel in drought or perish under rising ocean levels.

The diversity and complexity inherent in creation is a God-given gift that holds all things together. That truth is not a recent discovery of science, though science certainly undergirds it. That truth goes to the core of why the psalmist raises this song of blessing: "O LORD, how manifold are your works" (Psalm 104:24, today's key verse). "Manifold" underscores that magnitude and breadth of creation's elements. In the vision of the psalmist, and in the perception of any who live with senses wide open to the created order, that is cause for praise of the Creator.

### All Things Wise and Wonderful

The psalmist testifies to another decisive cause for our praise of God's creative work: "In wisdom you have made them all" (104:24). The complex diversity of creation, and the interdependence it results in for all earth's creatures, is seen by the psalmist as a sign of God's wisdom. It is a theme echoed in the line of the hymn that stands as this section's title: "all things wise and wonderful, the Lord God made them all."

While the diversity of creation may be obvious to our eyes and minds, asserting God's wisdom in the creation of all things may at times be more difficult, especially when individual elements of creation are seen in isolation. Do you easily admit to God's wisdom in creating mosquitoes or black widow spiders? Years ago, my wife and I attended a district gathering of clergy and laity offering a number of workshops. In the workshop my wife attended, a colleague and friend of mine was expounding on the sacredness of every element in creation. "Name one thing in the world that does not carry the sacred within it!" he exclaimed at the end to make his point. My wife spoke up: "kitty litter." At which point, Don became speechless (a rare thing!) and walked out of the room while everyone erupted in laughter.

Taken in isolation, lifted out of context from the whole picture of creation, there are likely many things we could single out and question as to their possessing any hint of God's wisdom. But to defend my friend Don's zeal, creation is not made of a zillion independent, stand-alone elements that have no relationship to the whole. We do not experience creation as single isolated pieces. Creation is a whole cloth. While we may question and struggle to see the wisdom of some individual element of creation, taken together all those individual elements testify to God's wisdom. Even the ones we tend to value less. Even the ones we may have phobias about. For in ways that we have only begun to understand, the diversity and complexity of creation actually underscore our interdependence for our well-being on the well-being of all of God's created order.

### Stewards of Creation

The wisdom of that interdependence is celebrated in the ways this psalm links human existence in particular to the rhythms of nature and harvest and our labors. Such wisdom seen in the balance of all things is the passion of folks who advocate for the health of the environment against abuses of individual elements of it. Of all persons, individuals and communities of faith bear a special calling for ecological advocacy. It derives, in part, from the vision and celebration of this psalm. It owes to the primal account of creation in Genesis 1, where every day of God's fashioning the earth and all its creatures—not just the day of human creation—is punctuated with God's valuation: "and God saw that it was good." One cannot despoil what God declares "good" without in some way acting contrary to God's purposes in creation.

Passages like Psalm 104 and Genesis 1 assert our calling to be stewards of creation, not simply consumers of its gifts. Some seek escape from this vocation by appealing to verses that speak of human "dominion" over creation (Genesis 1:26, 28). The problem with that attitude is this: Dominion is an idea associated with rule and authority. Not just in Genesis 1, but Psalm 104 and other creation allusions in Scripture: God is the one who holds final rule and sway. So if we are to exercise dominion faithfully in creation, our example must follow that of God's dominion. And the dominion of God in Psalm 104,

as in those other creation passages, is exercised in the bestowing of life, not life's abuse; it is in the fashioning of myriad species, not the systematic eradication of one or more. Faithful dominion is stewardship of the gifts of creation over time, not exacting what I can for me and my generation, and an attitude of "too bad for those who follow."

Whenever the language of faith is invoked to justify actions that diminish creation's diversity and complexity, simply to satisfy immediate wants, faith becomes a servant of greed. And the dominion of God is exchanged for the dominion of special interests willing to go to any lengths to excuse a failure of faithful stewardship.

Individuals and communities of faith are called not simply to praise the God who created all, but to carry on God's good work of nurturing the richness of creation. Ideally, the reason for doing so comes in the joyful recognition of God's wisdom in fashioning all things. Additionally, the reason for doing so comes in enlightened self-interest that recognizes the interdependence God has woven into creation. We cannot pollute the waters without the consequences showing up in our own bodies. We cannot strip or toxify the topsoil without harming the earth's ability to produce food. We cannot dump waste in the oceans unceasingly without creating dead zones where fish and crustaceans once thrived. And we cannot mask inattention to changes in climate and ecological balance with arguments that twist science as well as ignore the responsibility of faithful stewardship on behalf of the Creator whose wisdom made all things.

# SHARING THE SCRIPTURE

## PREPARING TO LEAD

### Preparing Our Hearts

Ponder this week's devotional reading from Psalm 8, where the writer acknowledges not only God's majesty but also the dignity and role of human beings in creation. How does the psalmist's depiction of humanity make you feel? What are you doing to take care of God's good creation?

Pray that you and the students will give thanks to God for the place of humanity within creation.

### Preparing Our Minds

Study the background Scripture from Psalm 104 and the lesson Scripture from Psalm 104:1-4, 24-30.

Consider this question: *What does the complexity and diversity of creation tell us about the world in which we live?*

Write on newsprint:
- ❏ questions for Goal 3 in Sharing the Scripture.
- ❏ information for next week's lesson, found under Continue the Journey.
- ❏ activities for further spiritual growth in Continue the Journey.

Determine how you might use any of the features that precede the first lesson of this quarter in today's session. Recommend one or more activities from Faith in Action: Acting as a Cocreator with God if you have not already done so.

## LEADING THE CLASS

### (1) Gather to Learn

❖ Welcome everyone and pray that those who have come today will give thanks for the wondrous diversity of God's creation.

❖ Form small groups and give each a sheet of newsprint and marker. Invite participants to list examples of God's creation that they were able to see, hear, taste, touch, or smell on their way to church this morning. Set a time limit and challenge the groups to list as many items as they can.

❖ Call the groups together to present their findings. Note that there will be differences, depending on the route and distance participants traveled to get here. Emphasize the number of different examples and their diversity by counting the different entries. Point out that some items may be small, like a pebble in the street, whereas others may be quite large, as a stand of tall trees or a towering mountain. Also note that some items may be seasonal, such as snowflakes on the windshield, while others are more permanent, such as a lake.

❖ Read aloud today's focus statement: **When we experience the vast diversity of creation we wonder how it is all held together. What does this complexity tell us about the world in which we live? The psalmist praises God for sustaining creation.**

### (2) Goal 1: Ponder the Diversity and Complexity of God's Creation

❖ Solicit a volunteer to read Psalm 104:1-4.

❖ Invite the group to identify the poetic images the writer uses to describe God and God's creation.

❖ Use The Weave of Creation in Interpreting the Scripture to help the adults recognize the diversity and interdependence of creation by relating that to weaving a rag rug.

❖ Call on another volunteer to read Psalm 104:24-30.

❖ Use information in Psalm 104:25-30 in Understanding the Scripture to discuss the dependency of all creation upon God.

❖ Challenge the class to "name one thing in the world that does not carry the sacred within it."

### (3) Goal 2: Affirm God's Wisdom in Ordering the World

❖ Focus on today's key verse, Psalm 104:24 by rereading this verse in unison.

❖ Note especially the reference to the role of God's wisdom in creating all things.

❖ Invite the students to identify examples of God's wisdom in creation. (They may think of things such as gills for breathing underwater or heavy coats of fur for surviving in cold climates or the ability to camouflage oneself to escape detection by predators.)

❖ Read or retell All Things Wise and Wonderful in Interpreting the Scripture to point out the diversity of creation, which the psalmist sees as a sign of God's wisdom.

❖ **Option:** Distribute hymnals and encourage the class to sing or read "All Things Bright and Beautiful" to emphasize the scope of God's creative power.

### (4) Goal 3: Honor God by Working to Preserve the World's Magnificent Diversity

❖ Read: **An ecosystem may be defined as "a complex set of** **relationships among the living resources, habitats, and residents of an area." Although ecosystems vary in size, everything that lives within that ecosystem is dependent on other parts of the ecosystem. When all the parts are in balance, the ecosystem is considered healthy and sustainable. When any parts are damaged or gone, everything else in the ecosystem feels the impact of the missing element.**

❖ Encourage the students to ponder silently the importance of ecosystems and their parts, all of which God has created.

❖ Bring everyone together and suggest that as the people of God we are called to be stewards of God's creation, to care for it in such a way that ecosystems can remain healthy and sustainable.

❖ Discuss these questions and list ideas on newsprint:

1. **Where in our community do you see healthy ecosystems?**
2. **Where in our community do you see damaged ecosystems that need the care of God's stewards to heal?** (Perhaps a river or streambed has become polluted with debris or unhealthy water containing toxins, or both. Possibly a wildfire has left soil vulnerable to erosion and mudslides. Maybe air is so full of smog that people find it difficult to breathe.)
3. **What actions can we, as either individual Christians or as members of this congregation, or both, take to help ailing ecosystems?**

❖ Spend some time working together or in small groups to brainstorm ideas for action and how the problem can be approached. The group(s) will need to answer questions, which you will write on newsprint, such as:

- Where can we find information about the problem and the solutions that have been—or are being—tried?
- Who can help us network with other interested parties?
- With which government agencies do we need to interact?
- How much might this project require in terms of time and money?

❖ Call the groups together to report on their findings. Take a poll to determine who is willing to make a commitment to take the next step.

*(5) Continue the Journey*

❖ Pray that as the learners depart they will take action to preserve and protect God's diverse creation.

❖ Post information for next week's session on newsprint for the students to copy:

- **Title: All Creation Praises God**
- **Background Scripture: Psalm 148**
- **Lesson Scripture: Psalm 148**
- **Focus of the Lesson: We think that nature exists for our benefit alone. For what purpose was the world created? The psalmist commands every element of creation to join the** chorus of praise for all that God has created.

❖ Challenge the adults to grow spiritually by completing one or more of these activities related to this week's session.

(1) **Research organizations that work to protect creation. Some examples include Creation Justice Ministries, Sierra Club, Oceana, Environmental Defense Fund, and League of Conservation Voters. Choose at least one that focuses on your concerns and support the organization as an advocate, volunteer, or financial contributor.**

(2) **Read a book about biodiversity, such as *The Diversity of Life* by Edward O. Wilson, to better understand the complexity and interdependence of God's good creation.**

(3) **Participate in a clean-up day in your community to rid streets and bodies of water of debris.**

❖ Sing or read aloud "Many and Great, O God."

❖ Conclude today's session by leading the class in this benediction, which is adapted from Galatians 5:22-23, the key verses for February 26: **Empower us to go forth to bear the fruit of the Spirit, which is love, joy, peace, patience, kindness, generosity, faithfulness, gentleness, and self-control. Amen.**

## UNIT 2: PRAISE FOR AND FROM GOD'S CREATION

# ALL CREATION PRAISES GOD

---

### PREVIEWING THE LESSON

**Lesson Scripture:** Psalm 148
**Background Scripture:** Psalm 148
**Key Verse:** Psalm 148:5

**Focus of the Lesson:**
We think that nature exists for our benefit alone. For what purpose was the world created? The psalmist commands every element of creation to join the chorus of praise for all that God has created.

**Goals for the Learners:**
(1) to acknowledge that creation exists primarily to praise God, not to meet our physical needs.
(2) to exult in the wonders of God's creation.
(3) to treat the things of nature with greater respect as befits their divine purpose.

**Supplies:**
Bibles, newsprint and marker, paper and pencils, hymnals

---

### READING THE SCRIPTURE

NRSV

Lesson Scripture: Psalm 148

¹Praise the LORD!

Praise the LORD from the heavens;
   praise him in the heights!

²Praise him, all his angels;
   praise him, all his host!

³Praise him, sun and moon;
   praise him, all you shining stars!

CEB

Lesson Scripture: Psalm 148

¹Praise the LORD!

Praise the LORD from heaven!
   Praise God on the heights!

²Praise God, all of you who are his
   messengers!

Praise God, all of you who
   comprise his heavenly forces!

⁴Praise him, you highest heavens,
and you waters above the heavens!
**⁵Let them praise the name of the
Lord,
for he commanded and they
were created.**
⁶He established them forever and
ever;
he fixed their bounds, which
cannot be passed.
⁷Praise the Lord from the earth,
you sea monsters and all deeps,
⁸fire and hail, snow and frost,
stormy wind fulfilling his
command!
⁹Mountains and all hills,
fruit trees and all cedars!
¹⁰Wild animals and all cattle,
creeping things and flying birds!
¹¹Kings of the earth and all peoples,
princes and all rulers of the earth!
¹²Young men and women alike,
old and young together!
¹³Let them praise the name of the
Lord,
for his name alone is exalted;
his glory is above earth and
heaven.
¹⁴He has raised up a horn for his
people,
praise for all his faithful,
for the people of Israel who are
close to him.
Praise the Lord!

³Sun and moon, praise God!
All of you bright stars, praise God!
⁴You highest heaven, praise God!
Do the same, you waters that are
above the sky!
**⁵Let all of these praise the Lord's
name
because God gave the command
and they were created!**
⁶God set them in place always and
forever.
God made a law that will not be
broken.
⁷Praise the Lord from the earth,
you sea monsters and all you
ocean depths!
⁸Do the same, fire and hail, snow
and smoke,
stormy wind that does what God
says!
⁹Do the same, you mountains,
every single hill,
fruit trees, and every single cedar!
¹⁰Do the same, you animals—wild
or tame—
you creatures that creep along and
you birds that fly!
¹¹Do the same, you kings of the earth
and every single person,
you princes and every single ruler
on earth!
¹²Do the same, you young men—
young women too!—
you who are old together with
you who are young!
¹³Let all of these praise the Lord's
name
because only God's name is high
over all.
Only God's majesty is over earth
and heaven.
¹⁴God raised the strength of his
people,
the praise of all his faithful ones—
that's the Israelites,
the people who are close to him.
Praise the Lord!

# UNDERSTANDING THE SCRIPTURE

**Introduction.** The 150 psalms in the Old Testament are a remarkably diverse collection of ancient Israel's worship resources. There are songs of praise, songs of thanksgiving, songs of trust, songs of lament—and single psalms frequently combine two or more of these elements. Each of those categories reflects both individual and communal expressions of these themes. This session's psalm, for example, is a song inviting praise not simply from the community of Israel but from all of creation. The Book of Psalms as a whole consists of five "books" (1–41, 42–72, 73–89, 90–106, and 107–150) that some traditions associate with the five books of the Pentateuch or Torah. Perhaps related to that, the final five psalms (of which today's is one) form a distinct subgroup in that fifth book of the psalms. All songs of praises, they are further linked by each one beginning and ending with the Hebrew *hallelujah*—literally, "Praise the LORD!"

**Psalm 148:1-4.** The psalm begins, as noted above, with the Hebrew exclamation that comes to us in English as *hallelujah*. The psalm's dominant call for praise of God is clearly established in these opening verbs. "Praise" occurs as an imperative verb eight times in these opening four verses, setting the tone for the summoning of creation's praise that follows. The inclusivity of the invitation extended to creation is reflected in these opening verses by the repeated use of "all" (in regards here to angels, hosts, and stars). These first four verses aim the invitation initially at elements of creation that are above the earth. "Heavens" is a term that

can be understood as both an astronomical reference (the "locale" of sky and celestial bodies as noted in the psalm with sun and moon and stars) and a theological referent (the realm of God and celestial beings as noted in the psalm by angels and hosts). Unlike our modern understanding of "host" as someone who welcomes others into home or some other place, "host" in the Old Testament and the ancient Middle East in general is a military term. Its reference to armies and soldiers came to be applied to the "legions" God has in command. Taken as a whole, the elements of creation summoned to praise in these verses hearken back to Genesis 1:6-8, 14-18, where they are fashioned by God as part of the created order.

**Psalm 148:5-6.** The heavenly beings and celestial bodies are now given reason for their summons to praise: God had created them. Verse 5 lifts up the linkage of their creation with God's "command." Command is a word frequently used in the Old Testament in reference to God's giving of law. While much of that usage occurs in the law-giving narratives following the Exodus from Egypt, this same word appears in the Genesis 2 creation narrative, when God commands Adam that he may eat fruit from all the trees in the garden except for the tree of knowledge (2:16). Linking command with creation also is suggestive of God's authoritative word in Genesis 1 where God speaks creation into being ("And God said . . ."). In verse 6, another detail of the creation of the "heavens" is declared that again traces back to the creation narrative in Genesis 1: "He [God] fixed their bounds which cannot be passed." Genesis 1:6-8 relates God's fashioning the "dome" that separates (fixes boundaries) between the waters above and those below, making life in between possible. The flood narrative describes the disastrous effects when those bounds are temporarily lifted, and the waters above and below are unleashed (Genesis 7:11).

**Psalm 148:7-12.** These verses in the psalm shift the chorus summoned to praise from the things above to all things on earth. Most of the elements of "earth" called to praise are framed in pairs throughout these verses, with one exception: "stormy wind fulfilling God's command" (148:8). The singularity of this expression among the pairs, intentionally or unintentionally, draws attention to the two Hebrew words used there. "Stormy "translates the same word used in 2 Kings 2:1 where the "whirlwind" takes Elijah up into heaven, and also in Job 38:1 as the "whirlwind" from which God answers Job. The word elicits an image of chaotic power, parallel to Canaanite deities (Baal in particular) associated with storms. Yet Psalm 148 joins this adjective with the Hebrew word translated here as "wind," but as noted in earlier sessions translated elsewhere as "breath" or "spirit." The irony in linking "storm" and "wind" in Psalm 148 arises out of the assertion in Genesis 1:2, where the wind/spirit of God moves over the face of the (chaotic) waters as the prelude to creation. Psalm 148:7-10 otherwise consists of pairings involving both animate and inanimate creations found on earth, including a mysterious reference to "sea monsters" (see also Genesis 1:21). Verses 11-12 shift to pairings of human life. The singling out of the most powerful of persons (kings, princes, rulers), who ordinarily might be seen as the recipients of praise, asserts that no one is above the summons to praise. This inclusiveness is further underscored by the concluding lines about men and women, young and old. No one is left out.

**Psalm 148:13-14.** These verses, similar to the function of verses 5-6, state the reasons for all of humanity's call to praise God. The first reason is a general assertion of God's glory and the greatness of God's name or renown. The second reason moves in the more specific direction of God's redemptive activity. In the symbolism of Judaism and the ancient near East, "horn" served as a symbol for power. (For example, Daniel 8 uses "horn" no less than nine times in reference to dynastic lines and kingdoms.) The declaration that God has "raised up a horn for his people" (148:14) is an allusion to God's acts of power exercised on behalf of Israel. The final verse of the psalm confirms the "closeness" existing between Israel and God, leaving it to the reader (or singer) of the psalm to wonder whether the closeness speaks more of a feeling of Israel for God, or God for Israel—or something of both. At the very end comes the *hallelujah* with which the psalm began.

# INTERPRETING THE SCRIPTURE

### *Part of the Hallelujah Chorus*

George Frideric Handel composed his "Hallelujah" chorus as part of a larger oratorio known as *Messiah*. But Handel's is not the first "Hallelujah" chorus. It could be argued that our psalm today is one of its most ancient predecessors, along with the Psalms 146, 147, 149, and 150 that all begin and end and are sprinkled throughout with the cry "praise the Lord!"

There are aspects of Handel's "Hallelujah" chorus that help unpack the meaning and implications of Psalm 148. First and foremost, Handel's work relies on a rich variety of voices: soprano, alto, tenor, and bass. I am aware of no version of the chorus that is written to be sung in unison. The chorus would simply not be the same without that diversity. The psalm makes that same point on a cosmic scale. The psalm does not just beckon the faithful alone to praise. The psalm does not just beckon humankind alone to praise. The psalm beckons all creation to praise—the voices so summoned belong to sea monsters and cedars, princes and stars, all peoples and all deeps. Handel's four-part harmonies are a mere hint of the myriad parts invited to lift their voices in God's praise.

Handel's "Hallelujah" chorus brings yet another insight into the breadth of this psalm's praise. As Handel's chorus begins and ends, all voices are singing the same words at the same time, albeit in parts. But then, something happens. The vocal parts split off, not only singing different words from one another but doing so in different timing. The result,

however, is not cacophony but symphony. The voices and times blend into a moving force of *hallelujahs* that reach an eventual crescendo. Consider that movement at work in the psalm— and in our own journeys of faith. Life does not come strictly metered, so that we all must fall lockstep into the same rhythm at every moment. The diversity of God's praise blends the slow quiet trust when grief is met with hope, along with the quickened pace of joy when we rejoice in a child's birth or at faith's confession.

The point of life and faith is not to force everything into feeling what we feel at the moment as cause for praise. And as the psalm underscores by its inclusion of all creation in the chorus and not just humankind: The point of life and faith is not for one part of creation to consider themselves (or ourselves) as superior to all other parts. Psalm 104's insight of "in wisdom God made them all" (104:24) is a note sounded in Psalm 148 by its making no distinctions between the value of praise summoned from "kings of the earth" and the praise summoned from "creeping things and flying birds" (148:11). Each part is valued. Each part is woven into the whole by God's hand. Our calling is not to distinguish between which part is needed most or least. Our calling is to sing our part, to render our praise in the times as they come to us, to cry out our *hallelujah* in praise of the One whose wisdom fashioned all. Hallelujah!

### *"Wow" as Prayer and Praise*

In an interview with NPR (National Public Radio), Anne Lamott offered these words about her book titled *Help, Thanks, Wow: The Three Essential Survival Prayers*: "Wow is the praise prayer. The prayer where we're finally speechless. . . . Wow is the prayer of wonder."

Psalm 148 is one extended "Wow!" uttered from a creation in awe of the Creator. "Wow" gets us closer to the meaning of *hallelujah*—and to its frequent use ("Praise the Lord") throughout this psalm. For what else can the psalmist finally say, and what else can we say, when the whole of creation comes into view with its God-given mystery and beauty in full bloom? Wow—*hallelujah!*

The first session of this unit on psalms that render praise for and from creation contained this quotation from the *Westminster Shorter Catechism*: "Man's chief end is to glorify God, and enjoy him forever." Psalm 148 could well be heard to add an addendum to the human purpose: to enjoy God's creation. For if faith calls upon us to honor God and rejoice in God's works, surely creation—the very handiwork of God—merits enjoyment grounded in praise.

God did not fashion us to be dour-faced ascetics who separate ourselves from all things material in a quest to center on the "spiritual." My working definition of spirituality is the awareness and responsiveness to the presence of God. If Genesis 1 and Psalm 148 are right, as I believe they are, discerning and responding to the presence of God leads us deeper into creation rather than out and away from it. Indeed, spirituality devoid of a delight in creation—the *hallelujah* of the psalmist, the "wow" of Anne Lamott—is a mere shadow of the real thing.

To confess God as Creator is to confess awe in the midst of creation. For in the rich diversity of creation—ranging from strands of DNA to glacial peaks, from the delicate intricacies of spiderwebs and snowflakes to the overwhelming sights of oceans stretching out of view or forests carpeting ridges upon ridges—we find ourselves standing on holy ground, our speech and faith reduced to the "wow" of praise.

### Praise Begets Ethics

To confess God as Creator has an aim in addition to awe and praise: to generate an ethic consistent with that confession. Once we confess God as Creator of all, we not only make a statement about creation's inherent value but we also acknowledge accountability to the One by whose hands all has come into being. And central to that accountability is how we, as one of God's creations, treat the rest of God's creations.

A key argument concerning what is entailed in human responsibility within and for creation arises in Genesis 1:26, 28, where God is said to grant dominion for creation to human hands. Too often, that endowment has been misunderstood as justifying an ethic of "anything goes" when it comes to human use—and abuse—of creation. But nowhere in Genesis or anywhere else does God indicate such dominion supersedes God's own dominion. Humanity is not given a higher authority than God when it comes to the treatment of creation. Indeed, the notion of God's dominion offers a helpful insight into what might be expected of the exercise of what authority has been entrusted into human hands. For when God exercises dominion, what happens? Life is called into being. Creation takes shape and is nurtured. The ethic of praise suggests those same ends and purposes for our treatment, our "dominion," of creation as those for whom creation in the image of God is not so much an entitlement as a responsibility.

The ethic generated by praise of God for creation summons us to ask: Do the things we do in and to this world further or endanger creation's life and diversity? Do we treat creation with the same respect and care with which God fashioned this marvelous world? To praise God with and for creation involves an ethic of respect and stewardship for all that God has fashioned, lest our praise ring hollow by our treatment of God's handiwork—including the way we treat one another.

---

# SHARING THE SCRIPTURE

## PREPARING TO LEAD

### Preparing Our Hearts

Ponder this week's devotional reading from Psalm 150. Read aloud these words of praise. Hear the instruments praising God. Imagine all living beings praising the God of creation. Ask yourself: Do I regularly praise God with such fervor? Does my congregation regularly lift such joyous praise?

Pray that you and the students will offer joyous praise that invites others to praise God as well.

### Preparing Our Minds

Study the background Scripture and the lesson Scripture, which are both from Psalm 148.

Consider this question: *For what purpose was the world created?*

Write on newsprint:

❏ information for next week's lesson, found under Continue the Journey.
❏ activities for further spiritual growth in Continue the Journey.

Determine how you might use any of the features that precede the first lesson of this quarter in today's session. This would be an appropriate week to suggest an activity from Faith in Action: Acting as a Cocreator with God.

## LEADING THE CLASS

### (1) Gather to Learn

❖ Welcome everyone and pray that those who have come today will praise God.

❖ Read this information from the May 1, 2011, blog, "The Ecologist": **According to philosopher Dr. Kate Rawls, the attempt by the United Kingdom's Department for Environment, Food and Rural Affairs "to put a price tag on nature with its National Ecosystem Assessment may reinforce the dangerous conceit that our own place in ecosystems is more important than any other. . . . Early environmental ethicist Aldo Leopold says "we abuse land because we see it as a commodity belonging to us. When we see land as a community to which we belong, we may begin to use it with love and respect."**

❖ Ask: **What kinds of shifts occur in our thinking and behavior when** we see that nature exists in its own right and not simply as a tool that humans can use, use up, and abuse?

❖ Read aloud today's focus statement: **We think that nature exists for our benefit alone. For what purpose was the world created? The psalmist commands every element of creation to join the chorus of praise for all that God has created.**

*(2) Goal 1: Acknowledge that Creation Exists Primarily to Praise God, Not to Meet Our Physical Needs*

❖ Distribute hymnals that include a Psalter and read Psalm 148 responsively. If you do not have access to such a Psalter, select one volunteer to read this psalm.

❖ Form two teams (or multiples of two if the group is large) and give each one a sheet of newsprint and marker. One team is to list all who are being called to praise God. The other is to list reasons for praising God.

❖ Call everyone together and ask a spokesperson from each group to report.

❖ Ask: **What does this psalm suggest to you about your relationship to the Creator and the Creator's relationship to creation?**

*(3) Goal 2: Exult in the Wonders of God's Creation*

❖ Read "Wow" as Prayer and Praise in Interpreting the Scripture. Invite participants to "talk back" to Anne Lamott by commenting on how her ideas on "wow" prayer reflect their own ideas regarding prayers of praise.

❖ Form small groups and encourage the adults to talk with a group about an experience of creation that truly "wowed" them. The experience might have been something commonplace though unforgettable, such as holding a newborn for the first time. It might have occurred in a backyard when the night sky was ablaze with a meteorite shower. Or it might have happened when a student visited a famous natural site, such as Niagara Falls or the Grand Canyon and was bowled over by the grandeur of the place.

❖ Bring everyone together and try to identify the types of experiences that seemed to cause class members to sing praise to God.

*(4) Goal 3: Treat Things of Nature with Greater Respect as Befits Their Divine Purpose*

❖ Read one or more of the following scenarios and invite participants to answer the questions:

• **Scenario 1: You live in a drought-stricken area where wildfires are a constant source of concern. Elected officials have curtailed water usage, but a neighbor is so proud of his stunning green lawn that he continues using water to irrigate it, simply because he has the money to do so. What will you say to help him understand that he cannot waste this precious resource? What alternatives might you offer to the green lawn he so cherishes?**

• **Scenario 2: You have a co-worker who brags about her dog. Yet she often mentions some action that clearly shows disrespect to this animal that is able to feel and experience emotions. She brags about how long the dog can sit in his crate without need-**

ing food, water, or a bathroom break, thereby allowing your coworker to arrive home very late. Moreover, she takes little time to interact with her dog, so SusieQ is neither exercised nor well trained. As a responsible dog owner, what do you tell her? What suggestions do you make? Are there steps you'd be willing to take if this dog is not treated more humanely?

- Scenario 3: You accept an invitation for a cruise with a friend who likes to go boating and are shocked to find that he just throws trash overboard into the river. He doesn't seem to care if the water is clean, as long as he doesn't have to haul trash back home for proper disposal. What do you tell him about how his behavior is affecting the water, the life that exists in the water, and other people who want to boat or swim?

*(5) Continue the Journey*

❖ Pray that as the learners depart, they will seek a greater reverence for the natural world that God has created.

❖ Post information for next week's session on newsprint for the students to copy:

- Title: Re-created to Live in Harmony
- Background Scripture: Galatians 3:26–4:7
- Lesson Scripture: Galatians 3:26–4:7
- Focus of the Lesson: Differences of race, class, and gender make it hard for people

to get along. How can we live in harmony? Paul tells the Galatians that through Christ we have received the Spirit, making us heirs of God and bringing us into a community of oneness where human differences are no longer divisive.

❖ Challenge the adults to grow spiritually by completing one or more of these activities related to this week's session.

(1) Notice media reports about nature. Is nature viewed as a commodity, which has economic value, to be used by humanity? Is nature understood as something having value in its own right? What might you imagine that God would be saying about the attitude of nature that predominates in these reports?

(2) Evaluate your own attitude toward nature: Does it exist primarily for the benefit of humans or does God have some other purpose for it? How do your behaviors reflect what you claim to be your attitude?

(3) Read one of the final five psalms each day this week. Let these words of praise remind you of God's goodness and greatness.

❖ Sing or read aloud "How Great Thou Art."

❖ Conclude today's session by leading the class in this benediction, which is adapted from Galatians 5:22-23, the key verses for February 26: Empower us to go forth to bear the fruit of the Spirit, which is love, joy, peace, patience, kindness, generosity, faithfulness, gentleness, and self-control. Amen.

## UNIT 3: THE BIRTHING OF A NEW COMMUNITY
# RE-CREATED TO LIVE IN HARMONY

---

### PREVIEWING THE LESSON

**Lesson Scripture:** Galatians 3:26–4:7
**Background Scripture:** Galatians 3:26–4:7
**Key Verse:** Galatians 3:28

**Focus of the Lesson:**
Differences of race, class, and gender make it hard for people to get along. How can we live in harmony? Paul tells the Galatians that through Christ we have received the Spirit, making us heirs of God and bringing us into a community of oneness where human differences are no longer divisive.

**Goals for the Learners:**
(1) to discover the unity of Christians based on the saving work of Christ and the Holy Spirit.
(2) to appreciate that through Christ believers are all one in the church.
(3) to examine themselves for biased attitudes toward other believers.

**Supplies:**
Bibles, newsprint and marker, paper and pencils, hymnals, clear glass or cup, water, vegetable oil, liquid food coloring, toothpick

---

### READING THE SCRIPTURE

**NRSV**
Lesson Scripture: Galatians 3:26–4:7
<sup>26</sup>[F]or in Christ Jesus you are all children of God through faith. <sup>27</sup>As many of you as were baptized into Christ have clothed yourselves with Christ. <sup>28</sup>**There is no longer Jew or Greek, there is no longer slave or free, there is no longer male and**

**CEB**
Lesson Scripture: Galatians 3:26–4:7
<sup>26</sup>You are all God's children through faith in Christ Jesus. <sup>27</sup>All of you who were baptized into Christ have clothed yourselves with Christ. <sup>28</sup>**There is neither Jew nor Greek; there is neither slave nor free; nor is there male and female, for you are**

**female; for all of you are one in Christ Jesus.** [29]And if you belong to Christ, then you are Abraham's offspring, heirs according to the promise.

[1]My point is this: heirs, as long as they are minors, are no better than slaves, though they are the owners of all the property; [2]but they remain under guardians and trustees until the date set by the father. [3]So with us; while we were minors, we were enslaved to the elemental spirits of the world. [4]But when the fullness of time had come, God sent his Son, born of a woman, born under the law, [5]in order to redeem those who were under the law, so that we might receive adoption as children. [6]And because you are children, God has sent the Spirit of his Son into our hearts, crying, "Abba! Father!" [7]So you are no longer a slave but a child, and if a child then also an heir, through God.

**all one in Christ Jesus.** [29]Now if you belong to Christ, then indeed you are Abraham's descendants, heirs according to the promise.

[1]I'm saying that as long as the heirs are minors, they are no different from slaves, though they really are the owners of everything. [2]However, they are placed under trustees and guardians until the date set by the parents. [3]In the same way, when we were minors, we were also enslaved by this world's system. [4]But when the fulfillment of the time came, God sent his Son, born through a woman, and born under the Law. [5]This was so he could redeem those under the Law so that we could be adopted. [6]Because you are sons and daughters, God sent the Spirit of his Son into our hearts, crying, "Abba, Father!" [7]Therefore, you are no longer a slave but a son or daughter, and if you are his child, then you are also an heir through God.

---

## UNDERSTANDING THE SCRIPTURE

**Introduction.** Galatia was not a single community or congregation being addressed by Paul. Galatia was an entire region in the center of what is now modern-day Turkey and a province of Rome administered from a city then called Ancyra (and now Ankara, the capital of Turkey). Paul does not name any Galatian cities in this epistle, so the letter apparently addresses some or all of the churches in this region. This plurality is underscored by Paul's opening line of "to the churches of Galatia" in 1:2. It is fitting to have portions of the Galatian correspondence selected to explore this unit's theme of The Birthing of a New Community. The pains of childbirth are very much evident in the opening chapters of Galatia, where Paul's ache at troubling developments in the Galatian churches leads to some of the most confrontational language in all of the Pauline Epistles. For example, in place of the usual opening thanksgiving for the church being addressed in Paul's other correspondence, Galatians moves directly from greetings (1:1-5) to the equivalent of *what are you doing?* (1:6-10). This opening salvo heightens the critical nature of Paul's ensuing passages in the epistle. Today's text regarding harmony and divisiveness is to be heard in the context of potentially fatal divisions that threaten the viability of these new communities being birthed in Galatia.

**Galatians 3:26.** Earlier in this chapter (3:6-7, 16-18), Paul touches on the themes of Abraham's offspring and inheritance. Now in 3:26, the connection of those earlier arguments with the Galatian communities is made clear. Those whom Paul addresses are identified as the children of God through their relationship with Christ. The word translated here as "children" will be used several more times, thus underscoring Paul's aim of establishing the unity of the Galatian believers in the metaphor of children within the same family. The assertion of their being children of God "in Christ Jesus" likewise draws a contrast with his earlier introduction of Abraham's descendants/offspring. This elevation of Christ above Abraham may owe to the general scholarly consensus that among the opponents Paul confronts in this epistle are some Jewish Christians who insist that Greek (Gentile) Christians must observe the law, including circumcision (see 2:1-14). Similarly, "through faith" in 3:26 furthers Paul's argument that even Abraham and those who are his true descendants demonstrate a life lived by faith rather than works of the law (3:6-9).

**Galatians 3:27-29.** Paul opens this section by asserting the shared experience of the Galatian Christians that marks them per the previous verse as "in Christ": baptism. Baptism thus lays the groundwork for Paul's ensuing declaration of the community's unity. The imagery of "clothing" oneself with Christ in baptism may reflect the practice in the early church of presenting new robes to those being baptized. Paul elsewhere uses the imagery of "clothing" oneself as a metaphor for taking on and practicing virtuous attributes (see Colossians 3:12-14). Paul's lifting up of Jew and Greek, male and female, slave and free, points to the very real diversity that is a given with the Galatian community. There is clearly conflict between the first two paired groups in this list within the Galatian communities. Otherwise, Paul would not elsewhere in this epistle have castigated those Jewish Christian who were advocating the necessity of circumcision for all believers. It is less clear if conflicts divided the other paired groups (male and female, slave and free). The closest parallel to such divisions Paul challenges elsewhere is 1 Corinthians 11:18-22. There, Paul condemns the abuse of the Lord's Supper that results from the rich feasting on food they bring to the meal preceding the sacrament while others go hungry. Paul's return in verse 29 to the themes of Abraham's offspring and heirs is used to set up what will be the focus of the opening verses of chapter 4.

**Galatians 4:1-3.** Underlying these verses was the relatively common custom in Hellenistic society of children coming under the care and tutelage of adult caretakers who were not their parents. The individuals charged with this responsibility could even be slaves. This helps one understand Paul's point in these verses as to how those who were "owners," in terms of an heir's future claim to inheritance, could be portrayed as under the supervision of individuals identified as "guardians" and "trustees" (both of those Greek words have uses specific to persons assigned to the care of children). In verse 3, Paul makes the comparison of this situation of heirs under guardians with the previous religious/spiritual status of the Galatians as under the authority of ("enslaved to") the "elemental spirits." There are several possibilities for what Paul means by this reference. It may refer to spiritual forces elsewhere described as "principalities" and "powers" (Ephesians 6:12 KJV; Colossians 1:16 KJV). More simply, it might mean that, before Christ, the Galatians were stuck in an immature phase of spiritual development.

**Galatians 4:4-7.** Paul uses the phrase "fullness of time" in Ephesians 1:10 to speak of God's plan of gathering all things in unity at the end of history. Here in Galatians 4:4, "fullness of time" is used in reference to God's sending of Christ as part of God's redemptive plan for unity asserted in 3:28. Verses 4b-6 reveal Paul's understanding of that redemptive purpose for the sake of our "adoption as children." "Redeem" is a term that indicates the making of a payment for the sake of recovering something (someone). The financial connection with this term can be seen in the Greek word, whose root *agora* literally referred to the public marketplace. Paul's use of "redeem" here is not in reference to sin but to the law. In the closing verses of this section, Paul identifies the consequences of this redemptive adoption as the bestowing of Christ's Spirit and our standing as heirs. The cry of Christ's Spirit of "Abba" uses a more familial address of "father," closer to an expression like "daddy" (see also Mark 14:36 and Romans 8:15 for the use of *abba*).

## INTERPRETING THE SCRIPTURE

### Unity in Christ

I remember an African American Lutheran pastor speaking to our seminary class on the theme of unity in the church. Those were the days when the worldwide ecumenical movement was in high gear, with high hopes of mergers and co-labors. It was also in the midst of the wind down of the Vietnam War and the stirrings of a scandal called Watergate. The country, and along with it the churches, was experiencing some deep fracture zones. Most appeals to church unity I had heard to that point emphasized the hard work it would take to achieve it. But what that Lutheran pastor asserted that day remains with me: Church unity is not a *task of* Christians; it is a *gift to* Christians. It is not so much up to us how we will create it, but rather how we will use (or ignore) it.

There is much that resonates between that message, seemingly so new to me then, and what Paul is trying to impress upon the Galatian community. Even the most superficial of readings of this epistle make clear that harmony is not the order of the day. Conflicts abound, not the least of which involve Paul and some whom he castigates for undermining that community. But at the core of what Paul says is this same notion of unity as a given. The determinative factor for harmony in the church and unity among its members do not trace to what we can hammer out in hard-fought agreements and not-always-easy compromises. Rather, unity in the church is what Christ has already bestowed upon us. Life in Christ is, by definition according to Paul, the basis for our unity. It is who Christ is that makes us who we are: one in Christ.

For Paul, we are marked by that truth in baptism. Sometimes, the argument that the early church only baptized those of sufficient age and understanding to profess faith, valid as it may be, has the detrimental effect of turning baptism into a human work. That is, who we are sets the parameters for its bestowal or not. But baptism, in the end, is not about what we bring to it. It is about the grace God freely bestows through its waters, a grace apprehended—not created—by faith. For that reason, Paul's choice of baptism as the primary mark of our unity in Christ is critical. It reminds us, as did that Lutheran pastor of my ministerial youth, that unity is a gracious given. We can be good or bad stewards of that unity, but we are not its creators. The creation of unity resides in the grace of Christ that makes us one. Like it or not, ready or not, we are one in Christ.

## Unity in the Midst of Diversity

Jew and Greek, slave and free, male and female: For Paul, those descriptions served as an accurate snapshot of the Galatian faith community. Even after Paul's startling litanies, "there is no longer . . ." in Galatians 3:28, you can be guaranteed that a snapshot taken of that community after hearing this verse would have shown the same view. Jews did not instantaneously become Greeks or vice versa. Sadly, Christian unity did not propel an emancipation of slaves in that age nor for many ages to come.

Men and women remained distinct, with some boundaries between them that Paul himself occasionally inexplicably continued to erect in spite of this verse in Galatians. The Galatians remained a diverse conglomeration in the midst of this unity that Paul declared and Christ made possible.

And that is good news for us. Because unless you live in a community that is utterly monotone and uniform to the point of dulling conformity, diversity remains the second-most basic fact of life in Christian community. In spite of those who would confuse lockstep conformity with Christian unity, diversity continues to remain the second-most basic fact of life in Christian community. Second-most because Paul has already asserted the fundamental truth of Christian community: We are *one* in Christ Jesus.

Just do not confuse "one" with necessitating "like me." That is, do not confuse unity in Christ with *that must mean everyone ought to believe the same way I do*. In place of "believe" in that previous sentence, feel free to substitute any number of verbs that still rise up to threaten the harmony of Christian community: for example, "vote" comes to mind; or perhaps "prefer worship to be done." For remember, as Paul strives to make clear: Christian unity is a Christ-given gift, not a human imposition of whatever our spiritual or political preferences happen to be.

Diversity, like unity, is God-given. The only matter to be settled by our efforts is how we will engage and nurture those gifts. How will we use the differing perspectives and experiences brought to the community by its varied members to enrich that unity, rather than being obsessed with how we will cajole or indoctrinate others to be as we are? Indeed, how will we appreciate what it means for Jews *and* Greeks, men *and* women—and feel free to add the pairings that sometimes are confused with polar opposites in our day—to belong to the one body in Christ Jesus?

### Looking in the Mirror

A long-ago advertisement for a tire manufacturer vaunted its products with the catchphrase: "where the rubber meets the road." It is well and good to speak glowingly of Christian unity and the values of diversity. The rubber meets the road when all of those lofty ideals come face to face with differences that inevitably arise in the midst of diversity—and when we see that it is not simply the prejudice of others that is the problem with holding to Christian unity, but the prejudices you and I bring to the table.

Who is it that you rail against: the fundamentalists, the liberals, the Bible-thumpers, the new-age-ists? One of my favorite targets is the intolerant. But in more reflective moments, I do need to ask: Is intolerance of the intolerant a virtue, or simply more of the same? And how is it for you? Who are the ones you would write out of the body of Christ? And

does it ever give you cause to consider how their longed-for absence from the body would diminish it . . . and might even diminish you?

Knowing one's own prejudices when it comes to our assessments of exceptions regarding our unity in Christ is a necessary first step before ever daring to charge the prejudice of others. That principle is akin to Jesus' teaching in both the Sermon on the Mount (Matthew 7:3-5) and the Sermon on the Plain (Luke 6:41-42). Failure to consider one's own distorted points of view is, in Jesus' assessment, hypocrisy—even if you have it right about another's failings. Why? Because change begins at home. Attitudes and actions that honor the church's unity and diversity are our responsibilities to keep, whether we perceive others doing so or not. We lead by example, not accusation.

Think of the ones in your particular community who may be at odds, as were the Galatians. With Paul as your guide, imagine what would result if "there is no longer . . . you are one in Christ Jesus" served as the byword for those parties, and for your part among them.

The thing is, you don't have to imagine it. You *are* one in Christ Jesus. That is the given. The task, the opportunity, is simply yet profoundly to live accordingly.

## SHARING THE SCRIPTURE

### PREPARING TO LEAD

#### Preparing Our Hearts

Ponder this week's devotional reading from Colossians 3:12-17. In verse 14 we are counseled to "clothe [ourselves] with love, which binds everything together in perfect harmony." What has been your experience in terms of love creating an atmosphere of harmony? How do compassion, kindness, humility, meekness, patience, and forgiveness reinforce harmony? What steps do you need to take to live more harmoniously with others?

Pray that you and the students will open your hearts and minds to all people in an attitude of love.

*Preparing Our Minds*

Study the background Scripture and the lesson Scripture, which are both from Galatians 3:26–4:7.

Consider this question: *How can you live in harmony, especially with people who are different from you?*

Write on newsprint:
❏ information for next week's lesson, found under Continue the Journey.
❏ activities for further spiritual growth in Continue the Journey.

Determine how you might use any of the features that precede the first lesson of this quarter in today's session.

Collect these supplies for the Gather to Learn activity: clear glass or cup, water, vegetable oil, liquid food coloring, and a toothpick.

Review information in Unity in the Midst of Diversity in Interpreting the Scripture for use with Goal 2.

## LEADING THE CLASS

*(1) Gather to Learn*

❖ Welcome everyone and pray that those who have come today will yearn for the unity that is theirs through Christ.

❖ Tell the class that you are going to do a scientific experiment, one that they may remember from school. Begin by pouring vegetable oil into a clear glass or measuring cup. Add an equal amount of water. (Just be sure

you have enough oil and water for people to see.) Ask the group to notice which liquid is on the top. (It will be the oil, since it is not as dense as water.) Then add one drop of food coloring. If it stays as a drop on top of the oil, move it with a toothpick until it dissipates into the water, thereby coloring the water.

❖ Ask: **What might this experiment suggest to us about how people interact with one another?**

❖ Read aloud today's focus statement: **Differences of race, class, and gender make it hard for people to get along. How can we live in harmony? Paul tells the Galatians that through Christ we have received the Spirit, making us heirs of God and bringing us into a community of oneness where human differences are no longer divisive.**

*(2) Goal 1: Discover the Unity of Christians Based on the Saving Work of Christ and the Holy Spirit*

❖ Read the Introduction in Understanding the Scripture to set the stage for our four-week study of Galatians.

❖ Enlist a volunteer to read Galatians 3:26–4:7.

❖ Discuss these questions:
1. **How does Paul use baptism to make his points about unity?** (See Galatians 3:27-29 in Understanding the Scripture.)
2. **What point is Paul making in Galatians 4:1-3?** (See these verses in Understanding the Scripture.)
3. **What are the consequences of our being redeemed by God?** (See Galatians 4:4-7 in Understanding the Scripture.)

**4. How would you summarize the connection Paul makes between unity among those who are in Christ and his saving work?**

*(3) Goal 2: Appreciate that Through Christ Believers Are All One in the Church*

❖ Read in unison today's key verse, Galatians 3:28.

❖ Use information from Unity in the Midst of Diversity in Interpreting the Scripture to help the class members recognize that although believers are all one in Christ, we are diverse people. Moreover, to be united in Christ does not mean that we all have to think and act alike. We can live harmoniously in love while also giving thanks for our differences.

❖ Post one or more sheets of newsprint and have markers available. Invite participants to make a graffiti board on which they randomly write characteristics of believers. Encourage as much diversity as possible. Examples include rich, poor, Republican, Democrat, Independent, names of racial or ethnic groups, children, teens, adults, workers, retirees.

❖ Direct the adults to step back to read the characteristics that have been noted. Ask:

**1. What do the characteristics that we have identified reveal about the nature of the church?**

**2. How can we affirm and expand this broad spectrum of characteristics while recognizing and appreciating that we are all one in Christ Jesus?**

*(4) Goal 3: Examine Oneself for Biased Attitudes Toward Other Believers*

❖ Read or retell Looking in the Mirror in Interpreting the Scripture.

❖ Distribute paper and pencils. Read the following questions, pausing for the class members to reflect silently and write brief answers. Note that participants will not be asked to read aloud their answers, so they need to be honest before God.

**1. Who is it that you rail against, even to the point of believing these groups should be excluded from the body of Christ?** (pause)

**2. Why do you believe such people should be excluded?** (pause)

**3. How might your attitude be changed if you really believed, as Paul wrote to the Galatians (3:28), that there are no divisions but rather "you are one in Christ Jesus"?** (pause)

❖ Bring everyone together and ask: **How can we as members of this class (or congregation) overcome our biases so as to be more open to and accepting of people who may in some way be different from us?**

*(5) Continue the Journey*

❖ Pray that as the learners depart, they will strive to put aside their biases and live in harmony with all.

❖ Post information for next week's session on newsprint for the students to copy:

■ **Title: New Birth Brings Freedom**
■ **Background Scripture: Galatians 4**

■ Lesson Scripture: Galatians 4:8-20

■ Focus of the Lesson: People are tempted to sacrifice freedom in order to gain a sense of security. What are the dangers of this trade-off? Paul rebuked the Galatians for trading the freedom Christ gives for slavery to religious legalism.

❖ Challenge the adults to grow spiritually by completing one or more of these activities related to this week's session.

(1) Plan to attend a service or event with a congregation that is different from yours, perhaps in terms of its racial or socioeconomic makeup or its theological leaning. The differences may be obvious, but look for similarities that you and this congregation share in Christ.

(2) Select one group of people you find difficult to relate to, perhaps by virtue of their race, language, gender identity, or theological leanings. Read about them. If possible, try to get to know someone in this group. How has your knowledge and relationship changed your attitude?

(3) Ponder what it means to be God's adopted child. How does this status affect your daily life?

❖ Sing or read aloud "Christ, from Whom All Blessings Flow."

❖ Conclude today's session by leading the class in this benediction, which is adapted from Galatians 5:22-23, the key verses for February 26: **Empower us to go forth to bear the fruit of the Spirit, which is love, joy, peace, patience, kindness, generosity, faithfulness, gentleness, and self-control. Amen.**

## UNIT 3: THE BIRTHING OF A NEW COMMUNITY
# NEW BIRTH
# BRINGS FREEDOM

### PREVIEWING THE LESSON

**Lesson Scripture:** Galatians 4:8-20
**Background Scripture:** Galatians 4
**Key Verse:** Galatians 4:9

### Focus of the Lesson:
People are tempted to sacrifice freedom in order to gain a sense of security. What are the dangers of this trade-off? Paul rebuked the Galatians for trading the freedom Christ gives for slavery to religious legalism.

### Goals for the Learners:
(1) to identify religious expectations and practices that diminish Christian freedom.
(2) to empathize with those who have been harmed by narrow religiosity.
(3) to challenge unhealthy attitudes toward religious practices or traditions.

### Supplies:
Bibles, newsprint and marker, paper and pencils, hymnals

### READING THE SCRIPTURE

NRSV
Lesson Scripture: Galatians 4:8-20

⁸Formerly, when you did not know God, you were enslaved to beings that by nature are not gods. ⁹Now, however, that you have come to know God, or rather to be known by God, how can you turn back again to the weak and beggarly elemental spirits? How can you want to be enslaved to them again? ¹⁰You are

CEB
Lesson Scripture: Galatians 4:8-20

⁸At the time, when you didn't know God, you were enslaved by things that aren't gods by nature. ⁹But now, after knowing God (or rather, being known by God), how can you turn back again to the weak and worthless world system? Do you want to be slaves to it again? ¹⁰You observe religious days and months

observing special days, and months, and seasons, and years. [11]I am afraid that my work for you may have been wasted.

[12]Friends I beg you, become as I am, for I also have become as you are. You have done me no wrong. [13]You know that it was because of a physical infirmity that I first announced the gospel to you; [14]though my condition put you to the test, you did not scorn or despise me, but welcomed me as an angel of God, as Christ Jesus. [15]What has become of the goodwill you felt? For I testify that, had it been possible, you would have torn out your eyes and given them to me. [16]Have I now become your enemy by telling you the truth? [17]They make much of you, but for no good purpose; they want to exclude you, so that you may make much of them. [18]It is good to be made much of for a good purpose at all times, and not only when I am present with you. [19]My little children, for whom I am again in the pain of childbirth until Christ is formed in you, [20]I wish I were present with you now and could change my tone, for I am perplexed about you.

and seasons and years. [11]I'm afraid for you! Perhaps my hard work for you has been for nothing.

[12]I beg you to be like me, brothers and sisters, because I have become like you! You haven't wronged me. [13]You know that I first preached the gospel to you because of an illness. [14]Though my poor health burdened you, you didn't look down on me or reject me, but you welcomed me as if I were an angel from God, or as if I were Christ Jesus! [15]Where then is the great attitude that you had? I swear that, if possible, you would have dug out your eyes and given them to me. [16]So then, have I become your enemy by telling you the truth? [17]They are so concerned about you, though not with good intentions. Rather, they want to shut you out so that you would run after them. [18]However, it's always good to have people concerned about you with good intentions, and not just when I'm there with you. [19]My little children, I'm going through labor pains again until Christ is formed in you. [20]But I wish I could be with you now and change how I sound, because I'm at a loss about you.

---

## UNDERSTANDING THE SCRIPTURE

**Galatians 4:1-7.** Please see comments on these verses in the previous session.

**Galatians 4:8-11.** "When you did not know God" (4:8) reminds the Galatians of their spiritual status as Gentiles, prior to their life in Christ which brought them into relationship with God (3:25-26). Returning to an assertion made in Galatians 4:3, Paul alludes to the prior "enslavement" of the Galatians to entities falsely elevated to the status of deity. That comment introduces a warning against another threat of enslavement facing the community. That appeal is being promoted by some Jewish-Christians who cajole the formerly enslaved Gentiles to embrace a new "enslavement" to the law. While Paul frames that argument elsewhere in terms of requiring circumcision (5:1-5), here he connects it to the observance of Jewish seasonal festivals. Writing in *The New Interpreter's Bible*, Richard B. Hays suggests a connection between these calendared observances and the "elemental spirits." These festivals were based on astronomical calendars that, in the ancient world, paralleled observances in pagan religions. Paul's issue with those who insist on strict observance of the "special days, and months, and seasons, and years" (4:10) is that they are "turning back" the Galatians into the same enslavement by elemental spirits that preceded their "turning" to Christ.

**Galatians 4:12-16.** Paul's invitation to the Galatians in verse 12 to "become as I am" echoes similar appeals to follow his example of faithful living (Philippians 3:17). Paul pairs that invitation here in verse 12 with his disclosure that he has "become as you are." This likely references Paul's decision to set aside any appeal he might have made previously to his Jewish orthodoxy (Philippians 3:4-6). His rationale was to radically identify with and live as a Gentile in order to further his mission among and on behalf of them (see 1 Corinthians 9:21). Paul's "physical infirmity" (4:13) is unknown to us, though the reference assumes the Galatians were acquainted with it and needed no explanation. Paul employs that detail here to both celebrate the Galatians' gracious acceptance of him in spite of it—and then to wonder openly what has become of such "welcome" by asking if he has become their enemy simply for telling the truth. That rhetorical question carries a subtle but distinct implication that those who oppose Paul are not telling the Galatians the truth when it comes to the "gospel" they pose as an alternative to Paul's.

**Galatians 4:17-20.** The verb "make much of" occurs three times in these verses to describe the efforts of his opponents to court the Galatians. The word is the origin of the English "zealous." The irony and force of Paul using it to indict his opponents is that he uses the adjective and noun forms of this word elsewhere to identify the zeal that drove his earlier persecution of the church. By implication, the opponents engage in the same zealotry that Paul did *prior* to his transformative experience on the Damascus road. The "exclusion" Paul alludes to in verse 17 likely is the attempt by his opponents to separate themselves from others in the community who do not follow their demand that the whole law must be observed to be one of Jesus' true followers. While much of Paul's Epistle to the Galatians carries a strident tone, verse 19 interjects a clear expression of Paul's fondness for the community as he addresses them as "my little children." It is to be noted that this same expression appears seven times in the First Letter of John. There, the author leans heavily on this familial expression to counter yet another instance of legalism threatening to divide the community (1 John 2:19). The intimacy Paul feels for the Galatians becomes even clearer in verse 19, when he invokes the imagery of being in the pain of childbirth in this crisis. His use of "again" in that imagery underscores Paul's experience of having been the one whose ministry among the Galatians resulted in the birthing of the church in that region.

**Galatians 4:21-26.** The core of Paul's message now comes to a head as he confronts those who wish to impose the law on the Gentile

Christians of Galatia by interpreting a critical narrative in that very law they would assert. The story of Sarah, Abraham, and Hagar can be reviewed in Genesis 16 and 21:1-21. That Paul does not recount the story, but simply interprets its meaning, presumes a close familiarity with the story that would be especially true for Jewish-Christians. That Paul's emphasis is upon the contrast of freedom and bondage is underscored by the fact that he never speaks of Sarah by name, but only as "the free woman" (4:23). Likewise, the children of these two women (Isaac and Ishmael) are never referred to by name, but only as the child of the promise or free woman and the child of the flesh or slave. The dual reference to "Jerusalem" in the interpretive teaching in verses 25-26 is intriguing. "Present" Jerusalem may subtly make reference to the Jerusalem church, some of whose leaders were at the forefront of Judaizing tendencies in the church that Paul has already confronted (2:11-12). Sinai is the place associated with the giving of law to Moses (Exodus 19:16-25). "New" Jerusalem had long-standing traditions in Judaism with the coming of the messianic age (Ezekiel 40 and following). The church would later incorporate these into its vision of the coming sovereign realm of God at the end of history (Revelation 21:2 and following).

**Galatians 4:27-31.** Paul now incorporates a quotation from Isaiah 54:1 in a further exaltation of the once-barren Sarah and her child. This verse in Isaiah opens the final of its "Zion" oracles that celebrate the restoration of Jerusalem following exile. Those who may have claimed the "authority" of Jerusalem are now confronted by Paul's appropriation of that symbol to buttress his own argument: the true children of Abraham and Sarah (3:29), the true heirs to the Abrahamic promise and freedom, are those born "according to the Spirit" (4:29; see also 4:6). Reflecting the ill feelings between Paul and the opponents, the quotation in verse 30 of Genesis 21:10 of the harsh judgment by Sarah against Hagar could be heard as Paul's implicit advice for the Galatians as to what they should do with his opponents.

## INTERPRETING THE SCRIPTURE

### Bad Trades

Have you ever made a trade or exchange that you lived to regret?

Examples abound. No true Chicago Cubs fan would ever repeat the trade that obtained Ernie Broglio, a decent but easily forgotten pitcher from the St. Louis Cardinals, in exchange for a young outfielder named Lou Brock, who went on to become a base-stealer extraordinaire and member of the Baseball Hall of Fame. Or, to cast this truth in Old Testament terms: had he known what his brother was up to, no matter how hungry he was, Esau would never have traded the family birthright to Jacob for a bowl of stew. Or perhaps closer in spirit to the crisis at the heart of this passage from Galatians is a quotation from Benjamin Franklin: "Those who would give up essential Liberty, to purchase a little temporary Safety, deserve neither Liberty nor Safety."

"Essential liberty." One might say that phrase could be an apt summary of Paul's central theme of his Epistle to the Galatians. For Paul, "essential liberty" was the essence of their new life in Christ. But now, the "essential liberty" of the Galatians was under siege.

In Paul's day, the threat to "essential liberty" issued from some who wished to compromise such liberty with the "safety" of reducing the life of faith to an observance of religious legalism. It is not that Paul had no idea what these opponents sought to do or had in mind. For much of his life Paul, like them, was a "zealot" (see the comments on 4:17-20 in Understanding the Scripture) who defined relationship with God through such meticulous observance. But Paul, owing to his transformative experience on the Damascus road, "traded" that religious path for another. And now, Paul weighs in against those who wanted to reinstate the performance of law for defining relationship with God over and above the baptismal marking of incorporation in Christ through grace (3:27).

Paul's perception that the key factor in this crisis involved "essential liberty" is asserted time and again in today's passage by repeatedly invoking its opposite: enslavement and bondage. Enslavement marked the Galatians' former status as Gentiles (4:8)—so why exchange that liberty found in Christ with a bondage to the law (4:9-10, 21-31)? That this liberty is essential to the Galatians' spirituality is made clear by Paul's declaration of his fear that these tendencies threaten to make a "waste" of Paul's labors among them (4:11). The law's premise that we can please God into a good relationship is a dead-end street

(as Paul discovered on the Damascus road). God's pleasure is the gracious gift of Christ to us. Our "right" (read, lawful) actions are how we respond to, not earn, that grace in the freedom Christ brings.

## Empathy for Casualties of Religion

On the one hand, the tone Paul frequently takes in Galatians, including in verses 9 and 20, might seem to justify viewing the Galatians with disdain. *Don't they get it? Can't they stand on their own two feet? What's wrong with them?* To do so, however, might mislead us into viewing Paul's epistle as a license to engage in the ridicule or condemnation of others. It is not ridicule Paul has in mind here, certainly not when we hear him address those who are being threatened as "my little children." In a way quite extraordinary when you think about this address and the imagery that follows it in verse 19, Paul is putting himself in the place of the Galatians' mother: one who has given birth to children now threatened, one who now feels again the pain of childbirth in their being formed in Christ once more. That is not ridicule. That is empathy. That is compassion, in the literal meaning of that word as "suffer with."

Paul's stance toward the Galatians is a helpful—and challenging—one for the church today. There continue to be casualties of religious legalism among us today. There continue to be victims buffeted about by voices that cajole and seduce with the tones of *you cannot be a Christian unless you do this first.* Sometimes the appeals to the new legalism are grounded in moralistic or political terms; sometimes the appeals are even more crudely fashioned in the materialistic terms of prosperity gospels. It may be that we see folks so swayed as deserving of the swindle being foisted upon them. Critique of such appeals, if Paul is to be followed, needs to be made. But like Paul, it is also imperative not to break the "family ties" with fellow siblings in Christ who come under the spell of such deceiving "gospels." Empathy and compassion, not scorn and excommunication, are the order of the day for those who confess our unity is in Christ Jesus, not in our opinions of one another.

### Saving Faith from Religiosity

My late father-in-law grew up in a small town in the Columbia Gorge of Oregon during the Depression. One of the bright spots there for Chuck as a young man was the youth program of the church in that community. Chuck and others in the group were especially appreciative of the youth pastor hired by the church. One week, the youth pastor organized a softball game for Sunday afternoon. It was after church, and all seemed fine. The next week, the church fired the youth pastor for encouraging Sabbath breaking. That experience shaped Chuck's view of the church the rest of his life. While he saw that his own children went to Sunday school and supported his wife in her involvement, Chuck retained a distrust of the church and the religion it practiced. Given his experience, I would sadly admit it was a healthy distrust for what had been done—not just to that youth pastor, but to those who were impacted first by his ministry and then by his firing.

The church has become quite adept at framing salvation in our need to be saved from sin. Unfortunately, the church has not been equally adept at framing salvation in our need to be saved from unhealthy religiosity. That is, from religion that devolves into either institutional maintenance or obsessive legalism, or both, and in the process loses touch with relationship with God as well as just and compassionate relationships with neighbor. Sometimes that tendency to get off track is much easier to see in others. We know the problem with those fundamentalists, or those liberals, or those—and you fill in the blank. The real crunch in listening to Paul address the Galatians comes in understanding that, in truth, he addresses us. He confronts us to examine the attitudes and actions by which legalistic or institutional religiosity may have supplanted the dynamics of faith and grace in our lives. He challenges us to consider what pain of childbirth may be needed if Christ is to be formed in our lives and communities by shedding unhealthy religious practices and traditions that get in the way of or become substitutes for the gospel.

The story at the beginning about my father-in-law is an illustration, and I do not believe an isolated one, of the decidedly un-evangelical consequences when narrow religiosity negatively impacts people's view of Christianity. Perhaps you have your own stories to tell. But even more important to the vocation we all share is to provide stories, and lives, that reveal the opposite: the grace to live freely and faithfully as children of God in Jesus Christ, with and on behalf of *all* of God's children.

# SHARING THE SCRIPTURE

## PREPARING TO LEAD

### Preparing Our Hearts

Ponder this week's devotional reading from Romans 8:1-11. What does this familiar passage say about freedom—and how we are able to attain it? How would you describe what it means to live in the flesh—versus what it means to live in the Spirit? What benefits do you experience because God's Spirit dwells in you?

Pray that you and the students will recognize and give thanks for the Spirit's activity in your lives.

### Preparing Our Minds

Study the background Scripture from Galatians 4 and the lesson Scripture from Galatians 4:8-20.

Consider this question: *What are the dangers in trading freedom in order to gain a sense of security?*

Write on newsprint:

❑ information for next week's lesson, found under Continue the Journey.

❑ activities for further spiritual growth in Continue the Journey.

Determine how you might use any of the features that precede the first lesson of this quarter in today's session.

## LEADING THE CLASS

### (1) Gather to Learn

❖ Welcome everyone and pray that those who have come today will treasure the freedom they have in Christ.

❖ Read the first portion of Bad Trades in Interpreting the Scripture (ending with "under siege"). Invite participants to identify other "bad trades" in sports or other areas of life. Discuss what, in their estimation, makes a trade bad or perhaps worthless.

❖ Read aloud today's focus statement: **People are tempted to sacrifice freedom in order to gain a sense of security. What are the dangers of this trade-off? Paul rebuked the Galatians for trading the freedom Christ gives for slavery to religious legalism.**

### (2) Goal 1: Identify Religious Expectations and Practices that Diminish Christian Freedom

❖ Read the final two paragraphs of Bad Trades in Interpreting the Scripture to introduce the lesson.

❖ Invite a volunteer to read Galatians 4:8-20. Remind the group that since many people were illiterate in the early church, letters were read aloud. Suggest that they listen as if a member were reading what Paul had written to their congregation.

❖ Discuss these questions:

1. **What is driving Paul's concern for the Galatians?** (See Galatians 4:8-11 in Understanding the Scripture.)

2. **How does their apparent willingness to fall back into spiritual slavery make Paul feel about his own work?** (See verse 11.)

3. **How would you have responded to Paul's invitation in verse 12 to follow his example in faithful living?**

4. **Why did he "become as [they] are"?** (See Galatians 4:12-16 in Understanding the Scripture.)

5. **Even after Paul asks if the Galatians have become his enemy (4:16), he refers to them as "my little children" (4:19). What do you think is Paul's real relationship with this church?** (See Galatians 4:17-20 in Understanding the Scripture.)

*(3) Goal 2: Empathize with Those Who Have Been Harmed by Narrow Religiosity*

❖ Read the first paragraph of Saving Faith from Religiosity in Interpreting the Scripture.

❖ Invite class members to comment of Chuck's experience and his response to it.

❖ Continue by reading the rest of Saving Faith from Religiosity.

❖ Encourage the adults to tell their own stories of any negative impact that unhealthy religiosity has had on them. For example, did they leave the church for some period, or continue attending while harboring resentment, or become angry with God? Since those responding are present in a Sunday school class today, something or someone must have prompted them to do whatever they needed to do to move beyond the harm they had experienced. What was that prompt? How free do they feel in Christ right now?

*(4) Goal 3: Challenge Unhealthy Attitudes Toward Religious Practices or Traditions*

❖ Read or retell Empathy for Casualties of Religion in Interpreting the Scripture.

❖ Reread: **Paul's stance toward the Galatians is a helpful—and challenging—one for the church today. There continue to be casualties of religious legalism among us today. There continue to be victims buffeted about by voices that cajole and seduce with the tones of** *you cannot be a Christian unless you do this first.*

❖ Post newsprint and encourage participants to call out behaviors, attitudes, or traditions that they personally or the congregation seems to insist that every Christian must observe. Point out that you are not talking about specific beliefs here, but rather practices or traditions that may be seen as unhealthy, often because they are rooted in legalism. Here's a true example: A customer in a Christian bookstore insisted that a clerk, who had short hair, could not possibly be a Christian because in 1 Corinthians 11:6 Paul claimed "it is disgraceful for a woman to have her hair cut off or to be shaved." This same customer was also horrified that a male youth minister, who walked in during her berating of the clerk, had long hair, which she found equally distasteful.

❖ Review the list. Are there examples here that at least some members of the class would challenge, that is, traditions they believe must be observed? If so, underline or check these items. Encourage the class to have a respectful discussion as to why such traditions must be observed or can be seen as optional.

❖ Conclude by asking: **Are there any traditions or attitudes that we need to work to change in ourselves or in our congregation so as to allow greater freedom for all?**

*(5) Continue the Journey*

❖ Pray that as the learners depart, they will keep open minds and hearts about the religious practices of others.

❖ Post information for next week's session on newsprint for the students to copy:

- Title: Freedom in Christ
- Background Scripture: Galatians 5:1-17
- Lesson Scripture: Galatians 5:1-17
- Focus of the Lesson: Rigorous self-discipline is appealing to some because it seems to promise mastery over temptation. What is the key to living a morally acceptable life? Paul urges the Galatians to stand firm in Christian freedom and to live by the Spirit, which leads to greater holiness, not greater self-indulgence.

❖ Challenge the adults to grow spiritually by completing one or more of these activities related to this week's session.

(1) Talk with someone who seems to have been negatively affected by narrow, legalistic religious beliefs or actions of another. What happened to cause harm? How was this person able to move beyond this situation to become reconnected with Christ and the church? If that has not yet been possible, what support might you offer so as to help this person?

(2) Examine the rules that you were taught to follow as a Christian. How are these rules a source of comfort or discomfort for you? Have you made any sacrifices for the sake of these rules?

(3) Identify at least one habit that "enslaves" you. Why does this habit have you so firmly in its grip? What steps have you taken to break this habit? Who might be able to help you if you have not been successful on your own?

❖ Sing or read aloud "Jesus, United by Thy Grace."

❖ Conclude today's session by leading the class in this benediction, which is adapted from Galatians 5:22-23, the key verses for February 26: **Empower us to go forth to bear the fruit of the Spirit, which is love, joy, peace, patience, kindness, generosity, faithfulness, gentleness, and self-control. Amen.**

UNIT 3: THE BIRTHING OF A NEW COMMUNITY
# FREEDOM IN CHRIST

---

## PREVIEWING THE LESSON

**Lesson Scripture:** Galatians 5:1-17
**Background Scripture:** Galatians 5:1-17
**Key Verse:** Galatians 5:13

### Focus of the Lesson:
Rigorous self-discipline is appealing to some because it seems to promise mastery over temptation. What is the key to living a morally acceptable life? Paul urges the Galatians to stand firm in Christian freedom and to live by the Spirit, which leads to greater holiness, not greater self-indulgence.

### Goals for the Learners:
(1) to understand Paul's teaching about life in the Spirit as foundational for Christian holiness.
(2) to celebrate the Holy Spirit's presence in their lives.
(3) to embrace new ways of creating openness to the Spirit's leading.

### Supplies:
Bibles, newsprint and marker, paper and pencils, hymnals

---

## READING THE SCRIPTURE

NRSV
Lesson Scripture: Galatians 5:1-17

¹For freedom Christ has set us free. Stand firm, therefore, and do not submit again to a yoke of slavery.

²Listen! I, Paul, am telling you that if you let yourselves be circumcised, Christ will be of no benefit to you. ³Once again I testify to every man who lets himself be circumcised that he is obliged to obey the entire law. ⁴You who want to be justified by the law have cut yourselves off

CEB
Lesson Scripture: Galatians 5:1-17

¹Christ has set us free for freedom. Therefore, stand firm and don't submit to the bondage of slavery again.

²Look, I, Paul, am telling you that if you have yourselves circumcised, having Christ won't help you. ³Again I swear to every man who has himself circumcised that he is required to do the whole Law. ⁴You people who are trying to be made righteous by the Law have been estranged from

from Christ; you have fallen away from grace. ⁵For through the Spirit, by faith, we eagerly wait for the hope of righteousness. ⁶For in Christ Jesus neither circumcision nor uncircumcision counts for anything; the only thing that counts is faith working through love.

⁷You were running well; who prevented you from obeying the truth? ⁸Such persuasion does not come from the one who calls you. ⁹A little yeast leavens the whole batch of dough. ¹⁰I am confident about you in the Lord that you will not think otherwise. But whoever it is that is confusing you will pay the penalty. ¹¹But my friends, why am I still being persecuted if I am still preaching circumcision? In that case the offense of the cross has been removed. ¹²I wish those who unsettle you would castrate themselves!

**¹³For you were called to freedom, brothers and sisters; only do not use your freedom as an opportunity for self-indulgence, but through love become slaves to one another.** ¹⁴For the whole law is summed up in a single commandment, "You shall love your neighbor as yourself." ¹⁵If, however, you bite and devour one another, take care that you are not consumed by one another.

¹⁶Live by the Spirit, I say, and do not gratify the desires of the flesh. ¹⁷For what the flesh desires is opposed to the Spirit, and what the Spirit desires is opposed to the flesh; for these are opposed to each other, to prevent you from doing what you want.

Christ. You have fallen away from grace! ⁵We eagerly wait for the hope of righteousness through the Spirit by faith. ⁶Being circumcised or not being circumcised doesn't matter in Christ Jesus, but faith working through love does matter.

⁷You were running well—who stopped you from obeying the truth? ⁸This line of reasoning doesn't come from the one who calls you. ⁹A little yeast works through the whole lump of dough. ¹⁰I'm convinced about you in the Lord that you won't think any other way. But the one who is confusing you will pay the penalty, whoever that may be. ¹¹Brothers and sisters, if I'm still preaching circumcision, why am I still being harassed? In that case, the offense of the cross would be canceled. ¹²I wish that the ones who are upsetting you would castrate themselves!

**¹³You were called to freedom, brothers and sisters; only don't let this freedom be an opportunity to indulge your selfish impulses, but serve each other through love.** ¹⁴All the Law has been fulfilled in a single statement: *Love your neighbor as yourself.* ¹⁵But if you bite and devour each other, be careful that you don't get eaten up by each other!

¹⁶I say be guided by the Spirit and you won't carry out your selfish desires. ¹⁷A person's selfish desires are set against the Spirit, and the Spirit is set against one's selfish desires. They are opposed to each other, so you shouldn't do whatever you want to do.

## UNDERSTANDING THE SCRIPTURE

**Galatians 5:1.** While some scholars judge this verse as a summary of the previous section (3:1–4:31), this session places it as the introduction to today's passage. Thematically, it expresses the core of the entire letter: freedom as both our gift from Christ and our vocation as Christians. The declaration of its gift from Christ provides in this verse the impetus for why our freedom must be held in the face of any attempts to dismiss or compromise it, which is precisely the conflict Paul confronts in this letter.

A yoke was typically a smooth wooden crosspiece used to harness together the shoulders of two draft animals for work. The imagery of a yoke, used negatively here as a means of enslavement, is elsewhere employed as a positive expression. For example, in Matthew 11:29-30, Jesus bids his followers to take his "yoke" upon them as a means of gaining rest from heavy labors. Galatians 5:1 speaks of a yoking that results in slavery. This not only hearkens back to Paul's previous warning in 4:8-10 but also sets up the argument he is about to make against those who insist that the Gentile Christians must be circumcised and thus "yoked" to the keeping of the law.

**Galatians 5:2-6.** Paul stamps his appeal to the Galatians with whatever personal authority he still holds in the community by introducing his argument with "I, Paul." The issue confronted in these verses is that of the alleged necessity of circumcision being insisted upon by Paul's opponents. The passion of Paul's personal appeal is matched by what he sees at stake for the Galatians in this matter: If they succumb to the demand of the circumcision party, then "Christ will be of no benefit to you" (5:2). "No benefit" employs the same pair of words as 1 Corinthians 13:3, where Paul writes that even the most sacrificial of actions, if they are devoid of love, "gain nothing." For Paul, one cannot undergo circumcision simply to please those who insist on it, and then be done with further encumbrances of the law. Paul, the once zealous Pharisee (1:14), understands that such observance cannot cherry-pick what commands they wish (such as circumcision) and discard the rest. The obligation is to keep the entire law (see Deuteronomy 27:26). The problem is that such obligation would cut off the Galatians from grace. As Paul declared earlier in 3:14, verse 5 in this passage asserts faith, not law, as the basis of our hope. Furthermore, he links God's Spirit with the effectiveness of such faith. Paul closes with a radical declaration that neither circumcision nor its absence is what counts for the hallmark of life in Christ. What counts is "faith working through love" (5:6). The Greek verb translated as "working" is *energeo*. Thus the phrase could more literally be heard as "faith *energizing* love." Paul uses that same word in 1 Corinthians 12:11 to speak of Spirit "activating" the gifts that build up the church for the common good.

**Galatians 5:7-12.** "Running" in verse 7 employs the imagery of an athletic contest, a metaphor Paul often uses in writings attributed to him (see, for example, 2 Timothy 4:7). The word translated in the NRSV as "obeying" is the same Greek word rendered in verse 10 as "am confident." In that sense, Paul's argument for what has impacted the Galatians' prior "running well" is an issue of confidence concerning the truth Paul proclaimed. Consequently, the opponents have been able to sow confusion (5:10) about the truth because of their insistence on circumcision. While Paul does not cite instances of it, verse 11 alludes to claims by the opponents that Paul himself preaches circumcision (see Acts 16:1-3 for an episode they might have claimed). For Paul, however, the evidence is clear: If he preached circumcision, why would he be persecuted by those who advocate it? Paul's identifying of his position/preaching with the offense (*skandalon*, the root of the English "scandal") of the cross parallels his use of the same word in a related argument (1 Corinthians 1:23, translated there as "stumbling block"), where his preaching of the cross is affirmed as a *skandalon* to the Jews. The vehemence of Paul's positions against his opponents in Galatians is not only implied in his threat that they will "pay the penalty" (5:10) but also expressed in the crass hyperbole of his wish in verse 12 that those who so trouble the Galatians would castrate themselves.

**Galatians 5:13-15.** These verses imply that Paul's opponents may have argued that failure to keep the law would inevitably result in an "anything goes" spirit of libertinism. Paul states his counterargument in two ways. First, he warns the Galatians against using their freedom in Christ as an excuse or rationale for "self-indulgence" (the Greek word is actually the same word translated in verses 16-17 as "flesh"). But beyond commanding what their freedom should not do, Paul goes on to identify what practices freedom should engage in: "through love become slaves to one another" and "love your neighbor as yourself." Note that the common denominator in those two assertions is "love." Significantly, Paul declares in verse 14 that love "summed up" (NRSV) or "fulfilled" (CEB) the law. That is, for all the opponents' ado about keeping the law, Paul argues that Christian freedom expressed in love is actually the highest expression of observing the law. It is ironic, though, given Paul's previous critique of how the opponents would "enslave" the Galatians (5:1, also 4:8-9), that Paul here urges the Galatians to become "slaves" to one another in love.

**Galatians 5:16-17.** In this final section, Paul delineates the opposing principles of Spirit and "flesh." In Pauline theology, "flesh" is not a mere synonym for "body" or even bodily existence. Its more significant function, particularly in this passage, is to serve as an image for that aspect of human nature that finds itself in opposition to God. Paul's overall assertion to the Galatians in this regard is to live (be guided) by the Spirit. In Galatians, Spirit is God's gift and God's promise come to them by faith (3:2, 14), even as the key verse for the next session will reveal the Spirit to be the source of "fruit" revealed in good character and works.

# INTERPRETING THE SCRIPTURE

### What Counts?

Ask yourself this question: What, for you, constitutes the "bottom line" of life in Christ? Take a moment to gather your thoughts. Is this bottom line encapsulated in formulas of creed or scriptural authority? Is it revealed in particular moral and ethical behaviors? Is it demonstrated in spiritual disciplines or liturgical practices or communal allegiances? In other words, what counts most for you as a reliable indicator that someone's life is grounded in Christ?

Paul's entire Epistle to the Galatians, and today's passage in particular, hinges on that issue. Apparently, a group of some Jewish-Christians has come into the Galatian communities and insisted that observing the Jewish law, including the rite of circumcision for men, is a prerequisite for life in Christ. That is what counts for them.

Paul counters their position with a very different baseline. For Paul, grace rules out righteousness obtained by observing the law as a basis for relationship with God in Christ. What counts for Paul, according to verse 6, is "faith working through love."

Paul's insistence on the primacy of faith above and beyond works as defining relationship with God (see also 2:15-16) has at times been caricatured and misrepresented to obliterate any role of works in the life of faith. Clearly from Paul's assertion here in 5:6, that is not the case. What counts is "faith *working through* love" (emphasis added). As noted in the comments in Understanding the Scripture, that phrase might be rendered more literally as faith *energizing* love. Faith does consist of a purely internal disposition requiring no outward expression. Faith aims to engage our lives in the practice of love. Paul returns to that point in verses 13-14 where he repeats not only the teaching of Leviticus 19:18 but also Jesus' own prioritizing of "what counts: "Love your neighbor as yourself" (Matthew 22:34-40).

Paul's argument and Jesus' priority continue to serve as the hallmark for what it means to live "in Christ." "What counts" for the church is to equip the people of God for engaging faith in the practice of love. Christian mission takes shape in giving free rein for our trust in God's grace to *energize* our practice of love. On an individual level, what counts for *you* and your Christian discipleship is allowing your trust in God to energize your practice of love.

Recall the opening question to this section: What, for you, constitutes the "bottom line" of life in Christ? As you consider the thoughts that first came to mind, let them all be shaped and challenged by the priority Paul places before the Galatians—and before us. What counts is faith energizing love. What might that priority seek from you, and make possible within you, this day?

### Spirit-ed Freedom

The date of my first Sunday in my first parish was July 4, 1976: the American bicentennial celebration! I have two distinct memories of that weekend. One was the church service we held at a member's home to observe that holiday. The second was a bicentennial parade held the day before in the small town where that church was located. What I remember most was not marching in my clergy collar along with a young child from the congregation dressed as a church mouse. What I remember most was a float emblazoned with the words: "God, guns, and guts made our country free!"

Ask ten people what "freedom" means, and you are liable to get a dozen or more answers. The ability to choose what we want, to do what we want, to be who we want to be would likely be some of the answers you would hear. Some theologians rightly focus on freedom's dual nature: that is, freedom "from" and freedom "for." "Freedom from" leans us in the direction of identifying what obligations or impositions are annulled by freedom. "Don't fence me in" might be a colloquial expression of such freedom, whether it be expressed politically ("no taxation without representation") or relationally ("I am the captain of my ship"). "Freedom for," on the other hand, moves us in the direction of responsibilities and opportunities made possible by freedom. Such freedom might be seen in the liberty to pursue one's vocation in an ethical manner or to live sacrificially rather than selfishly.

This dynamic of—and tension between—freedom that is at once liberty "from" and liberty "for" is clearly at work in today's passage in Galatians. Paul charges his opponents with stripping the community of its freedom by imposing the obligation to keep the law (circumcision in particular). Paul makes clear in verse 1 that freedom in the Christian community is nonnegotiable, precisely because it is a gift to us in Christ. But the meaning of life in Christ, and life in the Spirit, is not purely freedom "from" what Paul finds an imposition. Spirit-ed freedom finds its full expression in its adding what Christ has freed us "for." In this passage, as noted in the previous section, we are freed in Christ to exercise faith whose consequence is loving action.

Living by the Spirit is the ultimate freedom, precisely because it holds in dynamic tension our freedom *from* anything that would restrict the grace of Christ from us or others—and our freedom *for* giving witness to and thanksgiving for that grace in love embodied toward others. For such freedom, Christ has set you free!

*Embracing the Call to New Life*

Paul's earlier biographical narratives in Galatians (1:13-24 and 2:1-14) provide concrete instances of what it meant for Paul to embrace the call to new life—and to challenge those who sought to water down grace with legalistic demands. It is relatively easy to get a sense of Paul's earnestness and passion borne of those experiences as he addresses the Galatians. We clearly hear in his arguments and even in his hyperbolic exaggerations ("I wish those who unsettle you would castrate themselves!" [5:12]) that the new life and freedom in Christ is of utmost importance for the gospel. What is far from clear, however, is how the Galatians hear that passionate appeal—and how, or even if, they embraced these new ways with openness to the Spirit's leading or whether they followed the lead of Paul's opponents into the realm of legalism.

How the Galatians responded is, of course, a closed matter. We can conjecture what they decided, but that is not now the point. The point today is how (and whether) we will embrace the call to new life. Will we open ourselves to the Spirit's leading and our freedom in Christ, *freedom from* that which would restrict God's grace as well as *freedom for* living with "faith working through love?" (5:6). Or will we succumb to contemporary voices that bind the grace of God to scripted behaviors and legalistic attitudes?

As with Paul's exhortations to the Galatians, the freedom set before us is not a libertinism that allows anything under the sun in the name of free choice. Paul is clear in these verses with the Galatians, and with us, that freedom devoid of love—particularly love of neighbor—is a mere caricature of the freedom for which Christ has set us free. Paul is equally clear in his prioritization of "faith working through love" that embracing the new life in Christ is not exhausted by what we believe about Christ, but rather is fulfilled by how we live as Christ lived (Ephesians 5:2).

For such freedom, for such love, Christ has set us free.

---

## SHARING THE SCRIPTURE

### PREPARING TO LEAD

*Preparing Our Hearts*

Ponder this week's devotional reading from Galatians 5:22-26. These verses are part of next week's Scripture lesson. For today, try to memorize the nine fruit of the Spirit that Paul identifies. Think about how each "piece" of this fruit is made visible in your own life.

Pray that you and the students will live as holy people in whom the fruit of the Spirit is clearly evident.

*Preparing Our Minds*

Study the background Scripture and the lesson Scripture, which are both from Galatians 5:1-17.

Consider this question: *What is the key to living a morally acceptable life?*

Write on newsprint:
❏ questions for Goal 2 in Sharing the Scripture.
❏ information for next week's lesson, found under Continue the Journey.
❏ activities for further spiritual growth in Continue the Journey.

Determine how you might use any of the features that precede the first lesson of this quarter in today's session.

### LEADING THE CLASS

*(1) Gather to Learn*

❖ Welcome everyone and pray that those who have come today will find new meaning in Paul's teaching about Christian holiness.

❖ Post a sheet of newsprint and write the words "Freedom is" on it. Invite class members to call out words or phrases to complete the sentence.

❖ Read these words penned by pastor and writer Warren Wiersbe: **"Freedom does not mean I am able to do whatever I want to do. That's the worst kind of bondage. Freedom means I have been set free to** become all that God wants me to be, to achieve all that God wants me to achieve, to enjoy all that God wants me to enjoy." Invite the students to comment on Wiersbe's definition and how it may be similar to or different from their definitions.

❖ Read aloud today's focus statement: **Rigorous self-discipline is appealing to some because it seems to promise mastery over temptation. What is the key to living a morally acceptable life? Paul urges the Galatians to stand firm in Christian freedom and to live by the Spirit, which leads to greater holiness, not greater self-indulgence.**

*(2) Goal 1: Understand Paul's Teaching about Life in the Spirit as Foundational for Christian Holiness*

❖ Read the first two paragraphs of What Counts? in Interpreting the Scripture to set the stage for today's lesson.

❖ Solicit one or two volunteers to read Galatians 5:1-17.

❖ Ask these questions:

1. **Based on this passage, what would you say "counts" for Paul?** (Look at the third paragraph of What Counts? Refer the class to Galatians 5:6.)

2. **How does Paul differentiate between faith and works?** (See the fourth paragraph under What Counts?)

3. **What constitutes the "bottom line" for you in your relationship with Christ?**

4. **Beginning in verse 7, Paul writes about people who are "confusing" the Galatians. Who might be "confusing" Christians today—and with what kinds of teachings?**

5. **In verse 13, Paul makes the point that we are not to use our freedom for the purpose of self-indulgence. How would you define "self-indulgence"?**

6. **What do Paul's words in verse 15 suggest about how conflict affects believers?**

7. **What does Paul mean when he sets the words "Spirit" and "flesh" in opposition to one another?** (See Galatians 5:16-17 in Understanding the Scripture.)

*(3) Goal 2: Celebrate the Holy Spirit's Presence in the Lives of the Learners*

❖ Remind the students that freedom in the Spirit comes to us as a gift from Christ. It is not something we work for or earn.

❖ Distribute paper and pencils. Ask each participant to write one or two traits of people who are living holy lives in the Spirit. Collect the papers. Read as many answers as possible, trying to use all the sheets. Invite class members to comment on the ideas.

❖ Distribute a second sheet of paper to each person and provide time for the adults to write answers to these questions, which you will post on newsprint. Tell them that they will not be asked to share their answers.

1. **How do you experience the Spirit's presence in your life?**

2. **What facets of this experience are internal, known only to you?**

3. **How might others see the Spirit at work in you?**

❖ Conclude by reading in unison today's key verse, Galatians 5:13.

*(4) Goal 3: Embrace New Ways of Creating Openness to the Spirit's Leading*

❖ Read or retell Embracing the Call to New Life in Interpreting the Scripture.

❖ Form two groups and ask one to read Galatians 1:13-24 and the other to look at 2:1-14. Note that these passages provide biographical details of Paul's life. Direct the groups to look for concrete examples of how Paul embraced the Spirit's call to new life in Christ.

❖ Reconvene the class and invite speakers from both groups to report. See if you can find any common ground between Paul's experiences and those of the class members.

❖ Post newsprint and ask the students to call out answers to this question: **How might we help ourselves and other members of our congregation to be more open to the Spirit's leading?**

❖ Select one or two of the answers and try to pinpoint concrete steps that the class could take to help themselves and others be more open to the Spirit's leading. Here are three ideas: set up a short-term Bible study (perhaps led by your pastor) concerning the work and person of the Holy Spirit; agree to spend certain times at home in prayer, asking God to lead your church in new directions; form a covenant discipleship group in which members come together to watch over one in love and help them along their spiritual journeys.

*(5) Continue the Journey*

❖ Pray that as the learners depart, they will be aware of how and where the Spirit is leading them.

❖ Post information for next week's session on newsprint for the students to copy:

■ **Title: Christ Creates Holy Living**

■ **Background Scripture: Galatians 5:18–6:10**

■ **Lesson Scripture: Galatians 5:18–6:10**

■ **Focus of the Lesson: Many people reduce their religious obligations to fulfilling a set of legalistic requirements. What are the characteristics of an authentic Christian lifestyle? Paul sharply contrasts a Spirit-filled life with life in the flesh.**

❖ Challenge the adults to grow spiritually by completing one or more of these activities related to this week's session.

**(1) Identify rules or traditions that you think your congregation or denomination urges you to keep. Which of these, if any, cause frustration for you? Why?**

**(2) Discern how your freedom in the Spirit enables you to live according to biblical, moral, and ethical teachings because you want to, not because you must.**

**(3) Think about your spiritual journey in terms of running a race. What "baggage" do you need to get rid of in order to run faster?**

❖ Sing or read aloud "I Want a Principle Within."

❖ Conclude today's session by leading the class in this benediction, which is adapted from Galatians 5:22-23, the key verses for February 26: **Empower us to go forth to bear the fruit of the Spirit, which is love, joy, peace, patience, kindness, generosity, faithfulness, gentleness, and self-control. Amen.**

# UNIT 3: THE BIRTHING OF A NEW COMMUNITY
# CHRIST CREATES
# HOLY LIVING

---

## PREVIEWING THE LESSON

**Lesson Scripture:** Galatians 5:18–6:10
**Background Scripture:** Galatians 5:18–6:10
**Key Verses:** Galatians 5:22-23

**Focus of the Lesson:**
Many people reduce their religious obligations to fulfilling a set of legalistic requirements. What are the characteristics of an authentic Christian lifestyle? Paul sharply contrasts a Spirit-filled life with life in the flesh.

**Goals for the Learners:**
(1) to define characteristics Paul lists as fruit of the Spirit.
(2) to sense the needs of others in the church.
(3) to work, by the Spirit's empowerment, "for the good of all, especially for those of the family of faith."

**Supplies:**
Bibles, newsprint and marker, paper and pencils, hymnals, piece of poster board, table

---

## READING THE SCRIPTURE

**NRSV**

Lesson Scripture: Galatians 5:18–6:10

[18] But if you are led by the Spirit, you are not subject to the law. [19] Now the works of the flesh are obvious: fornication, impurity, licentiousness, [20] idolatry, sorcery, enmities, strife, jealousy, anger, quarrels, dissensions, factions, [21] envy, drunkenness, carousing, and things like these. I am warning you, as I warned you before:

**CEB**

Lesson Scripture: Galatians 5:18–6:10

[18] But if you are being led by the Spirit, you aren't under the Law. [19] The actions that are produced by selfish motives are obvious, since they include sexual immorality, moral corruption, doing whatever feels good, [20] idolatry, drug use and casting spells, hate, fighting, obsession, losing your temper, competitive opposition,

those who do such things will not inherit the kingdom of God.

²²By contrast, **the fruit of the Spirit is love, joy, peace, patience, kindness, generosity, faithfulness, ²³gentleness, and self-control. There is no law against such things.** ²⁴And those who belong to Christ Jesus have crucified the flesh with its passions and desires. ²⁵If we live by the Spirit, let us also be guided by the Spirit. ²⁶Let us not become conceited, competing against one another, envying one another.

¹My friends, if anyone is detected in a transgression, you who have received the Spirit should restore such a one in a spirit of gentleness. Take care that you yourselves are not tempted. ²Bear one another's burdens, and in this way you will fulfill the law of Christ. ³For if those who are nothing think they are something, they deceive themselves. ⁴All must test their own work; then that work, rather than their neighbor's work, will become a cause for pride. ⁵For all must carry their own loads.

⁶Those who are taught the word must share in all good things with their teacher.

⁷Do not be deceived; God is not mocked, for you reap whatever you sow. ⁸If you sow to your own flesh, you will reap corruption from the flesh; but if you sow to the Spirit, you will reap eternal life from the Spirit. ⁹So let us not grow weary in doing what is right, for we will reap at harvest time, if we do not give up. ¹⁰So then, whenever we have an opportunity, let us work for the good of all, and especially for those of the family of faith.

conflict, selfishness, group rivalry, ²¹jealousy, drunkenness, partying, and other things like that. I warn you as I have already warned you, that those who do these kinds of things won't inherit God's kingdom.

²²But **the fruit of the Spirit is love, joy, peace, patience, kindness, goodness, faithfulness, ²³gentleness, and self-control. There is no law against things like this.** ²⁴Those who belong to Christ Jesus have crucified self with its passions and its desires.

²⁵If we live by the Spirit, let's follow the Spirit. ²⁶Let's not become arrogant, make each other angry, or be jealous of each other.

¹Brothers and sisters, if a person is caught doing something wrong, you who are spiritual should restore someone like this with a spirit of gentleness. Watch out for yourselves so you won't be tempted too. ²Carry each other's burdens and so you will fulfill the law of Christ. ³If anyone thinks they are important when they aren't, they're fooling themselves. ⁴Each person should test their own work and be happy with doing a good job and not compare themselves with others. ⁵Each person will have to carry their own load.

⁶Those who are taught the word should share all good things with their teacher. ⁷Make no mistake, God is not mocked. A person will harvest what they plant. ⁸Those who plant only for their own benefit will harvest devastation from their selfishness, but those who plant for the benefit of the Spirit will harvest eternal life from the Spirit. ⁹Let's not get tired of doing good, because in time we'll have a harvest if we don't give up. ¹⁰So then, let's work for the good of all whenever we have an opportunity, and especially for those in the household of faith.

# UNDERSTANDING THE SCRIPTURE

**Galatians 5:18.** As this letter moves toward its end, Paul blends summaries of key elements from earlier sections into urgings for the community's Spirit-led living. This verse, along with verse 25, offers the overarching appeal to be led by the Spirit. The verb translated as "led" connotes an active, ongoing, personal involvement by the Holy Spirit in the lives of the Galatians. In 5:16, the closely related summons to "live by the Spirit" was coupled with not gratifying base desires. In 5:18, such leading by the Spirit is linked to Paul's earlier argument (3:23-25) of no longer being subject to the law.

**Galatians 5:19-21.** Paul earlier (5:16-17) framed in general terms how flesh and Spirit are opposed in their desires. Now he becomes specific, though it is not the desires, but their behavioral consequences, that Paul emphasizes. The bulk of verses 19-21 lists fifteen "works" of the flesh. The first three vices identify behaviors that are sexual/sensual in nature. The next two involve associations with worship of false gods. This includes the reference to sorceries—the Greek word is *pharmakeia*, related to the use of drugs in the magical arts. But it is critical to note that the predominant number of vices (eight of the fifteen) here highlight behaviors that specifically undermine life in community. The first of those listed, "enmities," is the same word Paul uses in Ephesians 2:15-16 (translated there as "hostility") to speak of the division between Jew and Gentile brought to an end by Jesus' cross. Verse 21 reveals that Paul has warned the Galatians before about these things. Paul elevates the stakes of this warning by returning to the theme of inheriting God's kingdom (3:18) and asserting that those who practice these vices in an ongoing way risk that inheritance.

**Galatians 5:22-23.** Continuing the contrast of Spirit and flesh (5:16-17), Paul now turns from the works of the flesh to the fruit of the Spirit. Note that "fruit" is singular; perhaps it is Paul's way of emphasizing the common source of all the qualities he will now list. As with the list of vices, Paul's listing of qualities generated by the Spirit is more a sampling than an exhausting of possibilities. That "love" (*agape*) heads this list is indicative of its importance in life led by the Spirit and in Christ, a point Paul makes even clearer in 1 Corinthians 13:13. It might also be telling that Paul lists "joy" as the second item. In an epistle noteworthy for its contentious and argumentative nature, this is the only occurrence of "joy" in this letter. Paul closes this listing of the Spirit's fruit with "there is no law against such things," a not so subtle verbal jab at his law-obsessed opponents.

**Galatians 5:24.** Both the NRSV and the CEB insert "belong" to clarify what the original Greek leaves vague (literally, "they that are Christ's"). Another uncertainty in this verse is what exactly is meant by "crucifying" the flesh and its desires. It is unlikely that it refers to some form of rigorous asceticism. That would, in essence, be another "works righteousness" effort that would contradict Paul's argument of freedom in Christ. More likely, "crucifying" represents a veiled reference to baptism, similar to Paul's teaching in Romans 6:3 that our baptism unites us in Christ's death and ends our enslavement to sin. In Galatians, "the flesh . . .with its desires" is akin to a synonym for sin, as that aspect of human nature that is in opposition to God (see the comments on Galatians 5:16-17 in last session's Understanding the Scripture).

**Galatians 5:25–6:5.** As with verse 18, verse 25 offers a summary statement on life in the Spirit. The disciplined and even communal consequence of such leading may be detected in the verb translated here as "guided." This word denotes "to go in order" or even "to proceed in a row as the march of a soldier." Having stated the general principle of such guidance, these next verses unpack how that guidance impacts the nature of and involvement in community. Bearing one another's burdens, caring for one another, is elevated by Paul into fulfilling the "law of Christ"—a phrase that most likely has in mind the command to love neighbor (see 5:14). Conceit, whether expressed in one-upmanship or jealousy, is to be avoided. The issue of how lapses (transgressions) are dealt with in community is next considered. Restoration of the offending party is the goal, along with an avoidance of falling into the same trap oneself. The resulting ethic of community blends individual responsibility for one's own actions with bearing one another's burdens.

**Galatians 6:6-8.** Verse 6 offers a practical instruction regarding the community's responsibility to support those who are its teachers. The instruction parallels a much more extended discourse in 1 Corinthians 9:3-14 regarding the material and financial support to be rendered to church leaders. Verse 7 states two proverb-like sayings regarding the impossibility of mocking God and reaping the consequences of one's own actions. It is unclear what specific situation Paul might have in mind regarding the mocking of God. It may simply serve as a qualifier to the following "reap whatever you sow" (6:7) comment. In that sense, the mocking of God might consist of presuming one can engage in actions (as in Paul's opponents preaching law versus grace?) without ever being held accountable. Whatever the situation evoking these words, Paul's implication is clear: God's judgment cannot be escaped.

**Galatians 6:9-10.** These closing verses of the passage serve as a commissioning of the community by Paul. Its encouragement of not growing weary in doing what is right underscores how Paul's defense of grace versus law in this letter does not reject the importance of works. Rather, it asserts the perspective that works are the fruit of grace rather than what deems us worthy of grace. In the final verse, Paul blends the missional task to work for the good of "all" with the task of the church to seek and do that same good for the community of faith, here described in the metaphor of household or family.

# INTERPRETING THE SCRIPTURE

*What a Spirit-led Life Produces*

Paul's listing of Spirit-led qualities is not a new law, but hallmarks of individuals and communities led by God's Spirit.

- **Love.** God's unconditional love revealed in the gift of Jesus provides example and challenge for how the community is to order its own life—not by the meticulous following of rules, but by the gracious exercise of love for one another.
- **Joy.** Why might a Spirit-led life be marked by joy? Because of the experience of God's presence manifest in grace. Such joy is not dependent on changing circumstances, but on the trustworthy presence of God in all times.
- **Peace.** Paul's inclusion of this was likely a challenging word for the Galatians, who face un-peaceful divisions in their midst. The hallmark of peace in troubled times calls to mind the risen Jesus twice pronouncing peace on fearful disciples huddled behind locked doors (John 20:19, 21).
- **Patience.** The literal meaning of this Greek word is "long-suffering." Patience is not merely waiting when we know everything will turn out right. Patience finds its virtue when waiting brings risk and cost—and yet is maintained.
- **Kindness.** To act kindly in

the face of personal attack is a demanding task. To reply in kind (a very different connotation of "kind") is the easier way. Unfortunately, it is also the way that allows opponents to change us, versus a witness that hopes to change them.
- **Generosity.** The CEB renders this word as "goodness," a more literal translation of the Greek. Goodness suggests not merely what a person is *like*, but more critically what a person (or community) *seeks and produces*.
- **Faithfulness.** This is the New Testament's basic expression for trust. Faith is not simply a body of beliefs but the active trust of one's life in God.
- **Gentleness.** This may be understood as less of *what* one does toward others (as the closely related virtue of kindness) but rather *how* one interacts. Gentleness thus relates to a quietness and mildness of spirit.
- **Self-control**. Paul's opponents may well have argued that failure to observe circumcision and the rest of the law threatened the community with libertinism (see Galatians 5:13). Listing self-control as the Spirit's fruit underscores Paul's position that freedom in Christ does not require legalism to exercise restraint when restraint is needed.

### The Close Quarters of Community

My childhood church concluded practically every worship service by singing the first verse of a hymn, whose opening words are these: "Blest be the tie that binds."

Ties. Bindings. Those are often heard as pejoratives, not affirmations, of life lived in community. They both can be expressions of restrictions on our freedom. And isn't Paul all about freedom in this passage. And aren't we, as a result, all about freedom in Christian community?

We are all about freedom . . . except. Except for this nagging tie to love. Except for this unyielding binding to bear one another's burdens. Unless we are willing to take up the life of hermits, living in caves or atop towers as hermits of old allegedly did in their spiritual escapes, faith ties and binds us to live in the close quarters of community. And it is close quarters, precisely because love binds us to the needs of others. For that, too, is how Paul unpacks what it practically means to stand firm in the freedom by which Christ has set us free: to stand firm with and by one another. To do so, even and especially when the easier route would be to cut our losses and head for communities less needy of our time and compassion, less bound to making commitments as to how we might be called upon to serve as Christ for others.

Christian community, Christian love, truly involves a balancing act. Paul did not say "bear somebody else's burdens," as if the bearing is all on one side. Paul's word is, "bear one another's burdens" (6:2, emphasis added). Which is to say: the ties and bindings of community are reciprocal.

There are two sets of challenges with that.

First, we might find those ties negatively binding us when it feels like we are always the ones on the giving side. *Why don't those people take care of themselves*, we might wonder. *Why don't they make better choices? Why aren't they more of the makers than the takers around here?* Before long, we are edging off the precipice of spiritual conceit, as if we know their lives from the inside out, as if we are in the place of God.

But second, the challenge of reciprocal ties and bindings in community can take shape in a fear of admitting our own need for help. We want to be self-made persons. We want to be the captains of our own ships, the masters of our own fates. But here comes Paul, and here comes life, reminding us there will be times and occasions when we stand in need of others to help us bear our burdens. Will we allow them to exercise their gift of caring? Or will we stand apart, solitary saints who are only there for others but not the other way around?

Either way is a challenge. Either way allows pride to muck up the reciprocity Paul understands at the heart of Christian community. Bear *one another's* burdens. Respond to human need around you—and allow others to grace you when the need is your own. For only in both can we find blessing in the ties that bind our hearts in Christian love.

### Workers for the Good

Do-gooder. Is that a compliment, or an epithet, to you? The truth that it is frequently used as an insult of those judged as naive reformers suggests that Galatians 6:10 may not always and everywhere be welcomed: "let us work for the good of all, and especially for those of the family of faith."

The scandal of working for the good "of all" may be resented or even rejected by those who take issue with "all." Keep in mind the grace that underlies the whole of this epistle. Where are the exceptions for God's grace? Is the exception, following the logic of those troubling the Galatians, the uncircumcised? Paul clearly argues: No exception there. And if grace is best revealed in the cross of Jesus, who are the exceptions to Christ's reach extended on the cross? Who are the ones "left behind," left out of Christ's saving act? Working for the good of all is not Pollyannaish optimism. It is the way of God's working in Christ—and by extension it is the way of God's working in us.

But Paul goes on to add beyond "the all" that we are to work for the good of those "in the family." Have you ever found it easier to help out strangers you don't know than seek the good of someone you know all too well? Is it easier for the church to support distant missions than to work face-to-face, hand in hand, with the homeless in our neighborhoods, or the victims of domestic violence in our communities? If familiarity can breed contempt, it also is true that anonymity can breed mere charity. But love bids us work in the closest of quarters, as well as out to the most distant of edges, to do good. To work good. Whenever, and with whomever, we have opportunity to do so.

## SHARING THE SCRIPTURE

### PREPARING TO LEAD

*Preparing Our Hearts*

Ponder this week's devotional reading from Romans 6:1-11. How does Paul view the purpose of baptism? How do you experience yourself as being freed from sin? What does it mean to you to be alive in Christ?

Pray that you and the students will walk with Jesus in newness of life.

*Preparing Our Minds*

Study the background Scripture and the lesson Scripture, which are both from Galatians 5:18–6:10.

Consider this question: *What are the characteristics of an authentic Christian lifestyle?*

Write on newsprint:
❏ information for next week's lesson, found under Continue the Journey.
❏ activities for further spiritual growth in Continue the Journey.

Determine how you might use any of the features that precede the first lesson of this quarter in today's session.

Create a picture puzzle prior to the session. Start by sketching a U-shaped line at the bottom of a piece of poster board to serve as a fruit bowl. Then, either sketch nine different pieces of fruit with the following words written, one per piece, or just write the words: love, joy, peace, patience, kindness, generosity, faithfulness, gentleness, self-control. Finally, cut the poster board into as many pieces as you choose.

Have a table handy so the puzzle can be constructed during the session.

## LEADING THE CLASS

### (1) Gather to Learn

❖ Welcome everyone and pray that those who have come today will seek to live as authentic Christians.

❖ Read: **Many of us know people who profess to be Christians but whose lives don't quite ring true. Sometimes these folks are, as one pastor often said, "sad, sour, and sanctimonious"—so much so that you would be hard-pressed ever to call them joyful. Others act in unloving ways, criticizing people for playing sports, watching television, wearing certain clothing or jewelry, or showing some other outward sign. These legalistic Christians are so bound by their religious traditions that they cannot imagine God doing anything new or reaching out to people whom they do not think deserve such grace. If you ever engage them in a conversation, you will likely find a "my way or the highway" view of belief. Either you agree with them— or you are wrong. Judgment abounds but grace seems to be in short supply.**

❖ Read aloud today's focus statement: **Many people reduce their religious obligations to fulfilling a set of legalistic requirements. What are the characteristics of an authentic Christian lifestyle? Paul sharply contrasts a Spirit-filled life with life in the flesh.**

### (2) Goal 1: Define Characteristics Paul Lists as the Fruit of the Spirit

❖ Choose a volunteer to read Galatians 5:18-21 and 5:24–6:10. For now, skip the key verses, 5:22-23.

❖ Place your puzzle pieces in random order on the table where many people can see them. Invite several participants to put the puzzle together. When the puzzle is assembled, read in unison Galatians 5:22-23.

❖ Invite class members to define each characteristic that is named. Use What a Spirit-led Life Produces in Interpreting the Scripture to add other points. The list you have is taken from the NRSV. Encourage people with other translations to note different words.

❖ Contrast believers who, according to Paul, have characteristics that enable them to live authentic, Spirit-led lives with those who, as we heard in the Gather to Learn portion, focus on legalism. (Note: The purpose here is not to judge the legalists but simply to show that Jesus calls us to be grace-filled, Spirit-led, fruitful believers who are a blessing to others.)

### (3) Goal 2: Sense the Needs of Others in the Church

❖ Direct attention to Galatians 5:25–6:5. Note that here we find a summary of how we are to live in the Spirit, especially as that pertains to living in the community of faith. (See these verses in Understanding the Scripture.)

❖ Add information from The Close Quarters of Community in Interpreting the Scripture to help class members answer these questions:

1. **How might you respond when you recognize that a church member needs help in bearing a burden?**
2. **How might you respond when you have a burden**

and a church member wants to help you?

3. **Do you find it more difficult to give or receive help? Why?**

*(4) Goal 3: Work, by the Spirit's Empowerment, "for the Good of All, Especially Those of the Family of Faith"*

❖ Look again at Galatians 6:6-10.

❖ Read Workers for the Good in Interpreting the Scripture. Discuss these questions:

1. **Why might a believer find it easier to help strangers than to seek the good of someone he or she knows all too well?**

2. **Why might some church members prefer to write a check to help those in need than to become involved in hands-on work in their own community?**

3. **Some Christians want to be sure that someone on the receiving end of help is not only in need but also worthy to receive such help. They may want to know, for example, if the potential recipient abuses drugs or alcohol or is unemployed or has a criminal history. What do you think Paul might say about such attitudes and questions?**

❖ **Option:** Invite the class to consider assisting with an outreach project that would enable them to "work for the good of all, and especially for those of the family of faith." Perhaps there is a church they could partner with so that each congregation could give and receive help that would be beneficial to it.

*(5) Continue the Journey*

❖ Pray that as the learners depart they will seek opportunities to work for the good of all this week.

❖ Post information for next week's session on newsprint for the students to copy:

- **Title: The Source of All Love**
- **Background Scripture: 1 John 4:7-19**
- **Lesson Scripture: 1 John 4:7-19**
- **Focus of the Lesson: Many search in all the wrong places for a perfect love in which to put their trust. Can other humans be trusted to love without blemish at all times? First John reminds us that God is love and those who abide in love have God's love perfected in them.**

❖ Challenge the adults to grow spiritually by completing one or more of these activities related to this week's session.

(1) **Review today's key verses, Galatians 5:22-23. Identify the specific fruit that you feel is mature within you. Then identify another fruit that is not "ripe." What steps can you take to nurture this particular fruit?**

(2) **Help someone who is struggling with a heavy load to bear this burden. Is there something you can do to help a family dealing with serious illness, or a major loss, or a serious financial reversal? If so, do whatever you can in the name of Jesus.**

(3) **Do something to show your Bible study teacher that you appreciate all that he or she**

does for the class. A note, small gift, or invitation to a meal would mean a great deal to your teacher, especially if he or she is a volunteer.

❖ Sing or read aloud "Spirit of God, Descend upon My Heart."

❖ Conclude today's session by leading the class in this benediction, which is adapted from Galatians 5:22-23, the key verses for today: **Empower us to go forth to bear the fruit of the Spirit, which is love, joy, peace, patience, kindness, generosity, faithfulness, gentleness, and self-control. Amen.**

# THIRD QUARTER
## God Loves Us

MARCH 5, 2017—MAY 28, 2017

God loves us. That astonishing fact that the Creator of heaven and earth loves us is evident in Scripture from the creation of the first humans and continues throughout the millennia as God intervenes in history and interacts with humanity. During the spring quarter we will be surveying selected passages from both the Old and New Testaments to reveal many facets of God's constant love for humanity.

The four sessions in Unit 1, God's Eternal, Preserving, Renewing Love, examine portions of 1 John, Ephesians, John, and Joel to discover that God's love for humanity in revealed in many ways. Throughout this quarter we will encounter God's redemptive, overflowing, uniting, restoring, and renewing love. The unit opens on March 5 to consider The Source of All Love, as discussed in 1 John 4:7-19. We move to Ephesians 2:1-10 on March 12 to examine the saving grace of God's Overflowing Love. Humans are empowered to love as we will learn in the session for March 19 from John 15:1-17, God's Love Manifested. Unit 2 ends on March 26 with God's Love Restores, a lesson concerning the reconciliation of relationships from Joel 2.

In Unit 2, God's Caring, Saving, and Upholding Love, we will explore selections from the Psalms, John, and Romans. These five sessions reveal God as protector, preserver, healer, comforter, and savior. The beloved Psalm 23 is the Scripture for God as Our Shepherd, the lesson for April 2. On Palm Sunday we turn to John 3:1-21 to encounter God's Saving Love in Christ. We will study three background Scriptures—John 19:38-42; 20:1-10; 1 Peter 1:3-9—on Easter to hear the incredible story of God's Love as Victory over Death. On April 23 we delve into Romans 5:1-11 and 8:31-39 to learn that because of God's Reconciling Love nothing will be able to separate us from God. For the final lesson in Unit 2 we will study John 10:1-15 on April 30 to learn about God's Preserving Love as enacted in Jesus the good shepherd.

The four sessions of the final unit, God's Pervasive and Sustaining Love, focus on the Book of Jonah to highlight God's unconditional love for humans and the natural world, as well as God's providential care for individuals and groups, including a nation of Gentiles. God's Sustaining Love is evident when calamity comes, as we see in Jonah 1:7-17, the lesson for May 7. Jonah 2, the Scripture for May 14, shows how God's Love Preserved Jonah when God rescued him from danger. Because of God's Love for Nineveh, God issues a wake-up call to this city through Jonah, as discussed in Jonah 3, with Nahum 1–3 serving as a second background Scripture. The quarter ends on May 28 with a study of Jonah 4 where we see how God's Pervasive Love spares the city of Nineveh.

# Meet Our Writer

## REV. DAVID KALAS

David Kalas is the pastor of First United Methodist Church in Green Bay, Wisconsin, where he has served since 2011.

David grew up as the son of a United Methodist minister, first in Madison, Wisconsin, and later in Cleveland, Ohio. After graduating from high school in Cleveland, he attended the University of Virginia, where he earned his bachelor's degree in English. He began his seminary work at Pittsburgh Theological Seminary and completed it at Union Theological Seminary of Virginia.

David felt his call to the ministry as a young teenager, and for the rest of his adolescent years his sense of purpose and preparation was for serving Christ and his church. He began his ministry while a college student, appointed as the student-pastor of two rural churches outside of Charlottesville, Virginia. He recalls with great fondness and gratitude the sweet and patient saints of Bingham's and Wesley Chapel United Methodist churches.

Because it was during his own teenage years that David came to Christ, began reading the Bible, and felt his calling, he has always had a heart for teens and for youth ministry. During the latter half of his college years and throughout his seminary training, David served as a youth minister. For six years, he worked with the youth of Church of the Saviour United Methodist Church in Cleveland, Ohio, followed by three years with the youth of Huguenot United Methodist Church in Richmond, Virginia. Even in his role as lead pastor of subsequent churches, he has made working with the youth of the church a personal priority.

Following seminary, David entered full-time pastoral ministry, serving a rural two-point charge in Virginia. A move to Wisconsin in 1996 was a happy return to his childhood home. For eight years, David served as pastor of Emmanuel United Methodist Church in Appleton, Wisconsin, followed by seven years in Whitewater, before moving to his current appointment in Green Bay.

In addition to *The New International Lesson Annual*, David has also contributed to a number of published sermon collections, and is a regular writer for *Emphasis*, a lectionary-based resource for preachers.

David and his wife, Karen, have been married for thirty years. They met in their home church youth group when they were just teenagers in Cleveland and have been together ever since. They are the proud parents of three daughters: Angela, Lydia, and Susanna.

Another great love of David's life is the Holy Land. He has made six trips to that part of the world and is always planning another pilgrimage. He has found his own reading of the Bible has been enriched by getting to know the land from which it came.

David is also an avid sports fan. He loves to play sports as recreation and to watch sports as relaxation. He is delighted to live and serve in Green Bay, the home of his beloved Packers. He also enjoys traveling, walking, tinkering with around-the-house projects, and spending as much time with his family as possible.

# THE BIG PICTURE: GOD'S LOVE FOR US

## A Daughter's Gift

When my oldest daughter turned twenty, I included a thank-you note in her birthday card. I was thanking her for all that she had given me and made me. Among other things, as our firstborn child, she was the one who made me a parent. And by making me a father, I told her, she had given me a better understanding of God than I had ever had before.

I wouldn't go so far as to say that a person cannot understand God apart from being a parent. I am quite certain, however, that we cannot understand God apart from love. And it was the experience of parental love that, for me, gave new insight into the nature of God.

A famous story is told of Karl Barth, the monumental early twentieth-century Swiss theologian. During a visit to America, he was asked if he could summarize in a few words the essence of his work. He had been a prolific author, whose published works were famously voluminous. The question seems, therefore, almost insulting. Yet Barth did not hesitate to answer it simply and directly. "Jesus loves me, this I know," Barth replied, "for the Bible tells me so."

Jesus loves me. For all of the theological sophistication, all of the nuances and complexities, still Barth concluded that it all comes down to the love of the Lord. And I'm sure that's correct. For that is the overwhelming testimony of Scripture.

Our great pleasure and privilege this quarter is to focus on God's love. Is there a better assignment than that? The curriculum could ask us to spend thirteen weeks contemplating the night sky, autumn leaves, ocean sunrises, and mountain views, and it wouldn't be as good. There is no subject more altogether lovely, entirely pure, and thoroughly good as the love of God.

Furthermore, this is an endeavor with very personal implications for us. To study the night sky might be fascinating and inspiring, but it is not personal. We have no meaningful relationship with those planets, stars, and galaxies that awe us. To study God, however, is to study someone whom we may know and with whom we may have a relationship. And our exploration together of God's love will no doubt invite us deeper into that relationship.

If I study the history of the Old Testament, the geography of the Holy Land, or the biography of Paul, then I will come away with greater knowledge. That knowledge will help me to read and understand Scripture. As a pastor, therefore, I do not hesitate to offer classes for my people to learn such things.

But to study the love of God is of a different order. This goes to the core of the divine nature, the heart of our faith, and the basis of our relationship with the Lord. And so, while a thirteen-week curriculum cannot do all that a daughter can, I hope that what follows will echo at least a part of my daughter's gift to me: that we will come to know and understand God better than we ever have before.

## The Great Commandment

We get a measure—an astonishing indication, really—of how central the issue of love is when a man asked Jesus which was the greatest commandment.

We are familiar, of course, with the Ten Commandments. The Old Testament law featured a total of 613 dos and don'ts. In the centuries between Moses' day and Jesus, many layers of traditions, explanations, and rabbinical teachings had been added onto those hundreds of laws. And so the inquirer wanted to know from Jesus which, of all of them, was the greatest.

"You shall love the Lord your God with all your heart, and with all your soul, and with all your mind," Jesus replied, quoting Deuteronomy 6:5. "This is the greatest and first commandment" (Matthew 22:37-38).

I wonder if we would have called that the greatest commandment. For myself, I would probably take a pragmatic approach and quote Moses: "Be careful to obey all these words that I command you" (Deuteronomy 12:28). A generic instruction to obey all of the commandments seems like the most sensible answer to me. It might seem like a cop-out answer to the man who asked Jesus the question, but at least it would be a comprehensive answer.

Yet that wasn't Jesus' answer. And it wouldn't have been, for it appears that obeying God is not the most important thing. At first blush, that seems like a heretical thing to say. But a closer review of Scripture tells me that obedience is not what is most important to God. Love is. That is what Jesus' answer to the question suggests. And that is what the creation story implies, as well.

Consider the choice that God made when creating human beings. I assume that the Lord could have created us in such a way that compliance with moral laws was as automatic as compliance with physical laws. That is to say, we human beings have no escape from the laws of physics. We do not choose whether to obey gravity or not. We are compelled.

Yet we are not compelled to obey the moral laws of God. That is our choice. The Lord wired us in such a way that we could choose to obey—or not obey—the divine will in matters of our lifestyle and the conduct of our relationships.

Because the Lord could have designed us to obey the moral laws as certainly as we do the physical laws but chose not to, that tells me that obedience is not what is most important. Rather, I gather that the Lord left us free so that we could do what is most important: love. The nature of our creation, therefore, confirms the answer that Jesus gave concerning the commandments. The most important thing to God is not mere obedience, but love.

We should not sell short obedience, of course. Disobedience is no small matter. Yet there is a lovely logic to God's design. For we know from the example of the Pharisees (and a great many other legalists through the ages) that it is theoretically possible to obey God without really loving God. Yet it is not truly possible to love God without also obeying. Jesus said, "If you love me, you will keep my commandments" (John 14:15). Since love does not automatically flow from obedience, but obedience should flow from love, we see again why love is the greatest and first commandment.

Jesus did not stop there, however. After answering the question about the greatest commandment, he added: "And a second is like it," he said. "You shall love your neighbor as yourself" (Matthew 22:39). And so the vertical commandment to love God is necessarily paired with the horizontal commandment to love neighbor. Love is the first commandment, as well as the second.

The logic of love continues. There is no need, it seems, to rank the rest of the commandments after identifying the first two. It's not as though the other several hundred laws are of subsequent importance. Rather, the other several hundred laws are all captured within these first two. "On these two commandments," Jesus concluded, "hang all the law and the prophets" (Matthew

22:40). Paul, likewise, taught the Christians in Rome that the commandments about adultery, murder, stealing, coveting, "and any other commandment, are summed up in this word, 'Lord your neighbor as yourself.' Love does no wrong to a neighbor; therefore, love is the fulfilling of the law" (Romans 13:9-10).

Love is the first commandment and the second commandment. Love fulfills all of the commandments. And love, we discover, is also the new commandment. "I give you a new commandment," Jesus told the disciples on the night prior to his crucifixion, "that you love one another. Just as I have loved you, you also should love one another" (John 13:34).

We cannot understand the nature of God apart from love. For love is the essence of God's will, as indicated by both the law and logic. And the will of God is an expression of the nature of God.

## The Great Attribute

The apostle John understood that love is the nature of God. He said it in the most simple and profound way imaginable. "God is love," John boldly wrote (1 John 4:8). I say "boldly" because there is something spectacular about John's grammar. For rather than using an adjective to describe God, John uses a noun.

If I say that God is holy, just, kind, or wise, I am employing adjectives to try to describe the nature of God. And no adjective pretends to be comprehensive. Each one may be used to help express a part of what God is like. John, however, uses a noun instead of an adjective. Where we might expect John to say, "God is loving," he says, instead, "God is love." Nowhere in Scripture does it say that God is holiness. Or justice. Or kindness. Or wisdom. That kind of one-to-one correlation is unparalleled. And it suggests to us that love, unlike anything else, is the essential attribute of God.

If we do not grasp love, then we will be doomed always to misunderstanding the Lord. Only when seen through the lens of love will we make sense of the words and deeds, the laws and will of God.

The parent recognizes what the child might not: namely, that rules are a function of love. The child hears no as an unhappy and limiting thing. Yet the parent knows better. All of our parental prohibitions are designed to keep our children safe and healthy. Our rules are to protect their best interests. And so, too, with the rules God has presented to humankind. They are an expression and extension of God's love, and we should embrace them as such.

Likewise, the parent understands the loving nature of punishment. Angry punishment, of course, is a terrible business, and most of us deeply regret the times that we have punished our children out of anger. Yet we know that punishing is a thing we do for their own good, not for our profit or convenience. The punishment is meant to guide them. It is designed to discourage what is wrong and redirect them to what is right. We too discover with the chastening of God in the lives of human beings. Divine punishment is an expression and extension of divine love.

Whatever comes from God must be understood as a function of love. It is the divine nature and the divine will. Because love is God's essential attribute, it is also meant to be the identifying attribute of God's people. "By this everyone will know that you are my disciples," Jesus said, "if you have love for one another" (John 13:35). As love is God's chief characteristic, so also it should be ours.

Jesus' teaching on this point is a remarkable one, for we might guess something else. If the text were blurred at that point, what would we presume he said? If we knew that Jesus had told his disciples, "By this everyone will know that you are my disciples," but the page was cut off at that point, how would we fill in the blank?

By what will the world recognize that we belong to and follow him? By our morality? That seems like a reasonable and appropriate answer. By our power? That would be consistent with the kinds of signs and wonders that characterized the early church. By our doctrine? That sort of definition of what it is to be a Christian has certainly prevailed in many generations of Western culture. Yet none of those good options were Jesus' point. No, the hallmark of his followers is meant to be love. The great attribute of God becomes the great attribute of the people of God.

## The Great Opportunity

See how everything springs from the love of God. That is the origin, the starting place, for everything that we have touched on thus far, as well as everything that we will explore together during this quarter. Law and gospel, human freedom and divine chastening, forgiveness and salvation, redemption and resurrection—trace each one back, and we find that it is rooted in God's love.

Our opportunity, then, is to live in response to that love. The relationship between us and God's law, for example, is a love relationship. The Lord gave the law as a function of love for us. And our obedience, in turn, is a function of our love for God.

Our exercise of our free will, likewise, becomes all about love. We recognize that the Lord made us free precisely so that we could love. To be free without loving, therefore, is to forfeit the very advantage we have been given. What is true of universal human freedom is more profoundly true of Christian freedom. "For you were called to freedom," Paul wrote to the Christians in Galatia. "Only do not use your freedom as an opportunity for self-indulgence, but through love become slaves to one another" (Galatians 5:13). Freedom that is not exercised in love has missed its purpose.

Jesus' parable of the unforgiving servant (Matthew 18:23-35) offers a compelling picture of this principle of living in response to God's love. The first servant was forgiven an enormous debt by his master. Yet when he encountered a fellow servant who owed him a comparatively small amount, that first servant was insistent and demanding, even to the point of having his debtor thrown in jail. The master was profoundly disappointed by this development, saying to that first servant, "Should you not have had mercy on your fellow slave, as I had mercy on you?" (Matthew 18:33). The servant missed an opportunity to live in response to his master's mercy.

Jesus' "new commandment" captures that truth most concisely:. "Just as I have loved you, you also should love one another" (John 13:34). We are set free from the unhappy cycle of constantly responding to others based on how they treat us, what they owe us, what they think of us or say about us. Rather, our love for them is a response to Christ's love for us, which is constant, joyful, and sure. Our love is a response to his.

And his love for us is an extension of the Father's. "As the Father has loved me," Jesus said, "so I have loved you" (John 15:9). Our love, therefore, is an extension of God's love. That, after all, is where everything begins. And our great opportunity is to live in that love.

# CLOSE-UP: JONAH AND HIS STORY

During this spring quarter we are seeing signs of God's love throughout the Scriptures. In the first two units we are surveying the New Testament and Psalm 23 to glimpse of a few of the many examples of God's love. The third unit, however, focuses exclusively on the Book of Jonah. You may remember the story well if you attended Sunday school as a child, but there's much more to learn about Jonah than his encounter with a large fish. Questions surround Jonah and his story.

Who was Jonah? Was he a historical person, as suggested by the reference in 2 Kings 14:25 to Jonah, the son of Amittai who hailed from Gath-hepher? Or was that reference in 2 Kings used only to tell an important story about God's love and compassion for all people by connecting it to a little known prophet?

When and where was the Book of Jonah written? Most prophetic books begin by mentioning the reign of a king (see Hosea 1:1; Amos 1:1) or the exile (see Ezekiel 1:1-3) or period after the exile (see Haggai 1:1; Zechariah 1:1) to set the book in a historical context for the prophecy. The Book of Jonah, however, includes no historical or geographical markers. Consequently, scholars have suggested dates for the writing of this book ranging across seven centuries—beginning as early as the eighth century b.c., which was when the Jonah in 2 Kings was prophesying.

Why is the Book of Jonah different from other biblical books of prophecy? Although Jonah is included with the Twelve Prophets, the book focuses on Jonah himself—how he relates to God and to the people to whom God has commissioned him to preach. All of the other prophetic books focus on the message of the prophets, rather than the prophets themselves, even if some biographical information is included.

How does Jonah relate to God and to the people to whom he is called to prophesy? Jonah knows God, for he remarks in 4:2 about God's graciousness, mercy, slowness to anger, love, and willingness to relent from punishing. After disobeying God's call and trying to flee from God, Jonah finally arrives in Nineveh, a "great city" where wickedness abounds. In contrast to the repeated, passionate speeches of most prophets, Jonah offers just five words in Hebrew, as recorded in 3:4: "Forty days more, and Nineveh shall be overthrown!" Also in contrast to other prophets whose words went unheeded, after hearing Jonah the Ninevites and their king immediately expressed contrition by fasting and donning sackcloth. The repentance of these powerful Assyrians, who are hated by Jonah but loved by God, differs sharply from Jonah's anger with God. The embittered prophet just cannot accept that God's compassionate love is freely available to all who repent, no matter how evil they have been. Despite Jonah's initial disobedience and halfhearted preaching, God deals graciously with Jonah too. Yet God also chastises him for his unwillingness to be concerned for the "hundred and twenty thousand" (4:11) lost souls of Nineveh.

# FAITH IN ACTION: REVEALING THE LOVE OF GOD

Throughout this quarter's study we encounter stories in which God's eternal, steadfast, saving love perseveres, renews, and upholds us. Just as God and Jesus act as the good shepherd, so we are to care for others who need to experience such love in their lives.

Post each of the following ideas on a separate sheet of newsprint. Begin with one idea and add others, one per week, throughout the quarter. Invite participants to choose those ideas that can help them reveal God's love to others. Suggest that the adults keep a journal about what they do to reveal God's love to others.

1.  Practice seeing and interacting with people with whom you usually have little contact. Talk with a server in a restaurant or clerk in a convenience store or a homeless person on the street. Take whatever action you can— tipping generously, buying lunch for a hungry person—as a means of revealing God's love.
2.  Invite a seeker to dialogue with you concerning what it means to live in relationship with God through Jesus Christ. Help this person to understand that being a child of God is about a loving relationship, not a list of do's and don'ts.
3.  Participate in a ministry of your church that shows God's love for other people. Perhaps you have a Good Samaritan fund that helps those who need assistance to avoid eviction or utility cutoff. In addition to writing a check to support this fund, volunteer time to assist those who come to the church in need of help.
4.  Try to act as a peacemaker between two people whose relationship has been broken. Do whatever you can to help bring about reconciliation.
5.  Act as a role model for others in times of stress and uncertainty. Tell people that you believe God is the good shepherd and will continue to love and care for you. Live in faith that God will provide for you and meet your needs.
6.  Stand in solidarity with Christians around the world by supporting a mission with your money and your prayers. Write a note, if possible, to let the people associated with this mission know that you are praying for their ministry.
7.  Ponder the stories of Jesus' resurrection as they appear in all four Gospels. Which one can you identify with most closely? Why? How do you especially see God's love poured out in this account?
8.  Recall from Paul's teachings in Romans 8:31-39 that nothing can separate

us from God's love. With whom can you share this good news? What can you do to help lighten this person's load?

9. Offer tangible assistance to someone who has been hurt by family or friends and needs to know that God loves and cares for them. A card with a heartfelt note or an invitation to a meal could really buoy someone's spirits.

10. Show God's love to someone who feels hopeless and perhaps is unwilling or unable to believe that God can help overcome a serious problem.

# PRONUNCIATION GUIDE

Arimathea (air uh muh thee' uh)
Bithynia (bi thin' ee uh)
Cappadocia (kap uh doh' shee uh)
*dikaioo* (dik ah yo' o)
*dikaios* (dik' ah yos)
*dikaiosune* (dik ah yos oo' nay)
eschatological (es kat uh loj' i kuhl)
*hupernikao* (hoop er nik ah' o )

*kathairo* (kath ah' ee ro)
Nicodemus (nik uh dee' muhs)
Nineveh (nin' uh vuh)
Ninevite (nin' uh vite)
*orge* (or gay')
Sheol (shee' ohl)
Tarshish (tahr' shish)

UNIT 1: GOD'S ETERNAL, PRESERVING, RENEWING LOVE

# THE SOURCE OF ALL LOVE

---

## PREVIEWING THE LESSON

**Lesson Scripture:** 1 John 4:7-19
**Background Scripture:** 1 John 4:7-19
**Key Verse:** 1 John 4:11

**Focus of the Lesson:**
Many search in all the wrong places for a perfect love in which to put their trust. Can other humans be trusted to love without blemish at all times? First John reminds us that God is love and those who abide in love have God's love perfected in them.

**Goals for the Learners:**
(1) to consider differences and similarities between God's love and human love.
(2) to reflect on how God's perfect love casts out fear in human life.
(3) to demonstrate what it means to love others the way God loves them.

**Supplies:**
Bibles, newsprint and marker, paper and pencils, hymnals

---

## READING THE SCRIPTURE

NRSV
Lesson Scripture: 1 John 4:7-19

⁷Beloved, let us love one another, because love is from God; everyone who loves is born of God and knows God. ⁸Whoever does not love does not know God, for God is love. ⁹God's love was revealed among us in this way: God sent his only Son into the

CEB
Lesson Scripture: 1 John 4:7-19

⁷Dear friends, let's love each other, because love is from God, and everyone who loves is born from God and knows God. ⁸The person who doesn't love does not know God, because God is love. ⁹This is how the love of God is revealed to us: God has sent

world so that we might live through him. [10]In this is love, not that we loved God but that he loved us and sent his Son to be the atoning sacrifice for our sins. **[11]Beloved, since God loved us so much, we also ought to love one another.** [12]No one has ever seen God; if we love one another, God lives in us, and his love is perfected in us.

[13]By this we know that we abide in him and he in us, because he has given us of his Spirit. [14]And we have seen and do testify that the Father has sent his Son as the Savior of the world. [15]God abides in those who confess that Jesus is the Son of God, and they abide in God. [16]So we have known and believe the love that God has for us.

God is love, and those who abide in love abide in God, and God abides in them. [17]Love has been perfected among us in this: that we may have boldness on the day of judgment, because as he is, so are we in this world. [18]There is no fear in love, but perfect love casts out fear; for fear has to do with punishment, and whoever fears has not reached perfection in love. [19]We love because he first loved us.

his only Son into the world so that we can live through him. [10]This is love: it is not that we loved God but that he loved us and sent his Son as the sacrifice that deals with our sins.

**[11]Dear friends, if God loved us this way, we also ought to love each other.** [12]No one has ever seen God. If we love each other, God remains in us and his love is made perfect in us. [13]This is how we know we remain in him and he remains in us, because he has given us a measure of his Spirit. [14]We have seen and testify that the Father has sent the Son to be the savior of the world. [15]If any of us confess that Jesus is God's Son, God remains in us and we remain in God. [16]We have known and have believed the love that God has for us.

God is love, and those who remain in love remain in God and God remains in them. [17]This is how love has been perfected in us, so that we can have confidence on the Judgment Day, because we are exactly the same as God is in this world. [18]There is no fear in love, but perfect love drives out fear, because fear expects punishment. The person who is afraid has not been made perfect in love. [19]We love because God first loved us.

---

## UNDERSTANDING THE SCRIPTURE

**Introduction.** We will discover that John's writing style reads like a piece of classical music. His flow of thought does not move linearly from A to B to C and so on. Rather, he introduces motifs, and he continues to weave them throughout his piece. As a result, his style can seem repetitive. In reality, there is genius in how he gradually develops each theme in relation to the others.

**1 John 4:7.** The chief concern is a pastoral one. John is writing to some group of believers that is near and dear to him, though the epistle does not contain enough detail to tell us much about them. New Testament scholars speculate about the audience of this epistle, yet still we can say very little with certainty about them. Whoever they are, the author is naturally concerned for their life together, and central to that common life is love for another.

**1 John 4:8.** New Testament ethics are always rooted in doctrine; what we believe guides how we live. The central point of doctrine for John is his affirmation that "God is love." If we are from God, then, it follows that our behavior will reflect God's nature. John specifically uses the image of being "born of God" (4:7), which invites some natural analogies for us. If I am born of my parents, then I will carry within myself many of their characteristics. And if you and I are born of God, then John reasons that we will reflect God's chief characteristic: love.

**1 John 4:9-10.** Love always shows itself. If it is never revealed, never manifested, it hardly qualifies as love. John wants his readers' love to show itself, and so he reminds them of how God's love showed itself. In the process, John briefly makes a distinction between love that initiates and love that responds. We know how that phenomenon works in our human relationships. In our relationship with God, it was God who took the initiative to love. You and I simply live in response to that love.

**1 John 4:11.** Here is the central logic of the text: God first loves us, and we live in response to that love. Our response to God's love is not merely that we love God in return. Rather, our love imitates and resembles God's love. Love increasingly becomes our nature. And we, like God, reach out in love to others.

**1 John 4:12-16.** The key motif of this section, reminiscent of a portion of Jesus' teaching in John 15:1-10, is *abiding*. Appropriately, the passage is overtly Trinitarian, with references to the love of God, faith in Jesus, and the indwelling of the Spirit. As we contemplate our relationships with both God and with other human beings, we are rightly reminded that God is innately relational and that the essence of the divine nature is love.

Meanwhile, the passage reveals again how inseparable doctrine and ethics are. We observe that testifying, confessing, and believing are intermingled with abiding and loving. The argument is not that those who do not believe certain elements of Christian doctrine are incapable of love. Rather, John's understanding is of a tightly knit system in which everything is interrelated. For John, there is only a very thin membrane that separates belief in God and relationship with God. To have one without the other is as illogical for John as separating works from faith is for James (2:14-20). A relationship with God, meanwhile, suggests an experience of God's love. For John, to experience God's love is to show and to share that love.

The goal is that we are to abide in God and God will abide in us. For John, that goal is a recipe with several ingredients. Having faith in Christ, living in love, loving one another, and acknowledging the presence of the Spirit—these all weave together in such a way that each one is cause, effect, and proof of God abiding in us.

**1 John 4:17.** In the previous section, John introduced the concept of love being "perfected in us" (4:12). He resumes that theme here, and then expands on it in the following verse. When he first mentioned it in verse 12, that perfected love was, in part, the product of our loving one another. John's paradigm is thus reminiscent of the old adage that practice makes perfect. Additionally, perfect love was associated with God abiding in us, and that is the principle that John picks up on here. Having just affirmed that "those who abide in love abide in God, and God abides in them" (4:16), John declares that this "love has been perfected among us" (4:17).

The New Testament concept of perfection deserves a moment's attention here. In our parlance, perfect is associated with being unblemished or error-free. The underlying Greek word that John uses, however, is the same one used by the writer of Hebrews to refer to those who are "mature" (Hebrews 5:14). Perfect love, therefore, is not so much love that never makes a mistake, but love that has ceased to be childish or adolescent. It is mature, full-grown love.

Such full-grown love, according to John, makes us like God. And, with that love, comes confidence. John introduces the prospect of Judgment Day, which is not a recurring theme for him, but it serves to illustrate his point about love.

**1 John 4:18.** The confidence of perfected love translates into fearlessness. And, more than that: Not only is perfect love free from fear but it also drives out fear. That is a remarkable claim to ponder. To say that a person is cancer-free, for example, is not nearly as potent as saying that this person drives out cancer. Such is the impact of perfect love in our lives.

**1 John 4:19.** John ends this section where he began. The concern is that we are to love one another. And both the source and the rationale for that love are reiterated: namely, God's love for us.

## INTERPRETING THE SCRIPTURE

### Love, American Style

Perhaps you remember the television comedy of the late 1960s and early 1970s called *Love, American Style.* Each episode featured a series of short vignettes about men and women involved in flirtatious and romantic situations. As I recall it, the show was more engaged in superficial humor than cultural commentary. Yet its title combined with its antics to prompt a serious question: What is the American style of love?

The preponderance of the theme in our popular music and movies might make an observer think that we are experts in love. But our statistics about broken homes suggest otherwise. The American style of love does not seem to be very durable.

Our very use of the word reveals our poverty. When we talk about loving a particular restaurant or food, a car, a singing group, a hairstyle, or a sports team, we betray a pervasive misunderstanding. Love has become confused with enthusiasm, which is a fleeting thing, indeed. And consider how often the word "love" could be replaced in a sentence with either "really enjoy" or "really want." Yet neither of those phrases appears in Paul's classic definition of love in 1 Corinthians 13.

In this regard, our common use of the word has become rather childish. We picture the child, pleading with his or her parents to get a pet. "I just love puppies," the child exclaims, as though excitement qualifies as reason.

And the parent predictably responds, "Yes, but who is going to feed it and take it for walks? Who is going to take care of it and clean up after it?"

In that familiar scenario, the parent and the child are functioning with two different definitions of love. The child thinks that loving a puppy means really wanting to have one. The parent knows that loving a pet means taking care of it. The former is more about personal enjoyment and satisfaction. The latter is more about commitment and sacrifice.

The child's understanding of love is immature. That's understandable for as long as he or she is young, of course. If we continue to mistake love for excitement and satisfaction as we grow up, however, we will ruin many relationships and disappoint many people. And so our love needs to mature. Indeed, John would say that it needs to be made perfect.

### What Do You Want to Be When You Grow Up?

Grown-up love is what John has in mind for his audience. Yet grown-up love may be hard to come by for human beings in general, and perhaps especially so for our present culture. After all, we all learn how to love from somewhere, from someone. And if the love that prevails around us is an immature love, then we are naturally handicapped in our ability to rise to something higher.

In 1996, Hillary Rodham Clinton wrote a book titled *It Takes a Village*, espousing the principle that it takes a village to raise a child. I presume that principle is correct. Yet just as surely as the "village" can raise a child, it can also be responsible for stunting a child's growth and development.

Specifically, it may be that some of the culture of our "village" keeps its residents from growing into a mature love.

The man or woman who has come to know the love of God, therefore, has a great advantage. We may learn about love from a better source and example than the world around us, or even our parents. We may learn about love from the author of love; indeed, from the One whose very nature is love.

John's repeated statement that "God is love" might easily be dismissed as sentimental or overlooked as simple. In truth, however, the author makes an astonishing claim. The grammatical pattern in Scripture, after all, is to describe God either with adjectives (for example, just, holy, righteous, mighty) or with metaphorical nouns (for example, shepherd, king, rock, refuge). But John steps out and makes an unprecedentedly bold assertion, for he makes a one-to-one correlation between God and an abstract noun. He does not merely claim that God is loving, but that God is love. More than holiness, wisdom, or might, love is God's very essence.

Consider, then, the logic of John's thought. Those who are "born of God" and "abide in God" become "as he is" (4:7, 13, 15, 17). Love increasingly becomes our nature and our practice. As we abide in love, and we abide in God, and God abides in us, love is perfected in us.

In the beginning, you recall, the divine design was that we should be like God, created in God's image (Genesis 1:26-27). Throughout the pages of Scripture, we see this recurring theme. It is God's continuing desire that we should be like our creator (see, for example, Leviticus 11:44-45; Matthew 5:43-48; John 13:34). Paul, likewise, understood that the goal is that we should come "to maturity, to the measure of the full stature of Christ" (Ephesians 4:13).

So when you ask the children of God what they want to be when they grow up, they should answer, "I want to be like God." It is both God's desire and ours. And the essence of growing into that likeness is to grow up into perfect love.

### The Look and Life of Perfect Love

For generations, trainers and coaches in a variety of fields have emphasized the importance of visualization. The techniques may vary, but the underlying principle remains basically the same. The idea is that, in part, succeeding depends upon being able to imagine or picture yourself succeeding.

At its core, this principle is as old as common sense. Being able to see myself doing something well, after all, is just a variation on the most basic method of training: namely, seeing someone else doing that thing well. We human beings have always learned how to do by watching how

things are done. That sort of attentive apprenticeship is the first step in becoming proficient in almost anything. We need to know what the process looks like, and we need to know what the finished product is meant to look like. Then we are prepared to do it ourselves.

So it is that you and I are prepared to love. We have seen the process. We have seen the finished product. And so we are trained to love.

"God's love was revealed among us in this way," John writes. "God sent his only Son into the world" (4:9). Thus we see God's initiative of love. Notably, it is initiative without the guarantee of a favorable response. Such is the extravagance of God's love that it is spent even though it may be for naught in a given individual's life.

Furthermore, God "sent his Son to be the atoning sacrifice for our sins" (4:10). The love we have seen from God is sacrificial love. It covers the distance in the broken relationship. It forgives at its own expense. It offers what is undeserved.

We learn how to do by seeing how it is done. And we have seen how perfect love is done. Therefore, "since God loved us so much, we also ought to love one another" (4:11, key verse).

---

## SHARING THE SCRIPTURE

### PREPARING TO LEAD

#### Preparing Our Hearts

Ponder this week's devotional reading from Psalm 40:1-10 in which the writer offers thanksgiving to God for deliverance. What situations have

caused you to feel as if you are trapped in a pit? How has God helped you? How did you offer thanks to God? What testimony can you give to help others who need to trust God for help?

Pray that you and the students will recognize and give thanks for God's saving love.

---

*Preparing Our Minds*

Study the background Scripture and the lesson Scripture, which are both from 1 John 4:7-19.

Consider this question: *Can humans be trusted to love at all times?*

Write on newsprint:

❏ information for next week's lesson, found under Continue the Journey.

❏ activities for further spiritual growth in Continue the Journey.

Determine how you might use any of the features that precede the first lesson of this quarter in today's session. Consider reading or retelling portions of The Big Picture: God's Love for Us to introduce this quarter's study.

## LEADING THE CLASS

*(1) Gather to Learn*

❖ Welcome everyone and pray that those who have come today will experience God's love and pass it on to others.

❖ Read: **In some countries potential couples are carefully matched on the basis of traditions or religious beliefs. In the United States, though, the majority of brides and grooms select their partners, usually based on love for each other. Despite a culture in which people are generally free to choose their mates, the reality is that a significant portion of these marriages will fail. Why does a once-promising relationship fall apart? Major reasons include incompatibility, infidelity, money issues, lack of commitment, unrealistic expectations, and lack of equality in the relationship. Tragically, the person that once seemed so right has, over time, become so wrong and love fades.**

❖ Read aloud today's focus statement: **Many search in all the wrong places for a perfect love in which to put their trust. Can other humans be trusted to love without blemish at all times? First John reminds us that God is love and those who abide in love have God's love perfected in them.**

*(2) Goal 1: Consider Differences and Similarities Between God's Love and Human Love*

❖ **Option:** Read or retell portions of The Big Picture: God's Love for Us to introduce the class to the theme of this quarter's study.

❖ Post a sheet of newsprint and invite the students to call out words or phrases they would use to describe God's love.

❖ Call on a volunteer to read 1 John 4:7-19.

❖ Ask these questions. Add information from Understanding the Scripture to expand the discussion.

1. **What evidence do we have that God loves us?**
2. **In whom does God abide?**
3. **How do you know if God abides in you?**
4. **What does John mean when he refers to "perfect love"?**
5. **Why, according to John, is it impossible for fear and love to coexist?**
6. **What does our treatment of our human brothers and sisters reveal about our relationship with God?**

*3) Goal 2: Reflect on How God's Perfect Love Casts Out Fear in Human Life*

❖ Read these words: **Meister Eckhart, a medieval theologian of the**

Dominican Order wrote: "Our Lord cannot endure that any who love him should be worried, for fear is painful. Thus St. John says: 'Love casteth out fear.' Love cannot put up with either fear or pain, and so, to grow in love is to diminish in fear, and when one has become a perfect lover, fear has gone out of him altogether. At the beginning of a good life, however, fear is useful. It is love's gateway. A punch or an awl makes a hole for the thread with which a shoe is sewed . . . and a bristle is put on the thread to get it through the hole, but when the thread does bind the shoe together, the bristle is out. So fear leads love at first, and when love has bound us to God, fear is done away."

❖ Note that Meister Eckhart goes beyond John's saying that "perfect love casts our fear" (1 John 4:18) by trying to explain how this "casting out" actually happens.

❖ Distribute paper and pencils. Invite participants to reflect on their understanding of how God's love is able to cast out fear. Do they agree with Eckhart that fear serves some initial purpose that helps drive us to be bound to God in love? What other descriptions, aside from sewing a shoe together, might describe their understanding of God's love casting out fear.

❖ Call everyone together and encourage volunteers to briefly state their ideas.

*(4) Goal 3: Demonstrate What It Means to Love Others the Way God Loves Them*

❖ Read The Look and Life of Perfect Love in Interpreting the Scripture.

❖ Note that the love we see in Jesus is sacrificial love, initiated by God who sent him with no guarantee that such love would be reciprocated.

❖ Form several small groups and give each one a sheet of newsprint and a marker. Direct each group to think of actions that Jesus took to reveal God's love that they could imitate. Recommend that they think big but also be realistic: They will not, for example, be able to feed five thousand with a few loaves of bread and some fish, but they may be able to provide a hot, nutritious meal for homeless people on a regular, ongoing basis. They may not be able to build a Habitat for Humanity home on their own, but it is possible to do that if several churches work together on all aspects of the project.

❖ Conclude by inviting those who are willing to make a commitment to follow through on any of the suggested actions to meet with others interested in the same project in order to make plans.

*(5) Continue the Journey*

❖ Pray that as the learners depart, they will grow closer to God and, in turn, share God's love with others.

❖ Post information for next week's session on newsprint for the students to copy:

- **Title: God's Overflowing Love**
- **Background Scripture: Ephesians 2:1-10**
- **Lesson Scripture: Ephesians 2:1-10**
- **Focus of the Lesson: Sometimes those who break the rules become outcasts in the group. Where can those who break rules find acceptance? Out of great love for us, God saved us by grace through faith and will show**

the immense richness of this grace in kindness to those who are in Christ Jesus.

❖ Challenge the adults to grow spiritually by completing one or more of these activities related to this week's session.

(1) Review your day as your prepare for bed each night this week. Where did you experience God's love? Where did you experience the love of other people? In what situations do you think others experienced God's love working through you?

(2) Participate in a church ministry that reveals God's love to people who may be "unseen" because they live on the margins of society. How do you perceive that the food, clothing, visitation, or whatever action this ministry engages in allows others to perceive God's love for them? How do the people who offer this ministry try to make clear that what they do for others is their way of showing God's love?

(3) Identify fears that keep you from showing love to certain groups or individuals. Pray that God's love will enable you to overcome these fears.

❖ Sing or read aloud "Where Charity and Love Prevail."

❖ Conclude today's session by leading the class in this benediction, which is adapted from John 15:12, the key verse for March 19: **Let us go forth obeying Jesus' commandment to love one another as he has loved us. Amen.**

UNIT 1: GOD'S ETERNAL, PRESERVING, RENEWING LOVE

# GOD'S OVERFLOWING LOVE

---

## PREVIEWING THE LESSON

**Lesson Scripture:** Ephesians 2:1-10
**Background Scripture:** Ephesians 2:1-10
**Key Verses:** Ephesians 2:4-5

### Focus of the Lesson:
Sometimes those who break the rules become outcasts in the group. Where can those who break rules find acceptance? Out of great love for us, God saved us by grace through faith and will show the immense richness of this grace in kindness to those who are in Christ Jesus.

### Goals for the Learners:
(1) to identify ways in which God's love addresses the separation of sin.
(2) to give thanks for God's grace that offers new possibilities for living in human community.
(3) to commit to expressing God's love in the world and the communities in which they live.

### Supplies:
Bibles, newsprint and marker, paper and pencils, hymnals

---

## READING THE SCRIPTURE

NRSV
Lesson Scripture: Ephesians 2:1-10

¹You were dead through the trespasses and sins ²in which you once lived, following the course of this world, following the ruler of the power of the air, the spirit that is now at work among those who are disobedient. ³All of us once lived among

CEB
Lesson Scripture: Ephesians 2:1-10

¹At one time you were like a dead person because of the things you did wrong and your offenses against God. ²You used to live like people of this world. You followed the rule of a destructive spiritual power. This is the spirit of disobedience to God's

them in the passions of our flesh, following the desires of flesh and senses, and we were by nature children of wrath, like everyone else. **⁴But God, who is rich in mercy, out of the great love with which he loved us ⁵even when we were dead through our trespasses, made us alive together with Christ—by grace you have been saved—** ⁶and raised us up with him and seated us with him in the heavenly places in Christ Jesus, ⁷so that in the ages to come he might show the immeasurable riches of his grace in kindness toward us in Christ Jesus. ⁸For by grace you have been saved through faith, and this is not your own doing; it is the gift of God— ⁹not the result of works, so that no one may boast. ¹⁰For we are what he has made us, created in Christ Jesus for good works, which God prepared beforehand to be our way of life.

will that is now at work in persons whose lives are characterized by disobedience. ³At one time you were like those persons. All of you used to do whatever felt good and whatever you thought you wanted so that you/ were children headed for punishment just like everyone else.

**⁴⁻⁵However, God is rich in mercy. He brought us to life with Christ while we were dead as a result of those things that we did wrong. He did this because of the great love that he has for us. You are saved by God's grace!** ⁶And God raised us up and seated us in the heavens with Christ Jesus. ⁷God did this to show future generations the greatness of his grace by the goodness that God has shown us in Christ Jesus.

⁸You are saved by God's grace because of your faith. This salvation is God's gift. It's not something you possessed. ⁹It's not something you did that you can be proud of. ¹⁰Instead, we are God's accomplishment, created in Christ Jesus to do good things. God planned for these good things to be the way that we live our lives.

## UNDERSTANDING THE SCRIPTURE

**Ephesians 2:1-3.** Paul operates with a different definition of "dead" than what is common in our vernacular. We might be tempted to dismiss his language as metaphorical. He might contend, however, that his definitions of life and death are more in touch with reality than ours. For while we tend to limit ourselves to the narrow confines of physical life and death, the New Testament bears witness to the weightier truths of spiritual death and eternal life.

In our common understanding, a

person begins alive but eventually dies. The people to whom Paul writes, on the other hand, started off dead, but have become alive. Not that those people are different from us. Rather, Paul is reflecting a different perception of the world and the human condition. It is entirely spiritual, involving "trespasses and sins," "the ruler of the power of the air," "the spirit that is now at work," and "children of wrath."

Paul is not singling out his Ephesian audience in these matters; his diagnosis is a universal one. "All of us once lived" in that condition, he affirms in verse 3. And in that state, we were "like everyone else."

**Ephesians 2:4.** "But God" is a beautiful way to begin a sentence. It reflects the intrusion of grace into a fallen world. Having defined the human condition in the preceding verses, Paul turns now to the attributes of God. Specifically, the apostle cites the rich "mercy" and "great love" that result in God acting in our favor.

Imagine two card players. The moment comes when each will show his hand. The first lays down his cards, and it appears to be a strong hand, indeed. But then, in response, the other player puts down a hand that completely trumps the previous one. So, too, when God's mercy and love answer human flesh and trespasses. What God is mercifully trumps what we are, and thus we are saved.

**Ephesians 2:5.** Paul returns to his spiritual life-and-death model. Formerly, "we were dead," and of course there is nothing that a dead person can do to help himself or herself. If a dead person is going to come back to life, it will require some outside intervention. Enter the grace of God. Meanwhile, the reference to being made "alive together with Christ" reflects Paul's understanding that we are crucified with Christ and raised with him (see Romans 6:3-11; Galatians 2:19-20).

**Ephesians 2:6-7.** Those of us with a concern for grammar and the tenses of verbs may raise our eyebrows as we read these verses. Exactly what has already been done and what is still in the plan for the future? But perhaps the present and future are blurred by the promise of God. Perhaps the promise of God is so strong and sure that it makes the future plan equivalent to a present certainty. Along these lines, Charles Spurgeon wrote, "We ought to treat the promise as in itself the substance of the thing promised, just as we look upon a man's check or note of hand as an actual payment."

Earlier in this same epistle, Paul affirmed that God had "seated [Christ] at his right hand in the heavenly places, far above all rule and authority and power and dominion" (Ephesians 1:20-21). In chapter 2 the same potent image is repeated, but we are included in the picture. And so the underlying principle of the preceding verse continues: namely, just as we are crucified and made alive with Christ, so we are also "raised up with him."

Finally, we note God's desire that "in the ages to come he might show the immeasurable riches of his grace in kindness toward us in Christ Jesus." The piling up of emphatic vocabulary reflects Paul's effort to express the inexpressible. Meanwhile, it seems that God has already overwhelmed us with grace and kindness in this age. Can we imagine what more awaits us?

**Ephesians 2:8-9.** The recipe for salvation features two ingredients: grace and faith. Grace is the part that comes from God, and that is what saves us. Faith, meanwhile, is our contribution to the recipe. It is not so much what saves us as it is what accesses that saving grace. Similarly, the electrical cord is not really the power that makes the appliance run, but it provides access to the power that does.

Paul juxtaposes "gift" and "works." Neither is a sophisticated theological term, but each combines to convey a profound doctrinal truth. A gift, we understand, is a reflection of the giver's heart and a product of the giver's generosity. If one works to receive a gift, however, then it would cease to be a gift. It would be something more like wages or compensation. Paul's insistent point is that we do not—indeed, we cannot—earn salvation. Rather, it is freely offered and available in Christ.

Boasting may not seem like much of a temptation to us when it comes to salvation. Perhaps we would do better, therefore, to think in terms of taking credit. You and I cannot take any credit for our salvation. If the player who comes in and pinch hits for me hits a game-winning home run, what is my part in that? I enjoy the victory, but I am not credited with the victory.

**Ephesians 2:10.** "We are what he has made us" appears, at first, to point back to Eden. Yet Paul does not seem to be referencing the original creation of humanity. Instead, "created in Christ Jesus" indicates that Paul has a different creation—perhaps the new creation (see 2 Corinthians 5:17)—in mind here.

The apostle is specific and clear about the purpose of this new creation. The Bible students and teachers through the years who have tried to gin up some argument between Paul and James about faith and works have missed this phrase. It turns out that Paul is not at all dismissive of works; on the contrary, he believes that you and I have been "created . . . for good works." Good works are not how we are saved; but good works are, arguably, why we are saved.

## INTERPRETING THE SCRIPTURE

*Our Preexisting Condition*

Theologians call it original sin. The apostle Paul captured it in his use of the term "flesh." In our modern parlance, we might be more inclined to categorize it in terms of various dysfunctions. Whatever you may call it, though, it is humanity's great ailment, and it is a preexisting condition.

Paul elaborates on and explains the human condition in his Letter to the Ephesians. While we think in terms of maladies being viral or bacterial, the apostle's diagnosis is that this soul-sickness is rooted in "trespasses and sins" (2:1). It is a handicapping condition, for its victims live "in the passions of our flesh, following the desires of flesh and senses" (2:3). And, worst of all, it is 100 percent fatal: "we

were dead," Paul says bluntly in verse 5.

He also says that we are all "children of wrath" (2:3). It's a strong image, and frankly an unpleasant one. We prefer to think of ourselves as children of God. Paul would contend, however, that children of God are what we become, not where we begin.

The underlying word that Paul uses is a telling one. The original Greek, which we translate "wrath," is *orge*, from which we get our English word "orgy." It connoted angry impulse, which is certainly consistent with living subject to the passions and desires of the flesh.

This malady, according to Paul, is a universal condition. He is not reflecting specifically on the biography of the Christians in Ephesus to whom he writes. Rather, he would have said the same thing to believers anywhere. For whatever guilt we earn by our choices and behavior, there is this underlying reality of brokenness that is not our choice. It is our condition, and we are born with it.

From our world of insurance policies and small-print legalities, of course, you and I know about pre-existing conditions. They are those maladies or disorders that might disqualify us from some sort of coverage or treatment. But can there be a more serious preexisting condition than being dead? Is there any state more disqualifying?

In our ordinary, physical life, our preexisting conditions disqualify us because our human legalities don't leave room for grace. Not so with God, however. As serious and seemingly hopeless as our human condition was, still we came under divine coverage. By grace, we were eligible for God's treatment, for "even when we were dead through our trespasses, [God] made us alive together with Christ" (2:5).

When Paul wrote to the Ephesians about the salvation that is offered in Christ, he taught them to recognize the prominence of grace. What else but grace would be willing to cover and to treat such a hopeless case as I? And, like any good doctor, Paul knew that it is essential to get the treatment right. The spiritual problem, however, is that there are other treatments that are very popular, even though they cannot cure.

### The Favorite Placebo

Many of us grew up with family cures. Knowing that you cannot go running to a doctor for every ache, pain, and injury, mom or dad probably had a few homegrown remedies. Some we enjoyed. Others were distasteful enough that we hesitated even to admit that we weren't feeling well. But the well-meaning intention was always to make us better.

Of course, *feeling* better and *being* better are not entirely the same thing. The mother kissing the small child's scraped knee typically makes the child feel better, but I'm not sure that there is anything truly curative in that kiss. In the moment, though, the child's first priority is to feel better.

As adults, too, we may make more of a priority of feeling better than actually being better. The phrases "comfort food" and "drowning one's sorrows" both reflect behaviors that are more about feeling better. We live in a pain-killing culture, and individuals may seek a lot of unhealthy ways of eliminating—or numbing—their pain.

Not surprisingly, what is true in the physical realm is also true in the spiritual realm. There, too, we have a malady. And there, too, we may be tempted to pursue what makes us feel better, even if it does not actually make us better.

Traditionally, there has been one, particular remedy that has enjoyed special popularity among good, religious folks. The diabolically deceptive treatment is works. Doing good works generally makes us feel better. In some cases, as in the notorious case of certain hypocritical Pharisees of Jesus' day, folks who emphasize good works may actually come to feel too good about themselves. But as we already noted, feeling good is not the same thing as being well.

The apostle Paul was as acquainted with this placebo as anyone else who ever lived. He was a Pharisee, and considered himself zealous and blameless (see Philippians 3:4-6). And so, while we do not see any evidence that he was prone to the kind of noxious hypocrisy that Jesus criticized, Paul did make a great deal of his works—that is, his own righteousness.

When he wrote to the Christians in Ephesus, therefore, Paul was eager to make clear to them the real way of salvation. It is "not your own doing" (2:8), he insisted. It is "not the result of works" (2:9). He didn't want those believers to settle for the placebo. He wanted them to know the real cure for our human condition.

### The Real Cure

Take a moment to imagine the preposterous. You apply for health insurance while in the hospital. You call an agent about acquiring homeowner's insurance from your basement while the tornado sirens are blaring and the windows are exploding. You try to purchase life insurance while on your deathbed.

What insurance agency takes on such a risk? No, these cases do not even qualify as risks anymore; they are pure liabilities. No one in their right mind offers these cases coverage. No one, that is, except God.

As soon as we can imagine the preposterous, we are in a position to think about God's grace. For as long as we are making reasonable calculations, we'll never reach grace. Only when we factor in what seems totally unreasonable will we arrive at the beauty of grace. And grace, according to Paul, is the real cure—the only cure—for the human condition.

Too often, it seems to me, the grace of God is shortchanged in people's minds. When we think of grace, we think of forgiveness. That is the truth, of course, but it is not the whole truth.

My concern is that so many folks underestimate the grace of God. They suppose that the best that God can do for us is to excuse us for being "dead through our trespasses" (2:5). That makes grace a rather weak player. The gospel that Paul preaches, however, reveals grace as a most powerful thing.

By God's grace we are saved. By grace, we are raised to new life in Christ. And by that grace, we are re-created to fully live the life that God intended. And so our salvation is not the result of good works, but our good works are the result of salvation.

---

## SHARING THE SCRIPTURE

### PREPARING TO LEAD

#### Preparing Our Hearts

Ponder this week's devotional reading from Ephesians 4:1-6. Paul, or someone writing in his name, calls on believers to live according to the calling they have in Christ Jesus. What are some of the attributes that Paul urges his readers to adopt? What role does love play within the body of Christ?

Pray that you and the students will bear with one another in love so as to maintain the unity of the church.

#### Preparing Our Minds

Study the background Scripture and the lesson Scripture, which are both from Ephesians 2:1-10.

Consider this question: *Where can those who break rules find acceptance?*

Write on newsprint:

❏ information for next week's lesson, found under Continue the Journey.

❏ activities for further spiritual growth in Continue the Journey.

Determine how you might use any of the features that precede the first lesson of this quarter in today's session.

Become familiar with the entire Interpreting the Scripture portion so that you can present the brief lecture suggested under Goal 1. You will likely want to prepare notes.

LEADING THE CLASS

*(1) Gather to Learn*

❖ Welcome everyone and pray that those who have come today will be open to the love and leading of God as they study together.

❖ Read: **Recall an incident during your youth when you broke the rules. Perhaps you tried to skirt rules to give yourself an advantage while playing a sport or game. Maybe you ignored household rules, such as a curfew. Possibly you tried to explain to a police officer why that speed limit sign did not apply to you. Share with the class what happened, the consequences of your action, and the lessons you learned from this experience.**

❖ Read aloud today's focus statement: **Sometimes those who break the rules become outcasts in the group. Where can those who break rules find acceptance? Out of great love for us, God saved us by grace through faith and will show the immense richness of this grace in kindness to those who are in Christ Jesus.**

*(2) Goal 1: Identify Ways in Which God's Love Addresses the Separation of Sin*

❖ Select a volunteer to read Ephesians 2:1-10.

❖ Use the three topics in the Interpreting the Scripture portion—Our Preexisting Condition, The Favorite Placebo, The Real Cure—to present a brief lecture concerning how God's love addresses the separation of sin.

❖ Discuss these questions:

1. **How is Paul's definition of "dead" different from our usual definition?** (See Ephesians 2:1-3 in Understanding the Scripture.)

2. **How do you interpret Paul's use of past verb tenses ("raised," "seated") in verse 6 when it seems obvious that you have not yet been "raised" or "seated"?** (See Ephesians 2:6-7 in Understanding the Scripture. Note the quotation by Charles Spurgeon at the end of the first paragraph in this section.)

3. **What roles do grace and faith play in salvation? How do works fit into the equation?** (See Ephesians 2:8-9 in Understanding the Scripture.)

4. **For what reason has God "created us in Christ"?** (See Ephesians 2:10 in Understanding the Scripture.)

*(3) Goal 2: Give Thanks for God's Grace that Offers New Possibilities for Living in Human Community*

❖ Read this quotation by John Baillie (1741–1806): **"A true Christian** is a man [or woman] who never for a moment forgets what God has done for him [or her] in Christ, and whose whole comportment and whole activity have their root in the sentiment of gratitude."

❖ Distribute paper and pencils and encourage participants to ponder what God has done for them in Christ that prompts them to feel gratitude. Then they are to write a letter of thanks to God, stating at least three reasons for their gratitude and explaining how God's lovingkindness and grace on their behalf opened new possibilities for living.

❖ Call everyone together. Invite volunteers to state briefly one reason for thanksgiving and how God's grace has changed their lives.

*(4) Goal 3: Describe How Christians Live Out God's Love in the World and in the Communities in which They Live*

❖ Form small groups and encourage participants to talk about situations in which the church reached out to others in ways that demonstrated the grace of God. Perhaps someone in the group is here now because the church stepped up to help in a time of need.

❖ Reconvene the groups and discuss these questions:
- **What does our congregation do to show others—believers and nonbelievers as well—that they can find God's grace and love here?** (Think about how the congregation generally greets visitors; how it accepts and ministers to those who may need life's basic necessities by having food, clothing, or money for urgent bills avail-

able; to which community groups that help individuals in need, such as Alcoholics Anonymous or Narcotics Anonymous, the church is willing to open its doors; and how it provides for guests and members who may need assistance to hear a service or read a bulletin.)
- **When you have visited other congregations, perhaps while on vacation, what evidence did you see that they were living out God's love for the world? What ideas that apparently worked for them could our congregation adopt? How might we do that?**

❖ Conclude this portion of the lesson by inviting those who are willing to make a commitment to being examples of God's love in the world to repeat after you this adaptation from a baptismal covenant. Read through the words of commitment once so that participants can hear what they are agreeing to do. Then read it again, this time stopping at the end of each line to allow time for students who want to commit themselves to repeat the words.

**With God's help we will proclaim the good news
and order our lives after the example of Christ
so that all those we meet
may experience God's steadfast love, forgiveness, and grace
through us.**

*(5) Continue the Journey*

❖ Pray that as the learners depart, they will be ready to share God's overflowing love and grace with everyone they encounter this week.

❖ Post information for next week's session on newsprint for the students to copy:

- **Title: God's Love Manifested**
- **Background Scripture: John 15:1-17**
- **Lesson Scripture: John 15:1-17**
- **Focus of the Lesson: In our human condition, we search for that which enables us to love and be loved by others. Where do we find the authentic source of this love? The writer of the Gospel says that God is the source of an all-encompassing love, which empowers us to love God and one another.**

❖ Challenge the adults to grow spiritually by completing one or more of these activities related to this week's session.

**(1) Respond to someone who** acts negatively toward you with a sign of God's grace and love. How does your response affect this person?

**(2) Do at least one good work each day this week. Recognize, as Saint Augustine has written, that "grace is given not because we have done good works, but in order that we may be able to do them."**

**(3) Offer a prayer in which you express thanks to God for the grace and love that has enabled you to have new life through Jesus Christ.**

❖ Sing or read aloud "Christ Is Made the Sure Foundation."

❖ Conclude today's session by leading the class in this benediction, which is adapted from John 15:12, the key verse for March 19: **Let us go forth obeying Jesus' commandment to love one another as he has loved us. Amen.**

UNIT 1: GOD'S ETERNAL, PRESERVING, RENEWING LOVE

# GOD'S LOVE MANIFESTED

## PREVIEWING THE LESSON

**Lesson Scripture:** John 15:1-17
**Background Scripture:** John 15:1-17
**Key Verse:** John 15:12

**Focus of the Lesson:**
In our human condition, we search for that which enables us to love and be loved by others. Where do we find the authentic source of this love? The writer of the Gospel says that God is the source of an all-encompassing love, which empowers us to love God and one another.

**Goals for the Learners:**
(1) to examine the role of love in human life and explore how God's love empowers and changes human love.
(2) to express the joy that is found in keeping God's commandment to love others.
(3) to reflect the love of God in ministries and lifestyles that grow from being called to be disciples.

**Supplies:**
Bibles, newsprint and marker, paper and pencils, hymnals, optional tree twigs

## READING THE SCRIPTURE

NRSV
Lesson Scripture: John 15:1-17
¹"I am the true vine, and my Father is the vinegrower. ²He removes every branch in me that bears no fruit. Every branch that bears fruit he prunes to make it bear more fruit. ³You have already been cleansed by

CEB
Lesson Scripture: John 15:1-17
¹"I am the true vine, and my Father is the vineyard keeper. ²He removes any of my branches that don't produce fruit, and he trims any branch that produces fruit so that it will produce even more fruit. ³You are

the word that I have spoken to you. [4]Abide in me as I abide in you. Just as the branch cannot bear fruit by itself unless it abides in the vine, neither can you unless you abide in me. [5]I am the vine, you are the branches. Those who abide in me and I in them bear much fruit, because apart from me you can do nothing. [6]Whoever does not abide in me is thrown away like a branch and withers; such branches are gathered, thrown into the fire, and burned. [7]If you abide in me, and my words abide in you, ask for whatever you wish, and it will be done for you. [8]My Father is glorified by this, that you bear much fruit and become my disciples. [9]As the Father has loved me, so I have loved you; abide in my love. [10]If you keep my commandments, you will abide in my love, just as I have kept my Father's commandments and abide in his love. [11]I have said these things to you so that my joy may be in you, and that your joy may be complete. [12]**"This is my commandment, that you love one another as I have loved you.** [13]No one has greater love than this, to lay down one's life for one's friends. [14]You are my friends if you do what I command you. [15]I do not call you servants any longer, because the servant does not know what the master is doing; but I have called you friends, because I have made known to you everything that I have heard from my Father. [16]You did not choose me but I chose you. And I appointed you to go and bear fruit, fruit that will last, so that the Father will give you whatever you ask him in my name. [17]I am giving you these commands so that you may love one another."

already trimmed because of the word I have spoken to you. [4]Remain in me, and I will remain in you. A branch can't produce fruit by itself, but must remain in the vine. Likewise, you can't produce fruit unless you remain in me. [5]I am the vine; you are the branches. If you remain in me and I in you, then you will produce much fruit. Without me, you can't do anything. [6]If you don't remain in me, you will be like a branch that is thrown out and dries up. Those branches are gathered up, thrown into a fire, and burned. [7]If you remain in me and my words remain in you, ask for whatever you want and it will be done for you. [8]My Father is glorified when you produce much fruit and in this way prove that you are my disciples.

[9]"As the Father loved me, I too have loved you. Remain in my love. [10]If you keep my commandments, you will remain in my love, just as I kept my Father's commandments and remain in his love. [11]I have said these things to you so that my joy will be in you and your joy will be complete. [12]**This is my commandment: love each other just as I have loved you.** [13]No one has greater love than to give up one's life for one's friends. [14]You are my friends if you do what I command you. [15]I don't call you servants any longer, because servants don't know what their master is doing. Instead, I call you friends, because everything I heard from my Father I have made known to you. [16]You didn't choose me, but I chose you and appointed you so that you could go and produce fruit and so that your fruit could last. As a result, whatever you ask the Father in my name, he will give you. [17]I give you these commandments so that you can love each other."

## UNDERSTANDING THE SCRIPTURE

**Introduction.** The Gospel of John boasts several distinctive elements, including its unusually long Last Supper scene. While Matthew, Mark, and Luke each devote less than a chapter to the setting of Jesus' Passover meal with his disciples, John devotes five of his chapters to that occasion. By volume, it is arguably the central event of the Fourth Gospel. Our selected passage is taken from that extended Last Supper scene.

**John 15:1.** Another distinctive feature of John's Gospel is its "I am" statements. Seven times in John, Jesus reveals something about himself by declaring what he is. "I am the vine" is the final one of the seven. And in this instance, the self-revelatory statement also includes a statement about the identity of God the Father: "my Father is the vinegrower."

**John 15:2.** A part of the divine vinegrower's work is to prune the branches. For a given branch or twig, that may seem like a painful thing. In the bigger picture, of course, it is a part of guaranteeing growth. God's desire is that we should thrive and be fruitful. We recognize pruning as a means to that good end.

**John 15:3.** The Greek word translated as "prune" in verse 2, *kathairo*, can also mean "cleanse." The reference in verse 3 to the disciples being cleansed, therefore, is continuing a motif, not departing from it. We also recognize our related English word, "catharsis," and understand more clearly the impact of Jesus' word on us.

**John 15:4-5.** God is consistently revealed in Scripture in relational titles, and relational titles have counterparts. As soon as I call the Lord "my shepherd," for example, I have an implied title and identity for myself as sheep. So Jesus' identity as vine gives rise to our identity as branches. His title tells us something about him, as well as something about ourselves.

**John 15:6.** The destruction of nonproductive trees is a recurring theme in the New Testament. John the Baptist also warns about fruitless trees being thrown into the fire (Luke 3:9). And Jesus makes the same sort of statement apart from his identity as the vine (Matthew 7:19).

**John 15:7.** This promise of answered prayer is one we are both eager and reluctant to believe. It falls into the category of things that seem too good to be true. Our first concern, of course, should not be with God's side of the bargain but with ours—learning to abide in Jesus and to have his words abide in us.

**John 15:8**. We are accustomed to seeing religious calendars and posters that feature magnificent scenes from nature as a testament to the Creator. We recognize that God is glorified by the majesty, beauty, and abundance of creation. Imagine, then, how much God is glorified when the human part of that creation is lush and laden with spiritual fruit!

**John 15:9-11.** Love originates with God. Tellingly, love does not merely reciprocate; it reproduces. That is to say, the Father loving the Son results not only in the Son loving the Father in return but also in loving us.

The correspondence between the two sets of relationships continues in the matter of obedience and love.

To obey the Lord is to abide in love. That principle would not apply to all human obedience, of course. Inasmuch as God's nature and chief commandment are love, however, then the correlation makes perfect sense.

**John 15:12-13.** Early in this extended Last Supper dialogue, Jesus introduces to his disciples "a new commandment" (John 13:34). The commandment to love is nothing new, of course. The standard and model for that love, however, is new: "as I have loved you" (15:12).

Then Jesus offers another measure of love: The greatest love is to lay down one's life for friends. This is not merely a theoretical thing for him to say, but instead carries the weight of what he and we know the very next day holds. In the end, therefore, the two standards for love are one. To love as he loved us and to lay down our lives are exactly the same.

**John 15:14-15.** Did the disciples know what was ahead? The reader knows, and so sees how poignant and compelling the transition from verse 13 to verse 14 is. Jesus has declared that the greatest love is to lay down one's life for a friend, and then he calls his disciples his friends.

These verses define the relationship between Jesus and the disciples. It is an evolving relationship, for he has moved from calling them servants to calling them friends. It's a lovely image that we may take too much for granted since we no longer live in a culture of masters and servants. Those disciples willingly called Jesus their master, and thus understood themselves as servants. It was his prerogative, not their right, to turn the relationship into a friendship.

Friendship with Jesus is indicated by two things. On our end, "you are my friends if you do what I command you" (15:14). Obeying sounds to us more like the stuff of servant than friend. When the chief command is to love, however, obedience is not so onerous. Also, consider his end: "I have called you friends, because I have made known to you everything that I have heard from my Father" (15:15), which makes the disciples different from the servant who "does not know what the master is doing" (15:15). It is precisely because the Lord brings us into his confidence that the friendship is characterized on our end by obedience. We demonstrate by our lives that we are with him or against him.

**John 15:16.** Jesus' statement that he chose us is an important word to hear in our age. By reflex, we treat virtually everything in our lives as our choice, and we resent experiences and obligations that may be involuntary. Yet here is a greater privilege than being the consumer who chooses Jesus: being chosen by Jesus.

**John 15:17.** The central issue with God is always love. It is the nature, the motivation, and the command of God. Here, it is the reason behind Jesus' words to his disciples.

## INTERPRETING THE SCRIPTURE

### What's a Cubit?

The cubit, you recall, was an old unit of measurement. Before human beings had standardized units—like inches, yards, meters, and such—they used what they had at hand, literally. In order to measure things, people used parts of their bodies. The "span" represented the distance from the thumb to the little finger of an open hand. The foot was, well, a foot. And the cubit was the distance from the top of the middle finger to the point of the elbow.

So what's a cubit? Well, that depends on who is doing the measuring. Modern translations of the term into more familiar units will often reckon a cubit to be eighteen inches, but that's an estimate of course. The length of the cubit will no doubt vary based upon whose arm is being used.

I had in one of my churches a former college basketball player who was 7'2" tall. Sometimes in our Wednesday night Bible study, he would sit down on the couch next to a woman who was barely five feet tall. They looked silly together, of course, his knees bent up like a grasshopper's as he sat there while her feet struggled to reach the floor. If he measured the sofa on which they were sitting in his cubits and she measured it in hers, she would end up describing a longer sofa.

So a cubit makes a rather variable unit of measure. If a cubit is your standard, it makes a great deal of difference whose cubit you're using. And when it comes to love, the disciples were introduced to a new cubit.

### The Standard Standard

In my observation, human beings operate with a certain, predictable standard when it comes to loving other people. It's natural reflex, though it is not a very commendable standard. The idea is that we love others the way that others love us.

Love begins, after all, as a responsive thing. The baby is not born loving. Indeed, the sad stories that some of us heard coming out of Romanian orphanages a few years ago was that babies who were not given adequate personal attention and love during their first years actually lost their capacity to receive and express love. That part of themselves was never fully developed, never formed. We have to be loved by others, it seems, in order to learn how to love others.

And so love begins as a responsive thing. Our parents love us from the beginning, and thus we learn how to love from them. We love in response. And, for good or ill, we tend to learn how to love based on the love that we received, which may have been beautiful or dysfunctional, conditional or free. Whatever the case, we love in response.

That can continue, then, into our behavior as children and adolescents. We just keep loving in response. We love the people who love us. And, conversely, we dislike the people who dislike us. We live and we love in response to how we are treated. That has become natural for us.

As adults, we do not automatically grow out of that style of love. Jesus identified the pattern in the Sermon on the Mount: "If you love those who love you, what reward do you have? (Matthew 5:46). That's the natural propensity, and it can spell doom for many of our relationships.

With strangers, or even circumstantial enemies, this childish form of love is disinclined to take any initiative. No love will develop if each party is simply mirroring the other. No love will form in many relationships if our love is only a response to the other person's love.

With people very dear to us, on the

other hand, the pattern can be devastating. It can be devastating because it is so deceptive, working so well at the beginning, and thus misleading us. Think of the enthusiastic love of young romance. The man and woman are so enthralled by each other that, to love in response, becomes a blissful cycle that just keeps taking them higher and higher.

But what happens when something interferes? A conflict, a distraction, some accidental hurt. He is busier than he used to be. She is more tired. They don't have the time and energy to invest in each other that they once did. She feels that he is being cool, and so she backs away emotionally to protect herself. He hears a different tone and feels a different vibe, and suddenly she seems very negative and high-maintenance to him. He's got enough problems at work. And now the same love-in-response cycle that functioned so deceptively well at the beginning becomes a painful, downward cycle for them.

Our standard standard is a product of our infancy. We learn to love in response to the people who are loving us. But we must grow out of that infantile love.

### The New Cubit

In contrast to the natural human instinct, God's law proposed a new standard for love. "You shall love your neighbor as yourself" (Leviticus 19:18). It was revolutionary, and Jesus later called it the second greatest of all the commandments (Mark 12:31). Instead of my loving you in response to how you love me, I am challenged to reach a higher bar. Let me endeavor to love you as I love myself.

This sort of love does not abandon our fallen, human selfishness, but it leverages it. In our sinful state, we may not know much about true love, but we do know about self-interest. We know how to take care of ourselves, protect our feelings, watch out for our own best interests, and such. And so let me apply that same set of caring skills to you. Let me protect your feelings as gently and seek your best interest as zealously as I do my own.

That's a high standard. The Old Testament law has given me a better, fairer cubit. Instead of measuring my love for you constantly by your love for me, let me instead measure it by my love for myself. That will guarantee that I love you rather well.

And then, on the night he was betrayed, the Lord gave to his disciples a new commandment: "that you love one another as I have loved you" (15:12). That's a higher standard, still. Now we are using Jesus' cubit!

Jesus' cubit for love is self-sacrifice. Jesus' cubit for love is the initiation of a relationship that risks rejection. Jesus' cubit for love is bottomless forgiveness. It is a daunting standard, to be sure.

Except that it is completely natural. Our natural instinct is to love in response, and Jesus merely redirects to whom we are responding. Rather than loving you in response to how you love me, I am invited to love you in response to how Jesus has loved me. And that's a happy assignment, indeed, to live in response to his love.

# SHARING THE SCRIPTURE

## PREPARING TO LEAD

### *Preparing Our Hearts*

Ponder this week's devotional reading from 1 John 4:16b-21, a passage that was also part of our lesson for March 5. What behaviors do people who truly love God exhibit? Do you agree with John's assessment of the relationship between love and fear? Why or why not? If there are people whom you claim not to love, what action will you take to reflect God's love for all?

Pray that you and the students will recognize God, who first loved you, as the source of all love.

### *Preparing Our Minds*

Study the background Scripture and the lesson Scripture, which are both from John 15:1-17.

Consider this question: *Where do we find the authentic source of love?*

Write on newsprint:
❏ information for next week's lesson, found under Continue the Journey.
❏ activities for further spiritual growth in Continue the Journey.

Determine how you might use any of the features that precede the first lesson of this quarter in today's session. You may want to use an activity from Faith in Action: Revealing the Love of God.

Collect, if possible, twigs from trees. If you have no access to trees, perhaps this optional task could be delegated to one or more class members who could secure enough twigs for the entire group.

## LEADING THE CLASS

### *(1) Gather to Learn*

❖ Welcome everyone and pray that those who have come will experience the joy of love as they gather together with brothers and sisters in Christ.

❖ Encourage participants to recall the lyrics for the 1980s hit, "Looking for Love," which was made popular in the movie *Urban Cowboy*. The singer admits to "lookin' for love in all the wrong places." Ask: **Where are some of the "wrong places" that people continue to look for lasting love but are unable to find it?**

❖ Read aloud today's focus statement: **In our human condition, we search for that which enables us to love and be loved by others. Where do we find the authentic source of this love? The writer of the Gospel says that God is the source of an all-encompassing love, which empowers us to love God and one another.**

### *(2) Goal 1: Examine the Role of Love in Human Life and Explore How God's Love Empowers and Changes Human Love*

❖ Read Introduction in Understanding the Scripture to segue into today's Bible lesson.

❖ **Optional:** If you were able to collect tree twigs, distribute them either one per person (if you have enough) or pass them around for students to hold momentarily. Think of these as branches that have been pruned from a tree. Invite the adults to handle the twigs and make comments on whatever value they see in them. Note that they can be used to start a fire, act as a spit for marshmallows, or perhaps create a sculpture, but they can never grow again and be part of the tree from which they came.

❖ Read or retell The Standard Standard in Interpreting the Scripture. Invite the students to comment on how they perceive this "standard" standard works in real life. Ask: **Why do you agree—or disagree—with what is written here about the role of human love in human life?**

❖ Choose one or more volunteers to read John 15:1-17 and then discuss these questions. Use information from Understanding the Scripture as you find it appropriate.

1. **What do you learn about God, especially in the role as the vinegrower?**
2. **What do you learn about Jesus?**
3. **What do you learn about the relationship between the Father and the Son?**
4. **What do you learn about Jesus' relationship with his followers?**
5. **What enables Jesus' followers to stay connected to him?**
6. **How does the image of the tree and branches help you to understand what Jesus wants from you?**

*(3) Goal 2: Express the Joy that Is Found in Keeping God's Commandment to Love Others*

❖ Read together today's key verse, John 15:12.

❖ Look at the verses that follow to note that Jesus considers self-sacrifice to be the greatest example of love. Read The New Cubit in Understanding the Scripture and then talk about how Jesus' revolutionary way brings him—and us—joy when we follow it.

❖ Invite class members to give examples of how keeping God's commandment to love other brings them great joy.

❖ Provide a few moments for the students to reflect silently on other actions they could take to show God's love for one another.

*(4) Goal 3: Reflect the Love of God in Ministries and Lifestyles that Grow from Being Called to Be Disciples*

❖ Distribute hymnals that include "Pass It On," which speaks of passing on God's love just as a spark creates a flame. This was a popular youth group song as far back as 1969, so class members may know it. Invite them to read the first verse in unison.

❖ Post a sheet of newsprint to record answers to this question: **What ministries does our church offer that enable us to pass on God's love in a tangible way?**

❖ Encourage individuals to speak about how their participation in one or more of the ministries that has been named gives them an outlet for passing God's love to other people. Discuss the benefits of a particular ministry, both for those who serve on behalf of the church and those who avail themselves of this ministry.

❖ Conclude this portion by inviting those who would like to participate in any current ministry—or start a new one—to raise their hands to signify their commitment to this way of sharing God's love.

*(5) Continue the Journey*

❖ Pray that as the learners depart, they will demonstrate love to one another just as God has demonstrated love for them.

❖ Post information for next week's session on newsprint for the students to copy:

- Title: God's Love Restores
- Background Scripture: Joel 2
- Lesson Scripture: Joel 2:12-13, 18-19, 28-32
- Focus of the Lesson: The rewards garnered from wholesome relationships may be shattered by unloving and unfaithful actions. How can these relationships be restored to their former glory? Joel recounts the benefits that emanate from a restored relationship with God.

❖ Challenge the adults to grow spiritually by completing one or more of these activities related to this week's session.

(1) Take a close look at several trees or vines. What do you notice about their roots, trunks, and branches? How do you perceive the relationship among the parts of a tree to be like your own relationship with God?

(2) Ponder how being an active member of a church influences—for better or worse—your ability to abide in Christ. What would you like your church to do to help you strengthen your relationship with Jesus?

(3) Identify various ways in which you demonstrate love for family, friends, and other church members. If there are changes you need to make to better fulfill Jesus' commandment to love one another as he has loved us, what steps will you take this week to bring about those changes?

❖ Sing or read aloud "Help Us Accept Each Other."

❖ Conclude today's session by leading the class in this benediction, which is adapted from John 15:12, the key verse for today's lesson: **Let us go forth obeying Jesus' commandment to love one another as he has loved us. Amen.**

UNIT 1: GOD'S ETERNAL, PRESERVING, RENEWING LOVE

# GOD'S LOVE RESTORES

---

## PREVIEWING THE LESSON

**Lesson Scripture:** Joel 2:12-13, 18-19, 28-32
**Background Scripture:** Joel 2
**Key Verse:** Joel 2:13

### Focus of the Lesson:
The rewards garnered from wholesome relationships may be shattered by unloving and unfaithful actions. How can these relationships be restored to their former glory? Joel recounts the benefits that emanate from a restored relationship with God.

### Goals for the Learners:
(1) to explore what motivates people to repent and seek restoration.
(2) to appreciate how God's love has equipped them to handle life's challenges.
(3) to seek restored relationships in personal and community life.

### Supplies:
Bibles, newsprint and marker, paper and pencils, hymnals

---

## READING THE SCRIPTURE

NRSV
Lesson Scripture: Joel 2:12-13, 18-19, 28-32

¹²Yet even now, says the LORD,
 return to me with all your heart,
with fasting, with weeping, and with
  mourning;
  ¹³rend your hearts and not your
  clothing.
Return to the LORD, your God,
 for he is gracious and merciful,
slow to anger, and abounding in
 steadfast love,

CEB
Lesson Scripture: Joel 2:12-13, 18-19, 28-32

¹²Yet even now, says the LORD,
  return to me with all your hearts,
   with fasting, with weeping, and
    with sorrow;
¹³tear your hearts
  and not your clothing.
 Return to the LORD your God,
  for he is merciful and
   compassionate,

**and relents from punishing.**

¹⁸Then the LORD became jealous for
　his land,
　and had pity on his people.
¹⁹In response to his people the
　LORD said:
I am sending you
　grain, wine, and oil,
　and you will be satisfied;
and I will no more make you
　a mockery among the nations.
²⁸Then afterward
　I will pour out my spirit on
　　all flesh;
your sons and your daughters shall
　prophesy,
　your old men shall dream dreams,
　and your young men shall see
　　visions.
²⁹Even on the male and female slaves,
　in those days, I will pour out my
　　spirit.
³⁰I will show portents in the heavens and on the earth, blood and fire
and columns of smoke. ³¹The sun
shall be turned to darkness, and the
moon to blood, before the great and
terrible day of the LORD comes. ³²Then
everyone who calls on the name of
the LORD shall be saved; for in Mount
Zion and in Jerusalem there shall be
those who escape, as the LORD has
said, and among the survivors shall
be those whom the LORD calls.

**very patient, full of faithful
　love,
　and ready to forgive.**

¹⁸Then the LORD became passionate
about this land, and had pity on his
people.
¹⁹The LORD responded to the people:
　See, I am sending you
　the corn, new wine, and fresh oil,
　　and you will be fully satisfied
　　　by it;
　and I will no longer make you
　　a disgrace among the nations.
²⁸After that I will pour out my spirit
　　upon everyone;
　your sons and your daughters
　　will prophesy,
　your old men will dream
　　dreams,
　and your young men will
　　see visions.
²⁹In those days, I will also pour out
　　my spirit on the male
　　and female slaves.
³⁰I will give signs in the heavens
and on the earth—blood and fire and
columns of smoke. ³¹The sun will be
turned to darkness, and the moon to
blood before the great and dreadful
day of the LORD comes. ³²But everyone who calls on the LORD's name
will be saved; for on Mount Zion and
in Jerusalem there will be security, as
the LORD has promised; and in Jerusalem, the LORD will summon those
who survive.

## UNDERSTANDING THE SCRIPTURE

**Joel 2:1-2a.** The trumpet served
several different functions in ancient
Israel's national life. We see it playing
two different roles even within the
scope of this one chapter. In this case,
we might think of it as Israel's Civil
Defense siren. We know the quicken-
ing heartbeat, the caution, and perhaps even the fright evoked by that
sound. So it was that the Lord wanted

"all the inhabitants of the land" to hear the prophet "sound the alarm."

We observe in the larger context of Scripture that the prospect of the day of Lord was a mixed bag. That "day" was not so much a date on a calendar as the moment when God would intervene in history to make things right. Whether that promise is a good thing or a bad thing, however, depends upon who you are. For Joel's audience, it is an unhappy prospect, for evidently they are among the things that are wrong and need to be made right.

**Joel 2:2b-3.** The blowing of the trumpet signaled the coming of the day of the Lord. And the judgment of the Lord on that day would be realized by a devastating army. That army is commonly interpreted as a plague of locusts, based upon an earlier reference (Joel 1:4), a later reference (2:25), and some of the descriptions of that army. Here that army is introduced as unprecedented in power and unmatched in destruction. The prophet paints both before and after pictures in order to illustrate the utter devastation that will occur.

**Joel 2:4-10.** Having pictured its devastating effects, now the prophet turns to a frightening description of the army itself. These troops are impersonal, machine-like, and unstoppable. They are everywhere, and they impact both heaven and earth. While locusts are not specifically mentioned in the text, it is easy to see how these descriptions might apply.

**Joel 2:11.** Lest there be any misunderstanding, the Lord is deliberately associated with the frightening army. While Israel's history was full of stories of God fighting enemy armies on their behalf, this army is under God's own command. Such is the nature of the judgment prophets' message. And so much greater is the dismay and fear of the people as a result.

**Joel 2:12.** "Yet even now" is grace pressing the pause button. Everything about the preceding verses suggests an inescapable doom. Destruction has been portrayed as fast moving and inevitable. Yet, still, there is hope, for the people have an option. "Return to me with all your heart" is the Lord's gracious invitation, even in the midst of a judgment message.

**Joel 2:13-14.** "Rend your hearts and not your clothing" (2:13) implores the people to repent where it counts. The temptation is always to be superficial, but torn clothes do not impress the Lord. And it is unsurprising that the people's hearts should be key to their repentance since the Lord's heart is key to their forgiveness.

The prophet reminds the people about the heart of God: "gracious and merciful, slow to anger, and abounding in steadfast love" (2:13). In truth, therefore, their encouragement to repent is more tied to God's love than God's power. It is the divine invitation rather than the divine warning that should compel their change of heart.

**Joel 2:15.** Once again, there is the call to "blow the trumpet in Zion." At the beginning of the chapter, the trumpet functions as a national siren. Here, however, it serves a different purpose, for the trumpet was also used to announce certain holidays and convocations. The first trumpet sent the people running for cover. This trumpet calls them together for worship.

**Joel 2:16.** The trumpet signals a kind of invitation, and in these verses we see how comprehensive that invitation is. The entire nation is summoned, from the youngest to the oldest. And the image of the bride and groom suggests the importance of the convocation, for it should interrupt every human activity.

**Joel 2:17.** Now the people's repentance turns to the priests' intercession. They cry out to God to spare the people. And, specifically, the attitudes and perceptions of other peoples are cited, which recalls Moses' earlier intercession on behalf of the Israelites of his day (Numbers 14:13-16).

**Joel 2:18-27.** "Land" and "people" are knit together in this passage. The Lord is said to be "jealous for his land" and to have "pity on his people." The promised rescue for the people, in turn, is manifested in blessings upon the land. The passage reminds us how tightly connected the land and the people are throughout the Old Testament, beginning with God's initial conversation with Abraham (Genesis 12:1-2).

The early part of this chapter is deliberately designed to frighten. From the alarming sound of the trumpet to the terrifying descriptions of the army and its destruction, we could hear the implicit message that the audience should be afraid. Now, in contrast, the Lord encourages even the soil and the animals not to be afraid. All the imagery is reversed, as the land is marked by abundance and fertility again.

In addition to nature being unafraid, the "children of Zion" themselves are encouraged to "be glad and rejoice." The Lord promises them both restoration and vindication. And, in the end, the real culmination of this lovely picture is the knowledge of God and God's presence in the midst of the people.

**Joel 2:28-29.** The earlier verses promised conventional, material blessings. Now the promises of God turn to spiritual blessings. More than mere rain, the Lord promises to "pour out my spirit," which is a whole other realm of grace and kindness.

**Joel 2:30-32.** The passage concludes where it began. Once again images point to the day of the Lord. And once again the tone surrounding that day is ominous and the events catastrophic.

This prediction about the day of the Lord seems different, however. Now the events are not as ordinary as locusts and armies. Now the cataclysm is in the heavens, which suggests a more eschatological version of the day of the Lord. Still, salvation is promised and available to "everyone who calls on the name of the LORD" (2:32).

## INTERPRETING THE SCRIPTURE

### If the Lord Wanted You Dead

From time to time, I have had folks ask me about the episode recorded in Exodus 4:24-26. They have been troubled by the report that the Lord "tried to kill" Moses. My response has always been that, if the Lord had really wanted to kill Moses, then Moses would have been dead.

The same logic applies to the messages of the Old Testament judgment prophets, of which Joel is one. He and the rest of that group are known for their words of warning, which include frightening details about the destruction that God intends to bring upon certain nations. The chapters of the judgment prophets in general read very much like the earlier part of Joel 2. It is a heavy, sober message.

Yet the very existence of a judgment prophet is a testimony to the kindness of God. After all, if the Lord really wanted the people to be destroyed, then no warning would have been given. The attacker does not notify the victim in advance. The thief does not ring the doorbell. The warning from God is a mercy of God.

That truth becomes apparent when the Lord implores the people, saying, "Even now, return to me with all your heart" (2:12). Redemption, not judgment, is the actual will of God. If the Lord were eager to judge, then there would be no warning, and there would certainly be no invitation to repent.

The will of God is an expression of the heart of God. It is by understanding the divine nature and character that we can understand God's will. And so the prophet proves God's desire for redemption by affirming God's nature: gracious, merciful, slow to anger, abounding in love. All of those arrows point the same direction, and each one directs the people to "return to the LORD, your God" (2:13).

The somber messages of frightening warning might have prompted the people to suspect that God wanted them dead. No, for if that's what the Lord wanted, they would have been dead already. Rather, what the Lord really wanted was for the people to be saved. And the first step toward that was repentance.

*Heart Condition*

Imagine a man who has grown distant from his wife. He is not antagonistic toward her; he is just not as attentive, as thoughtful, as interested as he once was. They are staying together, but their time together is bland and routine.

Imagine a woman who has lost all sense of passion and purpose for her job. She still gets up and goes in every day, but she feels no energy for it. Her creativity is gone. She doesn't have the eagerness to take on new things. She's just punching the clock.

We watch these two people, and we conclude, "Their hearts aren't in it. They're just going through the motions." And in that observation, we acknowledge the two-part composition of a human being. We have both an inside and an outside. And what we are visibly doing on the outside is not the real issue.

This was surely Jesus' point about the hopelessly superficial Pharisees of his day (for example, Matthew 23:23-28). In contrast to their fixation with "the outside of the cup" (23:25), Jesus turned the focus again and again to the human heart (Matthew 5:27-28; 15:10-20). And that focus is consistent with the reorienting lesson that Samuel learned so long ago: that "the LORD looks on the heart" (1 Samuel 16:7).

In our day, we know how cancer can spread from one part of a body to another. I heard recently about a woman who had been diagnosed and treated for breast cancer a year ago, but now the doctors have told her that the cancer has reappeared elsewhere. It is still breast cancer, but that is no longer where it is located.

So it is with us spiritually. Sin is

always a condition of the heart. It may manifest itself elsewhere—in our tongues, our eyes, our hands, and more—but at its core, sin is a heart condition.

Accordingly, the Lord urged the people of Joel's day, "Return to me with all your heart" and "rend your hearts and not your clothing" (Joel 2:12, 13).The problem has to be fixed at it source. We may lean toward treating the symptoms, for they are often bothersome or embarrassing. The real cure, however, is found in solving the heart condition. And so our invitation is to turn—or return—to the Lord with all our hearts.

### The Beauty of Jealousy

In our day, "jealous" is an almost exclusively negative term. The Old Testament, on the other hand, is unapologetic about applying the term to God (for example, Exodus 20:5; 34:14; Deuteronomy 4:24; Joshua 24:19; Nahum 1:2). The Lord is jealous, and the prophet Joel cites that jealousy as part of his good news for the land and its people.

We may think of the jealous person as selfish, insecure, and controlling. At its best, however, jealousy reflects a very natural instinct: namely, an unwillingness to share a person's affection. It indicates a desire that the beloved belong entirely and exclusively to the lover. In truth, it is what we all want and expect when we marry. And so, at its best, jealousy is a natural part of love.

The Scripture tells us that God is love (1 John 4:8), and so it should not surprise us to read that God is jealous.

And in that jealousy, the Lord pays a great compliment to us. Would we prefer for God to be indifferent about our affections and allegiances? Would it seem more loving if the Lord were more permissive and less protective?

Joel reports that God "became jealous for his land" (2:18), and what follows is a litany of blessing. The Lord promises to bless the land, as well as the people. And the blessings of God that Joel anticipates are both material and spiritual. Furthermore, as the prophet reveals God's perfect plan going forward, we see its global— even cosmic—reach. That land, for which God is jealous, proves to the epicenter of God's universal activity and perfect plan.

We are giving long and deep consideration this quarter to the love of God. Like a thing of beauty, the longer we gaze at it, the more carefully we examine it, the more we realize is in it. And Joel helps us to see more of the beauty of God's love than we might have recognized apart from his help.

We see that God's love includes a judgment message. Apart from love, it would be harshness. As a function of love, however, it is mercy.

We see, too, how redemptive God's love is. The Lord does not discard what is broken, but rather endeavors to make it whole and new. When God reveals a perfect plan that includes us, we hear that God loves us.

And, finally, we see that God's love is jealous. This is not lukewarm love. There is no indifference toward us in the heart of God. Rather, the Lord wants all the best from us and all the best for us.

## SHARING THE SCRIPTURE

### PREPARING TO LEAD

#### *Preparing Our Hearts*

Ponder this week's devotional reading from 2 Peter 3:1-10, which concerns the promise of the coming of the Lord. What do you learn about this judgment day? Why does God wait to bring about judgment, according to Peter? What words would you use to describe the events of this day?

Pray that you and the students will be prepared for God's judgment day.

#### *Preparing Our Minds*

Study the background Scripture from Joel 2 and the lesson Scripture from Joel 2:12-13, 18-19, 28-32.

Consider this question: *How can relationships that have been shattered by unloving and unfaithful actions be restored to their former glory?*

Write on newsprint:
❏ steps for resolving conflict in Goal 3.
❏ information for next week's lesson, found under "Continue the Journey."
❏ activities for further spiritual growth in "Continue the Journey."

Determine how you might use any of the features that precede the first lesson of this quarter in today's session.

Prepare a brief lecture using information for Joel 1:1-11 in Understanding the Scripture to set the context for today's session in Goal 1 in Sharing the Scripture.

Be prepared to read aloud Acts 2:1-4, 14-21 for Goal 2 in Sharing the Scripture.

### LEADING THE CLASS

#### *(1) Gather to Learn*

❖ Welcome everyone and pray that those who have come today will find evidence of God's love here.

❖ Read this information from the Council on Foreign Relations: **Following the 1959 overthrow of Cuban leader Fulgencio Batista by revolutionaries led by Fidel Castro and Cuba's subsequent closer relationships with the then Soviet Union, the United States severed all diplomatic ties with its neighbor in 1961. In an attempt to oust Fidel Castro, the US Central Intelligence Agency (CIA) mounted a failed operation, known as the Bay of Pigs Invasion in 1961. Tensions between the two countries escalated further when in 1962, after discovering Soviet plans to build a missile base on the island, the Cuban Missile Crisis brought the United States to the brink of a nuclear war. The United States tightened its economic sanctions with a strict embargo. Obstacles to normalizing relationships between the two countries that are situated just ninety miles apart continued to hamper negotiations over decades. In December 2014, after months of secret talks brokered by Pope Francis between officials of Cuba and the United States, leaders of both countries announced that full diplomatic ties would be restored for the first time in more than fifty years.**

❖ Ask: **How does the restoration of severed ties benefit two parties, whether they are nations, institutions, or individuals?**

❖ Read aloud today's focus

statement: **The rewards garnered from wholesome relationships may be shattered by unloving and unfaithful actions. How can these relationships be restored to their former glory? Joel recounts the benefits that emanate from a restored relationship with God.**

*(2) Goal 1: Explore What Motivates People to Repent and Seek Restoration*

❖ Present a brief lecture on information from Joel 1:1-11 in Understanding the Scripture to set the stage for today's reading.

❖ Select a volunteer to read Joel 2:12-13, 18-19, 28-32.

❖ Discuss these questions:
- **Often the tearing of garments is a sign of repentance. Why would God call people to return but "rend their hearts" rather than their garments?** (See Joel 2:12-13 and Heart Condition from Interpreting the Scripture.)
- **What do we learn about God's willingness to restore our broken relationship?** (See verses 13-14, Joel 2:13-14 in Understanding the Scripture, and If the Lord Wanted You Dead in Interpreting the Scripture.)
- **What does verse 19 mean when it refers to God's jealousy for the land?** (See The Beauty of Jealousy in Interpreting the Scripture.)

*(3) Goal 2: Appreciate How God's Love Has Equipped the Learners to Face Life's Challenges*

❖ Look again at Joel 2:28-32 and ask: **What has God provided to help** the Israelites—and us—to discern God's will so that we might be well equipped to face life's challenges? List ideas on newsprint. Be sure the group understands that God's Spirit will be poured out on all people. The means of discerning God's will—especially prophetic oracles, dreams, and visions—that were once the province of prophets will be made available to people of all ages, both male and female, both slaves and free persons.

❖ Form small groups and ask them to pray together that God's Spirit will be poured out on them and all people so that God's restoring love may be made known to all.

❖ Conclude by asking the groups to remain in an attitude of prayer as you read the events of Pentecost, after which Peter used Joel's prophecy to explain what was occurring. Read Acts 2:1-4, 14-21.

*(4) Goal 3: Seek Restored Relationships in Personal and Community Life*

❖ Observe that sometimes people who are struggling with broken relationships do not have the skills to bring about reconciliation, even if they would want to. For some, it's easier to keep silent and just ignore the ones with whom they are having difficulty. Other people will allow resentment and anger to fester while they put on a "happy face," rather than confront the problems and try to resolve them. Still others will be overtly angry, even acting aggressively to cause physical harm.

❖ Post on newsprint these steps for resolving a conflict, which have been adapted from information by Naomi Drew, author of *Hope and Healing*:

- Calm down before you try to resolve the issue.
- State the problem using "I messages," rather than making accusations.
- Use reflective listening by restating what the other person said.
- Take responsibility, since both parties usually have some part to play in the conflict.
- Brainstorm ideas to solve the problem and agree on one that satisfies both parties.
- Affirm, forgive, or thank.

❖ Distribute paper and pencils so that the class members can write these steps as you read them aloud. Talk with the group about how these steps could enable reconciliation. Challenge them to use these steps during the week to resolve a conflict and restore a relationship.

❖ Conclude by reading in unison Joel 2:13, today's key verse that calls us to return and be reconciled to God.

*(5) Continue the Journey*

❖ Pray that as the learners depart, they will seek, with God's help, to restore broken relationships.

❖ Post information for next week's session on newsprint for the students to copy:
- **Title: God as Our Shepherd**
- **Background Scripture: Psalm 23**
- **Lesson Scripture: Psalm 23**

■ **Focus of the Lesson: People face challenges that may seem too difficult to endure. Where can they find the support and reassurance to face these challenges? The psalmist promises that God's love provides what is necessary to confront any difficulties and to live in a fulfilling and intimate relationship with God.**

❖ Challenge the adults to grow spiritually by completing one or more of these activities related to this week's session.

(1) **Use the steps discussed in class to resolve a conflict and thereby restore a relationship.**

(2) **Research Bible passages in which God calls people to "return." Who is being called and under what circumstances? How do the called ones respond? Here are examples of texts to check: Isaiah 44:22; Jeremiah 3:7, 10; 4:1; 24:7; Hosea 11:5; Amos 4:6-9; Zechariah 1:3; Malachi 3:7.**

(3) **Act as a peacemaker to restore relationships within your family, church, or workplace.**

❖ Sing or read aloud "Forgive Our Sins as We Forgive."

❖ Conclude today's session by leading the class in this benediction, which is adapted from John 15:12, the key verse for March 19: **Let us go forth obeying Jesus' commandment to love one another as he has loved us. Amen.**

## UNIT 2: GOD'S CARING, SAVING, AND UPHOLDING LOVE
# GOD AS OUR SHEPHERD

---

### PREVIEWING THE LESSON

**Lesson Scripture:** Psalm 23
**Background Scripture:** Psalm 23
**Key Verse:** Psalm 23:1

### Focus of the Lesson:
People face challenges that may seem too difficult to endure. Where can they find the support and reassurance to face these challenges? The psalmist promises that God's love provides what is necessary to confront any difficulties and to live in a fulfilling and intimate relationship with God.

### Goals for the Learners:
(1) to explore Psalm 23's use of the metaphor of shepherding for trusting in God.
(2) to appreciate the ways that God's love provides goodness and mercy to people when they face challenges.
(3) to choose to trust God's leading, which transforms challenges and difficulties.

### Supplies:
Bibles, newsprint and marker, paper and pencils, hymnals

---

### READING THE SCRIPTURE

NRSV

Lesson Scripture: Psalm 23

¹The LORD is my shepherd, I shall not want.
²He makes me lie down in green pastures;
he leads me beside still waters;
³he restores my soul.
He leads me in right paths
for his name's sake.

CEB

Lesson Scripture: Psalm 23

¹The LORD is my shepherd.
I lack nothing.
²He lets me rest in grassy meadows;
he leads me to restful waters;
³he keeps me alive.
He guides me in proper paths
for the sake of his good name.
⁴Even when I walk through the
darkest valley,

⁴Even though I walk through the
  darkest valley,
 I fear no evil;
for you are with me;
  your rod and your staff—
  they comfort me.
⁵You prepare a table before me
  in the presence of my enemies;
you anoint my head with oil;
  my cup overflows.
⁶Surely goodness and mercy shall
  follow me
all the days of my life,
and I shall dwell in the house of the
  LORD
  my whole life long.

I fear no danger because you
  are with me.
Your rod and your staff—
  they protect me.
⁵You set a table for me
  right in front of my enemies.
You bathe my head in oil;
  my cup is so full it spills over!
⁶Yes, goodness and faithful love
  will pursue me all the days of
  my life,
  and I will live in the LORD's house
  as long as I live.

## UNDERSTANDING THE SCRIPTURE

**Psalm 23:1.** This familiar opening statement actually has an even more intimate quality than we might initially recognize. What we translate "the LORD" is not a title for God as it appears. Rather, the psalmist is using the name of God—Yahweh. The very personal testimony, therefore, begins with a very personal reference to God.

Both Old and New Testaments recognize that not all shepherds are created equal. There are good shepherds and bad shepherds. And if the author's own experience as a shepherd or exposure to shepherds had been negative, he might have been reluctant to summon this image for the Lord. As it is, however, it's clear that this author perceived the shepherd to be a source of protection and care, and so it is a beautiful and fitting metaphor for God.

The psalmist's declaration that "I shall not want" is a tremendous expression of trust. It is the kind of trust Jesus encouraged when he pointed to the flowers and the birds (Matthew 6:25-33). The psalmist was convinced that he would have everything he needed simply because of the Shepherd's providential care.

**Psalm 23:2-3a.** The expression of trust in verse 1 does not come out of a vacuum. The psalmist's certainty for the future is the natural product of his experience with the Lord in the past and present. And his next three statements reflect his experience with God.

The "green pastures" and "still waters" are pastoral images that may have sentimental appeal to us, but they had real-life, practical importance to a sheep. For a grazing, ruminant animal, those two images suggested having everything one needed. And while our human needs might not be so easily summarized, we may be just as confident that the Lord knows them all and will provide for them.

"He restores my soul," of course, goes beyond the basic needs of a sheep. It speaks, instead, a profound word to the fundamental needs of human beings. The underlying Hebrew word for "soul" is a robust one, which can refer to one's self, life, mind, desire, emotion, and passion. It is the word Genesis uses to capture the completion of Adam's creation after the Lord had breathed into the formed dust (Genesis 2:7). What a lovely tribute to the goodness and power of God. The one who created all that we are also restores all that we are.

**Psalm 23:3b.** The Bible makes frequent use of the image of paths. The people of Israel understood that life is full of various paths, and that not all paths are equal. One path may lead to destruction, while another leads to life (see, for example, Matthew 7:13-14). How important, then, it is for a person to choose "right paths." Of course, we cannot always see down the way to recognize where each path leads in the end. But we may feel secure for as long as we follow the Lord's lead in our lives, for "He leads me in right paths."

Specifically, the psalmist says that the Lord leads us in right paths "for his name's sake." Several times in the Old Testament, the Lord cites "for the sake of my name" as the divine motivation for a given choice or action (see, for example, Isaiah 48:9; Ezekiel 20:9). It is a recognition that what God's people do and what becomes of them accrue to the glory and praise of God.

**Psalm 23:4.** The earlier verses bear witness to where the Lord leads— "green pastures" and "still waters." Interestingly, the "darkest valley" is not identified as a place that the Lord leads, yet still it is recognized as a place that we go. And, mercifully, the Lord is there with us.

Especially noteworthy at this crucial juncture is the change in pronouns. Up until this point, the Lord has been referred to exclusively in the third-person. Now, however, the grammar shifts to second-person address. The writer does not say "I fear no evil because he is with me" but because "you are with me." In the darkest valley, the psalm becomes that much more personal.

Finally, a shepherd's rod and staff were not soft items. Still, they were an extension of the shepherd. We can imagine how routinely the feel of either was accompanied by the sound of his voice. And we may join the psalmist in being thankful for and comforted by all of the Lord's means of direction and correction.

**Psalm 23:5.** Again, the psalmist is not Pollyannaish about the events and circumstances of life. Life is not only lived in green pastures and by still waters. There is the "darkest valley" of the previous verse. And, here in verse 5, there is the reality of enemies.

Interestingly, an enemy of a sheep is likely to look at it as food. Yet the protection of the shepherd is so strong and sure that the sheep may graze while surrounded by its predators. The scene is a reminder to us of a larger biblical principle: namely, that we should not be afraid, not because there is nothing to be afraid of, but because the Lord is with us.

In our day, the prospect of having oil poured on our heads does not sound appealing. In Scripture, however, this was a luxuriant image (Psalm 133:1-2). Jesus identified it as an anticipated act of hospitality (Luke 7:46). He also associated oil with the care of wounds (Luke 10:34).

The cup that overflows is like our image of a cornucopia. It is reminiscent of Jesus' teaching about the generosity that awaits the generous

(Luke 6:38). It is the look of uncontainable blessing.

**Psalm 23:6.** The psalmist concludes his testimony with this grand affirmation about the future. The Hebrew word for what goodness and mercy will do can also mean "to pursue" or "to chase." There is a relentless, assertive quality to God's kindness.

Finally, we observe a lovely change of venue. The Lord's presence has been a central theme to the psalm, but it has always been portrayed as a presence wherever we are—pastures, valleys, amid enemies, and such. The beautiful forever prospect, however, is to "dwell in the house of the LORD."

---

## INTERPRETING THE SCRIPTURE

### If, Then

If the Lord is my shepherd, then what does that make me? One of the exquisite patterns of Scripture is that God is consistently revealed in relational terms. Father, Savior, Redeemer, Lord, King, Creator, Teacher, and so on: They are all terms that suggest a relationship. And one hallmark of the Bible's relational terms for God is that they all have counterparts.

Creator suggests creature. Lord implies servant. Teacher invites student. The terms we use for God go on to say something about us. Our theology yields our anthropology. And so if the Lord is my shepherd, then I must be a sheep.

To be a sheep suggests a tendency to follow, though not necessarily a discriminating tendency. We human beings may like to fancy ourselves more independent than that, but an objective look around reveals the hard truth. We follow the pack. What we wear, what we drive, how we decorate our homes, and how we spend our money are all heavily influenced by what we see those around us doing. We tell our children, "I don't care what other parents do," but we do care. It makes a great difference to us what other parents, families, neighbors, and coworkers do.

To be a sheep also suggests tremendous vulnerability. It's hard to imagine an animal less equipped to cope with its predators. The sheep isn't known for its getaway speed, its strong tail, or its protective shell. What marauder is kept at bay by the sheep's ferocious teeth, its inflated size, or its defensive odor? It is a helpless animal near the bottom of the food chain. And while human beings are not so defenseless, we admit our vulnerability every time we observe how fragile life is.

Finally, to be a sheep is to be dependent. Wild sheep may be more able to get by on their own, but the domesticated sheep that the psalmist had in mind were pretty helpless without their shepherds. Food, drink, shelter, health, and protection were all provided by a good shepherd. And apart from the shepherd's providential care, the sheep were in a desperate state.

The psalmist gladly claimed the Lord as his shepherd. And by doing so, he acknowledged his own similarities to a sheep. It is a testimony that rings true to me, for the longer I live, the better I know myself. I do tend to follow. I am terribly vulnerable. And I am learning more and more how much I depend upon our Shepherd.

## So Great a Cloud

Psalm 23 has an ancient attribution associating it with David, and his authorship is easy for us to imagine. We know that he grew up as a shepherd boy (1 Samuel 16:11), and that his experience as a shepherd helped to embolden him against Goliath (17:34-37). Furthermore, even when his heart had grown hard with sin, still a story about a lamb was able to break through and speak to him (2 Samuel 12:1-6). And so it is easy for us to hear this tender and informed portrait of a caring shepherd coming from both David's experience with sheep and David's experience with God.

Yet David's is far from being the only voice on this subject. We find the image of the Lord as a shepherd in Old and New Testament alike. Even though shepherds were often disrespected, and the biblical text itself recognizes the contempt of some for shepherds (Genesis 46:34), still the Lord is unapologetically associated with that group and their work.

The prophets portray both God and the promised Messiah as a shepherd for the people (Isaiah 40:10-11; Ezekiel 34:11-23; Micah 5:2-4). Jesus suggests the Lord as a shepherd in his teachings about a lost sheep (Matthew 18:12-14; Luke 15:3-7). He claims for himself the title of "the good shepherd" (John 10:11, 14). And the writer of Hebrews identifies Jesus as "the great shepherd of the sheep" (Hebrews 13:20). The imagery of Psalm 23, therefore, is part of a larger theme about the nature of God's relationship with people.

Meanwhile, the Lord's shepherding itself is also seen against a larger backdrop. All along, you see, there is the nagging reality of bad shepherds who fail their sheep. In Jeremiah, the Lord decries those shepherds—that is, the human leaders—who "destroy and scatter the sheep of my pasture" (Jeremiah 23:1) and who "have led them astray" (50:6). In Ezekiel, those shepherds are condemned for both exploiting and neglecting the sheep (Ezekiel 34:2-8). Likewise, Jesus critiques the hireling who does not care for the sheep, and therefore does not protect them (John 10:12-13).

In addition to the inadequate shepherds, there is the equally daunting reality of dangerous circumstances. The Bible acknowledges the threat of thieves and wolves. And the author of Psalm 23 is deeply aware of the dangerous circumstances that threaten a sheep. His testimony about the Lord as shepherd, therefore, is not a Norman Rockwell painting, full of harmlessness and innocence. On the contrary, it is a clear-eyed affirmation of God's goodness, strength, and faithfulness in the midst of life's very real dangers and difficulties.

## If the Shepherd Is Good

Perhaps you have been part of a worship service or fellowship setting where the leader has declared, "God is good," and the people have responded, "All the time." Then, in turn, the leader repeats, "All the time," and the people echo, "God is good." It is a popular affirmation that I have seen and heard many times in a variety of places.

Though it is a very simple statement, I believe the theology is sound. Jesus asserts the fundamental and incomparable goodness of God (Luke 18:19). And both the Old and New Testaments avow that the divine nature is unchanging (Malachi 3:6; Hebrews 13:8).

I am also fascinated by the insight of the simple refrain, for I wonder how people might respond if it were, instead, a fill-in-the-blank statement. If we presented folks, both inside and outside of the church, with a piece of paper that read, "All the time, \_\_\_\_\_ is good," what would they write in the blank? What do we experience or affirm as good all the time?

Certainly not life. Even if we know ourselves to be tremendously blessed in this life, still we recognize that life itself is not reliably good. It is fragile and often unfair. At times it is painfully hard. And, in some circumstances, it seems truly cruel.

The psalmist knew that life is not good all the time. He experienced goodness and blessing in life, to be sure, but even in the brevity of his testimony he acknowledged the troubles and threats of life. Yet in the midst of it all, God is always good.

Here is the great beauty of Psalm 23: not that the pastures are always green, but that God is always good. In every setting of life, the Lord's presence is sure; and in every circumstance, the divine providence is trustworthy. Even in the darkest valley, therefore, we do not fear. And even in the midst of enemies, we enjoy a feast.

Life is not good all of the time. The psalmist, you, and I all know it. But that's OK, for the Lord is always good. And the Lord is my shepherd.

## SHARING THE SCRIPTURE

### PREPARING TO LEAD

*Preparing Our Hearts*

Ponder this week's devotional reading from John 10:11-18, the familiar teaching of Jesus, who is the good shepherd. What are the traits of a good shepherd? How do these traits differ from those of someone simply hired to look after the sheep? How is Jesus the good shepherd in your life?

Pray that you and the students will be so intimately connected with the good shepherd that you know his voice and trust in his care.

*Preparing Our Minds*

Study the background Scripture and the lesson Scripture, which are both from Psalm 23.

Consider this question: *Where can you find support and reassurance when you face challenges?*

Write on newsprint:
❑ Bible verses for Goal 3 in Sharing the Scripture.
❑ information for next week's lesson, found under Continue the Journey.
❑ activities for further spiritual growth in Continue the Journey.

Determine how you might use any of the features that precede the first lesson of this quarter in today's session.

### LEADING THE CLASS

*(1) Gather to Learn*

❖ Welcome everyone and pray that those who have come today

will recognize how God's love is expressed in God's care for them.

❖ Read this story that appeared on September 3, 2015 in a *Washington Post* article by Michael Miller: **A Merino sheep, who apparently wandered away from his flock five or six years earlier, was found by a hiker in Canberra, Australia. "Chris," as the sheep was dubbed, had been living on his own and was in desperate need of shearing. Unlike wild sheep that shed every year, Merino sheep must be sheared. Chris was so heavy that had he fallen, he would have been unable to get up, leaving him in danger of being attacked by other animals or starving to death. Chris had to be sedated so that an expert shearer could get the massive coat off without cutting him. But Chris, who weighed just ninety-seven pounds after eighty-eight pounds of wool was removed, was miraculously saved. He had emerged from his ordeal, thanks to the aid of someone who knew how to care for sheep.**

❖ Read aloud today's focus statement: **People face challenges that may seem too difficult to endure. Where can they find the support and reassurance to face these challenges? The psalmist promises that God's love provides what is necessary to confront any difficulties and to live in a fulfilling and intimate relationship with God.**

*(2) Goal 1: Explore Psalm 23's Use of the Metaphor of Shepherding for Trusting in God*

❖ Read Psalm 23 responsively if you have hymnals available that include a Psalter. (Note that if you have *The United Methodist Hymnal*, Psalm 23 is found on page 754. The King James Version, which many older students likely would have memorized, is found on page 137 if you prefer to use that version.) If you do not have access to hymnals, invite several students who use the same Bible translation to read Psalm 23 in unison.

❖ Discuss these questions:
1. **What does it mean to you to say that the Lord is your shepherd?**
2. **If God is your shepherd, then you somehow understand yourself to be a sheep. What does that mean to you?** (See If, Then in Interpreting the Scripture.)
3. **How is the image of the shepherd used in other places in the Bible?** (See So Great a Cloud in Interpreting the Scripture.)
4. **What does the shepherd supply to meet the needs of the sheep?** (Review Understanding the Scripture.)
5. **Where do you see expressions of the psalmist's trust in the shepherd?** (Note that the psalmist apparently trusts God in all circumstances. He writes that he "shall not want," whether he is in green pastures or facing enemies.)
6. **Which image in this psalm is your favorite? Why?**

*(3) Goal 2: Appreciate Ways that God's Love Provides Goodness and Mercy to People When They Face Challenges*

❖ Read the last three paragraphs of If the Shepherd Is Good in Interpreting the Scripture. Note that we can count on the goodness of God, even when the circumstances of our lives are very difficult.

❖ Invite participants to tell brief stories of times when they experienced God's love in the midst of a challenge. Discuss how believing that God's love and mercy will support them enabled them to work through the situation they faced.

❖ Conclude by reciting in unison today's key verse, Psalm 23:1.

*(4) Goal 3: Choose to Trust God's Leading, Which Transforms Challenges and Difficulties*

❖ Assign individuals or groups to read the following verses, which you will write on newsprint, to discern what they teach about trusting in God:

Psalm 94:19-22
Psalm 118:5
Psalm 146:3-5
Jeremiah 17:5-6
Proverbs 3:5-8
Micah 7:5-6

❖ Bring the groups together and raise these questions. Recognize that some passages may provide more information than others.

1. **What did you learn from this passage about trusting God?**
2. **Why is it wiser to trust in God than in other people— or yourself?**
3. **What can those who trust in the Lord expect?**

❖ Form groups again to discuss why it can be difficult for people to trust completely in God. Suggest these questions: **What are the obstacles? How might they be overcome? How can the church help you to overcome cultural training that** claims that you are a self-made, independent individual who needs help from no one?

❖ Conclude by reading these words from Psalm 84:11-12 as a way for the class to affirm their trust in God:

**<sup></sup>¹¹For the L**ORD **God is a sun and shield;**

**he bestows favor and honor.**

**No good thing does the L**ORD **withhold**

**from those who walk uprightly.**

**¹²O L**ORD **of hosts,**

**happy is everyone who trusts in you.**

And all God's people said, "Amen."

*(5) Continue the Journey*

❖ Pray that as the learners depart, they will depend on God, the good shepherd, who can always be trusted to provide us with what we need.

❖ Post information for next week's session on newsprint for the students to copy:

■ **Title: God's Saving Love in Christ**
■ **Background Scripture: John 3:1-21**
■ **Lesson Scripture: John 3:1-16**
■ **Focus of the Lesson: A commitment to serve others may require more than what was anticipated. To what extent are we willing to sacrifice for the sake of others? God's love for the world is proved through the ultimate sacrifice of God's only Son so that all who believe in him will have eternal life.**

❖ Challenge the adults to grow spiritually by completing one or more of these activities related to this week's session.

(1) Research "sheep" and "shepherd" to learn what you can about the nature and ways of sheep, as well as the work of the shepherd.

(2) **Use a concordance to locate passages that refer to "shepherd(s)" in both the Old and New Testaments. What do you learn about how this word is used in a literal sense (that is, in relation to a person who tends sheep), as well as in a metaphorical sense where "shepherd" refers to God,** Jesus, or someone appointed to care for God's people.

(3) **Recall a funeral at which Psalm 23 was recited. What comfort did this psalm give you as a mourner?**

❖ Sing or read aloud "The King of Love My Shepherd Is."

❖ Conclude today's session by leading the class in this benediction, which is adapted from John 15:12, the key verse for March 19: **Let us go forth obeying Jesus' commandment to love one another as he has loved us. Amen.**

UNIT 2: GOD'S CARING, SAVING, AND UPHOLDING LOVE

# God's Saving Love in Christ

---

## PREVIEWING THE LESSON

**Lesson Scripture:** John 3:1-16
**Background Scripture:** John 3:1-21
**Key Verse:** John 3:16

### Focus of the Lesson:

A commitment to serve others may require more than what was anticipated. To what extent are we willing to sacrifice for the sake of others? God's love for the world is proved through the ultimate sacrifice of God's only Son so that all who believe in him will have eternal life.

### Goals for the Learners:

(1) to explore the story of Nicodemus, who learned from Jesus what it means "to be born from above."
(2) to appreciate how God's love offers salvation rather than condemnation.
(3) to seek to live as spiritually reborn persons who know and respond to God's love.

### Supplies:

Bibles, newsprint and marker, paper and pencils, hymnals

---

## READING THE SCRIPTURE

NRSV
Lesson Scripture: John 3:1-16

¹Now there was a Pharisee named Nicodemus, a leader of the Jews. ²He came to Jesus by night and said to him, "Rabbi, we know that you are a teacher who has come from God; for no one can do these signs that you do apart from the presence of God."

CEB
Lesson Scripture: John 3:1-16

¹There was a Pharisee named Nicodemus, a Jewish leader. ²He came to Jesus at night and said to him, "Rabbi, we know that you are a teacher who has come from God, for no one could do these miraculous signs that you do unless God is with him."

³Jesus answered him, "Very truly, I tell you, no one can see the kingdom of God without being born from above." ⁴Nicodemus said to him, "How can anyone be born after having grown old? Can one enter a second time into the mother's womb and be born?" ⁵Jesus answered, "Very truly, I tell you, no one can enter the kingdom of God without being born of water and Spirit. ⁶What is born of the flesh is flesh, and what is born of the Spirit is spirit. ⁷Do not be astonished that I said to you, 'You must be born from above.' ⁸The wind blows where it chooses, and you hear the sound of it, but you do not know where it comes from or where it goes. So it is with everyone who is born of the Spirit." ⁹Nicodemus said to him, "How can these things be?" ¹⁰Jesus answered him, "Are you a teacher of Israel, and yet you do not understand these things?

¹¹"Very truly, I tell you, we speak of what we know and testify to what we have seen; yet you do not receive our testimony. ¹²If I have told you about earthly things and you do not believe, how can you believe if I tell you about heavenly things? ¹³No one has ascended into heaven except the one who descended from heaven, the Son of Man. ¹⁴And just as Moses lifted up the serpent in the wilderness, so must the Son of Man be lifted up, ¹⁵that whoever believes in him may have eternal life.

¹⁶"For God so loved the world that he gave his only Son, so that everyone who believes in him may not perish but may have eternal life."

³Jesus answered, "I assure you, unless someone is born anew, it's not possible to see God's kingdom." ⁴Nicodemus asked, "How is it possible for an adult to be born? It's impossible to enter the mother's womb for a second time and be born, isn't it?" ⁵Jesus answered, "I assure you, unless someone is born of water and the Spirit, it's not possible to enter God's kingdom. ⁶Whatever is born of the flesh is flesh, and whatever is born of the Spirit is spirit. ⁷Don't be surprised that I said to you, 'You must be born anew.' ⁸God's Spirit blows wherever it wishes. You hear its sound, but you don't know where it comes from or where it is going. It's the same with everyone who is born of the Spirit."

⁹Nicodemus said, "How are these things possible?"

¹⁰"Jesus answered, "You are a teacher of Israel and you don't know these things? ¹¹I assure you that we speak about what we know and testify about what we have seen, but you don't receive our testimony. ¹²If I have told you about earthly things and you don't believe, how will you believe if I tell you about heavenly things? ¹³No one has gone up to heaven except the one who came down from heaven, the Human One. ¹⁴Just as Moses lifted up the snake in the wilderness, so must the Human One be lifted up ¹⁵so that everyone who believes in him will have eternal life. ¹⁶God so loved the world that he gave his only Son, so that everyone who believes in him won't perish but will have eternal life."

---

## UNDERSTANDING THE SCRIPTURE

**John 3:1.** Nicodemus is introduced with two credentials: He was "a Pharisee" and "a leader of the Jews." Although we Christians have a negative association with the Pharisees, they were known for their meticulous study and application of God's law. Meanwhile, the identification of Nicodemus as "a leader of the Jews" suggests that he may have been a member of the ruling council, before whom Jesus appeared on trial. In both cases, therefore, Nicodemus found himself in the midst of people who should have been better than they were and who were viciously opposed to Jesus.

**John 3:2.** That Nicodemus came to Jesus "by night" is generally understood as a negative detail about the man. It may indicate that he was afraid to be identified with Jesus. Also, we observe that the narrator not only includes the detail here but also reminds us of it when we see Nicodemus again at the time of Jesus' burial (John 19:39). Given John's symbolic use of light and dark, this element of Nicodemus's story suggests an unfavorable spiritual condition.

Nicodemus's greeting indicates his respect for Jesus. It is unclear, though, whom he means when he says "we know," for most of his associates refused to recognize these truths about Jesus. Meanwhile, because Nicodemus does not begin with a question or a request, we do not know what his purpose was in coming to Jesus.

**John 3:3.** The connection between Nicodemus's greeting and Jesus' response is not immediately clear. Jesus volunteers the subject of the kingdom of God, as well as the imagery of "being born from above." The underlying Greek adverb can be translated from above, again, or anew. Each is appropriately meaningful in this context.

**John 3:4.** Jesus and Nicodemus are clearly having parallel conversations.

Nicodemus is thinking literally and physically, while Jesus is speaking symbolically and spiritually. Consequently, Nicodemus cannot understand what Jesus is saying to him.

**John 3:5-8.** Jesus reiterates the "no one can see/enter the kingdom of God without" phrase from verse 3, but here it is tied to "being born of water and Spirit." Those two parts seem to correspond to the flesh and Spirit dichotomy that follows. The water and the flesh represent the physical birth that Nicodemus has in mind. The work of the Spirit, meanwhile, produces the birth Jesus has in mind.

**John 3:9-10.** The man who came to Jesus "by night" remains in darkness. After his initial greeting, all that we hear from Nicodemus is a series of questions. And this question—"How can these things be?"—is the last we hear from him. He exits the stage unnoticed.

Jesus chides Nicodemus for his failure to understand. We remember that two Gentiles impress Jesus with their faith (Matthew 15:28; Luke 7:9). This credentialed "teacher of Israel," however, is a great disappointment.

**John 3:11-13.** Three significant theological themes from John's Gospel are interwoven here. First, we are reminded of the importance of testimony. The gospel truth is not something worked out philosophically by an individual. Rather, it is revealed truth, rooted in historical events, and passed down by testimony from eyewitnesses.

Second, we see the dichotomy between things physical and things spiritual—or, here, earthly things and heavenly things. This distinction is central to the dialogue with Nicodemus. Although he is "a teacher of Israel," he seems unable to converse about heavenly, spiritual matters.

Third, there is Jesus' unique role as "the one who descended from heaven." In this case, it makes his testimony about heavenly things unmatched and reliable. In the larger scope of John, it also indicates the preexistent divinity of Christ.

**John 3:14-15.** Jesus makes reference to a brief, obscure story from Israel's generation of wandering in the wilderness. The story, tucked in Numbers (21:4-9), describes a plague of poisonous snakes that infested the Israelite camp. The people who had been bitten by the snakes were dying, and so there was a natural panic throughout the camp. When Moses prayed for help, God's prescription was to fashion a bronze image of a snake and hang it on a pole in the center of the camp. The Lord promised that anyone who had been bitten could look at the serpent on a pole and live.

Jesus identified himself with that serpent on a pole in the wilderness. The "lifted up" parallel anticipates the cross. The powerful implication is that we who are snakebitten by sin will find healing in looking to the one on the cross.

**John 3:16.** Often called "the gospel in a nutshell," this may be the most memorized verse in Scripture. It captures in just a few words the motivation and purpose of God in sending Jesus, as well as the desired human response and eternal result. Especially noteworthy is God's love for the world in light of the theme in this Gospel of the world's antagonism toward God and God's emissaries (7:7; 15:18-19; 17:14).

**John 3:17.** Here is the heart of God revealed. In contrast to any superstition, fear, or caricature that portrays God as angry and eager to judge, Jesus makes the divine desire clear. The guilt of humankind is a given. Accordingly, two options are available: condemnation or salvation. God's purpose in sending Jesus was to save.

Imagine a house that has been badly damaged by some natural disaster. Will we post on the door a "property condemned" sign or a construction permit? Shall we bulldoze or rebuild? God's choice is to rebuild.

**John 3:18.** We live in a culture where belief is a nearly inconsequential thing—a matter of personal opinion in a world without absolute truth. The Gospel of John presents belief as an enormously significant matter, however, for it marks the watershed between condemnation and salvation.

**John 3:19-21.** As previously noted, light and dark are prominent themes in John's Gospel. The former is associated with God, Jesus, life, openness, and truth. The latter is associated with sin, confusion, secrecy, and being lost. The logic here is that God's light has come into the world, and how people respond to that light is both their own choice and their own judgment.

---

## INTERPRETING THE SCRIPTURE

### Our Patron Saint

Play a word association game with two people. One is from first-century Palestine and the other from twenty-first-century America. Say the word "Pharisee," and see what their responses are. Chances are that the answers will be completely different.

The people of Jesus' day thought

of the Pharisees as scrupulously righteous. They were reputedly expert in knowing and understanding the laws of God, and they were famously careful about obeying them. They were not necessarily loved, but they were certainly respected.

The people in our day, however, have a very different impression of the Pharisees. We think of them as the worst kind of legalists: superficial, self-righteous, and hypocritical. We didn't know them personally, of course. Most of what we know about them, therefore, comes from Jesus' harsh critiques of them.

The fact is that the Pharisees were a mixed bag. Their legalism was probably an unfortunate mutation of an earlier earnestness. They should have been better than they were, and Jesus called them on it.

Nicodemus was a Pharisee. And Nicodemus, too, should have been better than he was. He was a leader of the people, yet too timid to come to Jesus in broad daylight. He was a teacher in Israel, yet in over his head when talking about spiritual matters. He skulked to Jesus secretly, and went away even more unnoticed. He was full of questions and confusion, and we never sense that his chord was resolved.

We must not be quick to dismiss or condemn Nicodemus, however, for he is a kindred spirit. He is the patron saint of all those who ought to be better than they are. And chances are that we know that that includes us.

Perhaps we sense that we should be better than we are because our generosity is not in proportion to our blessings. Perhaps our living is not in keeping with our understanding. Perhaps we underperform given our training and experience. Or, perhaps, we just chide ourselves at the end of some days, saying, "You know better than that."

Ever since the Fall, we human beings have been underperforming. We were given a perfect start and unimaginable advantage. Made in the image of God, yet preferring to believe the serpent, we did not live up to our Creator's design. We must not be too hard on Nicodemus, therefore, for he is one of us, and we are all in this together.

*The Math of the Kingdom*

The familiar maxim says that if A equals B and B equals C, then A must equal C. We see that principle at work in the things that Jesus endeavors to explain to Nicodemus about the kingdom. At one moment, Jesus says that "no one can see the kingdom of God without being born from above" (3:3). And then, a moment later, he says that "no one can enter the kingdom of God without being born of water and the Spirit" (3:5). Those statements are similar enough that we might use each to interpret the other.

The conversation begins with Nicodemus seeking out Jesus and greeting him admiringly. Jesus responds with an out-of-the-blue reference to the kingdom of God. There is no thematic antecedent within the conversation. Indeed, these two verses are the only times in the entire Gospel of John that Jesus uses the phrase "the kingdom of God." And his only other reference to "kingdom" at all in John comes when he is on trial before Pilate and he asserts that his kingdom is not of this world (18:36).

Likewise, this is the only reference in all of Jesus' teachings to this image of being born again, or anew, or from above. As we noted earlier, the Greek adverb could mean any of those things. It seems from Nicodemus's response that he interpreted Jesus to mean "again," for he asked about entering "a second time into his mother's womb" (3:4). He understood it to be a second, an "again," birth.

When Jesus restated and rephrased his teaching about entering the kingdom, however, he replaced the original adverb with the phrase "born of water and of Spirit" (3:5). He also echoed Nicodemus's word "enter," but redirected it. The issue is not about entering a womb, but entering the kingdom. It is not a going back but a moving forward.

Jesus' reference to being born of water has often been interpreted as an allusion to baptism. Within the context of this passage, however—both Nicodemus's question about the mother's womb and Jesus' subsequent comparisons of being born of flesh and being born of spirit—it seems more likely that the water image refers to our physical birth. The new birth, therefore, must be a birth "of the Spirit." That, combined with Jesus' later juxtaposition of earthly things with heavenly things, suggests that the adverb in verse 3 is perhaps best translated "from above."

So it is that there is a kingdom that is not of this world (18:36), and entering it requires a birth that is also not of this world. It is a new birth. It is a birth from above, just as it ushers us into a kingdom that is from above.

## Trinitarian Salvation

One of the distinctive benefits of John's Gospel is its attentiveness to the Trinity, though that word is never used. More than any of the other three, John offers a glimpse into the relationship between the Father, the Son, and the Spirit. And, in this brief passage, we see how each person of the Trinity is at work in our salvation.

The role of the Father is hinted at immediately in Nicodemus's insight about Jesus: "Rabbi, we know that you are a teacher who has come from God" (3:2). The "Rabbi" and "teacher" labels indicate an incomplete understanding of who Jesus is, of course, but Nicodemus was right that Jesus had come from God. And Jesus himself makes that point explicitly when he declares in verse 16 that "God so loved the world that he gave his only Son." Trace our salvation back to its origin—its point of departure, if you will—and you will find yourself at the heart of the Father.

Jesus also reveals the work of the Son to Nicodemus, and it is more than just rabbi and teacher. Jesus points back to the otherwise obscure story from Israel's wilderness era of the serpent on the pole. The reference suggests a malady, a prescription from God, a cross, and a cure that is attained by faith. Faith in the Son is the key to eternal life.

Finally, we reason that new life begins with a new birth. And that birth is the work of the Spirit. Jesus acknowledges the mysterious nature of the Spirit's work: invisible and unpredictable, on the one hand, yet apparent and undeniable in its impact.

The Father sent the Son because of love for the world. The Son became the prescription on a pole in order that we might be saved and have eternal life. And while the Father sent the Son once, and the Son was lifted up once, the Spirit is continuously doing a work in our lives.

So it was that Jesus told Nicodemus that he must be born from above. For the Spirit comes from above. As did the Son. As does our salvation.

# SHARING THE SCRIPTURE

## PREPARING TO LEAD

### Preparing Our Hearts

Ponder this week's devotional reading from Titus 3:1-7. How does recognition of the loving-kindness of God influence the behavior of a believer toward both nonbelievers and believers? What role does the Holy Spirit play in the life of a believer?

Pray that you and the students will be ready to do good works, not as a requirement for salvation but rather as a consequence of the saving grace you have experienced in Christ Jesus.

### Preparing Our Minds

Study the background Scripture from John 3:1-21 and the lesson Scripture from John 3:1-16.

Consider this question: *To what extent are you willing to sacrifice for the sake of others?*

Write on newsprint:

❏ questions for Goal 3 in Sharing the Scripture.
❏ information for next week's lesson, found under Continue the Journey.
❏ activities for further spiritual growth in Continue the Journey.

Determine how you might use any of the features that precede the first lesson of this quarter in today's session.

## LEADING THE CLASS

### (1) Gather to Learn

❖ Welcome everyone and pray that those who have come on this Palm Sunday will be open to receiving and sharing the saving love of Christ Jesus.

❖ Invite participants to call out brief answers to these questions. Write responses on newsprint.

1. **What sacrifices are parents willing to make for their children?**
2. **What sacrifices are adult children willing to make for their parents?**
3. **What sacrifices might members make on behalf of Christ for the church?**
4. **What sacrifices might one group make for another group that it considers an enemy?**

❖ Read aloud today's focus statement: **A commitment to serve others may require more than what was anticipated. To what extent are we willing to sacrifice for the sake of others? God's love for the world is proved through the ultimate sacrifice of God's only Son so that all who believe in him will have eternal life.**

### (2) Goal 1: Explore the Story of Nicodemus, Who Learned from Jesus What It Means "to Be Born from Above"

❖ Select three volunteers to read the parts of the narrator, Nicodemus, and Jesus in John 3:1-15.

❖ Discuss these questions:

1. **What do you learn about Nicodemus from this story?** (See Our Patron Saint in Interpreting the Scripture, as well as John 3:1 and 3:2 in Understanding the Scripture.)
2. **Why does Nicodemus seem to have so much difficulty understanding Jesus?** (Nicodemus is hearing the literal meaning of Jesus'

words, whereas Jesus is speaking symbolically. See John 3:4 in Understanding the Scripture.)

3. **What does Jesus teach about how one enters God's kingdom?** (See The Math of the Kingdom in Interpreting the Scripture. The concept of a second birth is particularly difficult for Nicodemus to grasp. Note that the Greek word translated in John 3:3 in the NRSV as "born from above" can also be translated "born again" or "born anew" as seen in the CEB)

4. **Where in this passage do you see evidence of how the Father, Son, and Holy Spirit work in concert to bring about our salvation?** (See Trinitarian Salvation in Interpreting the Scripture.)

5. **Two thousand years after Nicodemus talked with Jesus, we still have questions about the kingdom of God and how one can enter it. What question(s) would you want to ask Jesus?**

❖ **Option:** Investigate Jesus' reference in John 3:14-15 to Moses' having "lifted up the serpent in the wilderness" by reading Numbers 21:4-9. Also note Understanding the Scripture for verses 14-15. Mention that the Greek word used in John to translate "lift up" also means "exalt."

*(3) Goal 2: Appreciate How God's Love Offers Salvation Rather Than Condemnation*

❖ Read John 3:16-18 from today's key verse and partial background Scripture. Note that whereas some people emphasize God's judgment, John is underscoring that the purpose of Jesus' incarnation is to bring salvation rather than condemnation. God's ultimate purpose is that all people will be reconciled to God as a result of Jesus' coming.

❖ Discuss: **If you do an Internet search for "judgmental Christians," you'll find numerous research projects showing that a major reason people leave the church is that they find it too judgmental. What steps do you think the church—as an institution and as individual Christians—can take to create an atmosphere where God's loving offer of salvation overshadows judgment and condemnation? What changes could our congregation make to be more open and welcoming to all people who are seeking to know God?**

*(4) Goal 3: Seek to Live as Spiritually Reborn Persons Who Know and Respond to God's Love*

❖ Read John's definition of "eternal life" as found in *The New Interpreter's Study Bible*: **"'Eternal life' does not speak of immortality or a future life in heaven, but is a metaphor for living in the unending presence of God. . . . This is the new life Jesus promised Nicodemus in 3:3 and 5."**

❖ Ask: **What traits would you expect to see in people who are spiritually reborn and are now "living in the unending presence of God"?** List answers on newsprint, which you will leave posted.

❖ Distribute paper and pencils and invite the students to write responses to these questions, which you will write on newsprint. State in advance that they will not be asked to share their reflection.

1. **Which of these traits would others say they can see in me?**
2. **Which of these traits do I want or need to develop to live more fully as one who is spiritually reborn in Jesus?**
3. **How do my actions and attitudes reflect God's saving love so that others might see God's love in me?**

❖ Challenge participants to continue to reflect on and refine their answers as a means of living more fully as spiritually reborn persons.

### (5) Continue the Journey

❖ Pray that as the learners depart, they will give thanks for God's saving love as expressed through Jesus.

❖ Post information for next week's session on newsprint for the students to copy:

- Title: **God's Love as Victory over Death**
- Background Scripture: **John 19:38-42; 20:1-10; 1 Peter 1:3-9**
- Lesson Scripture: **John 20:1-10; 1 Peter 3–5, 8–9**
- Focus of the Lesson: **Although we are forewarned, some life events are beyond the realm of our imagination. How do we respond at these times? Even though the disciples were confounded when they entered the empty tomb, they experienced a new birth into a living hope through the Resurrection.**

❖ Challenge the adults to grow spiritually by completing one or more of these activities related to this week's session.

(1) **Research additional roles that Nicodemus plays in John's story. See John 7:45-52 and 19:38-42. What do Nicodemus's responses and actions suggest about how he viewed Jesus after his encounter with him at night?**

(2) **Brainstorm a list of three to five questions that you would have for Jesus. See what answers you can discern through reading, prayer, discussion with your pastor or other mature Christians. Recognize that the answer to some questions will remain a mystery in this life.**

(3) **Plan to attend services in your church or community to mark the events of Holy Week, beginning with today's Palm Sunday service. As you attend each service, ask yourself how God's love is made known to you in each event.**

❖ Sing or read aloud "Because He Lives."

❖ Conclude today's session by leading the class in this benediction, which is adapted from John 15:12, the key verse for March 19: **Let us go forth obeying Jesus' commandment to love one another as he has loved us. Amen.**

UNIT 2: GOD'S CARING, SAVING, AND UPHOLDING LOVE

# GOD'S LOVE AS VICTORY OVER DEATH

---

## PREVIEWING THE LESSON

**Lesson Scripture:** John 20:1-10; 1 Peter 1:3-5, 8-9
**Background Scripture:** John 19:38-42; 20:1-10; 1 Peter 1:3-9
**Key Verse:** John 20:8

**Focus of the Lesson:**
Although we are forewarned, some life events are beyond the realm of our imagination. How do we respond at these times? Even though the disciples were confounded when they entered the empty tomb, they experienced a new birth into a living hope through the Resurrection.

**Goals for the Learners:**
(1) to remember in the events of the Resurrection the power of God's love to overcome death.
(2) to celebrate the saving power of new life offered in the Resurrection.
(3) to share with others the power of God's love found in the good news of the Resurrection.

**Supplies:**
Bibles, newsprint and marker, paper and pencils, hymnals

---

## READING THE SCRIPTURE

NRSV
Lesson Scripture: John 20:1-10
¹Early on the first day of the week, while it was still dark, Mary Magdalene came to the tomb and saw that the stone had been removed from the tomb. ²So she ran and went to Simon Peter and the other disciple, the one whom Jesus loved, and said to them, "They have taken the Lord

CEB
Lesson Scripture: John 20:1-10
¹Early in the morning of the first day of the week, while it was still dark, Mary Magdalene came to the tomb and saw that the stone had been taken away from the tomb. ²She ran to Simon Peter and the other disciple, the one whom Jesus loved, and said, "They have taken the Lord from

out of the tomb, and we do not know where they have laid him." [3]Then Peter and the other disciple set out and went toward the tomb. [4]The two were running together, but the other disciple outran Peter and reached the tomb first. [5]He bent down to look in and saw the linen wrappings lying there, but he did not go in. [6]Then Simon Peter came, following him, and went into the tomb. He saw the linen wrappings lying there, [7]and the cloth that had been on Jesus' head, not lying with the linen wrappings but rolled up in a place by itself. **[8]Then the other disciple, who reached the tomb first, also went in, and he saw and believed;** [9]for as yet they did not understand the scripture, that he must rise from the dead. [10]Then the disciples returned to their homes.

the tomb, and we don't know where they've put him." [3]Peter and the other disciple left to go to the tomb. [4]They were running together, but the other disciple ran faster than Peter and was the first to arrive at the tomb. [5]Bending down to take a look, he saw the linen cloths lying there, but he didn't go in. [6]Following him, Simon Peter entered the tomb and saw the linen cloths lying there. [7]He also saw the face cloth that had been on Jesus' head. It wasn't with the other clothes but was folded up in its own place. **[8]Then the other disciple, the one who arrived at the tomb first, also went inside. He saw and believed.** [9]They didn't yet understand the scripture that Jesus must rise from the dead. [10]Then the disciples returned to the place where they were staying.

NRSV
Lesson Scripture: 1 Peter 1:3-5, 8-9

[3]Blessed be the God and Father of our Lord Jesus Christ! By his great mercy he has given us a new birth into a living hope through the resurrection of Jesus Christ from the dead, [4]and into an inheritance that is imperishable, undefiled, and unfading, kept in heaven for you, [5]who are being protected by the power of God through faith for a salvation ready to be revealed in the last time. [8]Although you have not seen him, you love him; and even though you do not see him now, you believe in him and rejoice with an indescribable and glorious joy, [9]for you are receiving the outcome of your faith, the salvation of your souls.

CEB
Lesson Scripture: 1 Peter 1:3-5, 8-9

[3]May the God and Father of our Lord Jesus Christ be blessed! On account of his vast mercy, he has given us new birth. You have been born anew into a living hope through the resurrection of Jesus Christ from the dead. [4]You have a pure and enduring inheritance that cannot perish—an inheritance that is presently kept safe in heaven for you. [5]Through his faithfulness, you are guarded by God's power so that you can receive the salvation he is ready to reveal in the last time.

[8]Although you've never seen him, you love him. Even though you don't see him now, you trust him and so rejoice with a glorious joy that is too much for words. [9]You are receiving the goal of your faith: your salvation.

# UNDERSTANDING THE SCRIPTURE

**Introduction.** Twenty-four hours earlier, Jesus was likely sitting down to supper with his disciples. The intervening hours have been eventful, and a large cast has crossed the stage. From the disciples at the supper to the mob in the garden, from the unjust and cowardly leaders to the cruel and mocking soldiers, and from the bloodthirsty crowd to the flanking criminals—we have seen a wide array of characters and actions. And now, as the sun sets on Friday, the stage is nearly empty and comparatively quiet. We see just two characters and a corpse.

**John 19:38-39.** The two characters are Joseph of Arimathea and Nicodemus. Each is laudable for his generosity and thoughtfulness in this moment, yet each is questionable because of his previous timidity. Joseph, we read, was a secret disciple, which seems oxymoronic, a contradiction in terms. He did not follow Jesus openly or boldly "because of his fear of the Jews." And we have the impression that Nicodemus, too, was cowed by peer pressure, having "at first come to Jesus by night."

**John 19:40-42.** All the details of John's account reflect standard Jewish practice for burial of a body, which was different from some other, nearby cultures. The hundred pounds of spices, though, would have been more than was customary. The burial may have been relatively hasty because of the Sabbath restrictions that would be in force beginning at sundown.

**John 20:1-2.** John paints a poignant picture: a grieving woman walking alone, in the dark, to the tomb. It is unclear from John's account what she intended to do since the stone would have prohibited her from accessing the corpse to care for it. She was surprised to find the stone already moved, and so she ran to tell Peter and another disciple, concerned that Jesus' body had been taken.

"The other disciple" is a phrase that appears five times in John's Gospel. Here he is also identified as the one "whom Jesus loved," which is the designation applied to this disciple on four other occasions in John. Near the end of the Gospel, that same disciple is recognized as the one "who is testifying to these things and has written them" (21:24), which gives rise to the common assumption that "the other disciple" was John.

**John 20:3-8.** Both disciples run to the tomb. John is evidently faster, yet Peter is (not surprisingly) more forward. And so, while John arrives at the tomb first, Peter goes into the tomb first. Eventually John also enters.

The tomb should not be confused with our traditional image of a grave. We traditionally dig deep holes in the ground, and then we cover with dirt the remains of the deceased. It would be nearly impossible for visitors to enter a grave. But we understand that the tomb in which Jesus was buried was more like a room that had been carved out of rock (see Matthew 27:60). The body was laid there, but not buried. And that is why the tomb could be entered by these visitors.

The arrangement of the linen coverings suggests a very calm departure. No thief who had stolen a body would leave behind such carefully set-aside wrappings. And perhaps that sight is what prompted belief rather than fear in "the other disciple." While Mary feared that the body had been stolen, this disciple evidently believed. Apparently, he believed that the empty tomb bore witness to Jesus' having conquered death.

**John 20:9.** Broadly speaking, it seems that the disciples did not anticipate events based on Scripture. Even though Jesus himself had foretold what would happen to him, they kept being surprised. It was only after events had occurred that they came to understand them in light of Scripture. This is standard human experience, of course.

**John 20:10.** No word for home or shelter or dwelling is used here in the original Greek. Instead, the text simply uses the third-person plural personal pronoun, suggesting that the disciples returned to "their" something. While most translators choose "homes," I prefer the *Young's Literal Translation*, which says that they "went away again unto their own friends." They were visitors in Jerusalem, and so it seems more likely to me that they would return to their group than to "their" homes.

**1 Peter 1:3-5.** After a customary greeting, Peter begins his letter with an expression of praise. Specifically, he praises God for what has been provided for us in Jesus Christ. We observe that Peter's list of what God has provided is rooted in the past and anticipated in the future. It was accomplished already "through the resurrection of Jesus Christ from the dead." Meanwhile, it is for us "a living hope" and "an inheritance" that is "kept in heaven for you" and a salvation that is "ready to be revealed in the last time." That all speaks of future prospects.

**1 Peter 1:6-7.** The beauty of that future prospect is quite different from the audience's present reality. While we don't know the exact audience to whom Peter wrote or the details of their circumstances, we surmise that the addressees were experiencing suffering, and perhaps specifically persecution for their faith.

Interestingly, the proposed response to sufferings is neither lament, nor revolt, nor even a plea for help. Instead, "in this you rejoice." Why? Because while the suffering itself is bad, it is instrumental in a good process and purpose.

**1 Peter 1:8-9.** The first words of verse 8 are especially lovely ones coming from Peter. To this next generation of believers, scattered across "Pontus, Galatia, Cappadocia, Asia, and Bithynia" (1:1), Peter writes: "Although you have not seen him, you love him" (1:8). They are removed by both time and space from the person that Peter had walked and talked with, beginning by the shores of Galilee. Peter had both seen and loved him, but his audience has loved Jesus without seeing him.

The theme of rejoicing continues. Indeed, it becomes more emphatic, as the apostle says in verse 8 that his readers "rejoice with an indescribable and glorious joy." This is quite independent of their difficult physical circumstances. This is a rejoicing rooted in "the salvation of [their] souls."

---

## INTERPRETING THE SCRIPTURE

*The Nature of the Victory*

I'm a big sports fan. When I have leisure time to watch television, I would rather watch a game than almost anything else. And it has also been my pleasure to attend in person a great many sporting events, where I cheer passionately.

Over the years of watching sports,

I have witnessed some remarkable comebacks. A few have been achieved by the team for which I was rooting. In some other, very painful instances, my teams have been the victims of a phenomenal comeback.

In either case, though, the comeback is a fascinating process to watch. A team that has been badly beaten throughout an entire game somehow rises up and begins to play brilliantly. They execute, they succeed, and they get a few lucky breaks. And the next thing you know, the team that was hopelessly behind as the game was nearing its end has the lead when the clock actually runs out. Fans and players alike walk away from the stadium in disbelief over what just occurred.

During the events of Holy Week, however, the scene is even more dramatic. The game is lost and the final gun has been sounded at the cross. Toward the end, the opponents taunted Jesus, challenging him to mount a comeback (see Matthew 27:39-44). They knew he couldn't, though. No one could come back from the cross.

After the game was over, the crowds dispersed. The antagonists went home happy. Their side had won. Jesus was finally dead and gone. The others went home mourning and beating their breasts.

Just a small handful of folks remain there on the field where the defeat occurred. A hillside that had been teeming with crowds and activity is now quiet and nearly vacant. Nicodemus and Joseph cooperate to manage the dead weight of Jesus' corpse. They dutifully do what little they can for him now.

By the time a sliver of light marks the horizon of Sunday morning's sky, all the crowds are at home. Most are still in bed. And all of them by now have probably come to terms with the events of Friday. The scoreboard is turned off. The loss is in the books.

But then Mary goes to the tomb. Then Peter. Then John. And with profound belief that flies in the face of their natural disbelief, they begin to realize what has happened. The greatest, most unthinkable comeback. The game that was already lost has been won, even after it was over. No one saw this coming, even though Jesus himself had predicted it. That is the remarkable nature of the victory.

### The Un-nature of the Victory

In Sunday school classes and children's sermons across the country today, I expect a lot of well-meaning teachers and preachers will point to the signs of spring outside and talk about the resurrection of Jesus. They will talk about flowers, leaves, and new life. And it will be undeniably lovely.

It will also, however, be somewhat misleading.

Nature does not provide an adequate analogy for the resurrection of Jesus. On the contrary, nature serves to highlight for us the remarkable victory of Christ's resurrection. After all, if what happened in that empty tomb happened in nature, then there would be no objections or skepticism from our scientifically-minded culture.

The trees in my yard do have new leaves today. They are beautiful signs of life, to be sure. And they are a welcome beauty after the bareness of winter. But those leaves are not resurrection.

Last fall, we raked up a great many leaves from our yard. I remember putting them in great piles and watching my children and dogs enjoying those piles. When they were on my trees, they were green at first, and then later yellow, orange, and red. By the time we finished piling them up, however, they were predominantly brown. Dead.

Where are those leaves now? What has become of them? Wherever they are, they are not green and growing on the branches of my trees. The leaves that were dead are still dead. Indeed, they are more dead and gone than they were last November. They did not come back to life. And those trees, meanwhile, that are adorned in new life were never dead. If the trees themselves had died last fall, then they wouldn't have leaves today.

What happened with Jesus does not happen in nature, you see. In nature, living things keep living until they die. And once they die, they stay dead. Jesus, on the other hand, died, and then he lived again. And having died, he now lives eternally. That is not natural, at all. Yet that is the remarkable nature of the victory.

*The Personal Nature of the Victory*

The many professional sporting events that I have watched, in the end, have nothing to do with me. As fond as I am of saying "We won" or "We lost," the truth is that "we" didn't do anything. I was not part of it. Even for all of the energy I may have expended, I didn't actually contribute anything to the win or the loss. All of my teams, as dear as I may hold them, are really, always "they."

We have been pondering the remarkable nature of the victory of Christ in the resurrection. And now we come upon one more remarkable aspect. It is personal.

The other disciple looked into the tomb, saw what was—and wasn't—there, and he believed. If, as we suspect, that other disciple was the author or source of the Gospel, then we have a measure of the significance of that moment and that account. For consider how John's Gospel understands belief.

The author explains that his whole purpose in writing is "so that you may come to believe" (20:31). Likewise, John the Baptist's testimony was "so that all might believe" (1:7). Time and again, the pivotal, personal question Jesus asks in John's Gospel is: "Do you believe?" (1:50; 9:35; 14:10; 16:31). Belief in Jesus leads to becoming children of God (1:12), eternal life (3:16; 6:40), and freedom from condemnation (3:18).

When the narrator says that the other disciple "saw and believed" (20:8), therefore, it is a moment of tremendous significance. The victory of Christ in the resurrection has personal consequence and impact when a person believes. Jesus' victory ceases to be a third-person, historical event. By faith, his victory becomes my victory, as it offers me freedom and life, and it makes me a child of God.

And this is the good news that Peter shared, too, with his audience. The resurrection is not a victory at a distance. Rather, through it, "he has given us a new birth into a living hope . . . [and] an inheritance that is imperishable, undefiled, unfading, and kept in heaven for you" (1 Peter 1:3, 4).

Jesus won the victory on Easter Sunday. You and I know that we contributed nothing to that victory. Yet we may partake of it, and by faith we may make it personal. And so, feel free to exclaim, "We won!" today. For that is the remarkable nature of the victory.

# SHARING THE SCRIPTURE

| PREPARING TO LEAD | LEADING THE CLASS |
|---|---|

### *Preparing Our Hearts*

Ponder this week's devotional reading from Luke 24:1-12. What insights do you gain from Luke's telling of the resurrection story? Compare his account with that of John 20:1-10. What similarities and differences do you notice? Even though these stories differ in details, why is it important for readers to have more than one version of this life-changing story?

Pray that you and the students will give thanks for the resurrection of Jesus and for the Gospel writers who preserved this story for you.

### *Preparing Our Minds*

Study the background Scripture from John 19:38-42; 20:1-10; 1 Peter 1:3-9 and the lesson Scripture from John 20:1-10; 1 Peter 1:3-5, 8-9.

Consider this question: *How do you respond when some life events are beyond the realm of your imagination?*

Write on newsprint:
❏ information for next week's lesson, found under Continue the Journey.
❏ activities for further spiritual growth in Continue the Journey.

Determine how you might use any of the features that precede the first lesson of this quarter in today's session.

**Option:** Create a brief lecture using the entries for 1 Peter 1:3-9 in Understanding the Scripture to answer the questions for Goal 1 in Sharing the Scripture.

### *(1) Gather to Learn*

❖ Welcome everyone and pray that those who have come today will celebrate God's love as revealed in Jesus' victory over death.

❖ Read aloud these headlines from 1917:
- **First U.S. combat troops arrive in France as U.S. declares war on Germany (April 6).**
- **World-wide influenza pandemic strikes; by 1920, nearly 20 million are dead. In U.S. alone, 500,000 perish.**
- **Dutch dancer Mata Hari is convicted and executed as a German spy.**
- **Government offices are seized and the Romanov's Winter Palace is stormed in Russian October Revolution.**

❖ Read: **World War I actually began about a month after a Serbian assassinated Archduke Franz Ferdinand in June 1914. Although tension in the Balkans had been escalating, the peace and prosperity in Europe made it difficult for people to believe that "the Great War" was imminent. This war seemed to come out of nowhere, surprising people across the globe.**

❖ Read aloud today's focus statement: **Although we are forewarned, some life events are beyond the realm of our imagination. How do we respond at these times? Even though the disciples were confounded when they entered the empty tomb, they experienced a new** birth into a living hope through the Resurrection.

*(2) Goal 1: Remember in the Events of the Resurrection the Power of God's Love to Overcome Death*

❖ Read Introduction from Understanding the Scripture to set the scene.

❖ Enlist a volunteer to read John 20:1-10 and then discuss these questions:

1. **Had you been Mary Magdalene, what emotions might you have experienced as you stood before the tomb?**

2. **What evidence might support Mary's assumption that Jesus' body had been stolen?** (Remember that she saw only that the stone had been removed. No one actually witnessed Jesus' resurrection.)

3. **What evidence did "the other disciple" (likely John) and Peter independently discover that would indicate Jesus's body, though missing, had not been stolen?** (It's highly unlikely that a thief would take the time to leave the linen wrappings and especially to roll up the face cloth and set it aside.)

4. **Although we are told that Simon Peter went in first and saw the scene, there is no mention of how he responded to it. The other disciple "believed" (20:8), but neither he nor the other disciples understood the Scripture that said Jesus "must rise from the dead" (20:9). If the other disciple did not yet believe in the resurrection,** what was it that he "believed"? (He likely had an understanding that Jesus had somehow overcome death, but did not yet know the full story.)

❖ Recruit a volunteer to read 1 Peter 1:3-9. Discuss these questions. See the entries for 1 Peter in Understanding the Scripture. Or, if you prefer, use these questions as a guide to create a brief lecture.

1. **For what reasons does Peter praise God?**

2. **What does Peter say about the circumstances under which his readers are living?**

3. **How does he recommend that they respond to their suffering? Why?**

4. **Peter speaks about rejoicing in verses 8-9. What would inspire these people who are suffering to rejoice?**

*(3) Goal 2: Celebrate the Saving Power of New Life Offered in the Resurrection*

❖ Read or retell The Nature of the Victory in Interpreting the Scripture.

❖ Discuss these questions:

1. **How do sports fans celebrate when their team wins, especially if the win was a World Series, Super Bowl, or other difficult to achieve victory?**

2. **How do Christians celebrate Jesus' victory over death, especially when all had apparently been lost?**

❖ Encourage class members to state how they celebrate and give thanks for the saving power of Jesus' resurrection not only on Easter but every day.

*(4) Goal 3: Share with Others the Power of God's Love Found in the Good News of the Resurrection*

❖ Read or retell The Personal Nature of the Victory in Interpreting the Scripture.

❖ Look together at John 20:30-31 where you will find John's purpose in writing his Gospel.

❖ Read these words of Belgian spiritual writer Louis Evely (1910–1985): **"The best proof that Christ has risen is that he is still alive. And for the immense majority of our contemporaries, the only way of seeing him alive is for us Christians to love one another."**

❖ Post a sheet of newsprint and invite the class to brainstorm answers to this question: **What can we do to share the good news of Jesus so that people "may come to believe that Jesus is the Messiah, the Son of God, and that through believing in him [they] may have life in his name" (John 20:31)?** (Suggest that the adults think not only of words they can say but also deeds they can do to encourage nonbelievers to recognize the inestimable value of Jesus in their lives.)

❖ Challenge participants to choose at least one of these ideas to implement during the coming week.

*(5) Continue the Journey*

❖ Pray that as the learners depart, they will go forth to spread the good news about the resurrection of Jesus and encourage others to make a commitment to the Savior who gives eternal life.

❖ Post information for next week's session on newsprint for the students to copy:

■ **Title: God's Reconciling Love**
■ **Background Scripture: Romans 5:1-11; 8:31-39**
■ **Lesson Scripture: Romans 5:6-11; 8:31-39**
■ **Focus of the Lesson: Hardship, distress, and separations of all kinds abound in human life. How can we face these difficulties? Paul is convinced that nothing in all creation is able to separate us from the love of God in Jesus Christ.**

❖ Challenge the adults to grow spiritually by completing one or more of these activities related to this week's session.

(1) **Read at least one of the Synoptic accounts of Jesus' resurrection: Matthew 28:1-15; Mark 16:1-8; Luke 24:1-12. Compare John with the account(s) you have read. What similarities and differences do you notice? What do you learn from one account that you did not read in another?**

(2) **Talk with someone who has not made a commitment to Christ about what his resurrection means to you. Explain how this life-changing event impacts your daily life.**

(3) **How does Jesus' resurrection affect your own expectations concerning death?**

❖ Sing or read aloud "The Strife Is O'er, the Battle Done."

❖ Conclude today's session by leading the class in this benediction, which is adapted from John 15:12, the key verse for March 19: **Let us go forth obeying Jesus' commandment to love one another as he has loved us. Amen.**

UNIT 2: GOD'S CARING, SAVING, AND UPHOLDING LOVE

# GOD'S RECONCILING LOVE

---

## PREVIEWING THE LESSON

**Lesson Scripture:** Romans 5:6-11; 8:31-39
**Background Scripture:** Romans 5:1-11; 8:31-39
**Key Verses:** Romans 8:38-39

### Focus of the Lesson:
Hardship, distress, and separations of all kinds abound in human life. How can we face these difficulties? Paul is convinced that nothing in all creation is able to separate us from the love of God in Jesus Christ.

### Goals for the Learners:
(1) to explain the meaning of justification by faith.
(2) to experience the joy of God's reconciling love.
(3) to live out God's reconciling love in the world.

### Supplies:
Bibles, newsprint and marker, paper and pencils, hymnals

---

## READING THE SCRIPTURE

NRSV
Lesson Scripture: Romans 5:6-11

⁶For while we were still weak, at the right time Christ died for the ungodly. ⁷Indeed, rarely will anyone die for a righteous person—though perhaps for a good person someone might actually dare to die. ⁸But God proves his love for us in that while we still were sinners Christ died for us. ⁹Much more surely then, now that we have been justified by his blood, will we be saved through him from

CEB
Lesson Scripture: Romans 5:6-11

⁶While we were still weak, at the right moment, Christ died for ungodly people. ⁷It isn't often that someone will die for a righteous person, though maybe someone might dare to die for a good person. ⁸But God shows his love for us, because while we were still sinners Christ died for us. ⁹So, now that we have been made righteous by his blood, we can be even more certain that we will be saved from God's

the wrath of God. [10]For if while we were enemies, we were reconciled to God through the death of his Son, much more surely, having been reconciled, will we be saved by his life. [11]But more than that, we even boast in God through our Lord Jesus Christ, through whom we have now received reconciliation.

NRSV

Scripture Lesson: Romans 8:31-39

[31]What then are we to say about these things? If God is for us, who is against us? [32]He who did not withhold his own Son, but gave him up for all of us, will he not with him also give us everything else? [33]Who will bring any charge against God's elect? It is God who justifies. [34]Who is to condemn? It is Christ Jesus, who died, yes, who was raised, who is at the right hand of God, who indeed intercedes for us. [35]Who will separate us from the love of Christ? Will hardship, or distress, or persecution, or famine, or nakedness, or peril, or sword? [36]As it is written,

"For your sake we are being killed
    all day long;
we are accounted as sheep to be
    slaughtered."

[37]No, in all these things we are more than conquerors through him who loved us. **[38]For I am convinced that neither death, nor life, nor angels, nor rulers, nor things present, nor things to come, nor powers, [39]nor height, nor depth, nor anything else in all creation, will be able to separate us from the love of God in Christ Jesus our Lord.**

wrath through him. [10]If we were reconciled to God through the death of his Son while we were still enemies, now that we have been reconciled, how much more certain is it that we will be saved by his life? [11]And not only that: we even take pride in God through our Lord Jesus Christ, the one through whom we now have a restored relationship with God.

CEB

Scripture Lesson: Romans 8:31-39

[31]So what are we going to say about these things? If God is for us, who is against us? [32]He didn't spare his own Son but gave him up for us all. Won't he also freely give us all things with him?

[33]Who will bring a charge against God's elect people? It is God who acquits them. [34]Who is going to convict them? It is Christ Jesus who died, even more, who was raised, and who also is at God's right side. It is Christ Jesus who also pleads our case for us. [35]Who will separate us from Christ's love? Will we be separated by trouble, or distress, or harassment, or famine, or nakedness, or danger, or sword? [36]As it is written,

*We are being put to death all day long*
    *for your sake.*

*We are treated like sheep for slaughter.*

[37]But in all these things we win a sweeping victory through the one who loved us. **[38]I'm convinced that nothing can separate us from God's love in Christ Jesus our Lord: not death or life, not angels or rulers, not present things or future things, not powers [39]or height or depth, or any other thing that is created.**

## UNDERSTANDING THE SCRIPTURE

**Romans 5:1-2.** Students of the Greek New Testament report that Paul is notorious for his long sentences. The grammatical complexity, however, may belie the theological simplicity. While the truth of what Paul declares is profound, it is not complicated. Our salvation features justification, peace, and hope. All these are ours by the grace of God. And we access that grace through faith in Christ.

Paul introduces a word that he will employ twice more in our passage. The NRSV and CEB translate it as "boast," though that may carry an unfortunate connotation for us. While for us, boasting is almost entirely negative, Paul's meaning is altogether positive, as we observe in the NASB's "exult" or the NKJV's "rejoice."

**Romans 5:3-5.** In verse 2, Paul says that "we boast in our hope." That seems much more palatable than verse 3's "we also boast in our sufferings." In truth, however, the latter is an extension of the former, for Paul is hopeful about his sufferings. He believes that they will produce good things, and he identifies the sequence of those good things "that suffering produces," namely, endurance, character, and hope.

**Romans 5:6-8.** The proof of God's love is its timing. Twice Paul uses the phrase "while we were still" (5:6, 8). The idea is that God's favorable actions toward us would have been more reasonable if our condition had been more favorable. But the mother hugged the child while he was still filthy and smelly. The buyer purchased the house while it was still decrepit and in need of repairs. And Christ died for us while we were still weak, ungodly sinners.

Paul's use of the "while we were still" phrase implies that our condition is different now. While we may have been weak before, the implication is that now we are strong. No longer are we ungodly, no longer sinners. Our condition has changed, but not by our own achievement. Rather, it is precisely because God loved us and Christ died for us "while we were still" that we can be different now.

**Romans 5:9-11.** Paul adds a new and dramatic word to describe our former state: "enemies." He reasons that God's favor toward us "while we were enemies" gives us even more reason for confidence now that we have been "reconciled to God." The use of "enemies" makes "reconciled" more compelling. We cherish the image of the lost sheep being recovered by the good shepherd. Yet here is the still stronger image of love that reaches out to save and embrace an adversary.

Finally, Paul boasts once more. First it was "in our hope," and then it was "in our sufferings." Now in verse 11 the boasting reaches its pinnacle as "we even boast in God through our Lord Jesus Christ." And Christ is identified as the agent of our reconciliation, just as he was the agent of God's grace above.

**Romans 8:31.** "These things" may hearken back to "the sufferings of this present time," which was Paul's subject, beginning in verse 18. Or the phrase may refer more broadly to the truths that the apostle had been affirming in the previous verses, including the providential and purposeful work of God in our lives. Meanwhile, Paul introduces the rhetorical technique of the entire passage:

asking a series of questions in order to lay the groundwork for the grand affirmation of answers with which the section concludes.

**Romans 8:32.** Here is the great logic behind our hope. We do not just keep our fingers crossed, full of wishful thinking about the nature of God and the divine attitude toward us. While the ancient pagans fretted under the frowns of their capricious gods, the apostle Paul lived with this rational confidence: if God "did not withhold his own Son," what would God withhold? Everything else is small by comparison. The incomparable gift of Jesus, therefore, gives us a bold hope for all the rest.

**Romans 8:33-34.** The apostle continues with a kind of doxology of logic. He asks more questions in order to offer the definitive gospel answers. The questions suggest some jeopardy or trouble for us. The answers, by contrast, become reminders of our security in Christ.

The only one truly eligible to bring a charge against us or to condemn us is the Lord. In the face of that, though, Paul reminds us that God is the one who justifies us and Jesus intercedes for us. The frightened defendant walks into the courtroom only to discover that the prosecuting attorney is pleading on his behalf with the judge, who has already declared him not guilty.

**Romans 8:35-36.** A review of Paul's biography reminds us that his list of troubles is not theoretical. He could attach a time and place to each of these words. And so it is with the credibility of personal experience that Paul writes. He introduces a question to which he will return in verses 37-39 with an emphatic answer.

Verse 35 recalled troubles that were part of Paul's own personal experience. In verse 36 he cites an Old Testament Scripture that gives voice and meaning to that personal experience. Psalm 44 is written as a national lament: Israel crying out to God for help in the midst of persecution and trouble. Paul borrows verse 22 from that psalm to express the persecution he has known for Christ's sake.

**Romans 8:37-39.** Finally comes the decisive answer to all of the questions. Paul's tone is triumphant and his claim is comprehensive. And the end result is one of the most cherished, comforting, and powerful passages in all of Scripture.

In order to express his robust confidence that we are "more than conquerors" (8:37), the apostle employs a marvelous compound word: *hupernikao*. We might recognize the two component parts, for they have worked their way into our vernacular. We use "hyper" as a prefix to suggest something excessive or extreme. Meanwhile, the shoe manufacturer *Nike* took its name from the Greek goddess of victory, and thus the Greek verb *nikao* means to conquer, overcome, or prevail. Paul's vigorous image, therefore, is of extremely overcoming, excessively prevailing. It's a strong word to portray a strong truth.

---

## INTERPRETING THE SCRIPTURE

*Making Things Right*

The old Fanny Crosby hymn declares, "Jesus doeth all things well." She borrows her declaration from the Gospel of Mark, where the crowds marvel at Jesus' healings, saying, "He hath done all things well" (Mark 7:37

---

KJV). In truth, though, Crosby could have made the same inference about the Lord from almost any point in Scripture.

The hallmark of the creation story is the recurring assessment that "it was good" (for example, Genesis 1:10). Whatever the Lord does, the Lord does well. And that is not merely a statement of skill, as it might be when applied to human beings. Rather, we affirm a moral quality when we say that what God makes is good and right.

The truth of that moral element is perhaps best revealed when things go wrong. When sin and unrighteousness prevail in a life or a land, the Lord is unwilling to chalk it up as ruined goodness. Rather, we see the recurring pattern of a God who sets out to make things right again. Creator becomes Redeemer, seeking to heal what has been broken and to restore what has been lost.

Even God's acts of judgment are part of this praiseworthy pattern. We sometimes misunderstand the acts or even the warnings of judgment as products of a God who is "fed up." Yet the Lord is "slow to anger" (Exodus 34:6), reluctant to destroy (Ezekiel 33:11), and "ready to relent from punishing" (Jonah 4:2). Even the judgment of God is an instrument of the larger divine purpose to make things right.

We understand the principle from the world of medicine. We know how severe some curative treatments can be. We recognize how dramatic certain surgical procedures are. Yet the doctors are not being cruel in these matters, but kind. You do what has to be done in order to set the body free from whatever is wrong with it.

So it is with the scalpel of God's judgment. The one who made everything good and right to begin with still endeavors to make things right. Even when they are wrong.

*The Semantics of Making Things Right*

In the Greek of the New Testament, we see a connection between words and concepts that is not automatically apparent in English. Because the gospel message was first written in that Greek, therefore, it is important to tap that resource in order to aide our understanding. If a connection was apparent to the author, then the reader needs to know about it as well.

The Greek word for right and righteous is *dikaios*. And when Paul writes about righteousness, his word is *dikaiosune*, an obvious cognate, that is, a related word that has the same root. These are the words that reflect the way things ought to be. To pay what is right, for example, is to pay what is fair. Societal righteousness means justice. And personal righteousness suggests a life lived God's way.

Meanwhile, when the apostle writes about the gospel principle of justification by faith, the underlying Greek word for justification is *dikaioo*. The word is a member of the same immediate family with the words for right, righteous, and righteousness. Yet that relationship may elude us in English.

There is a close and natural connection between justification and righteousness. To justify is to make right. And as we previously noted, it is always God's nature and will to make things right.

We have some sense of this from the vocabulary of text formatting. We speak of text being flush left or flush right, indicating the margin to which the text is aligned. When we center the text, then the imaginary line of alignment runs down the middle. And then there is that formatting that we call "justified" text. In this case, the left-to-right lines of text that would not reach to the right-hand margin are formatted so that they do. By themselves, they fall short. But once they are justified, they are made right.

## Making Us Right

By ourselves, we fall short (Romans 3:23), and our own righteousness, such as it is, is completely inadequate (Isaiah 64:6). Yet it is always God's desire to make things right. And so the Lord offers to make us right by means of what we call justifying grace.

The apostle Paul proclaimed that the righteousness that is available to us is a justification by faith. This idea gets at the great difference between God making me right and me trying to make myself right. If it is my doing, then righteousness is accessed by works. If it is God's doing, however, then it is accessed by faith.

We human beings tend toward two equally futile instincts in this regard. The one is to pretend that we already are right, and so no work is needed on anyone's part. But, as John bluntly writes: "If we say that we have no sin, we deceive ourselves, and the truth is not in us" (1 John 1:8). Paul reports that we were sinners (Romans 5:8), ungodly (5:6), and enemies (5:10). No, we were not already right.

The other futile instinct is the familiar works-righteousness trap of trying to make ourselves right. Perhaps Paul's image of "while we were still weak" (5:6) is a helpful reminder

in this respect. We do not have it within ourselves to do what needs to be done. We cannot save ourselves, and so we need a Savior.

God offers to do for us what we need but cannot do for ourselves. God makes us right—"justified by his blood" (5:9). It is a righteousness that flows from Christ's work rather than our own. And that righteousness flows to us when we believe God's promise and trust Christ's work. Thus, we are justified by faith.

The remaining question, then, is this: Why God would do all of this for us? What prompts the Lord to embrace an enemy? Why should I be justified at Christ's expense? The only possible answer is love, and Paul writes a majestic affirmation of God's love.

Notice that Paul asks what can separate us from God's love rather than what could make God stop loving us. This is a common fear among people, after all: that God doesn't or won't love them anymore. It's a fear born out of our experience of inconsistent human love. Yet for God to stop loving is not even a question raised by Paul, for such a conclusion does not logically follow what has already been said. Love is God's nature (1 John 4:8). It would make more sense to ask if the sun has stopped being hot than to ask if God has stopped loving.

No, the issue is not whether God stops loving, but whether anything can separate us from that love. And in response to that, the apostle pours forth a comprehensive litany, suggesting possible means by which we could become separated from God. He anticipates every direction and dimension, every factor and experience. And through it all he unblinkingly insists that nothing can separate us from the love of God that is available to us in Christ.

Sadly, many things can weaken and discourage human love. Tragically, many things can separate us from human love. But the love of God, which saves sinners, embraces enemies, and makes us right, is wonderfully invincible. Nothing can separate us from it.

---

# SHARING THE SCRIPTURE

## PREPARING TO LEAD

### Preparing Our Hearts

Ponder this week's devotional reading from Romans 1:1-15. What does Paul say about himself? What does he declare about Jesus? To whom is this letter addressed? For what reasons does Paul have to give thanks for this congregation, even though he has never visited it?

Pray that you and the students will receive and give thanks for God's grace in their lives.

### Preparing Our Minds

Study the background Scripture from Romans 5:1-11; 8:31-39 and the lesson Scripture from Romans 5:6-11; 8:31-39.

Consider this question: *How can you face the hardship, distress, and separations that abound in life?*

Write on newsprint:
❏ information for next week's lesson, found under Continue the Journey.
❏ activities for further spiritual growth in Continue the Journey.

Determine how you might use any of the features that precede the first lesson of this quarter in today's session.

Check the Pronunciation Guide at the beginning of this quarter for help with any Greek words you may encounter today.

## LEADING THE CLASS

### (1) Gather to Learn

❖ Welcome everyone and pray that those who have come today will experience God's reconciling love.

❖ Encourage participants to call out examples of hardships that they as individuals or as a community have experienced. Write these on newsprint. Answers could include the loss of a job; serious illness; flood or fire that destroyed their homes or businesses; war or civil unrest that caused injury, property damage, or tension among neighbors; economic hardship such as that caused by a recession. Leave the list posted for use with Goal 2.

❖ Read aloud today's focus statement: **Hardship, distress, and separations of all kinds abound in human life. How can we face these difficulties? Paul is convinced that nothing in all creation is able to separate us from the love of God in Jesus Christ.**

### (2) Goal 1: Explain the Meaning of Justification by Faith

❖ Read Romans 5:1, which refers to believers being "justified by faith."

❖ Ask: **What does it mean to say that we are "justified"?** Hear answers from the class and then add information by reading or retelling The Semantics of Making Things Right in Interpreting the Scripture.

❖ Enlist a volunteer to read about the results of justification from Romans 5:6-11 and then discuss these questions:

1. **What do the words "while we were still" (5:6) suggest to you about the timing of God's love?** (See Romans 5:6-8 in Understanding the Scripture.)

2. **Paul describes us as "ungodly" (5:6), "sinners" (5:8), and God's "enemies" (5:10)? What would you want to ask or say to Jesus in response to hearing that he died for us while we were estranged from God?** (See Romans 5:9-11 in Understanding the Scripture.)

❖ Choose a volunteer to read Romans 8:31-39.

❖ Read or retell the last four paragraphs of Making Us Right in Interpreting the Scripture to drive home the point that nothing can separate us from God's unconditional love.

❖ Encourage the adults to silently ponder these questions, which you will read aloud:

1. **What experiences with human love, which often has strings attached, have made it difficult to believe that God loves me unconditionally, in all circumstances?** (pause)

2. **How does Christ's sacrificial death on the cross when I was an unlovable sinner help to assure me that God will continue to love me unconditionally, no matter what?** (pause)

❖ Invite volunteers to comment on any insights they gleaned from this activity. Recognize that people may wish to keep their thoughts private, so do not press for responses.

*(3) Goal 2: Experience the Joy of God's Reconciling Love*

❖ Read or retell Making Things Right in Interpreting the Scripture.

❖ Point out that God's love empowers us to be "more than conquerors" (8:37). Read the definition of "conqueror" from the Greek as found in Understanding the Scripture, 8:37-39. Believers are able to overcome evil because of what Jesus has done for them. Ask:

1. **What words come to mind when you think of yourself as a "conqueror" in Christ?**

2. **Let's envision ourselves as spiritually victorious because of God's reconciling love. What might we do to celebrate that love?**

*(4) Goal 3: Live Out God's Reconciling Love in the World*

❖ Direct attention to the newsprint used in the Gather to Learn portion. Review those situations that are listed there. Go through each item on the list and ask the adults: **What might we be able to do to demonstrate God's reconciling love in this situation?**

❖ Form teams to further explore situations that the group believes they can address. Give each group a sheet of newsprint and marker. Tell them to develop a plan of action stating what they will do, for whom, when, how, and at what estimated cost. Make clear that they are not being asked to solve an entire problem, but rather, to find something they can do to demonstrate God's love. For example, if a family's home has been damaged by flood, perhaps class members could collect clothing and household goods. Maybe they could do some hands-on work by helping to remove furniture that cannot be salvaged if the building is safe to enter.

❖ Call on the teams to report their ideas. Challenge the teams to follow through on their ideas. Or, if one project seems to stand out, encourage the entire class to become involved.

### (5) Continue the Journey

❖ Pray that as the learners depart, they will experience God's reconciling love in their own lives and share that love with others.

❖ Post information for next week's session on newsprint for the students to copy:
- **Title: God's Preserving Love**
- **Background Scripture: John 10:1-15**
- **Lesson Scripture: John 10:1-15**
- **Focus of the Lesson: Everyone is looking for a leader who will solve all the problems of the world. Where can we find the leader we seek? Jesus, as the Good Shepherd, is the leader who shows and imparts God's love to those who follow.**

❖ Challenge the adults to grow spiritually by completing one or more of these activities related to this week's session.

(1) **Identify routine tasks that prompt you to think about justification. Each time you perform one of these tasks remember how through Jesus' sacrificial death you are justified—put right with—or reconciled to God. Typing a letter that is justified on the right margin would be one example. Reconciling your bank statement might be another. Use these opportunities to celebrate and give thanks for God's reconciling love for you.**

(2) **Practice saying this adaptation of today's key verses—"Nothing will be able to separate me from the love of God in Christ Jesus my Lord"—whenever you feel overwhelmed or threatened by a situation.**

(3) **Offer whatever support you can to someone who feels unloved and overcome by situations in life. Let this person know of God's love for him or her. Live out this reconciling love in ways that enable this person to see God's love through you.**

❖ Sing or read aloud "Close to Thee."

❖ Conclude today's session by leading the class in this benediction, which is adapted from John 15:12, the key verse for March 19: **Let us go forth obeying Jesus' commandment to love one another as he has loved us. Amen.**

UNIT 2: GOD'S CARING, SAVING, AND UPHOLDING LOVE

# GOD'S PRESERVING LOVE

---

## PREVIEWING THE LESSON

**Lesson Scripture:** John 10:1-15
**Background Scripture:** John 10:1-15
**Key Verses:** John 10:14-15

**Focus of the Lesson:**
Everyone is looking for a leader who will solve all the problems of the world. Where can we find the leader we seek? Jesus, as the Good Shepherd, is the leader who shows and imparts God's love to those who follow.

**Goals for the Learners:**
(1) to explore the metaphor of Jesus as the Good Shepherd who opens the gate for the sheep.
(2) to affirm the love of God expressed in the life and ministry of Jesus, the Good Shepherd.
(3) to respond to God's persevering love by loving others.

**Supplies:**
Bibles, newsprint and marker, paper and pencils, hymnals

---

## READING THE SCRIPTURE

NRSV
Lesson Scripture: John 10:1-15

¹"Very truly, I tell you, anyone who does not enter the sheepfold by the gate but climbs in by another way is a thief and a bandit. ²The one who enters by the gate is the shepherd of the sheep. ³The gatekeeper opens the gate for him, and the sheep hear his voice. He calls his own sheep by name and leads them out. ⁴When he

CEB
Lesson Scripture: John 10:1-15

¹I assure you that whoever doesn't enter into the sheep pen through the gate but climbs over the wall is a thief and an outlaw. ²The one who enters through the gate is the shepherd of the sheep. ³The guard at the gate opens the gate for him, and the sheep listen to his voice. He calls his own sheep by name and leads them out. ⁴Whenever

has brought out all his own, he goes ahead of them, and the sheep follow him because they know his voice. [5]They will not follow a stranger, but they will run from him because they do not know the voice of strangers." [6]Jesus used this figure of speech with them, but they did not understand what he was saying to them.

[7]So again Jesus said to them, "Very truly, I tell you, I am the gate for the sheep. [8]All who came before me are thieves and bandits; but the sheep did not listen to them. [9]I am the gate. Whoever enters by me will be saved, and will come in and go out and find pasture. [10]The thief comes only to steal and kill and destroy. I came that they may have life, and have it abundantly. [11]"I am the good shepherd. The good shepherd lays down his life for the sheep. [12]The hired hand, who is not the shepherd and does not own the sheep, sees the wolf coming and leaves the sheep and runs away—and the wolf snatches them and scatters them. [13]The hired hand runs away because a hired hand does not care for the sheep. [14]**I am the good shepherd. I know my own and my own know me,** [15]**just as the Father knows me and I know the Father. And I lay down my life for the sheep."**

he has gathered all of his sheep, he goes before them and they follow him, because they know his voice. [5]They won't follow a stranger but will run away because they don't know the stranger's voice." [6]Those who heard Jesus use this analogy didn't understand what he was saying.

[7]So Jesus spoke again, "I assure you that I am the gate of the sheep. [8]All who came before me were thieves and outlaws, but the sheep didn't listen to them. [9]I am the gate. Whoever enters through me will be saved. They will come in and go out and find pasture. [10]The thief enters only to steal, kill, and destroy. I came so that they could have life—indeed, so that they could live life to the fullest.

[11]"I am the good shepherd. The good shepherd lays down his life for the sheep. [12]When the hired hand sees the wolf coming, he leaves the sheep and runs away. That's because he isn't the shepherd; the sheep aren't really his. So the wolf attacks the sheep and scatters them. [13]He's only a hired hand and the sheep don't matter to him. [14]**"I am the good shepherd. I know my own sheep and they know me,** [15]**just as the Father knows me and I know the Father. I give up my life for the sheep."**

---

## UNDERSTANDING THE SCRIPTURE

**John 10:1.** The predominant image of this week's passage is of shepherds and sheep. Throughout the Old Testament, this metaphor was used to describe God's relationship to God's people. Here Jesus employs the same rich imagery to explain who he is and what he does.

While our prevailing association

with the shepherd-and-sheep image in Scripture is full of sweetness, the reality is that the world was full of hazards for the sheep. That is where Jesus begins, citing those who would sneak into the fold to steal the sheep. While no culprits are named here, it could probably be understood within its larger context, and the immediately preceding passage reported an episode of antagonism between the Pharisees and Jesus.

**John 10:2-3.** In contrast to the antagonists, Jesus describes the authentic shepherd for the sheep. He does not need to sneak into the fold, for he is known by both the gatekeeper and the flock. Further, there is a lovely intimacy suggested by the shepherd knowing and calling each sheep by name.

**John 10:4-5.** The contrast between the true shepherd and the antagonists is further developed. Here it is the sheep themselves that prove who is true and who is false, for they follow the familiar shepherd, but they run from the stranger. At this point, we may recall the poignant observation that animals sometimes know better than God's own people (Isaiah 1:3).

A key element of the relationship between the sheep and the shepherd is that "they know his voice," whereas "they do not know the voice of strangers." Surely the voice of its shepherd is what every sheep should know. And this becomes a beautiful ambition for our growing intimacy with the Lord: that amid the cacophony of voices calling out to us we would increasingly know, recognize, and respond exclusively to our Shepherd's voice.

**John 10:6.** Many times in the Gospels, Jesus' audience—including at times his own disciples—do not understand what he is saying to them. In this case, the metaphor may have been familiar, but the meaning was not immediately clear. And so, in the subsequent verses, Jesus explained the images more directly.

**John 10:7.** The role of the gate is made more explicit later. New Testament scholar and commentator

William Barclay suggests that Jesus' identification of himself as the gate is not separate from identifying himself as the shepherd in verse 11. Describing the nature of life out in the open, Barclay writes: "What happened was that at night the shepherd himself lay down across the opening [of the pen] and no sheep could get out or in except over his body. In the most literal sense the shepherd was the door."

**John 10:8.** Once again, the reality of thieves and bandits is affirmed, as is the litmus test of the sheep that refuse to listen to those whose voices they did not recognize.

**John 10:9.** Now we are offered greater insight into Jesus' role as gate. He is the one through whom we find salvation. And he is also the one who offers security and provision. Going in through the gate is the sheep's security. Going out through the gate is their access to pastureland. Meanwhile, Jesus' language here reminds us of his later statement that he is the way to the Father, and that no one comes to the Father except through him (John 14:6).

**John 10:10.** Once more, the authentic shepherd is juxtaposed with those who are enemies of the sheep. The highlighted difference is in their intent. What the thief intends is destructive and only in his own interest. What the shepherd intends is bountiful and in the best interest of the sheep.

Prior to verse 7, Jesus makes no direct reference to himself. Thieves, shepherds, gatekeepers, and sheep are all third person. In the second half of the passage, however, Jesus speaks in the first person as gate and shepherd. And here, in this specific verse, his first-person statement is especially profound, for he expresses the reason that he came.

This is an important theme in the Gospels. On a number of occasions, Jesus reveals a reason why he came (for example, Matthew 5:17; Mark 2:17; Luke 12:51; John 18:37). These statements are essential to our understanding of the person and work of Christ, for they reflect his own understanding of himself. And in many cases, as in this particular instance, the reason that he came becomes personal good news for us.

**John 10:11.** Here is a departure from the norm. We are accustomed to the imagery of sheep and shepherds in Scripture, and we cherish the truths embodied in the picture of the Lord as our shepherd. We are unaccustomed, however, to the prospect of the shepherd's death.

**John 10:12-13.** The good shepherd is seen in contrast to the hired hand who runs at the first sign of trouble. He is motivated entirely by self-interest, which is the opposite of self-sacrifice. His primary concern is not for the sheep, and so they are unprotected. His tragic example enables us to see the good shepherd more clearly.

We know who the good shepherd is in this passage. It is unclear, though, whom the hired hand and the wolf represent. As previously noted, the larger context features a controversy with the religious leaders of the land. Other critiques that Jesus levels against those leaders make them eligible to be either the hired hand or the wolf. They are both portrayed as negligent and predatory vis-à-vis the people in their care.

**John 10:14-15.** The concluding verses of this passage are rich with meaning. First, we observe again the quality of intimacy in the relationship between this shepherd and his sheep. Furthermore, we discover that the intimacy between Jesus and his sheep is an extension of the intimacy between Jesus and his Father. And, finally, we hear again the crucial statement of self-sacrifice. Jesus is no victim in his death: It is purposeful, and it is voluntary.

---

## INTERPRETING THE SCRIPTURE

### *A Familiar Picture*

If you grew up in the church, then you very likely grew up seeing a picture of the Lord as a shepherd. It is not the exact picture everywhere you go, of course. There are countless versions of it, which is itself a testament to how precious the image is to us. But in Sunday school classrooms, church hallways, Bible storybooks, church parlors, curriculum illustrations, and more, we have seen this kind of picture portrayed. It's appropriate that so many artists have undertaken to paint this picture, for visual images provide us with another way of connecting to the words we read in Scripture.

We have also heard the cherished image pictured in our music. From classical sacred music to contemporary praise and everything in between, we sing about the Lord as a shepherd. And it's appropriate, too, that we should sing the image, for before it was ever painted by an artist it was sung by the psalmist.

As we noted in our lesson on April 2, the Bible features many references to the Lord as a shepherd. Before it was a familiar picture for us as twenty-first-century Christians, it was a familiar image for the ancient Israelites and Jews. From the Psalms and the Prophets especially, the Old Testament people of God were well acquainted with the image of God as a shepherd for the people. Jesus was building on a well-established metaphor when he used this shepherd imagery, both here in John 10 and elsewhere (Matthew 18:12-14; Luke 15:3-7).

Of course, the picture that Jesus painted was familiar beyond just what the people read in the pages of Scripture. It was familiar from what they saw from their homes. It was familiar from what they saw as they traveled down the road or worked in the field.

For those of us who do not live on farms, the world of shepherds is as far removed from us as the worlds of knights or of pioneers in covered wagons. It's all from another time and another place. But for Jesus' original audience, the imagery of shepherds and sheep was neither sentimental nor foreign. They knew this stuff personally. And so this teaching of Jesus had the same close-to-home meaningfulness as parables about planting seeds, storing grain, adding yeast to dough, or attending a wedding.

From the fields and hillsides surrounding Jesus' audience to the preaching of the prophets, from the hymns of the church to the walls of our Sunday school classrooms, this is a familiar picture. It is the picture of the Lord as shepherd. We cherish it. And Jesus employs it to reveal truths about himself, about us, and about the world in which we live.

*An Unfamiliar Picture*

The biblical tradition of the shepherd metaphor had some standard elements. The good shepherd was a source of care, provision, and protection for the flock. The inadequate shepherd, by contrast, was negligent or exploitive. Also, there was a built-in recognition that the sheep were vulnerable, and that they were surrounded by a variety of hazards. The shepherd was essential, therefore, to the safety and survival of the flock.

In Jesus' teaching in John 10, however, he adds a new layer, unprecedented in the familiar, established tradition. Jesus says that the good shepherd "lays down his life for the sheep" (10:11). That's a different picture.

We recognize that the sheep are in jeopardy; that's obvious. Nothing about those cherished passages in the Psalms and the Prophets, however, suggested that the shepherd himself was in jeopardy. On the contrary, he is the one who is strong and in control. He is the one capable of providing safety for the sheep.

It's not until Jesus' teaching in John 10 that we are introduced to the prospect of the shepherd being in danger. Interestingly, Jesus refers to the one who is scared away by the arrival of a wolf as a "hired hand" (10:12). Jesus does not even honor those who run from danger with the title of "shepherd." The real shepherd of the sheep stays and faces the foe for the sake of his flock.

Let's return for a moment to the kinds of images that we probably grew up seeing in our Sunday school classrooms. First, we saw the portraits of Psalm 23. The shepherd there was strong, wise, and peaceful. And then, too, there were the portraits from the New Testament of the shepherd, who brings home the lost lamb. Again, we saw images of strength, love, and success. But none of those portrayals prompted us to imagine the shepherd bleeding and dying. That's a different picture.

Of course, that different picture is also a familiar one to us. It's the picture from Good Friday. It's the picture that features an arrest and trials, whips and mocking, nails and thorns. It's the picture of a cross.

In John 10, it's all the same picture. The Good Shepherd and Good Friday come together in this chapter. The shepherd lays down his life for the sheep.

### A Personal Picture

You and I have two different kinds of pictures in our homes. On the one hand, there are the kinds of pictures that we purchase. This is the art that hangs on our walls. It's very much a matter of personal taste, of course, but it is not usually the product of personal experience.

On the other hand, we also have those pictures that reflect our personal experience. They are photographs of ourselves, our families, and our friends. They are pictures of people we know, places we've been, and events we've attended. Each picture is a memory. It comes from some moment on our own personal time line.

Imagine, then, that we take all of the pictures in your home and divide them into those two categories. In one room, we put all of those pictures that are our chosen art, but do not come from our personal experience. In another room, we put all of the pictures that are the stuff of scrapbooks and photo albums: personal pictures.

Once the project has been completed—all of the pictures have been sorted and divided—someone brings into the house one final picture. It is the portrait of the Good Shepherd. In which room do you put it? Where does it belong?

The reason that our classrooms, hallways, parlors, storybooks, curricula, and music are filled with this picture is precisely because it is meant to be personal. It is the psalmist's personal testimony, after all. The writer does not merely say that the Lord is *a* shepherd, but rather, "The Lord is *my* shepherd." And that is inescapably the tone of Jesus' teaching in John 10, as well.

"I know my own and my own know me," Jesus says of his flock (10:14). He calls them by name, and they follow him because they know his voice. It is a beautifully intimate picture. It is a familiar picture because it is a picture of familiarity. One senses the mutual love and devotion that is shared between shepherd and sheep. And that love and devotion reach their climax when the shepherd lays down his life for their sake.

The picture of the Good Shepherd belongs with the personal pictures. It's a portrait of someone we know. It depicts a love and care we've experienced. And it recalls an event, Good Friday, which becomes part of our personal time line.

# SHARING THE SCRIPTURE

## PREPARING TO LEAD

### Preparing Our Hearts

Ponder this week's devotional reading from Matthew 18:1-5, 10-14. Although "greatness" usually refers to the power, status, or wealth that one has, Jesus defines this word another way. How do you understand Jesus' definition of greatness as embodied in a child? What do you think he means when he says "unless you change and become like children, you will never enter the kingdom of heaven" (18:3)? What do you learn about God's watchful care for the "little ones" by reading verses 10-14?

Pray that you and the students will embody the humility and vulnerability of children, who were powerless and had no access to economic resources.

### Preparing Our Minds

Study the background Scripture and the lesson Scripture, which are both from John 10:1-15.

Consider this question: *Where can you find a leader who will solve all of the world's problems?*

Write on newsprint:

❏ information for next week's lesson, found under Continue the Journey.

❏ activities for further spiritual growth in Continue the Journey.

Determine how you might use any of the features that precede the first lesson of this quarter in today's session.

Review the lesson for April 2, based on Psalm 23, which also uses the metaphor of the shepherd.

Select information from A Familiar Picture in Interpreting the Scripture that you will use to introduce today's lesson under Goal 1 in Sharing the Scripture.

## LEADING THE CLASS

### (1) Gather to Learn

❖ Welcome everyone and pray that those who have come today will seek out leaders who put their followers' best interests ahead of their own.

❖ Read: **As this lesson is being written, the political campaign bus has standing room only. Numerous candidates from the right and left compete for your vote and campaign contributions. Each one claims to know how to lead the United States in your best interest. By the time you read this lesson, the citizens will have made their choice and a new president will have been in office for about three months. That's hardly enough time to make a significant impact, but it may be enough time for you to decide whether you like the direction in which our new leader is headed. Depending on your perspective, you may or may not think this person can solve the problems that you see looming. Will you give this new leader a chance? Why or why not?**

❖ Read aloud today's focus statement: **Everyone is looking for a leader who will solve all the problems of the world. Where can we find the leader we seek? Jesus, as the Good Shepherd, is the leader who shows and imparts God's love to those who follow.**

*(2) Goal 1: Explore the Metaphor of Jesus as the Good Shepherd Who Opens the Gate for the Sheep*

❖ Introduce today's Scripture by using points from A Familiar Picture in Interpreting the Scripture to talk about how Jesus' audience would have been acquainted with sheep. Also consider how members of your class are acquainted with the image of the shepherd and the sheep.

❖ Select a volunteer to read John 10:1-15.

❖ Post a sheet of newsprint with a vertical line drawn down the center. On the left side, write "Jesus" and on the right side write "hired hand." Ask the students to identify traits for Jesus described in John 10 and write them under his name. Then ask the adults to describe the hired hand and write those traits under that name.

❖ Post another sheet of paper on which you have written "sheep" and ask the class to call out characteristics of the sheep.

❖ Review all of the traits that you have listed. Add information from Understanding the Scripture to create more complete pictures of Jesus, the hired hand, and the sheep and ask:

1. **Which of these traits surprises you? Why?**
2. **Even if you have no personal relationship with sheep, how does the metaphor of Jesus as the Good Shepherd help you to more fully experience Jesus' love for you?**

*(3) Goal 2: Affirm the Love of God Expressed in the Life and Ministry of Jesus, the Good Shepherd*

❖ Read: **Recall from John 10 that Jesus is not only the Good Shepherd** but also the gate to the sheep pen. The shepherd would lay across the opening so that anything coming in or out would have to pass over him. In his action we see a loving devotion to the care and protection of his flock.

❖ Lead the class in this guided imagery activity, which you will read aloud:

- **Envision yourself as a ewe or a ram bedding down for the night in your sheep pen. Think about how your shepherd takes care of you. Think about where and what you are guided to eat. Think about how the shepherd takes care of your wooly coat.** (pause)
- **Suddenly, you hear the howl of a nearby wolf, but have no means of self-defense. You are panic-stricken until you see that your shepherd Jesus is standing at the gate ready to protect you. How are you feeling now?** (pause)
- **Jesus has won! The wolf is running away. If you could talk, what would you say to Jesus?** (pause)
- **Open your eyes and talk with the person next to you about how you feel God's love expressed through Jesus the Good Shepherd.** (pause)

*(4) Goal 3: Respond to God's Persevering Love by Loving Others*

❖ Distribute paper and pencils and read these directions:

- **Draw a rectangle with an opening on one side. In that opening, which represents**

the gate of the sheep pen, you are to write your name.
- See yourself as a shepherd and write the names of people you consider as part of your "flock" within the rectangle.
- Select several of these "sheep" and write one act you will take this week to show God's love for them.

❖ Challenge participants to complete the actions they have noted on their papers.

*(5) Continue the Journey*

❖ Pray that as the learners depart, they will care for others in ways that show God's love.

❖ Post information for next week's session on newsprint for the students to copy:
- Title: God's Sustaining Love
- Background Scripture: Jonah 1
- Lesson Scripture: Jonah 1:7-17
- Focus of the Lesson: When calamity comes, people ask, "Why?" Can human behavior cause bad things to happen? In Jonah's case, human behavior did lead to calamity; however, Jonah discovered that God's love still surrounded him.

❖ Challenge the adults to grow spiritually by completing one or more of these activities related to this week's session.

(1) Try an experiment if you have a dog. Give your companion some simple instructions, such as sit, stay, or down. Now ask a friend to give the dog the same commands. Who does the dog listen to? Why do you suppose that the dog responds to your voice and not to the voice of someone else?

(2) Rewrite Jesus' message using an example that is more familiar to you than that of a shepherd.

(3) Identify by name the shepherds in your church—the pastor, teachers, and leaders—who care for you and the other members. Focus on one or two people. What traits do they share with Jesus? Which of these traits could you develop?

❖ Sing or read aloud "Savior, Like a Shepherd Lead Us."

❖ Conclude today's session by leading the class in this benediction, which is adapted from John 15:12, the key verse for March 19: **Let us go forth obeying Jesus' commandment to love one another as he has loved us. Amen.**

UNIT 3: GOD'S PERVASIVE AND SUSTAINING LOVE

# GOD'S SUSTAINING LOVE

---

## PREVIEWING THE LESSON

**Lesson Scripture:** Jonah 1:7-17
**Background Scripture:** Jonah 1
**Key Verse:** Jonah 1:10a

### Focus of the Lesson:
When calamity comes, people ask, "Why?" Can human behavior cause bad things to happen? In Jonah's case, human behavior did lead to calamity; however, Jonah discovered that God's love still surrounded him.

### Goals for the Learners:
(1) to explore the nature of God's love in the story of Jonah.
(2) to sense how people feel when faced with calamity and how they respond when others think they have caused the calamity.
(3) to pray for assurance of the presence of God's love in the midst of calamity.

### Supplies:
Bibles, newsprint and marker, paper and pencils, hymnals

---

## READING THE SCRIPTURE

**NRSV**
Lesson Scripture: Jonah 1:7-17

⁷The sailors said to one another, "Come, let us cast lots, so that we may know on whose account this calamity has come upon us." So they cast lots, and the lot fell on Jonah. ⁸Then they said to him, "Tell us why this calamity has come upon us. What is your occupation? Where do you come from? What is your country? And of what people are you?" ⁹"I am

**CEB**
Lesson Scripture: Jonah 1:7-17

⁷Meanwhile, the sailors said to each other, "Come on, let's cast lots so that we might learn who is to blame for this evil that's happening to us." They cast lots, and the lot fell on Jonah. ⁸So they said to him, "Tell us, since you're the cause of this evil happening to us: What do you do and where are you from? What's your country and of what people are you?"

a Hebrew," he replied. "I worship the LORD, the God of heaven, who made the sea and the dry land." **¹⁰Then the men were even more afraid, and said to him, "What is this that you have done!"** For the men knew that he was fleeing from the presence of the LORD, because he had told them so.

¹¹Then they said to him, "What shall we do to you, that the sea may quiet down for us?" For the sea was growing more and more tempestuous. ¹²He said to them, "Pick me up and throw me into the sea; then the sea will quiet down for you; for I know it is because of me that this great storm has come upon you." ¹³Nevertheless the men rowed hard to bring the ship back to land, but they could not, for the sea grew more and more stormy against them. ¹⁴Then they cried out to the LORD, "Please, O LORD, we pray, do not let us perish on account of this man's life. Do not make us guilty of innocent blood; for you, O LORD, have done as it pleased you." ¹⁵So they picked Jonah up and threw him into the sea; and the sea ceased from its raging. ¹⁶Then the men feared the LORD even more, and they offered a sacrifice to the LORD and made vows.

¹⁷But the LORD provided a large fish to swallow up Jonah; and Jonah was in the belly of the fish three days and three nights.

⁹He said to them, "I'm a Hebrew. I worship the LORD, the God of heaven—who made the sea and the dry land."

**¹⁰Then the men were terrified and said to him, "What have you done?"** (The men knew that Jonah was fleeing from the LORD, because he had told them.)

¹¹They said to him, "What will we do about you so that the sea will become calm around us?" (The sea was continuing to rage.)

¹²He said to them, "Pick me up and hurl me into the sea! Then the sea will become calm around you. I know it's my fault that this great storm has come upon you."

¹³The men rowed to reach dry land, but they couldn't manage it because the sea continued to rage against them. ¹⁴So they called on the LORD, saying, "Please, LORD, don't let us perish on account of this man's life, and don't blame us for innocent blood! You are the LORD: whatever you want, you can do." ¹⁵Then they picked up Jonah and hurled him into the sea, and the sea ceased its raging. ¹⁶The men worshipped the LORD with a profound reverence; they offered a sacrifice to the LORD and made solemn promises.

¹⁷Meanwhile, the LORD provided a great fish to swallow Jonah. Jonah was in the belly of the fish for three days and three nights.

---

## UNDERSTANDING THE SCRIPTURE

**Introduction.** Some Old Testament prophetic books, like Amos or Joel, comprise almost entirely message material, with very little biography. Others, like Isaiah and Jeremiah, feature a mixture of message and story. And Jonah is at the far end of the spectrum, focusing entirely on the prophet's story, with only a few words devoted to his message.

Many readers are inclined to write off the story of Jonah as fictitious. The series of events, including especially the role of the great fish, make it seem like a fable. Clearly he was a historical figure, however, since he was referenced in another context in one of ancient Israel's history books (2 Kings

14:25). And Jesus, too, seems to take Jonah's story as a matter of fact (for example, Matthew 12:38-41).

**Jonah 1:1-2.** "The word of the LORD came to" is a common phrase in the Old Testament prophets. It is an indicator of a "true" prophet, inasmuch as the message originates with God rather than with a human being. Sometimes the phrase introduces an instruction from God. More often, it is used to introduce the message itself. In this case, we have a little of both.

God's instruction is for Jonah to go to Nineveh. We discover shortly that he is unwilling to go there. Nineveh was the capital of the Assyrian Empire, and a Hebrew like Jonah might have felt fear, hatred, or contempt in response to the Assyrians.

God's message, meanwhile, is a crying out against the city of Nineveh and its great wickedness. While Jonah's succinct sermon (Jonah 3:4) was a promise of destruction, the very fact that God sent the prophet to cry out is a sign of divine mercy. If the Lord's real will was to destroy Nineveh, after all, no warning would have been necessary.

**Jonah 1:3.** The exact identity and location of Tarshish is unknown, but it is widely assumed to have been a destination in the western Mediterranean. Wherever Tarshish may have been, however, we do know that boarding a ship in Joppa is not the way to get to Nineveh. Joppa is on the Mediterranean coast of Israel; Nineveh was situated on the Tigris River in northern Mesopotamia, considerably northeast of Joppa. Instead of traveling by land to the east, Jonah boarded a ship heading west, presumably "away from the presence of the Lord." In contrast to Jonah, the psalmist knew that it was impossible to escape the presence of the Lord (Psalm 139:7-12).

**Jonah 1:4.** Although the prophet of God would not do the Lord's bidding, the forces of nature did. It is noteworthy that the Lord neither ignored Jonah's disobedience nor punished it. God was not indifferent, on the one hand, nor destructively angry, on the other. Rather, the Lord simply made Jonah's disobedience difficult, which is a beautiful thing. Meanwhile, as previously with respect to Nineveh, we assume that if the Lord really intended to destroy the ship, it would have been destroyed. The danger only serves to urge repentance and obedience.

**Jonah 1:5-6.** The stormy sea is an all-hands-on-deck moment, with the lone exception of Jonah. Everyone else on board is doing his part, while Jonah is conspicuously absent. The sailors seek both natural and supernatural rescue. The captain, meanwhile, insists that Jonah do his part as well.

The underlying paradigm was a world filled with many gods. There was no confidence about who was in charge of what. Accordingly, the logic was that every available god should be beseeched on behalf of the ship. The person who knows what works does what works. The person who doesn't know, however, will try everything. The captain and his crew were trying everything.

**Jonah 1:7-8.** Casting lots is represented in Scripture as a commonly accepted means of discernment. In this case, the sailors used the method to identify who was at fault for the storm. Jonah was found out, and so they interrogated him, desperate to find the reason for their trouble and, by extension, a solution for it.

**Jonah 1:9-12.** It's all very clear to Jonah, for he knows the whole truth.

He tells them who he is and who his God is. He acknowledges that he is the cause of the trouble, and he proposes the solution. The understanding is that God is targeting him, not the ship. As soon as Jonah is thrown overboard, therefore, the ship will be fine.

**Jonah 1:13-14.** Interestingly, the endangered men do not jump at the opportunity to escape from their troubles. They are not so interested in saving themselves that they will sacrifice this stranger, even with his permission. They willingly jettisoned cargo, but they would not throw overboard a fellow human being.

When it became clear that Jonah's proposal was the only solution, still the men performed the act reluctantly. And, as evidence of a certain conversion, they do not repent before their own gods for what they are about to do. Rather, they appeal to Jonah's God, acknowledging the Lord's sovereignty in the entire matter.

**Jonah 1:15-16.** The proposed solution works just as promised. When Jonah is jettisoned, the sea becomes calm and the ship is safe. And that culmination of events prompts those on board the ship to worship and make vows to the Lord.

Taken within the larger context of the whole story of Jonah, we observe that unbelievers are more responsive to the Lord than the prophet himself. Jonah was disobedient at the beginning and cranky at the end. The sailors with whom he had contact, however, came to faith and obedience. And, likewise as seen in chapter 3, the dreaded Ninevites were also quick to turn to the Lord in response to Jonah's message.

**Jonah 1:17.** Just as the wind, sea, and storm were at God's bidding, so, too, are the fish. All of creation is seen as under the Lord's authority and instruments of the divine will. Add to that the newfound faith and reverence of the previously pagan sailors, and we observe that it is Jonah, God's own prophet, who emerges from chapter 1 as the lone and ironic rebel against the will of God.

---

## INTERPRETING THE SCRIPTURE

### Lots of Causes

We've outgrown the answer, but not the question. The question is why?, and it seems that human beings have struggled with it forever. We moderns have tossed aside the ancients' practice of casting lots, but only because we don't think that's the way to find the answer; not because we have found it.

Why does this person enjoy good health all of their days, while that other poor soul suffers from one malady after another? Why does one have the Midas touch while the other can't catch a break? Why does he live to a ripe old age while she dies before her time? Diseases and accidents, natural disasters and unnatural disorders. So many troubles and surprises prompt us to wonder why.

The closer to home the trouble is, the more intense the question. When a disaster hits some island far away, the question is theoretical, and we manage to go about our business. When the calamity hits us or someone we love, however, then the need to know why is more urgent and the question more paralyzing.

We meet with two extremes in

trying to capture the role of God in the affairs of this world and of our lives. On the one end, there are those who believe that God causes everything. And, on the other end, those who believe God causes nothing.

That God causes nothing is the growing conviction of our modern and postmodern Western mind. Everything can be explained scientifically. The cause is found in astronomy or biology, plate tectonics or genetics. For this crowd, the explanation for the storm in Jonah 1 is meteorological, not theological.

At the other extreme are those folks who assume that God causes everything. I have known many folks in this camp, and I have heard them most often express their conviction at funerals. "The Lord took him," they'll say of the deceased, whether the cause of death was old age, cancer, or a drunk driver. The certainty that God causes whatever happens helps them to feel more at peace with events. It may prompt them to feel less at peace with God, however.

The sailors on Jonah's boat who cast their lots to find out why they were in peril didn't believe in chance. They believed that those ancient dice revealed real answers. And we, three thousand years later, don't want to believe in chance, either. We want to believe that there is some reason why things happen. But whether we look for the answer in lots, in science, or in the heavens, we all are asking why.

### The Human Why

The ancients were perhaps more inclined than our generation to attribute happenings to divine causation. Broadly speaking, the people of the ancient world believed in many gods, and those gods had their different spheres of influence. Yet the gods were not the only ones listed when it came time to roll the credits. The ancient peoples understood human responsibility and causation too.

"What is this that you have done?" the frightened sailors asked Jonah (1:10). They didn't doubt that the storm came from a god, but they reckoned that that god had a reason for sending the storm. And the lots had traced that reason back to Jonah.

This, too, is an ingredient of uncertain proportion in life's events. What role do we play in the troubles we experience? What is our level of culpability? How much of a cause are we in the effect?

We are at peace when there seems to be a correlation between human actions and consequences. When the good person fares well, that's as it should be. When the foolish or wicked person meets with disaster that at least seems just. But the flourishing wicked have always been a source of consternation, as have the suffering righteous.

The story of Jonah presents us with some interesting insights into this matter of the human role in calamities. Specifically, we are introduced to three different case studies. First, there is Jonah. Second, there are his traveling companions en route to Tarshish. And, third, there are the Ninevites.

Jonah's circumstance is the most straightforward. He disobeys God, and thus brings trouble on himself. We do not feel particularly sorry for Jonah, and our sense of justice is not offended by his plotline.

The sailors, on the other hand, are a different case. They face calamity, but they themselves are innocent. The Bible does not try to airbrush away this reality of life in this world. We know full well how the deeds of some can cause the suffering of others. Human wickedness or folly almost always has a victim, and too often it is an innocent victim.

Then we come to the case of the Ninevites. They are arguably the opposite of the sailors, and theirs is the situation most noxious to Jonah. They are a guilty people, notorious for the wickedness from the first verse of the story. And yet, as we shall see in the end, they are forgiven. They go unpunished, and it galls Jonah that they don't get what they have coming to them.

### The Best Reason Why

The story of Jonah is unapologetic about the role of God. The narrator does not flinch from attributing storms and fish, wind and waves, plants and worms to the work of the Lord. And the human players have no doubt about the divine involvement in their affairs.

Now the modern mind might balk at such assertions. Some mock the story of Jonah and its characters as primitively superstitious and woefully naive. Yet the objection is almost certainly rooted in a doubt about God's existence rather than a doubt about divine activity or a concern for the laws of nature. I break no laws of nature, after all, when I pick up a stone and throw it. Surely God has the prerogative and capacity, therefore, to hurl a great wind. And I do not interfere unreasonably with the natural order when I instruct my dog to come or to fetch. Why should it be unreasonable, therefore, for a fish to do God's bidding?

Of course, the affirmation that God causes some things does not automatically mean that God causes everything. The one need not follow from the other. We human beings ourselves prove every day our capacity to cause things that are contrary to God's will. Perhaps, therefore, we shouldn't struggle to find the divine purpose in every tragedy.

What we have in the story of Jonah is not merely a glimpse into the activity of God but into the heart of God. The Lord sends Jonah to Nineveh to warn the city, which, as we already noted, is an act of mercy. The Lord causes a storm to chasten Jonah. This, too, is a kindness, for either ignoring or destroying the disobedient prophet would have been unloving. The Lord spares the sailors, who turn into believers and worshipers. The Lord gives Jonah a second chance to obey. And the Lord pardons the penitent Ninevites (3:10).

In short, God is a very active cause of many effects in the story of Jonah. And as we discern the heart behind that divine activity, we discover the best answer to the most important "why." It is not necessarily an answer to why every single thing happens. But it is an answer to why God does everything that God does. Because of love.

---

## SHARING THE SCRIPTURE

### PREPARING TO LEAD

#### Preparing Our Hearts

Ponder this week's devotional reading from Psalm 139:1-12. As you read in verse 1 that God has "searched" and "known" you, do you find that assertion comforting or discomforting? Why? Have you ever had reasons to want to flee from God's presence?

What happened when you tried to do that?

Pray that you and the students will give thanks for divine love, which manifests itself in the closeness of God at all times.

### Preparing Our Minds

Study the background Scripture from Jonah 1 and the lesson Scripture from Jonah 1:7-17.

Consider this question: *How does God respond when human behavior causes calamity?*

Write on newsprint:

❏ information for next week's lesson, found under Continue the Journey.

❏ activities for further spiritual growth in Continue the Journey.

Consider using Close-up: Jonah—The Reluctant Prophet in this session or one of the three that follows.

### LEADING THE CLASS

#### (1) Gather to Learn

❖ Welcome everyone and pray that those who have come today will recognize that God sustains them even in the midst of a disaster.

❖ Read: **On April 26, 1986, in Pripyat, Ukraine, during a test at the Chernobyl nuclear power plant, a reactor core detonated, spewing radioactive materials in the air. Two people died that night and twenty-eight more died within several weeks due to acute radiation poisoning. Approximately 115,000 to 135,000 people lived within a 30 kilometer (about 19 mile) radius of the plant before the accident forced relocation. Although the power plant is now encased in concrete, the surrounding area is off limits, except to researchers and maintenance workers. This horrific accident was "the result of a flawed reactor design that was operated with inadequately trained personnel," according to the World Nuclear Association. Reportedly, an automatic shutdown mechanism had been disabled by an employee.**

❖ Read aloud today's focus statement: **When calamity comes, people ask, "Why?" Can human behavior cause bad things to happen? In Jonah's case, human behavior did lead to calamity; however, Jonah discovered that God's love still surrounded him.**

#### (2) Goal 1: Explore the Nature of God's Love in the Story of Jonah

❖ Select a volunteer to read Jonah 1:1-17.

❖ Form three groups and give each one a sheet of newsprint and a marker. Each group is to fold its paper into four sections and label them: *Attitudes, Expectations, Actions, Responses.* One group will look at the sailors, a second group at Jonah, and a third at God. Each group is to discern how each of these characters perceives what is happening. God, for example, *acted* by commissioning Jonah to prophesy the destruction of Nineveh. When the lot pointed to Jonah as the guilty party, he *responded* by saying that the sailors should throw him into the sea. Plagued by an *attitude* of fear, the sailors *expected* divine retribution if they were to toss Jonah overboard. (If you have additional copies of *The New International Lesson Annual*, distribute them among the groups so that they can check the Understanding the Scripture portion for ideas.)

❖ Call the groups together to report their findings. Ask: **Even though the situation is dire for Jonah, for the sailors, and for the Ninevites, where do you see God's love in this story?**

❖ Conclude by reading the final two paragraphs of The Best Reason Why from Interpreting the Scripture.

*(3) Goal 2: Sense How People Feel When Faced with Calamity and How They Respond When Others Think They Have Caused the Calamity*

❖ Read Lots of Causes in Interpreting the Scripture. Encourage the students to talk about the role that they feel God plays in catastrophes. Do they believe that God causes everything—or nothing—or some things but not others? Ask them to explain their answers.

❖ Recall the information from Gather to Learn concerning the Chernobyl disaster and ask:

1. **Had you been the employee who caused this catastrophe, what would you have wanted to say to the families of those who died and the thousands who had to be relocated?**

2. **Had you been one of the people whose life was turned upside down by this tragedy, what would you want to say to the person whose actions caused the disaster?**

❖ Turn attention to the story of Jonah and the sailors in the storm. Ask:

1. **Had you been Jonah, what would you have said to the sailors after they agreed to throw you overboard?**

2. **Had you been the sailors, what would you have**

**wanted to do when you realized that Jonah was the one whose behavior had brought this terrible storm?**

*(4) Goal 3: Pray for Assurance of the Presence of God's Love in the Midst of Calamity*

❖ Post a sheet of newsprint and invite participants to call out calamities that recently have been in the news. These may be natural disasters, but especially encourage mention of catastrophes that were caused by human error or sin. Think of such things as refugees having to leave their homes due to war, a town terrorized by gunmen on the loose, the collapse of a business and loss of jobs because of unscrupulous owners, a terrorist attack.

❖ Write this prayer response on the newsprint as well: **Lord, let your love shine brightly in the midst of those who are hurting.**

❖ Form a circle. Starting with you and moving clockwise, invite each person to offer prayer for those who are in the midst of one of the situations that has been identified. Encourage everyone to pray aloud by limiting the prayers to one or two sentences. After each sentence prayer is spoken, lead the class in reading in unison the prayer response.

*(5) Continue the Journey*

❖ Conclude the prayer time by praying that as the learners depart, they will cherish the love of God that sustains them even in the direst of circumstances.

❖ Post information for next week's session on newsprint for the students to copy:

- Title: God's Love Preserved Jonah
- Background Scripture: Jonah 2
- Lesson Scripture: Jonah 2
- Focus of the Lesson: People experience being rescued from dire circumstances and are thankful. Whom do we thank in these circumstances? Jonah acknowledges with thanksgiving that it is God's love that protects and offers deliverance.

❖ Challenge the adults to grow spiritually by completing one or more of these activities related to this week's session.

(1) **Research the Assyrian Empire. What do you learn about this dominant power of the Near East that might help you to understand Jonah's negative response to God's commissioning of him to prophesy in the capital city of Nineveh?**

(2) **Reread Jonah 1:3, 10. When have you wanted to flee from God's presence? What did you do? How did things work out for you? What did you learn about God?**

(3) **Ponder the reactions of the sailors. What do their actions suggest about their spirituality, even though they were not Jews? Did their response to the drawing of lots that indicated Jonah's guilt surprise you? Why or why not? How might you have reacted?**

❖ Sing or read aloud "Great Is Thy Faithfulness."

❖ Conclude today's session by leading the class in this benediction, which is adapted from John 15:12, the key verse for March 19: **Let us go forth obeying Jesus' commandment to love one another as he has loved us. Amen.**

UNIT 3: GOD'S PERVASIVE AND SUSTAINING LOVE
# God's Love
# Preserved Jonah

---

## PREVIEWING THE LESSON

**Lesson Scripture:** Jonah 2
**Background Scripture:** Jonah 2
**Key Verse:** Jonah 2:9

### Focus of the Lesson:
People experience being rescued from dire circumstances and are thankful. Whom do we thank in these circumstances? Jonah acknowledges with thanksgiving that it is God's love that protects and offers deliverance.

### Goals for the Learners:
(1) to discover with Jonah that God's love protects and preserves when people make decisions to do God's will.
(2) to feel grateful for times God rescued or protected them.
(3) to explore how God's love is expressed when they accept the mission God gives them.

### Supplies:
Bibles, newsprint and marker, paper and pencils, hymnals

---

## READING THE SCRIPTURE

NRSV
Lesson Scripture: Jonah 2
  ¹Then Jonah prayed to the LORD his God from the belly of the fish, ²saying,
    "I called to the LORD out of my distress,
    and he answered me;
  out of the belly of Sheol I cried,
    and you heard my voice.
  ³You cast me into the deep,

CEB
Lesson Scripture: Jonah 2
  ¹Jonah prayed to the LORD his God from the belly of the fish:
  ²"I called out to the LORD in my distress, and he answered me.
    From the belly of the underworld I cried out for help;
    you have heard my voice.
  ³You had cast me into the depths in the heart of the seas,

into the heart of the seas,
and the flood surrounded me;
all your waves and your billows
passed over me.
⁴Then I said, 'I am driven away
from your sight;
how shall I look again
upon your holy temple?'
⁵The waters closed in over me;
the deep surrounded me;
weeds were wrapped around my
head
⁶at the roots of the mountains.
I went down to the land
whose bars closed upon me
forever;
yet you brought up my life from
the Pit,
O LORD my God.
⁷As my life was ebbing away,
I remembered the LORD;
and my prayer came to you,
into your holy temple.
⁸Those who worship vain idols
forsake their true loyalty.
⁹But I with the voice of thanksgiving
will sacrifice to you;
what I have vowed I will pay.
Deliverance belongs to the LORD!"
¹⁰Then the LORD spoke to the fish, and
it spewed Jonah out upon the dry
land.

and the flood surrounds me.
All your strong waves and
rushing water passed over me.
⁴So I said, 'I have been driven away
from your sight.
Will I ever again look on your
holy temple?
⁵Waters have grasped me to the
point of death;
the deep surrounds me.
Seaweed is wrapped around my
head
⁶at the base of the undersea
mountains.
I have sunk down to the underworld;
its bars held me with no end in
sight.
But you brought me out of the
pit.'
⁷When my endurance was
weakening,
I remembered the LORD,
and my prayer came to you,
to your holy temple.
⁸Those deceived by worthless things
lose their chance for mercy.
⁹But me, I will offer a sacrifice to
you with a voice of thanks.
That which I have promised,
I will pay.
Deliverance belongs to
the LORD!"
¹⁰Then the LORD spoke to the fish, and
it vomited Jonah onto the dry land.

## UNDERSTANDING THE SCRIPTURE

**Jonah 2:1.** Like a serial television show, perhaps we should begin with a few scenes from last week's program, for we left off in the middle of a story. Last week, we saw Jonah resist a call from God to go and preach in Nineveh. He traveled in the opposite direction instead, but the Lord sent a frightening storm to trouble the ship that the recalcitrant prophet had chosen for his getaway vehicle. Jonah recognized the hand of God in it all, and so he advised his fellow travelers to throw him into the sea, which did prove to quell the storm. Meanwhile, the Lord sent a great fish to swallow

Jonah. This would be the prophet's transport back to where he belonged.

The trip back to where Jonah belonged was not merely geographical. Indeed, it was not even primarily geographical. It was spiritual. Even if Jonah had never left his house, the reality was that he had walked away from God. He needed to come back.

The old adage notes that there are no atheists in foxholes. Similarly, perhaps there are no atheists in fish bellies, either. Peril inspires prayer.

**Jonah 2:2.** Jonah's prayer is written in poetic form, and the chief hallmark of Hebrew poetry is parallelism. That stylistic convention takes several forms, but it always involves the repetition of an idea. We see that technique here in the phrases of verse 2. "I called" is paralleled by "I cried." "Out of my distress" is matched by "out of the belly of Sheol." And "he answered me" is balanced by "you heard my voice."

"Out of my distress," of course, is so often the place from which we call out to the Lord. Then, in an interesting turn of phrase, Jonah characterizes that distress as "the belly of Sheol." Belly, indeed. Sheol, meanwhile, was the Hebrew term for the place of the dead. While some translations render it "hell," it was not generally understood as a place of punishment so much as a place of nothingness. "Sheol" is also sometimes translated grave, which is probably where Jonah reckoned himself to be.

**Jonah 2:3.** Jonah acknowledges that his situation is the chastening work of God. While the psalmist sometimes uses the imagery of storms and waters figuratively to represent his troubles (for example, Psalm 18:16; 69:1-2), the images are quite literal for Jonah. The prophet's language may sound accusatory, but at some level it is a very positive affirmation. Just as King David wanted only a calamity that put him in the hands of the Lord (2 Samuel 24:14), Jonah was in the good place of knowing that God was in charge of his fate.

**Jonah 2:4.** I wonder how often we have assumed the passive voice like Jonah. "I am driven away," he prayed, yet we know that was not the reality of his state at all. He was no more driven away from God's presence than the prodigal son was driven away from his father's house.

The longing for God's Temple is a common expression in the Old Testament. It was the place especially associated with the presence of the Lord. In Jonah's case, therefore, the matters are synonymous in his heart. He feels that he is at a distance from God, and he cannot imagine ever getting back to the Temple again from where he is.

**Jonah 2:5-6.** Read in the setting of the belly, these verses clearly understand the fish as an agent of God's deliverance. We hear the descriptive, picturesque language, and we can see Jonah sinking deep into the waters of the Mediterranean. He reckons that he is a goner. But then the Lord spared Jonah, delivering his life from the Pit. Inasmuch as this testimony does not come from dry land, then, we see that the fish was God's means of salvation.

**Jonah 2:7.** "Remembered" is a richly meaningful term in Scripture. It is not merely the opposite of forgetting. Rather, it assumes the actions that naturally follow from what is being remembered. Hence it is sufficient for the Lord to command Israel to "remember the Sabbath day" (Exodus 20:8). That is not merely making a mental note of the Sabbath, but living out a conscious recognition and practice of the Sabbath.

For Jonah to remember the Lord, therefore, is for Jonah to turn back to God. He prayed to the Lord. And while the prophet had earlier despaired of seeing the "holy temple" again, still he affirms that his prayer reached God there.

**Jonah 2:8.** The Hebrew in this verse is unclear. The NRSV renders it: "Those who worship vain idols forsake their true loyalty." The CEB, meanwhile, offers: "Those deceived by worthless things lose their chance for mercy." And the KJV reads: "They that observe lying vanities forsake their own mercy."

We do not know, therefore, precisely what Jonah was saying. We do understand, however, the spirit of what he meant. Ever since Eden, humankind has been faced with a choice. That choice is a theme that runs all through Scripture (Deuteronomy 30:19; Proverbs 4:14-19; Matthew 7:13-14; Romans 8:5-6). And one element of that choice has always been deceptive, empty, and ultimately very costly.

**Jonah 2:9.** It is part of the human reflex to complement repentance with promises. When we say we're sorry to one another for something past, we almost always add a promise that we'll do better in the future. I don't think that is a prerequisite for God's forgiveness. While it is not necessary for the Lord, however, it is necessary for us. It is right and good that contrition should be accompanied by new resolve. And so Jonah looks hopefully forward, and he promises to God his thanksgiving, his sacrifices, and his obedience.

**Jonah 2:10.** God's mission and the fish's purpose are accomplished. Jonah is back where he belongs. He is compliant with the will and call of God, and he is back on land. Next stop: Nineveh.

---

## INTERPRETING THE SCRIPTURE

### A Place to Pray

The billboard was an advertisement for a maker of hot dogs and brats, which were pictured on a grill. The printed message was simple: "Another perfect day for cooking out." But the real genius of the advertisement was that the billboard also sported a thermometer. The passerby was being educated, you see, that it is a perfect day for cooking out these hot dogs and brats no matter what the weather.

I believe that prayer is the spiritual version of that principle. Whatever the temperature, whatever the circumstance, it is the perfect time and place for prayer. And Jonah discovered and bore witness to that truth.

In the midst of the fish's belly, the prophet despaired that he might never again see the Lord's holy Temple. Surely the Temple is the appropriate and the inspiring place for prayer. Its architecture, its elements, and its symbols all point to God. The worshiper senses the very presence of the Lord, just beyond the altar, hallowed behind the curtain.

But Jonah was very far from the Temple. He was not surrounded by the ornately adorned priests, the grand architecture, and the sights and sounds of worship. Quite the contrary, Jonah was surrounded by the sights and sounds of digestion. His setting was dark and unbearably smelly. What sort of a place for prayer is that?

It was a perfect place for prayer.

Trouble is a perfect place for prayer. So is need. So is desperation. Indeed, I have often felt that I am at my best when I am desperate, for it is at those times that I abandon all self-reliance and lean entirely upon the Lord.

George Matheson knew the truth of that. "I sink in life's alarms," he sang, "when by myself I stand." Jonah had tried to go it alone, to be by himself without the Lord. When he began to sink, however, he reached out to God once again.

The belly of the fish was, in many respects, a long way from the Temple in Jerusalem. And that unpleasant place, like the prodigal's pigsty (Luke 15:15-19), became a catalyst for a change of heart. It was, therefore, a perfect place of prayer.

The belly of the fish was a long way from the Temple in Jerusalem. But God was not far away. So Jonah turned to the Lord there in that unlikely, yet perfect, place of prayer.

### Deliver Us from Evil

We are constantly praying for deliverance.

As previously noted, peril inspires prayer. And so when we face trouble, when we feel threatened, when we are worried or overwrought, we naturally turn to prayer. In some instances, that praying is not even the product of a very deep personal faith. Rather, it is simply the impulse of logic, when circumstances are too big to handle, to turn to someone who is big enough to handle them.

But we are also constantly praying for deliverance beyond those times when we are feeling endangered. For many of us, praying The Lord's Prayer is a standard part of our worship services, and perhaps even our private prayer lives. And built right into the framework of that model prayer is this familiar petition: "Deliver us from evil."

There is something quite right, of course, about praying for deliverance even when we don't see or sense any trouble. Our senses are not infallible, after all, and our very perception of evil is clouded. There is, therefore, more evil from which we need to be delivered than we likely know. And the story of Jonah illustrates very effectively for us how God endeavors to deliver us from all kinds of evil.

Jonah's prayer for deliverance came in the belly of the great fish. That unpleasant and frightening place was the "evil" from which he longed to be saved. But that is a bit like calling 911 from the back of the ambulance. For the fish was already part of God's project to save Jonah.

Turn the lens on the camera to see the bigger picture. Back away from the narrow focus on the episode in the fish's belly and see how God worked to deliver from evil. The very first words of the story, after all, reflect God's heart in this matter.

The first order of divine business, you see, was to deliver the people of Nineveh from their evil. To that end, God sent Jonah to preach to them. But next thing we know, Jonah himself needs to be delivered from evil. And that evil is not the fish, but his disobedience and attempted distance from God.

The storm is a part of God trying to save Jonah. The fish is part of God trying to save Jonah. And Jonah is meant to be an instrumental part of God trying to save Nineveh.

Jesus taught the disciples to pray, among other things, that the Lord would deliver us from evil. The instructional prayer reflects an ongoing need. And it also reflects the heart of God, for delivering us from evil is what the Lord is doing more than we know.

### Can I Get a Witness?

I recently preached a sermon that began with an illustration from my own experience. I told a story from twenty-five years ago about an old car I was driving that gave me trouble. And after that Sunday morning's services, a great number of folks in my congregation regaled me with stories of car troubles that they had had along the way. Everybody has a car story.

At some level, I expect that everyone has a fish-belly story too. The details are not going to be the same as Jonah's, of course, but his experience serves as a metaphor for us. You and I could go around the room and share our individual versions of it. We know about living through a terrible time. We know about being in a frightening place. We know about calling out to the Lord for help. And we have stories about God's deliverance.

The interesting thing I noted about the car stories was that they were all told with smiles. Even though they were filled with details of inconvenience, expense, and even danger, still they were told with smiles and laughter. Why? Because the people had come out of the other side of those troubles, and the passage of time had turned broken cars into funny stories.

For us, meanwhile, the final product is something even better than a funny story. We, too, can look back and tell about certain, serious troubles in our experience—our versions of Jonah's terrible fish belly. And perhaps we may also smile as we recall them. But those experiences are of a higher order than just a funny story. The deliverance of God turns our troubles into testimonies.

Toward the end of his prayer, Jonah speaks "with the voice of thanksgiving" (2:9). Thanksgiving is always the tone of testimony, you see. It may be accompanied by smiles or by tears, but it always points to loving intervention of God. And in the end, Jonah makes a declaration that can be echoed by multitudes. Jonah, his fellow sailors, the people of Nineveh, you, and I—we may all join together in affirming, "Deliverance belongs to the Lord!" (2:9).

---

## SHARING THE SCRIPTURE

### PREPARING TO LEAD

#### Preparing Our Hearts

Ponder this week's devotional reading from Psalm 116:1-14. What does the psalmist say about God, who saved him from a near-fatal illness? He asks the question: "What shall I return to the Lord for all his bounty to me?" (116:12). As you think about times when God has rescued you, what have you returned unto God?

Pray that you and the students will

recognize that even in the depths of a life-threatening situation God is there for you.

### Preparing Our Minds

Study the background Scripture and the lesson Scripture, which are both from Jonah 2.

Consider this question: *Whom do you thank when you are rescued from difficult circumstances?*

Write on newsprint:

❏ words for "Love Lifted Me" under Goal 2 in Sharing the Scripture.

❏ information for next week's lesson, found under Continue the Journey.

❏ activities for further spiritual growth in Continue the Journey.

Determine how you might use any of the features that precede the first lesson of this quarter in today's session.

## LEADING THE CLASS

### (1) Gather to Learn

❖ Welcome everyone and pray that those who have come today will recall with gratitude times when God has rescued them from physical, emotional, or spiritual danger.

❖ Read: **On April 12, 1912, the purportedly unsinkable *Titanic* suffered a catastrophic failure after colliding with an iceberg. People were helped to the lifeboats, but 1,517 lives were lost as the ship broke in two and quickly sank. Second-class passenger Lillian Bentham, who was in one of those lifeboats, helped to pull twenty men from atop a collapsible lifeboat that had overturned. She wrapped her fur coat around freezing crewman Cecil Fitzpatrick. To show his gratitude to the woman who had saved his life, Cecil gave her the whistle he had used in an effort to call another boat to assist them. Captain Arthur Henry Rostron of the *Carpathia*, the only ship to respond to the *Titanic*'s distress calls, was presented with a trophy from the survivors and the Medal of Honor from President Taft as a token of gratitude for his rescue of hundreds of survivors.**

❖ Read aloud today's focus statement: **People experience being rescued from dire circumstances and are thankful. Whom do we thank in these circumstances? Jonah acknowledges with thanksgiving that it is God's love that protects and offers deliverance.**

### (2) Goal 1: Discover with Jonah that God's Love Protects and Preserves When People Make Decisions to Do God's Will

❖ Read Jonah 2:1 in Understanding the Scripture to set the stage for today's scene by recalling the events of last week.

❖ Recruit a volunteer to read Jonah 2. Note that the entire chapter comprises Jonah's prayer of thanksgiving. Although this prayer is unique to Jonah, most of its lines can be found within the psalms.

❖ Discuss these questions:

1. **Being swallowed by a large fish would seem to signify that God is punishing Jonah. But that's not the case. What is the real purpose of the fish?** (See Jonah 2:5-6 in Understanding the Scripture).

2. **Jonah does more than simply *recall* when he says,**

"I remembered the LORD" (2:7). What is he really saying? (See Jonah 2:7 in Understanding the Scripture.)

3. What does Jonah's prayer of thanksgiving, rather than a lament or cry for deliverance as we might expect to hear in this situation, say about what Jonah believes? (He is praying as if he believes that God has already delivered him.)

4. Given that Jonah has prayed believing that God has already rescued him, and Jonah has promised to uphold his vows to God, what would you expect to happen next? (See Jonah 2:10 in Understanding the Scripture. Also suggest that as the class reads the Scripture for next week's lesson they pay attention to Jonah's attitude as he answers God's second call and goes to Nineveh.)

*(3) Goal 2: Feel Grateful for Times When God Rescued or Protected the Learners*

❖ Read or retell Deliver Us from Evil in Interpreting the Scripture.

❖ Invite the adults to talk with a small group about their gratitude for God's rescue of them in a difficult situation.

❖ Conclude this portion of the lesson by leading the class in a unison reading of James Rowe's 1912 hymn, "Love Lifted Me." Post the words on newsprint. Note the depth of gratitude for God's protection and rescue from deep waters expressed here.

I was sinking deep in sin, far from the peaceful shore,

Very deeply stained within, sinking to rise no more,
But the Master of the sea heard my despairing cry,
From the waters lifted me, now safe am I.

*Refrain:*
Love lifted me!
Love lifted me!
When nothing else could help,
Love lifted me!

All my heart to Him I give, ever to Him I'll cling,
In His blessed presence live, ever His praises sing,
Love so mighty and so true, merits my soul's best songs,
Faithful, loving service, too, to Him belongs.

*Refrain*

*(4) Goal 3: Explore How God's Love Is Expressed When the Learners Accept the Mission God Gives Them*

❖ Invite the students to trace Jonah's change of heart in chapter 2. Notice that once inside the fish, he begins to pray, crying out to God in his distress. As the waters and weeds wash over him, he realizes that he is near death. Still inside the fish, he says that he will sacrifice with thanksgiving and declares that "deliverance belongs to the LORD" (2:9).

❖ Read or retell A Place to Pray in Interpreting the Scripture. Ask:

1. Why do we often find it so hard to seek God and accept God's mission for us until we are pushed to the edge?

2. Where do you see God's love in today's portion of Jonah's story?

3. **God never abandoned Jonah, as evidenced by the sending of a great fish to rescue him. What experiences have you had that assure you that God loves you and will never abandon you?**

❖ Challenge participants to be mindful of how they experience God's love when they answer the call to undertake God's mission for them.

*(5) Continue the Journey*

❖ Pray that as the learners depart, they will be as ready to thank God for loving protection as they are to ask for and receive it.

❖ Post information for next week's session on newsprint for the students to copy:

- **Title: God's Love for Nineveh**
- **Background Scripture: Jonah 3; Nahum 1–3**
- **Lesson Scripture: Jonah 3**
- **Focus of the Lesson: Communities today are wracked with separation and violence. What can bring people together to live in wholeness and peace? When the people of Nineveh repented, God brought peace and wholeness through divine love.**

❖ Challenge the adults to grow spiritually by completing one or more of these activities related to this week's session.

(1) **Write your own prayer to thank God for rescue or protection during a time of difficulty.**

(2) **Meet with someone who is in the throes of a difficult situation. Listen to his or her concerns. Where natural in the conversation mention how God has worked in a difficult situation in your own life.**

(3) **Talk with a child about Jonah and how God showed love and grace to him even when Jonah was trying to run away. Search the Internet for pictures to color and activities, such as crossword puzzles, that the child might do independently to reinforce your discussion.**

❖ Sing or read aloud "Praise, My Soul, the King of Heaven."

❖ Conclude today's session by leading the class in this benediction, which is adapted from John 15:12, the key verse for March 19: **Let us go forth obeying Jesus' commandment to love one another as he has loved us. Amen.**

## UNIT 3: GOD'S PERVASIVE AND SUSTAINING LOVE
# GOD'S LOVE FOR NINEVEH

---

## PREVIEWING THE LESSON

**Lesson Scripture:** Jonah 3
**Background Scripture:** Jonah 3; Nahum 1–3
**Key Verse:** Jonah 3:10

### Focus of the Lesson:
Communities today are wracked with separation and violence. What can bring people together to live in wholeness and peace? When the people of Nineveh repented, God brought peace and wholeness through divine love.

### Goals for the Learners:
(1) to explore how repentance is related to God's love.
(2) to sense the joy that comes when forgiven a wrong.
(3) to share examples of times when wholeness and peace are the result of God's intervening love.

### Supplies:
Bibles, newsprint and marker, paper and pencils, hymnals

---

## READING THE SCRIPTURE

**NRSV**

Lesson Scripture: Jonah 3

¹The word of the LORD came to Jonah a second time, saying, ²"Get up, go to Nineveh, that great city, and proclaim to it the message that I tell you." ³So Jonah set out and went to Nineveh, according to the word of the Lord. Now Nineveh was an exceedingly large city, a three days' walk across. ⁴Jonah began to go into

**CEB**

Lesson Scripture: Jonah 3

¹The LORD's word came to Jonah a second time: ²"Get up and go to Nineveh, that great city, and declare against it the proclamation that I am commanding you." ³And Jonah got up and went to Nineveh, according to the LORD's word. (Now Nineveh was indeed an enormous city, a three days' walk across.)

the city, going a day's walk. And he cried out, "Forty days more, and Nineveh shall be overthrown!" [5]And the people of Nineveh believed God; they proclaimed a fast, and everyone, great and small, put on sackcloth.

[6]When the news reached the king of Nineveh, he rose from his throne, removed his robe, covered himself with sackcloth, and sat in ashes. [7]Then he had a proclamation made in Nineveh: "By the decree of the king and his nobles: No human being or animal, no herd or flock, shall taste anything. They shall not feed, nor shall they drink water. [8]Human beings and animals shall be covered with sackcloth, and they shall cry mightily to God. All shall turn from their evil ways and from the violence that is in their hands. [9]Who knows? God may relent and change his mind; he may turn from his fierce anger, so that we do not perish."

**[10]When God saw what they did, how they turned from their evil ways, God changed his mind about the calamity that he had said he would bring upon them; and he did not do it.**

[4]Jonah started into the city, walking one day, and he cried out, "Just forty days more and Nineveh will be overthrown!" [5]And the people of Nineveh believed God. They proclaimed a fast and put on mourning clothes, from the greatest of them to the least significant.

[6]When word of it reached the king of Nineveh, he got up from his throne, stripped himself of his robe, covered himself with mourning clothes, and sat in ashes. [7]Then he announced, "In Nineveh, by decree of the king and his officials: Neither human nor animal, cattle nor flock, will taste anything! No grazing and no drinking water! [8]Let humans and animals alike put on mourning clothes, and let them call upon God forcefully! And let all persons stop their evil behavior and the violence that's under their control!" [9]He thought, Who knows? God may see this and turn from his wrath, so that we might not perish.

**[10]God saw what they were doing—that they had ceased their evil behavior. So God stopped planning to destroy them, and he didn't do it.**

## UNDERSTANDING THE SCRIPTURE

**Jonah 3:1-3.** That the word of the Lord came to Jonah a second time is emblematic of the entire story. Jonah did not respond properly the first time, yet still God spoke to him a second time. And the second chance given to Jonah anticipates the second chance given to the city of Nineveh.

Three different times in the book, the Lord identifies Nineveh as a "great city" (1:2; 3:2; 4:11). The phrase seems to refer to both the physical size (3:3) and the population (4:11) of the city.

Also, during its golden age, Nineveh was evidently a great city in terms of its fabulous wealth, architecture, and culture.

**Jonah 3:4-9.** Jonah's message seems quite terse, yet it evokes a tremendous response within the city of Nineveh. Fasting and wearing sackcloth are common symbols of both mourning and repentance in Scripture. As with any external or physical act, it is not worth much if it remains superficial. In the case of the people of Nineveh, however, it appears to be a sincere reflection of their hearts. We observe, too, how comprehensive their response is, ranging all the way from their king to their animals. And it is the king who gives expression to the communal hope and purpose: "God may relent and change his mind; he may turn from his fierce anger, so that we do not perish" (3:9).

**Jonah 3:10**. The king's hope was realized. The narrator reports that "God saw what they did." See how reasonable the divine judgment is. Just as God had seen their wickedness before, so God sees their repentance now. With the people's change of heart came a change of behavior, and with the change in behavior came a change in their fate.

**Nahum 1:1**. Nahum serves as a kind of counterpart to Jonah in the writings of the Old Testament prophets. Both men are assigned messages concerning Nineveh, the capital of Assyria. Neither text contains enough internal evidence to date precisely, but conventional wisdom puts Nahum in the era of the Babylonian Empire's ascendency. Nineveh fell to a coalition of Babylonians and Medes in 612 B.C.

**Nahum 1:2-8**. Nahum's mission is to announce the judgment of Nineveh. Tellingly, the starting place for that message is not the wickedness of the people but the character of God. Lest we suspect that the Lord acts in response to us and what we do, Nahum reminds us that human beings ought to live in response to who God is and what God does.

**Nahum 1:9-11**. Now the human audience is addressed directly, and the message is a question. We are conscious of how often we would like to ask God "Why?" Perhaps it is even more common that the Lord wants to ask us "Why?" In the case of Nineveh, given the justice and the power of God, the question is why the people would presume to oppose the Lord.

**Nahum 1:12-13**. The personal pronouns change freely in this passage. Suddenly, in the midst of a message to Nineveh, we meet these words of comfort that are evidently meant for the inhabitants of Judah and Jerusalem. The Lord assures those people that their oppressive enemy, the Assyrians, will be defeated and that their affliction and bondage will come to an end.

**Nahum 1:14**. Another ominous word for Nineveh is inserted here. Just as the promise of a great and lasting name accompanies God's favor (see Genesis 12:2; 2 Samuel 7:9), so the termination of a name is a part of divine judgment. Also, in judgment, God puts an end to what God hates, which includes all idolatry.

**Nahum 1:15–2:10**. The messages continue to toggle between two audiences: Nineveh and Judah. The word to Judah is one of encouragement and hope for the future. The word to Nineveh is full of sober warning. Quick-hitting images of warfare morph into pictures of fear and trouble, climaxing finally with scenes of total devastation and despair.

**Nahum 2:11-13**. Nineveh is compared to a lion: powerful, destructive, ravaging, and at peace in his own preeminent strength. By itself, that comparison might be flattering. But it is introduced with a disquieting question: "What became of the lions' den?" All of the flattery about the lion's prevailing strength, therefore, is cast instead as a thing of the past.

**Nahum 3:1-7**. Chapter 3 opens

with a powerful passage, full of strong and vivid language. First, we encounter a flurry of phrases that serve as broad brushstrokes to paint the wickedness of Nineveh. In response, the Lord declares opposition to Nineveh. In contrast to Paul's cherished question, "If God is for us, who is against us?" (Romans 8:31), Nahum communicates this devastating word from God: "I am against you" (Nahum 3:5). And, to add insult to injury, the devastation of Nineveh will not even be mourned.

**Nahum 3:8-10**. God's sobering message to Nineveh challenges them to look around in several directions. The Lord directs their attention to other cities and countries, each of which was splendid and powerful in its own way, but each of which had fallen. Their destruction is a cautionary tale to Nineveh.

**Nahum 3:11-13**. A series of quick metaphors follows—drunkenness, hiding, ripe figs, inadequate troops, vulnerable gates, and destructive fire. Each one describes the state of affairs. And each one spells doom for the city.

**Nahum 3:14-16**. Nineveh is challenged to prepare for the coming assault, though assured that their preparations will be futile. Meanwhile, the image of locusts is intricately employed. First, it represents the coming, total destruction. Next, it is used to represent prolific reproduction. Nineveh is dared to reproduce like that, though again it will be futile, for "the locust sheds its skin and flies away" (3:16).

**Nahum 3:17-19**. More picturesque language is employed to illustrate Nineveh's plight. In this case, leaders, guards, nobles, scribes, and the general population are all referenced disparagingly. The itemization suggests a comprehensive vulnerability and total calamity. The scene everywhere else, however, is just the opposite, as "all who hear the news about you clap their hands" (3:19).

---

## INTERPRETING THE SCRIPTURE

### The Anatomy of Repentance

Jonah's recorded message is hardly a rhetorical masterpiece. We see in other prophets more impassioned exhortations, as well as more frighteningly detailed warnings. Compared to some of the messages preached by Isaiah, Jeremiah, Amos, and Haggai, Jonah's effort seems like an embarrassment.

It may be that Jonah's whole message is not recorded. It may be that his paltry effort is a reflection of the fact that his heart was never in this mission. But whatever he preached, the people of Nineveh responded commendably. When setting Jonah and Jeremiah next to each other, therefore, we conclude that it doesn't matter how good the preaching is if the audience is unresponsive. And, conversely, it may not matter how average the preaching is if the people's hearts are inclined to respond.

The people of Nineveh responded, and that is to their credit. The Book of Jonah offers a quick summary of how Nineveh responded. And their response is a model for us all.

The starting point is the heart of God, which dispatches a prophet to proclaim the word of the Lord. Paul's words are appropriate to the case: "How are they to hear without someone to proclaim [Jesus]? And how are they to proclaim him unless they are sent?" (Romans 10:14b-15a).

The next step is the receptive and responsive heart of the audience. The narrator reports that "the people of Nineveh believed God" (Nahum 3:5). The brief declaration is reminiscent of Abraham (Genesis 15:6), and thus the New Testament's gospel message of justification by faith (Romans 4:3-5).

Next comes the fasting and the command to "turn from their evil ways and from the violence that is in their hands" (3:8). Fasting and turning, of course, are the stuff of repentance. And the change of lifestyle recalls John the Baptist's challenge to "bear fruit worthy of repentance" (Matthew 3:8).

The command to turn came from the king. That sort of royal leadership is often a part of national repentance and revival in the Old Testament. We think especially of Hezekiah and Josiah. It does not have a natural parallel in our modern experience, of course, except to recognize the potentially important spiritual role of whoever is "at the top" in any organization or situation.

Finally, we note the comprehensive compliance that characterized Nineveh's repentance. By the king's command, both human beings and animals—all the creatures within his jurisdiction—were to participate in this humble fast. It is the same kind of thoroughgoing observance of all people and creatures that we see required in the Sabbath commandment: "you, your son or your daughter, your male or female slave, your livestock, or the alien resident in your towns" (Exodus 20:10). It is the sort of total obedience and complete response that honors God.

### Perhaps God Will Relent

"Who knows?" reasoned the king of Nineveh. "God may relent and change his mind" (3:9). It was an audacious hope, yet it was exactly what happened. The narrator reports that "when God saw what they did, how they turned from their evil ways, God changed his mind about the calamity that he had said he would bring upon them; and he did not do it" (3:10, key verse).

What are we to make of this episode? Is it possible to change the mind of God? On the one hand, we read, "I the LORD do not change" (Malachi 3:6). On the other hand, Moses' experience echoes the episode from Jonah. After Moses interceded on behalf of the people: "The LORD changed his mind about the disaster that he planned to bring on his people" (Exodus 32:14).

Is it possible for one who is omniscient to think differently? Is it conceivable for one who is immutable to "change his mind"? And if it is, then can we rely on God, or are we left with a capricious, unpredictable deity?

A closer look at Jonah's story reveals both an important theological point and a lovely truth about God. For God's mind to change is not the same as God's nature or will changing. In fact, the change of mind actually reveals the consistency of the divine character and will.

The question to ask, from start to finish, is "What does God want?" And the answer, from start to finish, is that God desires our salvation, our wholeness, and our love. Both the judgment and the forgiveness of God serve those purposes. The judgment pushes us back toward the wholeness of God's design. The forgiveness welcomes us back to God and provides that wholeness.

While the prophet's message is one of coming judgment, the prophet's presence is a proof of mercy. If the real desire was to destroy Nineveh, after all, then no warning would be needed or given. But the very fact of the warning proves that God would rather not do it.

When the narrator reports that "God changed his mind," therefore, there is no actual change in the nature or will of God. Indeed, the inconsistency would have been if God had not changed his mind. If the Lord had persisted in destroying a repentant people, that would have reflected an inconsistency in the divine character.

This truth is revealed beyond just the story of Jonah. The instance from the time of Moses, for example, follows the same pattern. There, too, the Scripture reports that the Lord changed his mind, but it was the same change: a decision not to destroy people.

Interestingly, even the Lord's own statement about not changing fits this same pattern. "I the LORD do not change," God says to the people of Malachi's day, "therefore you, O children of Jacob, have not perished" (Malachi 3:6). It is precisely because God doesn't change that the people were not destroyed.

## A Recurring Story

The Book of Jonah is like a piece of classical music, with recurring motifs woven throughout the piece. And, specifically for our purposes this week, we note the motif of human repentance and God's forgiveness. That theme reaches its climax in Nineveh, but the motif was introduced in the experience of Jonah himself.

Before the people of Nineveh had the opportunity to hear and respond to God's word, the courier of that word foretold their experience. Jonah disobeyed God, and God did not ignore it. Divine pressure brought Jonah back to his senses, and within the belly of the great fish, Jonah repented. The prophet was himself the beneficiary of the mercy and forgiveness of God.

Even after the Book of Jonah is closed, the music keeps playing. The same motif is woven throughout all of Scripture, and it resonates in our own lives and experiences, as well. The story of Jonah is familiar, not simply because we know it, but because we know personally the forgiveness at the heart of the story too.

What was true for Jonah was true for Nineveh. And what was true for Nineveh is true for us. The Lord urges, invites, and welcomes us back. When we come to our senses, we too walk through the steps of repentance that the Ninevites model for us. And as we do, we meet the same love and grace of the forgiving God who does not change.

## SHARING THE SCRIPTURE

### PREPARING TO LEAD

#### Preparing Our Hearts

Ponder this week's devotional reading from Acts 11:11-18. Here you will find a situation similar to that of Jonah. In this case Peter reports to the church at Jerusalem that he went on a mission to the home of the Gentile soldier named Cornelius. Like Jonah, Peter had been reluctant to go. What changed his mind? What was the result of his trip? (The entire story is told in Acts 10:1–11:18.)

Pray that you and the students will be open to following wherever God may lead you.

#### Preparing Our Minds

Study the background Scripture from Jonah 3; Nahum 1–3 and the lesson Scripture from Jonah 3.

Consider this question: *What can bring together people who are wracked with separation and violence to live together in wholeness and peace?*

Write on newsprint:

❏ the list of Bible passages under Goal 3 in Sharing the Scripture.
❏ questions under Goal 3 in Sharing the Scripture.
❏ information for next week's lesson, found under Continue the Journey.
❏ activities for further spiritual growth in Continue the Journey.

Determine how you might use any of the features that precede the first lesson of this quarter in today's session.

Take the time to explore the three chapters of the prophet Nahum. This difficult book has inspired many questions among scholars and also raises perplexing questions about the nature of God. Yet this book appears in today's background Scripture because it portrays the destruction of Nineveh (2:1–3:19) at the hands of a coalition of soldiers from Babylon and Mede in 612 B.C. See the Understanding the Scripture portion for help in comprehending this book.

### LEADING THE CLASS

#### (1) Gather to Learn

❖ Welcome everyone and pray that those who have come today will be mindful of God's loving call for repentance in their lives.

❖ Read: **Ferguson, Missouri, and Baltimore, Maryland—just two of the communities wracked by violence following the death of an African American male at the hands of police officers. What can be done to quell the unrest that devastates communities and address its root causes? Proposals include having police officers wear body cameras, training officers to be more sensitive to racial tensions, conducting independent investigations when an incident occurs, and working with the community to win trust and cooperation between the residents and law enforcement officials. As helpful as these ideas may be, people from across each community also need to come together to address the underlying issues of unemployment, poverty, crime, and ineffective education.**

❖ Read aloud today's focus statement: **Communities today are wracked with separation and violence. What can bring people together to live in wholeness and peace? When the people of Nineveh repented, God brought peace and wholeness through divine love.**

*(2) Goal 1: Explore How Repentance Is Related to God's Love*

❖ Enlist a volunteer to read the story of Nineveh's repentance in Jonah 3:1-10.

❖ Discuss these four questions:

1. **What does God tell Jonah to do?** (See Jonah 3:1-3 in Understanding the Scripture.)
2. **What does Jonah tell the people?** (See Jonah 3:4-9 in Understanding the Scripture. Look at verse 4 and note how brief and uninspired Jonah's message is, at least as it is recorded. Ask the students to comment on how they might have responded to Jonah's few words, which number only five in Hebrew.)
3. **How do the people and the king of Nineveh respond?** (See Jonah 3:4-9 in Understanding the Scripture. Also take note of the steps outlined in The Anatomy of Repentance in Interpreting the Scripture, beginning with "The starting point.")
4. **How does God respond to the actions of the Ninevites?** (See Jonah 3:10 in Understanding the Scripture and Perhaps God Will Relent in Interpreting the Scripture.)

*(3) Goal 2: Sense the Joy that Comes When Forgiven a Wrong*

❖ Read these questions and ask the students to reflect silently on them:

1. **Recall a time when you were forgiven. What emotions did you express. Joy, relief, disbelief, gratitude, or other feelings?** (pause)
2. **How did these feelings come into play when someone asked for your forgiveness?** (pause)
3. **Based on your own experience, how would you expect the Ninevites to react to God's change of heart that allowed them to remain whole?** (pause)

❖ Note that chapter 3 ends with God's decision not to destroy Nineveh. We do not have any record of how the Ninevites responded to that news. Form two or three groups and ask each group to create a short drama showing how the forgiven people might have reacted when they realized that God was not going to rain down destruction upon them. Provide time for each group to present its drama.

❖ Encourage students to comment on these brief dramas by asking: **If you were to visit Nineveh a year after Jonah had been there, do you think you would find a penitent, peaceful society—or a different situation? Explain the reasons for your speculation.**

*(4) Goal 3: Share Examples of Times When Wholeness and Peace Are the Result of God's Intervening Love*

❖ Read or retell A Recurring Story from Interpreting the Scripture.

Observe that the story of Jonah and the Ninevites is but one example of God's gracious love under circumstances where, by human standards, punishment would be expected.

❖ Post these Bible passages on newsprint:

- Exodus 32:1-14 (Golden Calf incident)
- Jeremiah 18:1-11 (God the potter)
- Joel 2:12-17 (God's people still have a window of opportunity to repent)
- Amos 7:1-9 (God shows Amos a vision)

❖ Form up to four groups and assign each group a different passage. Tell the groups to read their passage together and answer these questions, which you will also post on newsprint:

1. **What do you learn about how God responds to sin?**
2. **What do you think motivates God's response?**

❖ Call the groups together to report their findings.

❖ Point out that God's love motivates God's openness to human repentance and then ask: **How can these Bible stories help you to express God's forgiving love in difficult situations so that the peace and wholeness God intends can prevail?**

*(5) Continue the Journey*

❖ Pray that as the learners depart, they will remember that out of love God gives us wake-up calls when we have strayed in order to set us back on the path of peace and wholeness.

❖ Post information for next week's session on newsprint for the students to copy:

■ **Title: God's Pervasive Love**

■ **Background Scripture: Jonah 4**

■ **Lesson Scripture: Jonah 4**

■ **Focus of the Lesson: People become displeased and angry when things do not go their way. How can they gain a larger perspective? Jonah discovers the wide breadth of God's pervasive love.**

❖ Challenge the adults to grow spiritually by completing one or more of these activities related to this week's session.

(1) **Review today's key verse, Jonah 3:10. Use a concordance to find other examples of God changing God's mind or repenting. What does this idea suggest to you about God's love? What does it suggest about human ability to change God's mind? What action might you take on your findings?**

(2) **Try to see yourself as God sees you. For what reasons do you need to repent? Do you believe that your repentance precedes God's forgiveness, or does God's love precede human repentance? What does your answer reveal about your understanding of sin and forgiveness?**

(3) **Offer forgiveness to someone who has wronged you so as to bring peace and reconciliation to your relationship.**

❖ Sing or read aloud "Love Divine, All Loves Excelling."

❖ Conclude today's session by leading the class in this benediction, which is adapted from John 15:12, the key verse for March 19: **Let us go forth obeying Jesus' commandment to love one another as he has loved us. Amen.**

UNIT 3: GOD'S PERVASIVE AND SUSTAINING LOVE
# GOD'S PERVASIVE LOVE

---

## PREVIEWING THE LESSON

**Lesson Scripture:** Jonah 4
**Background Scripture:** Jonah 4
**Key Verse:** Jonah 4:11

**Focus of the Lesson:**
People become displeased and angry when things do not go their way. How can they gain a larger perspective? Jonah discovers the wide breadth of God's pervasive love.

**Goals for the Learners:**
(1) to understand why God's love for Nineveh caused Jonah to become irate.
(2) to reflect on anger that results when one's perspective is limited.
(3) to learn strategies for expressing God's pervasive love.

**Supplies:**
Bibles, newsprint and marker, paper and pencils, hymnals

---

## READING THE SCRIPTURE

NRSV
Lesson Scripture: Jonah 4

¹But this was very displeasing to Jonah, and he became angry. ²He prayed to the LORD and said, "O LORD! Is not this what I said while I was still in my own country? That is why I fled to Tarshish at the beginning; for I knew that you are a gracious God and merciful, slow to anger, and abounding in steadfast love, and ready to relent from punishing. ³And now, O LORD, please take my life from me, for it is better for me to die than to live."

CEB
Lesson Scripture: Jonah 4

¹But Jonah thought this was utterly wrong, and he became angry. ²He prayed to the LORD, "Come on, LORD! Wasn't this precisely my point when I was back in my own land? This is why I fled to Tarshish earlier! I know that you are a merciful and compassionate God, very patient, full of faithful love, and willing not to destroy. ³At this point, LORD, you may as well take my life from me, because it would be better for me to die than to live."

⁴And the LORD said, "Is it right for you to be angry?" ⁵Then Jonah went out of the city and sat down east of the city, and made a booth for himself there. He sat under it in the shade, waiting to see what would become of the city.

⁶The LORD God appointed a bush, and made it come up over Jonah, to give shade over his head, to save him from his discomfort; so Jonah was very happy about the bush. ⁷But when dawn came up the next day, God appointed a worm that attacked the bush, so that it withered. ⁸When the sun rose, God prepared a sultry east wind, and the sun beat down on the head of Jonah so that he was faint and asked that he might die. He said, "It is better for me to die than to live."

⁹But God said to Jonah, "Is it right for you to be angry about the bush?" And he said, "Yes, angry enough to die." ¹⁰Then the LORD said, "You are concerned about the bush, for which you did not labor and which you did not grow; it came into being in a night and perished in a night. **¹¹And should I not be concerned about Nineveh, that great city, in which there are more than a hundred and twenty thousand persons who do not know their right hand from their left, and also many animals?"**

⁴The LORD responded, "Is your anger a good thing?" ⁵But Jonah went out from the city and sat down east of the city. There he made himself a hut and sat under it, in the shade, to see what would happen to the city.

⁶Then the LORD God provided a shrub, and it grew up over Jonah, providing shade for his head and saving him from his misery. Jonah was very happy about the shrub. ⁷But God provided a worm the next day at dawn, and it attacked the shrub so that it died. ⁸Then as the sun rose God provided a dry east wind, and the sun beat down on Jonah's head so that he became faint. He begged that he might die, saying, "It's better for me to die than to live."

⁹God said to Jonah, "Is your anger about the shrub a good thing?"

Jonah said, "Yes, my anger is good—even to the point of death!"

¹⁰But the LORD said, "You 'pitied' the shrub, for which you didn't work and which you didn't raise; it grew in a night and perished in a night. **¹¹Yet for my part, can't I pity Nineveh, that great city, in which there are more than one hundred twenty thousand people who can't tell their right hand from their left, and also many animals?"**

---

## UNDERSTANDING THE SCRIPTURE

**Jonah 4:1.** As we read the final chapter in Jonah's story, we sense that he may have been a rather unpleasant fellow. He was unwilling to serve God in the lives of the Ninevites. He complacently slept while everyone else on board ship was laboring to survive. And now he is displeased and angry about the good thing that has transpired between God and Nineveh.

Originally, the wickedness of Nineveh was so great that God had pronounced judgment against that city. When the people heard that sober message, however, they repented. And their change of heart led to God's change of mind. Jonah, however, was more interested in their destruction than their salvation.

**Jonah 4:2.** Read aloud the second half of this verse apart from its context, and ask some hearer from which book of the Bible it comes. Most listeners will guess Psalms, for what Jonah says about God has that quality of praise. Yet the very thing for which any sensible person would praise and thank God is, for Jonah, a point of criticism. He is unhappy with God's forgiving nature.

Interestingly, God's nature comes as no surprise to Jonah. In fact, it seems that he fully expected God to forgive the people of Nineveh. That, he claims, is why he "fled to Tarshish at the beginning." In the content of his lament, of course, Jonah only indicts himself, not God.

**Jonah 4:3.** It is difficult to take Jonah seriously at this moment. One pictures the child threatening to hold his breath until he gets his way with his parents. It is a self-important, self-pitying tantrum.

**Jonah 4:4.** The Lord knows that Jonah's anger is misplaced. The fact that God responds with a question rather than a condemnation, however, is further evidence of divine mercy. The question invites Jonah to reconsider. It allows Jonah the room to come back to his senses on his own. There is a world of difference between God declaring, "You're wrong" and God asking, "Is it right?"

Meanwhile, we do well to think about on which side of the table our chair may be found. We are inclined to side with God in this episode, for it is so clear to us that Jonah is in the wrong here. Yet we might wonder, instead, about the times we are on Jonah's side of the table. When might God ask us, "Is it right for you to be angry?"

**Jonah 4:5.** The man so reluctant to go to Nineveh now seems unwilling to leave. Both reflexes stem from the same core unwholesomeness, of course: namely, how Jonah feels about Nineveh. It was likely his distaste for that place and its people made him reluctant to go there in the beginning. And now, in this moment, it is his disdain for Nineveh that prompts him to camp out nearby, seeking a front-row seat from which to view the city's destruction.

Meanwhile, the fact that Jonah erected for himself a booth is an important detail. On the one hand, it paints a more complete and damning picture of this prophet's heart that he seeks to make himself as comfortable as possible to watch a city being destroyed. In addition, it introduces the reader to Jonah's need for shade in that climate.

**Jonah 4:6-8.** Now it is God who makes provision for Jonah's shade and comfort, though the Lord has a bigger purpose in mind than mere comfort. After providing the bush, God also provides for that bush to be destroyed. And then the Lord turns up the heat on Jonah so much that, again, this unhappy soul declares that it would be better to die than to live.

Seen against the larger backdrop of Jonah's whole story, this passage reveals to us the patient and providential work of God in one person's life. Earlier, God had provided a storm and a fish. Now God provides a bush, a worm, and a hot wind. Most of these are not particularly desirable, of course, but Jonah brings them on himself. They are all designed to teach and to grow the man of God.

**Jonah 4:9.** The Lord returns to the earlier question, which Jonah evidently had not condescended to answer. With this additional, divine kindling of Jonah's anger, the prophet is ready to answer God's question. Indeed, he is emphatic in his answer. Yes, he is right to be angry, and he reiterates that he is angry enough to die.

**Jonah 4:10-11.** Like a good teacher, the Lord has asked questions of Jonah in order to lead this stubborn student to a better answer. First, God asked him about his anger, in general. Then God asked about his anger over the plant. And now God turns that disproportionate concern for a mere plant into an object lesson for Jonah.

The transition from "angry about" to "concerned about" is a stroke of genius on the part of the Lord. The fact is that Jonah's anger was mostly born out of self-interest and self-concern. For God to interpret Jonah's anger as concern, however, elevates the discussion and flatters the prophet. It also sets the stage for the larger point that the Lord wants to make, for whether the attitude is "anger" or "concern," the issue is that Jonah feels strongly about the plant, while God feels strongly about the city.

The object lesson shows that this debate is a matter of perspective. The Lord reminds Jonah how ultimately inconsequential the plant is, as well as how little Jonah had invested in it. By contrast, however, Nineveh has tremendous value. It has value as a place, as a population of people, and even as the home of many animals.

Interestingly, the Lord does not assume or assert that Jonah ought to be concerned about Nineveh. We know that he should, but God does not even require him to reach that high bar. Instead, the logic is simple and irrefutable: If Jonah feels strongly about a mere plant, shouldn't the Lord feel strongly about a great city?

---

## INTERPRETING THE SCRIPTURE

### Heart Problem

The empirical evidence suggests that Jonah was a remarkable man. He enjoyed clear communication from God. Even Matthew and Luke remark on the success of Jonah's preaching in Nineveh. He accurately recognized the Lord's activity in nature and events. And he had a profound understanding of God's character and will.

With all of that going for him, then, what was the matter with him? Clearly he is a disappointing character and a substandard prophet. I've never heard a preacher hold him up as a role model. So what was wrong with Jonah?

I believe that Jonah had a heart problem. He had the word of God, but he did not have the heart of God. And the one divorced from the other becomes a terrible aberration.

The heart of God desired Nineveh's redemption. Even though it was the Lord who initiated the judgment message, the purpose of the message was to bring about salvation. And so, when the people of Nineveh repented and changed their ways, God was pleased. Jonah was not.

The phenomenon does not belong to Jonah alone. We think, for example, of the prodigal's older brother, who did not share their father's enthusiasm for the wayward boy's return. While the father was evidently watching for the prodigal, the brother was oblivious. And while their father showered the prodigal with a hearty welcome, the older brother resented him.

Jonah is the older brother. While God rejoiced at the "return" of the Ninevites, Jonah sulked. The prodigal didn't deserve a party, and Nineveh didn't deserve forgiveness.

What people deserve is the issue. God, Jonah, the prodigal's father, and the older brother are all acutely aware of what is deserved. Yet in some hearts, there is an eagerness to offer more than what is deserved. In others, there is a stingy version of fairness.

We see the same principle at work in Jesus' parable of the workers in the vineyard (Matthew 20:1-16). The property owner hires workers throughout the course of a day to labor in his vineyard. At the end of the day, he calls them forward to pay them their wages. The folks hired first were paid the agreed upon amount. Yet all of the rest of the workers, including those who had barely broken a sweat, were also paid that same amount.

Interestingly, the first workers were content with their pay until they saw other workers who had labored far fewer hours getting the same amount. The owner calls them on it, asking, "Am I not allowed to do what I choose with what belongs to me? Or are you envious because I am generous?" (Matthew 20:15).

God's grace to Nineveh didn't cost Jonah a thing. Still, he fumed about it, right along with the older brother and the workers who began the earliest. God is never less than fair, mind you, but we see how often God is more than fair. That is the nature of grace,

and it reflects the heart of God. But Jonah didn't have a heart like that.

*Big Enough to Love*

During one scene in the 1963 movie *Cleopatra*, Julius Caesar overhears a young man reciting the Roman poet Catullus. Caesar speaks appreciatively of the recitation. Cleopatra challenges Caesar, saying, "Catullus doesn't approve of you. Why haven't you had him killed?" And Caesar coolly replies, "Because I approve of him."

It does not take much strength or character to dislike someone. Children on the playground reveal just how easy and accessible it is to dislike and disapprove, to mistreat and to tease. But it takes a bigger, more secure individual to like someone else, especially if that someone else is unlikable. This is the stature of Caesar in the movie: He is strong enough and secure enough to approve of someone who did not approve of him.

So it is with God. God is big enough, strong enough, and secure enough to like the unlikable, to love the unlovable, and to reach out even to those who do not believe or approve. Jesus encourages the same bigness of love in us (for example, Matthew 5:43-44). And he, not Caesar, is our model (John 13:34). We are to love as he loves.

Our choice to dislike someone, or our unwillingness to forgive others, is often just a monument to our pain. That is to say, when we feel that no one else takes seriously how we have been hurt or wronged, then we try to establish a permanent memorial to our pain by declaring that we never will forget and we never will forgive.

In the story of Jonah, that human

weakness and smallness is juxtaposed with God's generosity and greatness. Jonah never did like those Ninevites—and he never would. They had probably been responsible for inflicting some pain on Jonah and his people. And so we envision him there with his arms crossed and his back turned stubbornly away from the city. God, however, turned toward that city with arms open wide.

We can imagine the movie's conversation between Jonah and the Lord. "The Ninevites don't love you," Jonah declares. "Why haven't you had them killed?" And God gently replies, "Because I love them."

### Jonah in the Mirror

"How did he miss that?" the indignant sports fan yells at the television. It looks so easy to us from where we sit in the comfort of our living rooms. We wonder how the player could fail so badly.

And we wonder the same thing about certain characters in Scripture. We are armchair quarterbacks with the Bible. We shake our heads disapprovingly at the faithlessness of the Israelites, the fearfulness of the disciples, and the insensitivity of the priest and the Levite. And it is likewise easy for us to feel condescending toward Jonah, who is so obviously disobedient, petty, and petulant.

In the case of the player who failed on the field, we have the luxury of never having to perform in his place. Not so with Jonah, however. While I will never be asked to catch a pass from an NFL quarterback or hit a ball thrown by a major league pitcher, I will stand in Jonah's place. So will you.

We are not sent to Nineveh, yet we are God's emissaries. Specifically, we carry God's word and reflect God's love. Unless we do not.

Our first order of business is to recognize God's heart. Inasmuch as the Lord does not change, we may assume that the divine purpose is still for people to repent and turn to the Lord. And in order for that to happen, someone must represent God to the fallen world. Is that you? Is that me?

The second consideration, then, is whether we will, like Jonah, flee from our responsibility. We, too, may have a variety of reasons why we'd rather not do what God asks us to do. Will we abdicate like Jonah?

Finally, we must be candid about the people we dislike. Candidly admit to God our qualms, hurts, fears, resentments, and prejudices. And then candidly admit to ourselves that God still loves them. The Lord is as eager to extend the same grace and forgiveness to them that we have received and enjoyed.

## SHARING THE SCRIPTURE

### PREPARING TO LEAD

#### Preparing Our Hearts

Ponder this week's devotional reading from Psalm 86:8-13. In this portion of David's prayer in a time of trouble, he extols the virtues of God and asks for divine help in becoming more faithful. What virtues do you see here? What others might you add?

Pray that you and the students

will, like the psalmist, ask God for "an undivided heart to revere your name" (86:11).

### Preparing Our Minds

Study the background Scripture and the lesson Scripture, which are both from Jonah 4.

Consider this question: *How can you gain a larger perspective when things do not go the way you had hoped?*

Write on newsprint:
- ❏ information for next week's lesson, found under Continue the Journey.
- ❏ activities for further spiritual growth in Continue the Journey.

Determine how you might use any of the features that precede the first lesson of this quarter in today's session.

### LEADING THE CLASS

#### (1) Gather to Learn

❖ Welcome everyone and pray that those who have come today will be able to see God's love all around them, even in people and places where they would least expect it.

❖ Read: *The First 48* is a critically acclaimed and widely watched documentary show that has aired since 2004. There are neither actors nor scripts. Instead, detectives in cities across the United States are filmed as they work to find clues to solve murders. According to the show's introduction, if the investigators do not get a lead within the first 48 hours after the crime, their chances of solving it are cut in half. All too often a senseless murder was committed because someone said something that enraged someone else who was armed with a gun or knife.

**Many times drugs are involved, frequently leading to drug deals gone bad or robberies committed to fund a drug habit that leaves innocent store clerks or bystanders dead. It seems as if perpetrators unthinkingly shoot to vent their anger without considering the consequences. Even if the murderer is later sorry, it's too late for the victim and the victim's family and friends. It's also too late for the criminal, who usually is sentenced to decades in jail. Many lives are shattered when anger goes unchecked.**

❖ Read aloud today's focus statement: **People become displeased and angry when things do not go their way. How can they gain a larger perspective? Jonah discovers the wide breadth of God's pervasive love.**

#### (2) Goal 1: Understand Why God's Love for Nineveh Caused Jonah to Become Irate

❖ Choose a volunteer to read Jonah 4:1-8 and discuss these questions:
1. **As a result of Jonah's preaching, halfhearted as it was, the Ninevites repented and God "changed his mind about the calamity" intended for them (3:10). Chapter 4 begins: "But this was very displeasing to Jonah." Why is Jonah so upset—and with whom?** (See Jonah 4:1, 2, 3 in Understanding the Scripture and Heart Problem in Interpreting the Scripture.)
2. **How does God try to calm Jonah's anger?** (See Jonah 4:4, 5 in Understanding the Scripture and Big Enough to Love in Interpreting the Scripture.)

3. **How does Jonah respond to God concerning the bush that withered soon after it appeared?** (See Jonah 4:6-8 in Understanding the Scripture.)

❖ Select a volunteer to finish the story of Jonah by reading verses 9-11. Ask:

1. **What would you have said to Jonah when he claimed that he was angry enough to die because the bush had withered, leaving him exposed to the sun?**
2. **How did God handle the situation?** (See Jonah 4:10-11 in Understanding the Scripture.)
3. **Jonah's response to God's question in verse 11 is not recorded here. After God's discussion with him and the object lesson of the bush, what might Jonah have said in answer to God's question?**

*(3) Goal 2: Reflect on Anger that Results When One's Perspective Is Limited*

❖ Read: **We've all done it. We've become very angry because of words spoken or actions taken. Sometimes we strike back verbally with hurtful words. Some people routinely lash out physically. Others, even if they are able to appear calm outwardly, are boiling inside. And then, sometime later, we learn the rest of the story and can understand (if not approve of) why the other person acted as he or she did. We recognize now that our perspective was limited because we did not know all the facts. Sure, those facts may not excuse the other individual's behavior, but they** do temper our response. If we had known, for example, that the "opponent" had recently received bad news, we could have waited to air our grievance, which in comparison may be trivial.

❖ Distribute paper and pencils. Invite participants to reflect on a time when they lashed out in anger only to later learn that their perspective on the situation had been very limited. Suggest that they write their response to the anger at the time—and how they would have responded if they had known all the facts.

❖ Bring the students together and ask: **What changes might you make in the future to curb your own anger?**

*(4) Goal 3: Learn Strategies for Expressing God's Pervasive Love*

❖ Invite the students to review all four chapters of Jonah's story to see examples of God's love, both toward Jonah and the Ninevites. Post on newsprint examples of God's love. (Some ideas may include God commissioning Jonah to call the Ninevites to repentance, God sending a big fish to deliver Jonah, God giving the disobedient Jonah a second chance to obey, God having a change of heart concerning the destruction of Nineveh.)

❖ Ask: **Using God's methods as our example, what strategies can we use to express God's love for all people?** (Possibilities include offering opportunities for others to say "I'm sorry and be forgiven," act in obedience to God so that others may see our witness, want the best for others.)

*(5) Continue the Journey*

❖ Pray that as the learners depart they will do all that they can, even in the midst of a situation that has aroused their anger, to let the love of God shine through them.

❖ Post information for next week's session on newsprint for the students to copy:

- **Title: Deborah and Barak**
- **Background Scripture: Judges 4–5**
- **Lesson Scripture: Judges 4:1-10**
- **Focus of the Lesson: People called to be leaders may doubt their capabilities. How do leaders deal with their doubts? Barak willingly went into battle after the prophetess Deborah agreed to accompany him.**

❖ Challenge the adults to grow spiritually by completing one or more of these activities related to this week's session.

(1) **Review other stories of God's grace that offended someone who did not view the recipient(s) as deserving such favor. Compare the characters in** two parables, Matthew 20:1-16 (laborers in the vineyard) and Luke 15:11-32 (the prodigal and his brother), with Jonah. How are these stories and their characters similar? Why do we sometimes resist extending the grace we have received to other people?

(2) **Monitor your response in situations that might anger you. How did you keep your temper under control? How were you able to show God's love and grace even in a tense situation?**

(3) **Write a paragraph about what you have learned from Jonah during this four-week study that can help you to be more loving and compassionate. Put into practice whatever you have learned.**

❖ Sing or read aloud "Depth of Mercy."

❖ Conclude today's session by leading the class in this benediction, which is adapted from John 15:12, the key verse for March 19: **Let us go forth obeying Jesus' commandment to love one another as he has loved us. Amen.**

# FOURTH QUARTER
## God's Urgent Call

JUNE 4, 2017—AUGUST 27, 2017

Our course during the summer quarter, God's Urgent Call, investigates who God calls and how they have responded. The three units probe God's call from the days of the judges through the era of selected Old Testament prophets into the New Testament as God calls ordinary people from diverse backgrounds to lead the church. Those who answer the call are able to make a difference because God promises to be with each one.

The first unit, Called to Be Strong, explores the era of the judges, who led Israel from the period after Joshua died until the anointing of Israel's first king, Saul. In Judges 4–5, which we will encounter on June 4, we see the interaction between Deborah and Barak—the prophetess and judge who gives confidence to the military leader. On June 11 we read in Judges 6–8 about Gideon's Call and how he wrestles with doubt about this call. Before Jephthah Answers the Call, as we will discover in Judges 11 on June 18, he needs to reestablish trust with the people of Gilead. Samson's Call, the lesson for June 25 from Judges 13–16, tells the story of an unborn child destined for greatness.

Unit 2, Calling of Prophets, looks at how God called Moses, Isaiah, Jeremiah, Ezekiel, and Amos to bring divine messages at different times for specific purposes. Exodus 3, the Scripture for July 2, delves into the encounter between Moses and the Burning Bush to hear God's call on the life of the one chosen to lead the Hebrew slaves out of Egypt. One July 9 we encounter Isaiah in the Temple and learn how he answers God's call, according to Isaiah 6. In Jeremiah's Call and Commission, the lesson on July 16, we overhear God's call in Jeremiah 1 to a prophet who was to bring a challenging message during a difficult time. Ezekiel 1–3, which we will study on July 23, spotlights Ezekiel's Call to speak truth to the Israelites held captive in Babylon. The eighth-century prophet Amos faced hostility, as we read in Amos 7 when we study Amos's Call on July 30.

In Unit 3, Calls in the New Testament, we will examine the lives of Stephen, , Philip, Ananias, Paul, and Peter who each answered God's call and in turn helped the fledgling church to develop and move forward. The unit opens on August 6 with Called to Witness, based on readings from Acts 1, 6, and 7 that deal with the call of people, particularly Stephen, to meet needs within the early church. Acts 8, the Scripture for August 13, follows Philip the evangelist who is Called to Break Down Barriers. On August 20 we hear the story recorded in Acts 9:1-31 of Ananias, who was Called to Preach and minister to Saul (Paul) soon after his Damascus road experience. Called to Be Inclusive, the lesson for August 27 rooted in Acts 10, concerns Peter's vision and subsequent trip to the home of Cornelius.

# MEET OUR WRITER

## DR. JEROME F. D. CREACH

Jerome F. D. Creach is the Robert C. Holland Professor of Old Testament at Pittsburgh Theological Seminary (PTS) where he has taught since 2000. Before accepting his current post he taught at Barton College in Wilson, North Carolina (1994–2000), The College of William & Mary (1993–94), and the Baptist Theological Seminary at Richmond (1991–92). In addition to his work at PTS, Dr. Creach preaches and teaches frequently in churches in the Pittsburgh area. He has also taught and lectured at many retreat centers, churches, and other academic institutions.

Dr. Creach earned his Ph.D. at Union Presbyterian Theological Seminary (Richmond, Virginia) in 1994. His work there focused on the Book of Psalms. He has published three books on the Psalter: *Yahweh as Refuge and the Editing of the Hebrew Psalter* (Sheffield: Sheffield Academic Press, 1996); *Psalms* (Interpretation Bible Studies; Louisville: Geneva Press, 1998); *The Destiny of the Righteous in the Psalms* (St. Louis: Chalice Press, 2008). He has also written a commentary on the book of Joshua in the series *Interpretation: A Commentary for Teaching and Preaching* (Louisville: Westminster John Knox Press, 2003) and *Violence in Scripture: Interpretation: Resources for the Use of Scripture in the Church* (Louisville: Westminster John Knox Press, 2013). He is active in the Society of Biblical Literature.

Dr. Creach is a minister of the Word and Sacrament in the Presbyterian Church (U.S.A.). He is married to Page L. D. Creach, who is pastor of the United Presbyterian Church of Freeport, Pennsylvania. They have two children. In his spare time Dr. Creach enjoys hiking, camping, and fishing. He is an avid fan of the Pittsburgh Steelers. He enjoys watching *The Andy Griffith Show* and listening to the music of Bruce Springsteen, Johnny Cash, and U2.

# THE BIG PICTURE: THE CALL OF GOD

The lessons during this summer quarter focus on God calling individuals to do certain work or to take on certain vocations. One of the basic features of the stories, therefore, is that each person called is engaged in work set forth by God to accomplish divine purposes. In the course of the lessons we will examine key questions about the call of God such as: how does God present a call to a person and how do people typically receive it; what types of tasks does God call a person to do; and what challenges does God's call introduce into a person's life? As we study how God's call played out in the lives of biblical characters, we will also consider how God might call us to a particular action, job, or vocation. We will see that God's call comes to a variety of different types of people and presents a myriad of possible actions God desires people to perform. Our lessons include people who fall into three categories. We will begin with four stories from the Book of Judges that involve Deborah and Barak (Judges 4–5), Gideon (Judges 6–8), Jephthah (Judges 11), and Samson (Judges 13–16). Each of these people is called to free the Israelites from their oppressors. Then we turn to five prophetic figures: Moses who is also like the judges in that he delivers Israel from bondage (Exodus 3); Isaiah (Isaiah 6); Jeremiah (Jeremiah 1); Ezekiel (Ezekiel 1–3); and Amos (Amos 7). Finally, we will consider prominent figures in the book of Acts: Stephen and the others chosen to serve the needs of widows (Acts 6); Philip (Acts 8); Saul and Ananias (Acts 9); and Peter and Cornelius (Acts 10).

## The Pattern of God's Call

Although the call God gives to each person is distinct, many of the stories of God calling individuals into service have a recognizable pattern that reveals much about the nature of that call. In such stories: (1) the person being called meets God or an angel and reacts with fear. This reaction shows proper reverence when encountering the divine, a necessary prerequisite for answering God's call. (2) God commissions the person to a special task or vocation. Thus, God takes the initiative and sets the agenda; the call represents something other than the person's own personal interests. (3) The person being commissioned expresses doubt or questions whether the task can be accomplished. In some cases the doubts reflect a lack of faith or a reluctance to answer God's call. In other cases the person's objections are due to feelings of inferiority or lack of preparation. Finally, (4) God gives a sign of assurance that the task will be successful. Often the assurance God gives is only that God will be with the person who answers the call. So the role God gives the person to fill requires faith first and foremost. We will recognize in our lessons that some people answer a call that does not come through an established pattern such as the one just described. In such cases God's purpose is accomplished in more indirect or subtle ways and the person may not always show awareness of doing something specifically for God. But this feature of some of the stories reminds us of another important truth: Every part of our lives is sacred and God may use anything we do or say to accomplish a higher purpose.

## God's Call as Intrusion

Most of the characters in our lessons illustrate the point that God's call comes as an intrusion and disruption. It is an intrusion in that the person called is jolted into the reality of the work of God's kingdom that was not previously their interest. For instance, some of the prophets testify to God giving them a message to deliver they would not have considered or embraced if God had not given it. Isaiah, Jeremiah, Ezekiel, and Amos fit this description. God's call is a disruption because it typically changes the direction of a person's life, away from their pursuits of their own interests and toward God's interests. God takes Moses and Gideon away from their daily work of farming and sends them to deliver Israel. Amos declares that he was not a prophet, but a sheep breeder and cultivator of sycamore trees until God gave him the order to prophesy to Israel (Amos 7:10-17). In Acts 9 God turns Saul's life around completely. He was persecuting the church before God called him; God's call changed his entire perspective on Jesus and the church and turned him into the church's greatest missionary and ambassador.

As a result of God interrupting and disrupting their lives, the people in our lessons often have lives fraught with challenge and hardship. For example, Jeremiah makes enemies of his closest family and friends because they hate the message he delivers. Likewise Amos is rejected and chastised for preaching against Israel. Saul, later to be called Paul, will have his life threatened so that his allies have to lower him in a basket over the city wall. In other words, those called to God's service don't have problems solved and receive blessings because God calls them; instead, they often have more difficulty.

Perhaps the key feature of the people in our lessons who answer God's call is that they do not live for themselves but for the One who called them. This characteristic of the lives of those who fulfill God's call reveals something essential about being in relationship with God more generally: God requires attention to God's will, which bends the human will toward God's vision for the world.

In this sense it is appropriate for all Christians to consider how God has called them with the belief that God calls everyone to something for the sake of the Kingdom. Thinking this way, it is appropriate to consider a life in relationship with God as a "called life," and to note that it stands in marked contrast with what Walter Brueggemann terms an "uncalled" life. The uncalled life is one in which a person pursues certain activities or takes certain paths only because they bring pleasure, make money, or fulfill the person's interests. By contrast, the called life is marked by an awareness of God's holiness and is directed by God's agenda. The one called thinks differently about everything: The comfortable routines of life are now cast off and all energy is spent seeking to know the direction God is leading. The call leads to a redefinition of happiness, success, and fulfillment. Now the only success that matters is the accomplishment of God's purpose. God's vision becomes the guide to everything in the life of the one called.

# The Call of the Judges

Our lessons begin with four sessions from the Book of Judges. Deborah and Barak, Gideon, Jephthah, and Samson are each featured in one of the lessons. The stories of these judges (and in the case of Barak, one who supports a judge) are unique call accounts represented in the quarter. Gideon is the only one of the group who has a typical call experience. He meets an angel who commissions him to God's service. The others, however, answer God's call simply by responding to the need of the Israelites to be freed from the oppression of their enemies. As we will see, there are summary statements in the Book of Judges that indicate God appointed judges to deliver Israel after God gave them over to enemies because of Israel's rebellion (Judges 2:16). But the specific actions of the other judges are just part of the work they are already doing. There is no record of a dramatic call to service.

Jephthah and Samson are particularly strange examples of people who answered the call of God. Neither of them has an encounter with God in which God commissions them, and neither of them particularly lives as though God's call guides their actions. Nevertheless, there are significant times when God's spirit guides them. As a result they both free God's people from oppression. For this reason Hebrews 11 lists them both as examples of faith. Jephthah and Samson also have women in their lives who show great faithfulness and who have their own calls to answer. Although they are secondary characters in Judges, they are important in that they help redeem the flaws of the primary characters. Thus, the stories of Jephthah and Samson should create in us some sense of caution in making judgments about who lives a called life and who does not and how the call of God is actually being worked out. It is possible God is working in someone's life and we simply cannot recognize it. It is also possible that someone is working behind the scenes whose work will only be seen in a later and fuller telling of the story.

# The Call of the Prophets

Five of the lessons in this quarter deal with the call of Old Testament prophets: Moses, Isaiah, Jeremiah, Ezekiel, and Amos. Moses is unique in this group in that his call account appears in a larger narrative, whereas Isaiah, Jeremiah, Ezekiel, and Amos include call stories before or in the midst of prophetic oracles. But Moses is often considered the ideal prophet after whose ministry other prophets will pattern their ministries (Deuteronomy 18) and thus his story fits together nicely with the others.

The call stories that appear in books that bear the names of those prophets have at least two common characteristics: (1) God's call is definitive. In the case of Isaiah and Ezekiel it occurs in the context of great visions in which the prophets see God's throne in the heavens and hear God speaking. For Jeremiah and Amos there is no call vision, but the prophet testifies to God singling him out to be a prophet and taking him from what he would otherwise be doing. (2) God warns the prophet the message will not be received well. Each of these prophets is called to proclaim the message to a stubborn and rebellious people. Perhaps if this were not the case there would be no need for a prophet! But it makes the prophet's life extremely difficult. For Jeremiah and Amos it means they will be rejected by the people. For all of the prophets the call story seems to strengthen them and their disciples for the opposition and resistance they will face.

The calls of Jeremiah and Ezekiel show how the personal life of the prophet is taken over by God and used as part of the prophetic message. Jeremiah's message is completely rejected by the people. His own mistreatment at the hands of those who refuse to hear will symbolize the people's turning away from God. So too Ezekiel will embody his message through his inability to speak (Ezekiel 3:22-27).

Amos presents the classic case of a prophetic call. Like Moses, he is tending to pastoral work as "a herdsman and a dresser of sycamore trees" (Amos 7:14) when God calls him to prophesy. As Amos recalls how God commissioned him he makes clear that he was appointed to speak only for God, not for a king or other human agent. Thus, Amos's life also was not his own and it created great trouble for him.

It is important to note also that the call to prophesy was not a call for the prophet to separate from the people. To the contrary, each of the prophets included in this unit lives in the midst of the people and cares for them deeply. The primary sign of this caring is that the prophet intercedes for the people when God is angry with them. In this way the prophets Isaiah, Jeremiah, Ezekiel, and Amos fit with Moses. One of the main features of Moses' prophetic work was that he spoke to God on behalf of the people, as well as speaking to the people on behalf of God (for example, Exodus 32:12). Thus the prophets were called to minister to the people with compassion and to be part of the people. This even applies to Amos who seems not to be part of the people of Israel when he is called (he is from a small town in Judah, at some distance from the place he prophesies; Amos 1:1). Amos does not proclaim destruction with joy, but with sorrow. Moreover, like Moses, he pleads with God to allow Israel to survive (Amos 7:1-6).

## God's Call in Acts

The lessons from the Book of Acts for the most part focus on stories that continue the stereotypical call stories found in the prophetic books. Saul, Ananias, Peter, and Cornelius have visions in which God speaks to them and commissions them for service. These figures experience God's call as a profound disruption, as noted above, as each of them is forced not only to change the path he is taking in life but also to change the way he thinks about people in general. Saul (later, Paul) must come to terms with the fact that his life to that point has been aimed against God's will. Now God's call gives him new clear vision that will lead him to embrace the very people he once thought were enemies of God. Ananias is called in a vision to embrace and support Saul, whom he once feared. In a similar way God reveals to Peter that the Gentiles whom he once thought were unfit to be in God's presence are actually objects of God's care and compassion, and Cornelius provides him with an immediate example. For each of these people God's call is dramatic and life-changing.

Two of the lessons from Acts show God's call coming in a different, yet equally important way. Philip does not receive a vision; he is simply led by the Spirit to travel a road he would not ordinarily travel. As a result he meets the Ethiopian eunuch and baptizes him. Thus God's call may come through the leading of the Spirit that requires openness and imagination to see where it might lead. Finally, the call of Stephen in Acts 6 comes by an election the people hold to appoint new leaders for service. To be sure, they go about the election by seeking the will of God through prayer (Acts 6:6). But this shows another important way God's call appears in Scripture. Sometimes the call of God comes because the people of God recognize a person's gifts and affirm that person as one whom God is calling. Even in the case of those who have dramatic visions in which God calls them, they are in turn affirmed by the larger community. So the Book of Acts shows us that God's call is finally a community matter. The call is affirmed by the community and the community then benefits from the work of the ones who are called.

# CLOSE-UP: THE JUDGES

The first unit of the summer quarter will focus on the era of the Judges, which extended from about 1200 until 1020 B.C. During this transitional period between the death of Joshua and the installation of Israel's first king, Saul, God periodically raised up leaders to deliver Israel when the people sinned. These deliverers were called judges, though only Deborah was said to perform the kind of work that we associate with a courtroom judge (Judges 4:5). The Hebrew word translated as "judge" can also mean "rule" or "ruler," which best describes the people we will meet this quarter. Their role was to resolve internal disputes, as well as external conflicts with the Canaanites, Midianites, Moabites, and Ammonites.

Although the stories we will encounter have their roots in this ancient period, scholars believe that independent accounts were gathered together and edited during the sixth century B.C. to create the Book of Judges as we know it. Viewed together, these stories present a repetitive pattern as Israel disobeyed God by failing both to conquer Canaan and to remain faithful to their covenant. This pattern is clearly and succinctly seen in 2:11-19: the apostate Israelites worship other gods, God hands them over to enemies who punish and oppress them, God mercifully responds to Israel's cries for help by sending a military leader—a judge—to free them from their enemies, the cycle begins anew after the judge dies. The named judges, whose stories are told in 3:7—16:31, are Othniel (3:7-11), Ehud (3:12-30), Shamgar (3:31), Deborah (4–5), Gideon (6:11–8:35), Abimelech (9:1-57), Tola (10:1-2), Jair (10:3-5); Jephthah (11:1–12:7), Iban (12:8-10), Elon (12:11-12), Abdon (12:13-15), and Samson (13:1–16:31). Reading through the entire book, it becomes clear that there is a downward spiral from the first judge Othniel, considered a model judge, to the last judge Samson. During this quarter we will be looking at selected passages of the stories of Deborah (and Barak), Gideon, Jephthah, and Samson to explore God's call on their lives and their responses.

Although the stories of these judges likely contain snippets of Israel's historical memory, the editing of these stories during the period of the Babylonian captivity has likely obscured these references as the Deuteronomistic History that emerged during this period reflected on what appeared to be total defeat and irrevocable loss of the Promised Land. Thus, in Judges we see Israel slowly declining as a society and as the people of God. By the time the Book of Judges ends, it is clear that the use of judges to lead the people has not worked. A new way of leading God's people is needed. God, of course, could choose to abandon Israel, but God's love for the people means that abandonment is not an option. Their next leader will be a king.

# FAITH IN ACTION: HEARING AND HEEDING THE CALL

Distribute paper and pencils so that the students may copy the five questions. Read the rest of this page aloud. The theme for this quarter's lessons is "call." We are studying how God called strong leaders, who in the early days of Israel's life together in the Promised Land were known as judges. We will also see how God called prophets to fulfill specific tasks and proclaim difficult messages. In the final unit we will encounter those whom we might label as "ordinary" going about the extraordinary work of shaping and serving the early church. We'll read the stories of people such as Deborah and Gideon, Isaiah and Jeremiah, Stephen and Philip who all answered God's call on their lives. God not only called these servants of millennia ago but also continues to call each of us to certain tasks, some big, some small, all important. Our challenge is to be ready to listen for God's call and then to respond so as to heed that call.

During this quarter we are being challenged to keep a spiritual journal about what we believe God is asking us to do. On this newsprint are five questions for you to copy on your paper. Over the course of this quarter, write answers to these questions in a spiritual journal, which can simply be some sheets of notebook paper.

1. As I look at my church, community, and family, where do I see unmet needs?
2. In what ways do I hear God calling me to address any of these needs?
3. What skills, talents, or other resources has God given me to make a difference in these situations?
4. How can I use these resources?
5. What are my motives for becoming involved?

After you have identified a need and prayerfully considered how you might meet it, begin to take action. Continue seeking God's leading as to the people or agencies you might work with to fulfill your calling. Determine how you may raise money if funds are needed to support a project.

As you work to address this need, keep your heart and mind open as God leads you through answered prayer, Scripture passages, sermons that may seem as if they were preached just for you, words of encouragement from others, new ideas and possibly even a "thank you" from whomever you are trying to serve.

You may reach a point where you think the need has been met and you can begin to listen for a new calling. Or you may feel even though the need is great you have now done all you can do and God will be sending others to pick up as you leave to engage in other ministries.

Replay your call and response by summing it up in your spiritual journal. Review what you learned about how God calls and equips you. Listen for God's words "well done, good and faithful servant" and give thanks that God chose to call you and that you heeded this call.

# PRONUNCIATION GUIDE

Abiezrite (ay bi ez' rite)
Abimelech (uh bim' uh lek)
Abinoam (uh bin' oh uhm)
Achsah (ak' suh)
*adamah* (ad aw maw')
Amalekite (uh mal' uh kite)
Amaziah (am uh zi' uh)
Ammonite (am' uh nite)
Amorite (am' uh rite)
*anak* (an awk')
Ananias (an uh ni' uhs)
Anathoth (an' uh thoth)
Asherah (uh shihr' uh)
Ashkelon (ash' kuh lon)
Azariah (az uh ri' uh)
Barak (bair' ak)
Candace (kan' duh see)
Dagon (day' gon)
Danite (dan' ite)
Ehud (ee' huhd)
ephah (ee' fuh)
ephod (ee' fod)
Ephraim (ee' fray im)
Eshtaol (esh' tay uhl)
Eusebius (yoo see' bee uhs)
Harosheth-ha-goiim
     (huh roh shith huh goin' im)
Hazor (hay' zor)
Hilkiah (hil ki' uh)
Hittite (hit' tite)
Hivite (hiv' ite)
Hobab (hoh' bab)
Horeb (hor' eb)
Jabin (jay' bin)
Jael (jay' uhl)
Jebusite (jeb' yoo site)
Jehoiachin (ji hoi' uh kin)
Jehoiakim (ji hoi' uh kim)
Jephthah (jef' thuh)
Jeroboam (jer uh boh' uhm)
Jerubbaal (ji ruhb bay' uhl)
Joash (joh' ash)
Kedesh (kee' dish)

Kenite (ken' ite)
Kishon (ki' shon)
Lappidoth (lap' i doth)
Mahaneh-dan (may hun uh dan')
Manasseh (muh nas' uh)
Manoah (muh noh' uh)
Meggido (mi gid' oh)
Meroz (mee' roz)
Midianite (mid' ee uh nite)
Mizpah (miz' puh)
Naphtali (naf' tuh li)
nazarite (naz" uh rite)
Nicanor (ni kay' nuhr)
Nicolaus (nik uh lay' uhs)
Ophrah (of' ruh)
Othniel (oth' nee uhl)
Parmenas (pahr' huh nuhs)
Perizzite (per' i zite)
Prochorus (prok' uh ruhs)
Ramah (ray' muh)
Sadducee (sad' joo see)
Sanhedrin (san hee' druhn)
Seir (see' uhr)
Seraph (ser' uf)
Shamgar (sham' gahr)
*shaqed* (shaw kade')
*shoqed* (show kade')
Sisera (sis' uh ruh)
Taanach (tay' uh nak)
Tekoa (tuh koh' uh)
theophany (thee of' uh nee)
Theophilus (thee of' uh luhs)
Timnah (tim' nuh)
Timon (ti' muhn)
Tob (tob)
Uzziah (uh zi' uh)
Wadi (wah' dee)
Zalmunna (zal muhn' uh)
Zebah (zee' buh)
Zebulun (zeb' yuh luhn)
Zedekiah (zed uh ki' uh)
Zorah (zor' uh)

## UNIT 1: CALLED TO BE STRONG
# DEBORAH AND BARAK

---

### PREVIEWING THE LESSON

**Lesson Scripture:** Judges 4:1-10
**Background Scripture:** Judges 4–5
**Key Verse:** Judges 4:9a

**Focus of the Lesson:**
People called to be leaders may doubt their capabilities. How do leaders deal with their doubts? Barak willingly went into battle after the prophetess Deborah agreed to accompany him.

**Goals for the Learners:**
(1) to grasp the status of Israel and its changing leadership dynamics during the time of Deborah.
(2) to identify with Barak's sense of inadequacy and Deborah's sense of confidence and pragmatism.
(3) to welcome godly counsel and be willing to share such wisdom with others.

**Supplies:**
Bibles, newsprint and marker, paper and pencils, hymnals

---

### READING THE SCRIPTURE

**NRSV**
Lesson Scripture: Judges 4:1-10
¹The Israelites again did what was evil in the sight of the Lord, after Ehud died. ²So the Lord sold them into the hand of King Jabin of Canaan, who reigned in Hazor; the commander of his army was Sisera, who lived in Harosheth-ha-goiim. ³Then the Israelites cried out to the Lord for help; for he had nine hundred chariots of

**CEB**
Lesson Scripture: Judges 4:1-10
¹After Ehud had died, the Israelites again did things that the Lord saw as evil. ²So the Lord gave them over to King Jabin of Canaan, who reigned in Hazor. The commander of his army was Sisera, and he was stationed in Harosheth-ha-goiim. ³The Israelites cried out to the Lord because Sisera had nine hundred iron chariots and

iron, and had oppressed the Israelites cruelly twenty years.

⁴At that time Deborah, a prophetess, wife of Lappidoth, was judging Israel. ⁵She used to sit under the palm of Deborah between Ramah and Bethel in the hill country of Ephraim; and the Israelites came up to her for judgment. ⁶She sent and summoned Barak son of Abinoam from Kedesh in Naphtali, and said to him, "The Lord, the God of Israel, commands you, 'Go, take position at Mount Tabor, bringing ten thousand from the tribe of Naphtali and the tribe of Zebulun. ⁷I will draw out Sisera, the general of Jabin's army, to meet you by the Wadi Kishon with his chariots and his troops; and I will give him into your hand.'" ⁸Barak said to her, "If you will go with me, I will go; but if you will not go with me, I will not go." ⁹**And she said, "I will surely go with you; nevertheless, the road on which you are going will not lead to your glory, for the Lord will sell Sisera into the hand of a woman."** Then Deborah got up and went with Barak to Kedesh. ¹⁰Barak summoned Zebulun and Naphtali to Kedesh; and ten thousand warriors went up behind him; and Deborah went up with him.

had oppressed the Israelites cruelly for twenty years.

⁴Now Deborah, a prophet, the wife of Lappidoth, was a leader of Israel at that time. ⁵She would sit under Deborah's palm tree between Ramah and Bethel in the Ephraim highlands, and the Israelites would come to her to settle disputes. ⁶She sent word to Barak, Abinoam's son, from Kedesh in Naphtali and said to him, "Hasn't the Lord, Israel's God, issued you a command? 'Go and assemble at Mount Tabor, taking ten thousand men from the people of Naphtali and Zebulun with you. ⁷I'll lure Sisera, the commander of Jabin's army, to assemble with his chariots and troops against you at the Kishon River, and then I'll help you overpower him.'"

⁸Barak replied to her, "If you'll go with me, I'll go; but if not, I won't go." ⁹**Deborah answered, "I'll definitely go with you. However, the path you're taking won't bring honor to you, because the Lord will hand over Sisera to a woman."** Then Deborah got up and went with Barak to Kedesh. ¹⁰He summoned Zebulun and Naphtali to Kedesh, and ten thousand men marched out behind him. Deborah marched out with him too.

---

## UNDERSTANDING THE SCRIPTURE

**Introduction.** Judges 4–5 tells the story of Deborah and Barak leading the Israelites into battle against the forces of Jabin, king of Canaan. This is perhaps the same Jabin mentioned in Joshua 11:1. The account focuses, however, on the encounter between Deborah and Barak and Jabin's general, Sisera. Chapter 4 is a narrative that gives the account in story-form.

Chapter 5 is a poem that tells the same story. Most scholars believe the poem is older and that the narrative is based on it (see a similar case with the poem in Exodus 15 and the narrative in Exodus 14). Both chapters emphasize Deborah's fiery leadership and Barak's dutiful assistance.

**Judges 4:1-3.** The introduction to Deborah's leadership in chapter

4 is part of a pattern in Judges first introduced in Judges 2:11-23: Israel "did what was evil in the sight of the LORD" (2:11-13); the LORD gave them over to enemies (2:14-15); "then the LORD raised up judges, who delivered them" (2:16). Like Othniel (3:7-11) and Ehud (3:12-30), Deborah leads an effort to free the Israelites from oppression. The role of the judge was primarily that of charismatic military leader, though some judges had other roles as well.

**Judges 4:4-10.** Deborah's leadership includes two roles other than that of military leader: She is also a prophet and a judge in the traditional sense of that term. As a prophet she stands as mediator between God and humans. Perhaps as an extension of that role, she also acts as arbiter of disputes. In verse 5 she is identified with a tree where the Israelites seek her for "judgment." Deborah summoned Barak to lead the forces in battle. His insistence that she go with him testifies to Deborah's charismatic leadership. Verse 9 includes the ironic statement that "the LORD will sell Sisera into the hand of a woman." The reader might assume "the hand of a woman" refers to Deborah, but it actually refers to Jael the Kenite.

**Judges 4:11-24.** Verse 11 explains how a group of Kenites came to reside so far north of their original territory (see Judges 1:16). Verses 12-23 then report how Barak routed the forces of Sisera with the help of a Kenite woman. Sisera escaped on foot while Barak pursued Sisera's chariots in another direction. Sisera's retreat to the "tent of Jael, wife of Heber the Kenite" (or "a woman of the Kenite community") assumes a world dominated by tribal chieftains (4:17). Sisera believed Heber was sympathetic to him, and Jael gave that impression by welcoming Sisera into the tent (4:18). Jael here is portrayed in language that suggests either a mother who dotes over a child or as a lover, or perhaps as an ambiguous mix of the two. She extended hospitality to Sisera by giving him milk to drink when asked only for water (4:19). The milk caused him to sleep. When he fell asleep beneath the cover Jael placed over him she approached him "softly" (4:21, stealthily). She then took in her hands a tent stake and mallet and drove the stake through Sisera's temple.

**Judges 5:1-5.** "When locks are long" may refer to the long hair of soldiers, a sign of fierceness and wildness (5:1). The poetic version of the battle is a hymn of praise ("I will make melody to the LORD," 5:3). Verses 4-5 are similar to ancient poetry that speaks of God on the march to God's mountain abode (Psalm 68:7). Seir is another name for the territory of Edom. It sounds like the word for "hairy" (*sear*), which aided the association of this territory with Esau (Genesis 25:25).

**Judges 5:6-11.** Shamgar was judge before Deborah (see Judges 3:31). The picture of caravans ceasing and new gods being chosen is one of anarchy and disorder (5:6, 8). The label "mother" for Deborah refers to her authority and may apply to her prophetic identity, just as Elisha called Elijah "father" (2 Kings 2:12).

**Judges 5:12-23.** Only some of the Israelite tribes participated in the battle. The others are criticized. Note that Gilead and Meroz are not tribes, but they are counted here as Israelite territories that did not come to the aid of the others. Taanach and Megiddo were two major fortresses in northern Israel.

**Judges 5:24-27.** This portion of the hymn focuses on Jael and her encounter with Sisera. The poetic version of Jael killing Sisera differs from the narrative in some details. For example, verse 26 suggests Jael hit Sisera with a blunt object, probably while he consumed the drink she had given him. Tent pegs could be substantial (Isaiah 33:20) and might well have been an object tent-dwellers would have grabbed in an act of self-defense. This picture of the event is confirmed by verse 27, which indicates Sisera fell at Jael's feet after she hit him (rather than Sisera lying under a carpet when Jael struck the blow, as in 4:18, 21). These differences may be largely explained, however, as the differences between poetry and prose and the way the two genres report an event.

**Judges 5:28-31.** The song's final section portrays Sisera's mother waiting for her son to return from battle with the spoil. Her role here, however, probably involves more than merely her motherly concern for her son. She was likely an advisor to the king and a powerful member of his court. She also probably represented a religious faith opposed to the faith of the Israelites. Numerous Canaanite ivory carvings with depictions of women looking out the window have been discovered and the woman in each case seems to represent the goddess Asherah. Hence, Sisera's mother probably represents a religious faith that promoted a way of life characterized by oppressive hierarchical relationships. This understanding of Sisera's mother is borne out by the response she and her attendants make to Sisera's delay in returning from battle. The word her attendants use for "girl" actually means something like "womb" (5:30). It is a crude term that presents female captives as objects. This is an example of the values Deborah and Barak fought to overcome.

## INTERPRETING THE SCRIPTURE

### God's Call to Relieve Oppression

If there is one subject that dominates the Bible it might be freedom. From the story of the Exodus through most of the rest of the Bible, a primary concern is that God's people are victims of oppressive powers and God works to liberate them. One of the "oppressive powers" Scripture is concerned about is sinfulness; thus, oppression from within. But there is arguably a greater concern with oppression from without. We see this in Luke 4:18-19 where Jesus declares that his purpose is to "bring good news to the poor," "release to the captives, and recovery of sight to the blind" and "to let the oppressed go free." Hence, God cares deeply about human freedom and works actively against the powers that hinder freedom.

If God is this concerned with freeing people from oppression, it follows that many of the people God calls into service will be called to take on this concern as well. This is certainly true in the Book of Judges. As we observed in Judges 4:1-3 in Understanding the Scripture, each of the judges appears as part of a pattern in which the Israelites disobey God, God gives them over to their enemies, and the Israelites cry out to God for deliverance. God hears their cries and answers by sending judges to liberate them. Each judge is evaluated, in turn, on the degree to which the judge subdued Israel's enemies and "the land had rest" from war (Judges 3:30; 5:31; 8:28).

So also Deborah's calling should be understood primarily in terms of freeing the oppressed. According to Judges 4:3, when Deborah came to power, King Jabin of Canaan had "oppressed the Israelites cruelly twenty years." What is more, Jabin represents a reliance on force and cruelty that the Israelites are to reject when they settle in the land. Jabin's instruments of cruelty were his military forces. He had "nine hundred chariots of iron" (4:3). Israel was to operate on different principles and was to reject military might as the basis of their power (Deuteronomy 17:14-20; Psalm 20:7).

Since Deborah is the instrument of God's deliverance from Jabin's oppressive forces, it might seem that Deborah's actions merely counter Jabin and Sisera with more military might. Judges 4 makes clear, however, that God fought for Israel and this was the source of Israel's strength. Indeed, God's call to Barak declares, "I will draw out Sisera" and "I will give him into your hand" (4:7). The emphasis in the story in Judges 4 is that not that Deborah and Barak defeated Sisera but that God delivered him to them. This point is even clearer in Judges 5, which is a hymn of praise to God for the victory over the Canaanite forces. Judges 5:20 even says "the stars fought from heaven, from their courses they fought against Sisera." In other words, the main calling of Deborah and Barak is to trust in God to deliver God's promises.

### A Fiery Leader

Although the primary call for Deborah and Barak is to trust in God, they still have gifts and talents to be used in God's service. The character of Deborah is particularly important in that regard. Many leaders who are called to special tasks have charisma and passion. That certainly seems to be the case with Deborah. In fact, Deborah's name may indicate something about her fiery character. According to most translations, Judges 4:4 identifies her as the "wife of Lappidoth." This expression, however, could be translated at least two other ways. It could be rendered "woman of Lappidoth" thus identifying her with a place rather than with a husband. But even more intriguing is the translation "woman of fire." Lappidoth means "torches" and it could well refer to Deborah's personality and character. If understood this way, the focus is on Deborah's charisma. She is a fiery figure, like Elijah, one chosen by God and endowed with extraordinary gifts. Whether this is the intention of the label or not, Deborah is a prime example of a leader who draws people to her and motivates them by the force of her personality.

The force of Deborah's personality is apparent in at least two ways in Judges 4. First, she has an expanded role in comparison to many of the other judges. Deborah not only leads the Israelites in battle, she also settles disputes between fellow Israelites (4:5) and she delivers messages from God as a prophet (4:4). She is the epitome of charisma, and God uses that trait to meet the needs of the people. Second, when Deborah delivers the divine message to Barak that he is to lead the army into battle, Barak responds that he will answer the call only if Deborah will go with him (4:8). God uses Deborah's fiery personality to lead the Israelites in general and to assist Barak in particular in responding faithfully to his own call. So although we acknowledge that God calls, empowers, and ultimately accomplishes God's purpose, we must also recognize that an individual who uses his or her gifts fully in response to God's call can make a dramatic impact on the world.

### Not for Your Glory

One of the most intriguing themes of Judges 4 and 5 is the unexpected triumph by people who would normally take a secondary role or no role at all. An important part of this theme is the fact that Barak, Deborah's general, takes a back seat to her and to another woman, Jael. He shows dependence on Deborah when he declares that he will not go to battle if she does not go with him. But more important, Deborah declares to him that the battle will not bring him glory (4:9). In other words, Barak's call is to fill a supportive role or at least one that does not garner the most attention. If God calls charismatic figures like Deborah who take leading roles, God also calls people who will be part of a supporting cast. In Judges 4 and 5, the leading roles go to two women, which may come as a surprise to many modern readers of the Bible. It did not seem to surprise Barak. Perhaps that is because early Israelite society was quite open to women's leadership (see the prominent role of Achsah in Judges 1:11-15). Whatever the reason, Barak was faithful in answering his call because he accepted the secondary role God had for him.

In his commentary on the Book of Judges, Clinton McCann labels his comments on chapters 4 and 5 "Women to the Rescue." Indeed, Barak, whose name means "lightning," was content not only not to be the greatest flash in the story but also to see a woman get the greatest share of glory. But the issue of who received the greatest accolades has another important twist. When Deborah declared to Barak "the LORD will sell Sisera into the hand of a woman" (4:9), readers might expect the woman to be Deborah. But as we know, it is another woman, Jael, who kills Sisera (4:17-22). Hence, the greatest point about receiving glory might be that when it comes to answering God's call it is God who receives the glory and *all* human actors play supporting roles.

## SHARING THE SCRIPTURE

### PREPARING TO LEAD

#### Preparing Our Hearts

Ponder this week's devotional reading from Hebrews 11:29-40. Here the writer continues a roll call of the faithful, where Barak is mentioned (11:32), but not Deborah. Speculate as to why she may be omitted. What do you learn about these Israelite servants of God? How might their stories of faithfulness motivate you in your own faith journey?

Pray that you and the students will be strong and confident in your faith in the Lord.

*Preparing Our Minds*

Study the background Scripture from Judges 4–5 and the lesson Scripture from Judges 4:1-10.

Consider this question: *How do leaders deal with their doubts?*

Write on newsprint:

❏ questions for Goal 3 in Sharing the Scripture.

❏ information for next week's lesson, found under Continue the Journey.

❏ activities for further spiritual growth in Continue the Journey.

Familiarize yourself with Close-up: The Judges, which you will use for Goal 1 in Sharing the Scripture.

## LEADING THE CLASS

*(1) Gather to Learn*

❖ Welcome everyone and pray that those who have come today will find the strength and confidence to answer God's call on their lives.

❖ Read this quotation from A. W. Tozer (1897–1963): **"A true and safe leader is likely to be one who has no desire to lead but is forced into a position of leadership by the inward pressure of the Holy Spirit and the press of the external situation."**

❖ Encourage the participants to debate Tozer's point. You may want to use these questions to spark discussion: How does the Holy Spirit press people to see a need and step up to lead? Why might people not want to assume a leadership role, or feel unfit to take on such responsibility? If Tozer is correct, what might we say about leaders who jump at the chance to assume power, especially those who must spend huge sums to be elected to public office?

❖ Read aloud today's focus statement: **People called to be leaders may doubt their capabilities. How do leaders deal with their doubts? Barak willingly went into battle after the prophetess Deborah agreed to accompany him.**

*(2) Goal 1: Grasp the Status of Israel and Its Changing Leadership Dynamics During the Time of Deborah*

❖ Introduce the first unit of this summer's quarter by reading all or portions of Close-up: The Judges. Focus especially on the role of the judge and the cycle that begins with apostasy, which calls forth the need for a judge.

❖ Choose a volunteer to read Judges 4:1-10.

❖ Discuss these questions:

1. **What aspects of the cycle that is repeated in Judges do you see in this passage?** (See Judges 4:1-3 in Understanding the Scripture, as well as the second paragraph of Close-up: The Judges to review the cycle.)

2. **Why was Deborah raised up as a judge?** (See God's Call to Relieve Oppression in Interpreting the Scripture.)

3. **How would you describe Deborah as a leader?** (See Judges 4:4-10 in Understanding the Scripture and A Fiery Leader in Interpreting the Scripture.)

4. **What was Barak called to do?** (See Judges 4:6-7.)

5. **How did Barak respond when Deborah told him what God had commanded him to do?** (See Judges 4:8. Note that his request for

Deborah to accompany him and the troops may be seen as a sign of weakness, but it may also be understood as Barak's desire to continue to receive God's direction through Deborah.)

6. **Deborah told Barak that what he was doing would not lead to his glory, because God would give King Jabin's commander, Sisera, "into the hand of a woman" (4:9.) A reader may assume that Deborah was referring to herself as that woman. Scan the rest of chapter 4 to see to whom Deborah was referring.**

❖ Conclude by reading the final paragraph from God's Call to Relieve Oppression in Interpreting the Scripture to emphasize that God was the main actor in this story.

*(3) Goal 2: Identify with Barak's Sense of Inadequacy and Deborah's Sense of Confidence and Pragmatism*

❖ Read: **We can find reluctant leaders in the Bible and throughout history. Perhaps Moses is the perfect model for such a leader. He was content shepherding sheep in the back country and was not seeking a leadership role; he gave God a long list of reasons why he was not the right person to lead the Hebrew people out of Egypt; and throughout the sojourn in the wilderness Moses had to contend with complainers who really did not want him as their leader. Barak, likewise, felt inadequate to lead, but God used him to accomplish God's purposes.**

❖ Invite the students to talk with a partner or threesome about a situation in which they felt inadequate to take responsibility. This situation could be in the church, the workplace, the community, or home. Suggest that they answer questions such as: How did you move from a sense of "I can't do this" to "with God's help all things are possible"? Perhaps something you read or a person you talked with or a prayer that you knew was answered pushed you forward. How did this boost of confidence empower you to do what needed to be done, despite your feelings of inadequacy?

*(4) Goal 3: Welcome Godly Counsel and Share Such Wisdom with Others*

❖ Observe that Deborah gave Barak godly counsel, which he accepted.

❖ Form small groups to discuss these questions, which you will post on newsprint:

1. **What, for you, are the marks of godly counsel?**
2. **Where or to whom do you look to find such counsel?**
3. **How do you share godly counsel with others?**

❖ Reconvene the class and ask a spokesperson to give a summary of his or her group's discussion.

❖ Distribute paper and pencils. Read these additional questions aloud and invite the students to jot down responses, which they will not be asked to share with the class:

1. **What situation in my own life is causing me doubt or uncertainty?** (pause)
2. **What will I do this week to seek godly counsel?** (pause)

*(5) Continue the Journey*

❖ Pray that as the learners depart, they will be open to seeking out others for help with their doubts, even as they are open to others who seek them out for counsel.

❖ Post information for next week's session on newsprint for the students to copy:
- Title: Gideon's Call
- Background Scripture: Judges 6–8
- Lesson Scripture: Judges 6:11-18
- Focus of the Lesson: People sometimes view their circumstances as a hindrance to being effective leaders. How do they deal with their doubts? Gideon voiced his doubts and requested a miraculous sign.

❖ Challenge the adults to grow spiritually by completing one or more of these activities related to this week's session.

(1) Compare Judges 4, a prose account, with Judges 5, a poetic account often referred to as The Song of Deborah. How are these accounts similar and different? Which one do you find most inspiring? Why?

(2) Look for opportunities to bolster someone who may have doubts by sharing a pertinent experience of your own.

(3) Build up your own confidence by reading about biblical characters or historical figures (for example, George Washington) who really did not want the jobs they were called to do. How did they manage? What lessons can you learn from them?

❖ Sing or read aloud "¡Canta, Débora, Canta!"

❖ Conclude today's session by leading the class in this benediction, which is adapted from Isaiah 6:8, the key verse for July 9: **In response to your call, O God, I say, "Here am I, send me!" Amen.**

## UNIT 2: CALLED TO BE STRONG
# GIDEON'S CALL

---

### PREVIEWING THE LESSON

**Lesson Scripture:** Judges 6:11-18
**Background Scripture:** Judges 6–8
**Key Verse:** Judges 6:12

#### Focus of the Lesson:
People sometimes view their circumstances as a hindrance to being effective leaders. How do they deal with their doubts? Gideon voiced his doubts and requested a miraculous sign.

#### Goals for the Learners:
(1) to understand that God's criteria for choosing leaders differ from those set by humans.
(2) to reexperience a time of feeling unqualified for a task because of perceived inadequacies in "pedigree."
(3) to embrace the call of God in building personal confidence.

#### Supplies:
Bibles, newsprint and marker, paper and pencils, hymnals

---

### READING THE SCRIPTURE

NRSV
Lesson Scripture: Judges 6:11-18

¹¹Now the angel of the LORD came and sat under the oak at Ophrah, which belonged to Joash the Abiezrite, as his son Gideon was beating out wheat in the wine press, to hide it from the Midianites. **¹²The angel of the LORD appeared to him and said to him, "The LORD is with you, you mighty warrior."** ¹³Gideon answered him, "But sir, if the LORD is with us,

CEB
Lesson Scripture: Judges 6:11-18

¹¹Then the LORD's messenger came and sat under the oak at Ophrah that belonged to Joash the Abiezrite. His son Gideon was threshing wheat in a winepress to hide it from the Midianites. **¹²The LORD's messenger appeared to him and said, "The LORD is with you, mighty warrior!"**

¹³But Gideon replied to him, "With all due respect, my Lord, if the LORD

why then has all this happened to us? And where are all his wonderful deeds that our ancestors recounted to us, saying, 'Did not the LORD bring us up from Egypt?' But now the LORD has cast us off, and given us into the hand of Midian." ¹⁴Then the LORD turned to him and said, "Go in this might of yours and deliver Israel from the hand of Midian; I hereby commission you." ¹⁵He responded, "But sir, how can I deliver Israel? My clan is the weakest in Manasseh, and I am the least in my family." ¹⁶The LORD said to him, "But I will be with you, and you shall strike down the Midianites, every one of them." ¹⁷Then he said to him, "If now I have found favor with you, then show me a sign that it is you who speak with me. ¹⁸Do not depart from here until I come to you, and bring out my present, and set it before you." And he said, "I will stay until you return."

is with us, why has all this happened to us? Where are all his amazing works that our ancestors recounted to us, saying, 'Didn't the LORD bring us up from Egypt?' But now the LORD has abandoned us and allowed Midian to overpower us."

¹⁴Then the LORD turned to him and said, "You have strength, so go and rescue Israel from the power of Midian. Am I not personally sending you?"

¹⁵But again Gideon said to him, "With all due respect, my Lord, how can I rescue Israel? My clan is the weakest in Manasseh, and I'm the youngest in my household."

¹⁶The LORD replied, "Because I'm with you, you'll defeat the Midianites as if they were just one person."

¹⁷Then Gideon said to him, "If I've gained your approval, please show me a sign that it's really you speaking with me. ¹⁸Don't leave here until I return, bring out my offering, and set it in front of you."

The LORD replied, "I'll stay until you return."

---

## UNDERSTANDING THE SCRIPTURE

**Introduction.** The story of Gideon is one of mostly positive leadership. As a devoted follower of Israel's God, Gideon destroys idols and helps the Israelites worship faithfully. But Gideon also does some very bad things at the end of his career as judge, most notably reintroducing idolatry, as reported in Judges 8:22-28. This mix of good and bad is typical of human leadership.

**Judges 6:1-10.** The introduction to the story of Gideon records the pattern that preceded previous judges: Israel is unfaithful; God gives Israel into the hand of enemies; Israel cries to the Lord. The details of oppression here are new, with the enemies being the Midianites and Amalekites. The prophet mentioned in verse 8 delivers a message about pure worship that is typical of many prophets. It is not unusual for a prophet with such a message to be anonymous (2 Kings 21:10-15).

**Judges 6:11-18.** The story of the call of Gideon follows a pattern like that of many other call stories in the Bible: In such stories (1) the person being called meets God or an angel (6:11-13);

(2) God commissions the person to a special task (6:14); (3) the person being commissioned expresses doubt or questions the task (6:15); (4) God gives a sign of assurance that the task will be successful (6:16). Gideon's commissioning is particularly like that of Moses (Exodus 3). Both men protest the call by saying essentially, "I do not have the authority to do this" (Exodus 3:11; Judges 6:15). Also, God assures both men they will be able to answer the call with the promise, "I will be with you" (Exodus 3:12; Judges 6:16). Although God gives signs to Gideon (and Moses) to show further that he will succeed, the main promise remains God's presence and Gideon's main challenge is to go in faith.

**Judges 6:19-27.** In response to the encounter with the angel of the Lord Gideon prepares a ritual meal. An ephah is approximately a bushel, so he prepares enough to feed a crowd. This is perhaps a way of saying Gideon responded in an exaggerated manner. Afterward the Lord ordered Gideon to tear down the image of Baal that belonged to his father. Baal was a fertility god, believed to be responsible for the production of crops and reproduction of animals. Therefore, the bull was an appropriate symbol. The word "Baal" means "husband." As such Baal was thought to partner sexually with the ground to produce crops. The Asherah was a sacred pole that probably represented a goddess who was Baal's consort. Thus this worship involved both sexes and had at its center their sexual union. Israel's God was thought to give the produce of the ground, but not to be of the same substance with the ground. This distance from creation made Israel's God somewhat unique among the deities of the day.

**Judges 6:28-35.** The people of the town are angry when they discover the sacred items have been destroyed. Their anger is understandable from an economic point of view. Baal represented wealth (the growth of crops). Therefore, the destruction of the image of Baal was thought to be bad for the economy. It helps Gideon that his father, who owns the idol, defends his son. Because of his battle against Baal, Gideon received the nickname Jerubbaal, which means "let Baal contend" (6:32).

**Judges 6:36-40.** Gideon's request for a sign seems to show a lack of faith. The two signs with fleece show an increasing need for certainty. The first sign is that fleece on the ground would be wet from the dew, but the ground around it would be dry. This is not hard to accomplish since the fleece could soak up the dew around it. But the second sign Gideon requests is much harder. If the dew wet the ground, surely the fleece would not be dry. But God gives both signs just as Gideon asks.

**Judges 7:1-25.** The story of the battle against the Midianites is testimony to how Israel is to understand military might. The Israelites will win the battle because God is going to "give" the Midianites into their hands (7:2). Hence, God declares to Gideon there are too many soldiers. The problem is they may say after victory that their might gave them the battle. So Gideon sends soldiers home in groups until only three hundred are left. The battle itself is also unusual. Gideon uses torches, jars, and trumpets as weapons. The main point is that Gideon approaches the battle with confidence in God and God gives the victory. Gideon moves from fear and uncertainty (seen in

Judges 6:36-40) to faith in the battle (7:24).

**Judges 8:1-21.** Despite Gideon's good start in Judges 7, now he seems to turn from humility to pride, from dependence on God to self-reliance. If Judges 7 was all about God giving victory to Gideon, Judges 8 is about Gideon claiming victory for himself. Note Gideon's language: "I am pursuing Zebah and Zalmunna, the kings of Midian" (8:5); "When I come back victorious, I will break down this tower" (8:9). Thus Gideon speaks of winning, not receiving the battle from God.

**Judges 8:22-28.** After boasting of winning victory himself, Gideon returns to humility and to correct theology when the Israelites ask him to rule over them. In Hebrew the word for "rule" comes from the same root as the word "king." Essentially Gideon is turning down the offer to be king because he recognizes that God alone is Israel's king. Nevertheless, Gideon then makes an ephod that leads the people into idolatry. An ephod was an elaborate vestment normally worn by a priest. It was perhaps thought to have magical power. The object became a snare to Gideon because it became a means by which he controlled the people. Thus, while Gideon formally rejected the role of king, he could not resist the power to rule that came through the ephod.

**Judges 8:29-35.** Upon Gideon's death his son took control. Ironically, the son's name, Abimelech means "my father is king." The Israelites fell further into idolatry despite the good that Gideon did to point them to the true God.

---

## INTERPRETING THE SCRIPTURE

### The Lord Is with You

Gideon was an unlikely candidate to rescue Israel. As Gideon's objections to his call indicate, he is not from a privileged family: "My clan is the weakest in Manasseh, and I am the least in my family" (Judges 6:15). But God's call to Gideon is not based on Gideon's greatness, wealth, or family influence. Rather, it is based on God's choice to support him and to be present to strengthen him. Twice the promise of the Lord's presence comes to Gideon. First the angel tells him "The LORD is with you" (6:12), and then the Lord says it directly, "I will be with you" (6:16).

Throughout Scripture this promise of the Lord's presence is the most important promise for those God calls. It is the key promise to Moses (Exodus 3:12) and Joshua (Joshua 1:5). In the New Testament it is the main promise given to Mary (Luke 1:28). So also the "the LORD is with you" is meant to stir and support Gideon as he answers the call to lead the Israelites. If this is the most essential promise in the call or commissioning, however, it is also the most difficult to believe. Both Moses and Gideon need and ask for more. Gideon asks for tangible signs, not once but twice, in order to go forward into his call. He needs to see God make the fleece wet, then dry (Judges 6:36-40). But it is just this difficulty of resting in the promise of God's presence that makes it so important. The primary requirement to embrace God's call is faith. It is crucial to trust that God's call is real, that God will not abandon the one God calls. We see why this is difficult when Gideon asks the angel, "If the LORD is with us, why then has all this happened to us?" (6:13).

Indeed, the promise that God is with us sometimes requires us to look to the future with the belief that the present trouble will end. It does not give us constant comfort that all is well at the moment. In fact, this promise perhaps more often than not comes in the midst of hardship and uncertainty. This was the case when God promised the people of Judah through Isaiah they would know "God with us" (Immanuel; Isaiah 7:14; 8:8, 10). The promise of a child named "God with us" was really a promise that the present trouble would soon end (Isaiah 8:10). So also Gideon had to believe God would bring him and his people through the trouble they experienced, not that they would be free from it altogether. This assurance for those called by God culminates in the ministry of Jesus, the ultimate sign that God is with us. That one took pain, brokenness, and hardship on himself to show us finally that we are not alone. So the calling upon our lives, as upon Gideon's life, is finally a calling to enter the pain of others, as Christ did for us.

### Go in This Might of Yours

When Gideon complains that his people have been cast off by God and that he is inadequate to lead them, the angel's words to him may seem rather strange: "Go in this might of yours and deliver Israel" (Judges 6:14). The angel had earlier addressed Gideon as a "mighty warrior" (6:12), but there is nothing yet in the story to suggest he is in any sense mighty.

The problem, however, is that Gideon does not see the might that is within him. Gideon's reluctance to recognize his strength shows humility, which is essential for answering God's call to serve others. But one who answers such a call must also realize that he or she is created in the image of God and therefore has potential for greatness.

Believing that God has given us potential for greatness may be the scariest part of God's promises for us to embrace. As Marianne Williamson famously says, "Our deepest fear is not that we are inadequate. Our deepest fear is that we are powerful beyond measure." She goes on to say, "We ask ourselves, 'Who am I to be brilliant, gorgeous, talented, fabulous?' Actually, who are you not to be? You are a child of God. Your playing small does not serve the world. There is nothing enlightened about shrinking so that people won't feel insecure around you. We were born to make manifest the glory of God that is within us."

The call of God thus requires us to assert our strengths so God can use us, but without deluding ourselves into thinking we can act out of an inherent strength. Our might is in knowing we are children of God and allowing the glory of God to show through us. The rise and fall of Gideon's leadership shows how delicate the balance can be. Gideon begins with doubts about the gifts God gave him to lead the people. But when Gideon tasted success in leadership he went too far. The key to answering God's call, which Gideon did not perfectly realize, is to learn to reflect the glory of God, but not our own glory.

### A Warrior for God?

The angel of the Lord who addressed Gideon called him "mighty warrior" (Judges 6:12) and the Lord commissioned him to deliver Israel from the hand of Midian (6:14). That raises the question of whether God's call is ever issued in a way that promotes violence. Such a call would seem to be at odds with the gospel, which promotes love of enemies and nonviolence. The call of Gideon has two dimensions that help address the question. First, it occurs when the Midianites are cruelly oppressing the Israelites. The angel appears to Gideon while he is beating out wheat in secret, lest the Midianites capture it. This enemy would literally starve the people of Israel. So the call of Gideon, like the call of the other judges and like the call of Moses is to bring freedom to people who are in bondage. That is also part of Jesus'

vision of the kingdom of God (Matthew 6:10).

Second, although Gideon must serve as a military leader to answer his call, God is the one who really does the fighting, as we observed in Judges 7. This may seem like a hair-splitting distinction, but it is actually quite important. Violence is imposing one's will on another by force. *That* is absolutely not what Gideon is called to do. Rather, he is called to submit to God's will. When Gideon begins to tout his will, his abilities, and his plans he falls from God's call into idolatry (Judges 8). As observed, the command to "go in this might of yours" (6:14) is a command to reflect the glory of God. Gideon's might is evident only to the extent that he gives his life over to the work of God. For Christians this work is always shaped by the life and teachings of Jesus.

---

## SHARING THE SCRIPTURE

### PREPARING TO LEAD

#### Preparing Our Hearts

Ponder this week's devotional reading from Psalm 83:1-12, 18, which is a communal lament. Although no particular situation has been identified as the impetus for writing this psalm, the psalmist describes a conspiracy among Israel's enemies to destroy God's people. Which countries are involved in this plot? What incidents do verses 9-12 call to mind? What does verse 18 suggest about what the poet hopes will happen to Israel's enemies?

Pray that you and the students will be strong in the face of tribulations caused by foes.

#### Preparing Our Minds

Study the background Scripture from Judges 6–8 and the lesson Scripture from Judges 6:11-18.

Consider this question: *How do leaders deal with their doubts about the impact of their circumstances on their abilities to be effective leaders?*

Write on newsprint:
❏ information for next week's lesson, found under Continue the Journey.
❏ activities for further spiritual growth in Continue the Journey.

Determine how you might use any of the features that precede the first lesson of this quarter in today's session. Familiarize yourself with the suggested portions of The Big Picture: The Call of God for Goal 1 in Sharing the Scripture.

## LEADING THE CLASS

### (1) Gather to Learn

❖ Welcome everyone and pray that those who have come today will bring their doubts before God.

❖ Read: **The critically acclaimed 2010 movie *The King's Speech* is based on the true story of King George VI of England. After his father, King George V died and his brother, King Edward VIII, abdicated the throne to marry American socialite Wallis Simpson, George VI found himself as the ruling monarch of a country on the brink of war. George VI had a stuttering problem that an unorthodox practitioner helped him to overcome, despite the king's many doubts. After much hard work, this reluctant leader, who previously was very inept as a public speaker, was able to deliver an inspiring radio address that helped to unite his people for battle.**

❖ Read aloud today's focus statement: **People sometimes view their circumstances as a hindrance to being effective leaders. How do they deal with their doubts? Gideon voiced his doubts and requested a miraculous sign.**

### (2) Goal 1: Understand that God's Criteria for Choosing Leaders Differ from Those Set by Humans

❖ Read or retell The Big Picture: The Call of God, beginning with the first paragraph and concluding at the end of The Call of the Judges.

❖ Recap Introduction and Judges 6:1-10 in Understanding the Scripture to set the scene for Gideon's call.

❖ Select a volunteer to read Judges 6:11-18.

❖ Discuss these questions:
1. **How does Gideon respond to his call?** (See Judges 6:11-18 in Understanding the Scripture.)
2. **Why is Gideon an unlikely person to lead his people?** (See the first paragraph of The Lord Is with You in Interpreting the Scripture.)
3. **The angel refers to Gideon as a "mighty warrior" (6:12), a description that Gideon cannot fathom. How does God make it possible for Gideon to take on the responsibility of leadership?** (See Go in This Might of Yours and The Lord Is with You, both found in Interpreting the Scripture.)

❖ Tell "the rest of the story" by using information in Understanding the Scripture, beginning with verses 6:19-27, and then assess together the effectiveness of Gideon's leadership. Point out how God's promise to be with Gideon was fulfilled as God gave the victory to the Israelites.

### (3) Goal 2: Reexperience a Time of Feeling Unqualified for a Task Because of Perceived Inadequacies in "Pedigree"

❖ Read this information about Mother Teresa, the widely known and admired nun who ministered to the poorest of the poor in India: **A collection of letters written to spiritual advisors, *Mother Teresa: Come**

*Be My Light,* was released ten years after her death, despite her wish that they be destroyed. These letters revealed that Teresa wrestled with feelings that Jesus, who she passionately loved and served with devotion, was absent from her. According to Rev. James Martin, a Jesuit priest, "this [book] is a real treasure for not only believers, but even doubters and skeptics. . . I think it also makes her much more accessible to the everyday believer. It shows that even the saints struggle in their spiritual lives and that they don't have it easier than we do. They sometimes have it harder than we do."

❖ Encourage the students to speculate about how difficult it might be to pursue a calling for which they may have felt unqualified and/or failed to experience the presence of Christ as they attempted to fulfill their calling.

❖ Provide a few moments of silence during which the students are to reflect on a time when they felt they were unequal to a challenge. How did this situation end? How did they experience God's presence and leading in the midst of this situation?

### (4) Goal 3: Embrace the Call of God in Building Personal Confidence

❖ Post a sheet of newsprint and invite the students to brainstorm answers to this question: **Why do people lack confidence, especially when they feel God is calling them to do something?** Possible answers include fear of failing, fear of succeeding, feelings of inadequacy, unwillingness to appear stupid or foolish, lack of self-esteem, belief that the task cannot be achieved, unwillingness to take a risk.

❖ Review the list and ask: **Are any of the reasons we have suggested similar to ones that you have heard Bible characters use when called by God? If so, who—and how did God alleviate this lack of confidence?**

❖ Distribute paper and pencils. Encourage the students to jot down reasons why they lack confidence about answering God's call to do a specific task. Here are some examples: "I don't want to witness to someone because I don't know what to say," "I can't teach Sunday school because I don't know my Bible that well," "I can't answer God's call to give more financial resources to the church because an emergency may come up and I may need that money."

❖ Suggest that the adults take home their papers and review them throughout the week, prayerfully asking for the confidence and courage to do whatever God calls them to do.

### (5) Continue the Journey

❖ Pray that as the learners depart they will feel confident that God is with them at all times.

❖ Post information for next week's session on newsprint for the students to copy:

- **Title: Jephthah Answers the Call**
- **Background Scripture: Judges 11**
- **Lesson Scripture: Judges 11:4-11, 29-31**
- **Focus of the Lesson: People called to be leaders may question the motives of their supporters. How do these leaders know if their supporters' motives are sincere? Jephthah discussed the**

inconsistencies in the behavior of his supporters and established conditions for his leadership.

❖ Challenge the adults to grow spiritually by completing one or more of these activities related to this week's session.

(1) Identify contemporary leaders who strike you as shocking choices. What traits did these people have that impelled people to support these unlikely leaders? What lessons can you learn from them about your own possibilities as a leader?

(2) Keep a journal of "God sightings," that is, revelations of God that you experienced through other people, prayer, situations, worship, or by other means. How does an awareness of these encounters with God empower you to make faithful decisions concerning what God wants for—and from—you?

(3) Talk with a trusted mature Christian about a call you are currently experiencing. Enlist this person to help you test the validity of this call and determine what your next steps might be.

❖ Sing or read aloud "Praise the Lord Who Reigns Above."

❖ Conclude today's session by leading the class in this benediction, which is adapted from Isaiah 6:8, the key verse for July 9: **In response to your call, O God, I say, "Here am I, send me!" Amen.**

## UNIT 1: CALLED TO BE STRONG
# JEPHTHAH ANSWERS THE CALL

---

### PREVIEWING THE LESSON

**Lesson Scripture:** Judges 11:4-11, 29-31
**Background Scripture:** Judges 11
**Key Verse:** Judges 11:9

**Focus of the Lesson:**
People called to be leaders may question the motives of their supporters. How do these leaders know if their supporters' motives are sincere?
Jephthah discussed the inconsistencies in the behavior of his supporters
and established conditions for his leadership.

**Goals for the Learners:**
(1) to acknowledge that people who have had disagreements can unite to
    defeat a common foe.
(2) to feel remorse for alienating others.
(3) to consider the importance of reaching "a meeting of the minds" on
    motives and expected outcomes before accepting a leadership role.

**Supplies:**
Bibles, newsprint and marker, paper and pencils, hymnals

---

### READING THE SCRIPTURE

**NRSV**
Lesson Scripture: Judges 11:4-11, 29-31

⁴After a time the Ammonites made war against Israel. ⁵And when the Ammonites made war against Israel, the elders of Gilead went to bring Jephthah from the land of Tob. ⁶They said to Jephthah, "Come and be our commander, so that we may fight with the Ammonites." ⁷But Jephthah

**CEB**
Lesson Scripture: Judges 11:4-11, 29-31

⁴Sometime afterward, the Ammonites made war against Israel. ⁵And when the Ammonites attacked Israel, Gilead's elders went to bring Jephthah back from the land of Tob. ⁶They said to him, "Come be our commander so we can fight against the Ammonites." ⁷But Jephthah replied to Gilead's

said to the elders of Gilead, "Are you not the very ones who rejected me and drove me out of my father's house? So why do you come to me now when you are in trouble?" ⁸The elders of Gilead said to Jephthah, "Nevertheless, we have now turned back to you, so that you may go with us and fight with the Ammonites, and become head over us, over all the inhabitants of Gilead." ⁹**Jephthah said to the elders of Gilead, "If you bring me home again to fight with the Ammonites, and the Lord gives them over to me, I will be your head."** ¹⁰And the elders of Gilead said to Jephthah, "The Lord will be witness between us; we will surely do as you say." ¹¹So Jephthah went with the elders of Gilead, and the people made him head and commander over them; and Jephthah spoke all his words before the Lord at Mizpah.

²⁹Then the spirit of the Lord came upon Jephthah, and he passed through Gilead and Manasseh. He passed on to Mizpah of Gilead, and from Mizpah of Gilead he passed on to the Ammonites. ³⁰And Jephthah made a vow to the Lord, and said, "If you will give the Ammonites into my hand, ³¹then whoever comes out of the doors of my house to meet me, when I return victorious from the Ammonites, shall be the Lord's, to be offered up by me as a burnt offering."

elders, "Aren't you the ones who hated me and drove me away from my father's household? Why are you coming to me now when you're in trouble?"

⁸Gilead's elders answered Jephthah, "That may be, but now we're turning back to you, so come with us and fight the Ammonites. Then you'll become the leader over us and everyone who lives in Gilead."

⁹**And Jephthah said to Gilead's elders, "If you bring me back to fight the Ammonites and the Lord gives them over to me, I alone will be your leader."**

¹⁰Gilead's elders replied to him, "The Lord is our witness; we will surely do what you've said." ¹¹So Jephthah went with Gilead's elders, and the people made him leader and commander over them. At Mizpah before the Lord, Jephthah repeated everything he had said.

²⁹Then the Lord's spirit came on Jephthah. He passed through Gilead and Manasseh, then through Mizpah in Gilead, and from there he crossed over to the Ammonites. ³⁰Jephthah made a solemn promise to the Lord: "If you will decisively hand over the Ammonites to me, ³¹then whatever comes out the doors of my house to meet me when I return victorious from the Ammonites will be given over to the Lord. I will sacrifice it as an entirely burned offering."

---

## UNDERSTANDING THE SCRIPTURE

**Introduction.** The story of Jephthah is the story of an unlikely hero who rises to a position of great power and accomplishment. But the story is also like a Greek tragedy. Jephthah begins with nothing and he works his way into power and wealth by means of his military and negotiating skills. He uses those skills too readily, however, by "negotiating" with God and thereby loses his most prized possession: his daughter. One challenge in reading this story is to understand how Jephthah answers a call and acts to redeem God's people, while he also fails at the most personal level of his life. Jephthah appears as one of the examples of living by faith mentioned in Hebrews 11:32, though he is a flawed character.

**Judges 11:1-3.** The opening of the story of Jephthah reveals something important about his character and how he will answer the call to lead God's people. Jephthah was born and grew up in hardship. As the son of a prostitute, his brothers push him out of the family inheritance since inheritance was based on certainty about the identity of the father. Jephthah was thus left to fend for himself in the world. Ironically he flees to the land of Tob, a name that means "good." What he experienced is obviously not good, but he makes the most of it. He gathers around him disaffected men and they hire themselves out as mercenaries. David will later do a similar thing (1 Samuel 22:2).

**Judges 11:4-11.** The elders of Gilead seek out Jephthah for protection against the Ammonites. Jephthah has them pledge to make him their ruler if he defeats their enemy. So Jephthah wins the support of the elders of Gilead and he then leads them successfully against the Ammonites. In this encounter Jephthah's negotiating skills first appear and lead him to success.

**Judges 11:12-28.** Jephthah again shows himself particularly adept at negotiation. At issue is Israel's possession of traditional Ammonite territory. The Ammonites claim that Israel took the land illegally when coming from Egypt; therefore, Israel's claim on the land is illegitimate. Jephthah adroitly argues that the Israelites took

possession of such territory during the Exodus only because the kings who lived there launched unprovoked attacks on them (11:12-28). He makes the point that the Israelites did not even enter Ammonite territory, but sent envoys to ask for permission. The Ammonite king responded with the unnecessary attack. In response to such unjust action God gave Israel the land. Thus, Jephthah argues that the Israelites have rights to the land and now the Ammonites are in the wrong by trying to recapture it.

**Judges 11:29-33.** Jephthah's making of a vow in itself is not unusual. Numbers 21:1-3, for example, tells of the Israelites making a vow to God in order to seek God's help in battle. What is unusual is the open-ended nature of Jephthah's vow. The expression, "whoever comes out" could be translated just as accurately *"whatever comes out."* Thus, it is possible to speculate that Jephthah assumed a domestic animal would come out of the house. The first floor of houses in this period typically had a central courtyard where domestic animals were kept and a second floor that served as the family's domestic quarters. It was possible that the one "coming out" of the house would be a sheep or goat. But the courtyard was also used for cooking and other domestic chores and would have been a typical workplace for women.

**Judges 11:34-35.** Jephthah's daughter performed a role that was typical in her day, leading a celebration for the army's victory (compare Exodus 15:20-21; 1 Samuel 18:6-7). The note that she was an only child creates an important parallel with Genesis 22:1-19, the story of the sacrifice of Isaac. The label given to Jephthah's daughter (Judges 11:34) is the same term used for Isaac (Genesis 22:2, 12, 16). The emphasis on his daughter being his "only" child suggests this point is primary. She is valued because she is the only child and through her Jephthah will pass on his inheritance and his name. Jephthah's comment to his daughter when he sees her coming out of his house should be understood in this light ("Alas, my daughter! You have brought me very low; you have become the cause of great trouble to me"; 11:35). His "great trouble" refers to the loss of his progeny. Thus, Jephthah, who had worked so hard to overcome his lack of inheritance, now has no one to inherit what he has gained. The label of the daughter as the only child also relates to common ideas about child sacrifice. Where this horrifying practice existed, it was based on the notion that the one who sacrificed a child was giving the very best, the most meaningful thing (the "only") to the deity. In the case of Jephthah as of Abraham, the sacrifice of the child does not mean the child is not valued. To the contrary, the child is most precious. A vow was an irrevocable pledge that carried with it a self-curse. Jephthah is now bound by his promise.

**Judges 11:36-40.** Amazingly, Jephthah's daughter agrees that the vow must be kept. She understands the seriousness of a vow and the necessity of keeping it even though it costs her life. Her desire to "mourn her virginity" refers to the fact that she will die childless. What Jephthah does to himself as a result of the vow (taking away his only child and heir) prevents his daughter from possessing heirs as well. The account of the daughter closes with reference to a mourning rite that is otherwise unknown. But the mourning of childlessness reveals the point of greatest anxiety in this society, namely, the need for children to inherit property and pass on the family name. The greatest tragedy for Jephthah and his daughter is that they possessed this great prize and then lost it because of Jephthah's foolish vow.

---

## INTERPRETING THE SCRIPTURE

### A Nitty Gritty Call

God's call is often presented in Scripture as a profound event, filled with God's holy presence, the recognition on the part of the one called of a need for justice, and the leader's intense desire to fulfill God's purpose. The call of Moses and many of the prophets includes these features. But God's call to other leaders is more practically oriented. In the case of Jephthah, the call is characterized by his negotiation for a position of leadership with people he has reason not to trust. The leaders of Gilead are the very people who cast him out in order to prevent him from gaining an inheritance. But when they are threatened by a foreign military power, they seek out Jephthah for help. Jephthah, in turn, sees this as an opportunity to gain something for himself he would not have otherwise. He says to the elders of Gilead, "If you bring me home again to fight with the Ammonites, and the LORD gives them over to me, I will be your head" (Judges 11:9, key verse).

The story of Jephthah is similar

to the story of Abimelech (Judges 9) and David (1 Samuel 16:1-13) who were forced to find wealth and position apart from the resources of the household of the father (David, being the youngest son, was thus virtually assured of inheriting nothing). Jephthah gathers around him others who were similarly disadvantaged economically and they "went raiding," that is, they became essentially mercenaries or guerrilla fighters. Jephthah acts in this manner like David (1 Samuel 22:2), as well as Jeroboam (2 Chronicles 13:6-7) and Abimelech (Judges 9:4). There is nothing particularly pious about Jephthah in this regard, but God was able to use this mercenary fighter to bring relief from oppression. Sometimes the call of God does not look particularly religious in nature. Yet God is often at work in ordinary and secular contexts to bring about God's purpose.

### Casualties of a Call

God calls imperfect people to accomplish divine purpose, and they in turn bring their flawed character to the task God gives them. It is not surprising, therefore, that many people called into God's service hurt themselves and people close to them as they try to serve God. Jephthah is an extreme case, but he illustrates well how this occurs.

The primary flaw that led to Jephthah's trouble is his willingness to negotiate for success at any cost. At first Jephthah's negotiating skills are quite helpful. He works his way into power and wealth by negotiating with the people of Gilead to be their ruler. Then he negotiates with the Ammonites to establish that his people are in the right. But Jephthah oversteps his bounds when he tries to negotiate with God by making a vow. In the biblical world a vow was a sacred pledge that a person typically made to show devotion to God. It often involved giving something or some service to God in thanksgiving for God's help. For example, Hannah gave her son, Samuel, to God's service because God blessed her with the child (1 Samuel 1–2). But Jephthah makes an open-ended vow to give "whoever" (or whatever) comes out of his house as a sacrifice. Whatever Jephthah may have intended by the language of the vow, he clearly offers more than he should in an attempt to gain God's help in battle. As a result he loses his daughter.

Some readers of this story have also tried to blame God for the death of Jephthah's daughter. They point out that the story is very similar to the story of the sacrifice of Isaac in Genesis 22. In that account, a voice from heaven directs Abraham not to sacrifice Isaac. In Judges 11:34-40, however, God does not speak to Jephthah. This has led some to conclude that God favors the sacrifice of the daughter. This seems an unfair burden to place on the Judges passage, however, for two reasons. First, the story of the sacrifice of Jephthah's daughter seems not to be about God or God's take on the sacrifice of this child, or any child. This part of the story is about Jephthah and his failure.

Second, although the story does not speak specifically against Jephthah's actions in making the vow, it clearly does not show approval of it either. On the other hand, the story does seem to show approval for the daughter. The story ends with the daughter taking initiative and giving herself over to her father's vow. Because of the character of the daughter, although presented briefly in the story, she became a heroic figure in Jewish and Christian tradition. In some Jewish legends, for example, the daughter is held up as a model of self-sacrifice for the good of the community. In fact, in these later reflections the daughter symbolizes Jerusalem, which remains precious to God when destroyed by the enemy.

### The Last Becomes First

Despite Jephthah's tragic miscalculation that resulted in the loss of his daughter, there are redeeming aspects of Jephthah's career that are worth noting. Perhaps chief among them is that Jephthah represents the idea that God chooses those we might least expect to accomplish God's purposes. The story of Jephthah opens with a key piece of information: He is the son of a prostitute. For the original audience of the story this information is not primarily related to the moral issue of prostitution (and Jephthah's father's participation) or to a stigma attached to Jephthah as a child from such a union. Rather, it suggests Jephthah's chances of inheriting property from his father are slim and, therefore, he will have to live by his wits since he will have no economic foundation on which to build. Indeed, when Jephthah's half-brothers reject him, they do so precisely so the inheritance will not be further divided by including him (11:2).

The issue at the beginning of the story is not so much with Jephthah's mother as with the inability to validate that Gilead is his father. In ancient Israelite society the certain identity of the father was crucial for determining rights of inheritance. This issue is at the heart of Old Testament laws concerning virginity and adultery (for example, see Deuteronomy 22:13-30). Because Jephthah had no inheritance he became a kind of Robin Hood, much like David before he became king (1 Samuel 22:1-2).

It should not come as a surprise that God uses someone like Jephthah to accomplish God's purpose. One of the major themes of Scripture is that those who are lowly and overlooked become the focus of God's purposes. Joseph, for example, was the youngest son and cast out by his brothers, but God used him to save them all (Genesis 37–50). Perhaps this is because God favors the lowly, or perhaps the lowly are more readily available to answer God's call. The good news in the story of Jephthah and for all who desire a place in God's work is that God chooses humble people. As the apostle Paul says to the Corinthians, "Consider your own call, brothers and sisters: not many of you were wise by human standards, not many were powerful, not many were of noble birth. But God chose what is foolish in the world to shame the wise; God chose what is weak in the world to shame the strong" (1 Corinthians 1:26-27).

# SHARING THE SCRIPTURE

## PREPARING TO LEAD

### *Preparing Our Hearts*

Ponder this week's devotional reading from Acts 15:6-21 where we hear Paul speaking before the Jewish council concerning how Gentiles were to be included in the church. What arguments does Paul make? What issues of trust do you discern here? Had you been a faithful Jew who heard Paul, what conclusion would you have come to?

Pray that you and the students will be open to people who, from your perspective, are outsiders to the church.

### *Preparing Our Minds*

Study the background Scripture from Judges 11 and the lesson Scripture from Judges 11:4-11, 29-31.

Consider this question: *How can leaders who question the motives of their supporters know if their motives are sincere?*

Write on newsprint:
- ❏ five questions found in Faith in Action: Hearing and Heeding the Call.
- ❏ information for next week's lesson, found under Continue the Journey.
- ❏ activities for further spiritual growth in Continue the Journey.

Plan to use Faith in Action: Hearing and Heeding the Call for the Gather to Learn portion.

Determine how much of the story of Jephthah you wish to tell. You will find options under Goal 1. Remember that even though class members may want to know what happens as a result of his vow, mentioned in verses 30-31 that are part of today's lesson Scripture, the focus of the lesson is on how Jephthah answers the Lord's call.

## LEADING THE CLASS

### *(1) Gather to Learn*

❖ Welcome everyone and pray that those who have come today will be open to answering God's call to serve.

❖ Distribute paper and pencils as students gather. Post the sheet on which you have written the five questions found in Faith in Action: Hearing and Heeding the Call. Provide a few moments for the students to write the questions and then read this activity aloud. Allow time for the adults to talk with a partner or threesome about unmet needs that they see in the community to spark their thinking about what could be done and how they may take a leadership role.

❖ Read aloud today's focus statement: **People called to be leaders may question the motives of their supporters. How do these leaders know if their supporters' motives are sincere? Jephthah discussed the inconsistencies in the behavior of his supporters and established conditions for his leadership.**

### *(2) Goal 1: Acknowledge that People Who Have Had Disagreements Can Unite to Defeat a Common Foe*

❖ Read Introduction and Judges 11:1-3 from Understanding the Scripture to set the stage.

❖ Solicit a volunteer to read Judges 11:4-11 and then summarize these verses by reading or retelling Judges 11:4-11 in Understanding the Scripture.

❖ Also read or retell what happens in this story from Judges 11:12-28 in Understanding the Scripture.

❖ Read Judges 11:29-31 from your Bible. As an option, you may want to retell the rest of the story through verse 40 by referring to Understanding the Scripture.

❖ Read A Nitty Gritty Call from Interpreting the Scripture and ask:

1. **Had you been one of the people of Gilead, would you have supported Jephthah as a leader? Why or why not?**
2. **Had you been Jephthah, who has previously been rejected by the people of Gilead, why would you trust—or distrust—those leaders who are now enlisting your aid?**

*(3) Goal 2: Feel Remorse for Alienating Others*

❖ Form several small groups and read this scenario: **You chair your church's worship committee. Three members have come to you to ask the committee to consider some changes in the Sunday morning schedule. Without consulting the pastor or committee you reply that the schedule is set, so this is not a topic for discussion. After thinking about how you handled the situation, you realize that even though you were polite, members went away feeling that they were not heard and that their idea was stonewalled even before it could be considered. Word trickles back to you that these people, who apparently spoke for a larger group, feel they cannot trust you.**

❖ Invite the groups to discuss how they would feel, knowing they had alienated parishioners. How would they express their remorse and try to rebuild trust?

*(4) Goal 3: Consider the Importance of Reaching "a Meeting of the Minds" on Motives and Expected Outcomes Before Accepting a Leadership Role*

❖ Read this excerpt from Robert K. Greenleaf's influential book *Servant Leadership: A Journey into the Nature of Legitimate Power and Greatness* (1977): **A new moral principle is emerging which holds that the only authority deserving one's allegiance is that which is freely and knowingly granted to the leader in response to, and in proportion to, the clearly evident servant stature of the leader. Those who choose to follow this principle will not casually accept the authority of existing institutions. Rather, they will freely respond only to individuals who are chosen as leaders because they are proven and trusted as servants.**

❖ Invite the students to comment on how people view the motives and demeanor of a leader. Encourage them to state why they think that Greenleaf's observations are—or are not—still valid.

❖ Discuss these questions as they relate to the church:

1. **What steps can you take to learn what is expected of you before you agree to assume a leadership role?** (At the least you should have a job description and an understanding of how

your work supports the vision and mission of your congregation.)

2. **What skills do you think a good church leader should have?**

3. **How is your congregation helping leaders to develop these skills?**

4. **What do you believe are appropriate motives for accepting a leadership position within the church?**

### (5) Continue the Journey

❖ Pray that as the learners depart, they will build trust with the people they lead by acting as servants on their behalf.

❖ Post information for next week's session on newsprint for the students to copy:

- Title: Samson's Call
- Background Scripture: Judges 13–16
- Lesson Scripture: Judges 13:1-7, 24-25
- Focus of the Lesson: Preparation for leadership may involve life circumstances not of one's own choosing. How do we respond when we find ourselves in such circumstances? Even before birth, Samson's call was assured as shown by the instructions the Lord's angel gave to his mother.

❖ Challenge the adults to grow spiritually by completing one or more of these activities related to this week's session.

(1) **Keep an eye on issues causing gridlock in local or national politics, especially where elected officials with polarized views are unable to compromise to serve the common good. Do you see any current examples of such a failure in leadership? If so, how might an understanding of godly ways to trust people with whom they have disagreed enable elected officials to move forward?**

(2) **Read *Violence in Scripture* by Jerome F. D. Creach, who is the writer of this quarter's lessons. Chapter 5, "Judges' Use of Violence," includes a discussion of "Jephthah and the Sacrifice of His Daughter." This insightful book is part of the Interpretation series, published by Westminster John Knox Press.**

(3) **Take steps to rebuild trust with a person from whom you have been alienated. Perhaps this person is a leader with whom you have had disagreements.**

❖ Sing or read aloud "God Will Take Care of You."

❖ Conclude today's session by leading the class in this benediction, which is adapted from Isaiah 6:8, the key verse for July 9: **In response to your call, O God, I say, "Here am I, send me!" Amen.**

# UNIT 1: CALLED TO BE STRONG
# Samson's Call

---

## PREVIEWING THE LESSON

**Lesson Scripture:** Judges 13:1-7, 24-25
**Background Scripture:** Judges 13–16
**Key Verse:** Judges 13:5

### Focus of the Lesson:

Preparation for leadership may involve life circumstances not of one's own choosing. How do we respond when we find ourselves in such circumstances? Even before birth, Samson's call was assured as shown by the instructions the Lord's angel gave to his mother.

### Goals for the Learners:

(1) to recount the details of Samson's birth and call.
(2) to empathize with the emotions Samson probably experienced regarding lifestyle restrictions imposed on him by others.
(3) to identify some ways that unforeseen circumstances prepare people for leadership roles today.

### Supplies:

Bibles, newsprint and marker, paper and pencils, hymnals

---

## READING THE SCRIPTURE

NRSV
Lesson Scripture: Judges 13:1-7, 24-25

¹The Israelites again did what was evil in the sight of the LORD, and the LORD gave them into the hand of the Philistines forty years.

²There was a certain man of Zorah, of the tribe of the Danites, whose name was Manoah. His wife was barren, having borne no children. ³And the angel of the LORD appeared to the woman and said to her, "Although

CEB
Lesson Scripture: Judges 13:1-7, 24-25

¹The Israelites again did things that the LORD saw as evil, and he handed them over to the Philistines for forty years.

²Now there was a certain man from Zorah, from the Danite clan, whose name was Manoah. His wife was unable to become pregnant and had not given birth to any children. ³The LORD's messenger appeared to the

you are barren, having borne no children, you shall conceive and bear a son. ⁴Now be careful not to drink wine or strong drink, or to eat anything unclean, **⁵for you shall conceive and bear a son. No razor is to come on his head, for the boy shall be a nazirite to God from birth. It is he who shall begin to deliver Israel from the hand of the Philistines."** ⁶Then the woman came and told her husband, "A man of God came to me, and his appearance was like that of an angel of God, most awe-inspiring; I did not ask him where he came from, and he did not tell me his name; ⁷but he said to me, 'You shall conceive and bear a son. So then drink no wine or strong drink, and eat nothing unclean, for the boy shall be a nazirite to God from birth to the day of his death.'"

²⁴The woman bore a son, and named him Samson. The boy grew, and the Lord blessed him. ²⁵The spirit of the Lord began to stir him in Mahaneh-dan, between Zorah and Eshtaol.

woman and said to her, "Even though you've been unable to become pregnant and haven't given birth, you are now pregnant and will give birth to a son! ⁴Now be careful not to drink wine or brandy or to eat anything that is ritually unclean, **⁵because you are pregnant and will give birth to a son. Don't allow a razor to shave his head, because the boy is going to be a nazirite for God from birth. He'll be the one who begins Israel's rescue from the power of the Philistines."**

⁶Then the woman went and told her husband, "A man of God came to me, and he looked like God's messenger—very scary! I didn't ask him where he was from, and he didn't tell me his name. ⁷He said to me, 'You are pregnant and will give birth to a son, so don't drink wine or brandy or eat anything that is ritually unclean, because the boy is going to be a nazirite for God from birth until the day he dies.'"

²⁴The woman gave birth to a son and named him Samson. The boy grew up, and the Lord blessed him. ²⁵The Lord's spirit began to move him when he was in Mahaneh-dan, between Zorah and Eshtaol.

## UNDERSTANDING THE SCRIPTURE

**Introduction.** Samson is a much more ambiguous figure than most of the judges who went before him. The announcement of his birth is filled with promise that he will be a devout and effective deliverer. His mother dedicates him to God before his birth, but he never lives up to the vows she makes for him. He also embodies much of what is wrong with Israel in the Book of Judges. Nevertheless, God does use Samson for some positive purposes. Samson's life is framed by the Philistine conflict (13:1; 16:23-30) and Samson acts against them to deliver Israel.

**Judges 13:1.** The setting of Samson's work as judge is much like that of the judges before him. The Israelites rebel against God and God gives them over to their enemies. In this case the enemy is the Philistines.

**Judges 13:2-7.** The story of Samson is set in Zorah, a town on the border between Israelite and Philistine territory. The family's proximity to Philistine towns is a major theme as Samson is attracted to Philistine women.

The account of Samson's birth raises great expectations for him to deliver Israel. His parents are devout but his mother is barren. As many other stories in the Old Testament illustrate, however, this is merely the setting for God's call of the mother to faithfulness and God's promise of a child who will do great things (see also 1 Samuel 1). The angel who appears to the woman charges her to devote herself as a nazirite. The word "nazirite" derives from a root that means "to consecrate." Hence a nazirite was a man or woman who devoted himself or herself to God for a period of time. Nazirites showed evidence of their consecration by refusing alcoholic beverages, avoiding anything unclean, and not cutting their hair (see Numbers 6:1-21). In this story the angel tells Samson's mother to become a nazirite during pregnancy in order to prepare her son to be a nazirite for life.

**Judges 13:8-25.** After the angel appears to Samson's mother, the information is essentially repeated at the father's request. The irony of this repetition is that Manoah does not learn anything his wife does not already know. He seems to need confirmation of the encounter, but his wife has more insight into the meaning of the angel's message and she has already responded faithfully (see 13:23). Despite her insight and faithfulness, however, she remains unnamed throughout the story. She is simply called "the woman."

**Judges 14:1-4.** Samson's first act is to request his father and mother to arrange a marriage with a Philistine woman at Timnah, another town on the border between Philistia and Judah. Recognizing the covenantal implications, his parents suggest marriage to an Israelite woman, but Samson refuses. When Samson declares, "she pleases me" (14:3) the word translated "please" is from the same root as the word translated "what seemed right" in the refrain that structures the final portion of the book, "all the people did what was right in their own eyes" (17:6; 21:25). Samson's declaration for the Philistine wife, therefore, echoes the narrator's judgment on Israel's behavior.

**Judges 14:5-9.** En route to and during his wedding he breaks one, and possibly two, of his nazirite vows: He eats honey from the carcass of a dead animal, thus rendering the honey unclean (14:9); his proximity to the vineyards (14:5) and the seven feast days (14:12) suggest that he drank wine as well. Samson's great physical strength, attributed to "the spirit of the Lord" rushing on him (14:6) appears here for the first time as he kills a lion with his bare hands.

**Judges 14:10-20.** Samson proposes a riddle based on his discovery of the honey in the lion's carcass (14:14). The riddle in turn is the center of a wager of sixty garments. When the Philistines cannot solve the riddle, they threaten Samson's wife and her family. She then nags him for the length of the festival until he reveals the solution to the riddle. When she discovers the answer to the riddle and provides it to the thirty Philistines they give Samson the answer just before their time is up (14:18). Their response is formed as a question,

"What is sweeter than honey? What is stronger than a lion?" (14:18). Samson gives a response filled with sexual and chauvinistic overtones: "If you had not plowed with my heifer, you would not have found out my riddle" (14:18). After being bested by the Philistines at Timnah, Samson goes into a rage, attributed again to the spirit of the Lord (14:19), and kills thirty men at Ashkelon, one of Philistia's major cities (see Joshua 13:3). Then Samson abandons his wife, an act tantamount to divorce. So her father gives her to Samson's best man.

**Judges 15:1-8.** Chapter 15 continues the story of Samson's wedding at Timnah with Samson returning to reclaim his wife whom he left earlier. Verses 4-8 tell of Samson's Herculean strength. Samson again attacks the Philistines and the Philistines respond by killing Samson's wife and her father (15:6).

**Judges 15:9-20.** In one of Samson's best-known exploits he kills a thousand Philistines with the jawbone of an ass. This act, however, is attributed to the spirit of the Lord that "rushed on him" (15:14).

**Judges 16:1-3.** Samson shows himself again unfaithful by sleeping with a prostitute. The strength he shows in carrying the gate of the city is cartoon-like.

**Judges 16:4-22.** Samson marries Delilah. Whether she is Philistine or Israelite is uncertain, but the Philistines try to use her to capture Samson as they had used the wife at Timnah. The cycle of being bound and escaping illustrates how clueless Samson is to what Delilah is doing. The result is that Samson gives away his secret, Delilah cuts his hair, and the Philistines capture and blind him.

**Judges 16:23-31.** The Philistines take Samson to the temple of Dagon, a fertility god. They celebrate their belief that Dagon delivered Samson to them. In his last heroic act Samson regains his strength and pulls down the pillar of Dagon's house, thus killing everyone inside.

## INTERPRETING THE SCRIPTURE

*Called Before Birth*

While leading a group of college students on a tour of the Middle East I noticed that two of our students, an Indian American woman and a Caucasian man, enjoyed each other's company very much. The two of them sat together on the tour bus and in the evening during our free time they walked hand-in-hand through the cities we visited. After a few days of seeing how close they appeared to be, I commented to another student, "They seem pretty serious." The student replied, "Oh no. They like being together, but they know it won't last." "What do you mean?" I asked. "They seem to love being together." "You see," the student said, "her parents have already promised her to a man in California, an arranged marriage the families set up when they were babies."

My immediate reaction to this news, was "How unfair!" American culture emphasizes the rights and freedom of an individual to choose his or her own path in life. But people from other cultures remind us that our lives are not completely our own, as we would like to imagine. The story of Samson's call illustrates well how someone's life can be given direction and purpose and commitments without their deciding on any of it. In the case of Samson, the commitments made for him transcended any personal considerations. His people were oppressed and he was to be devoted to the task of freeing them. As the angel said to his mother, "It is he who shall begin to deliver Israel from the hand of the Philistines" (Judges 13:5). Samson's call to be a nazirite, one consecrated to God, also reminds us of another point: The Israelites suffered at the hands of enemies in the first place because they were not faithful to God. Samson's dedication would represent their renewed commitment to the one who saved them.

If this type of call seems unfair, it is helpful to remember two points about the Samson story. First, Samson was called to embody the God-directed character of the nation as a whole. His call was essentially that of every other Israelite, but the nazirite vow focused attention on it in a particular way. So his prebirth calling was to satisfy much more than a family's commitment (as was the commitment to marriage of my student). Samson was called to be front and center in the restoration of the nation. Second, although Samson is called to conform to certain restrictions outlined in the vow his mother makes for him, the primary commitment is made by God. When God chooses us, as God chose Samson, it is without any promise of faithfulness on our part. So while Samson's call illustrates a call of a child that is accepted by his parents, it also illustrates God's grace that is extended without the child's promise of obedience or commitment. The greatest lesson for us to learn about our lives not being completely our own is that

they are governed by God, and God's reign over them begins with God's grace extended to us before birth.

### The Mother as Hero

If we read the Samson story without the introduction, we might conclude that the story is about one of the greatest hedonists of all time. Samson often appears as an oversexed jerk who goes from one woman to another in search of self-gratification. Much of the time he seems only concerned for his own pleasure. In the first episode of the story of Samson as an adult, he sees a Philistine woman and demands that his parents get her as his wife. When his parents counsel him against it, he says, "Get her for me, because she pleases me" (Judges 14:2). This attitude dominates most of Samson's life. So we might wonder why God would choose to use someone like Samson.

Throughout the Samson story there is evidence that God uses him for good. This strongman uses his great strength to defeat the Philistines and he helps free the Israelites from their yoke. But the real hero in the story is Samson's mother who dedicated him to God while he was in the womb. In every way she acted faithfully and thus set an example for her son, which he unfortunately did not follow. When the angel appears to her and gives her the mission of being a nazirite and then bearing the child Samson, she gladly accepts the call and is faithful to it. She reports all of this to her husband and then she leads him as they accept the task placed upon them.

For anyone who reads the Book of Judges closely, it should not come as a surprise that a woman appears in a prominent role like the one given to Samson's mother. Achsah (1:11-15), Deborah (chapters 4 and 5), and Jael (4:11-22; 5:24-27) play prominent roles in restoring Israel's fortunes and freeing the people from their enemies. Compared to these other women, however, Samson's mother is distinct in that she remains unnamed in the story. Despite her faithfulness and insight, we do not even know what to call her. She is simply called "the woman." But perhaps her anonymous character serves a larger purpose in the story. The story of Samson's failure is largely a story of women: The wife at Timnah (Judges 14–15), the prostitute at Gaza (Judges 16:1-3), and Delilah (Judges 16:4-22) all participate in his downfall. So perhaps by not naming Samson's mother the narrator is telling us at the beginning that the best chance Samson has for covenant fidelity is to follow the lead of this woman who bore him. Without a name, his mother is perhaps better able to serve in the story as a symbol of faithfulness. Indeed, she is like Lady Wisdom in Proverbs who calls to the foolish to get wisdom and insight (Proverbs 8:1–9:6). Often in that book Wisdom calls young men to bind themselves to her and not with women who will lead them astray (Proverbs 9:13-18). Lady Wisdom is like a mother or a good wife who keeps close to God (Proverbs 31:10-31). The greatest tragedy in Judges 13–16 is that Samson never quite learns this lesson. His mother, however, was there at the beginning to set him on the right path.

### Stirred by the Spirit

Despite Samson's manly failures with the women in his life, and despite his inclination to seek self-gratification above all else, Samson was able to accomplish some of the purpose for which he was called. In his last act he destroyed the temple of Dagon and all those gathered to worship and make claims that this fertility god ruled over the world (Judges 16:23-31). Samson is a prime example that God sometimes uses people despite themselves. Judges 13:24-25 anticipates that this will be the case.

At the end of the account of Samson's mother accepting the angel's call the text says, "The spirit of the Lord began to stir him" (13:25). We might well judge that the spirit of God was hindered by Samson's own unfaithfulness and so the spirit only "began to stir him." Nevertheless, the work of the spirit of God punctuates the story (Judges 14:6, 19; 15:14). This is wonderful evidence that God does not abandon those whom God calls even if they fail in faithfully answering that call.

---

## SHARING THE SCRIPTURE

### PREPARING TO LEAD

#### Preparing Our Hearts

Ponder this week's devotional reading from Judges 13:19-23. This portion of today's background Scripture fits between the first and second readings from the lesson Scripture. What danger does Manoah, Samson's father, allude to here? Why does Samson's mother remain calm? What do you learn about Samson?

Pray that you and the students will be prepared at all times to meet God.

*Preparing Our Minds*

Study the background Scripture from Judges 13–16 and the lesson Scripture from Judges 13:1-7, 24-25.

Consider this question: *How do you respond when you find yourself in circumstances not of your own choosing?*

Write on newsprint:
❏ information for next week's lesson, found under Continue the Journey.
❏ activities for further spiritual growth in Continue the Journey.

Determine how you might use any of the features that precede the first lesson of this quarter in today's session.

Prepare to tell the rest of Samson's story, beginning with Judges 13:8-25 and going through to Judges 16:23-31 in the Understanding the Scripture portion. Keep this summary in Goal 1 brief, remembering that the thrust of the lesson is on the call of Samson given to his mother before he was born.

LEADING THE CLASS

*(1) Gather to Learn*

❖ Welcome everyone and pray that those who have come today will prepare themselves and the next generation to answer God's call for leaders.

❖ Read the first two paragraphs of Called Before Birth in Interpreting the Scripture.

❖ Invite the students to comment on other circumstances people find themselves in that are not of their own choosing. Here are examples: the

student in a substandard school; the worker who has lost a job and then home and now depends upon a shelter for a home and meals; the older employee whose company closed, leaving him with poor prospects for future work.

❖ Read aloud today's focus statement: **Preparation for leadership may involve life circumstances not of one's own choosing. How do we respond when we find ourselves in such circumstances? Even before birth, Samson's call was assured as shown by the instructions the Lord's angel gave to his mother.**

*(2) Goal 1: Recount the Details of Samson's Birth and Call*

❖ Read Introduction in Understanding the Scripture to set the stage.

❖ Recruit a volunteer to read Judges 13:1-7, 24-25.

❖ Follow up the Scripture by reading the third paragraph of Called Before Birth in Interpreting the Scripture. Then ask:

1. **What do you learn about the angel's visit to Samson's mother and the instructions given to this unnamed woman?** (See Judges 13:2-7 in Understanding the Scripture and The Mother as Hero in Interpreting the Scripture.)
2. **Judges 13:24-25 tells us about the child who was born. What inferences can you draw concerning how God acted in Samson's life from these two verses?** (See Stirred by the Spirit in Interpreting the Scripture.)

❖ Tell the rest of Samson's story by hitting highlights from

Understanding the Scripture, beginning with Judges 13:8-25 and going through the end of Judges 16. Observe that Samson does not always act with the purity expected of one under a nazarite vow. He especially gets himself into difficulty with women. Note differences between what you would expect of one under a vow to God (13:5) and the footloose character described in chapters 14–16.

*(3) Goal 2: Empathize with the Emotions Samson Probably Experienced Regarding Lifestyle Restrictions Imposed on Him by Others*

❖ Invite three volunteers to role-play a discussion between Samson as a boy of about ten, his father, and his mother. His mom and dad are to explain to him the circumstances of his birth and the rules that the angel made clear they were to follow. Samson is to ask questions and respond with his feelings about the restrictions that are placed upon him.

❖ Encourage the class members to add to—or question—ideas from the roleplay and then ask: **How would you feel if others imposed lifestyle restrictions on you? Or, if you have lived with such restrictions, what difference did they make in your outlook on life?**

*(4) Goal 3: Identify Some Ways that Unforeseen Circumstances Prepare People for Leadership Roles Today*

❖ Read this story about Francis Asbury: **Born in 1745 in Great Barr, England, Francis Asbury grew up in a rough neighborhood. The family's small cottage was owned by a brewery, so the unspecified problems of Francis's father, Joseph, may have** been drinking and gambling. Francis attended a nearby school until the age of twelve when he quit because of the master's cruel behavior. He apprenticed to a local metalworker, likely expecting to be a tradesperson and remain within his small village. After the death of his sister Sarah, Francis often went to Methodist meetings, where he was converted at about age fifteen. He joined a class meeting, began to preach at age seventeen, and at age twenty-one was a traveling preacher. At age twenty-six he answered John Wesley's call for volunteers to preach in America, but even Wesley had no inkling what Asbury would accomplish. Although his formal education ended in the sixth grade, Asbury's upbringing enabled him to relate well to the people. According to observers, he was not at all a good preacher. Yet this uneducated, mediocre preacher was able to inspire and convince people, as well as organize and build consensus. He was spiritually disciplined and lived very simply. Under his leadership, American Methodism grew from a few hundred in 1771 to more than two hundred thousand by 1816.

❖ Discuss these questions:

1. **What were some factors that apparently helped to prepare an unlikely candidate for ministry to become such an outstanding leader?**

2. **How does Asbury's story motivate and inspire you to take a leadership position, even if you feel unprepared?**

3. **What does Asbury's leadership suggest about what God can do through people who are willing to answer God's call?**

*(5) Continue the Journey*

❖ Pray that as the learners depart, they will sense God's call on their lives and follow God's directions for fulfilling that call.

❖ Post information for next week's session on newsprint for the students to copy:

- Title: Moses and the Burning Bush
- Background Scripture: Exodus 3
- Lesson Scripture: Exodus 3:1-12
- Focus of the Lesson: People get accustomed to living with the injustices that prevail in society. What does it take to address injustice? God called Moses to address injustice and empowered him with the knowledge of God's identity, purpose, and presence.

❖ Challenge the adults to grow spiritually by completing one or more of these activities related to this week's session.

(1) Compare the "birth announcement" story found in Judges with the announcements in Genesis 16–18, 1 Samuel 1, and Luke 1. What similarities and differences do you observe concerning the mother, the child, and the one who brings the announcement?

(2) Review the specifics of the nazarite vows as found in Numbers 6:1-21, as well as Samson's story in Judges. How does he uphold—or fail to uphold—these vows? How difficult would you find it to live such an austere, highly disciplined life?

(3) Read John Milton's "Samson Agonistes" for a poetic account of the biblical story. What insights do you glean from Milton's retelling of Samson's story? (See: https://www.dartmouth.edu/~milton/reading_room/samson/drama/text.shtml).

❖ Sing or read aloud "If Thou But Suffer God to Guide Thee."

❖ Conclude today's session by leading the class in this benediction, which is adapted from Isaiah 6:8, the key verse for July 9: **In response to your call, O God, I say, "Here am I, send me!" Amen.**

## UNIT 2: CALLING OF PROPHETS
# MOSES AND THE BURNING BUSH

---

### PREVIEWING THE LESSON

**Lesson Scripture:** Exodus 3:1-12
**Background Scripture:** Exodus 3
**Key Verses:** Exodus 3:9-10

### Focus of the Lesson:
People get accustomed to living with the injustices that prevail in society. What does it take to address injustice? God called Moses to address injustice and empowered him with the knowledge of God's identity, purpose, and presence.

### Goals for the Learners:
(1) to examine the details of how Moses was called and the self-revealed nature of God, who called him.
(2) to empathize with God's awareness of injustice and desire to correct it.
(3) to address injustice in ways that honor God's identity, purpose, and presence.

### Supplies:
Bibles, newsprint and marker, paper and pencils, hymnals

---

### READING THE SCRIPTURE

NRSV
Lesson Scripture: Exodus 3:1-12

¹Moses was keeping the flock of his father-in-law Jethro, the priest of Midian; he led his flock beyond the wilderness, and came to Horeb, the mountain of God. ²There the angel of the LORD appeared to him in a flame of fire out of a bush; he looked, and the bush was blazing, yet it was not

CEB
Lesson Scripture: Exodus 3:1-12

¹Moses was taking care of the flock for his father-in-law Jethro, Midian's priest. He led his flock out to the edge of the desert, and he came to God's mountain called Horeb. ²The LORD's messenger appeared to him in a flame of fire in the middle of a bush. Moses saw that the bush was in flames, but

consumed. [3]Then Moses said, "I must turn aside and look at this great sight, and see why the bush is not burned up." [4]When the LORD saw that he had turned aside to see, God called to him out of the bush, "Moses, Moses!" And he said, "Here I am." [5]Then he said, "Come no closer! Remove the sandals from your feet, for the place on which you are standing is holy ground." [6]He said further, "I am the God of your father, the God of Abraham, the God of Isaac, and the God of Jacob." And Moses hid his face, for he was afraid to look at God.

[7]Then the LORD said, "I have observed the misery of my people who are in Egypt; I have heard their cry on account of their taskmasters. Indeed, I know their sufferings, [8]and I have come down to deliver them from the Egyptians, and to bring them up out of that land to a good and broad land, a land flowing with milk and honey, to the country of the Canaanites, the Hittites, the Amorites, the Perizzites, the Hivites, and the Jebusites. [9]**The cry of the Israelites has now come to me; I have also seen how the Egyptians oppress them. [10]So come, I will send you to Pharaoh to bring my people, the Israelites, out of Egypt."** [11]But Moses said to God, "Who am I that I should go to Pharaoh, and bring the Israelites out of Egypt?" [12]He said, "I will be with you; and this shall be the sign for you that it is I who sent you: when you have brought the people out of Egypt, you shall worship God on this mountain."

it didn't burn up. [3]Then Moses said to himself, Let me check out this amazing sight and find out why the bush isn't burning up.

[4]When the LORD saw that he was coming to look, God called to him out of the bush, "Moses, Moses!"

Moses said, "I'm here."

[5]Then the LORD said, "Don't come any closer! Take off your sandals, because you are standing on holy ground." [6]He continued, "I am the God of your father, Abraham's God, Isaac's God, and Jacob's God." Moses hid his face because he was afraid to look at God.

[7]Then the LORD said, "I've clearly seen my people oppressed in Egypt. I've heard their cry of injustice because of their slave masters. I know about their pain. [8]I've come down to rescue them from the Egyptians in order to take them out of that land and bring them to a good and broad land, a land that's full of milk and honey, a place where the Canaanites, the Hittites, the Amorites, the Perizzites, the Hivites, and the Jebusites all live. [9]**Now the Israelites' cries of injustice have reached me. I've seen just how much the Egyptians have oppressed them. [10]So get going. I'm sending you to Pharaoh to bring my people, the Israelites, out of Egypt."** [11]But Moses said to God, "Who am I to go to Pharaoh and to bring the Israelites out of Egypt?"

[12]God said, "I'll be with you. And this will show you that I'm the one who sent you. After you bring the people out of Egypt, you will come back here and worship God on this mountain."

## UNDERSTANDING THE SCRIPTURE

**Introduction.** Exodus 3 begins the story of God's call to Moses to lead the Israelites out of slavery in Egypt. The story follows a pattern found in many other call stories in the Bible (the story of Gideon in Judges 6, for example). In such stories (1) the person being called meets God or an angel (3:2), (2) God commissions the person to a special task (3:10), (3) the person being commissioned expresses doubt or questions the task (3:11, 13; 4:1, 10), (4) God gives a sign of assurance that the task will be successful (3:12, 14-15; 4:2-9, 15-16).

**Exodus 3:1-6.** Moses was shepherding the flocks of his father-in-law near the mountain of God when God appeared to him and called him to lead the Israelites out of Egypt. Here the holy mountain is called Horeb. In other texts, however, the same location is known as Sinai (Exodus 19:1). Moses' father-in-law is here named Jethro, though he was called Ruel in 2:18 and will be called Hobab in Numbers 10:29. The memory of these different place names and personal names may indicate there were different local memories of these names and the written records from those different places were combined to create the Book of Exodus.

Moses draws near the place where he meets God because he sees a bush that is burning but not consumed. God's appearance in some feature of nature is a common motif in the Old Testament (1 Kings 19:1-18; Psalm 29:3-9; Ezekiel 1). Such appearances of God are called "theophanies," which signify the revelation of God through natural phenomenon.

Exodus 3:2 says God's messenger, "the angel of the Lord" appeared to Moses in the burning bush. Verse 4, however, identifies the voice from the bush as being directly from God. This type of interplay between God and the angel shows the reluctance of the biblical writer to say matter-of-factly that God appeared and spoke (see also Gideon's call in Judges 6:12, 14). God's command for Moses to remove his shoes (3:5) indicates the seriousness and holiness of the place because of God's presence. Moses shows awareness of God's holiness by hiding his face (3:6).

In Exodus 3:6 God expresses the divine identity by saying, "I am the God of your father." "Father" here could be translated generically "ancestor," but when this formula specifies the ancestor it is always Abraham (and Isaac and Jacob).

**Exodus 3:7-12.** God introduces the call to Moses by first expressing concern for the Israelites' condition in Egypt (3:7). God is passionate about people and about justice. This chapter also begins to show Moses' doubts about his calling, something that continues into Exodus 4. In 3:11 Moses raises the first, and most general, objection to God's call: "Who am I that I should go to Pharaoh?" The other objections are really an expansion of this one. God then gives a sign of assurance to Moses, but ironically, the sign of assurance God gives can only be seen after Moses answers the call (3:12).

**Exodus 3:13-22.** Parts of the exchange between God and Moses in 3:13-15 are difficult to understand. Moses asks God to reveal God's name. It is not certain why Moses asks for this. As Exodus 3:13 indicates, the Hebrews had known this

God previously as the God of their ancestors. So perhaps it would have been necessary for Moses to tell this generation what this God will be to them. The name of God would help them understand, since the name would indicate something of God's character. Although this is possible, Moses' inquiry about the divine name appears in a string of objections to Moses' call and should perhaps be taken simply as one more stall tactic.

It is also not certain what God's response in verse 14 to Moses means. The sentence, "I AM WHO I AM" is actually one of several possible translations of this line. In Hebrew the sentence consists of three words. It has two forms of the verb "to be" ("I am") connected by a relative particle ("who"). But the verb in Hebrew has no inherent tense as verbs in English do. So the sentence could also be translated, "I will be who I will be," or "I am who I will be," or any number of other possible combinations of verb tense. We can only guess at the meaning of the answer God gives Moses concerning the significance of the divine name. Some have proposed that the answer is essentially evasive. More likely, however, God is simply telling Moses that he and the people will know who God is by seeing what God does.

In Exodus 3:15 God's statement "I AM WHO I AM" (3:14) is linked to the name of God frequently used in the Old Testament. It is translated "the LORD." But the Hebrew word that stands behind the translation is actually a third-person form of the verb, "to be." Christians sometimes translate this name as it perhaps sounded, Yahweh. The name is formally translated "LORD," however, because Jews in the ancient world held it to be so sacred that it was not pronounced. And the scribes who passed on the Old Testament put signals in the text that instructed readers to say the word Adonai, which refers simply to one who has authority over another (hence, a "lord"). Since this name appears in verse 15 as God instructs Moses on how to address the Israelites, it seems that God's answer to Moses in 3:13-14 is meant to explain the divine name (Yahweh). Here "the LORD" is identified as the God of Israel's ancestors, "the God of Abraham, the God of Isaac, and the God of Jacob" (3:15). The passage ends with this same identity and linked to the promise that the Lord will bring the Israelites out of slavery and to "a land flowing with milk and honey" (3:17). Hence, the divine name may suggest that God is known both for what God has done in the past and what God will do in the future. The main point though is that God is one who acts, particularly in response to the cries of the needy.

## INTERPRETING THE SCRIPTURE

*Their Cries Have Come to Me*

Exodus 3 reveals an essential feature of the character of God: God is moved by human suffering; God acts within human history and enters human experience to relieve the suffering God sees. We might also say that God's compassion for human beings is the basis of God's calling human beings to be part of God's purpose. That is certainly the case with the call of Moses.

This dual focus on the character of God and the call of human beings in turn reveals an important feature of both. First, it indicates that the God of the Bible and of the Christian faith is different from the God many modern Western people invoke. It is common to think of God as the sum of all the good and just actions in the world, or as the Prime Mover who set the world in motion. To be sure, God may be understood in these ways. But the biblical God is much more. Exodus 3 depicts God as one who seeks a relationship with people, especially with a particular people, Israel. God works for them and through them to bring justice to the world. Thus God responds to their cries with action meant to relieve them.

Second, this portion of the story not only tells us about God's character; it also defines God's calling upon the lives of human beings. The specific calling varies from person to person. Everyone God calls is called to show God's compassion, whether it is to relieve hunger or pain, or to free people from oppression as Moses did. In fact, a good way to discern whether some urge or impulse reflects the call of God is to ask if that urge or impulse leads to the increased welfare of others. Is its aim to create peace and well-being, or just to satisfy the desires of the one who is discerning the call? God's call typically leads to the former and if the latter also occurs, it should be considered icing on the cake.

### Who Am I, Lord?

God's promise to rescue the Israelites from slavery in Egypt is as clear as any promise in Scripture. The problem for Moses in Exodus 3 is that God declares that Moses will be the instrument through whom God will accomplish this. God says, "So come, I will send you to Pharaoh to bring my people, the Israelites, out of Egypt" (3:10).

Moses responds to God's call with a logical question: "Who am I that I should go to Pharaoh, and bring the Israelites out of Egypt?" (3:11) .The question is essentially the same question Gideon raises in Judges 6:15. Gideon protests because his family is the least important in the tribe and he is the least in his family. So also Moses seems to have no pedigree or inherent authority. To add to this general weakness, he is a murderer and now a fugitive (Exodus 2:11-15). As the larger story in Exodus 3–4 makes clear, Moses raises numerous objections to God as to his ability to answer God's call. It is understandable that Moses might feel inadequate for such a task. So why would God choose to use this particular person to rescue the Israelites? One answer is that such is the nature of God's work in our world. God works through frail creatures to accomplish the divine purpose. God's work through Moses is a perfect example of the fact.

This dimension of the story reminds us that God is the main actor in the story of the Exodus and in our story. The point is not so much that we are weak and inadequate. Our abilities are never enough to deliver us or anybody else. God knows already that our efforts alone will fail (3:19). Ultimately, only God can save us. So while Exodus 3 focuses on Moses as God's agent, it also reminds us that Moses is an ordinary human being chosen by God to show God's extraordinary deeds. God's call of Moses is yet another example in Scripture of what the apostle Paul said about how God works: "God chose what is weak in the world to shame the strong" (1 Corinthians 1:27).

### God's Sign of Assurance

In response to Moses' objection to God's call in verse 11 ("Who am I that I should go?"), God offers Moses a sign of assurance that what God called Moses to do would indeed come to pass. But notice that the "sign" is something that will happen in the future. God tells Moses the Israelites will worship God on the mountain where Moses is now standing (3:12). What kind of sign is this? It is as though God is saying to Moses, "you will know for sure this will all come to pass when it comes to pass!" It may seem a ridiculous response to Moses' question. It may not be so ridiculous, however, if the real message behind the sign is that Moses will have to live by faith. Perhaps God is saying that Moses will have to trust in the call God has given him and in God's ability and willingness to accomplish the task at hand.

There are at least two features of Moses' call story that suggest the assurance God gives Moses is really a call for Moses to rely on God. First, God does not respond to Moses' question immediately with the "sign," but with the simple promise: "I will be with you" (3:12). Throughout the Old Testament this promise, in one form or another, is given to God's people as a promise intended to lead them through all hardship. For example, God gave this promise to King Ahaz through the prophet Isaiah to assure him his people would be kept safe from their enemies (Isaiah 7:14). But Ahaz and his people insisted on seeking protection through foreign alliances; they would not live by faith (Isaiah 8:5-8). Moses also has trouble answering his call with this promise of God's presence, but God seems to understand. So as Moses continues to object to God's call, God gives increasingly concrete signs of divine help. He provides a staff that turns into a serpent (Exodus 4:1-5) and the ability to turn his hand leprous and then to make it normal again (4:6-8). God tells Moses he will be able to take water from the Nile and turn it into blood (4:9). But Moses still doubts (4:10)! Finally God sends Aaron with Moses so he will have the most tangible sign of God's presence: another person (4:14-16).

Moses seems to fail the test of faith that he needs to answer God's call. But amazingly, God does not give up on Moses. Perhaps this is the most comforting message in this passage. God takes whatever faith we have, however small it may be, and fills in the gaps as we try to serve.

---

## SHARING THE SCRIPTURE

### PREPARING TO LEAD

#### Preparing Our Hearts

Ponder this week's devotional reading from 2 Chronicles 19:4-7.

Jehoshaphat ruled in Judah from 873 to 849 B.C. What do you learn from these verses about this king's judicial reforms? What expectations are there of those who judge on behalf of God? (Observe that "judges" here carries the meaning that we usually associate with a courtroom judge.)

Pray that you and the students will confront injustice wherever you find it.

### Preparing Our Minds

Study the background Scripture from Exodus 3 and the lesson Scripture from Exodus 3:1-12.

Consider this question: *What does it take to address the injustices that prevail in society?*

Write on newsprint:
- ❏ information for next week's lesson, found under Continue the Journey.
- ❏ activities for further spiritual growth in Continue the Journey.

Determine how you might use any of the features that precede the first lesson of this quarter in today's session. Plan to use The Call of the Prophets, found in The Big Picture: The Call of God.

### LEADING THE CLASS

#### (1) Gather to Learn

❖ Welcome everyone and pray that those who have come today will become more keenly aware of the injustices that pervade society and be willing to challenge them.

❖ Read: **As this lesson is being written, numerous instances have been reported in the media concerning tensions between law enforcement officers and citizens. Based on what they see happening around them and to them, these citizens believe that some officers act unfairly toward certain populations, especially younger African American males. Tempers have boiled over to the point where there have been major clashes between the police and those who feel unjustifiably targeted. And these citizens' feelings cannot be brushed aside, for in some cases the police have shot and killed people for reasons that are not apparent even when video footage is viewed. On the other hand, officers who have had no role in violence have also been targeted simply because they were wearing uniforms. The American public is outraged by this senseless violence. In God's kingdom all lives matter—and all people must be treated with respect, dignity, and justice.**

❖ Read aloud today's focus statement: **People get accustomed to living with the injustices that prevail in society. What does it take to address injustice? God called Moses to address injustice and empowered him with the knowledge of God's identity, purpose, and presence.**

#### (2) Goal 1: Examine the Details of How Moses Was Called and the Self-Revealed Nature of God, Who Called Him

❖ Read or retell Their Cries Have Come to Me in Interpreting the Scripture to provide a context and reason for Moses to be called from his work as a shepherd.

❖ Select three volunteers to read the parts of the narrator, Moses, and an angel/God from Exodus 3:1-12.

❖ Discuss these questions:
1. **What do you learn about who God is?**
2. **What do you learn about why God is calling Moses?**
3. **What do you learn about Moses' response to God's call?** (See Who Am I, Lord? in Interpreting the Scripture.)

4. **What sign does God offer to assure Moses?** (See verse 12 and God's Sign of Assurance in Interpreting the Scripture.)

5. **What, if anything, puzzles or surprises you about God's call or Moses' response?**

### (3) Goal 2: Empathize with God's Awareness of Injustice and Desire to Correct It

❖ Read this quotation from theologian Ronald Sider: **"[God's] freedom from bias does not mean that he maintains neutrality in the struggle for justice. He is indeed on the side of the poor! The Bible clearly and repeatedly teaches that God is at work in history casting down the rich and exalting the poor because frequently the rich are wealthy precisely because they have oppressed the poor or have neglected to aid the needy. God also sides with the poor because of their special vulnerability."**

❖ Discuss these questions:

1. **This quotation from Sider, as well as God's words to Moses in Exodus 3:7-9, makes clear that God is not only aware of injustice on earth but also takes action to correct it. In what situations today do you want to see God act to correct an injustice?**

2. **Where is the church currently involved in God's name in action to bring about justice?**

3. **Are there any issues of injustice that you think the church should be addressing but is not? Why is the church failing to take**

meaningful action? What can be done to remove barriers to action?

### (4) Goal 3: Address Injustice in Ways that Honor God's Identity, Purpose, and Presence

❖ Direct attention again to Exodus 3:1-12 and ask:

1. **What words or phrases come to mind to describe the God revealed in these verses?** List ideas on newsprint. (Make sure to include the ideas of holiness; empathy with humans; desire to be in relation with humans; willingness and power to act; readiness to deliver those who suffer; desire to work with humans to bring about the divine will; presence with people, especially those who are called to work for God.)

2. **What examples of oppressed peoples can you think of in today's world?** List ideas on newsprint. (Ideas may include slaves, children forced to work because the family must have the money, women who are silenced and kept under the control of their husbands, laborers who are not paid fairly for what they do, poor people who live in substandard housing sometimes near dumps or other environmentally hazardous areas, families that are food insecure.)

3. **What actions can we take to address these injustices in ways that would honor**

God? List ideas on newsprint. (For example, write letters to newspapers about the issue(s); join groups that are concerned about the same issue(s) that you are; lobby local, state, and national officials to bring about change; provide short-term assistance to people, such as food, while you continue to advocate for them in the long term.)

❖ Distribute paper and pencils. Encourage the students to answer these questions, which you will read aloud, and take their papers home for review:

1. What issues do I believe God is calling me to address?
2. What steps can I take to address these issues in ways that call forth just resolution and honor God?

*(5) Continue the Journey*

❖ Pray that as the learners depart they will be willing to identify and address injustice just as God would.

❖ Post information for next week's session on newsprint for the students to copy:

- **Title: Isaiah in the Temple**
- **Background Scripture: Isaiah 6**
- **Lesson Scripture: Isaiah 6:1-8**
- **Focus of the Lesson: Unex-**

pected circumstances can lead us into paths we do not anticipate. Where do we gain confidence to undertake these unexpected tasks? Isaiah's confidence came from the unusual and compelling events of his call.

❖ Challenge the adults to grow spiritually by completing one or more of these activities related to this week's session.

**(1) Use a concordance or do an Internet search for the words "I will be with you Bible." Check out several passages. Under what circumstances does God promise to be with people? Claim the promise of God's presence for yourself.**

**(2) Observe that unlike Gideon who set out fleece not once but twice as he asked for a sign from God, the sign Moses would receive would not come until after he had fulfilled his call by bringing people out of Egypt. Rate yourself on your willingness to move forward in answer to God's call, even without a tangible sign.**

**(3) Identify and address an injustice you see.**

❖ Sing or read aloud "Go Down, Moses."

❖ Conclude today's session by leading the class in this benediction, which is adapted from Isaiah 6:8, the key verse for July 9: **In response to your call, O God, I say, "Here am I, send me!" Amen.**

## UNIT 2: CALLING OF PROPHETS
# ISAIAH IN THE TEMPLE

---

### PREVIEWING THE LESSON

**Lesson Scripture:** Isaiah 6:1-8
**Background Scripture:** Isaiah 6
**Key Verse:** Isaiah 6:8

**Focus of the Lesson:**
Unexpected circumstances can lead us into paths we do not anticipate. Where do we gain confidence to undertake these unexpected tasks? Isaiah's confidence came from the unusual and compelling events of his call.

**Goals for the Learners:**
(1) to explore the circumstances of Isaiah's call and his reaction to it.
(2) to sense Isaiah's emotions as he reacted to his call.
(3) to answer God's call to service.

**Supplies:**
Bibles, newsprint and marker, paper and pencils, hymnals

---

### READING THE SCRIPTURE

**NRSV**
Lesson Scripture: Isaiah 6:1-8
¹In the year that King Uzziah died, I saw the Lord sitting on a throne, high and lofty; and the hem of his robe filled the temple. ²Seraphs were in attendance above him; each had six wings: with two they covered their faces, and with two they covered their feet, and with two they flew. ³And one called to another and said:
"Holy, holy, holy is the LORD of hosts;
the whole earth is full of his glory."
⁴The pivots on the thresholds shook

**CEB**
Lesson Scripture: Isaiah 6:1-8
¹In the year of King Uzziah's death, I saw the Lord sitting on a high and exalted throne, the edges of his robe filling the temple. ²Winged creatures were stationed around him. Each had six wings: with two they veiled their faces, with two their feet, and with two they flew about. ³They shouted to each other, saying:
"Holy, holy, holy is the LORD of
heavenly forces!

at the voices of those who called, and the house filled with smoke. ⁵And I said: "Woe is me! I am lost, for I am a man of unclean lips, and I live among a people of unclean lips; yet my eyes have seen the King, the LORD of hosts!"

⁶Then one of the seraphs flew to me, holding a live coal that had been taken from the altar with a pair of tongs. ⁷The seraph touched my mouth with it and said: "Now that this has touched your lips, your guilt has departed and your sin is blotted out." **⁸Then I heard the voice of the Lord saying, "Whom shall I send, and who will go for us?" And I said, "Here am I; send me!"**

All the earth is filled with God's glory!"

⁴The doorframe shook at the sound of their shouting, and the house was filled with smoke.

⁵I said, "Mourn for me; I'm ruined! I'm a man with unclean lips, and I live among a people with unclean lips. Yet I've seen the king, the LORD of heavenly forces!"

⁶Then one of the winged creatures flew to me, holding a glowing coal that he had taken from the altar with tongs. ⁷He touched my mouth and said, "See, this has touched your lips. Your guilt has departed, and your sin is removed."

**⁸Then I heard the Lord's voice saying, "Whom should I send, and who will go for us?"**
**I said, "I'm here; send me."**

---

## UNDERSTANDING THE SCRIPTURE

**Introduction.** Isaiah 6 reports the call of the prophet Isaiah. Most prophetic books in the Old Testament do not include a call story like this, but enough do include such a story to indicate this experience was very important to the prophets and their followers. Similar stories appear in Ezekiel 1:1–3:11; Jeremiah 1:4-10; and 1 Kings 22:19-23. The prophets likely told these stories (and their disciples passed them on) in order to validate their words. The call story was a way of saying "this person's message and ministry is from God."

**Isaiah 6:1.** The call of Isaiah took place in 742 B.C. in the year King Uzziah died. Uzziah helped lead Judah to an economic resurgence and a time of peace during his fifty-two-year reign (2 Kings 15:1-7, 32). Second Kings 15:1-7 calls him Azariah,

which was perhaps a throne name (or perhaps this version of his name was the result of a copying error since in Hebrew the two names differ in only one letter). In the year of Uzziah's death Isaiah "saw the Lord," that is, he saw a vision of God. The vision took place in the Jerusalem Temple, but God was seated on a heavenly throne. The people of Judah experienced the Temple as the connecting point between heaven and earth so, even though God was enthroned in heaven "the hem of his robe filled the temple."

**Isaiah 6:2-3.** Seraphs were figures who attended God's throne. The word in Hebrew is related to the word for serpent. In some ancient Near Eastern myths the temples of the gods were thought to be guarded by serpent-like creatures. Thus the name of these creatures reflects the mystery of God's throne in the heavens. The description of six wings is similar to the description of creatures in Ezekiel's call vision, who had four wings (Ezekiel 1:6, 11). The creatures cover their faces with two wings because they cannot look on the face of God. The reference to covering their feet is a euphemism for covering the private parts (see Ruth 3:7). Modesty is required when in proximity to God who is most holy. The role of the seraphs participating in the scene through singing (6:3) and speaking to the prophet being commissioned (6:7) is like the participation of the spirits in 1 Kings 22:19-23. The song of the seraphs echoes one of Isaiah's favorite titles for God, "Holy One" (Isaiah 12:6; 29:23; 30:12).

**Isaiah 6:4-5.** The expression "pivots on the thresholds" translates a difficult expression. The word for "pivot" may come from the same root word that also gives us the word "mother." If so, the RSV's translation "foundations" makes sense. Another possibility is that the word comes from a root with the sense of "holder." In that case NRSV's "pivots" would seem best. The main point, however, is that the voices of the heavenly beings caused the Temple entrance to shake. "The house" refers to the Jerusalem Temple in which Isaiah saw the vision of God. Isaiah's words in verse 5 reveal a concern for ritual purity, like the earlier reference to the seraphs covering their feet.

The word "unclean" is the typical term used to refer to the condition of ritual impurity that would prevent a priest from serving in the Temple (see Leviticus 11–15 for a sample of such conditions). But here the word "unclean" is a metaphor for "unworthy" or "unrighteous." Before God's

holiness Isaiah recognizes that his speech is not adequate. It is not clear what "my eyes have seen the King" means (6:5). Some biblical traditions declare that humans cannot see God and live (Exodus 33:20). In some prophetic visions the prophet sees God on a throne (1 Kings 22:19) or in heavenly visions (Ezekiel 1:1). Exodus 33:20 may offer a solution; it specifies that humans cannot see God's face. But Moses is allowed to see God's backside (Exodus 33:23). Perhaps Isaiah sees a vision of God, but does not see the essence of God, God's face.

**Isaiah 6:6-7.** In response to Isaiah's complaint about having unclean lips, a seraph touches his tongue with a coal from the altar and purifies Isaiah. This theme of the prophet's mouth being prepared to speak God's word appears also in Jeremiah 1:9 and Ezekiel 3:1-3.

**Isaiah 6:8.** To this point Isaiah has only seen God. Now he hears God's voice. The sentence God speaks is simple, yet profound: "Whom shall I send, and who will go for us?" The first part of the question asks who is able to do the job. It is not clear if God is including Isaiah as part of the audience or not. In 1 Kings 22:20 the same question is spoken to the beings around God's throne, not to the prophet. The second part of the question asks who is willing to go. "For us" is typical language God uses when speaking as the head of the heavenly court (as in Genesis 1:26). Isaiah's response indicates his willingness to answer the call. Since the seraph just cleansed him and prepared his mouth, he is also able to perform the task.

**Isaiah 6:9-13.** Verses 9-13 contain a further interchange between God and Isaiah. This section makes clear that answering God's call may be difficult. Now God reveals what the call involves. God tells Isaiah to prophesy destruction. The message is cast as sarcasm: "Keep listening, but do not comprehend; keep looking, but do not understand" (6:9). If the people really comprehended God's message and understood what it meant they would turn to God and be healed. But God knows they will not. So the message has no hope in it. Isaiah responds, "How long, O Lord?" (6:11). These words are typical of laments in which the speaker cries out in desperation to God (as in Psalm 13:1). God answers that Judah will be almost completely destroyed like a tree cut down to its stump (6:13). The last line of the passage is difficult to translate, but it leaves a glimmer of hope for God's people and for the prophet.

---

## INTERPRETING THE SCRIPTURE

### God the True King

One striking feature of Isaiah's call to prophesy is that it came during a time when the people of Judah were discouraged and their future seemed bleak. They had been devastated by the loss of King Uzziah, who had rebuilt their nation and given its people hope for the future. He came to the throne in the wake of a very dark period of time when the people of Judah, like the people of Israel (the northern tribes governed from Samaria), were struggling under the burden of Assyrian domination. But when Assyria's own internal strife weakened them, Uzziah strengthened the people of Judah. Basically the same scenario had played out in the Northern Kingdom under the reign of King Jeroboam II. Both kingdoms that identified with the God of Abraham and Moses showed signs of prosperity. But now the gains made during Uzziah's reign were threatened. What would become of the nation without King Uzziah?

The account of Isaiah's call to prophesy includes a subtle yet profound answer to this question in the vision of God's throne room. When the people of Judah felt hopeless because they had lost their king, Isaiah saw the one who really delivered prosperity and hope: Judah's Lord, the God who reigns over the world. The opening reference to the year that King Uzziah died recognizes a human monarch, but after seeing the vision Isaiah reports, "my eyes have seen *the* King, the LORD of hosts" (6:5, emphasis added). This label Isaiah gives for God provides a most important perspective on Isaiah's call to prophesy and to the message God calls him to deliver. The message carries two primary points: First, it identifies the true ruler of the world. For those who place their hopes in a human ruler, or human resources in general, Isaiah's vision recognizes that the real power belongs to God. Second, the vision reminds God's people that God is still in control even when circumstances seem bleak. In a time when the world seemed to be in chaos, Isaiah "saw the Lord sitting on a throne" (6:1). Throughout Scripture a similar truth appears again and again. The apostle Paul delivers a similar message when he speaks of creation groaning in the present time as it awaits God's fulfillment (Romans 8:18-25). The point is that God is leading the world to its conclusion even if it seems that other forces are in control.

Because of this message of hope in the true ruler of the universe, Isaiah 6 is appropriate for times of great transition and tragedy. When John F. Kennedy was assassinated, insightful preachers might have chosen Isaiah 6 as their text the following Sunday. The passage would have been perfect for the chaotic time after terrorists attacked the United States on September 11, 2001. The belief that God still reigns is at the heart of the Christian faith.

### The Call as God's Intrusion

The call of Isaiah occurs within a dramatic vision of God that prompted Isaiah to proclaim, "I am a man of unclean lips!" (6:5). The story reveals the important truth that a "call" is marked by God intruding on the life of the one who is called. Isaiah's story shows this in two very important ways. First, Isaiah is granted the vision of God and then is overwhelmed by it. The sight of God on the throne in heaven was beyond what he could have imagined, and it was surely more than he ever would have asked to see. Second, Isaiah hears God's call and that call is something he could not have dreamed up on his own. This is apparent by the fact that the message Isaiah is given to preach will not lead to success. He must bear bad news, at least mostly bad news. But the point of the call was not Isaiah's success, or his happiness; it was rather God's message delivered faithfully. Thus Isaiah's life was taken over by God, and such is

the nature of one who answers God's call.

The life lived in response to God's call may not be easy. It is certainly not a life lived for the sake of the person called. Such a life lived in response to God's call stands in marked contrast to an "uncalled" life. Walter Brueggemann puts it this way: "An uncalled life is an autonomous existence in which there is no intrusion, disruption, or redefinition, no appearance or utterance of the Holy." Brueggemann's words concerning what happens in the presence of the Holy are fitting for the call of Isaiah, and the call of any of us. As noted already, the call of God is an intrusion into the life being planned and lived according to human desires. God's intrusion naturally leads to disruption. The one called suddenly must think differently about everything: The comfortable routines of life are now cast off and all energy is spent seeking to know the direction God is leading. Finally, the call leads to a redefinition of happiness, success, and fulfillment. Now the only success that matters is the accomplishment of God's purpose. God's vision becomes the guide to everything in the life of the one called.

### Hearing and Answering the Call

A retired schoolteacher was sitting in worship, listening attentively to the sermon. Earlier in the service a child was baptized and the congregation recited vows to nurture the child in her faith. In the sermon the preacher continued this theme. He mentioned how crucial Sunday school is to the children of the congregation, for in that setting their lives are shaped by Scripture and they are equipped to live the Christian life. As the former teacher listened she thought, "That's exactly right! And who better to teach the children than me?" After the service she spoke to an elder who served on the church's Christian Education Committee. She told him she wanted to volunteer. The elder was thrilled because in fact they had been struggling to find teachers. This woman's volunteering marked the beginning of the congregation's growth and revitalization. No one asked her directly to do anything, but in the sermon and in the baptismal liturgy she heard God's call for her.

This scenario is very much in line with the account of the call of the prophet Isaiah. Unlike Jeremiah, who complained that God forced him into his role as a prophet (Jeremiah 20:7), Isaiah seems to be a bystander, just one in God's audience when God asks, "Whom shall I send, and who will go for us?" (6:8). As noted earlier, it is not even certain that God intends to include Isaiah in the group being addressed. Isaiah, however, is overwhelmed with the presence of God. The vision of the heavenly king changes him. So he cries out, "Here am I; send me!" (6:8). This response to God's question is a model for people through the ages when they perceive a need God is trying to meet or a hurt God is trying to heal. Whether directed at them or not, they hear the call "who will go for us?" as a question for them. So also in every age people have responded to the call with the surrendering words of commitment, "Here am I; send me!"

## SHARING THE SCRIPTURE

### PREPARING TO LEAD

#### *Preparing Our Hearts*

Ponder this week's devotional reading from Isaiah 66:18-23. What do you learn about the coming reign of God? What surprises you about this passage, especially in relation to foreign nations? What are your hopes and dreams for the new heavens and the new earth that God promises to make?

Pray that you and the students will live in light of God's promises, especially those concerning the end days.

#### *Preparing Our Minds*

Study the background Scripture from Isaiah 6 and the lesson Scripture from Isaiah 6:1-8.

Consider this question: *Where do you gain confidence to undertake unexpected tasks?*

Write on newsprint:
- ❏ questions for Goal 2 in Sharing the Scripture.
- ❏ information for next week's lesson, found under Continue the Journey."
- ❏ activities for further spiritual growth in Continue the Journey.

Determine how you might use any of the features that precede the first lesson of this quarter in today's session.

Select a hymn for study under Goal 3 in Sharing the Scripture.

### LEADING THE CLASS

#### *(1) Gather to Learn*

❖ Welcome everyone and pray that those who have come today will be open to the call of God on their lives.

❖ Read this information from Dr. Justo González's book *The History of Theological Education*: **In writing about what seminary students who are preparing for ministry need to know, Dr. González points out "that it is much easier to teach people what they ought to think than to teach them to think." He argues that teaching people to think is essential because no professor or church leader "knows what will be the new circumstances that the church and its members will face in the near future. If we are to prepare leaders for a future that we cannot envision, it does not suffice to teach them how to think and what to do. They also have to be trained in such a way that they will know how to respond to unexpected circumstances and challenges on the basis of solid theological and biblical principles."**

❖ Ask: **How might the method of preparation suggested here help church leaders to gain confidence to respond effectively to unexpected circumstances?**

❖ Read aloud today's focus statement: **Unexpected circumstances can lead us into paths we do not anticipate. Where do we gain confidence to undertake these unexpected tasks? Isaiah's confidence came from the unusual and compelling events of his call.**

*(2) Goal 1: Explore the Circumstances of Isaiah's Call and His Reaction to It*

❖ Use the Introduction and Isaiah 6:1 in Understanding the Scripture to provide a context for today's lesson.

❖ Recruit a volunteer to read the call story from Isaiah 6:1-8. Encourage participants to be especially aware of what Isaiah might have sensed during his vision.

❖ Discuss these questions:
1. **What did Isaiah see, hear, taste, touch, or smell?** (This passage is filled with images that appeal to the senses. Enter into the vision by being aware of the sight of God and the seraphs, and sounds of flapping wings and the voice of God, the smell of smoke, the taste of the coal on Isaiah's lips, the feel of the Temple shaking.)
2. **Who are seraphs?** (See Isaiah 6:2-3 in Understanding the Scripture.)
3. **Why is Isaiah afraid when he realizes what's happening?** (See the second paragraph of Isaiah 6:4-5 in Understanding the Scripture. Be sure to contrast the holiness of God with the uncleanness/unworthiness of Isaiah.)
4. **Do you think Isaiah, who was likely a priest before God called him to be a prophet, expected to encounter God as he was doing his routine tasks in the Temple? Explain your answer.** (See The Call as God's Intrusion in Interpreting the Scripture.)
5. **Notice that God asks, "Whom shall I send," but does not single out Isaiah, as was the case with Moses, Jeremiah, and other prophets. What might have prompted Isaiah to volunteer so quickly?** (See the second paragraph of Hearing and Answering the Call in Interpreting the Scripture.)

### (3) Goal 2: Sense Isaiah's Emotions as He Reacted to His Call

❖ Post a sheet of newsprint on which you will write answers to this question: **What emotions do you think Isaiah would have experienced during this vision?** (for example: fear, awe, wonder, sense of doom, amazement)

❖ Form small groups to talk about how they might have reacted to this vision. Post these questions on newsprint:

1. **Why would you have answered God's call, which was not specifically directed to you, with a resounding yes—or no, or silence?**
2. **Recall that Isaiah was already doing the work of the Lord when he was called to do something else. What questions might Isaiah have wanted to ask God about this change in his life's work? What questions might you have wanted to ask God?**
3. **Although Isaiah immediately volunteered, many people would have said "Who, me?" Why is it difficult for us to imagine that God would call us to serve?**

❖ Reconvene the group and invite volunteers to report on any insights they gleaned.

### (4) Goal 3: Answer God's Call to Service

❖ Read the first paragraph of Hearing and Answering the Call in Interpreting the Scripture.

❖ Distribute hymnals and direct the students' attention to the section concerning "call." In *The United*

*Methodist Hymnal*, for example, that section is labeled "Called to God's Mission" (numbers 567–593). Choose one hymn in advance and look together at it to see (1) the kinds of work to which God calls people, and (2) the tools God gives to enable believers to fulfill their calls.

❖ Distribute paper and pencils. Encourage the adults to scan the pertinent pages of their hymnals and jot down the types of work and the tools.

❖ Bring everyone together after allowing the students several minutes to work. Encourage volunteers to name the work and tools they have found in any of the hymns they scanned. Emphasize the scope of the work and the many tools God provides.

❖ Provide time for the adults to reflect silently on these questions:

1. **To what kind of work do I hear God calling me?** (pause)
2. **How will I answer the call?** (pause)
3. **What tools will I need from God?** (pause)

### (5) Continue the Journey

❖ Break the silence by praying that as the learners depart, they will continue to listen for God's call and be ready to answer with Isaiah, "Here am I; send me!"

❖ Post information for next week's session on newsprint for the students to copy:

- **Title: Jeremiah's Call and Commission**
- **Background Scripture: Jeremiah 1**
- **Lesson Scripture: Jeremiah 1:4-10**

■ Focus of the Lesson: Each of us has some aspect of our lives that might convince us that we have nothing to give others. How do we overcome these perceived shortcomings? Jeremiah's response was based on God's promise to be with the prophet as he carried out his calling.

❖ Challenge the adults to grow spiritually by completing one or more of these activities related to this week's session.

(1) Be alert for ways in which you can hear and respond to the call of God. Helping a lost stranger or providing money for a shopper who is a bit short of funds are modest examples of ways you can respond to a call.

(2) Pray about ways that you can answer a call to serve God within the church or community.

(3) Research what it means to say that God is holy.

❖ Sing or read aloud "Here I Am, Lord."

❖ Conclude today's session by leading the class in this benediction, which is adapted from Isaiah 6:8, the key verse for today's lesson: **In response to your call, O God, I say, "Here am I, send me!" Amen.**

UNIT 2: CALLING OF PROPHETS

# Jeremiah's Call and Commission

---

## PREVIEWING THE LESSON

**Lesson Scripture:** Jeremiah 1:4-10
**Background Scripture:** Jeremiah 1
**Key Verse:** Jeremiah 1:8

### Focus of the Lesson:

Each of us has some aspect of our lives that might convince us that we have nothing to give others. How do we overcome these perceived shortcomings? Jeremiah's response was based on God's promise to be with the prophet as he carried out his calling.

### Goals for the Learners:

(1) to investigate the story of Jeremiah's call and recount the details of the promises God made to Jeremiah.
(2) to identify feelings of personal inadequacy.
(3) to respond to a call from God despite feelings of personal inadequacy.

### Supplies:

Bibles, newsprint and marker, paper and pencils, hymnals

---

## READING THE SCRIPTURE

**NRSV**

Lesson Scripture: Jeremiah 1:4-10
⁴Now the word of the Lord came to me saying,
⁵"Before I formed you in the womb
    I knew you,
and before you were born I
    consecrated you;
I appointed you a prophet to the
    nations."

**CEB**

Lesson Scripture: Jeremiah 1:4-10
⁴The Lord's word came to me:
⁵"Before I created you in the womb
    I knew you;
before you were born I set
    you apart;
I made you a prophet to the
    nations."

⁶Then I said, "Ah, Lord GOD! Truly I do not know how to speak, for I am only a boy." ⁷But the LORD said to me, "Do not say, 'I am only a boy'; for you shall go to all to whom I send you, and you shall speak whatever I command you. ⁸Do not be afraid of them, for I am with you to deliver you, says the LORD." ⁹Then the LORD put out his hand and touched my mouth; and the LORD said to me, "Now I have put my words in your mouth. ¹⁰See, today I appoint you over nations and over kingdoms, to pluck up and to pull down, to destroy and to overthrow, to build and to plant."

⁶"Ah, LORD God," I said, "I don't know how to speak because I'm only a child." ⁷The LORD responded, "Don't say, 'I'm only a child.' Where I send you, you must go; what I tell you, you must say. ⁸Don't be afraid of them, because I'm with you to rescue you," declares the LORD. ⁹Then the LORD stretched out his hand, touched my mouth, and said to me, "I'm putting my words in your mouth. ¹⁰This very day I appoint you over nations and empires, to dig up and pull down, to destroy and demolish, to build and plant."

## UNDERSTANDING THE SCRIPTURE

**Introduction.** The first chapter of the Book of Jeremiah contains Jeremiah's own testimony about his call to be a prophet and the basic contents of the message he will preach. Jeremiah does not describe his call as coming in the midst of a dramatic vision like some other prophets (Moses, Isaiah, and Amos, for example). Nevertheless, his call is as direct and inescapable as that of any prophet. He describes his calling as God's clear choice of him for particular service as though he was created for that purpose (Jeremiah 1:4-5). Later in the Book of Jeremiah the prophet complains about the hardships this call places upon his life (Jeremiah 12). In chapter 1 God prepares Jeremiah for the difficulties of prophetic ministry by promising him his enemies will not get the best of him (1:18-19).

**Jeremiah 1:1-3.** The setting of Jeremiah's prophetic work has two dimensions. First, his prophecy is set in a particular time. King Josiah reigned from 640 to 609 B.C., so the thirteenth year of his reign puts Jeremiah's prophecy beginning in 627 B.C. As noted in verse 3, his ministry would continue through the tumultuous reigns of Jehoiakim and Zedekiah. As 2 Kings 24–25 recounts, in 598 B.C. Babylon installed Zedekiah as a puppet king, and exiled a portion of the Jerusalem population in order to assure Judah's loyalty. Then in 587 B.C., when Zedekiah also rebelled against Babylon, the Babylonians returned to destroy Jerusalem and take away more exiles.

Second, Jeremiah's prophecy takes place in a circle of "priests who were in Anathoth" (Jeremiah 1:1). Anathoth was a city given to the Levites who did not possess territory in the Promised Land (Joshua 21:18). Hence, Jeremiah was from a family of Levites. His father, Hilkiah, may be the same Hilkiah who served King Josiah (2 Kings 22–23). Josiah instituted religious reforms that began in 622 B.C. and the Levites of Anathoth seem to have been important leaders in that reform movement (2 Kings 23:4-25). Despite the religious purity of these Levites, however, Jeremiah will later complain that the people of Anathoth tried to kill him because of his unpopular message of destruction for Judah (Jeremiah 11:21-23).

**Jeremiah 1:4-5.** "The word of the LORD came to me" is a common expression the prophets use to introduce God's message delivered to them. (See Ezekiel 6:1; 7:1; 15:1; Hosea 1:1; Joel 1:1; Micah 1:1; Zephaniah 1:1.) In this case it introduces God's call of Jeremiah. God's knowledge of the prophet before birth shows intimacy and purpose like the psalmist's description of God's knowledge in Psalm 139:13-16. "Prophet to the nations" anticipates Jeremiah's sweeping message that includes prophecy against foreign nations (Jeremiah 46–51).

**Jeremiah 1:6-10.** Jeremiah's complaint that he is only a "boy" may mean he is a child, like Samuel, at the time of his commissioning (1 Samuel 3), or it may simply mean he is a young man with little experience. "Ah, Lord GOD" introduces a formal complaint and objection similar to the one Ezekiel lodges in Ezekiel 4:14. God's response to Jeremiah has two parts. First, God assures Jeremiah that

he will be able to accomplish his task because "I am with you" (Jeremiah 1:8). God gave the same promise to Moses (Exodus 3:12) and Gideon (Judges 6:16). God's command "do not be afraid of them" (Jeremiah 1:8) refers to the ones who will hear Jeremiah's message (1:7); it also anticipates the opposition Jeremiah will face, which will be largely the subject of his laments (11:18–12:6). The message he will preach will be mainly one of destruction and devastation (1:9-10). But the words will be from God, who had prepared Jeremiah's mouth. The idea that God will put words in the prophet's mouth is similar to the promise to Moses that God would raise up a prophet like Moses and give him the message he should speak (Deuteronomy 18:18).

**Jeremiah 1:11-12.** Jeremiah reports a vision, which serves as a medium for the "word of the LORD" that came to him. The vision operates on a wordplay. God asks Jeremiah what he sees. He responds, "a branch of an almond tree." The Hebrew word for almond tree in Hebrew is *shaqed*. Then God says, "I am watching over my word to perform it." The Hebrew word for "watching" is *shoqed*. What Jeremiah sees is not significant here. It is the sound of the word for the object he sees that is important. This type of wordplay appears also in Amos 8:1-3.

**Jeremiah 1:13-16.** A second vision reveals directly what will happen in the future. Jeremiah sees "a boiling pot tilted away from the north." God interprets the vision to mean that tribes from the north will invade Judah and overtake it. The vision is about the Babylonians. Technically Babylon was to the east, but their armies could not march directly through the desert areas that separated them from Judah. They traveled northwest and then turned south. So the enemy did come from the north. This judgment comes on Judah for Judah's disobedience and idolatry. The expression they "worshiped the works of their own hands" (1:16) refers to the worship of idols and religious objects associated with other deities. Idol worship in this case was not really the worship of a humanly made object. Rather it was worship of a god connected directly to the worshiper's quest of wealth and material prosperity. Worship of the true God demanded obedience that produced justice and

righteousness and the well-being of the community.

**Jeremiah 1:17-19.** God assures Jeremiah that the people who try to threaten him will not succeed. The promise that Jeremiah will be like a bronze wall uses a metaphor inspired by the defensive structures of cities in the ancient Near East. City walls were designed to prevent invaders from breaching the wall. Often an attacking army used a battering ram or other methods of destruction to break through the wall. A city might enhance the wall's strength by covering it with metal. Thus God tells Jeremiah he will be able to withstand any attack.

---

## INTERPRETING THE SCRIPTURE

### Providence and the Prophetic Call

The Christian doctrine of Providence holds that God is the sovereign ruler of the world who is involved at every level of existence to bring the world to fruition. This does not mean that God controls every minute detail of existence—certainly God's creation is free to rebel—and does rebel— against God's intentions. But it does mean that, in the big picture, God is bringing all things to God's self. As the apostle Paul puts it, "all things work together for good for those who love God, who are called according to his purpose" (Romans 8:28).

The testimony Jeremiah gives of his call is a grand statement about the providence of God. Divine Providence is not predeterminism, the idea that all human actions are programmed by God ahead of time. Rather, Providence has to do with God's constant engagement with humankind to bring about

good. The doctrine is about humankind not being alone, but having God as a partner in all aspects of life. Jeremiah expresses this beautifully in the opening testimony of his call in terms of being known by God. His description is much like that of the psalmist in Psalm 139. The psalmist declares he or she was formed by God in the womb and now can go nowhere away from God's presence. So also Jeremiah was known completely by his Maker. In this way of expressing his call, Jeremiah says that his call to be a prophet is the natural outcome of God's love and guidance. So also will be the course of his ministry. God will never leave him, and that is the most important aspect of what we call Providence.

### Facing Opposition

Perhaps more than any other prophet, Jeremiah's call required him to face bitter opposition from those who disagreed with his message. Later in the book, Jeremiah will complain numerous times to God about the terrible conflict he faces. At one point he says "I was like a gentle lamb led to the slaughter" (Jeremiah 11:19). But the conflict looms already when God commissions Jeremiah. When God says "do not be afraid of them" (1:8) it is more than the general assurance that appears in some call stories (see Joshua 1:6). "Of them" refers to a specific group of people who will oppose Jeremiah. What is more, the people who will give him the greatest problem are those from his own hometown of Anathoth (Jeremiah 11:21-23). Although Amos also was rejected when he preached his message, his opponents were government officials with whom he had no prior contact (Amos 7:10-17). But Jeremiah's very own people rejected him and threatened his life.

Jeremiah's greatest complaint may be that God is his adversary for giving him such a call. Although Jeremiah does not say this in his call account, he will say it later (Jeremiah 20:7). Furthermore, there are signs in Jeremiah's report of his commissioning that this feeling will come upon him eventually. For example, God calls Jeremiah and he has no choice but to answer the call. God appointed him before birth for this role, so what can he do but fulfill it? But there are also signs here and elsewhere in the Book of Jeremiah that the prophet cannot resist the call. Even if he wanted to flee like Jonah to a far country, he would be miserable. Later Jeremiah will say that God's word is like a fire shut up in his bones and he can do nothing but let it out (20:9). Many people who answer God's call to ministry experience the call just this

way. Though the mantle of ministry is difficult to wear at times, they simply cannot take it off. It is as much a part of their identity as the members of their family or the sound of their voice.

Although Jeremiah's call is fraught with internal conflict over how inescapable the call is, the nature of the call also gives strength to persevere. One of the subtle messages of Jeremiah's call account is that the strength of the call and the certainty of God's presence will carry this prophet through all the storms of his ministry. The commissioning appears at the beginning of the Book of Jeremiah to prepare the reader of the rest of the book with this perspective: God's call is certain; Jeremiah cannot reject the call, as much as he might wish to do so; God will protect Jeremiah and see him through all the hardships that come. Many people who feel called to some service in God's name also draw strength from articulating the origin and nature of that call. It stands as a constant reminder in difficult times of why they continue to speak and act in God's name.

### God's Call and Human Politics

The call of Jeremiah plunges him directly into the political issues of his time. This may seem at odds with the nature of being called today. Indeed, the call to speak for God, especially in pastoral ministry, is often thought to be apolitical. But as Robert Laha says, "Contrary to most people's understanding of 'call' today, Jeremiah's calling involves him in the political affairs of his day. God sets him over and against nations and kingdoms." This is true of most of the Old Testament prophets. They brought a message about God's kingdom that inevitably bumped up against the aspirations of human rulers and their kingdoms. Often their prophecies contained predictions of destruction and defeat that were quite unpopular, that went directly against the desires of political figures.

One of the reasons people in contemporary American society have concluded their religious calling must avoid politics is they have too narrow an understanding of what is political and how Christian faith engages politics. Jeremiah recognizes politics for what it is: a human attempt to garner support for certain causes. He also recognizes that human political leaders always seek support for ventures that establish or enhance their own power, often at the expense of others. God's call to Jeremiah was to proclaim truths about what God's rule means for human beings. This is the gist of what Jeremiah was called "to build and to plant" (1:10)—a community shaped by God's desires, not human aspirations. But building a community around divine values means that many human political goals must be rejected. Thus, Jeremiah's words would go out to "pluck up" and "overthrow" (1:10) human kingdoms in order for God's kingdom to be a reality.

If we take Jeremiah's call seriously as a model for what God's call on our lives might be, we must recognize that Jeremiah's opposition to "nations and kingdoms" (1:10) is opposition to all human political systems to some degree. In our world, political parties divide up values so that one party looks out for the poor but ignores basic social morality and another does the opposite. God's kingdom calls all such limited and self-serving systems into question. So the question is not whether we will be involved in politics, but whether we will join Jeremiah in opposing nations and kingdoms when their actions contradict the justice and righteousness of God's kingdom.

---

## SHARING THE SCRIPTURE

### PREPARING TO LEAD

#### *Preparing Our Hearts*

Ponder this week's devotional reading from Psalm 75, a song of communal thanksgiving. For what reasons do God's people give thanks? What wondrous deeds has God done in your own life and in the life of your church? What does the psalmist proclaim about God's judgment?

Pray that you and the students will give thanks and praise to God for all that God has done for them.

#### *Preparing Our Minds*

Study the background Scripture from Jeremiah 1 and the lesson Scripture from Jeremiah 1:4-10.

Consider this question: *How do you overcome the shortcomings that you perceive yourself to have?*

Write on newsprint:
- ❏ information for next week's lesson, found under Continue the Journey.
- ❏ activities for further spiritual growth in Continue the Journey.

Determine how you might use any of the features that precede the first lesson of this quarter in today's session.

## LEADING THE CLASS

### (1) Gather to Learn

❖ Welcome everyone and pray that those who have come today will feel encouraged to take on whatever task God calls them to do.

❖ Read: **Sometimes we don't think we have much to offer the world, or at least much that the world cares about receiving from us. Writer and musician Michael Konik addressed this problem in "Encouraging Words for Despairing Artists" written in 2012. Konik realizes that many artists despair, because their work is undervalued. But, he insists, their gifts are important and, therefore, they need to keep making and sharing their art. He urges artists to "understand that the gift is not theirs; they are merely the vessel through which the divine energy flows, and they are meant to, they are** *obligated*, **to share it with the world. It's a heavy responsibility."** And he recognizes that it's difficult to keep moving forward when no one else seems to care about what you have to offer and the things that are important to you. Still, he argues, "your gifts matter . . . to us and to God."

❖ Read aloud today's focus statement: **Each of us has some aspect of our lives that might convince us that we have nothing to give others. How do we overcome these perceived shortcomings? Jeremiah's response was based on God's promise to be with the prophet as he carried out his calling.**

### (2) Goal 1: Investigate the Story of Jeremiah's Call and Recount the Details of the Promises God Made to Jeremiah

❖ Set the stage for today's lesson by reading or retelling Introduction and Jeremiah 1:1-3 in Understanding the Scripture.

❖ Select two people to read the roles of Jeremiah and God as found in Jeremiah 1:4-10.

❖ Discuss these questions:

1. **What is God's plan for Jeremiah's life?** (See Jeremiah 1:4-5, 10.)
2. **How does this prophet's call relate to what we often call Providence?** (See Providence and the Prophetic Call in Interpreting the Scripture.)
3. **How does Jeremiah respond to God? How does God respond to Jeremiah's objections?** (See Jeremiah 1:6-10 in Understanding the Scripture.)
4. **What similarities do you see between the call of Jeremiah and the calls of other biblical characters we have studied thus far this quarter?**
5. **Jeremiah faced strong opposition during his ministry. What role might this call story play as he is criticized by people who disagree with his message?** (See Facing Opposition in Interpreting the Scripture.)
6. **Some people insist there is no connection between the Bible and politics. Do you think Jeremiah would—or would not—agree? Why?** (See God's Call and Human Politics in Interpreting the Scripture.)

### (3) Goal 2: Identify Feelings of Personal Inadequacy

❖ Distribute paper and pencils. Let the students know that what you are asking them to write will be kept confidential. Note that Jeremiah initially responded to his call by expressing feelings of inadequacy that made him believe he was not up to the job. Encourage the students to make a list of things, specifically related to the mission and ministry of the church, they feel that they are inadequate to handle. They might want to write their concerns in this format: I feel inadequate to greet people I don't know because I'm shy; I feel inadequate to take on tasks that I could do because I think other people could do these jobs better; I feel inadequate to serve on a committee because other people have more experience than I do. Set a time limit for the students to work independently.

❖ Reconvene the class and read: **God has given everyone gifts, although different ones, to build up the church. We all cannot do the same things, nor should we. But many Christians do not engage in ministry at all because of feelings of personal inadequacy such as those that you have identified. Silently ponder these questions as I read each one:**

1. **Review your list. Which one item would you like to focus on?** (pause)
2. **Envision yourself as being adequate to perform this task. What skill or information do you need to master in order to feel adequate to assume this job?** (pause)
3. **Where can you get the training or information or spiritual boost you need?** (pause)
4. **What are you willing to do this week to try to rise above these feelings of inadequacy? For example, if you feel you are too shy to greet worshipers you do not know well, would you be willing to greet just one unfamiliar person?**

### (4) Goal 3: Respond to a Call from God Despite Feelings of Personal Inadequacy

❖ Invite the students to add these words to the papers they wrote on earlier: **Write one action you will take in response to God's call, despite your feelings of inadequacy.** Suggest that they make an effort, with God's help, to complete this action.

❖ Conclude this portion of the lesson by inviting the class to dispel their feelings of inadequacy by repeating after you these words of Paul from Philippians 4:13: **I can do all things through [Christ] who strengthens me.**

### (5) Continue the Journey

❖ Pray that as the learners depart, they will be ready to respond to God's call in spite of their feelings of inadequacy because they know God can equip and empower them for the task at hand.

❖ Post information for next week's session on newsprint for the students to copy:

- **Title: Ezekiel's Call**
- **Background Scripture: Ezekiel 1–3**
- **Lesson Scripture: Ezekiel 3:1-11**
- **Focus of the Lesson:**

Discouragement and doubt can be hindrances to what we hope to achieve. What concrete action can help us get beyond our fears? Ezekiel's call involved eating a scroll that sweetened the bitter taste of his mission and receiving from God extra strength and protection for the challenges that lay ahead.

❖ Challenge the adults to grow spiritually by completing one or more of these activities related to this week's session.

(1) Take on a small challenge that is outside of your comfort zone this week. Perhaps you will volunteer to pray at the opening of a meeting, if praying aloud is difficult for you.

(2) Compare the excuses that Moses (Exodus 3–4) and Jeremiah give for not wanting to respond to God's call. What common themes do you notice?

(3) Help someone, perhaps a younger Christian, who feels that he or she has nothing useful to offer to the church to recognize that God calls a wide variety of people. Tell the story of the young Jeremiah being used mightily by God during a very difficult time in Israelite history.

❖ Sing or read aloud "Whom Shall I Send?"

❖ Conclude today's session by leading the class in this benediction, which is adapted from Isaiah 6:8, the key verse for July 9: **In response to your call, O God, I say, "Here am I, send me!" Amen.**

## UNIT 2: CALLING OF PROPHETS
# EZEKIEL'S CALL

---

### PREVIEWING THE LESSON

**Lesson Scripture:** Ezekiel 3:1-11
**Background Scripture:** Ezekiel 1–3
**Key Verses:** Ezekiel 3:10-11

### Focus of the Lesson:

Discouragement and doubt can be hindrances to what we hope to achieve. What concrete action can help us get beyond our fears? Ezekiel's call involved eating a scroll that sweetened the bitter taste of his mission and receiving from God extra strength and protection for the challenges that lay ahead.

### Goals for the Learners:

(1) to explore God's call of Ezekiel in terms of Ezekiel's eating of a scroll.
(2) to relate Ezekiel's experience with people who do not want to listen to their own experiences.
(3) to identify ways to be "harder than flint" in obeying God's call in a hostile context.

### Supplies:

Bibles, newsprint and marker, paper and pencils, hymnals, scroll-like cookies

---

### READING THE SCRIPTURE

NRSV
Lesson Scripture: Ezekiel 3:1-11

¹He said to me, O mortal, eat what is offered to you; eat this scroll, and go, speak to the house of Israel. ²So I opened my mouth, and he gave me the scroll to eat. ³He said to me, Mortal, eat this scroll that I give you and fill your stomach with it. Then I ate it; and in my mouth it was as sweet as honey.

CEB
Lesson Scripture: Ezekiel 3:1-11

¹Then he said to me: Human one, eat this thing that you've found. Eat this scroll and go, speak to the house of Israel. ²So I opened my mouth, and he fed me the scroll. ³He said to me: Human one, feed your belly and fill your stomach with this scroll that I give you. So I ate it, and in my mouth it became as sweet as honey.

⁴He said to me: Mortal, go to the house of Israel and speak my very words to them. ⁵For you are not sent to a people of obscure speech and difficult language, but to the house of Israel— ⁶not to many peoples of obscure speech and difficult language, whose words you cannot understand. Surely, if I sent you to them, they would listen to you. ⁷But the house of Israel will not listen to you, for they are not willing to listen to me; because all the house of Israel have a hard forehead and a stubborn heart. ⁸See, I have made your face hard against their faces, and your forehead hard against their foreheads. ⁹Like the hardest stone, harder than flint, I have made your forehead; do not fear them or be dismayed at their looks, for they are a rebellious house. **¹⁰He said to me: Mortal, all my words that I shall speak to you receive in your heart and hear with your ears; ¹¹then go to the exiles, to your people, and speak to them. Say to them, "Thus says the Lord God"; whether they hear or refuse to hear.**

⁴Then he said to me: Human one, go! Go to the house of Israel and speak my words to them. ⁵You aren't being sent to a people whose language and speech are difficult and obscure but to the house of Israel. ⁶No, not to many peoples who speak difficult and obscure languages, whose words you wouldn't understand. If I did send you to them, they would listen to you. ⁷But the house of Israel—they will refuse to listen to you because they refuse to listen to me. The whole house of Israel is hardheaded and hard-hearted too. ⁸I've now hardened your face so that you can meet them head-on. ⁹I've made your forehead like a diamond, harder than stone. Don't be afraid of them or shrink away from them, because they are a household of rebels.

**¹⁰He said to me: Human one, listen closely, and take to heart every word I say to you. ¹¹Then go to the exiles, to your people's children. Whether they listen or not, speak to them and say: The Lord God proclaims!**

## UNDERSTANDING THE SCRIPTURE

**Introduction.** The call vision of Ezekiel takes place in Babylon. Ezekiel was part of a wave of exiles taken from Jerusalem in 597 B.C. that included King Jehoiachin. In an effort to manage a local population, the Babylonians first deposed the native king and removed wealthy and educated citizens. Since Ezekiel was from a priestly family, he was considered a most prominent citizen. If further rebellion occurred, the Babylonians attacked and took more exiles, as they did in 587 B.C. Most of Ezekiel's prophecy in chapters 1–24 predicts this event and the hardships it will bring.

**Ezekiel 1:1-3.** Ezekiel's vision takes place in Babylon among the exiles from Judah. The reference to the thirtieth year is uncertain. The additional information on date clarifies that the vision takes place in the fifth year of the exile of King Jehoiachin (593 B.C.). So Ezekiel is not referring to the thirtieth year of exile. Therefore, it seems most likely that "thirtieth year" refers to Ezekiel's age. Since priests began serving in the Temple at age thirty, this would have been a key time for

Ezekiel. But instead of beginning priestly service in the Jerusalem Temple he is far removed in Babylon, an unclean land.

**Ezekiel 1:4-14.** God's presence is frequently described as a storm with thunder and lightning (Exodus 19:16; Psalm 29:3-5). The four creatures Ezekiel sees are similar to the creatures in other prophetic visions (Isaiah 6), but Ezekiel's description is much more elaborate. In this vision the creatures are guardians of God's throne; they do not participate in the vision or go forth to do God's service as in Isaiah 6. As in Isaiah 6:2, however, the creatures use one pair of wings to cover their "bodies" or "feet" in Isaiah (a euphemism for private parts) because of the holiness of God.

**Ezekiel 1:15-21.** The wheels move the throne of God along as if on a chariot, but the wheels can move in any direction, unlike chariots that are unidirectional.

**Ezekiel 1:22-25.** The vision of God's throne looks like a microcosm of the entire cosmos. The dome was believed to separate heaven from earth and to hold back water above the earth (Genesis 1:6-8). God's voice sounds like thunder. This is another common way of describing God's overwhelming presence.

**Ezekiel 1:26-28.** The centerpiece of the vision is the throne of God. Ezekiel's description is at once reserved and outlandishly bold. He uses terms like "likeness" and "appearance of" to say with some caution how the vision of God looked. But his description of brightness ("like gleaming amber") above the loins seems to be describing the appearance of the face of God. Not even Moses was allowed to see God's face (Exodus 33:20). But Ezekiel seems to be saying he did,

albeit through the storm cloud. The rainbow is a sign of God's covenant with Noah that the earth will never again be destroyed by a flood (1:28; see also Genesis 9:13). Thus, the rainbow is a sign of God's peace with God's people, a welcome sign for people in exile. The natural reaction to such a vision of God's glory is to fall down prostrate in worship.

**Ezekiel 2:1-7.** God addresses Ezekiel as "mortal." The Hebrew expression is *ben adam*, literally "son of humankind." The word *adam*, the name given to human beings in Genesis 1:26 and 2:7, derives from the same root as the word for "ground" (*adamah*). Thus a human being is one taken from the dust or soil and the label "son of humankind" emphasizes Ezekiel's frailty.

**Ezekiel 2:8–3:3.** As in the calls of Isaiah and Jeremiah, God prepares Ezekiel to speak God's word. Typical of Ezekiel, however, the way God prepares Ezekiel's mouth is more elaborate than in other prophetic call accounts. God gives Ezekiel a scroll and commands him to eat. Only one side of a scroll was generally used, so the description in verse 10 of writing on both sides is also outlandish. It seems to symbolize the fullness of the message. The content of the scroll is lamentation, mourning, and woe. Much of Ezekiel's early prophecy will point forward to the destruction of Jerusalem in 587 B.C. Ezekiel and his fellow exiles will not be able to prevent the trauma, but only to mourn when it occurs. It may seem odd that the scroll filled with lamentation is sweet. This description does not refer to the sweetness of the message itself. Rather, as God's word, it is to be desired for it contains the truth (see Psalm 19:7-10).

**Ezekiel 3:4-11.** The call of Ezekiel is to speak God's word to his own people. The irony is that these people, who speak the same language and have the same religious beliefs, will not listen to the word from Ezekiel. If God sent Ezekiel to a foreign people, as God sent Jonah, those people would probably heed the prophet's word. The promise that the people will not heed the prophet's word is a common theme in prophetic calls (Isaiah 6:9-10; Jeremiah 1). God does not prevent the people from hearing; rather, God simply tells the prophet what is sure to be the case.

**Ezekiel 3:12-15.** The theme of the spirit transporting Ezekiel is common in the book (Ezekiel 8:3; 37:1). Ezekiel now returns from the visionary state to the company of exiles.

**Ezekiel 3:16-21.** As a watchman, Ezekiel will be a lookout. This role is applied here to Ezekiel's preaching of personal responsibility. His main task is to warn the wicked of the consequences of their actions. Ezekiel's audience is divided into two groups: righteous and wicked. This is a common way Scripture speaks of those who depend on God and those who do not (see Psalm 1).

**Ezekiel 3:22-27.** Ezekiel's inability to speak is a major theme in the book (Ezekiel 33:21-22). At times it seems to be accompanied by paralysis (4:4-8). The main point of his speechlessness may be that he can only speak when God opens his mouth to utter words about Jerusalem's destruction. Once the city had fallen, the prophet reports that he was "no longer unable to speak" (33:22).

---

## INTERPRETING THE SCRIPTURE

*To Speak the Truth in Love*

The call of Ezekiel and other prophets is rightly characterized by the expression "speaking the truth in love" from Ephesians 4:15. The first part of the expression ("speaking the truth") is often associated with the prophets and it certainly applies to Ezekiel. When God commissions Ezekiel it is not with a specific message, but only "speak my very words to them" (Ezekiel 3:4) and say to them "Thus says the Lord GOD" (3:11). As Ezekiel begins his work, however, it becomes apparent that God's word will often be very hard for the people to hear. There is a hint of the difficulty of the message in the description of the scroll Ezekiel is given to swallow (2:10) and in the description of Ezekiel's audience as having a "hard forehead and a stubborn heart" (3:7). Indeed, Ezekiel's job will sometimes be hard and God prepares Ezekiel for that. This is what is often meant by "speaking the truth."

In relation to the prophets, however, speaking the truth is often conceived as something harsh, done in opposition to the people who receive the message. A surface reading of Ezekiel 3:1-11 might give that impression as well, but a close reading reveals that indeed Ezekiel is called to speak the truth in love. In God's call of Ezekiel, God prepares the prophet for the people not to listen to him. But one simple feature of Ezekiel's call includes the injunction to speak in love. God tells him to "go to the exiles, to *your* people" (3:11, emphasis added). Prophets like Ezekiel are, for the most part, not called to speak to strangers, but to the people of their own communities. Ezekiel is sent to minister to family and friends. Over and over the Book of Ezekiel refers to the prophet being "among the exiles" (1:1), not separate from them. Hence, the hard truth Ezekiel must sometimes speak is as painful for him as for his audience. This kind of pain is at the heart of what it means to speak the truth in love, and it is at the heart of the prophetic call.

### Called in Our Mortality

The label "mortal" ("Human one" in CEB) God uses for Ezekiel is an important marker of the prophet's limitations and how those limits will be used to communicate the truth of God's word. As the Book of Ezekiel unfolds, his limitations become instruments for God to deliver the divine message. As noted already, the silence of Ezekiel may indicate a bodily ailment, perhaps paralysis. If so, God used it as a symbolic gesture to deliver a message to the exiles. In Ezekiel 24:15-27 the death of Ezekiel's wife becomes a symbol of the destruction of Jerusalem. Ezekiel's great personal loss communicated profoundly the great loss the exiles would experience. Ezekiel's identity as a weak mortal did not hinder his work as a prophet. It became part of the message itself. This is important for one to remember if he or she feels inadequate to answer God's call. God is able to use frailty and weakness to accomplish God's purpose in ways the one called could not have imagined.

Once in college I participated in a youth rally organized by our campus minister. I was asked to share my experience with Christ from the perspective of a student. There was also to be music and a sermon. The preacher was an evangelist named David Ring, who I only knew by name. When I arrived at the event I was introduced to the preacher. He walked toward me with a limp, held out a disfigured hand, and said hello with slurred speech. I later learned David has cerebral palsy, which had altered his body and impaired his speech significantly. I appreciated his willingness to preach despite these limitations, but I wondered how a gym full of high school students would be able to listen closely enough to understand him since his speech was so impaired. I was amazed at what happened. As he spoke, you could hear a pin drop in the gym. The kids hung on his every word. He preached on Paul's thorn in the flesh that God would not take away, about God's power made evident in weakness (2 Corinthians 12:5-10). David Ring's limitations made him the perfect embodiment of the message. He was not effective *in spite of* his cerebral palsy but *because of* it. Suffice it to say that everyone present that night got the message that even our weaknesses, when turned over to God, can become something useful for God's purpose.

### Sustained by God's Word

The call of Ezekiel includes the strange episode of God presenting a scroll and telling Ezekiel to eat it. When Ezekiel eats the scroll he says, "Then I ate it; and in my mouth it was as sweet as honey" (Ezekiel 3:3). When the scroll was mentioned in Ezekiel 2:8-10 the prophet described it as containing words of "lamentation and mourning and woe" (2:10). How could Ezekiel then say it was as sweet as honey? The writer of Revelation has a similar vision in which he is told to eat a little scroll. When he eats it, it is first sweet, but then his stomach becomes bitter (Revelation 10:10). Is this not what we expect for Ezekiel also?

The sweetness of the scroll Ezekiel eats makes sense if we consider three points about the scroll. First, the scroll represents the word of God given to Ezekiel to deliver. When Ezekiel says it is sweet he is perhaps alluding to the description of Torah in Psalm 19:10: "sweeter also than honey, and the drippings of the honeycomb." God's word orders the world, provides good news of God's grace, and promises God's people that God will always be with them. This is sweet indeed. From Ezekiel's perspective, a scroll containing God's word is sweet, regardless of the exact content.

Second, since the scroll is given as God's word to prepare Ezekiel to speak to God's people, it is part of the commissioning of the prophet. The sweetness of the scroll may therefore refer to the pleasure of answering the call of God. As Walter Eichrodt says, the commands God gives as part of our call "when they are once fulfilled by us, bestow an inward satisfaction which takes away all their bitterness."

Finally, a scroll containing words of lament and predictions of destruction can be sweet in and of itself if we consider how such words were meant to be received by Ezekiel's audience. Predictions of woe in the prophets are almost never meant to be final pronouncements of what will occur. Rather, they are warnings of what will be if the people do not change their ways. Thus, even predictions of doom can be considered sweet when received as part of God's larger purpose to restore and heal. To be sure, lamentation refers to a complaint over disaster that has already occurred. But this too can be understood as good news when we realize that complaint offered to God assumes God hears and will respond and those issuing the complaint have not lost faith. Therefore, it makes sense that Ezekiel received the scroll gladly and was sustained and even pleased by it.

---

## SHARING THE SCRIPTURE

### PREPARING TO LEAD

#### Preparing Our Hearts

Ponder this week's devotional reading from Ezekiel 17:22-24. In this passage the importance and effectiveness of God's word is highlighted. The passage also makes reference to an image known as the "cosmic tree," which was widely used in mythology. What do you learn here about this tree?

Pray that you and the students will recognize the sovereignty and might of God, whose very word can accomplish great things.

#### Preparing Our Minds

Study the background Scripture from Ezekiel 1–3 and the lesson Scripture from Ezekiel 3:1-11.

Consider this question: *What concrete action can help you get beyond your fears when discouragement and doubt hinder what you hope to achieve?*

Write on newsprint:
- ❏ information for next week's lesson, found under Continue the Journey.
- ❏ activities for further spiritual growth in Continue the Journey.

Determine how you might use any of the features that precede the first lesson of this quarter in today's session.

Purchase or bake enough scroll-like cookies, such as Pepperidge Farm® Pirouettes, so that each student has one cookie for Goal 1 in Sharing the Scripture. Use a plain, sweet cookie if you cannot find any scroll-shaped ones.

## LEADING THE CLASS

### (1) Gather to Learn

❖ Welcome everyone and pray that those who have come today will open their hearts and minds to receive God's word for them from today's session.

❖ Read: **Many authors who eventually earn critical acclaim and adoring readers have had their work rejected, often numerous times. Would you have felt discouraged and just given up dreams of being a writer had you been**

- **Herman Melville? Melville reportedly received a letter asking, "Does it have to be a whale?" The rejection notice went on to suggest that Melville choose "an antagonist with a more popular visage among the younger readers." He did not, and *Moby Dick* became a classic in American literature.**
- **John le Carré, whose book *The Spy Who Came in from**

*the Cold* **was turned down with a rejection note stating that the author "hasn't got any future"?**
- **Stephen King, who in response to his manuscript for *Carrie* was told that "science fiction which deals with negative utopias . . . do not sell"?**
- **Ernest Hemingway, who was chided for his "tedious and offensive" prose in *The Sun Also Rises*?**

❖ Read aloud today's focus statement: **Discouragement and doubt can be hindrances to what we hope to achieve. What concrete action can help us get beyond our fears? Ezekiel's call involved eating a scroll that sweetened the bitter taste of his mission and receiving from God extra strength and protection for the challenges that lay ahead.**

### (2) Goal 1: Explore God's Call of Ezekiel in Terms of Ezekiel's Eating of a Scroll

❖ Read or retell Introduction and Ezekiel 3:1-2 in Understanding the Scripture to set the stage for today's lesson.

❖ Distribute the cookies you have brought so that each person has one. Tell them that as you read Ezekiel 3:1-3 they are to eat their cookie slowly, noticing the taste and texture. Pause briefly after verse 3. Then continue reading verses 4-11.

❖ Discuss these questions:
1. How did your cookie taste to you?
2. What parallels can you draw between the taste of the cookie and the word of God? (See Sustained by God's Word in Interpreting the Scripture.)

3. **What did God commission Ezekiel to do?** (See Ezekiel 3:4-11 in Understanding the Scripture and To Speak the Truth in Love in Interpreting the Scripture.)
4. **Why was Ezekiel a good choice for the job that God called him to do?** (See the first paragraph of Called in Our Mortality in Interpreting the Scripture.)

*(3) Goal 2: Relate Ezekiel's Experience with People Who Do Not Want to Listen to the Learners' Experiences*

❖ Distribute paper and pencils. Invite participants to imagine themselves as Ezekiel the day after he heard God's call. They are to write a journal entry concerning the positive and negative reactions he might have to his call, as well as any questions they might have about this work.

❖ Bring everyone together and call on several volunteers to read or retell their journal entries.

❖ Encourage the adults to tell stories to the class (or a small group) of times when they tried to speak God's truth to someone who clearly was not interested in listening. Could the class member discern reasons for this "turn off"? If so, what steps did they take to try to reach this person? Note that even if they did not "feel" successful, they were faithful if they made the attempt. The Holy Spirit is ultimately responsible for how the person responds.

*(4) Goal 3: Identify Ways to Be "Harder than Flint" in Obeying God's Call in a Hostile Context*

❖ Read: **Often people say nothing because they fear speaking to** others in a public setting. **If we are going to obey God's call to speak truth, we must be willing to speak, even if the listeners seem hostile or we're simply afraid. Writer of the highly influential book,** *How to Win Friends and Influence People* **(first published in 1936), Dale Carnegie claimed, "A book may give you excellent suggestions on how best to conduct yourself in the water, but sooner or later you must get wet, perhaps even strangle and be 'half scared to death.' There are a great many 'wet less' bathing suits worn at the seashore, but no one ever learns to swim in them. To plunge is the only way."**

❖ Form small groups and distribute newsprint and markers. Ask each group to brainstorm ways that they can plunge into situations where they feel God has called them to act, even if they are "half scared to death."

❖ Call the groups together to hear their ideas. (Some possible ideas include: relying on the Holy Spirit; listening for God's word in Scripture, prayer, and sermons; continuing to obey God whether people embrace your message or are hostile to it.)

*(5) Continue the Journey*

❖ Pray that as the learners depart, they will resolve to speak God's truth openly and honestly, no matter how people respond.

❖ Post information for next week's session on newsprint for the students to copy:
- **Title: Amos's Call**
- **Background Scripture: Amos 7**
- **Lesson Scripture: Amos 7:10-17**

■ Focus of the Lesson: At times we find obeying God's direction to be in direct contrast to what others think we should do. Is it possible to remain determined despite the opposition? Amos committed to serving even in the face of negativity.

❖ Challenge the adults to grow spiritually by completing one or more of these activities related to this week's session.

(1) Make a commitment to continue "talking the talk" and "walking the walk" as a Christian even when people rebuff your words and deeds.

(2) Consider the strategies you use to witness to God's truth. Do you come across as a know-it-all? Do you try to insist on your way of understanding God's Word? Are you willing to do humble deeds that truly help others? Try to identify any areas of your witness (not just how you talk but what you do) that may turn people away from Christ—and then make necessary changes.

(3) Try to say and enact God's Word in a winsome way in your workplace. How do people respond?

❖ Sing or read aloud "Trust and Obey."

❖ Conclude today's session by leading the class in this benediction, which is adapted from Isaiah 6:8, the key verse for July 9: In response to your call, O God, I say, "Here am I, send me!" Amen.

## UNIT 2: CALLING OF PROPHETS
# AMOS'S CALL

---

### PREVIEWING THE LESSON

**Lesson Scripture:** Amos 7:10-17
**Background Scripture:** Amos 7
**Key Verses:** Amos 7:14-15

### Focus of the Lesson:
At times we find obeying God's direction to be in direct contrast to what others think we should do. Is it possible to remain determined despite the opposition? Amos committed to serving even in the face of negativity.

### Goals for the Learners:
(1) to discover how Amaziah and Jeroboam challenged Amos's prophetic ministry.
(2) to sense instances of God's calling to serve in unfamiliar places and capacities.
(3) to commit to serving God in spite of opposition.

### Supplies:
Bibles, newsprint and marker, paper and pencils, hymnals

---

### READING THE SCRIPTURE

NRSV
Lesson Scripture: Amos 7:10-17

¹⁰Then Amaziah, the priest of Bethel, sent to King Jeroboam of Israel, saying, "Amos has conspired against you in the very center of the house of Israel; the land is not able to bear all his words. ¹¹For thus Amos has said,
'Jeroboam shall die by the sword,
and Israel must go into exile
away from his land.'"

CEB
Lesson Scripture: Amos 7:1-17

¹⁰Then Amaziah, the priest of Bethel, reported to Israel's King Jeroboam, "Amos has plotted against you within the house of Israel. The land isn't able to cope with everything that he is saying. ¹¹Amos has said, 'Jeroboam will die by the sword, and Israel will be forced out of its land.' "

¹²Amaziah said to Amos, "You who see things, go, run away to the land of Judah, eat your bread there, and

¹²And Amaziah said to Amos, "O seer, go, flee away to the land of Judah, earn your bread there, and prophesy there; ¹³but never again prophesy at Bethel, for it is the king's sanctuary, and it is a temple of the kingdom."

**¹⁴Then Amos answered Amaziah, "I am no prophet, nor a prophet's son; but I am a herdsman, and a dresser of sycamore trees, ¹⁵and the LORD took me from following the flock, and the LORD said to me, 'Go, prophesy to my people Israel.'**

¹⁶"Now therefore hear the word of the LORD.
You say, 'Do not prophesy against Israel,
and do not preach against the house of Isaac.'
¹⁷Therefore thus says the LORD:
'Your wife shall become a prostitute in the city,
and your sons and your daughters shall fall by the sword,
and your land shall be parceled out by line;
you yourself shall die in an unclean land,
and Israel shall surely go into exile away from its land.'"

prophesy there; ¹³but never again prophesy at Bethel, for it is the king's holy place and his royal house."

**¹⁴Amos answered Amaziah, "I am not a prophet, nor am I a prophet's son; but I am a shepherd, and a trimmer of sycamore trees. ¹⁵But the LORD took me from shepherding the flock, and the LORD said to me, 'Go, prophesy to my people Israel.'**

¹⁶"Now then hear the LORD's word.
You say, 'Don't prophesy against Israel, and don't preach against the house of Isaac.'
¹⁷"Therefore, the LORD proclaims:
'Your wife will become a prostitute in the city,
and your sons and your daughters will fall by the sword,
and your land will be measured and divided up;
you yourself will die in an unclean land,
and Israel will surely be taken away from its land.'"

---

## UNDERSTANDING THE SCRIPTURE

**Introduction.** In Amos 7 the prophet reports three visions (7:1-3, 4-6, and 7-9) that are nearly identical in form. Another vision in Amos 8:1-3 also has the same structure and should be included with those in chapter 7. But this group of visions is interrupted by a narrative in Amos 7:10-17. The narrative tells the story of Amos's encounter with Amaziah, the priest who is in charge of the sanctuary at Bethel. Amaziah orders Amos to cease his message of judgment on Israel and to return to his home in Judah. Together, the visions and the narrative show both the unique and costly calling of prophets in ancient Israel and the cost of speaking the hard truth in any time or place.

**Amos 7:1-3.** In his first vision Amos reports that the Lord showed him something. As Amos 7:12 indicates, prophets were often called "seers" because they had visions of things that would happen in the future. Prophetic vision reports typically include an account of seeing or being shown something (Ezekiel 1:1). In Amos 7:1 the Lord showed Amos a locust swarm that was forming. Amos notes it was after "the king's mowing," that is, the first mowing of grain the king exacted as a tax. Now, as the people are about to harvest the grain that would provide their food and income, a swarm of locusts threatens to destroy the crop. Amos responds, "O Lord, please forgive! How can Jacob stand. He is so small" (paraphrase). God answers with a promise that the vision will not come to pass.

This vision report reveals two crucial characteristics of prophets. First, they were intermediaries and they often made intercession for the people to God. Some casual readers of the prophets have the impression that Israel's prophets mainly lambasted the people with words of doom. But true prophets were pained by the prospect of disaster for the people. This is one of the main problems with Jonah, who did not want to answer God's call because he feared God would not carry through with threats. Jonah wanted to see destruction, but Amos did not. Second, God listened to the prophet. God cared about the prophet's prayers for the people. Like Moses in Exodus 32–34 (the golden calf story), Amos pleads to God on behalf of the people and God "relented" and did not to bring disaster on Israel.

**Amos 7:4-6.** The second vision report is identical to the first in form and it has very similar content. Amos sees another disaster coming for Israel. This time it is a devouring fire that will wipe out everything. "Great deep" refers to the ocean ancient Israelites believed surrounded and

flowed under earth (Genesis 1:2). It was often a symbol of chaos and disorder. But the devastating fire Amos saw would trump it. Again Amos asks God not to let it be, and God again listens to Amos's plea.

**Amos 7:7-9.** The third vision changes slightly in form. Instead of Amos simply reporting what he sees, God asks Amos what he sees. When Amos answers, God responds with a pronouncement of judgment. The key line is "I will never again pass them by" (7:8). God has ceased listening to Amos's intercession, it seems. Now God will bring punishment. The final vision in Amos 8:1-3 makes this clear: "The end has come upon my people Israel" (8:2).

Most translations of the third vision report follow a tradition that developed in the Middle Ages wherein Amos is understood to see "a wall built with a plumb line" (7:7). A plumb line is a builder's tool used to determine if a wall is perpendicular or not. According to this tradition, Amos reports that he sees a plumb line (7:8). Then God declares, "I am setting a plumb line in the midst of my people Israel" (7:8). The plumb line represents judgment, for Israel is surely not straight. Thus, God cannot pass it by any longer.

This traditional translation captures the essence of Amos 7:7-9. There is another way of reading this passage, however, that may be more accurate and may reveal more about the calling of the prophet Amos. As noted, our translation of this vision reflects an interpretation that dates to the Middle Ages. Until then, however, there was great disagreement about what the translation should be. The main problem was the word rendered "plumb line." The problem is that the word literally means "tin" (Hebrew *anak*). Furthermore, the description of what Amos sees is better translated "a wall of tin." Walls were sometimes covered with metals to make them better able to withstand attack. So this makes sense as something Amos might see. The notion that the wall was "built with" a plumb line is difficult to get from the Hebrew construction. For centuries translators and scholars did not know what to make of the word *anak*. The ancient Aramaic version, for example, translated with a word that means "judgment." The translators thought the word must be symbolic. They could make no sense of it otherwise. Finally in the Middle Ages someone proposed that the word referred to another metal-like lead that could be shaped into a plummet, attached to a line, and then used as a carpenter's tool. This was based on a misunderstanding of the meaning of the word *anak*; it also required a great leap in interpretation. Nevertheless, the translation stuck.

Modern scholars, however, have recognized that the meaning "plumb line" is not accurate, but they have not come to any agreement on what the meaning is. They have noticed, however, that this vision is identical in form to the vision in Amos 8:1-3, which works on a word play based on the sounds of two words.

Most scholars now think Amos 7:7-9 also originally had a word-play that carried the meaning of the vision report, but the word play was lost, perhaps because of mistakes in the manuscript. One interesting point, however, is that the word for tin (*anak*) is similar in sound to the Hebrew pronoun meaning "you" (the *k* sound is characteristic of this pronoun). Therefore, it is possible that God's response to Amos intends to say "I am putting *you* in the midst of my people Israel." If so, this translation would explain why the narrative about Amos preaching at Bethel comes next. Here we see the prophet "in the midst of" Israel. Since intercession is no longer possible, Amos now preaches judgment and is rejected.

**Amos 7:10-17.** The narrative about Amos preaching at Bethel shows exactly what happened when God put Amos in the midst of Israel to deliver God's message. Amaziah reported to King Jeroboam that Amos proclaimed a message directly against him in the Bethel sanctuary. He then commands Amos to "flee away to the land of Judah," perhaps referring to Amos's home in Tekoa, a village south of Jerusalem (Amos 1:1). Amos's response to Amaziah in verse 14, "I am no prophet, nor a prophet's son" may seem curious since Amos obviously was a prophet! By "prophet's son," however, Amos means he was not part of a prophetic guild, not a professional prophet. Also, this sentence in Hebrew has no verbs. The construction requires the verb "to be" to be supplied. But the tense of the verb is uncertain. So Amos could actually be saying, "I was no prophet" (until the Lord called me). Regardless of how we read this verse, Amos's emphasis is clearly on God calling him. He is not a prophet who existed to serve the king of Israel, but only to serve the king of Glory, the Lord.

## INTERPRETING THE SCRIPTURE

### The King's Sanctuary

The encounter between Amos and Amaziah took place in the sanctuary at Bethel, a place that held great religious importance for the people of Israel. The place of worship traced its roots to the patriarch Jacob and to the time he dreamed of a stairway coming down from the heavens (Genesis 28). One of the points of that story of origins was that this place that God chose was under divine control. It was not to be manipulated by human beings. But now the Bethel sanctuary was completely under the control of the monarchy. Thus Amaziah said, "It is the king's sanctuary, and it is a temple of the kingdom" (Amos 7:13). On the basis of that claim Amaziah ordered Amos not to preach there again but to return to his home where he might find a more sympathetic audience.

Everyone who answers God's call eventually runs into this kind of resistance if she or he follows God's direction. The designation of Bethel as the king's sanctuary was really an order for Amos to conform his message to the powers represented there so as not to offend them and to pay homage to those powers. What appeared to Amos as an order, however, often takes the form of a subtle temptation to those who are trying to answer God's call. It is often like the temptations of Jesus. Satan encouraged Jesus to care for himself, perhaps with the idea that he could then care for others (Matthew 4:3-4). Satan also suggested that Jesus would have to acknowledge the one who controls the kingdoms of this world in order to accomplish his mission (Matthew 4:8-10). Jesus refused, however, as did Amos, to compromise the message of God's kingdom in order to placate the kingdoms of this world. For all who answer God's call to live the Christian life and to proclaim the gospel, there will be a persistent struggle not to submit to the ways things are done and said in "the king's sanctuary."

### The Lord Took Me

Amos's testimony about how he ended up preaching at Bethel includes an enduring description of the call to prophetic ministry. Amaziah tries to dismiss Amos by lumping him together with the professional prophets ("O seer," 7:12). The idea Amaziah puts forth is that Amos is just rebellious. Perhaps he has his own agenda and is trying to promote it by preaching against King Jeroboam. Or perhaps Amos is supported by anti-Jeroboam political figures who want to control the throne. Prophets were sometimes used by various political parties for such purposes. But Amos responds by refuting these accusations. He declares that his call came from God alone and his message is the word of God, not a humanly shaped political message.

The kind of calling Amos describes is perhaps necessary to preach the message Amos preached. He must have known that his message would be unpopular in the Bethel sanctuary. He must have also known that prophets who proclaimed messages against the king might be risking their lives to do so. Indeed, Amaziah essentially charges Amos with treason when he reports to the king that "Amos has conspired against you" (7:10). About a century later Jeremiah will be brought to trial on just such charges because he predicted Judah would be destroyed (Jeremiah 26:7-9). Amos must know he preaches at his own peril. In such circumstances the only strength the one who answers the call may have is the conviction that God has really issued the call.

We should note that no one who speaks as Amos spoke can do so completely without any human support. Amos must have had some followers, even if only a small group of disciples. Otherwise, his message would have been lost. But many figures like Amos are peripheral to the powers of society. Their strength comes from the absolute conviction that what they are saying and doing is right. We see this in contemporary society in figures like Martin Luther King Jr., who described hearing a voice at midnight that urged him to stand up for justice. Not everyone who answers God's call hears such a voice. But for those who face opposition as Amos did, it is a key factor in shaping the person's identity and giving her or him courage to answer the call.

### The Cost of Opposing God's Call

Amaziah opposed Amos with the direct instructions: "Do not prophesy against Israel" (Amos 7:16). Amos answered with an equally clear word from God: "Thus says the LORD . . ." (7:17). The message Amos then proclaimed was devastating. He declared to Amaziah that his wife would become a prostitute in the desperate times after an enemy invasion, his children would be killed, his property confiscated, and he would be sent into exile. But it did not have to be so.

The structure of this part of the passage carries an important message. Note that it actually begins with Amos reporting God's word: "Therefore hear the word of the LORD" (7:16). But that word begins with a quotation of Amaziah's rebuke of Amos ("do not prophesy").

In other words, Amaziah's order for Amos not to prophesy seems to be the direct cause of the devastating message that follows. In verse 11, Amos had prophesied that King Jeroboam would die and Israel would go into exile. Now Amos prophesies about Amaziah because of his refusal to hear God's word.

It should be said clearly that God does not punish someone directly in such a horrible way simply for being disobedient. The point is that Amaziah is working directly against God's word that would heal and correct Israelite society, that would prevent the disaster predicted in verse 11. By shutting up the prophet, however, Amaziah brings the full brunt of God's word on himself and on the society. This says something crucially important about repentance.

---

## SHARING THE SCRIPTURE

### PREPARING TO LEAD

#### Preparing Our Hearts

Ponder this week's devotional reading from Psalm 119:1-8. What do verses 1-3 state about those who are happy (or blessed)? For what does the psalmist pray? Clearly, the psalmist is extolling the glories of God's law. He wants to learn and keep God's law. Do you?

Pray that you and the students will make a commitment to study God's Word on a daily basis.

*Preparing Our Minds*

Study the background Scripture from Amos 7 and the lesson Scripture from Amos 7:10-17.

Consider this question: *Is it possible to remain committed to obeying God's direction when other people oppose us?*

Write on newsprint:
❏ information for next week's lesson, found under Continue the Journey.
❏ activities for further spiritual growth in Continue the Journey.

Determine how you might use any of the features that precede the first lesson of this quarter in today's session.

LEADING THE CLASS

*(1) Gather to Learn*

❖ Welcome everyone and pray that those who have come today will be open to hearing and heeding the word of the Lord.

❖ Read: **In 2015, Kim Davis, clerk of Rowan County, Kentucky, refused to issue marriage licenses to same-sex couples, despite a ruling from the United States Supreme Court that made such marriages legal across the country. She held fast to her position that same-sex marriages were contrary to God's will and, therefore, she could not sign licenses validating these marriages. Davis was jailed for five days for her refusal to issue these licenses. From a Christian perspective this situation is not easy to sort out, because there are valid arguments on both sides. Had she been a private citizen, Mrs. Davis certainly could have exercised her freedom of religion and peacefully protested the court's ruling. However, as an elected official, she had an obligation to uphold the oath of her office and provide legal services to all citizens of Rowan County—or resign, which she was unwilling to do. Obeying God does come at a price, but it also requires careful discernment.**

❖ Read aloud today's focus statement: **At times we find obeying God's direction to be in direct contrast to what others think we should do. Is it possible to remain determined despite the opposition? Amos committed to serving even in the face of negativity.**

*(2) Goal 1: Discover How Amaziah and Jeroboam Challenged Amos's Prophetic Ministry*

❖ Read or retell Introduction in Understanding the Scripture to set the stage.

❖ Choose two volunteers, one to read Amos 7:10-13 and another to read verses 14-17.

❖ Discuss these questions:
1. **What do you know about Amos and his background, especially since he insists in verse 14 that he is neither a prophet nor a prophet's son?** (See Amos 7:10-17 in Understanding the Scripture and The Lord Took Me in Interpreting the Scripture.)
2. **We know that Amos came from Judah in the south but was preaching at Bethel in the north. Based on Amaziah's words to Amos, what tension was this outsider's message causing?** (See The

King's Sanctuary in Interpreting the Scripture.)

3. **Amaziah did not simply disagree with Amos; rather, he opposed him and told him to stop preaching at Bethel and go home to Judah. How did Amos respond to the priest's order?** (See The Cost of Opposing God's Call in Interpreting the Scripture.)

❖ **Option:** Invite two volunteers to roleplay a discussion between Amaziah and Amos after the prophet unleashes his terrifying prophecy. The student playing Amaziah may—or may not—back off or change his attitude toward Amos.

*(3) Goal 2: Sense Instances of God's Calling to Serve in Unfamiliar Places and Capacities*

❖ Ask class members to identify examples of when God calls people to serve in unfamiliar settings. Here are some ideas: an older person who has always lived in the city has been called into ministry as a second career and now works in a very rural area; a young adult feels called to serve a two-year stint as a missionary in a country where the language, climate, and customs are quite different from his or her own; a suburban family moves to the inner city to help establish and support a new congregation that is much needed in this area.

❖ Encourage the students to give examples from their own lives of serving in situations that were unfamiliar or uncomfortable for them. For example, a teacher may agree to take on a challenging assignment in a school with a bad reputation and witness for God through her actions, or a member of the armed forces may find opportunities to witness to local people.

❖ Observe that sometimes we prefer to ignore God's call to go into unfamiliar places. Ask:

1. **What prevents us from answering God's call to bear witness in new and different territory?**
2. **How can we overcome our fears?**

*(4) Goal 3: Commit to Serving God in Spite of Opposition*

❖ Read: **It would be easy for us to think that the total commitment Amos made is only for God's chosen few—those prophets who were called to take incredible risks and preach with passion despite opposition. Yet Jesus calls his disciples to this same level of commitment. After he foretells his own death and resurrection, he gives account of the cost of discipleship: "If any want to become my followers, let them deny themselves and take up their cross daily and follow me" (Luke 9:23). Commitment is not a one-time affair; nor is it lightly done. This kind of commitment is life-changing, for we are putting ourselves at the complete disposal of our Lord.**

❖ Distribute paper and pencils. Challenge the participants to complete this sentence, which you will read aloud for them to copy: **As a disciple of Jesus Christ, I am willing to . . . in order to serve the One who gave his life for me.**

*(5) Continue the Journey*

❖ Pray that as the learners depart, they will affirm their willingness to go wherever God sends them, despite any opposition they may encounter.

❖ Post information for next week's session on newsprint for the students to copy:

- **Title: Called to Witness**
- **Background Scripture: Acts 1; 6; 7**
- **Lesson Scripture: Acts 6:1-8**
- **Focus of the Lesson: Recognizing priorities is a continuing challenge. How do we allocate resources in such a way that these priorities are appropriately addressed? The apostles realized that God calls us to make the best use of our specific gifts so that the witness of God can be accomplished.**

❖ Challenge the adults to grow spiritually by completing one or more of these activities related to this week's session.

(1) Research the sanctuary at Bethel in the northern region of the Promised Land. What was its relationship with the Temple at Jerusalem in the south? Who are some of the familiar biblical figures who went to Bethel?

(2) Act in a situation where you feel God is calling you to act, even if you feel opposed.

(3) Pray for those people who face hostile circumstances on account of their faith in Jesus. Ask God to give them boldness to continue to act according to their beliefs.

❖ Sing or read aloud "The Voice of God Is Calling."

❖ Conclude today's session by leading the class in this benediction, which is adapted from Isaiah 6:8, the key verse for July 9: **In response to your call, O God, I say, "Here am I, send me!" Amen.**

# UNIT 3: CALLS IN THE NEW TESTAMENT
# CALLED TO WITNESS

## PREVIEWING THE LESSON

**Lesson Scripture:** Acts 6:1-8
**Background Scripture:** Acts 1; 6; 7
**Key Verse:** Acts 6:3

**Focus of the Lesson:**
Recognizing priorities is a continuing challenge. How do we allocate resources in such a way that these priorities are appropriately addressed? The apostles realized that God calls us to make the best use of our specific gifts so that the witness of God can be accomplished.

**Goals for the Learners:**
(1) to explain the ministry challenges of evangelism and benevolence in the first-century church in Jerusalem.
(2) to sense the ministry challenges of evangelism and benevolence in the twenty-first-century church.
(3) to establish ministry priorities and act to meet them.

**Supplies:**
Bibles, newsprint and marker, paper and pencils, hymnals

## READING THE SCRIPTURE

**NRSV**
Lesson Scripture: Acts 6:1-8
¹Now during those days, when the disciples were increasing in number, the Hellenists complained against the Hebrews because their widows were being neglected in the daily distribution of food. ²And the twelve called together the whole community of the disciples and said, "It is not right that we should neglect the word of God

**CEB**
Lesson Scripture: Acts 6:1-8
¹About that time, while the number of disciples continued to increase, a complaint arose. Greek-speaking disciples accused the Aramaic-speaking disciples because their widows were being overlooked in the daily food service. ²The Twelve called a meeting of all the disciples and said, "It isn't right for us to set aside proclamation

in order to wait on tables. ³Therefore, friends, **select from among yourselves seven men of good standing, full of the Spirit and of wisdom, whom we may appoint to this task,** ⁴while we, for our part, will devote ourselves to prayer and to serving the word." ⁵What they said pleased the whole community, and they chose Stephen, a man full of faith and the Holy Spirit, together with Philip, Prochorus, Nicanor, Timon, Parmenas, and Nicolaus, a proselyte of Antioch. ⁶They had these men stand before the apostles, who prayed and laid their hands on them.

⁷The word of God continued to spread; the number of the disciples increased greatly in Jerusalem, and a great many of the priests became obedient to the faith.

⁸Stephen, full of grace and power, did great wonders and signs among the people.

of God's word in order to serve tables. ³Brothers and sisters, **carefully choose seven well-respected men from among you. They must be well-respected and endowed by the Spirit with exceptional wisdom. We will put them in charge of this concern.** ⁴As for us, we will devote ourselves to prayer and the service of proclaiming the word." ⁵This proposal pleased the entire community. They selected Stephen, a man endowed by the Holy Spirit with exceptional faith, Philip, Prochorus, Nicanor, Timon, Parmenas, and Nicolaus from Antioch, a convert to Judaism. ⁶The community presented these seven to the apostles, who prayed and laid their hands on them. ⁷God's word continued to grow. The number of disciples in Jerusalem increased significantly. Even a large group of priests embraced the faith. ⁸Stephen, who stood out among the believers for the way God's grace was at work in his life and for his exceptional endowment with divine power, was doing great wonders and signs among the people.

## UNDERSTANDING THE SCRIPTURE

**Introduction.** This lesson considers the need for a new kind of leadership. This need arose when the demands of ministry in the burgeoning church were simply overwhelming the appointed leaders.

**Acts 1:1-11.** Acts opens with the author addressing someone called Theophilus. The author refers to a previous book that recorded the teachings and deeds of Jesus. The previous book is the Gospel of Luke which also mentions Theophilus (Luke 1:1-4). The name is Greek, so it is possible the

name refers to a Roman official or to a wealthy patron of the church. The name means "lover of God." Therefore, it could be symbolic of the Christians in the church being addressed and not refer to a single person. After this introduction to Theophilus, the book repeats basically the ending of Luke, the account of Jesus' ascension into heaven.

**Acts 1:12-14.** The Ascension took place on the Mount of Olives, which is a "sabbath day's journey" from Jerusalem. That is, it lies within about one thousand yards of the city, the maximum distance a Jew could travel on Sabbath and remain obedient to the law (Exodus 16:29). The Ascension did not occur on the Sabbath, but reference to Sabbath day's journey is typical of the biblical language that dominates the story of Acts. The disciples returned to an upper room. This may be the place they gathered with Jesus for the Last Supper (Luke 22:12), but this is not certain. The disciples were of one accord. As is typical of Luke, the writer mentions the women who are present, including the mother of Jesus (1:14).

**Acts 1:15-26.** Peter recalls the death of Judas with reference in verse 20 to Psalms 69:25 and 109:8 that the early church understood spoke of the fate of the one who betrayed the Son of God. As a result of Judas's death the number of apostles is now incomplete. So those gathered cast lots to decide whether to choose Justus or Matthias. Lots were implements used by priests in the Old Testament to seek an objective yes or no answer from God. In this case the lot fell upon Matthias, that is, it pointed to him as God's choice for the twelfth apostle.

**Acts 6:1-6.** The Hellenists were probably Greek-speaking Jews, as opposed to Jews who spoke Aramaic, the more common language of Jews in Palestine. The Hellenists were one subgroup of Christians in the Jerusalem church. Their complaint was that their widows were neglected. Widows were women who had lost their husbands and had no other relatives to care for them. They depended on the mercy of people in the community to survive (see the Book of Ruth). The twelve apostles determined, however, they could not spend their time meeting this need. The expression "to wait on tables" could also be translated "to keep accounts." Regardless of the exact meaning, these leaders knew they could not do the everyday work of feeding people because they would then neglect the larger task of preaching. So they appointed seven men to take on this responsibility.

**Acts 6:7.** The statement that the word of God spread and increased appears frequently in Acts to show that opposition, conflict, and challenges do not hinder the gospel. (See, for example, Acts 5:14; 9:31; 12:24; 16:5; and 19:20.)

**Acts 6:8-15.** Stephen is the most prominent of the seven appointed to wait tables. Ironically, the seven are identified for this service so the apostles would not neglect the word. But here Stephen performs miracles and preaches. In a synagogue attended by freed slaves (Freedmen), those attending the synagogue argue with Stephen and bring him up on false charges. He comes before the Sanhedrin, the official Jewish court located in the Temple. The specific charge against him is that he spoke against the Temple by repeating the words of Jesus concerning the destruction of the holy place. The shining of Stephen's face shows he is innocent of the charges of blasphemy.

**Acts 7:1-53.** Stephen responds to the charges against him with a speech that rehearses the history of God's people. He focuses the speech so that he recalls every event related to the establishment of a permanent worship site in Jerusalem. The majority of the history occurred without a sanctuary or temple. God's people wandered about, being led by God. God led Abraham through the land of Canaan. Then God used Moses to deliver the Israelites from bondage and took them through the wilderness. Finally a Temple was established in Jerusalem. But, Stephen points out, it was not to be understood as a building that contained God or limited God. In verse 49 he cites Isaiah 66:1-2 in which God declares, "Heaven is my throne, and the earth is my footstool." This brings Stephen's speech to a sharp conclusion: The Jewish officials who derive their power from the Temple have institutionalized the Creator, as though God is bound to the house in Jerusalem. By quoting from Isaiah 66, Stephen draws from a part of the Old Testament that declares openness and inclusiveness in God's Temple. Stephen charges the keepers of the Temple, therefore, with working against the very purpose of God. Their attempts to maintain their own power and to control the Temple practices are directly linked to the betrayal and killing of Jesus.

**Acts 7:54-60.** The crowd responds to Stephen with outrage. They take up stones to kill him. They follow a tradition recorded in Leviticus 24:14 of stoning a blasphemer outside the camp or city. But Stephen speaks twice more with important words that interpret his death even as it is occurring. First, he declares that he sees in the heavens "the Son of Man standing at the right hand of God" (7:56). In this statement he recognizes the true court of justice, convened by God. The court that has convicted him is a false authority. Second, he prays, "Lord Jesus, receive my spirit" (7:59). In saying this, Stephen alludes to Jesus' own words on the cross (Luke 23:46) and thus links his death with Jesus' death.

---

## INTERPRETING THE SCRIPTURE

### A Family Table

The church depicted in Acts is characterized by a radical sharing of all property. Acts 4:34 declares, "There was not a needy person among them, for as many as owned lands or houses sold them and brought the proceeds of what was sold." In Acts 5:1-11 a couple named Ananias and Sapphira withheld some of the proceeds from the sale of property and then lied to the apostles about it. When confronted, Ananias and Sapphira fell over dead! This is the backdrop for the story in Acts 6. The members of the church are holding everything in common and out of the common goods they are feeding the hungry and caring for the weakest among them. The appointing of seven people to feed the poor is part of this recognition that the church is responsible for the daily distribution of food.

This picture of the church raises the question of why these early Christians participated in such communal living. What was their reasoning for this type of arrangement and should the church today emulate it? How does the sharing of goods in common fit with the larger calling to proclaim the gospel?

There are three primary ways of answering these questions. First, some might argue that the fledgling church exhibited an early form of communism in which there was no private ownership of property. This conclusion might be drawn from Acts 4:32 that says, "no one claimed private ownership of any possessions, but everything they owned was held in common." The comparison to communism, however, is not really appropriate since communism is an economic system put in place by governments. Acts portrays members of a community voluntarily sharing their wealth. Ananias and Sapphira die because they lie to the Spirit of God (Acts 5:4). The comparison to communism also allows those who oppose such an economic system to dismiss the sharing of the church's goods and declare the church today free of such responsibility.

A second way of explaining the common sharing of goods in the early church is to say these Christians believed the end of time would come soon and their manner of living was an "interim" measure. That is, if not for the belief in the imminent coming of Christ, the church would not have lived in this way. But there is little in Acts to suggest the members of the church are motivated by this idea. In fact, there seems to be every expectation they will see the gospel reach all the way to Rome and then the Gentile mission will continue into the future (Acts 28:17-31).

The third and best way to understand the sharing of resources in the early church is that they were called to live as a single family. As N. T. Wright says, "Like any family in that world, and many in today's world, they would all own everything together." This way of thinking of the early church not only best explains the common sharing of property but it also informs the church today as to its identity and calling. The church is not like a business called to balance its books or show a profit. It is also not like a civic organization that must be concerned primarily with proper allocation of resources as it answers to the public. Rather, the church is like—it is—a family. Though a family must plan and care well for its resources, it puts those resources to use wherever there is a need. No one person in the family reserves part of the goods for his or her own benefit. So also the church uses its resources to feed, support, heal, and minister wherever there is need.

### Community and Communion

The table fellowship of early Christians served the practical needs of poor widows. But the serving of food in the church also has overtones of the Last Supper. Eating together in such settings, though perhaps intended only to serve a practical need, connects participants to the sharing of the spiritual food in communion. Thus, eating in Christian fellowship should never be reduced to just satisfying bodily needs.

Fred Craddock tells a story of an occasion on which eating and communion came together for him. He had traveled to Winnipeg, in Canada in the early fall to give lectures, but the lectures had to be canceled due to an unexpected snowstorm. With all transportation stalled and his host unable to pick him up for a meal, Craddock walked to the nearest open restaurant for breakfast. It was filled with stranded travelers. When he sat down the proprietor told him the only item left from the menu was soup. The soup arrived and Craddock tasted it. It was not appetizing at all. Just then the door opened and a homeless woman entered and sat in the only empty seat. She asked for water. The proprietor demanded that she order food or leave. When the others in the restaurant heard what he said, they all in unison got up to leave in protest. The proprietor responded apologetically, "All right, all right, all right, she can stay." He brought her water, and soup, and told her there was no charge. The people in the restaurant cheered. Craddock tasted his soup again and this time he thought it was not so bad. He ate some more and said that, in fact, "it tasted a little bit like bread and wine."

## Allocating Resources

The story of feeding the widows in Acts 6:1-8 raises a very practical issue of how the early church's resources would be divided. The question of material wealth was not an issue. Acts has already said the members of the church shared everything in common. But who would ensure the resources were divided so as to meet the increasing needs of the people?

The problem for the twelve apostles is similar to the problem Moses faced in Exodus 18. Moses was confronted with a crisis when he sat all day settling disputes among the people. This took Moses away from key activities of leadership, so his father-in-law wisely advised him to delegate responsibility. So also the twelve apostles determined they could not spend their time waiting on tables (Acts 6:2). The community chose seven people to take on that duty. The apostles appropriately laid hands on the new servants and prayed over them to empower them in their new roles. As a result of this wise administration of duties "the word of God continued to spread" (Acts 6:7).

The issue facing the apostles is one all churches face and the solutions are not always easy. A comparable situation in the church today would be a congregation that has a food pantry but no one to staff it. A pastor might serve in that role for a day or two, but if she or he continued in this role there would be no time for sermon preparation or hospital visitation. The latter duties are not higher or more important than the former, but they are more crucial to the work the church needs the pastor to do. Freeing the pastor to do the work of preaching, teaching, and spiritually guiding the congregation is necessary if the gospel is to flourish, as it did in Acts.

---

# SHARING THE SCRIPTURE

## PREPARING TO LEAD

### Preparing Our Hearts

Ponder this week's devotional reading from Acts 2:14-28. Since this passage is written in the form of a speech, try reading it aloud. Which points stand out as most important for you? How would you have responded to the witness that Peter made?

Pray that you and the students will be ready and eager to witness for Jesus as opportunities present themselves.

### Preparing Our Minds

Study the background Scripture from Acts 1; 6; 7 and the lesson Scripture from Acts 6:1-8.

Consider this question: *How do we allocate resources according to appropriate priorities?*

---

Write on newsprint:

❏ information for next week's lesson, found under Continue the Journey.

❏ activities for further spiritual growth in Continue the Journey.

Determine how you might use any of the features that precede the first lesson of this quarter in today's session. Prepare to use God's Call in Acts, found in The Big Picture: The Call of God, for Goal 1 in Sharing the Scripture.

## LEADING THE CLASS

### (1) Gather to Learn

❖ Welcome everyone and pray that those who have come today will be open to the needs around them and do whatever they can to meet those needs.

❖ Read this scenario and then invite the adults to express ideas: **The pastor of Ruralsville Community Church also serves another, which means that Sunday mornings are very hectic. Pastor Deere has little time to greet people at County Line Church before rushing to Ruralsville, where he also lacks time to greet folks and hear their needs. What might these churches do to ensure that people are welcomed and made to feel at home, even though the pastor cannot do this important work due to time constraints?** (Hear several ideas.)

❖ Read aloud today's focus statement: **Recognizing priorities is a continuing challenge. How do we allocate resources in such a way that these priorities are appropriately addressed? The apostles realized that God calls us to make the best use of our specific gifts so that the witness of God can be accomplished.**

*(2) Goal 1: Explain the Ministry Challenges of Evangelism and Benevolence in the First-century Church*

❖ Introduce Unit 3 by reading or retelling God's Call in Acts, which you will find in The Big Picture: The Call of God. Observe that the calls we will study in Acts concern people who are called within the church community.

❖ Set the stage for today's lesson by reading the first paragraph of A Family Table in Interpreting the Scripture.

❖ Select a volunteer to read Acts 6:1-8 and discuss these questions:

1. **What do we know about the way the people of the early church in Acts lived in community? Why did they live that way?** (See the rest of A Family Table in Interpreting the Scripture.)

2. **Who is having a problem in the church, and what is the problem?** (See Acts 6:1-6 in Understanding the Scripture.)

3. **What do the apostles do to alleviate this problem?** (See Allocating Resources in Interpreting the Scripture.)

4. **How might the new arrangement have helped both those in need and the apostles?**

5. **What challenges do you think the early church encountered in terms of taking care of its members? How might these challenges be similar to and different from challenges we currently encounter?**

*(3) Goal 2: Sense the Ministry Challenges of Evangelism and Benevolence in the Twenty-first-century Church*

❖ Observe that the proper allocation of staff, volunteers, and available resources is just as important today as it was two thousand years ago.

❖ Write these headings on one sheet of newsprint:

Problem/Issue
Possible Causes
Possible Solutions

Form small groups and give each group a sheet of newsprint and a marker. Ask each group to identify one Problem/Issue that challenges the church today. Invite each group to brainstorm ideas for each category. Here is a brief sample of what the chart could look like:

| Problem/Issue | Possible Causes | Possible Solutions |
| --- | --- | --- |
| Low attendance at 11:00 on Sunday morning | Competing activities on Sunday morning | Schedule church at a different time |
| Low attendance at 11:00 on Sunday morning | Lack of parking | Provide a church bus; set up carpools; see about using the lot of a nearby business or school that is closed during worship time |
| Low attendance at 11:00 on Sunday morning | Worship service is not connecting with people | Talk with those who participate and those who have stopped coming to see what changes they would like to see; encourage lay involvement in the service; train people to more actively participate |

❖ Call everyone back together to hear their ideas. Provide time for feedback from the class by discussing these questions:

1. **Which cause seems most important?** (Note that usually if one or two causes can be identified as major and then addressed, most of the problem will be solved, even if there are other causes.)
2. **What solutions would you favor for solving the problem?**

*(4) Goal 3: Establish Ministry Priorities and Act to Meet Them*

❖ Take a poll of class members to see who serves on teams or committees in ministry areas. These folks are likely part of what many congregations call a Church Council. Ask them to state briefly the primary focal points for ministry in your congregation and/or denomination.

❖ Recall that people in the church in Acts who felt they were being neglected asked for help so that their needs would be met. Ask: **Based on our discussion, what other priorities would you like to see our church focus on in order to meet additional needs?** List ideas on newsprint.

❖ Poll the class to see who would be willing to make a commitment to work on a particular priority. To ensure that action is taken, ask the class to identify any group within the church that would normally take responsibility for such a priority. Also invite volunteers to take the class's concerns to the appropriate committee or ministry team.

*(5) Continue the Journey*

❖ Pray that as the learners depart, they will work to meet their congregation's priorities for ministry.

❖ Post information for next week's session on newsprint for the students to copy:

- **Title: Called to Break Down Barriers**
- **Background Scripture: Acts 8**
- **Lesson Scripture: Acts 8:26-39**
- **Focus of the Lesson: People rarely cross cultural boundaries in significant ways. What should motivate us to do so? Acts 8 records a cross-cultural encounter where Philip is called by God to bear witness concerning** Jesus, the Son of God, as the basis of true meaning and purpose.

❖ Challenge the adults to grow spiritually by completing one or more of these activities related to this week's session.

**(1) Identify tasks that other people could do for you so that you could spend more time in ministry and mission. What specific tasks would you take on if you could free up enough time to do them?**

**(2) Think about people in your congregation who are underserved in some way. Perhaps they need transportation or child care or help with errands. What could you—or you and your group—do to better serve these people?**

**(3) Identify a problem your congregation is having. What are the issues? What needs to happen for the problem to be solved in a way that works for everyone? What can you contribute to the solution?**

❖ Sing or read aloud "Tú Has Venido a la Orilla (Lord, You Have Come to the Lakeshore)."

❖ Conclude today's session by leading the class in this benediction, which is adapted from Isaiah 6:8, the key verse for July 9: **In response to your call, O God, I say, "Here am I, send me!" Amen.**

## UNIT 3: CALLS IN THE NEW TESTAMENT
# CALLED TO BREAK DOWN BARRIERS

---

### PREVIEWING THE LESSON

**Lesson Scripture:** Acts 8:26-39
**Background Scripture:** Acts 8
**Key Verse:** Acts 8:35

### Focus of the Lesson:
People rarely cross cultural boundaries in significant ways. What should motivate us to do so? Acts 8 records a cross-cultural encounter where Philip is called by God to bear witness concerning Jesus, the Son of God, as the basis of true meaning and purpose.

### Goals for the Learners:
(1) to realize that the encounter between Philip and the Ethiopian represented a cross-cultural recognition of Jesus' identity.
(2) to value the need for cross-cultural evangelism.
(3) to plan to participate in cross-cultural evangelism.

### Supplies:
Bibles, newsprint and marker, paper and pencils, hymnals

---

### READING THE SCRIPTURE

**NRSV**
Lesson Scripture: Acts 8:26-39
  26Then an angel of the Lord said to Philip, "Get up and go toward the south to the road that goes down from Jerusalem to Gaza." (This is a wilderness road.) 27So he got up and went. Now there was an Ethiopian eunuch, a court official of the Candace, queen of the Ethiopians, in charge of her entire treasury. He had

**CEB**
Lesson Scripture: Acts 8:26-39
  26An angel from the Lord spoke to Philip, "At noon, take the road that leads from Jerusalem to Gaza." (This is a desert road.) 27So he did. Meanwhile, an Ethiopian man was on his way home from Jerusalem, where he had come to worship. He was a eunuch and an official responsible for the entire treasury of Candace.

come to Jerusalem to worship ²⁸and was returning home; seated in his chariot, he was reading the prophet Isaiah. ²⁹Then the Spirit said to Philip, "Go over to this chariot and join it." ³⁰So Philip ran up to it and heard him reading the prophet Isaiah. He asked, "Do you understand what you are reading?" ³¹He replied, "How can I, unless someone guides me?" And he invited Philip to get in and sit beside him. ³²Now the passage of the scripture that he was reading was this:
"Like a sheep he was led to the
　　slaughter,
　and like a lamb silent before its
　　shearer,
　　so he does not open his mouth.
³³In his humiliation justice was
　　denied him.
　Who can describe his generation?
　For his life is taken away from
　　the earth."
³⁴The eunuch asked Philip, "About whom, may I ask you, does the prophet say this, about himself or about someone else?" **³⁵Then Philip began to speak, and starting with this scripture, he proclaimed to him the good news about Jesus.** ³⁶As they were going along the road, they came to some water; and the eunuch said, "Look, here is water! What is to prevent me from being baptized?" ³⁸He commanded the chariot to stop, and both of them, Philip and the eunuch, went down into the water, and Philip baptized him. ³⁹When they came up out of the water, the Spirit of the Lord snatched Philip away; the eunuch saw him no more, and went on his way rejoicing.

(Candace is the title given to the Ethiopian queen.) ²⁸He was reading the prophet Isaiah while sitting in his carriage. ²⁹The Spirit told Philip, "Approach this carriage and stay with it."

³⁰Running up to the carriage, Philip heard the man reading the prophet Isaiah. He asked, "Do you really understand what you are reading?" ³¹The man replied, "Without someone to guide me, how could I?" Then he invited Philip to climb up and sit with him. ³²This was the passage of scripture he was reading:
*Like a sheep he was led to the slaughter*
　*and like a lamb before its shearer*
　　*is silent*
　*so he didn't open his mouth.*
³³*In his humiliation justice was taken*
　　*away from him.*
　*Who can tell the story of his*
　　*descendants*
　*because his life was taken from*
　　*the earth?*
³⁴The eunuch asked Philip, "Tell me, about whom does the prophet say this? Is he talking about himself or someone else?" **³⁵Starting with that passage, Philip proclaimed the good news about Jesus to him.** ³⁶As they went down the road, they came to some water.

The eunuch said, "Look! Water! What would keep me from being baptized?" ³⁸He ordered that the carriage halt. Both Philip and the eunuch went down to the water, where Philip baptized him. ³⁹When they came up out of the water, the Lord's Spirit suddenly took Philip away. The eunuch never saw him again but went on his way rejoicing.

## UNDERSTANDING THE SCRIPTURE

**Introduction.** Acts 8 tells the story of the beginning of the church's expansion beyond Jerusalem and beyond the Jewish community in which it began. The chapter may be summed up by the notion that the gospel was not hindered. When the church faced violent opposition in Jewish circles, its preachers simply moved out to Samaria. By the end of the chapter Philip will share the good news with and convert a man from the farthest reaches of the earth. Hence, Acts 8 marks a major turning point in the story of the church. The unhindered gospel spreads throughout the world despite attempts of some Jewish officials to squelch it.

**Acts 8:1-3.** The previous chapter reported the stoning of Stephen. Now the opening of chapter 8 concludes the story, first with a note that Saul of Tarsus approved of Stephen's death and then with the further comment that Saul was bringing Christians up on trial. As a result, all leaders of the church except the twelve apostles of Jesus were scattered throughout the surrounding region.

**Acts 8:4-8.** Philip went to Samaria when the Christians were scattered away from Jerusalem. Samaria was a city located thirty-five miles north of Jerusalem. It was the capital of the old Northern Kingdom of Israel, built by King Omri (1 Kings 16:23-24). The name of the city became the name of the region around the city well before the New Testament period. The Samaritans recognized some of the Jewish Scriptures as authoritative, but they worshiped on the mountains around Shechem in northern Israel rather than in Jerusalem. As the story of the good Samaritan illustrates (Luke 10:25-37), most Jews hated Samaritans. Philip's preaching to them is the first of many signs that the gospel will go beyond the Jews and embrace all people.

**Acts 8:9-13.** In the New Testament world, miracle workers and magicians were common and many thought people like this had power that came from God. The man named Simon in this story is often called Simon Magus since the Latin word "magus" means "magician." Simon is also called "Great" (9:10). Interestingly, the Latin word for "great" is "magnus." But Philip showed him an even greater power, the power of the gospel, and Simon was greatly impressed. He was converted and baptized along with a host of others. But there are signs he did not understand this new faith he was embracing.

**Acts 8:14-25.** The Samaritan believers were baptized, but the Holy Spirit was not upon them. Although the Holy Spirit came from God and God alone determined who would receive it, in Acts the apostles help mediate the presence of the Spirit. This is similar to the practice in the modern church of laying hands on those ordained for Christian service or confirmed as new Christians. John and Peter came to Samaria and laid hands on the ones who were baptized and they received the Spirit. As a result, they probably demonstrated the same power as those in Jerusalem on the day of Pentecost (Acts 2).

Upon seeing the power of those who received the Holy Spirit, and that Peter and John conferred the Spirit upon them, Simon Magus saw the great potential of a power like this. He wanted the ability the two apostles had to bestow the Spirit on others. He offered to pay them for the ability. Peter strongly rebuked him, however, saying it was blasphemous to suggest anyone could buy the Holy Spirit. He declared Simon was in no way straight about how to relate to God in this new life of faith. Simon quickly repented and asked to be restored to the Christian community.

**Acts 8:26-40.** The conclusion to the background Scripture turns attention once again to Philip. The Spirit, which has been moving in the church and among those preaching the gospel, sent him to a wilderness area, a road that leads from Jerusalem to Gaza. There he met the Ethiopian eunuch. In New Testament times Ethiopia was thought of as the end of the earth, like we think of Timbuktu. Ethiopia was located in the Upper Nile area, about as far as one could imagine traveling from Jerusalem. The people there were darker-complexioned, as compared with the bronze or brown-complexioned people in the region of Judea. Hence, Ethiopia came to designate an exotic, faraway place. The Ethiopian may have seemed exotic, but he was also a very important government official, in charge of a queen's treasury, and traveling in luxury, in a chariot. The passage gives two additional points about him that are crucial to the story. First, he had been to Jerusalem to worship. This probably meant he was a "God-fearer," a Gentile who adopted the Jewish faith and actively attended a synagogue.

According to Acts, this was the primary source of Gentile converts to Christianity (Acts 10:2). Second, the Ethiopian was a eunuch. This probably meant the man was rendered sexless, either because of an accident or as part of a vow of chastity. Regardless of the reason, such persons were often used as government officials, especially working with harems and other members of a royal court. The detail is important for this story since Jewish law prohibited eunuchs from entering the Temple (Deuteronomy 23:1). To the ancient priestly way of thinking, this condition placed a man outside the bodily norm and made him ritually unclean. So, although the Ethiopian had been to Jerusalem to worship, he would not have been admitted to the Temple. The Scripture passage he was reading was from Isaiah 53, part of a larger poem about a servant-figure who suffered on behalf of others (Isaiah 52:13–53:12). There is no agreement as to the identity of the servant in the time the poem was written. It is possible the passage is about the prophet, as the Ethiopian suggests (one popular interpretation). It is also possible that the servant represents the suffering Israelite people in exile. According to Acts, Philip does not suggest one answer that explains what Isaiah was thinking. Rather, Philip starts with this passage and shows the Ethiopian how the description of suffering points us to the suffering and death of Jesus.

---

## INTERPRETING THE SCRIPTURE

*Called to the Wilderness*

The call of Philip is set when the gospel is spreading like wildfire and multitudes of people are coming into the church. According to Acts 8:4-7, he had preached in Samaria about Jesus and also did deeds of great power there. The people of Samaria "had accepted the word of God" (8:14) and were baptized (8:12). So it may come as a surprise to read that an angel appeared to Philip and commanded him to leave the cities and villages where this fruitful ministry occurred and travel the lonely road from Jerusalem to Gaza. At the end of verse 26 the author of Acts adds the comment, "This is a wilderness road."

Such a road does not seem like a fortuitous place for a gifted and successful preacher like Philip to be sent. Indeed, for people in the ancient world the wilderness was a place of disorder and lifelessness, a place where evil spirits flourished. It is no accident that Jesus went into the wilderness to be tempted (Matthew 4:1-11; Mark 1:12-13; Luke 4:1-13). But for a preacher to be sent to such a place seems most strange at this juncture in Acts because a wilderness road is likely to be empty.

Although these possible objections to a call to go into the wilderness seem logical, Philip did not express any of them. Instead, he went on the lonely road toward Gaza as the angel commanded him. Philip then discovered what many people called to faraway places discover: There was great and rewarding work to do! Suddenly on this wilderness road was an Ethiopian eunuch who needed someone like Philip to help him understand the passage from Isaiah he was reading. Philip talked with him, and the eunuch was baptized.

Two remarkable things happened in Philip's encounter with the Ethiopian eunuch that illustrate why ministry in a wilderness can have untold rewards. First, the Ethiopian was an important and talented man. Although Philip met only one person on this wilderness road, the person he encountered was more fascinating than perhaps anyone he could have met elsewhere. The ancient church historian Eusebius said that the Ethiopian returned home and became an evangelist. Although there is no way to verify this information, it testifies to how important Philip's encounter was. Second, when the Ethiopian received the good news about Jesus, suddenly there was water for baptism. Water was there in the wilderness! The writer of Acts perhaps meant this as a straightforward observation. But it is important to note that Philip discovered the wilderness to be a place where there was life.

*Interpreting Scripture*

By all accounts Philip was a gifted preacher and he had exercised his gifts in the cities and villages of the Samaritans. But now on the wilderness road his role changes to something much more basic. He is called simply to interpret Scripture. When Philip meets the Ethiopian he is reading a portion of Isaiah 52:13–53:12. This is one of the so-called servant songs, each of which focuses on an anonymous figure simply called "the servant of the Lord." (The others are Isaiah 42:1-4; 49:1-6; and 50:4-9a). The Ethiopian reads that the servant was deemed accursed by God (Isaiah 53:4), but now we know God chose him to bear the sins of others and to redeem his people (Isaiah 53:10-12). As the Ethiopian eunuch reads this, however, he is confused as to what it means. Who is this despised and rejected one whom God vindicated? Was it the prophet Isaiah or someone else? Since ancient times interpreters of the Bible have been trying to answer these questions, but they continue to be among the most difficult problems in the study of Scripture.

Philip's calling at the moment of the Ethiopian's question was reduced to explaining this one passage of Scripture. For all who are called by God this scene offers two very important principles. First, reading and studying Scripture is the most basic preparation to answer God's call. Scripture is the starting point of our faith, the basic source that tells us what God is like. So we cannot possibly answer a call of God for service—whatever that service is— without learning the Bible well. We will be called on to answer questions about what we are doing and why, and the answers must come for us, as they did for Philip, from Scripture. Second, Philip gives us a wonderful example of how to interpret Scripture. Philip assumed that all Scripture points to Jesus Christ, even if it does not speak of him directly. Notice that Philip does not answer the Ethiopian's question by saying, "The passage is talking about Jesus." Rather it says, "starting with this Scripture, he proclaimed to him the good news about Jesus" (8:35). Philip told him good news (the meaning of "gospel"), and he got that good news by relating the suffering servant passage to the suffering, death, and resurrection of Jesus. The interpretation of Scripture is a complicated endeavor, but Philip provides a great example of how it should be done: connect the words of Scripture to the truth of God in Jesus Christ.

### Including the Excluded

Before meeting the Ethiopian Philip preached to Samaritans and

they received the gospel. This was a major turning point in the early church. The first Christians were Jewish and the questions of *who* would be included in the new religious movement and *how* they would be included were critical. The answer came in the form of radical openness to all people who believed in Jesus. In the case of the Ethiopian yet another barrier was broken. The Ethiopian is described as a eunuch. A eunuch was a person rendered sexless. In ancient monarchies such persons were often used as officials to serve the female members of the court. He was a very important and powerful government official. In Jewish thought, however, he was ritually unclean. According to Deuteronomy 23:1 he could not enter the Temple to make sacrifices or pray. So even though he had been to Jerusalem to worship, he likely stood outside the main Temple building, listening in, but unable to participate fully.

This background makes it very interesting that the Ethiopian is reading from the portion of Isaiah that comes from the time of the Babylonian exile (Isaiah 40–66). Isaiah imagined a time of restoration when a new Temple would be constructed in which eunuchs who observed the Sabbath would be included. Isaiah 56:3b-5 declares, "Do not let the eunuch say, 'I am just a dry tree'" (56:3b). "I will give them [eunuchs] an everlasting name that shall not be cut off" (56:5). The suffering servant in Isaiah 53 has also been "cut off" from the community (56:5). Acts does not tell us specifically that Philip makes these connections for the eunuch, but it is clear that the eunuch found in this passage a message that was important for him. It is also not clear how Philip drew a line from the suffering servant in Isaiah to Jesus. But Jesus was like the servant in that he was cut off from the living through an act of injustice and God affirmed him as righteous. In so doing, Jesus identified with all people, including this Ethiopian eunuch, and welcomed them into full fellowship in the family of God. This radical openness was and is an essential feature of the faith founded on the sacrificial love of Jesus.

---

# SHARING THE SCRIPTURE

## PREPARING TO LEAD

### *Preparing Our Hearts*

Ponder this week's devotional reading from Romans 10:9-15. Here Paul emphasizes the universal availability of salvation. There are no barriers to God because "everyone who calls on the name of the Lord shall be saved" (10:13). What barriers seem to exist today in terms of welcoming people in the name of Jesus? How are you and your congregation working to tear down these barriers?

Pray that you and the students will encourage all people to come to know Jesus and accept him as their Savior.

### *Preparing Our Minds*

Study the background Scripture from Acts 8 and the lesson Scripture from Acts 8:26-39.

Consider this question: *What could motivate you to cross cultural boundaries in a significant way?*

Write on newsprint:

❏ information for next week's lesson, found under Continue the Journey.

❏ activities for further spiritual growth in Continue the Journey.

Determine how you might use any of the features that precede the first lesson of this quarter in today's session.

Create a brief lecture as suggested under Goal 1 in Sharing the Scripture to introduce the events of Acts 8.

Make a list of missionaries your congregation supports. Where and with whom are they working? Also make a list of ministries your church engages in that reach across cultural and ethnic lines. Check with your pastor or mission chair if you need help creating these lists.

## LEADING THE CLASS

### *(1) Gather to Learn*

❖ Welcome everyone and pray that those who have come today will participate with open hearts and minds.

❖ Read: **When many of us hear the word "missionary," we think of a person called from the United States to go to a foreign country to preach, teach, or perform other tasks that allow this individual to witness for Jesus. To be prepared for such an undertaking, the candidate must not only be a committed Christian but also must learn the language and become sensitive to the culture of the people with whom he or she will work. Moreover, the missionary must be able to frame the gospel message in terms that can be understood within the cultural context. Today some countries that have received missionaries for decades or** longer, including those in Africa, are now sending people into a cross-cultural mission field in the United States.

❖ Read aloud today's focus statement: **People rarely cross cultural boundaries in significant ways. What should motivate us to do so? Acts 8 records a cross-cultural encounter where Philip is called by God to witness to Jesus, the Son of God, as the basis of true meaning and purpose.**

*(2) Goal 1: Realize that the Encounter Between Philip and the Ethiopian Presented a Cross-cultural Recognition of Jesus' Identity*

❖ Use the information in Understanding the Scripture from Introduction through Acts 8:14-25 to create a brief lecture that you will present to introduce today's lesson. Be sure to note that cultural boundaries were crossed when Philip, a Jewish Christian from Jerusalem, preached in Samaria. As a result of Philip's ministry, people not only heard about Jesus but they also accepted him.

❖ Select a volunteer to read Acts 8:26-39.

❖ Discuss these questions:
   1. **Philip was a successful evangelist who was winning souls for Christ in Samaria. Yet when God called him to a "wilderness road" where there would be few people, Philip "got up and went" (8:27). What does his willingness to follow what must have seemed like a questionable commission say to you about Philip— and about how God works?**

2. **What do you learn about the man whom Philip encounters?** (See Acts 8:26-40 in Understanding the Scripture and Including the Excluded in Interpreting the Scripture.)
3. **How does Philip help the man?** (See Interpreting Scripture in Interpreting the Scripture. If time permits, look at the Fourth Servant Song in Isaiah 52:13–53:12.)
4. **Why did Philip's call from fruitful ministry to what seemed like a barren place, prove to be fruitful after all?** (Observe that not only was the Ethiopian man baptized but he also "went on his way rejoicing" according to verse 39. From this we can conjecture that he returned to tell others in Ethiopia about his life-changing experience.)

*(3) Goal 2: Value the Need for Cross-cultural Evangelism*

❖ Discuss these questions:
   1. **What are the names and locations of the missionaries that our congregation supports?** (List on newsprint information you gathered.)
   2. **What mission projects do we support in our community or country that likely help people who are of a different racial, ethnic, or national background than most of our congregation is?** (List on newsprint.)
❖ Invite the adults to tell stories of how they have personally been enriched by working with people of different cultural backgrounds.

❖ **Option:** If the congregation is not currently engaged in cross-cultural ministry, encourage the class to state why that might be and how they could go about getting involved in such ministry.

*(4) Goal 3: Plan to Participate in Cross-cultural Evangelism*

❖ Post a sheet of newsprint and invite participants to identify congregations in your area that are of a different culture or ethnic background than your own.

❖ Ask: **How might our congregation partner with a church from a different culture background to reach out to our community with the love of Jesus?** (Here are several possibilities: a multicultural vacation Bible school, a joint effort to benefit the community such as a homeless shelter or food pantry, a revival sponsored by several churches representing different cultures.)

❖ Designate a representative or two to talk with your pastor about the class's ideas and then approach the other church(es) to see what kind of joint ventures the congregations could create.

*(5) Continue the Journey*

❖ Pray that as the learners depart, they will be open to the responsibility and joy of working in ministry with others whose backgrounds are different from theirs to reach people for Christ.

❖ Post information for next week's session on newsprint for the students to copy:

■ **Title: Called to Preach**
■ **Background Scripture: Acts 9:1-31**

■ **Lesson Scripture: Acts 9:10-20**
■ **Focus of the Lesson: We often feel urges to act in certain ways. Is it acceptable to question those urges? Acts 9 describes God's call to Ananias and Saul, Ananias's questioning reaction, and God's firm response.**

❖ Challenge the adults to grow spiritually by completing one or more of these activities related to this week's session.

(1) **Recall a time when you felt excluded by a church. Why did you feel left out? How did you overcome this barrier? What steps can you take to help people who seem to be excluded to feel included?**

(2) **Visit a church whose majority membership is of a different cultural, racial, or language makeup than your own congregation. How were you welcomed? What did you learn from this experience?**

(3) **Recognize that Philip could help the Ethiopian man because the evangelist knew the story of Jesus. If called upon to help someone understand the Scriptures, what would be your response? Why? If you do not feel up to the task, what can you do to be better prepared?**

❖ Sing or read aloud "In Christ There Is No East or West."

❖ Conclude today's session by leading the class in this benediction, which is adapted from Isaiah 6:8, the key verse for July 9: **In response to your call, O God, I say, "Here am I, send me!" Amen.**

UNIT 3: CALLS IN THE NEW TESTAMENT
# CALLED TO PREACH

---

## PREVIEWING THE LESSON

**Lesson Scripture:** Acts 9:10-20
**Background Scripture:** Acts 9:1-31
**Key Verse:** Acts 9:17

### Focus of the Lesson:
We often feel urges to act in certain ways. Is it acceptable to question those urges? Acts 9 describes God's call to Ananias and Saul, Ananias's questioning reaction, and God's firm response.

### Goals for the Learners:
(1) to analyze the sequence of events before and during Ananias's witness to Saul.
(2) to reflect on times of questioning and resisting God's call.
(3) to develop spiritual maturity that breaks down one's resistance to calls of God.

### Supplies:
Bibles, newsprint and marker, paper and pencils, hymnals

---

## READING THE SCRIPTURE

NRSV
Lesson Scripture: Acts 9:10-20

¹⁰Now there was a disciple in Damascus named Ananias. The Lord said to him in a vision, "Ananias." He answered, "Here I am, Lord." ¹¹The Lord said to him, "Get up and go to the street called Straight, and at the house of Judas look for a man of Tarsus named Saul. At this moment he is praying, ¹²and he has seen in a vision a man named Ananias come in

CEB
Lesson Scripture: Acts 9:10-20

¹⁰In Damascus there was a certain disciple named Ananias. The Lord spoke to him in a vision, "Ananias!" He answered, "Yes, Lord." ¹¹The Lord instructed him, "Go to Judas' house on Straight Street and ask for a man from Tarsus named Saul. He is praying. ¹²In a vision he has seen a man named Ananias enter and put his hands on him to restore his sight."

and lay his hands on him so that he might regain his sight." [13]But Ananias answered, "Lord, I have heard from many about this man, how much evil he has done to your saints in Jerusalem; [14]and here he has authority from the chief priests to bind all who invoke your name." [15]But the Lord said to him, "Go, for he is an instrument whom I have chosen to bring my name before Gentiles and kings and before the people of Israel; [16]I myself will show him how much he must suffer for the sake of my name." **[17]So Ananias went and entered the house. He laid his hands on Saul and said, "Brother Saul, the Lord Jesus, who appeared to you on your way here, has sent me so that you may regain your sight and be filled with the Holy Spirit."** [18]And immediately something like scales fell from his eyes, and his sight was restored. Then he got up and was baptized, [19]and after taking some food, he regained his strength.

For several days he was with the disciples in Damascus, [20]and immediately he began to proclaim Jesus in the synagogues, saying, "He is the Son of God."

[13]Ananias countered, "Lord, I have heard many reports about this man. People say he has done horrible things to your holy people in Jerusalem. [14]He's here with authority from the chief priests to arrest everyone who calls on your name."

[15]The Lord replied, "Go! This man is the agent I have chosen to carry my name before Gentiles, kings, and Israelites. [16]I will show him how much he must suffer for the sake of my name." **[17]Ananias went to the house. He placed his hands on Saul and said, "Brother Saul, the Lord sent me— Jesus, who appeared to you on the way as you were coming here. He sent me so that you could see again and be filled with the Holy Spirit."** [18]Instantly, flakes fell from Saul's eyes and he could see again. He got up and was baptized. [19]After eating, he regained his strength.

He stayed with the disciples in Damascus for several days. [20]Right away, he began to preach about Jesus in the synagogues. "He is God's Son," he declared.

---

## UNDERSTANDING THE SCRIPTURE

**Introduction.** The story of the conversion and call of Saul—later known as Paul—is as dramatic as any call story in Scripture. In the beginning of the chapter Saul is persecuting the church, but Acts 9 reports his complete transformation into not only a member of the church but also its greatest spokesperson. The story also includes an account of God calling another man named Ananias who is crucial to Saul's conversion and early success. Ananias is a Christian leader in Damascus who knows of Saul's fierce persecution of Christians. God asks Ananias to embrace Saul and care for him so Saul may accomplish the mission God has appointed for him. So this chapter is really about two calls, one for Saul who will gain most attention, but also a call for Ananias who nurtures Saul in the Christian faith and leads him to the church. When Saul returns to Jerusalem, another Christian, Barnabas, introduces Saul to the apostles and serves as his mediator there.

**Acts 9:1-2.** Saul was one of the Pharisees, part of a lay movement in Judaism that began in the second century B.C. Pharisees were concerned to make the Mosaic law, which was largely written for priests to regulate their service in the Temple or sanctuary, accessible to the common person. For example, they translated dietary laws and Sabbath laws into numerous, unofficial laws they passed on orally. They defined the allowable work of the Sabbath so that farmers and ordinary citizens could observe these laws and still be considered ritually clean. The synagogue was the main forum for the Pharisees. That was the place where Scripture was read and interpreted. The official political power in Judaism was held among the priests who ran the Temple. They are known in the New Testament as Sadducees. So Saul sought approval and sanction from the high priest to bring Christians (who were also Jewish) to trial. The first name for members of the church was "The Way." They would only later be called "Christians," a pejorative name given to these people who focused on the Messiah (the Christ, or anointed one).

**Acts 9:3-9.** Saul sees a blinding light and falls to the ground. He then hears a voice he will learn is the voice of Jesus. Saul is suddenly confronted with the horror of knowing he has been persecuting members of the church for preaching that Jesus was raised from the dead and that what they are saying is true. This transforming event occurs on the way to Damascus, the capital of Syria.

**Acts 9:10-19.** The Lord appears also to a Christian named Ananias who is in Damascus. The appearance has all the hallmarks of a call story: The Lord appears and gives a commission; Ananias objects and expresses doubts; the Lord gives assurance the mission will be successful. Ananias's objections are understandable: Saul has been killing members of the church! But God reveals that Saul is a chosen vessel; God will work through this unlikely agent, as is often the case. When Ananias arrives at the house where Saul is staying, he lays hands on him as a sign of official approval by the church. With the laying on of hands the Holy Spirit comes upon Saul just as it had come upon the Samaritans in Acts 8. Saul then regains his sight as well. Baptism, the laying on of hands, and the coming of the Holy Spirit all appear together in Acts, though not always in the same order. Saul receives all three and thus becomes a full member of the church.

**Acts 9:20-22.** Saul now goes, as a good Pharisee would, to the synagogue to teach. But now he teaches that Jesus is the Messiah, the Son of God. This confounds both traditional Jews and the Jews who have become part of The Way. Members of The Way know Saul has been persecuting members of the church. Perhaps this is a trick, they must be thinking. The traditional Jews continue not to believe that anyone convicted of a capital crime and crucified could be an agent of God.

**Acts 9:23-25.** The beginning of Saul's missionary work does not exactly seem auspicious. The Jews in Damascus are trying to kill Saul, so the followers of Jesus lower him in a basket to safety, outside the city walls. But as Saul, later known as Paul, writes in

2 Corinthians 11, events like this are not signs of failure, but of success. Just as Jesus was rejected and killed, so also Saul must be rejected and have his life threatened as well. This initial escape from danger would be the first sign for Saul that God would work in his weakness to bring about good.

**Acts 9:26-30.** After his encounter with the members of The Way in Damascus, Saul's next step was clear: He would have to return to Jerusalem. Jerusalem was his spiritual home as a Jew, but it was also the hub of the new movement that proclaimed Jesus as the Messiah. When Saul arrives in Jerusalem he relies on yet another welcoming soul, Barnabas, to get access to the apostles. After getting acquainted with them in Jerusalem, Saul travels to his birthplace, his other home in Tarsus.

**Acts 9:31.** The conversion of Saul marks an important transition in the development of the new faith. The summary statement at the end of chapter 9 gives an appropriate statement of what has occurred: The church is at peace, due undoubtedly in part to the fact that the church's greatest detractor and fiercest opponent is now one of them. Saul is firmly in the fellowship of those who believe in Jesus. But this final statement also anticipates what will soon come for the church. The message of Jesus has spread from Jerusalem to Judea and into Samaria, just as Jesus said it would (Acts 1:8). Now the new convert Saul is at home reflecting on what has happened to him. When he emerges he will take the gospel to the ends of the earth.

---

## INTERPRETING THE SCRIPTURE

*A Vision of God and the Face of Jesus*

When Saul had his conversion experience it became a model for dramatic changes in life. Anyone who has an encounter with God that changes his or her life might call it a "Damascus road experience." Ananias also experiences a radical change of perspective as God calls him to minister to Saul. Experiences like this may seem to come out of the blue. But they are typically rooted in some set of beliefs or experiences already present in a person's life. What prepared Saul for his meeting with Jesus on the road to Damascus? What, in turn, prepared Ananias to accept Saul as his Christian brother and partner in ministry?

We cannot answer these questions with certainty. It is clear, however, that Saul's mind was changed about the nature of God and the nature of Jesus. Saul had certain ideas about God from his reading and studying of Scripture: God is holy, powerful, just, and righteous, for example. Jesus, so Saul thought, was a criminal executed by Rome and his followers were blasphemers who claimed Jesus was the closest expression of God anyone had ever known. When Jesus appeared to Saul on the road to Damascus he knew immediately he was wrong about Jesus and, therefore, he was also wrong about God.

N. T. Wright suggests a way this transformation could have happened. Although it is only a guess, it is certainly plausible and it might help us better understand Saul's conversion and commissioning. Wright notes there was in Judaism of Saul's day a meditation practice Saul probably knew in which the person focused on the great vision of God described in Ezekiel 1. In the report of the vision Ezekiel gives stunning detail about the appearance of God's glory. Ezekiel saw something like God's throne with mysterious creatures supporting it and the whole thing moved on wheels. Ezekiel even comes close to saying he sees God's face, but he uses reserved language, saying only it looked like "gleaming amber" (Ezekiel 1:27). The ones who meditated on this language from Ezekiel hoped to gain such spiritual clarity that they saw what Ezekiel saw, the throne of God and perhaps even God's face.

Wright asks us to imagine Saul on his way to Damascus meditating in this very way. Saul is deep in spiritual contemplation as he sees in his mind's eye the vision of God's throne. He moves on in meditation until he looks closely at the throne of God, the appearance of one sitting there, and then, the face. It is the face of Jesus! Then he hears the voice, "Saul, Saul, why are you persecuting me?" Saul's view of the world and of God has changed forever.

Although this scenario is only a guess at what might have been going on when Saul met the risen Christ, it is helpful as an illustration of how we may be changed as God calls us. We may hold strongly to certain beliefs about God or about what God expects of us and we may reject others who think differently. Then, we encounter someone with beliefs or practices we reject, but we see God at work in them. Suddenly we must face the fact that we have been wrong in our narrowly held views of God and the world. As a result, we go about the work of God with a different outlook, with more compassion and grace than before. After Saul's conversion, Ananias also makes a dramatic change in his way of seeing the world. Now he is called to embrace Saul, whom he once feared, as a brother in Christ.

### From Enemy to Brother

"If you can't beat them, join them." So the old saying goes. Most of us have seen or experienced rivals or opponents becoming partners in some endeavor. Two fourth-grade boys get into a scuffle on the playground. They do not like each other. The one thinks the other brags too much about what a star he is in sports. The self-acclaimed sports star thinks the other boy is arrogant because he is a straight-A student. The rivalry continues until the boys find themselves on the same soccer team. In practice the coach praises them both as team leaders. They begin to see that together they can make the team quite good. Suddenly they see each other differently. They become close friends as well as teammates.

God calls Ananias to accept Saul and welcome him into his religious world. But the reason Ananias is able to do what God asks involves something more profoundly spiritual than discovering a partnership like the two soccer players had. When God calls Ananias to meet Saul, Ananias does not know about Saul's dramatic conversion (at least the passage does not tell us he knows this). Ananias has not encountered Saul personally so as to find camaraderie with him. Rather, Ananias accepts this call based on one thing God tells him: "He is an instrument whom I have chosen to bring my name before Gentiles and kings and before the people of Israel" (Acts 9:15). Perhaps it is important to Ananias that Saul has an essential job to do for the kingdom of God. But the most basic realization Ananias has is that God chose Saul. We often keep our distance from others because we think of them as evil, as people God has rejected. When we see them as children of God, however, we are forced to find kinship with them for we see that they are objects of God's grace just as we are. We see a sign of this awareness when Ananias meets Saul and greets him as "Brother Saul" (Acts 9:17).

### A Call to Promote Another

As we learn later in Acts 10 and in the rest of the Book of Acts, Saul becomes one of the most import-ant figures in the spread of the gos-pel. Ananias is completely different in this regard. After this chapter in Acts we do not meet him again. He recedes into the background as Saul proclaims the message about Jesus throughout the Gentile world. It is easy to imagine, therefore, that

Ananias might have rejected the task God gave him. His only objection to God's call is that he knows Saul as an enemy of the church (Acts 9:13). But after he was assured Saul had become part of The Way he might well have felt resentment. "This Saul has perse-cuted the church while I have labored faithfully, and in fear of people like him," he may have thought, "and now God appoints *him* as the chief messenger of the gospel?"

Nevertheless, Ananias accepts the role God gives him. As he does, he demonstrates two very important qualities. First, he shows that he is will-ing to accept a supporting role, rather than a leading role, in God's work. He seems ready to let God do the choos-ing and he follows obediently. Sec-ond, instead of resentment for Saul, Ananias shows joy. In responding this way Ananias welcomes Saul just as the prodigal son's father welcomed him, thus following God's own example (Luke 15:11-32). It would have been easy for Ananias to respond like the prodigal's older brother. By welcoming Saul, Ananias shows himself capable of assuming a crucial role in God's work.

---

## SHARING THE SCRIPTURE

### PREPARING TO LEAD

#### Preparing Our Hearts

Ponder this week's devotional read-ing from 1 Timothy 4:6-16. What does Paul, writing to his protégé Timothy, say about how he as a faithful servant of God is to conduct himself? What are the main tasks of his ministry?

Pray that you and the students will follow Paul's instructions so that you are well prepared to serve and

be faithful to whatever tasks God has called you.

#### Preparing Our Minds

Study the background Scripture from Acts 9:1-31 and the lesson Scrip-ture from Acts 9:10-20.

Consider this question: *When you feel urges to act in certain ways and are not sure if you are being led by God, is it acceptable to question those urges?*

Write on newsprint:

❏ information for next week's lesson, found under Continue the Journey.

❏ activities for further spiritual growth in Continue the Journey.

Determine how you might use any of the features that precede the first lesson of this quarter in today's session.

## LEADING THE CLASS

### (1) Gather to Learn

❖ Welcome everyone and pray that those who have come today will be open to God's call on their lives.

❖ Invite the students to share stories of times when they felt God calling them. Before they responded with a final yes or no, what questions did they ask of God?

❖ Read aloud today's focus statement: We often feel urges to act in certain ways. Is it acceptable to question those urges? Acts 9 describes God's call to Ananias and Saul, Ananias's questioning reaction, and God's firm response.

### (2) Goal 1: Analyze the Sequence of Events Before and During Ananias's Witness to Saul

❖ Create the context for today's lesson by reading or retelling the Introduction, Acts 9:1-2, and Acts 9:3-9 in Understanding the Scripture.

❖ Choose a volunteer to read Acts 9:10-20.

❖ Discuss these questions:
1. **What do you know about Saul's Damascus road experience?** (See Acts 9:1-9 and A Vision of God and the Face of Jesus in Interpreting the Scripture.)

2. **What does God tell Ananias to do? How does he respond to God? How does God reassure Ananias?** (See From Enemy to Brother in Interpreting the Scripture.)

3. **Ananias is obviously a faithful follower of Jesus, yet God calls him to play a supporting role, whereas Saul, who persecuted the church, was destined for greatness. How do you think Ananias may have felt about helping Saul? How do you think Saul may have felt when he realized that one whom he would have persecuted has come to his aid?** (See A Call to Promote Another in Interpreting the Scripture.)

### (3) Goal 2: Reflect on Times of Questioning and Resisting God's Call

❖ Invite the students to reflect on the calls and responses of some biblical characters we have encountered this quarter: Gideon, Samson, Moses, Isaiah, Jeremiah, Ezekiel, Amos, Philip. Ask:
1. **Which of these characters questioned, even resisted God's call?**
2. **Why do you think that in the end they said yes?**
3. **Which of these characters would you compare to Ananias or to Saul?**

❖ Read: **Resistance to God's call is not limited to characters we meet in the Bible. Some persons who enter ordained ministry as a second or third career report that they have known for years, perhaps decades, that God was calling them into this work, but they procrastinated until** they felt they could no longer resist this call. Oh sure, there were many good excuses: I have a wife and family to support; I own a small business that cannot survive without me; I have two children to put through college; I have a mortgage and cannot afford to attend seminary; getting through school would be difficult for me. At some point those who were called could not continue to say no and took a leap of faith to do God's will.

❖ Form small groups and encourage each person to remember aloud a time when God was calling him or her to a task, large or small. Ask the students to consider how this call came, how they knew it was from God, and how and when they responded.

*(4) Goal 3: Develop Spiritual Maturity that Breaks Down One's Resistance to the Calls of God*

❖ Read: **God can certainly call anyone, but those who have been on the Christian journey longer are more likely to have the spiritual maturity to say yes. People define "spiritual maturity" in various ways, and it is not an easy concept to nail down. Broadly speaking, a mature person is one who is more conformed to the image of Jesus than people who are not as mature. The mature person will, like Jesus, act out of love for others and put their needs first. This person will be open to the call of God and willing to say yes to God, even when circumstances would argue for a response of no. Charles Swindoll observes, "One of the marks of spiritual maturity is the quiet confidence that God is in control . . . without the need to understand why he does what he**

does." The question for us becomes: How do we develop such maturity, which is not an end point but a process, so that we may be ready to hear and respond with a resounding yes when God calls?

❖ Provide time for participants to suggest ways in which people can grow and become more like Christ. Certain actions, such as regular Bible study, prayer, worship, and service may top their list. But be sure to note that maturity comes as a result of a close, personal relationship with Jesus. It's not just what we do but rather who we are and ways in which who we are shows forth the love of God.

❖ Challenge participants to make a silent commitment to grow as Christians.

*(5) Continue the Journey*

❖ Pray that as the learners depart, they will seek ways to be more closely connected to Jesus.

❖ Post information for next week's session on newsprint for the students to copy:
- **Title: Called to Be Inclusive**
- **Background Scripture: Acts 10**
- **Lesson Scripture: Acts 10:19-33**
- **Focus of the Lesson: Traditions and cultural understandings often shape our view of the world and others in ways that limit our interactions. How do we overcome the limitations of such understandings? Through a vision and the Spirit, Peter learned how and why to witness to Cornelius and his household.**

❖ Challenge the adults to grow spiritually by completing one or more of these activities related to this week's session.

(1) Practice a spiritual discipline so as to grow in your faith and move toward spiritual maturity. Consult one of the many books that will help you understand and practice building your faith. *Celebration of Discipline* by Richard Foster is a modern classic on this important topic.

(2) Review the Book of Esther, about a woman who, like Ananias, took a huge risk to act in a desperate situation. What lessons can Esther teach you about speaking up on behalf of God and God's people?

(3) Listen to someone who is trying to discern God's call. Ask questions that may help this person discern what he or she needs to do without actually offering advice. Tell this person that you care and are praying.

❖ Sing or read aloud "Lord, Speak to Me."

❖ Conclude today's session by leading the class in this benediction, which is adapted from Isaiah 6:8, the key verse for July 9: **In response to your call, O God, I say, "Here am I, send me!" Amen.**

## UNIT 3: CALLS IN THE NEW TESTAMENT
# CALLED TO BE INCLUSIVE

---

### PREVIEWING THE LESSON

**Lesson Scripture:** Acts 10:19-33
**Background Scripture:** Acts 10
**Key Verse:** Acts 10:28

**Focus of the Lesson:**
Traditions and cultural understandings often shape our view of the world and others in ways that limit our interactions. How do we overcome the limitations of such understandings? Through a vision and the Spirit, Peter learned how and why to witness to Cornelius and his household.

**Goals for the Learners:**
(1) to read the story of Cornelius's meeting with Peter
(2) to appreciate that the gospel is for everyone and so desire to reach others with the gospel message.
(3) to commit to enhancing the church's cross-cultural mission outreach.

**Supplies:**
Bibles, newsprint and marker, paper and pencils, hymnals

---

### READING THE SCRIPTURE

NRSV
Lesson Scripture: Acts 10:19-33

¹⁹While Peter was still thinking about the vision, the Spirit said to him, "Look, three men are searching for you. ²⁰Now get up, go down, and go with them without hesitation; for I have sent them." ²¹So Peter went down to the men and said, "I am the one you are looking for; what is the reason for your coming?" ²²They

CEB
Lesson Scripture: Acts 10:19-33

¹⁹While Peter was brooding over the vision, the Spirit interrupted him, "Look! Three people are looking for you. ²⁰Go downstairs. Don't ask questions; just go with them because I have sent them."

²¹So Peter went downstairs and told them, "I'm the one you are looking for. Why have you come?"

answered, "Cornelius, a centurion, an upright and God-fearing man, who is well spoken of by the whole Jewish nation, was directed by a holy angel to send for you to come to his house and to hear what you have to say." <sup>23</sup>So Peter invited them in and gave them lodging.

The next day he got up and went with them, and some of the believers from Joppa accompanied him. <sup>24</sup>The following day they came to Caesarea. Cornelius was expecting them and had called together his relatives and close friends. <sup>25</sup>On Peter's arrival Cornelius met him, and falling at his feet, worshiped him. <sup>26</sup>But Peter made him get up, saying, "Stand up; I am only a mortal." <sup>27</sup>And as he talked with him, he went in and found that many had assembled; <sup>28</sup>**and he said to them, "You yourselves know that it is unlawful for a Jew to associate with or to visit a Gentile; but God has shown me that I should not call anyone profane or unclean.** <sup>29</sup>So when I was sent for, I came without objection. Now may I ask why you sent for me?"

<sup>30</sup>Cornelius replied, "Four days ago at this very hour, at three o'clock, I was praying in my house when suddenly a man in dazzling clothes stood before me. <sup>31</sup>He said, 'Cornelius, your prayer has been heard and your alms have been remembered before God. <sup>32</sup>Send therefore to Joppa and ask for Simon, who is called Peter; he is staying in the home of Simon, a tanner, by the sea.' <sup>33</sup>Therefore I sent for you immediately, and you have been kind enough to come. So now all of us are here in the presence of God to listen to all that the Lord has commanded you to say."

<sup>22</sup>They replied, "We've come on behalf of Cornelius, a centurion and righteous man, a God-worshipper who is well-respected by all Jewish people. A holy angel directed him to summon you to his house and to hear what you have to say." <sup>23</sup>Peter invited them into the house as his guests.

The next day he got up and went with them, together with some of the believers from Joppa. <sup>24</sup>They arrived in Caesarea the following day. Anticipating their arrival, Cornelius had gathered his relatives and close friends. <sup>25</sup>As Peter entered the house, Cornelius met him and fell at his feet in order to honor him. <sup>26</sup>But Peter lifted him up, saying, "Get up! Like you, I'm just a human." <sup>27</sup>As they continued to talk, Peter went inside and found a large gathering of people. <sup>28</sup>**He said to them, "You all realize that it is forbidden for a Jew to associate or visit with outsiders. However, God has shown me that I should never call a person impure or unclean.** <sup>29</sup>For this reason, when you sent for me, I came without objection. I want to know, then, why you sent for me."

<sup>30</sup>Cornelius answered, "Four days ago at this same time, three o'clock in the afternoon, I was praying at home. Suddenly a man in radiant clothing stood before me. <sup>31</sup>He said, 'Cornelius, God has heard your prayers, and your compassionate acts are like a memorial offering to him. <sup>32</sup>Therefore, send someone to Joppa and summon Simon, who is known as Peter. He is a guest in the home of Simon the tanner, located near the seacoast.' <sup>33</sup>I sent for you right away, and you were kind enough to come. Now, here we are, gathered in the presence of God to listen to everything the Lord has directed you to say."

# UNDERSTANDING THE SCRIPTURE

**Introduction.** The story in Acts 10 continues the account of the church's growth. In this chapter the idea of ritual purity that separates the Jews from the Gentiles will be called into question. This, in turn, will open the door to the Gentile mission that will be led by the apostle Paul. Eventually Paul will take the gospel to Rome, the capital of the empire. In Acts 10 we have a first glimpse of this eventual spread of the faith as a Roman military officer is welcomed into the church.

**Acts 10:1-2.** Caesarea was a prominent Roman city on the Mediterranean coast, about thirty miles north of Joppa. It was an important port, built by Herod the Great that served as a hub of Roman governmental activity in the Middle East. Cornelius was a centurion, that is, a mid-level officer who was in charge of one hundred soldiers. The fact that he was stationed at Caesarea where the governor of Judea resided indicates he was very successful and well respected in Rome. The note that he and his family were God-fearers means they were attached to a Jewish synagogue and were devoted to the story and ethics of Judaism, but Cornelius had not been circumcised to become a full convert.

**Acts 10:3-8.** The angel commends Cornelius for his faithfulness to God. The angel highlights Cornelius's acts of prayer and compassion to the poor. Ritual purity, which will soon be rejected as a test of godliness, is not mentioned at all. Simon is the leading disciple's given name. This is a common name, as illustrated by the fact that the man who is hosting him is also named Simon. Simon the tanner is distinguished by his profession. Peter means "rock," which denotes his strength and his crucial role as head of the church.

**Acts 10:9-16.** Peter's vision is related directly to Jewish dietary laws. Many of the restrictions are described in Leviticus 11. These laws were meant to ensure ritual purity and thus to make a person fit to appear in the presence of God. Over time, the dietary laws also set the Jewish people apart from non-Jews and became a primary sign of their devotion to God (see Daniel 1). The most famous restriction is the prohibition against eating pork, but there are a host of other animals considered unclean. The rationale for why certain animals are clean and others are not is uncertain. For example, why are locusts good for food, but shellfish are not? The best guess is that the ancient Jewish priests concluded that certain animals had developed contrary to God's intentions in creation. So, they perhaps determined, anything that lives in water should have fins and scales and should swim. Thus, clams and oysters seemed out of sync. Most important to the story in Acts 10 is the fact that Jews also developed an idea about people with whom they could share food. Jews not only were forbidden to eat certain foods, they also were forbidden to eat with non-Jews who did partake of food that was unclean. Peter's vision directly calls into question the idea that certain foods are unclean. It also anticipates the more important message that no person is unclean.

**Acts 10:17-23**. Peter is puzzled about the meaning of his vision. The messengers from Cornelius prompt an interpretation. The Spirit declares that Peter is to go with these Gentiles who have arrived. Peter is to have fellowship with them because God has declared them clean. So Peter and an entourage from Joppa go to Caesarea.

**Acts 10:24-33**. The meeting between Peter and Cornelius reveals important aspects of the character of both men. Cornelius has devoted himself to Jewish Scripture and its teachings about showing kindness to the poor. Nevertheless, he is excluded from full fellowship with the Jewish community because he is not circumcised. This must have been difficult for Cornelius. In his military work he commanded troops and had the respect of Roman officials. Yet in this religious life he was treated as a second-class citizen. Despite this exclusion from full participation in Jewish life, Cornelius was humble. He bows to Peter as to a great authority figure. Peter, for his part, is obedient to God by going against every impulse of his Jewish upbringing. He follows the leading of the Holy Spirit into a completely new experience of what God is doing with the Gentiles.

**Acts 10:34-43**. Peter preaches a sermon that summarizes the life and teachings of Jesus and their meaning for humankind. The message begins with the point that God chose the Israelites to carry the message of Jesus Christ to the world. He ties together the Old Testament witness to God's work with Israel and the experience with Jesus. Indeed, Peter declares, "All the prophets testify about him" (Acts 10:43). Like Philip in Acts 8, Peter shows how all of Scripture points to God's work in Jesus. Even though God chose Israel to bear the good news, however, it was intended as good news for everyone ("everyone who believes in him receives forgiveness of sins through his name," 10:43). Thus, Peter for the first time articulates how the Gentiles are recipients of God's love through Jesus, which was God's plan from the beginning.

**Acts 10:44-48**. As Peter is preaching, the Holy Spirit comes upon Cornelius and all those gathered to hear the sermon. In Acts 8:14-17 the Samaritans believed, were baptized, and then received the Holy Spirit. Here, however, the Spirit comes first and the Gentiles who receive it speak in foreign tongues like the apostles on the day of Pentecost. The reason for the Spirit coming first seems to be that God wanted to show the Jewish Christians that the Gentiles were just as worthy to be part of the family of God as they. So, Peter asked, "Can anyone withhold the water for baptizing these people who have received the Holy Spirit just as we have?" (10:47).

---

## INTERPRETING THE SCRIPTURE

### The Conversion of Peter

The Book of Acts is about the growth of the church from its beginnings in the circle of Jesus' disciples in Jerusalem stretching to the end of the known world. As the story unfolds it focuses on the conversion of people who encounter the Gospel: the conversion of three thousand Jews in

Jerusalem on Pentecost (Acts 2); the conversion of Samaritans and the Ethiopian eunuch (Acts 8); and the conversion of Saul, who once persecuted the church (Acts 9). Now in Acts 10 there is a story of the conversion of the first Gentiles. To this point no one who has come into the church has clearly been non-Jewish (the Ethiopian eunuch may be an exception, but he is not identified as a Gentile in the story). But after Peter's preaching in Caesarea, the first group of Gentiles professes faith in Jesus.

Although the conversion of Gentiles marks a major development in the story, the main subject of Acts 10 is the conversion of Peter. As a devout Jew, Peter assumed the Gentiles were outside the will of God and therefore outside God's plan for spreading the news of Christ to the world. So Peter was surprised when the messengers from Cornelius showed up asking for the apostle and the Spirit declared, "go with them without hesitation; for I have sent them" (10:20). Peter was suddenly confronted with the reality that God was at work among these Gentiles. The vision that preceded the appearance of these visitors was giving the message already, and now the implications of the vision become clear. Among the Gentiles Peter would discover sisters and brothers in Christ. Peter testifies to this conversion experience in Acts 10:28: "You yourselves know that it is unlawful for a Jew to associate with or to visit a Gentile; but God has shown me that I should not call anyone profane or unclean." So also those who were with Peter "were astounded that the gift of the Holy Spirit had been poured out even on the Gentiles" (10:45).

God's call to Peter was to spread the gospel of Jesus Christ. But for Peter to be prepared to do so, his own heart had to be radically changed. Peter had surely heard Jesus teach in ways that pointed to the openness to people outside his own religious circle (for example, in the story of the good Samaritan in Luke 10:25-37). He had also witnessed Jesus embracing centurions and other Gentiles (7:1-17). But the full conversion did not take place until he saw the vision on Simon the tanner's rooftop and met the representatives from Cornelius. This is often the way such "conversions" take place for all of us in the midst of answering God's call: We encounter people who are different from us and we discover that the Holy Spirit is moving in them. When we have such an experience we are confronted with a new way of seeing such persons and God's work in the world.

### Jesus Christ Is the Center

What Peter discovered through his meeting with the Gentiles in Caesarea is that God does not favor any one group of people over another (Acts 10:34). The lesson, however, was not primarily about the equality of people of different backgrounds. Rather, it was that God desires to bind people together through faith in Jesus Christ rather than through ethnic identity or rituals associated with one religious group. Before meeting the Gentiles, Peter thought very narrowly about people: They were either circumcised (Jewish) and therefore in God's favor, or uncircumcised and therefore unclean and unfit to be in God's presence. To be sure, circumcision and other identity-shaping acts of the

Jews had been appropriate outward signs of faithfulness to God. God had chosen these people as instruments to bring blessing on the entire world, and their testimony to what God had done was crucial (Genesis 12:3). But by the time Peter met the Gentiles in Caesarea, many Jews had come to believe these outward signs of identity with God were ends in themselves. The end, or goal, however, was God's work of mercy and grace made known fully in Jesus Christ (Acts 10:36). Peter learned that people were not supposed to be bound together primarily by circumcision, but by Jesus Christ. Anyone who had faith in Christ was a brother or sister.

The kind of conversion Peter had in Caesarea may happen to anyone as he or she encounters people who are different and discovers a bond with them in Jesus Christ. I once lived in a city that was rife with racial tension. The divide between African Americans and Caucasians was as great as I have ever experienced it. One day I went to a large home improvement store to pick up a piece of furniture my wife had purchased. I took it to my vehicle only to discover it would not fit inside no matter how I turned it. Then I heard a man behind me ask, "Do you need some help?" I turned around to meet an African American man about my age. He asked where I lived and I told him it was only a mile or two away. He then offered to take the furniture there in his truck. I thanked him profusely and offered to pay him, which he refused. When we arrived at my home we unloaded the furniture and then we talked for a few minutes. He shared with me that he was a Christian and that when he saw me wrestling with the furniture he felt God telling him to help me. Given the racial tension in the city, I was surprised that he stopped to help me. He was equally surprised that I received his help. But we confessed to each other a new awareness, that we had a bond of faith in Christ that transcended our racial differences. Peter discovered something like this too. The divide between Jew and Gentile was humanly created and sustained. God's goal all along was to bring them together. Now in Christ this began to happen.

### What About the Law?

One of the biggest questions the story of Peter in Acts 10 raises is this: How are we to understand the Jewish law that shaped Peter and created his initial hesitation to associate with Gentiles? God's message to Peter that he should not "call anyone profane or unclean" (10:28) seems to nullify the Law of Moses completely. The answer to the question is complex, but three points are essential. First, the law Moses received from God was never intended as a means to salvation. Rather, God's salvation came first, and the law simply gave God's people opportunity to respond in faithfulness. Second, the law became for some Jews (particularly the Pharisees) a dividing line between Jews and Gentiles when the Jews were living as an oppressed and powerless minority in the midst of great political powers such as Babylon and Rome. It was a way of preventing them from compromising their faith in such an environment. Finally, God's special care for the Jews was always for the purpose of blessing the whole world (Genesis 12:1-3). So Acts 10 does not so much declare that the law is null and void as it returns to God's original purpose of choosing the Jews.

# SHARING THE SCRIPTURE

## PREPARING TO LEAD

### Preparing Our Hearts

Ponder this week's devotional reading from Psalm 15. In answer to the question concerning who may come into the presence of God, the psalmist offers ten conditions for admission. As a Christian why do you—or don't you—believe adherence to these conditions is necessary? Even if these conditions are unnecessary, what purpose do you believe they could serve in the life of a Christian?

Pray that you and the students will be held fast by God so as not to stumble.

### Preparing Our Minds

Study the background Scripture from Acts 10 and the lesson Scripture from Acts 10:19-33.

Consider this question: *How do you overcome the limits of the traditions and cultural understandings that have shaped your worldview in ways that limit your interactions with others?*

Write on newsprint:
❑ questions for Goal 2 in Sharing the Scripture..
❑ activities for further spiritual growth in Continue the Journey.

Determine how you might use any of the features that precede the first lesson of this quarter in today's session.

Prepare a brief lecture to use with Goal 1 in Sharing the Scripture as an introduction to today's session.

Learn about cross-cultural outreach opportunities sponsored by your congregation and/or denomination for Goal 3 in Sharing the Scripture.

## LEADING THE CLASS

### (1) Gather to Learn

❖ Welcome everyone and pray that those who have come today will feel the desire to tell the story of Jesus' love for all people.

❖ Option: If you have not yet used Faith in Action: Hearing and Heeding the Call, plan to use this activity to lead into this final lesson.

❖ Read these words by Charles (Chuck) Colson (1931–2012): **"When the church fails to break the [cultural] barrier, both sides lose. Those who need the gospel message of hope and the reality of love, don't get it, and the isolated church keeps evangelizing the same people over and over until its only mission finally is to entertain itself."**

❖ Ask: What perils does Colson imply if the church limits its interactions with people of other cultures?

❖ Read aloud today's focus statement: **Traditions and cultural understandings often shape our view of the world and others in ways that limit our interactions. How do we overcome the limitations of such understandings? Through a vision and the Spirit, Peter learned how and why to witness to Cornelius and his household.**

### (2) Goal 1: Read the Story of Cornelius's Meeting with Peter

❖ Present a brief lecture using the portions labeled Introduction, Acts

10:1-2, 3-8, 9-16 in Understanding the Scripture and The Conversion of Peter in Interpreting the Scripture to help participants understand why Peter, an observant Jew, would consider going to the home of a Roman soldier.

❖ Recruit a volunteer to read Acts 10:19-33.

❖ Point out that from his perspective, Peter had valid concerns about breaking the law that was so dear to him. (See What About the Law? in Interpreting the Scripture.) Despite these concerns he allowed himself to be taught by the vision and thereby was free to go and witness to people with whom he would not otherwise have interacted.

❖ Choose two volunteers to role-play an imaginary scene after Peter returned to the home of Simon, a tanner who also would have been a Jewish Christian. Have "Peter" explain to "Simon" what prompted him to go with men he didn't know to Joppa and how "Peter" was changed by this experience. Encourage "Simon" to raise questions, especially about "Peter's" apparent failure to observe the law.

### (3) Goal 2: Appreciate that the Gospel Is for Everyone and So Desire to Reach Others with the Gospel Message

❖ Distribute hymnals and form teams of three or four people. Assign to each team one hymn that speaks about being called to tell the story of Jesus to people who are unlike themselves. Some useful examples would be "We've a Story to Tell to the Nations," "Go, Make of All Disciples," "O Zion, Haste," or "Lord, You Give the Great Commission." Post these questions on newsprint for the teams to answer, though note that not every question will apply to every hymn:

1. **To whom does the hymn call people to go?**
2. **For what reason are people to go?**
3. **What outcome does the hymn writer expect as a result of people going to tell the story of Jesus?**

❖ Reconvene the class. Call on a spokesperson from each group to report their findings.

❖ Try to summarize what the students learned from these hymns about reaching out in the name of Christ to people who are somehow different from them.

### (4) Goal 3: Commit to Enhancing the Church's Cross-cultural Mission Outreach

❖ Recall that we have talked earlier in our study of Acts about the need to go places and meet people who do not share our cultural perspectives but who are just as valuable in the sight of God as we are.

❖ Offer information you have located concerning cross-cultural outreach projects. In The United Methodist Church, for example, such projects can be found through Global Ministries (http://www.umcmission.org/Give-to-Mission/Search-for-Projects). Bring to the class's attention several projects you located during the week to see if they feel called to become involved.

❖ Option: Talk about one specific project: Stop Hunger Now, founded in 1998, has as its objective the feeding of hungry people with the ultimate goal of ending hunger. This agency goes to local churches with supplies to package rice, soy, dehydrated vegetables and a flavoring mix including twenty-three essential vitamins and minerals into small meal packets that can be stored and delivered to areas outside the United States hit by disaster, schools, and other places where such meals may be all that one person, especially a child, has to eat for the entire day. This is a great project that relies on fund-raising within the church as well as an intergenerational work day to do the actual packing. (See more at: http://www.umcmission.org/Give-to-Mission/Search-for-Projects/Projects/982795.)

❖ Encourage each student to make a commitment to at least one cross-cultural outreach project.

### (5) Continue the Journey

❖ Pray that as the learners depart, they will pray for greater inclusiveness within the church.

❖ Tell the students that this is the last lesson from *The New International Lesson Annual*, which is being retired with this volume. You may continue to follow the International Lesson Series (ILS) as a class by using *Adult Bible Studies* and *Adult Bible Studies Teacher*. For individual study, students may want to purchase *Daily Bible Lessons* and/or *Christian Living in the Mature Years*. All of these quarterly resources are available through Cokesbury online at https://www.cokesbury.com or by calling toll-free at 800-672-1789.

❖ Challenge the adults to grow spiritually by completing one or more of these activities related to this week's session.

**(1) Check with the appropriate office in your denomination to see if there are short-term mission trips you could go on to broaden your spiritual horizons.**

**(2) Recall that God used a vision of food that included "unclean" animals to help Peter see that people who were very different from him were included within God's realm. What images could you imagine that would open vistas of inclusiveness for members of the contemporary church?**

**(3) Write a spiritual journal entry about the different people we have studied this quarter. Why were they called? How did God call them? How did they respond? How might they be role models for you?**

❖ Sing or read aloud "We Are the Church."

❖ Conclude today's session by leading the class in this benediction, which is adapted from Isaiah 6:8, the key verse for July 9: **In response to your call, O God, I say, "Here am I, send me!" Amen.**